GARFIELD AT 25
In Dog Years
I'd Be Dead

GARFIELD AT 25
In Dog Years I'd Be Dead

JIM DAVIS

Edited by Mark Acey and Scott Nickel

BALLANTINE BOOKS ❖ NEW YORK

A Ballantine Book
Published by The Random House Publishing Group
Foreword copyright © 2002 by Dave Barry
Afterword copyright © 2002 by Lynn Johnston

All rights reserved under International and Pan-American
Copyright Conventions. Published in the United States by
The Random House Publishing Group, a division of Random House,
Inc., New York, and simultaneously in Canada by Random House
of Canada Limited, Toronto.

www.ballantinebooks.com

www.garfield.com

Library of Congress Control Number: 2004092324

ISBN 0-345-45204-6

Manufactured in the United States of America

First Edition: November 2002

First Trade Paperback Edition: June 2004

10 9 8 7 6 5 4 3 2 1

Credits

WRITERS Mark Acey and Scott Nickel

ART DIRECTOR Betsy Knotts

DESIGNERS Kenny Goetzinger, Brad Hill,
Tom Howard, Betsy Knotts

ILLUSTRATORS Gary Barker, Lori Barker,
Larry Fentz, Mike Fentz, Brett Koth, Lynette Nuding

PRODUCTION ARTISTS Linda Duell, Kenny Goetzinger

PHOTOGRAPHER Jon Barnard

Acknowledgments

Bob Beasley, Karen Blank, Sheila Bolduc, Kim Campbell,
Marty Campisi, Mary Carr, David "Doc" Davis,
James William Davis, Jill Davis, Linda Davis, Madelyn Ferris,
Gretchen and Robert Gipson, Neil Greer, Sherri Greer,
Cliff Hackney, Frieda Howard, Jugnoo Husain, John Jones,
Dave Kuhn, Bobby Nickel, David Nickel, Karen Nickel,
Marvin Porter, Karla Powell, Eric Reaves, Michael Shermis,
Jeff Wesley, Glenn Zimmerman.

Special thanks to Betty Davis for the use of her
photographs, letters, and archival material.

Growing old is inevitable.
Growing up is optional.

—Garfield

To all the Garfield fans around the world:
This one's for you!

—Jim Davis

Garfield's 25th Birthday Celebration:

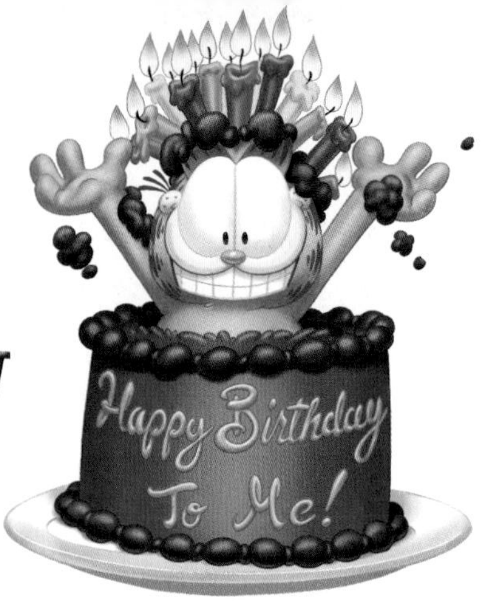
Happy Birthday
To Me!

One Continuous Party!

They came. They partied. They ate cake. Garfield's fans came out in force to celebrate the fabulous feline's 25th. They celebrated with a book tour, a weeklong Garfield-theme cruise, and a Birthday Bash that lasted three days. Garfield, elated by the outpouring of fan love, said, "Whoop-de-doo."

Garfield Book Tour

The furry feline was in the news in 2003, beginning with the debut of a new book, *Garfield at 25: In Dog Years I'd Be Dead*. Garfield's right-hand man, Jim Davis, toured the nation, signing autographs for about 15,000 fans at 14 different locations. Additionally, Jim was interviewed by journalists from 30 newspapers, 35 radio stations, and 20 TV stations, including Al Roker from NBC'S *Today Show*. The 12-city book tour conjured up publicity from Sao Paulo to San Francisco to Singapore, and Garfield basked in the glow of the limelight, while Jim discovered the true meaning of the term "writer's cramp."

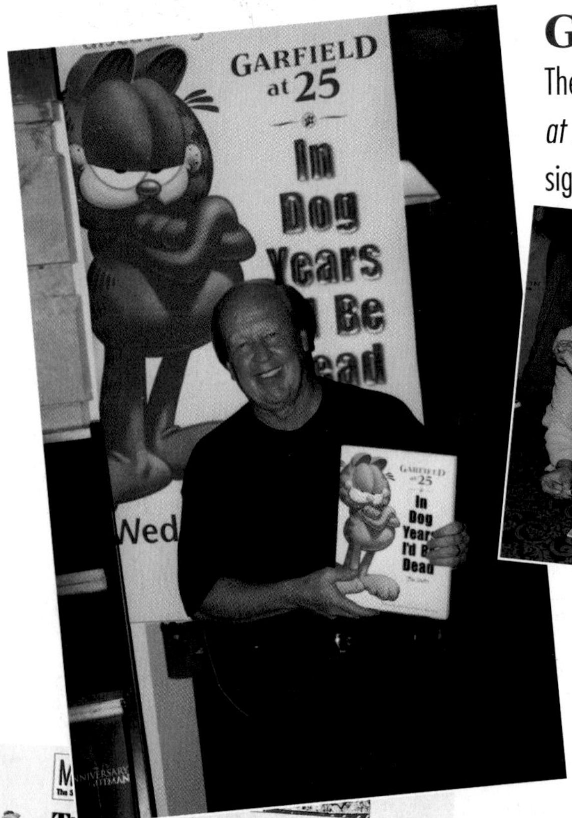
GARFIELD
at 25
In
Dog
Years

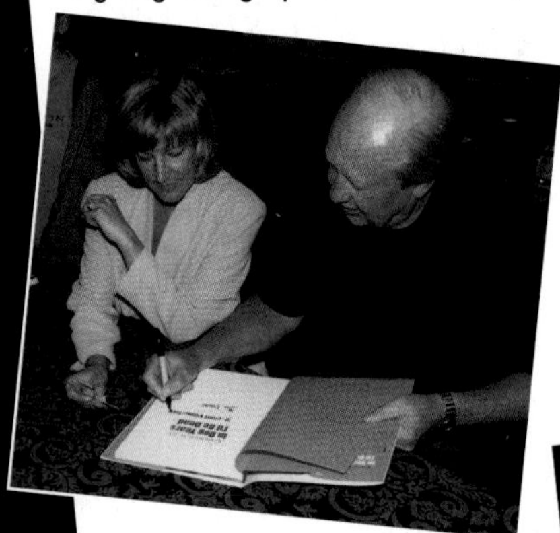

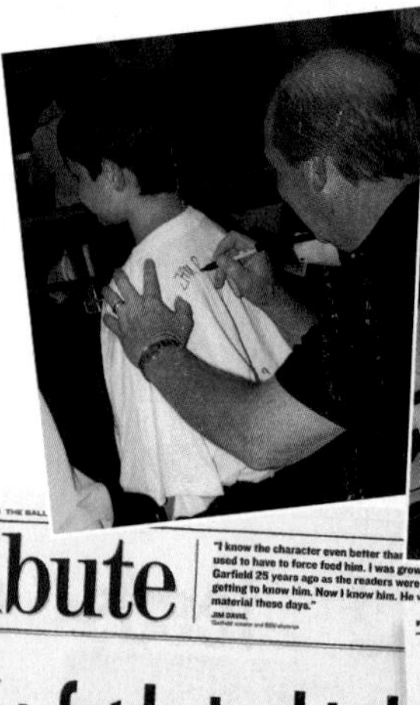

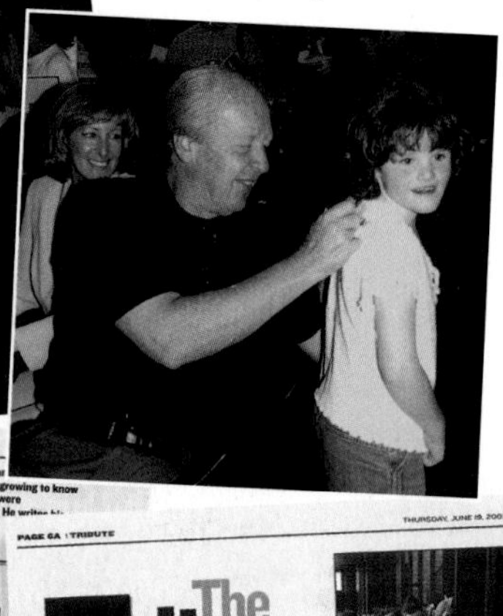

LEFT: If it's Wednesday, it must be Cleveland. Jim poses with a poster promoting one of the book signings on his 12-stop tour.
ABOVE: Jill makes sure her husband spells "Davis" correctly.
RIGHT: Back-to-back book signings.

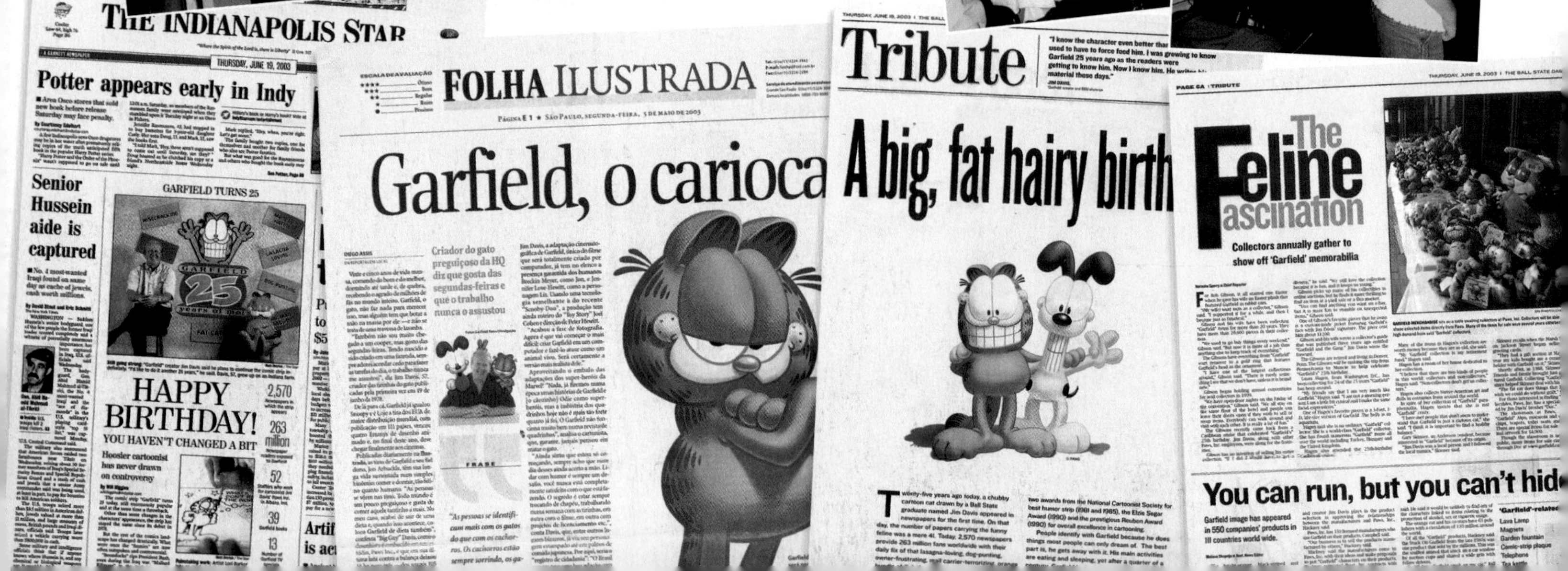
THE INDIANAPOLIS STAR
Potter appears early in Indy
Senior Hussein aide is captured
GARFIELD TURNS 25
HAPPY BIRTHDAY!
YOU HAVEN'T CHANGED A BIT
Hoosier cartoonist has never drawn on controversy
FOLHA ILUSTRADA
Garfield, o carioca
Criador do gato preguiçoso da HQ diz que gosta das segundas-feiras e que o trabalho nunca o assustou
Tribute
A big, fat hairy birth
The Feline Fascination
Collectors annually gather to show off 'Garfield' memorabilia
You can run, but you can't hid

Garfield Cruise

Garfield's It's All About Me at Sea in 2003 cruise was a blast. Three-hundred fifty fat-cat fanatics spent the week partying with Garfield, Odie, and Jim, all the while soaking up the sun, the sea, and the endless buffet on the *Zuiderdam*.

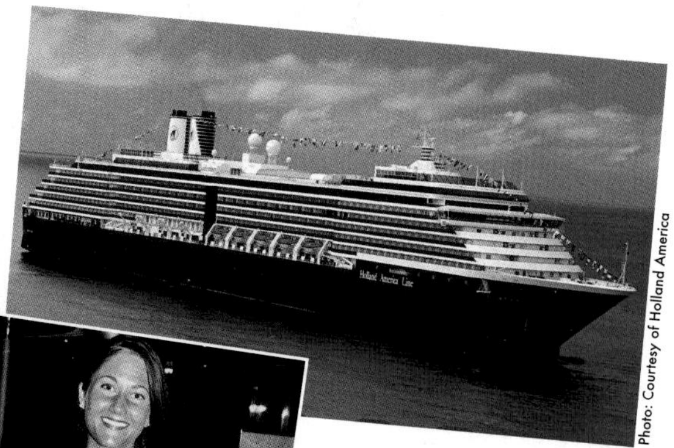

Photo: Courtesy of Holland America

ABOVE: Holland America's Zuiderdam.

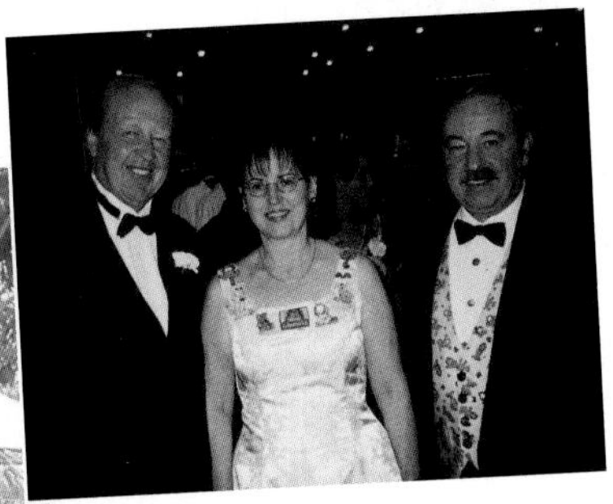

ABOVE: Jim and friends put on the dog-and-cat for black-tie night.

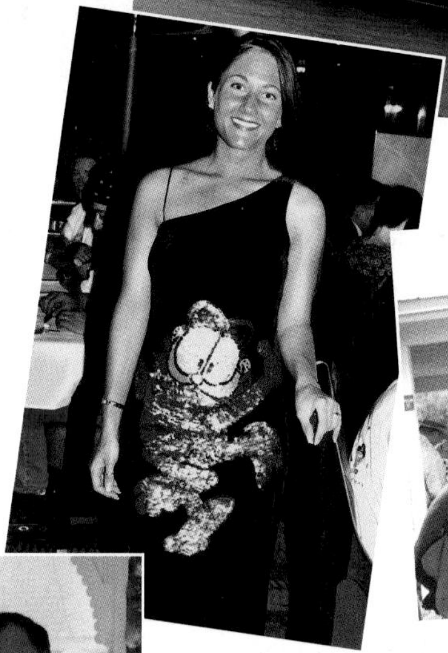

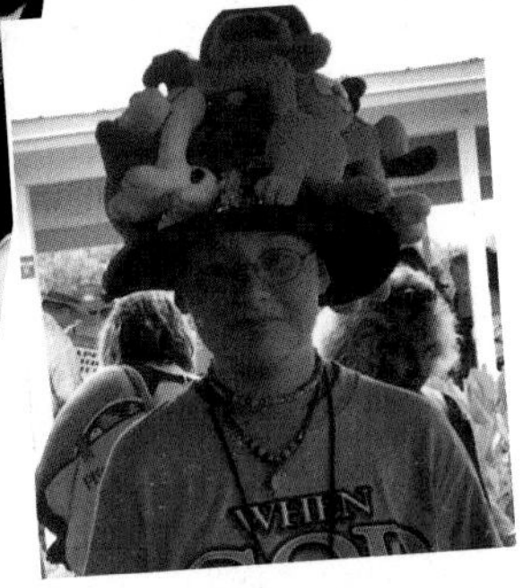

ABOVE LEFT: This lovely Garfield fan models her hand-sequined formal, made especially for the black-tie Garfield Garb dinner.
ABOVE RIGHT: Cruise trivia king Sean Farrell eliminated hundreds of would-be Garfield trivia buffs to win the coveted kitty crown.

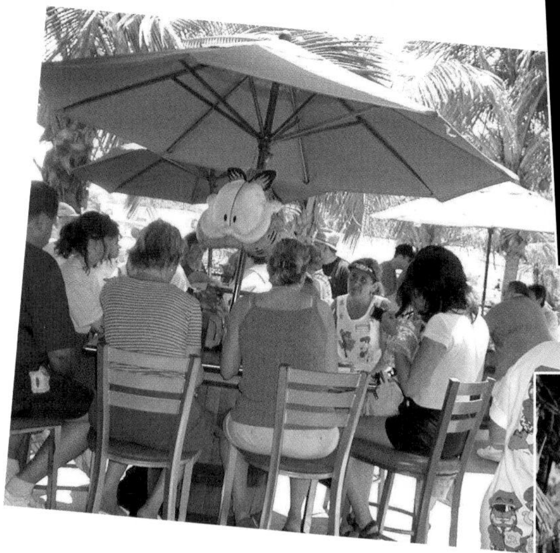

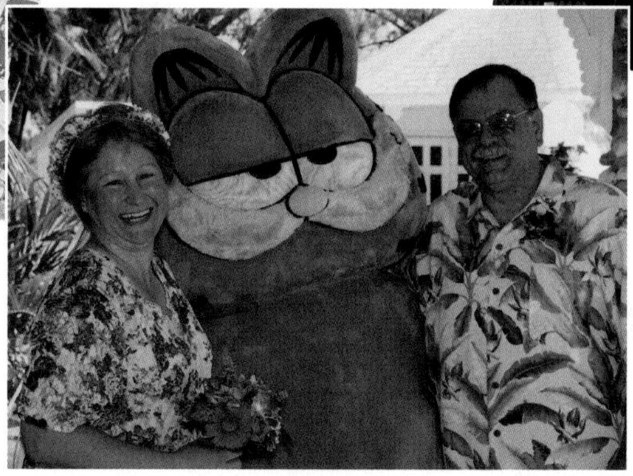

Day 2 of cruise called for a Garfield Scavenger Hunt in Key West, Florida. Thirteen teams competed for the grand prize.
ABOVE: A weary scavenger-hunt team huddles while contemplating their next move.
RIGHT: Garfield fans Arthur and Cindy Williams tie the knot in Cozumel during the Garfield Cruise. A very proud Garfield gave away the lovely bride.

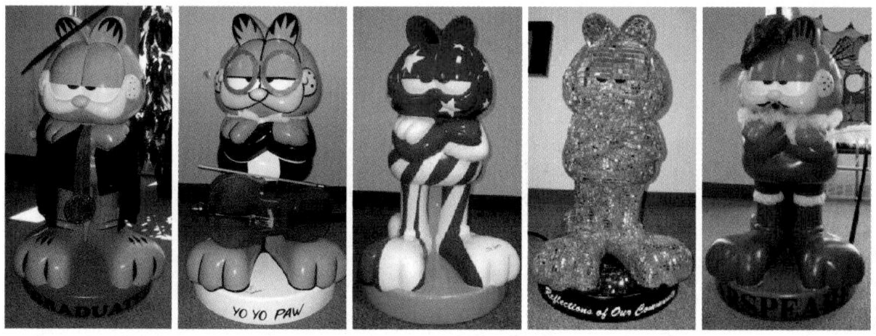
YO YO PAW

Photo: Ron Groves

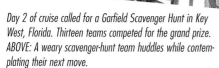

ABOVE: Garfield gets an Extreme Makeover. Twenty-five 4-foot Garfield statues were designed and decorated by local artisans in celebration of the kitty's 25th. The statues were auctioned with proceeds benefitting area not-for-profits.

Garfield Birthday Bash

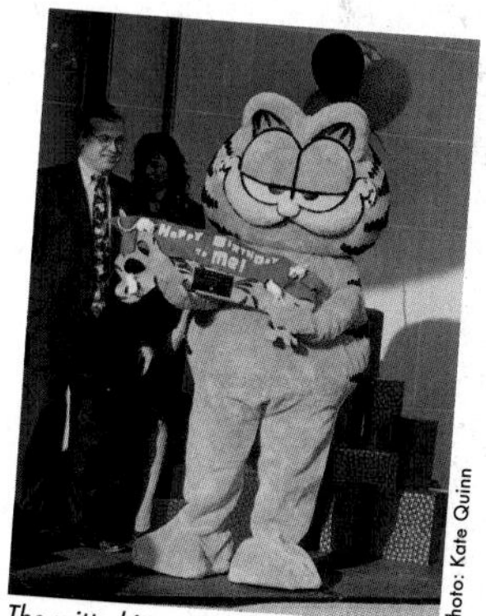

Photo: Kate Quinn

The witty kitty gets the key to the city.

Fans from Switzerland, Denmark, Japan, and from all points in-between traveled to Garfield's hometown to celebrate Garfield's big day, at the Garfield Birthday Bash, June 19–21. The out-of-this-world festivities included a cake and ice cream kickoff, a Fat Cat run, a Fur Ball dance, a spectacularly wacky parade, and a 3-day street fair. As Garfield says, "Too much celebrating is never enough!"

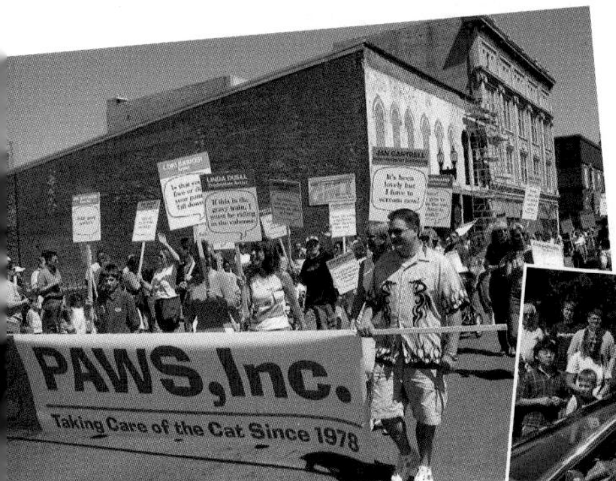
PAWS, Inc.
Taking Care of the Cat Since 1978

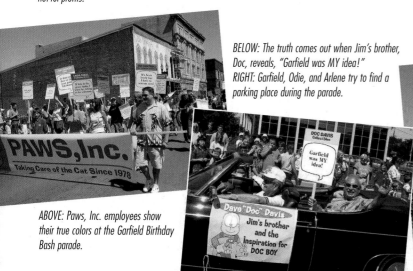

ABOVE: Paws, Inc. employees show their true colors at the Garfield Birthday Bash parade.

BELOW: The truth comes out when Jim's brother, Doc, reveals, "Garfield was MY idea!"
RIGHT: Garfield, Odie, and Arlene try to find a parking place during the parade.

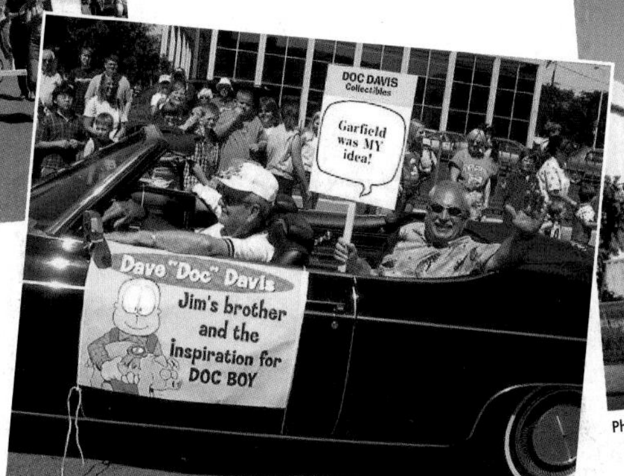
Garfield was MY idea!
Dave "Doc" Davis
Jim's brother and the inspiration for DOC BOY

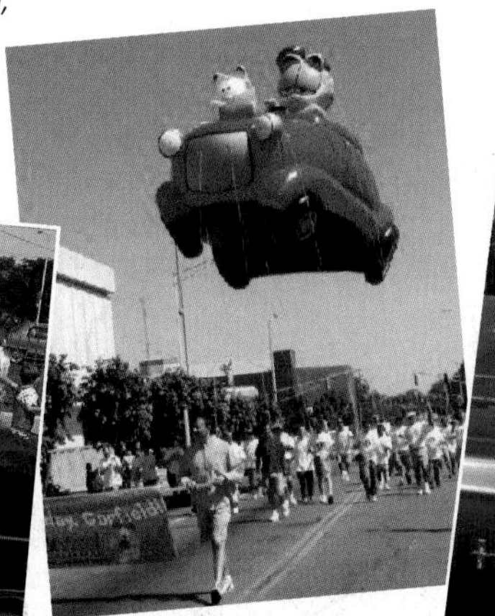

Photo: Ron Groves

BELOW: Muncie Mayor Dan Canan throws Garfield's hat into the ring.

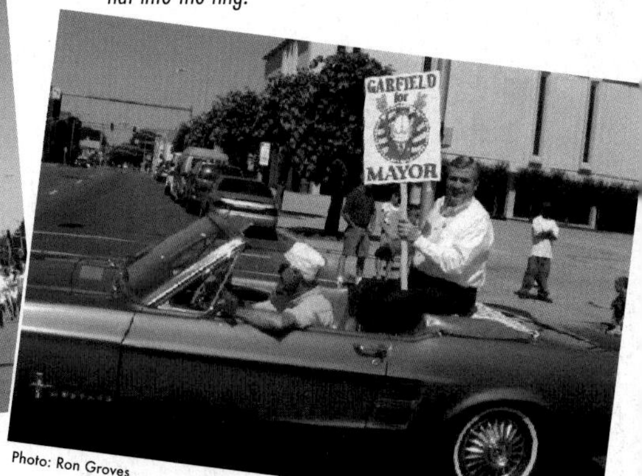
GARFIELD for MAYOR

Photo: Ron Groves

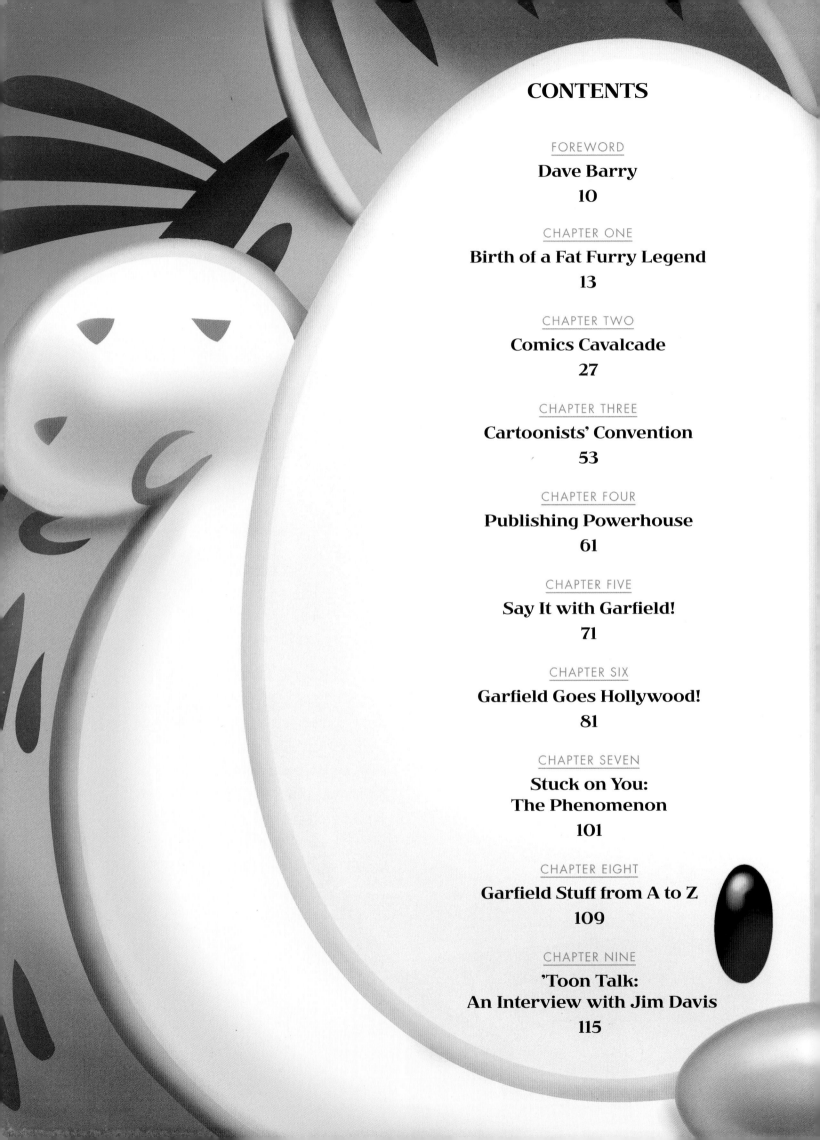

CONTENTS

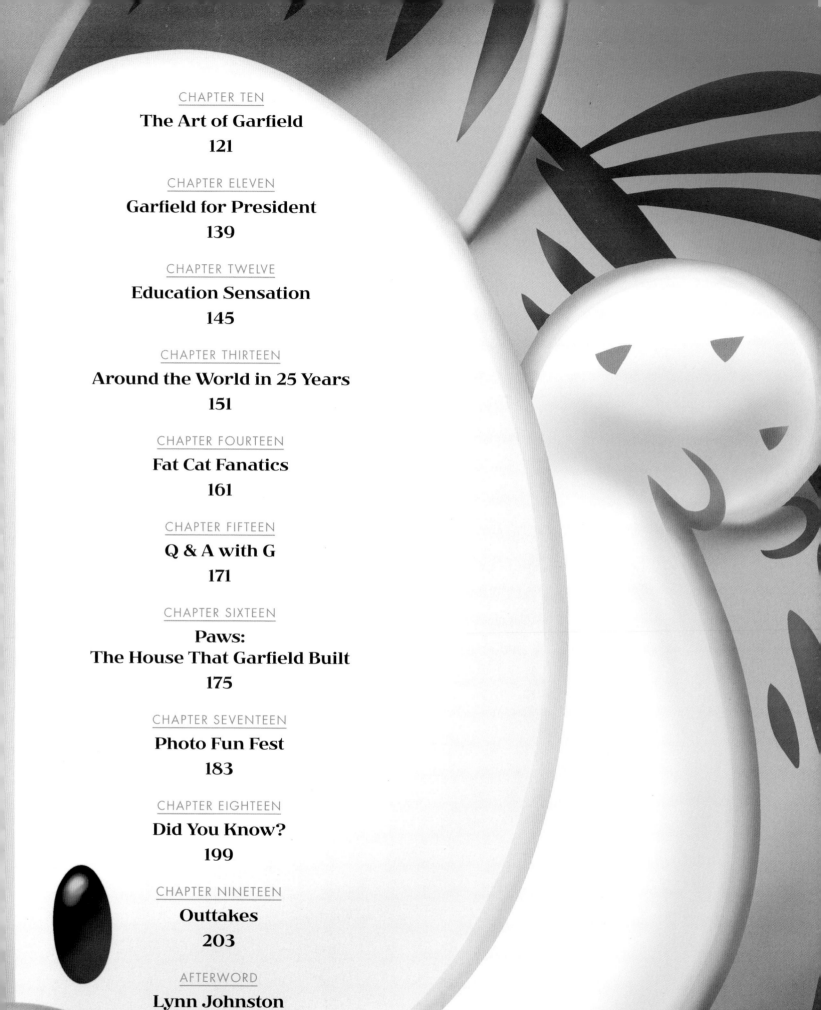

FOREWORD BY DAVE BARRY

I'll be honest here: I'm not a cat guy. I'm a dog guy.

I love dogs because they're loyal. I'm using "loyal" here in the sense of "not the rocket scientists of the animal kingdom." If you have a dog, no matter how pathetic you are, and no matter WHAT you do, your dog will be impressed. You could leap from the edge of the Grand Canyon, and your dog would happily leap right along with you. On the way down, it would be thinking: "What a GREAT idea! At the bottom, maybe there will be food!"

A cat would not do this. A cat would calmly watch you fall, and it would be thinking: "What a *moron*."

So, as I say, I've always been partial to dogs. And thus when the Garfield comic strip started running twenty-five years ago, I skipped it. I continued to skip it until 1984, when my son, Rob, was starting to learn to read.

Rob was not interested in the usual children's books, the ones with titles like *Walter Worm's Big Surprise*, where nothing interesting

ever happens. (Page one: "One day Walter Worm went outside." Page two: "Walter Worm saw Arnold Ant." Page three: "'Hi, Arnold Ant!' said Walter Worm." Page four: "'Hi, Walter Worm!' said Arnold Ant." Page five: "Then Walter Worm saw Marge Moth." Page six: "'Hi, Marge Moth!' said Walter Worm." Etc.)

Then one day when we were in a bookstore Rob picked up a Garfield Treasury Book, and started reading it and laughing. He struggled with some of the words, but he got most of the jokes. He devoured that book and wanted more, so I got him more. I ended up buying him every Garfield book there was, which required me to take out a second mortgage, because at the time there were roughly 73,000 Garfield titles (today the figure is closer to 14 million).

Rob became obsessed with Garfield. It seemed that whenever anything happened, it reminded him of a Garfield strip, which he would repeat verbatim. And the more Garfield jokes he told me, the more I found myself thinking: "Hey, that's FUNNY."

That's when I started reading Garfield regularly, and I've been reading it ever since. I'm still amazed at how consistently good it is—the comic timing; the economy and skill of the writing; the perfect blend of goofiness, cynicism, and slapstick; the way that every now and then, something truly warped pops up; and, of course, the profound yet totally believable stupidity of Odie the dog.

A few years after Rob and I started reading Garfield, we got a chance to meet Jim Davis. For Rob, this was like meeting Elvis. The three of us spent an afternoon talking and fishing off a dock on the west coast of Florida. What I remember best about that afternoon is how much we laughed. In part, this was because a very large manatee surfaced near the dock and emitted a huge bubble of manatee flatulence. But mainly it was because Jim is one of those people who can find humor everywhere.

That's a great gift, and one that Jim has been generously sharing with the world for twenty-five years. On behalf of his zillions of fans, I thank him for creating Garfield.

Not that Garfield would be grateful.

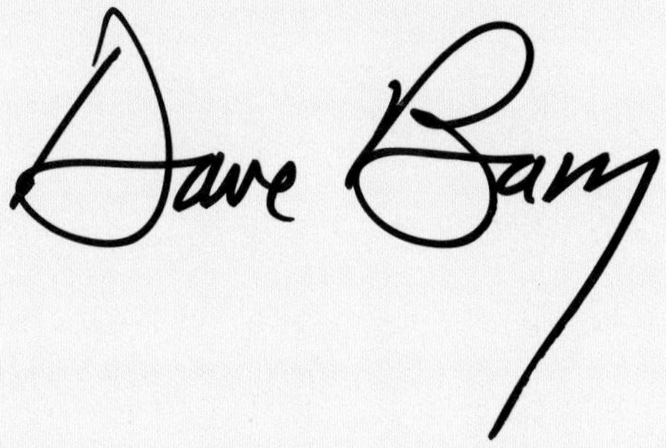

Dave Barry is a humor columnist for the *Miami Herald.* His column appears in more than 500 newspapers in the United States and abroad. In 1988 he won the Pulitzer Prize for Commentary. Many people are still trying to figure out how this happened.

Dave has also written a total of 24 books, although virtually none of them contain useful information. Two of his books were used as the basis for the CBS-TV sitcom *Dave's World,* in which Harry Anderson played a much taller version of Dave.

CHAPTER ONE

Birth of a Fat Furry Legend

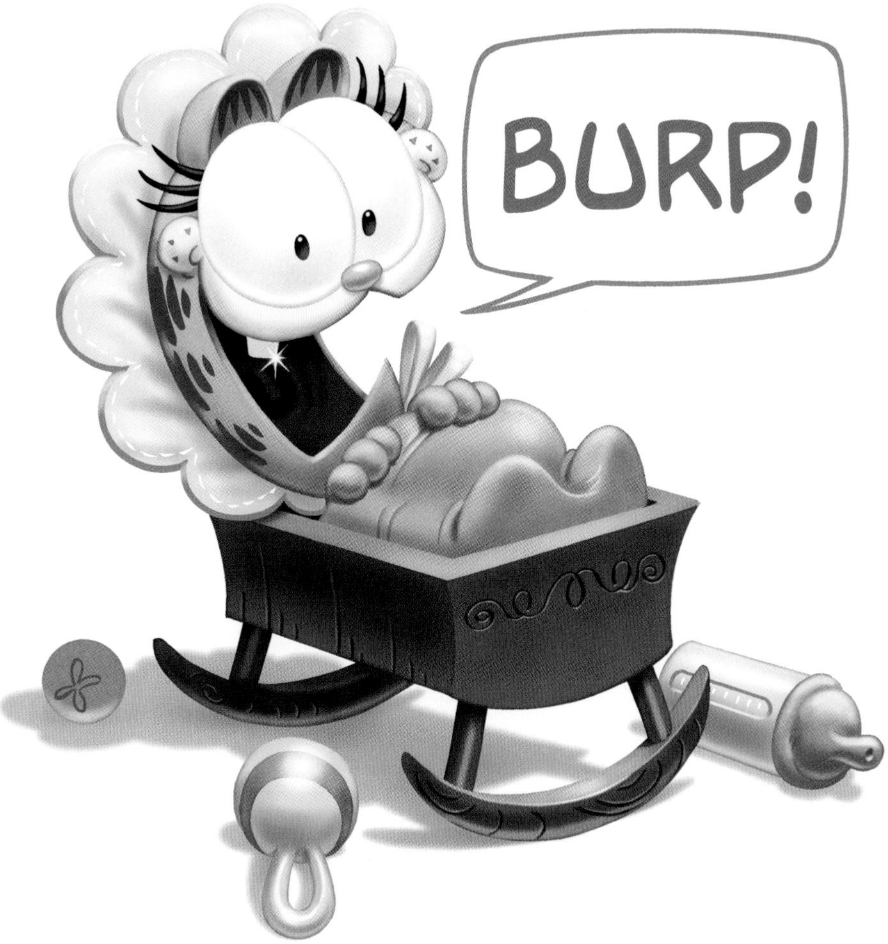
BURP!

Jim Davis gave birth to Garfield, and he has the stretch marks on his brain to prove it. On June 19, 1978, the lasagna-loving fat cat waddled onto the comics page and changed comic strip history. Originally syndicated in just forty-one newspapers, *Garfield* would eventually appear in more than 2,500 papers around the world—not bad for a lazy orange furball.

In the mid-1970s, Jim Davis was an assistant on the popular *Tumbleweeds* comic strip. Jim was also working on his own comic strip called *Gnorm Gnat*. *Gnorm* featured an all-insect cast drawn in a simple, humorous style. Unfortunately, Jim couldn't get the comic-strip syndicates interested in Gnorm and his bug buddies, and after years of rejection slips, abandoned the strip.

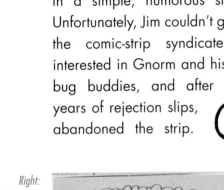

Garfield sketch, circa 1976.

Jim then began work on another strip idea, one that featured a bachelor cartoonist and his cat. After months of development, Jim shopped the new comic around to syndicates and received some encouraging responses. Editors liked the strip, but there was just one problem: The cat kept getting all the good lines. Jim wisely changed the focus of the feature and gave the spotlight to Garfield. Thus, a comic-strip legend was born!

I WISHED I LIVED IN 6TH CENTURY BRITAIN DURING THE TIME OF KING ARTHUR
1-31-74
© Jim Davis. All rights reserved.
I CAN SEE ME NOW...
A GNAT IN SHINING ARMOR
JIM DAVIS

HI FREDDY. GOT A MINUTE?
THAT MAY BE JUST ABOUT IT GNORM
OH, COME ON NOW. JUST BECAUSE THE LIFE SPAN OF A FRUIT FLY IS ONE WEEK, YOU SHOULDN'T BE DEPRESSED. LIVE IT UP! HAVE A FLING! ENJOY EVERY MOMENT!
I CAN'T AFFORD TO
© Jim Davis. All rights reserved.
YOU SHOULD SEE MY LIFE INSURANCE PREMIUM
JIM DAVIS

Right: Jim's first strip, *Gnorm Gnat*. Editors liked the drawing and humor but felt that readers couldn't relate to bugs.

Pictured here are original newspaper clippings from the scrapbook of Betty Davis, Jim's mom. Betty saved nearly all of her son's published work.

While developing *Garfield*, Jim kept a sketchbook in which he jotted down ideas, drew character studies, and roughed out individual strips.

Jim worked on the feature for nearly eighteen months before it was finally accepted for syndication. Over that time, the look of the characters evolved and changed. Here are some early sketches of Garfield and friends.

Garfield trying to
look cute

Garfield

oh look
a cat who
likes mickey
mouse
SHAKE IT,
ANNETTE

Odie (then called Spot)

Jon

Lyman

Liz

Right: Page from Jim's sketchbook showing some of the strips he submitted to the syndicate. As part of the development process, an editor graded the submissions, helping Jim pick the best gags. (Note the letter grades on the top and bottom strips.)

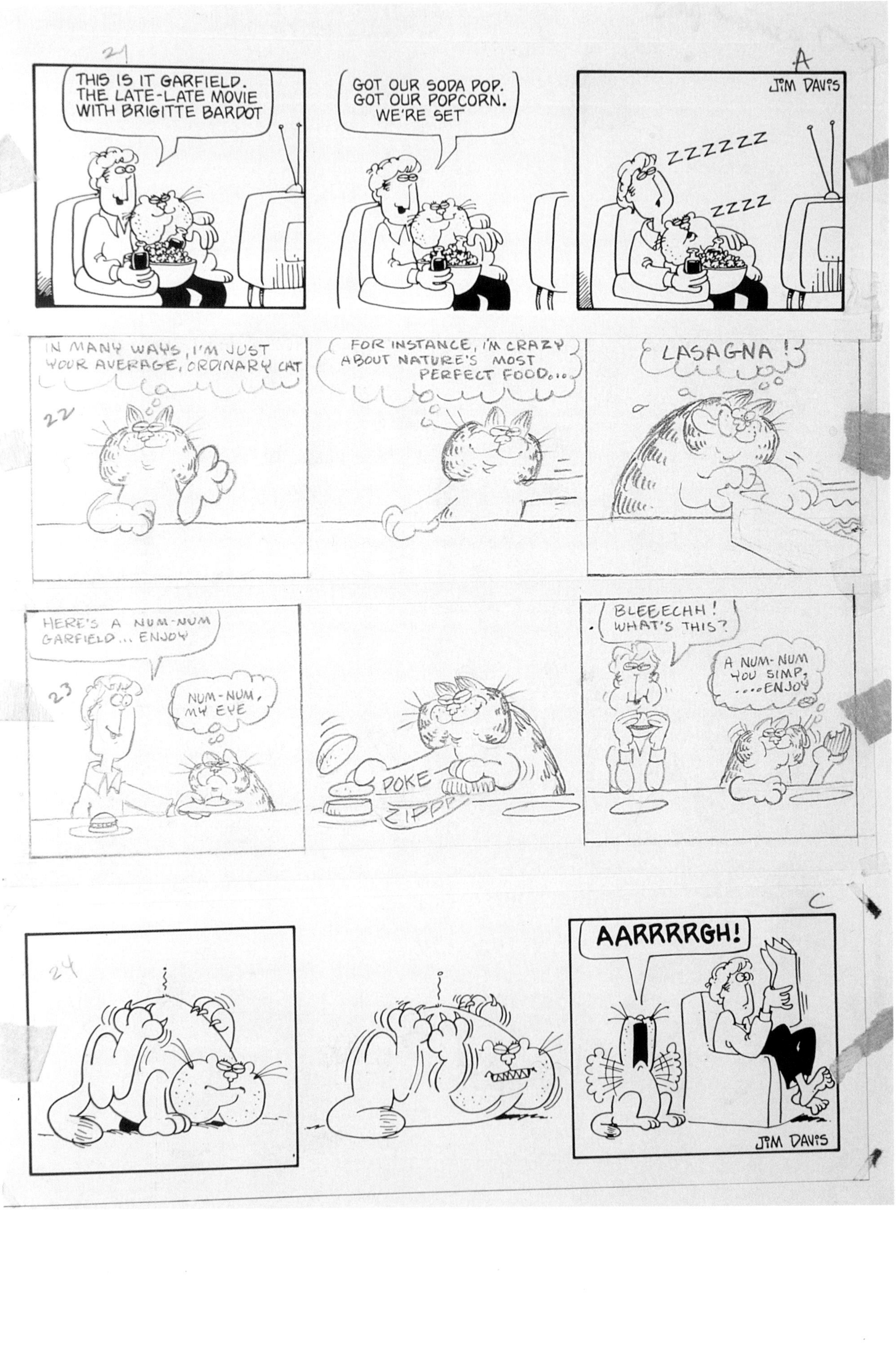
21
A
THIS IS IT GARFIELD. THE LATE-LATE MOVIE WITH BRIGITTE BARDOT
GOT OUR SODA POP. GOT OUR POPCORN. WE'RE SET
JIM DAVIS
ZZZZZZ
ZZZZ
22
IN MANY WAYS, I'M JUST YOUR AVERAGE, ORDINARY CAT
FOR INSTANCE, I'M CRAZY ABOUT NATURE'S MOST PERFECT FOOD...
LASAGNA!
23
HERE'S A NUM-NUM GARFIELD... ENJOY
NUM-NUM, MY EYE
POKE
ZIPPP
BLEEECHH! WHAT'S THIS?
A NUM-NUM YOU SIMP, ...ENJOY
C
24
AARRRRGH!
JIM DAVIS

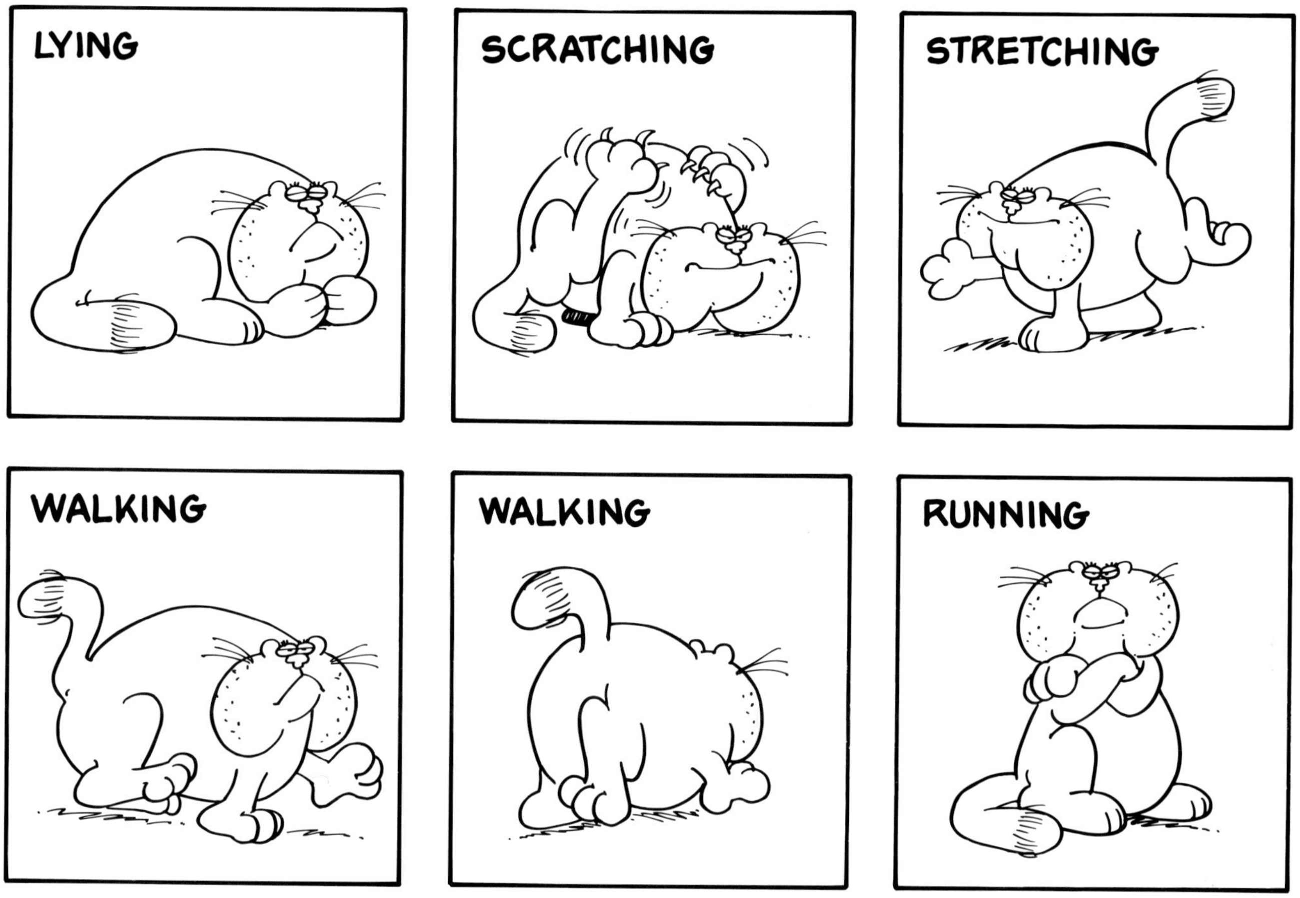
LYING
SCRATCHING
STRETCHING
WALKING
WALKING
RUNNING

Left: The first version of Garfield was decidedly different. The cat was fatter and had no stripes. But the rude 'tude was just the same.

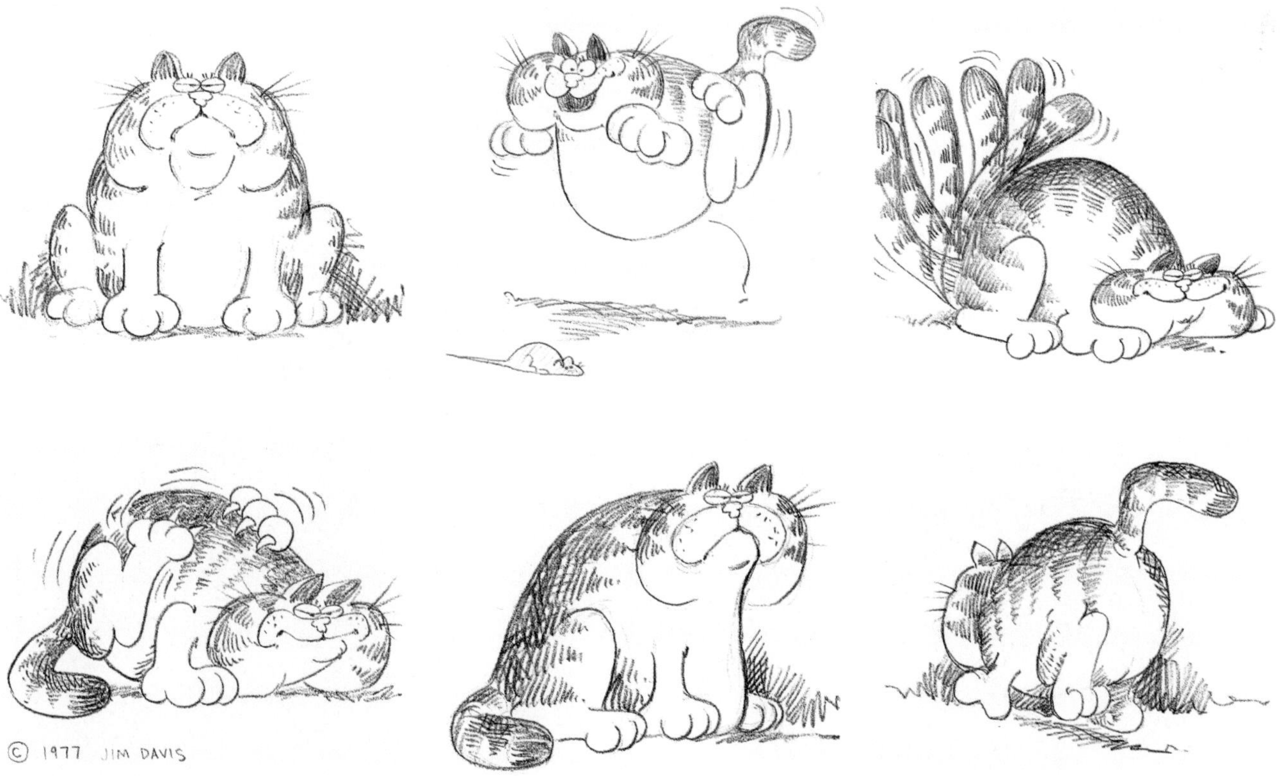
© 1977 JIM DAVIS

Left: Working with syndicate editors, Jim refined the look of the character, adding stripes, sharpening facial features, and making the ears more prominent.

Right:
BOOB-TUBE TABBY
A sketchbook rough and the final published strip.

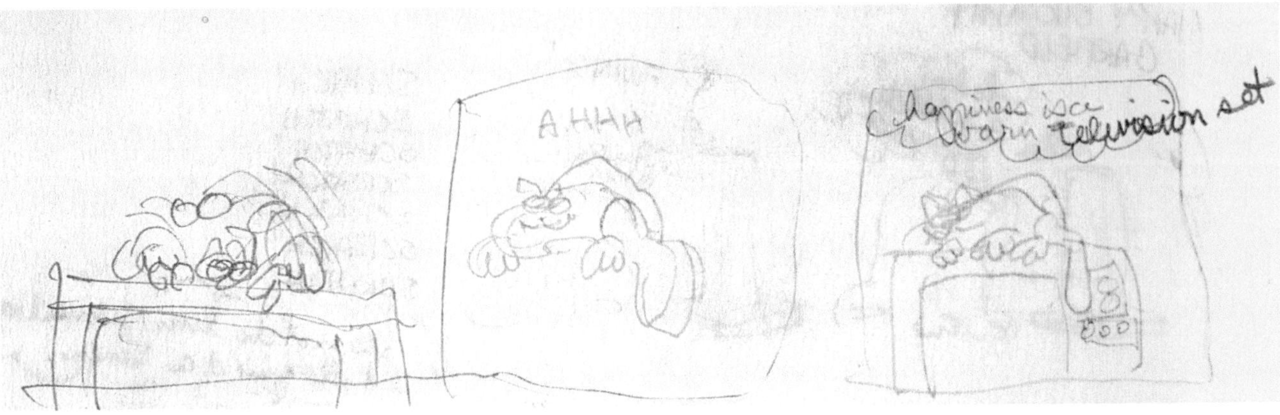
A.HHH

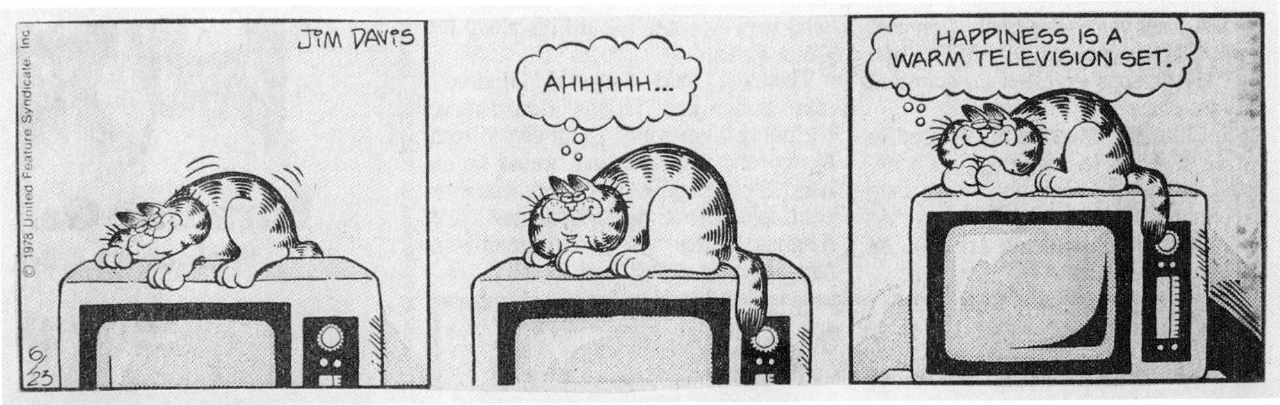
JIM DAVIS
AHHHHH...
HAPPINESS IS A WARM TELEVISION SET.
© 1978 United Feature Syndicate, Inc
6/23

Below:
The cartoonist in his natural habitat: Thirty-two-year-old Jim Davis poses for an early publicity photo.

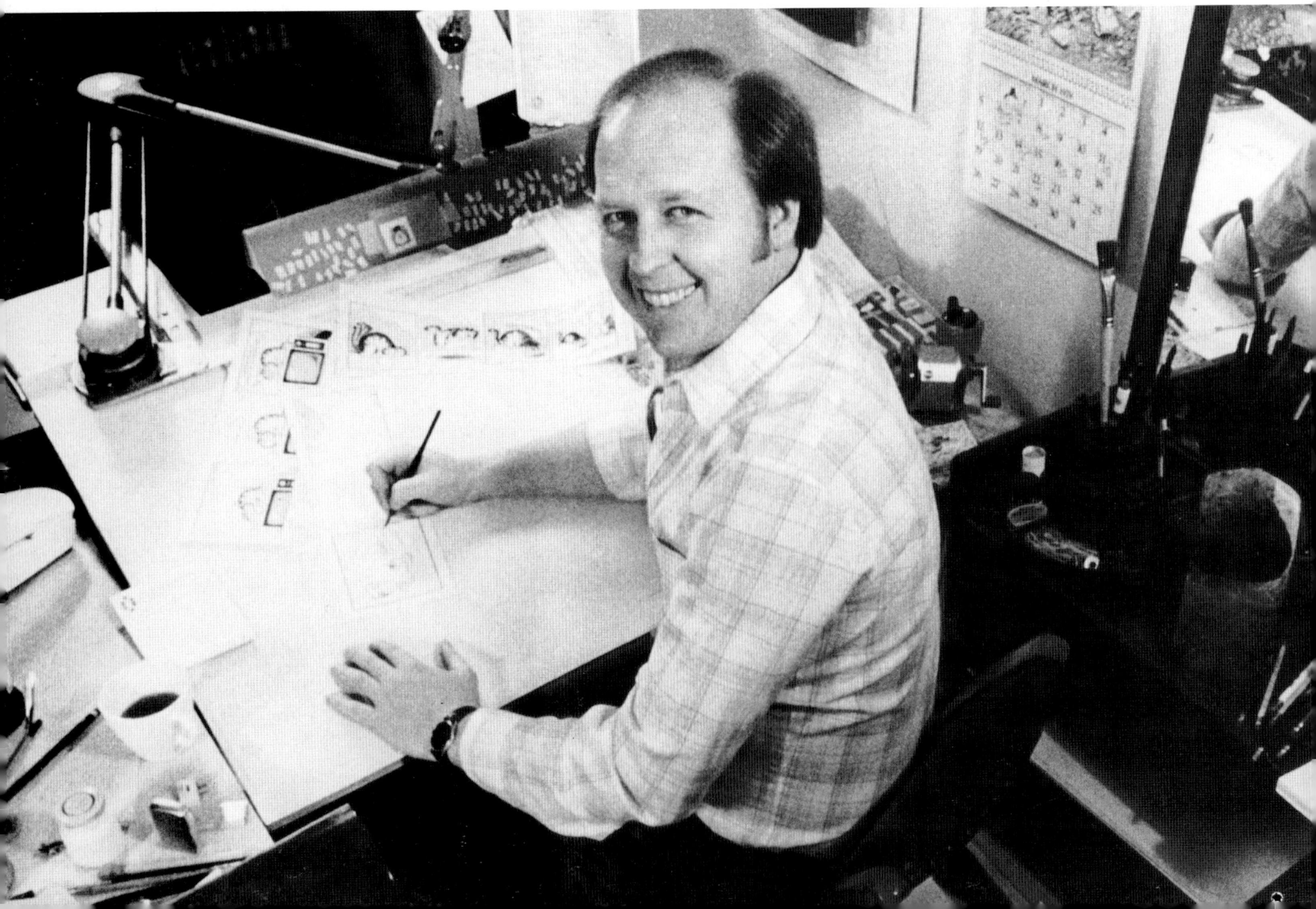

A star is syndicated! United Feature Syndicate accepted *Garfield* on January 24, 1978. Jim had just a few short months to produce the initial strips and create the sales kit.

Originally, the comic was going to be called *Garfield and Friends.* This title would later be used for Garfield's animated TV series.

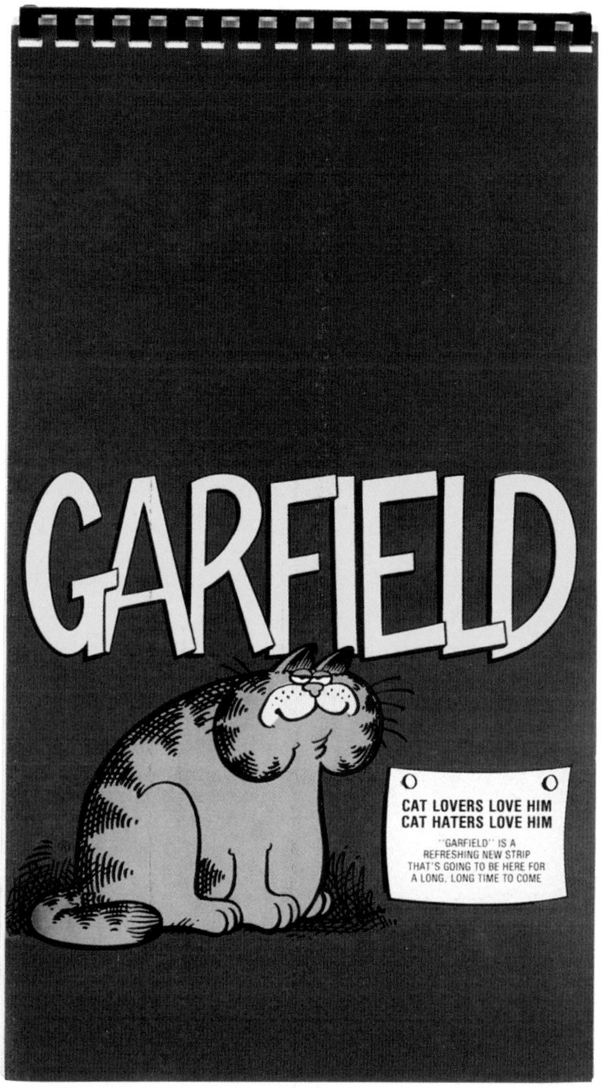
GARFIELD
CAT LOVERS LOVE HIM
CAT HATERS LOVE HIM
"GARFIELD" IS A REFRESHING NEW STRIP THAT'S GOING TO BE HERE FOR A LONG, LONG TIME TO COME

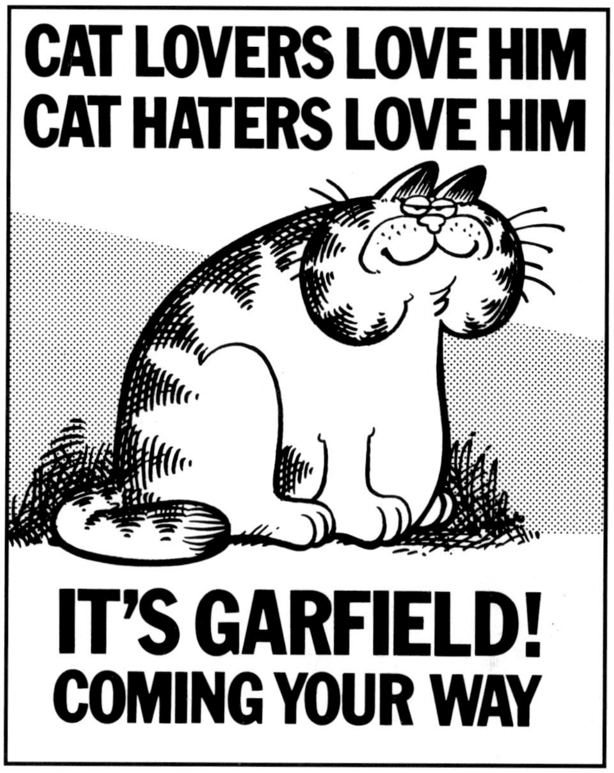
CAT LOVERS LOVE HIM
CAT HATERS LOVE HIM
IT'S GARFIELD!
COMING YOUR WAY

Far left:
The first sales kit.

Left:
Promotional ad created for the sales kit emphasizing Garfield's universal appeal.

Below:
Character sheet from 1978.

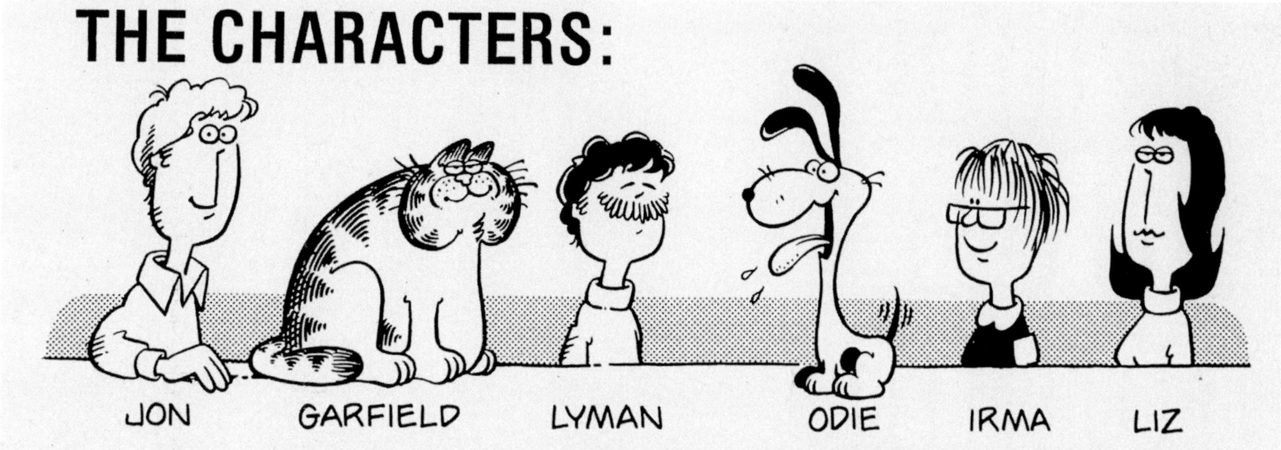
THE CHARACTERS:
JON
GARFIELD
LYMAN
ODIE
IRMA
LIZ

JON: A cartoonist, GARFIELD's daydreaming owner.

GARFIELD: A fat, lazy, cynical, endearing cat.

LYMAN: Nutty, flighty, excitable. Jon's eventual roommate.

ODIE: Lyman's mindless dog. A hapless foe of GARFIELD.

IRMA: An opinionated, klutzy, man-hungry waitress at the coffee shop.

LIZ: Jon's unattainable Venus. Eventually, his girlfriend. Then?... Who knows.

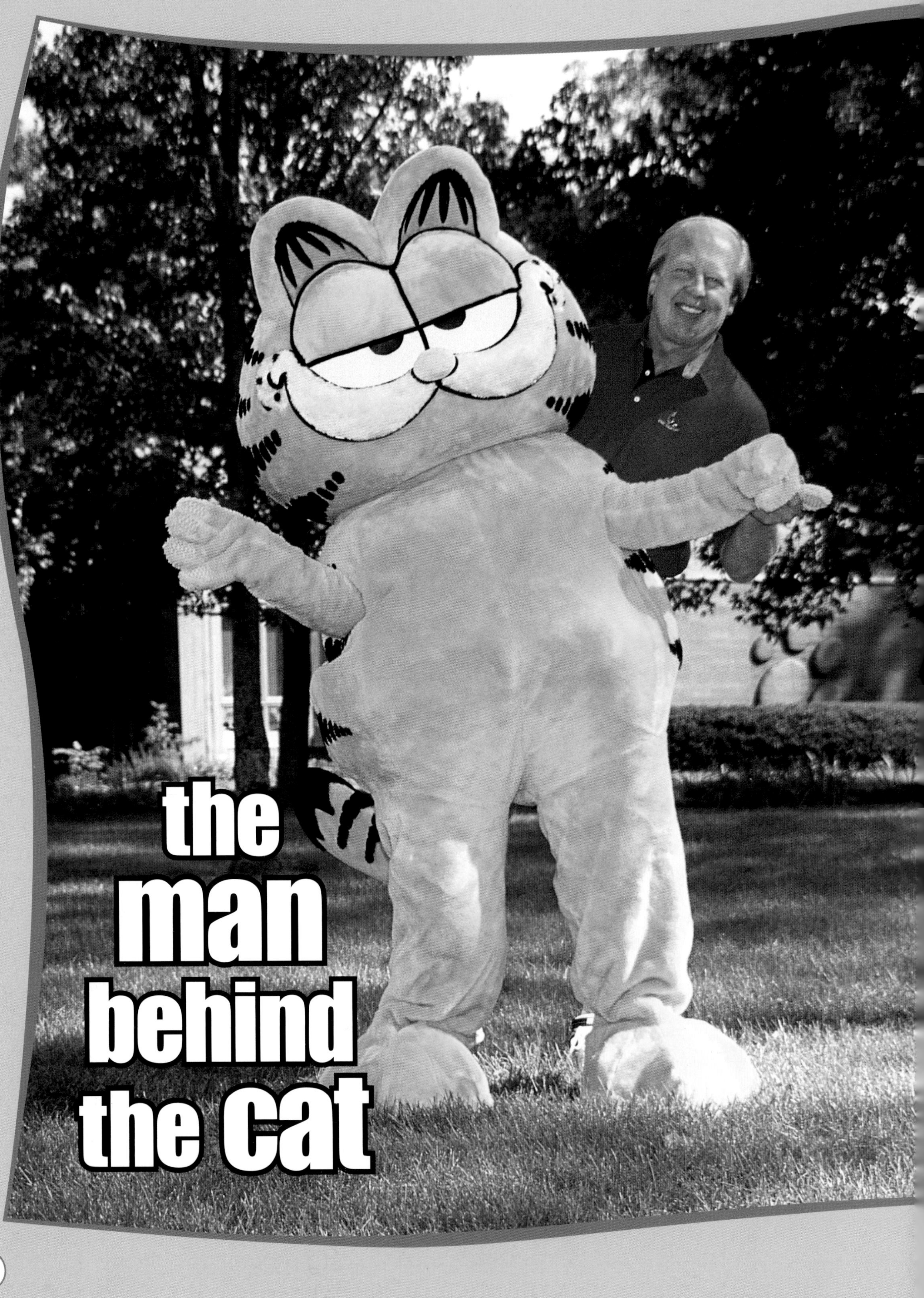

the man behind the cat

The Davis Dossier

TAKE CARE OF THE CAT ...
... AND THE CAT WILL TAKE CARE OF YOUR STUFF!

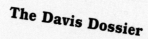

NAME: James Robert Davis

NICKNAMES: Jim Dandy, Jim Boy, The Great Catsby, Big Guy

BIRTHPLACE: Marion, Indiana

BIRTH DATE: July 28, 1945

HEIGHT: About yay-high

WEIGHT: Bigger than a breadbox

EYES: Two

HAIR: Shedding

FAVORITE COLOR: PMS 137 (Garfield orange)

OCCUPATION: Cartoon guy

HOBBIES: Golf, fine wine, cow tipping

FAVORITE FOOD: Lasagna is a fave, but the top spot goes to hamburgers . . . big, little, burnt, sloppy—I love 'em all!

LEAST FAVORITE FOOD: Raisins

FAVORITE FARM ANIMAL: Cows. As a kid I raised 'em—and ate many of my faves.

LEAST FAVORITE FARM ANIMAL: Goat/chicken (tie)

FAVORITE MOVIE: *Airplane* (love those fighting Girl Scouts!)

FAVORITE TV SHOW: *Walt Disney's Wonderful World of Color* (even though we only had a black-and-white TV)

FAVORITE SONG: "Shout" ('cause it makes me wanna shout!)

FAVORITE CAR: Viper (it's a retro muscle car . . . an engine with seats)

THREE THINGS YOU'D TAKE TO A DESERT ISLAND: A hamburger, a bun, and some ketchup

BIGGEST PET PEEVE: Getting that pesky ball of cotton out of the baby aspirin bottles

ULTIMATE DREAM: To write that one gag that makes the whole world laugh

BOXERS OR BRIEFS: Neither. I'm a bloomers man.

OH, BABY!
Jim grew up on a farm in Fairmount, Indiana (birthplace of actor James Dean!), where his family raised Black Angus cows . . . and twenty-five assorted cats.

BUDDING ARTIST
An early drawing by Jim, age two.

Grant Co. Fair Pepper Grand Champion heifer

DRESSED TO THRILL
School picture taken in 1954 when Jim was nine. As a child, Jim suffered from severe asthma and spent many hours away from farm chores, drawing and sketching.

FARM BOY
Jim was a member of 4-H and won many a competition with Pepper, his prize heifer.

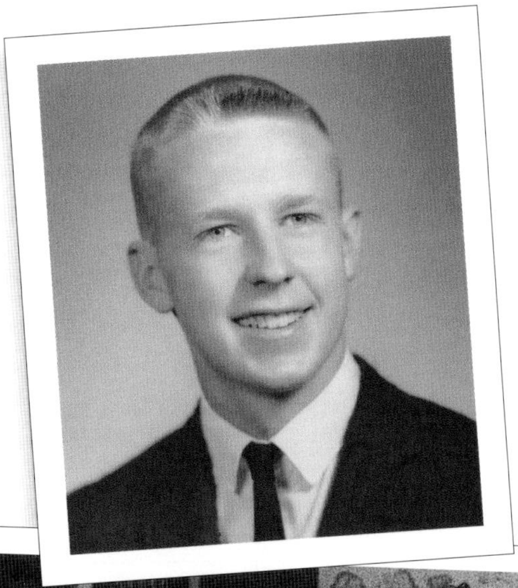

BIG MAN ON CAMPUS

Look at all that hair! After graduating from Fairmount High in 1963, Jim enrolled in Muncie, Indiana's Ball State University (where David Letterman was also a student). As Jim laughingly puts it, "I distinguished myself by earning one of the lowest cumulative grade point averages in the history of the university."

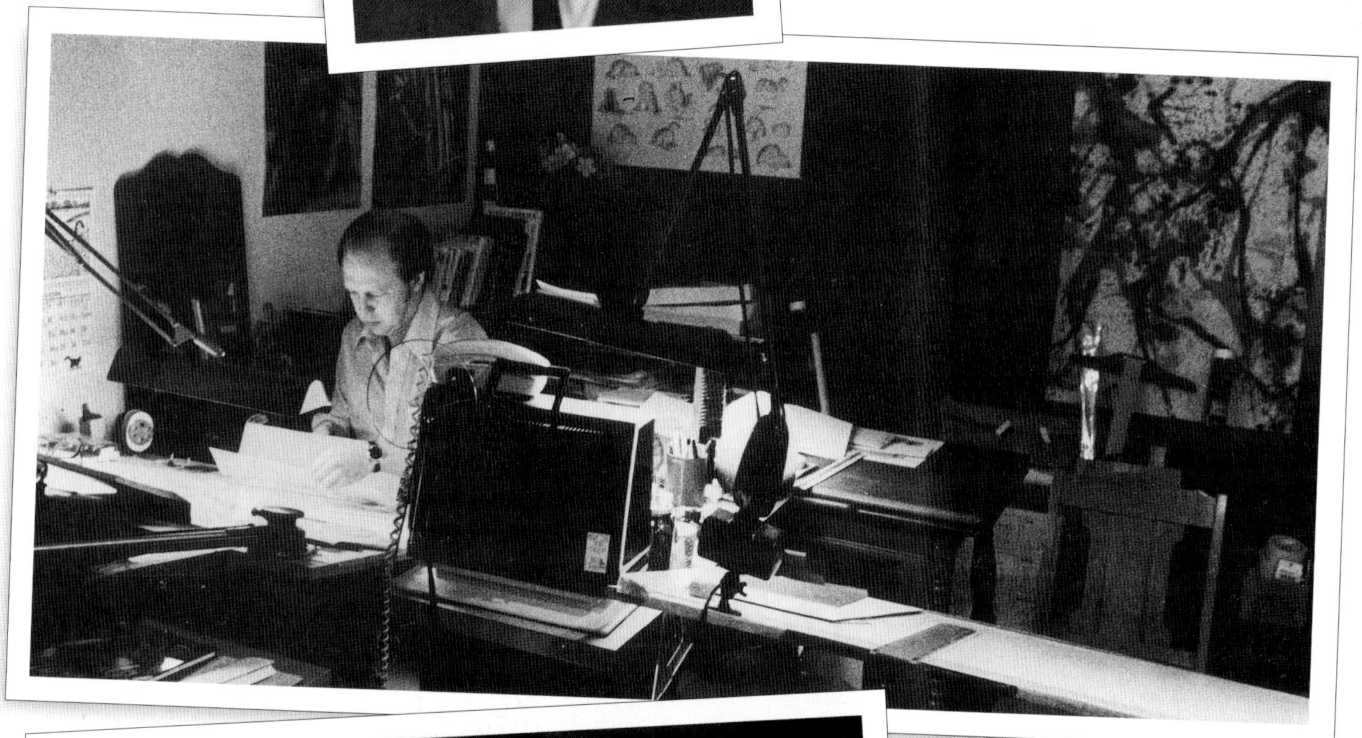

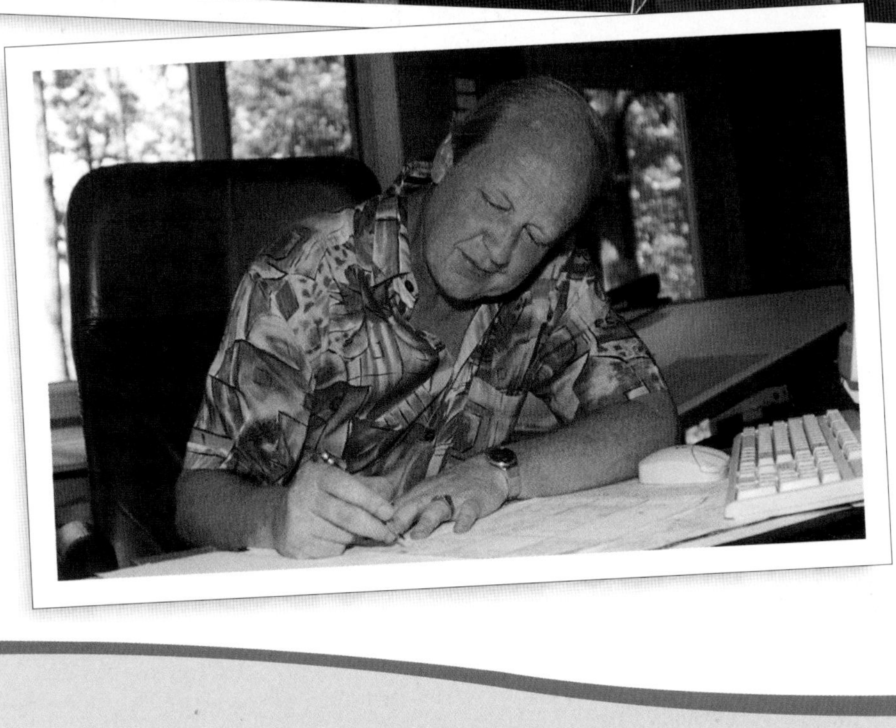

Above:

TAKING CARE OF THE CAT

From the beginning, Jim worked tirelessly on the comic strip and related products, helping Garfield claw his way to superstardom.

Left:

KING OF CARTOONS

Today, Jim still keeps his paw, er, hand in the business, producing the daily strip and providing creative direction for the feisty orange feline.

Cartoon Counterparts

It's a family affair: Jim named Garfield after his grandfather, James A. Garfield Davis, and modeled Jon Arbuckle's family after his own mother, father, and brother.

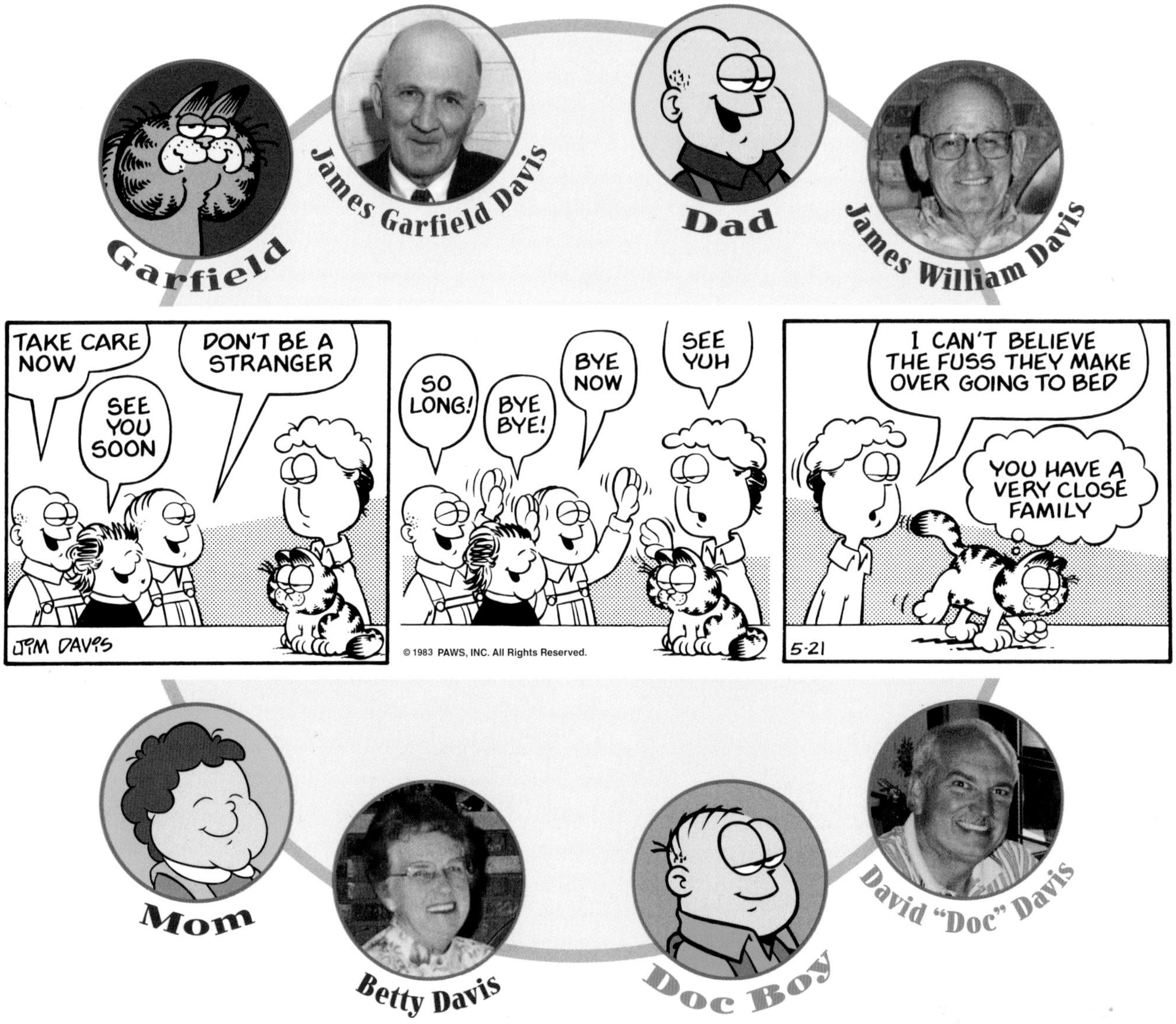
Garfield
James Garfield Davis
Dad
James William Davis
TAKE CARE NOW
SEE YOU SOON
DON'T BE A STRANGER
JIM DAVIS
SO LONG!
BYE BYE!
BYE NOW
SEE YUH
© 1983 PAWS, INC. All Rights Reserved.
I CAN'T BELIEVE THE FUSS THEY MAKE OVER GOING TO BED
YOU HAVE A VERY CLOSE FAMILY
5-21
Mom
Betty Davis
Doc Boy
David "Doc" Davis

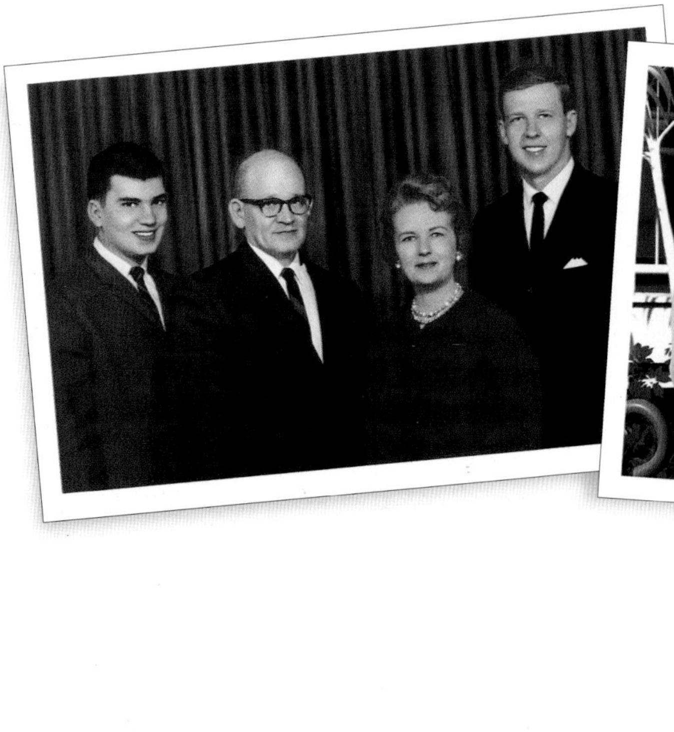

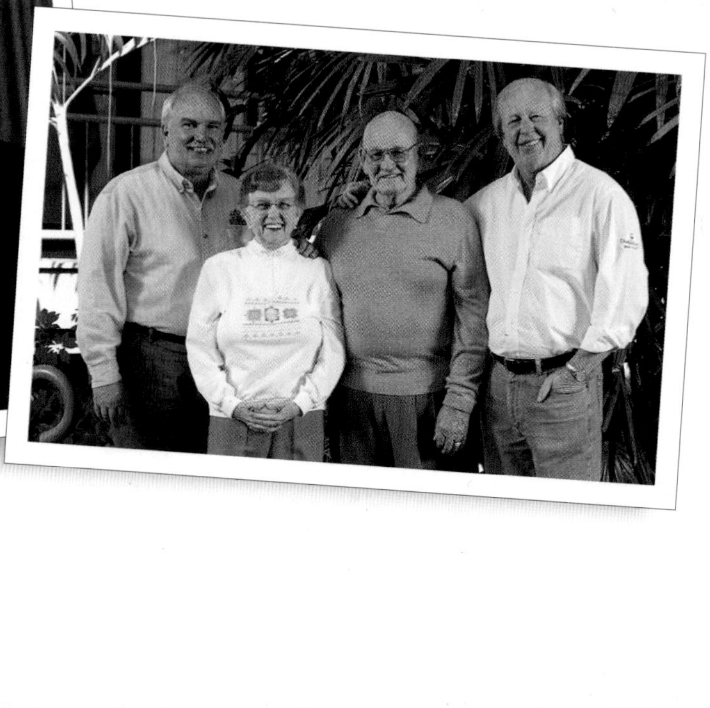

Right and far right: The Davis clan in 1965 and 2002.

The Creative Process

"When I write the comic strip, it's like watching a TV in my head. I put Garfield into a situation—on a diet, camping, something—and I watch him, and ask myself, 'What would he do? Where would he go? What would he say? What would the other characters do and say?' I watch Garfield until he does something funny, back up three frames, and cut it off."

–Jim Davis

RELEASE MY HAND, GARFIELD
YOU RELEASE HAMBURGER, I RELEASE HAND

JIM DAVIS
5-5
© 1983 PAWS, INC. All Rights Reserved.
RELEASE MY HAND, GARFIELD
YOU RELEASE HAMBURGER, I RELEASE HAND

Left and below: Jim's roughs were created directly on bond paper using a felt-tip pen, without the aid of penciled guidelines or an eraser. Garfield's humor, personality, and charm really shine through in these simplified, spontaneous drawings.

Z
Z
WHIMPER
NO, ODIE, GARFIELD ISN'T DEAD. HE'S JUST A HARD CORE SLEEPER
Z

Z
JIM DAVIS
© 1984 PAWS, INC. All Rights Reserved.
Z
WHIMPER
NO, ODIE, GARFIELD ISN'T DEAD. HE'S JUST A HARD-CORE SLEEPER
7-26

Z

Here's to Garfield

In 1982 *Garfield* joined an elite few comic strips syndicated in more than 1,000 newspapers. Five years later, *Garfield* became one of only four strips to run in more than 2,000 papers. Today, the cat is the undisputed king of the comic-strip jungle, running in more than 2,500 newspapers worldwide.

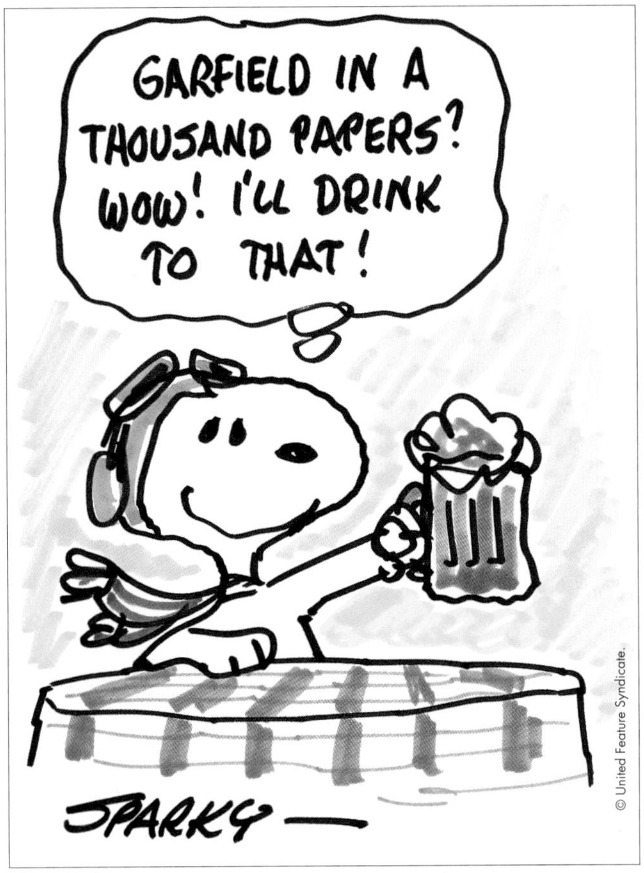
GARFIELD IN A THOUSAND PAPERS? WOW! I'LL DRINK TO THAT!
SPARKY

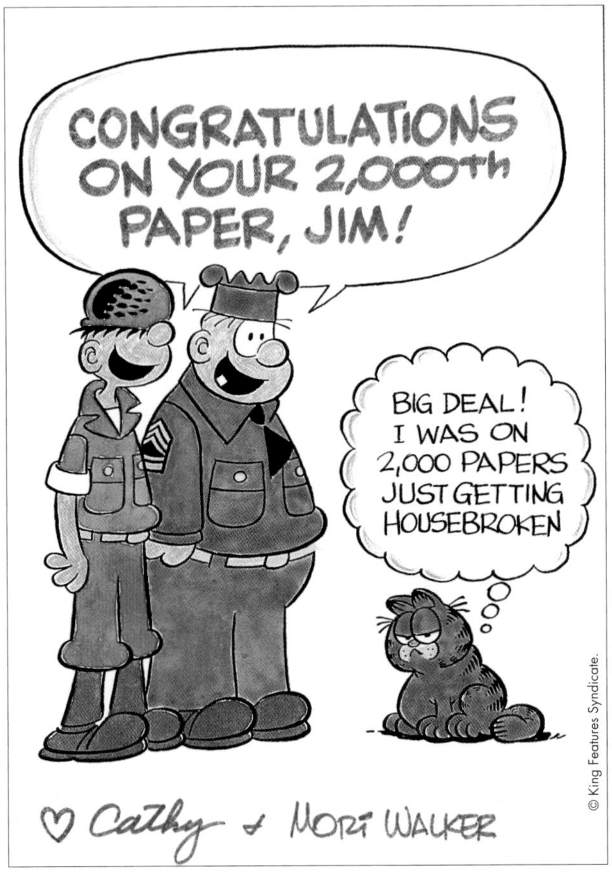
CONGRATULATIONS ON YOUR 2,000th PAPER, JIM!
BIG DEAL! I WAS ON 2,000 PAPERS JUST GETTING HOUSEBROKEN
♡ Cathy + MORT WALKER

Peanuts creator Charles M. Schulz and *Beetle Bailey* cartoonist Mort Walker pay tribute to the titanic tabby.

You've Come a Long Way, Kitty!

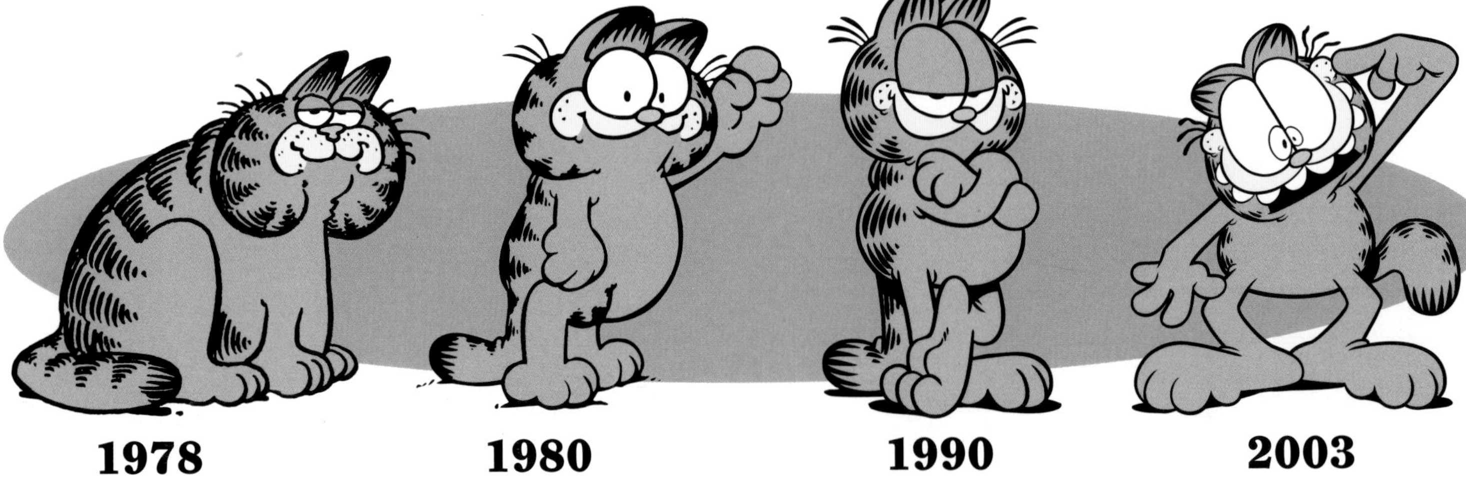
1978
1980
1990
2003

CHAPTER TWO

Comics Cavalcade

Here's a sampler platter of Garfield strips from the past twenty-five years, complete with a side order of comments and quips from the chef, Jim Davis. Dig in!

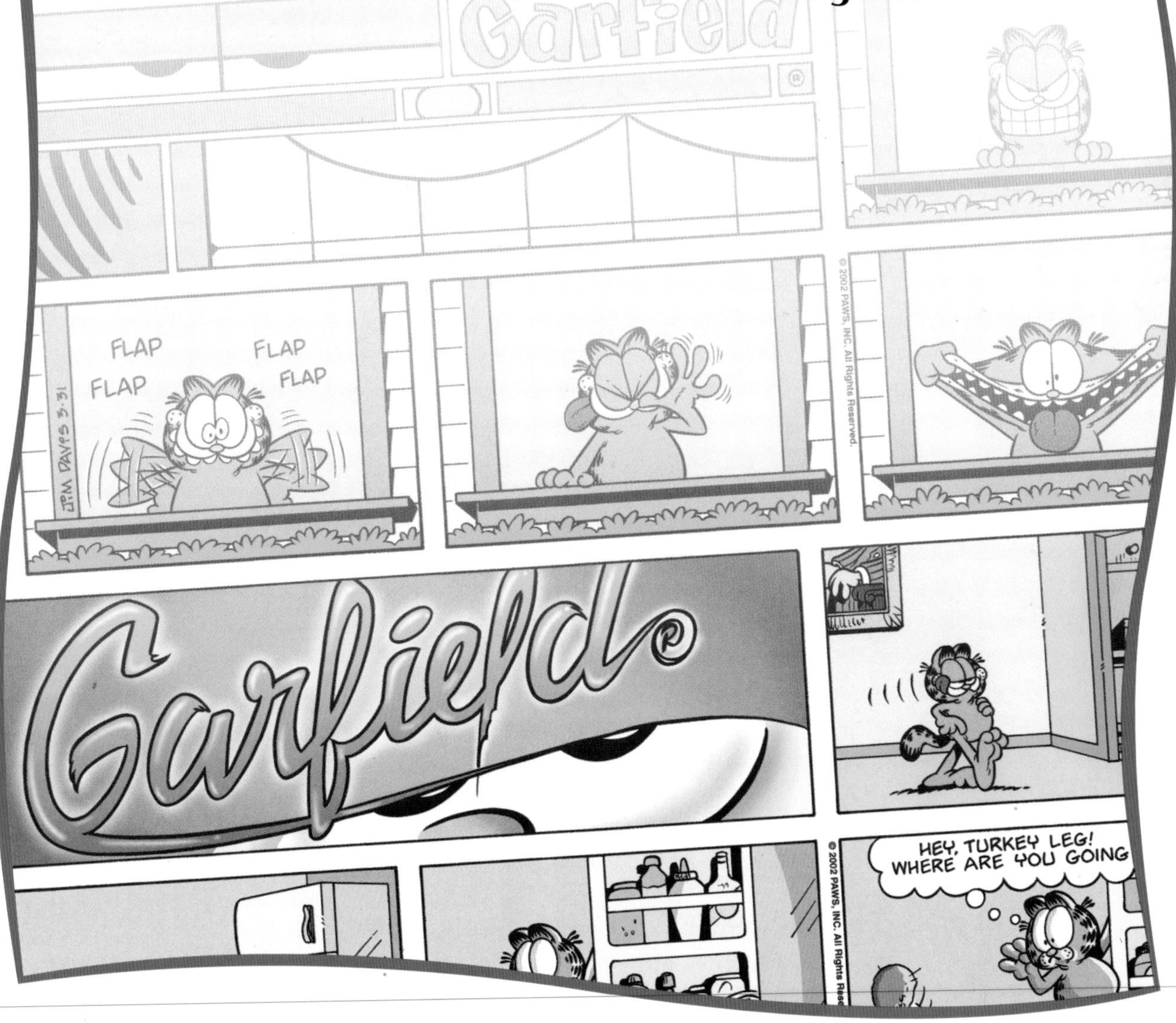
FLAP
FLAP
FLAP
FLAP
JPM DAVPS 3-31
© 2002 PAWS, INC. All Rights Reserved.
Garfield
HEY, TURKEY LEG! WHERE ARE YOU GOING

1978

HERE, GARFIELD, ...BEG.
6/28
EEYOUCH!!
SWIPE!
GROVELING IS NOT ONE OF MY STRONG SUITS.
© 1978 PAWS, INC. All Rights Reserved.
JIM DAVIS

"From the outset, Garfield established who the real master was in this relationship."

IS THAT ALL YOU HAVE, THE ONE SUITCASE?
NOT EXACTLY
HERE BOY!
© 1978 PAWS, INC. All Rights Reserved.
OH, LAWSEY, LAWSEY, LAWSEY.
8-8
JIM DAVIS

"Odie first slobbers onto the scene. Originally, Odie was Lyman's dog. I introduced Lyman to give Jon someone to talk to, but found that device unnecessary after a while. People still ask whatever happened to Lyman. I'll just say this: Don't look in Jon's basement!"

SOME PEOPLE HAVE ANXIETY ATTACKS. SOME PEOPLE HAVE GAS ATTACKS
JIM DAVIS
I HAVE NAP ATTACKS
© 1978 PAWS, INC. All Rights Reserved.
11-6
ZZZZZ

"In the early days of the strip, I'd work for long stretches and get so tired that I'd literally fall asleep in the middle of a drawing. I thought these 'nap attacks' would be funny to use in the strip. I started getting positive fan mail about them, so I did more strips."

SPRING IS HERE
THE WARM SPRING SUN IS COAXING TREES TO BUD AND FLOWERS TO BLOOM. FLEDGLING SONGBIRDS ARE TESTING THEIR LILTING VOICES. SOFT SPRING ZEPHYRS ARE WAFTING THE SWEET SCENT OF LILACS. SPRING IS HERE
© 1979 PAWS, INC. All Rights Reserved.
BIG, FAT HAIRY DEAL
4-3
JIM DAVIS

"The phrase that pays: The first appearance of this famous 'Garfism.' Those words did as much as anything to establish Garfield's personality."

PURRRR
PURRR
TAPPITY TAPPITY TAPPITY
TAPPITY TAPPITY TAPPITY
© 1979 PAWS, INC. All Rights Reserved.
5-6
SCRATCH! SCRATCH! SCRATCH! SCRATCH!
GOOD MORNING, SUNSHINE. WELCOME TO ANOTHER GLORIOUS, FUN-FILLED DAY WITH YOUR FAVORITE PET!
I'M SO HAPPY TO OWN A CAT, I COULD JUST THROW UP
JIM DAVIS

"We used this for the opening sequence of Garfield's first TV special, *Here Comes Garfield*—although with one minor change. The network wouldn't let us show Garfield putting his paws around Jon's neck, so I changed the visual to Garfield grabbing and shaking Jon's cheeks."

1980

I KNOW YOU CATS ARE INQUISITIVE BY NATURE, GARFIELD
© 1980 PAWS, INC. All Rights Reserved.
AND I KNOW THIS IS YOUR HOME AS WELL AS MINE...
BUT STAY OUT OF MY UNDERWEAR DRAWER!!
3-19
JIM DAVIS

"I wrote this in my underwear."

GRAB!
STRETCH
PTING!
© 1980 PAWS, INC. All Rights Reserved.
KABOING!
ZOOM!
FLAP
FLAP
FLAP
THAT'S THE DARNDEST THING I'VE EVER SEEN
JIM DAVIS
5-25

"I worked really hard to get the drawing and action right on this strip. I love the deadpan humor of the last line."

MY, MY, A CHOCOLATE COVERED PEANUT
2-12
RIP!
JIM DAVIS
I THINK I NEED A BIGGER CAT SUIT
© 1981 PAWS, INC. All Rights Reserved.

"I always tell people Garfield is a human in a cat suit."

ONCE AGAIN I VENTURE INTO THE WILDERNESS IN SEARCH OF QUARRY
JIM DAVIS
4-30
I SPOT MY PREY, BUT I MUST MAKE A CLEAN KILL
HAMBURGERS CAN BE VICIOUS IF THEY'RE ONLY WOUNDED
© 1981 PAWS, INC. All Rights Reserved.

"Forget the mice; Garfield's after bigger game."

JIM DAVIS
SCRATCH SCRATCH SCRATCH
SCRATCH SCRATCH
© 1981 PAWS, INC. All Rights Reserved.
TIMBER
10-22

"I love visual humor."

1982

JIM DAVIS
1-11
GARFIELD! WHAT HAPPENED!
QUICK! GET THE LICENSE NUMBER OF THAT DOG!
© 1982 PAWS, INC. All Rights Reserved.

"Every dog has his day: Odie finally gets the upper paw."

I LOVE SHOW BUSINESS. GIMME THE FULL MOON. GIMME THE FENCE
3-24
© 1982 PAWS, INC. All Rights Reserved.
KAWHOCK!
JIM DAVIS
GIMME THE BROKEN TEETH. GIMME THE MULTIPLE LACERATIONS

"A little vaudeville goes a long way."

UH-OH
JIM DAVIS
4-9
© 1982 PAWS, INC. All Rights Reserved.

"When I go on a diet, Garfield goes on one, too."

JIM DAVIS
DINNERTIME, GARFIELD!
BANZAI
GARFIELD
3-26
© 1983 PAWS, INC. All Rights Reserved.

"Another defining moment in Garfield's love for lasagna, nature's most perfect food."

GARFIELD
SKITTER SKITTER SKITTER
THAT'S ODD... TWO LITTLE BUGS IN FULL SHAKESPEAREAN DRESS
ROMEO, ROMEO, WHEREFORE ART THOU, ROMEO?
I'M RIGHT HERE, JULIET
I BRING BAD NEWS, JULIE BABY. OUR FAMILIES ARE FEUDING AND DON'T WANT US TO DATE ANYMORE
OH NO!
THAT DOES IT! LET'S DIE IN EACH OTHER'S ARMS AND LIVE TOGETHER IN ETERNITY
HOW DO WE DO THAT?
JIM DAVIS
5-22
HERE'S HOW
SQUASH
I'M NOT ONE TO FOOL WITH GREAT LITERATURE
© 1983 PAWS, INC. All Rights Reserved.

"To squash, or not to squash? *That* is a stupid question."

1984

I AM PROUD TO BE A PET. PETS LEND A TOUCH OF ELEGANCE TO A HOME
SLUP SLUP
JIM DAVIS
© 1984 PAWS, INC. All Rights Reserved.
I AM PROUD TO BE A CAT
SLUP SLUP
3-7

"You can lead a dog to water, but you can't make him think."

GARFIELD
YAWN
IT'S BEDDY-BYE TIME AGAIN
TONIGHT I THINK I'LL TAKE A DEEP BREATH, SLOWLY CLOSE MY EYES AND SAVOR THE HEAVY FEELING OF SLEEP GRADUALLY OVERTAKING MY BODY
PAT! PAT! PAT!
THEN AGAIN IT WOULD BE FUN TO HAVE A CUP OF COFFEE AND TOSS AND TURN FOR A COUPLE OF HOURS, THEN SLEEP 'TIL NOON
© 1984 PAWS, INC. All Rights Reserved.
OR MAYBE I'LL RUN AROUND THE BLOCK, COLLAPSE INTO BED EXHAUSTED AND FALL ASLEEP INSTANTLY
OR I COULD WATCH THE ALL-NIGHT MOVIES ON TV UNTIL MY EYELIDS GET SO HEAVY I COULDN'T POSSIBLY HOLD THEM OPEN ANY LONGER
SIGH... SO MUCH SLEEPING TO DO AND SO FEW NIGHTS
JIM DAVIS
6-24

"Sleep. The best eighteen hours of Garfield's day."

I HAVE A DATE WITH MARY LOU TONIGHT AND I'M GOING TO CHARM HER OUT OF HER SOCKS
I'M GOING TO PLAY IT REAL COOL. I'M GOING TO QUOTE POETRY AND BE REAL SUAVE
SHE'LL BE PUTTY IN MY HANDS
YOUR TIE IS IN YOUR COFFEE
JIM DAVIS 4-25
© 1985 PAWS, INC. All Rights Reserved.

"Classic Jon."

I THINK I'LL EXERCISE
I'D BETTER START SLOWLY
TODAY I SHALL ATTEMPT TO REGISTER A PULSE
JIM DAVIS 5-27
© 1985 PAWS, INC. All Rights Reserved.

"Exercise is one of my favorite spectator sports."

THERE'S NOTHING MORE ANNOYING THAN A LEAKY FAUCET
DRIP
DRIP
DRIP
DRIP
DRIP
DRIP
DRIP
UNLESS IT'S A LEAKY DOG
DRIP
DRIP
DRIP
JIM DAVIS 7-17
© 1985 PAWS, INC. All Rights Reserved.

"Fun Fact: Dogs contain 90% of the world's drool supply."

1986

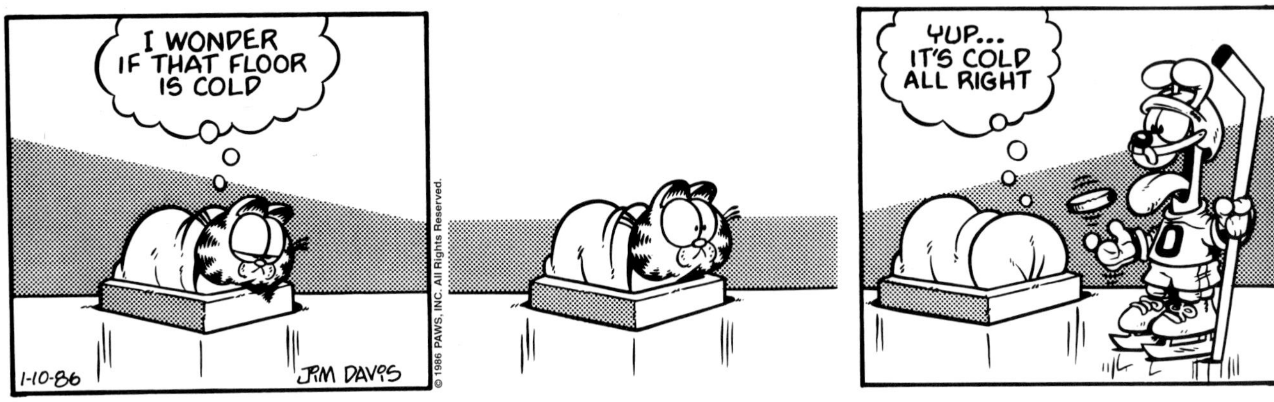
I WONDER IF THAT FLOOR IS COLD
1-10-86
JIM DAVIS
© 1986 PAWS, INC. All Rights Reserved.
YUP... IT'S COLD ALL RIGHT

"Absurd is the word. I like to keep the readers on their toes by playing with the strip's reality."

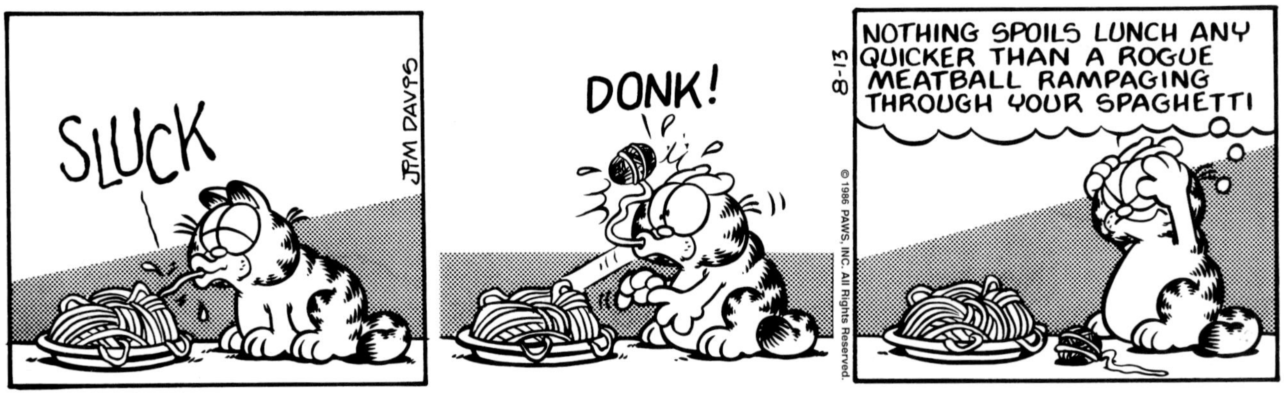
SLUCK
JIM DAVIS
DONK!
8-13
© 1986 PAWS, INC. All Rights Reserved.
NOTHING SPOILS LUNCH ANY QUICKER THAN A ROGUE MEATBALL RAMPAGING THROUGH YOUR SPAGHETTI

"'Rogue meatball rampaging' . . . full of sound and fury—signifying silliness."

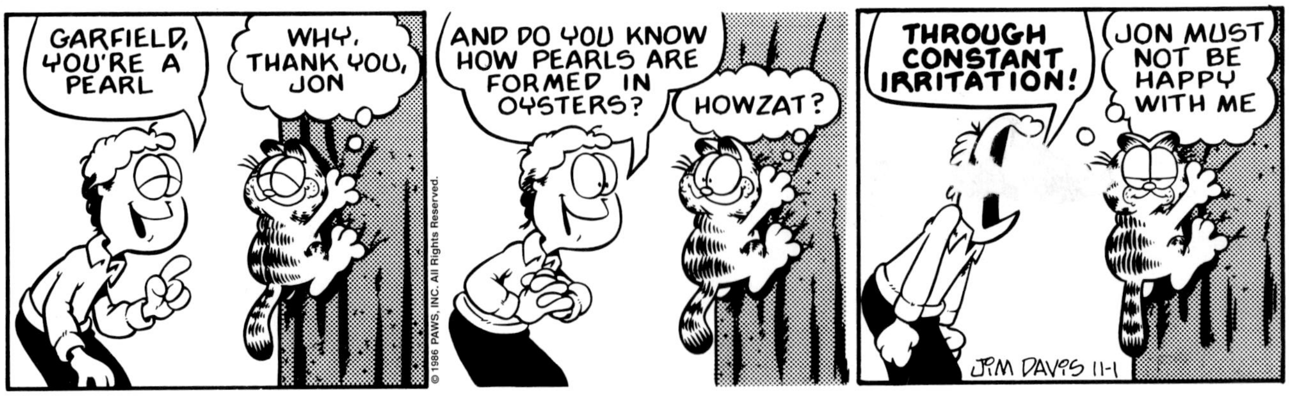
GARFIELD, YOU'RE A PEARL
WHY, THANK YOU, JON
© 1986 PAWS, INC. All Rights Reserved.
AND DO YOU KNOW HOW PEARLS ARE FORMED IN OYSTERS?
HOWZAT?
THROUGH CONSTANT IRRITATION!
JON MUST NOT BE HAPPY WITH ME
JIM DAVIS 11-1

"One of your basic science-based gags."

ISN'T THIS GREAT, GARFIELD? WE HAVE A WHOLE DAY OF FISHING AHEAD OF US!
HOTCHA
HEY! WHERE'S THE BAIT?
BAIT?
GARFIELD!
I THOUGHT IT WAS SUSHI
JIM DAVIS 1-12
© 1987 PAWS, INC. All Rights Reserved.

"The only sports I feature in the strip are golf and fishing, which, not coincidentally, are my two favorite pastimes."

GARFIELD
© 1987 PAWS, INC. All Rights Reserved.
JIM DAVIS 5-31

"Kids tend to read the Sunday comics more than the dailies, so I try to throw in a lot of sight gags to appeal to them."

1988

DO YOU KNOW HOW TO SPOT A LAZY PERSON?
A TRULY LAZY PERSON NEVER FINISHES ANY...
Z
JIM DAVIS 5-28
© 1988 PAWS, INC. All Rights Reserved.

"Garfield is so lazy, he thinks yawning is an exercise."

GARFIELD
WHEW! I WAS BEGINNING TO THINK I'D NEVER GET FULL. BURP!
LAH-LAH-LAH-LAH-LAH LAH-LAAAAAAHHH
I HOPE THE WRITERS' STRIKE ENDS SOON
AND NOW, BACK TO THE BINKY THE CLOWN SHOW!
HEEEEEEEY, KIDS!!!
GOOD MORNING, BINKY!
IT'S A BEAUTIFUL DAY IN BINKYLAND. LET'S SAY HELLO TO MR. SUN!
HELLO, MR. SUN
OH LOOK! HERE COMES MR. FISH TO VISIT US!
GOOD MORNING, MR. FISH. KIDS, CAN YOU SAY HELLO TO...
© 1988 PAWS, INC. All Rights Reserved.
AAAYIEEEEE!!!
HELLO, MR. PIRANHA
JIM DAVIS 9-4

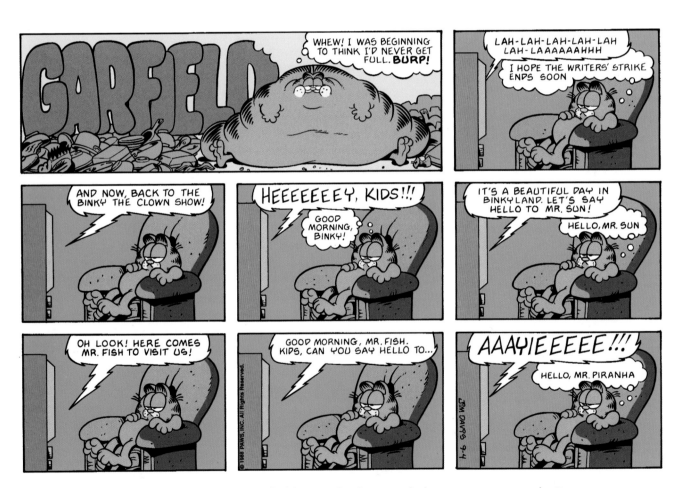

"In this logo box, Garfield is so fat he needs his own area code."

© 1989 PAWS, INC. All Rights Reserved.
WHIRR
2-14
JIM DAVIS

"Cartoony, ain't it?"

SO LONG, SPIDER
FLINK
© 1989 PAWS, INC. All Rights Reserved.
GARFIELD
JIM DAVIS
3-15

"Garfield hates it when that happens . . . and so does the spider."

SHOULD I BE MEAN OR LAZY TODAY?...
© 1989 PAWS, INC. All Rights Reserved.
OR, MAYBE A HAPPY MEDIUM...
I'LL JUST LIE HERE AND BITE ANYONE WHO TRIPS OVER ME
JIM DAVIS
9-12

"That's Garfield in a nutshell."

1990

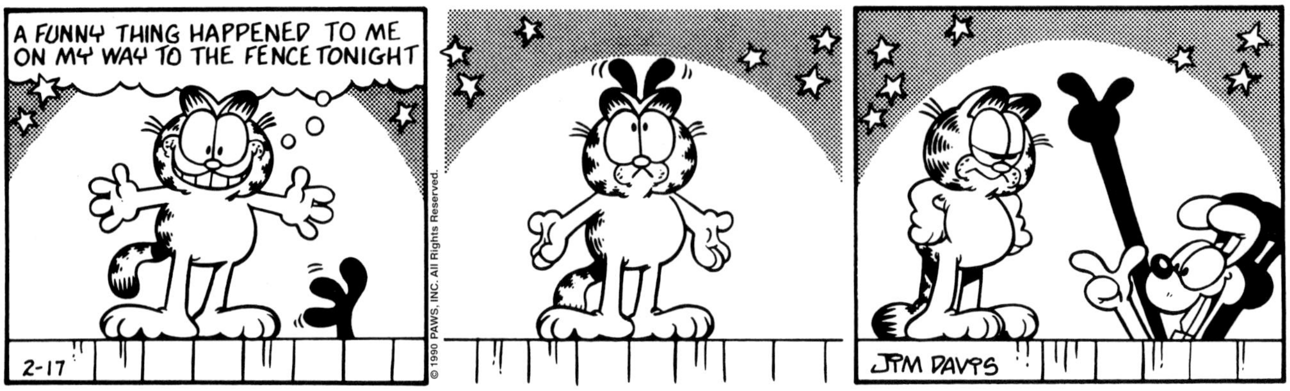
A FUNNY THING HAPPENED TO ME ON MY WAY TO THE FENCE TONIGHT
© 1990 PAWS, INC. All Rights Reserved.

"I thought this was funny in grade school, and I still think it's funny today."

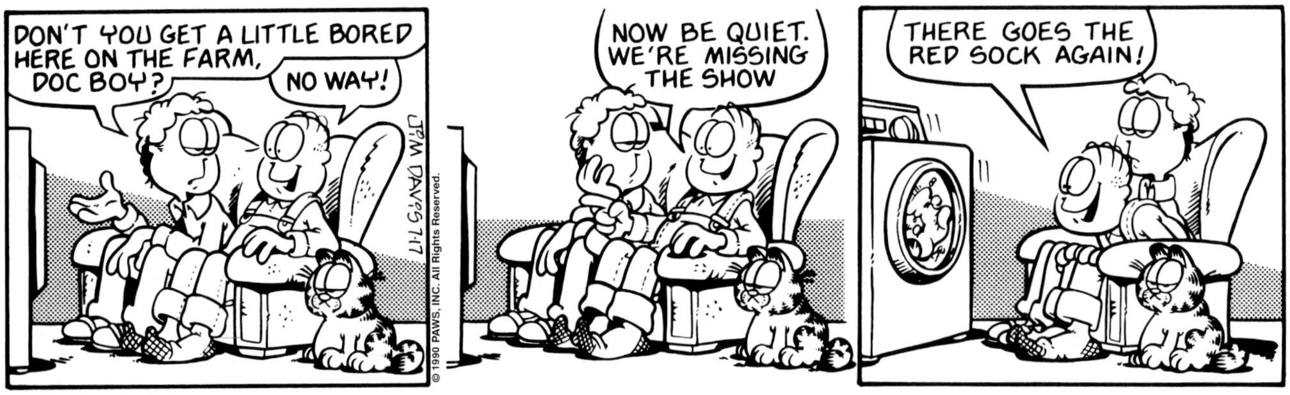
DON'T YOU GET A LITTLE BORED HERE ON THE FARM, DOC BOY?
NO WAY!
© 1990 PAWS, INC. All Rights Reserved.
NOW BE QUIET. WE'RE MISSING THE SHOW
THERE GOES THE RED SOCK AGAIN!

"Brother, can you spare a brain? Doc Boy is based on my own brother, Dave 'Doc' Davis."

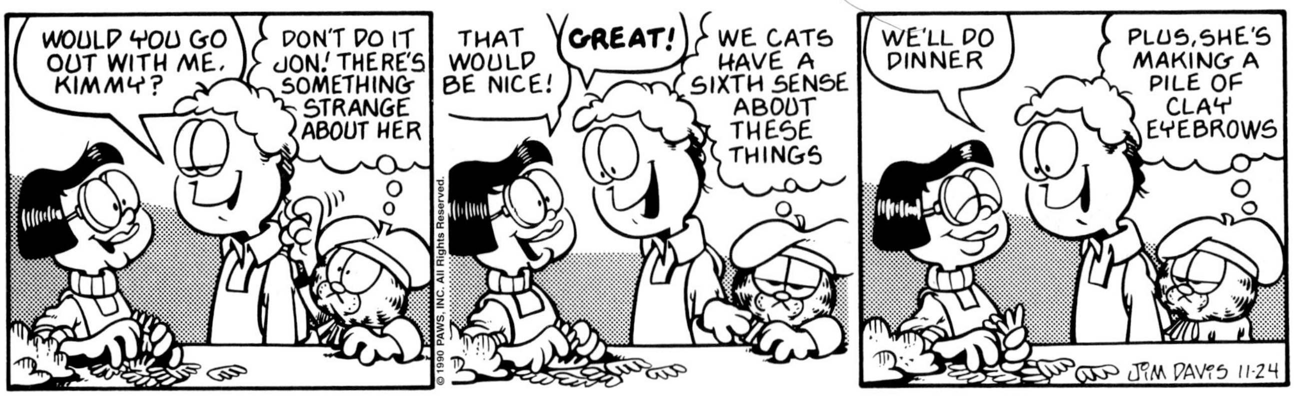
WOULD YOU GO OUT WITH ME, KIMMY?
DON'T DO IT JON! THERE'S SOMETHING STRANGE ABOUT HER
© 1990 PAWS, INC. All Rights Reserved.
THAT WOULD BE NICE!
GREAT!
WE CATS HAVE A SIXTH SENSE ABOUT THESE THINGS
WE'LL DO DINNER
PLUS, SHE'S MAKING A PILE OF CLAY EYEBROWS

"Love is blind . . . and weird, too."

I WISH I HAD A LITTLE PIECE OF LAND...
ABOUT A MILE LONG, AND AN INCH WIDE
YESSIR, MY VERY OWN SPAGHETTI FARM
© 1991 PAWS, INC. All Rights Reserved.
JIM DAVIS 11-1

" . . . with a silo full of puttanesca sauce!"

Garfield
SLURK!
10-9-8-7-6-5...
4-3-2-1...
PONG!
IGNITION...
GOOD MORNING, JON!
LIFT-OFF... WE HAVE LIFT-OFF
© 1991 PAWS, INC. All Rights Reserved.
JIM DAVIS 2-3

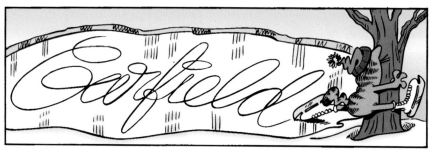

"Garfield's up for a cup! I think more cats would drink coffee if they, like Garfield, had opposable thumbs."

1992

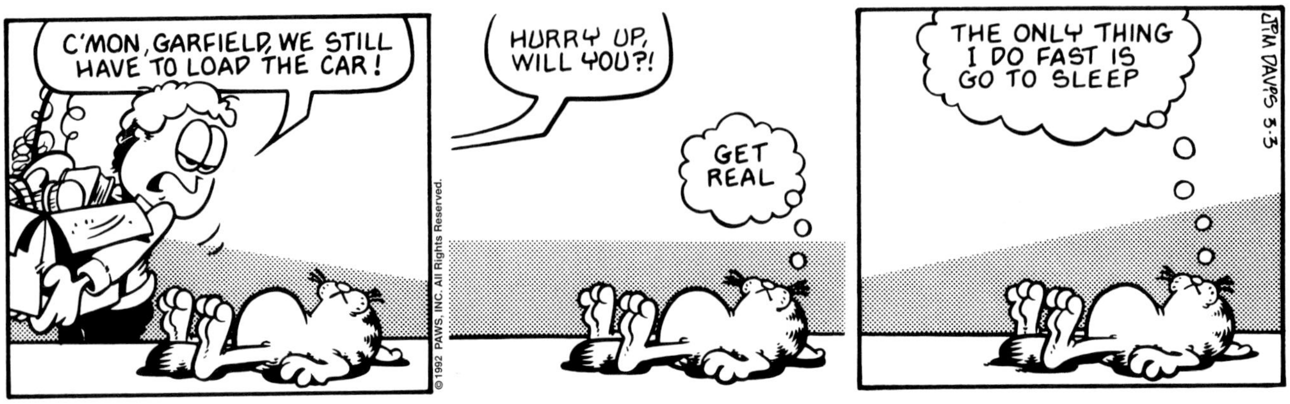
C'MON, GARFIELD, WE STILL HAVE TO LOAD THE CAR!
HURRY UP, WILL YOU?!
GET REAL
THE ONLY THING I DO FAST IS GO TO SLEEP
JIM DAVIS 5-3
© 1992 PAWS, INC. All Rights Reserved.

"I sometimes structure the strip so that the last panel is a stand-alone 'Garfism.'"

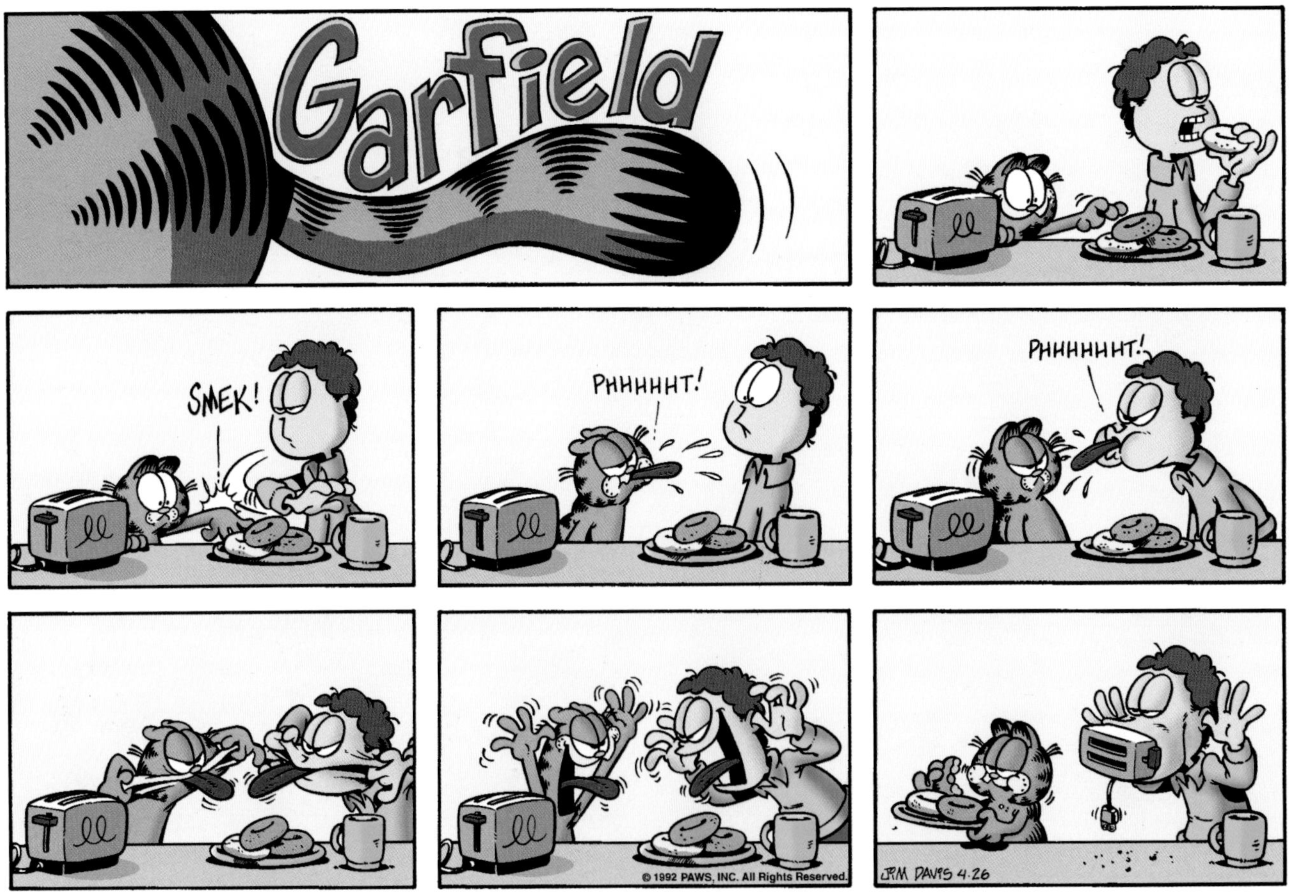
Garfield
SMEK!
PHHHHHT!
PHHHHHHHT!
© 1992 PAWS, INC. All Rights Reserved.
JIM DAVIS 4-26

"A little in-your-face humor . . . "

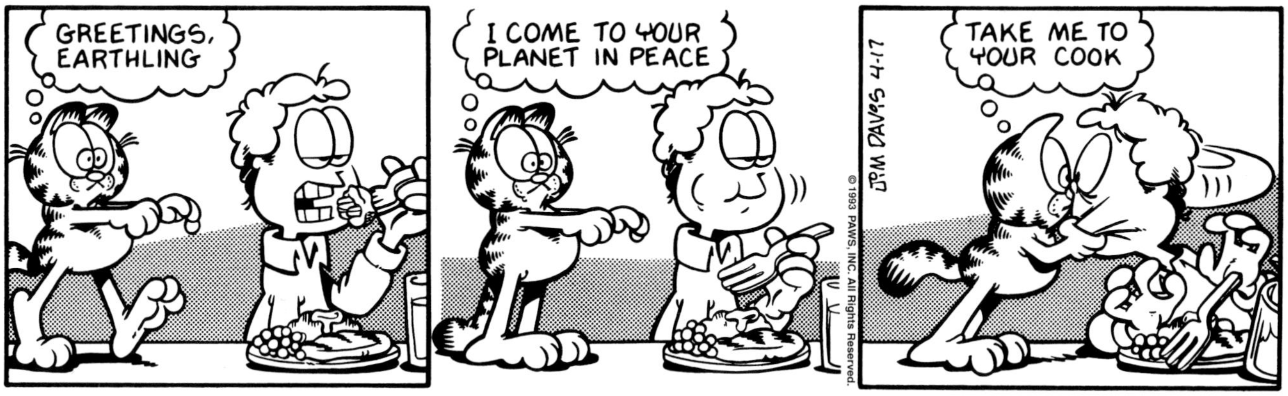
GREETINGS, EARTHLING
I COME TO YOUR PLANET IN PEACE
TAKE ME TO YOUR COOK
JIM DAVIS 4-17
© 1993 PAWS, INC. All Rights Reserved.

"One of my guilty pleasures is watching schlocky old B movies."

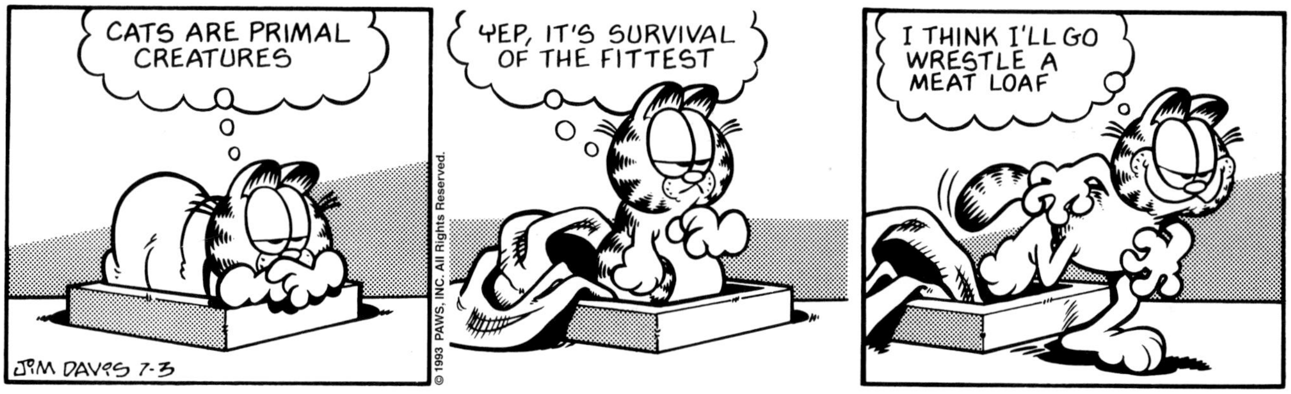
CATS ARE PRIMAL CREATURES
YEP, IT'S SURVIVAL OF THE FITTEST
I THINK I'LL GO WRESTLE A MEAT LOAF
JIM DAVIS 7-3
© 1993 PAWS, INC. All Rights Reserved.

"Make that survival of the fattest."

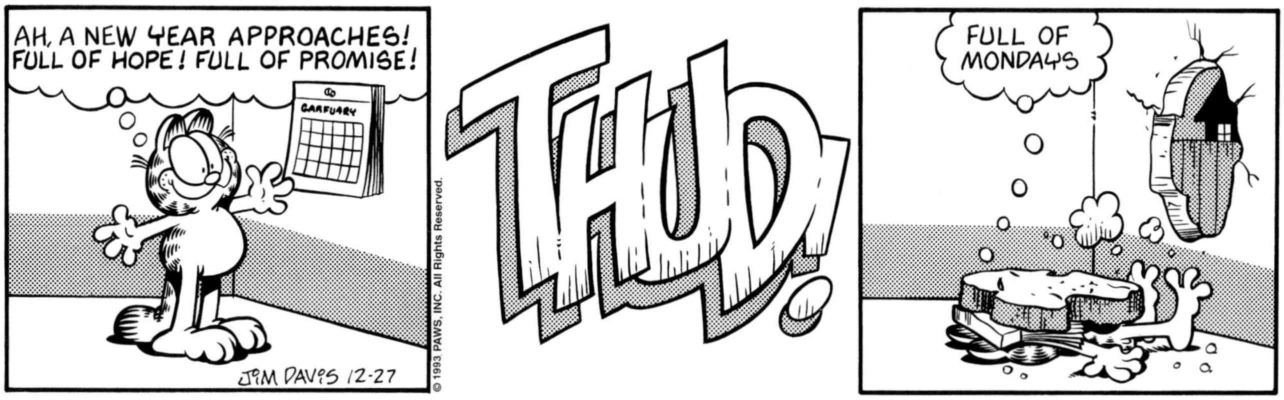
AH, A NEW YEAR APPROACHES! FULL OF HOPE! FULL OF PROMISE!
GARFUARY
JIM DAVIS 12-27
© 1993 PAWS, INC. All Rights Reserved.
THUD!
FULL OF MONDAYS

"Garfield hates Mondays so much that we actually created a 'No Mondays' calendar."

1994

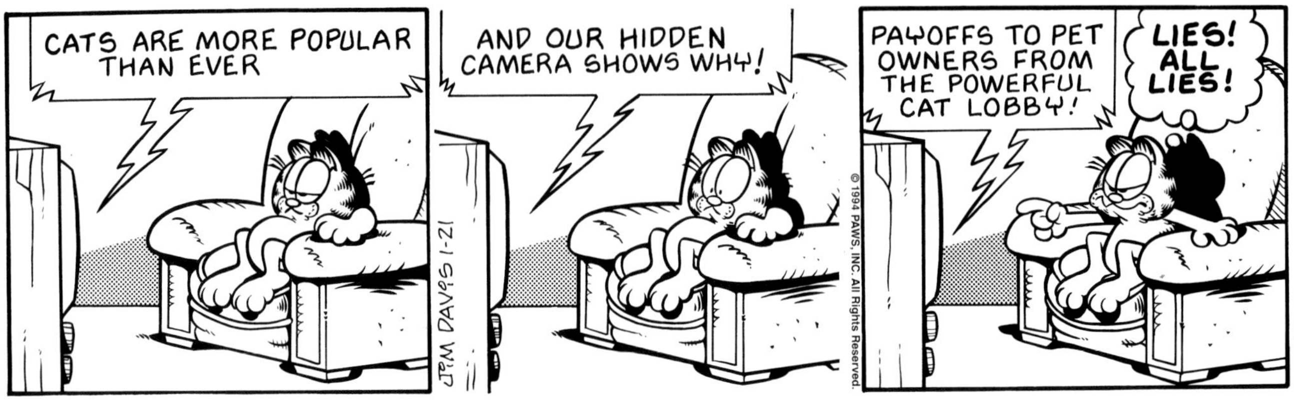
CATS ARE MORE POPULAR THAN EVER
JIM DAVIS 1-21
AND OUR HIDDEN CAMERA SHOWS WHY!
© 1994 PAWS, INC. All Rights Reserved.
PAYOFFS TO PET OWNERS FROM THE POWERFUL CAT LOBBY!
LIES! ALL LIES!

"This is about as political as I get in the strip."

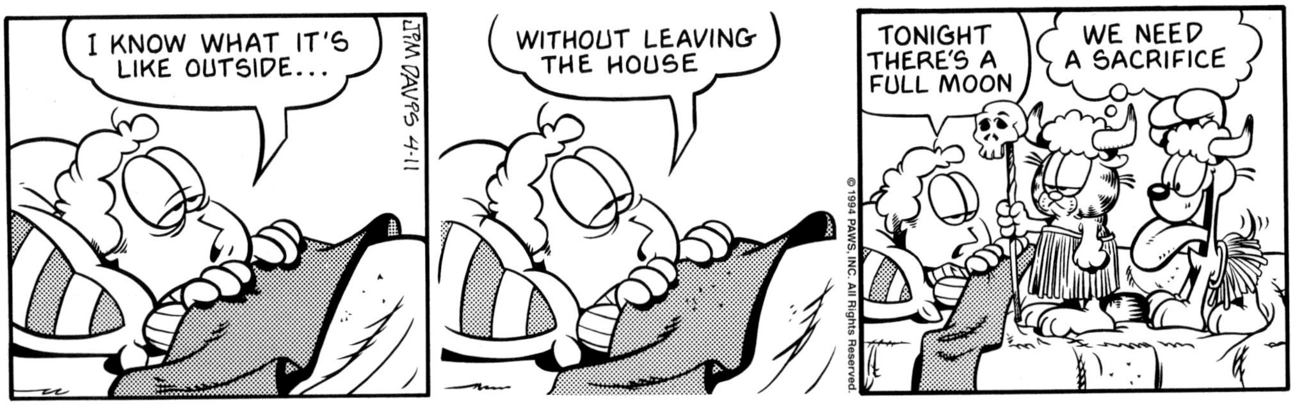
I KNOW WHAT IT'S LIKE OUTSIDE...
JIM DAVIS 4-11
WITHOUT LEAVING THE HOUSE
© 1994 PAWS, INC. All Rights Reserved.
TONIGHT THERE'S A FULL MOON
WE NEED A SACRIFICE

"Dressing the pets up is always a guaranteed laugh."

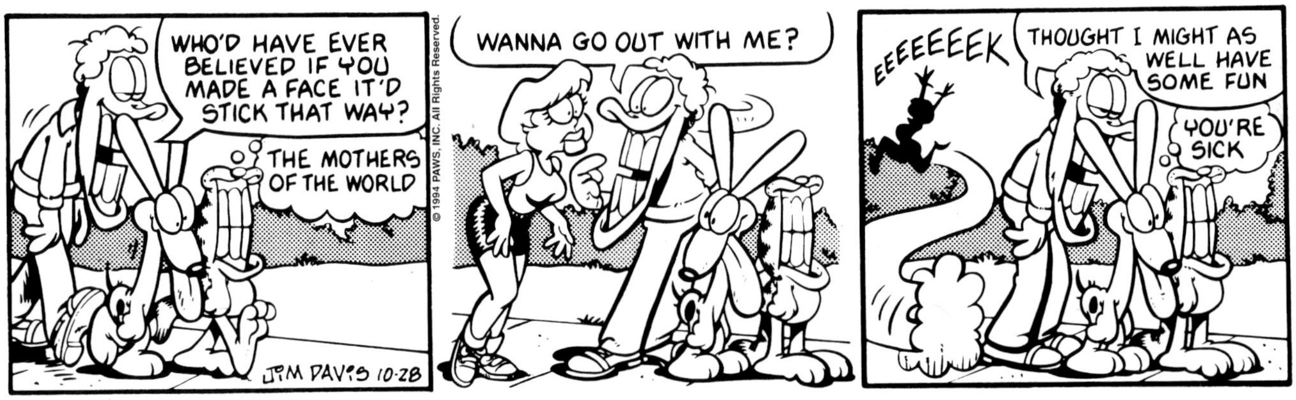
WHO'D HAVE EVER BELIEVED IF YOU MADE A FACE IT'D STICK THAT WAY?
THE MOTHERS OF THE WORLD
JIM DAVIS 10-28
© 1994 PAWS, INC. All Rights Reserved.
WANNA GO OUT WITH ME?
EEEEEEEK
THOUGHT I MIGHT AS WELL HAVE SOME FUN
YOU'RE SICK

"Sometimes it's good to stretch as an artist."

YOU'RE LAZY, GARFIELD
I HAPPEN TO BE CONDUCTING A SCIENTIFIC EXPERIMENT, THANK YOU
© 1995 PAWS, INC. All Rights Reserved.
LAZY, LAZY
I'M TESTING THE FIRST LAW OF PHYSICS...
LAZY, LAZY, LAZY, LAZY!
"BODIES AT REST TEND TO STAY AT REST"
JIM DAVIS 3-2

"Who says science isn't funny?"

GARFIELD
SPROING
TWANG
THOT!
SPROING
TWANG
THOT!
JIM DAVIS 7-23
SPROING
TWANG
THOT!
SPROING
TWANG
©1995 PAWS, INC. All Rights Reserved.
THOT
PULL!
GARFIELD!!
SPROING
BREAD

"Just another example of pets' inhumanity to man."

1996

NICE HAT
HAT?
YOU MUST BE REFERRING TO MY HAM HOLDER
JIM DAVIS 2-13
© 1996 PAWS, INC. All Rights Reserved.

"Pork is the funniest of meats."

GARFIELD®
SO YOU'RE GOING TO BE EIGHTEEN SOON, HUH GARFIELD?
THANKS FOR THE REMINDER
I REMEMBER BACK ON THE FARM, WHEN I TURNED EIGHTEEN I REALLY CUT LOOSE
UH-HUH
MY BUDDIES AND I WENT OUT COW TIPPING
PANT PANT PANT PANT
TIP
HUH? HUH? WAS THAT FUN OR WHAT?
WHATEVER MILKS YOUR GUERNSEY
PANT PANT PANT

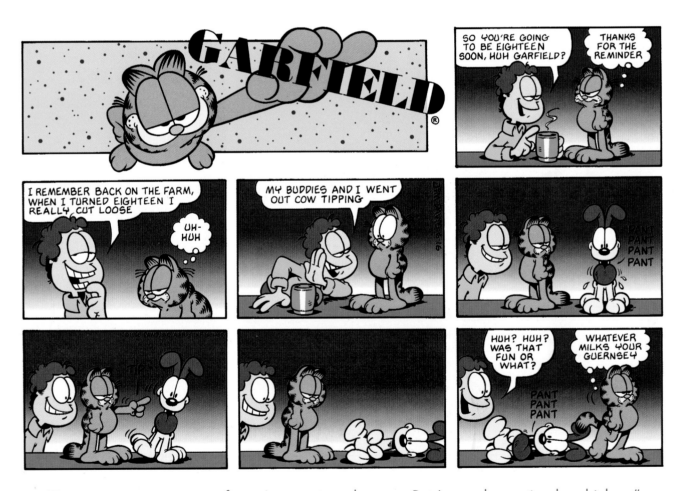

"Despite growing up on a farm, I never tipped a cow. But I once hypnotized a chicken."

HEY....THIS ISN'T WATER...
IT'S CHICKEN STOCK!
THERE GOES MY SPARROW GUMBO
JIM DAVIS 7-8
© 1997 PAWS, INC. All Rights Reserved.

"I'm a sucker for snappy wordplay."

CHECK OUT THAT CUTE GIRL OVER THERE!
JIM DAVIS 7-15
AND CHECK OUT HER BIG BOYFRIEND RETURNING WITH ICE CREAM!
© 1997 PAWS, INC. All Rights Reserved.
ACTUALLY, IT'S KIND OF REFRESHING

"Eat your heart out, Madonna!"

JIM DAVIS 11-18
PUMPA
PUMPA
PUMPA
© 1997 PAWS, INC. All Rights Reserved.
IDLE PAWS ARE THE DEVIL'S WORKSHOP

"Don't try this at home, kids."

Editor's note: Garfield daily strips began appearing in color in 1997.

1998

GARFIELD, ALL YOU THINK ABOUT IS FOOD
ME, I'M READING A BOOK
"MOBY DICK"
WE'RE OUT OF TARTAR SAUCE
© 1998 PAWS, INC. All Rights Reserved.
JIM DAVIS 5-18

"Two things I like: great literature and condiments (though not necessarily in that order)."

JIM DAVIS 7-29
© 1998 PAWS, INC. All Rights Reserved.
GARFIELD!
I DON'T RECALL YOU APPLYING FOR A PERMIT TO BUILD A BAY WINDOW...

"The mousehole strips afford the opportunity to do a lot of funny sight gags."

WHEN JON HAS A BAD HAIR DAY, HE WEARS A HAT
© 1998 PAWS, INC. All Rights Reserved.
J
MUST BE HAVING A BAD **FACE** DAY
JIM DAVIS 11-18

"The best of both worlds: visual *and* verbal humor."

GARFIELD, HOW WOULD YOU LIKE A NICE TREAT?
LAY IT ON ME!
IT'S SORT OF A RAP POLKA THING
SUCKERED AGAIN!
© 1999 PAWS, INC. All Rights Reserved.
JIM DAVIS 3-29

"Rap polka. Get jiggy wit' it!"

GARFIELD
I SUPPOSE YOU'RE WONDERING WHY I HAVE THIS SACK ON MY HEAD
WELL, I HAVE THIS BIG, UGLY ZIT ON MY FACE...
AND IT LOOKS SO HORRIFIC I DON'T WANT IT SEEN
© 1999 PAWS, INC. All Rights Reserved.
DING-DONG
THAT'S MY DATE
JIM DAVIS 6-13
I HOPE SHE UNDERSTANDS

"I love the last panel. Sometimes a visual is so strong, you don't need any words."

2000

www.coffeequick.com
TIC TIC TIC
CLICK
DING-DONG
I NOW OFFICIALLY LOVE THE INTERNET
© 2000 PAWS, INC. All Rights Reserved.
JIM DAVIS 9-7

"We created an actual coffeequick.com site for this strip, just in case readers typed in the address. Sure enough, the day the strip appeared, thousands of curious fans visited the site."

GARFIELD
HOT PEPPER EATING CONTEST!
JALAPEÑO!
© 2000 PAWS, INC. All Rights Reserved.
CAYENNE!
HABANERO!
PERUVIAN DEATH PEPPER!
FOOM
YOU WIN...
THEN WHY AM I NOT HAPPY?
JIM DAVIS 9-17

"Gonna be a hot time in the ol' mouth tonight! We researched various peppers for this strip (and have the burnt taste buds to prove it)."

HOME IS WHERE YOU CAN WALK AROUND IN YOUR UNDERWEAR
HOME IS WHERE YOU CAN DRINK MILK OUT OF THE CARTON
© 2001 PAWS, INC. All Rights Reserved.
HOME IS WHERE YOU CAN SCRATCH WHERE IT ITCHES
HOME IS DISGUSTING

"The true stuff is the funniest."

GOOD TO SEE YOU AGAIN, SON. YOU'RE LOOKING WELL
THANKS... YOU TOO, DAD
© 2001 PAWS, INC. All Rights Reserved.
WELL, GOT CHORES TO DO
BETTER GO UNPACK
(SNIFF) A REAL FATHER-SON MOMENT

"It's a guy thing. This seems to have struck a chord with readers. Many fans saw themselves and their dads in this strip."

HMM...THE THREE-BEAN BURRITO LOOKS GOOD...
© 2001 PAWS, INC. All Rights Reserved.
SORRY, WE'RE OUT OF THAT
I OWE YOU ONE, IRMA

"I've always had a soft spot in my heart (and stomach) for diners. In fact, I was born with a greasy spoon in my mouth! Don't stop me, I'm on a roll! A KAISER ROLL!"

2002

I'M GOING TO MAKE A LIST OF THINGS I CAN DO TO IMPRESS WOMEN
"CAN MAKE A LIST..."
HE'S WRITING THAT IN **INK**, LADIES!
JIM DAVIS 1-9
© 2002 PAWS, INC. All Rights Reserved.

"Jon, the babe magnet, in action."

GARFIELD, HOW DO YOU EXPLAIN THIS?
HMMM...NEW MOUSE, HIGHER-THAN-AVERAGE DISPOSABLE INCOME, HEAVILY INTO BAROQUE ROCOCO, I'D SAY
JIM DAVIS 1-23
© 2002 PAWS, INC. All Rights Reserved.

"'Baroque rococo' is a funny phrase. I'm a sucker for a hard *k* sound. 'Cabbage' is funny; 'lettuce'—not funny."

LISTEN TO ODIE HOWL LIKE ONE OF HIS WOLF ANCESTORS
EVEN AFTER YEARS OF DOMESTICATION, A DOG IS STILL IN TOUCH WITH PRIMAL URGES A THOUSAND YEARS OLD
LOST HIS INTERNET CONNECTION
JIM DAVIS 2-12
© 2002 PAWS, INC. All Rights Reserved.

"Little-known fact: Odie once spent six hours watching live WebCam footage of a fire hydrant."

CHAPTER THREE

Cartoonists' Convention

Jim's fellow 'toonsmiths get together to toast—and occasionally roast—the famous feline.

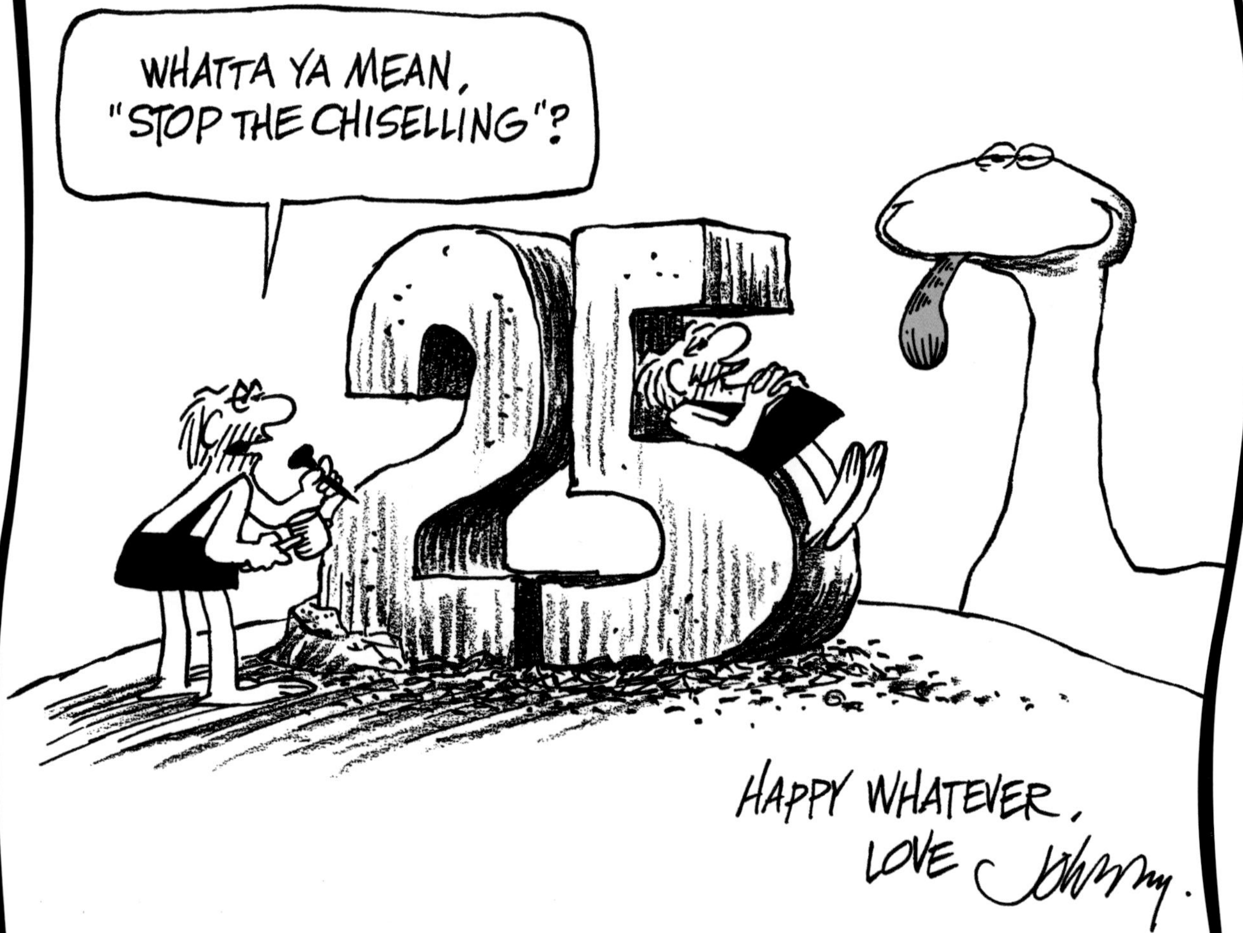
WHATTA YA MEAN, "STOP THE CHISELLING"?
HAPPY WHATEVER. LOVE Johnny.

Beetle Bailey

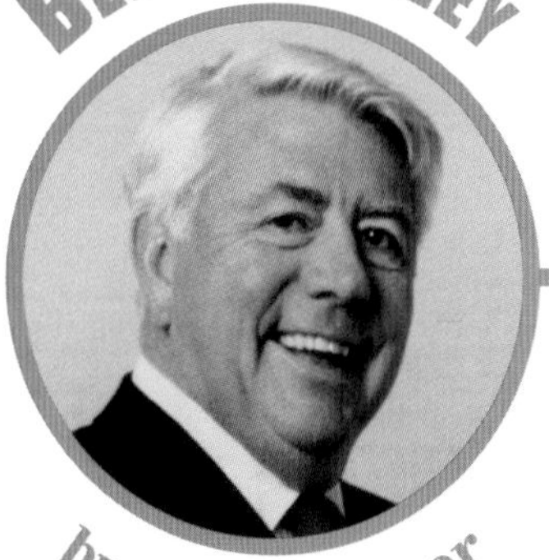

by Mort Walker

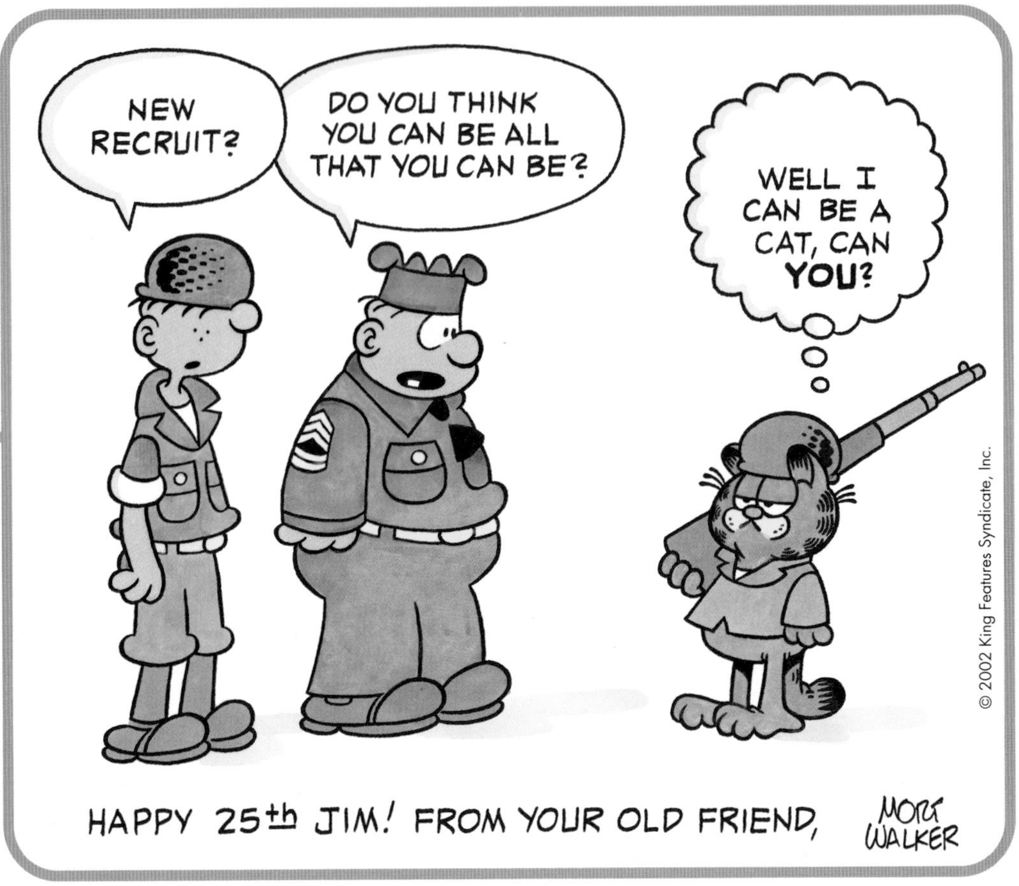
NEW RECRUIT?
DO YOU THINK YOU CAN BE ALL THAT YOU CAN BE?
WELL I CAN BE A CAT, CAN YOU?
HAPPY 25th JIM! FROM YOUR OLD FRIEND, MORT WALKER

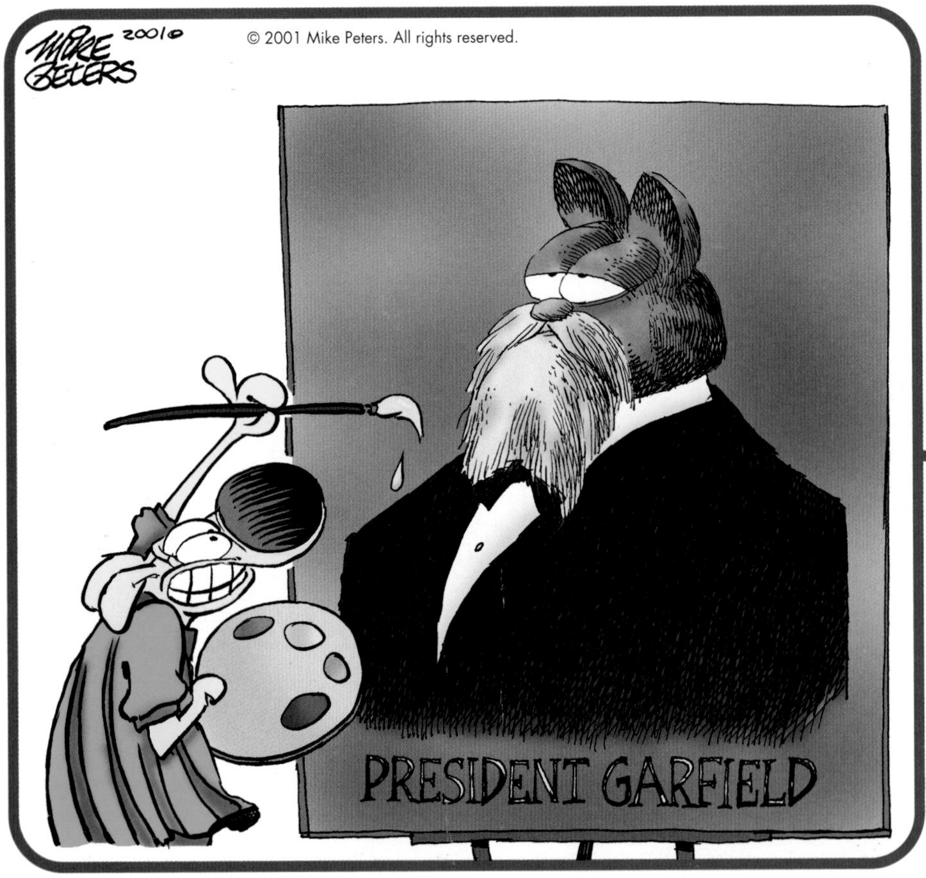
MIKE PETERS 2001©
PRESIDENT GARFIELD

Mother Goose & Grimm

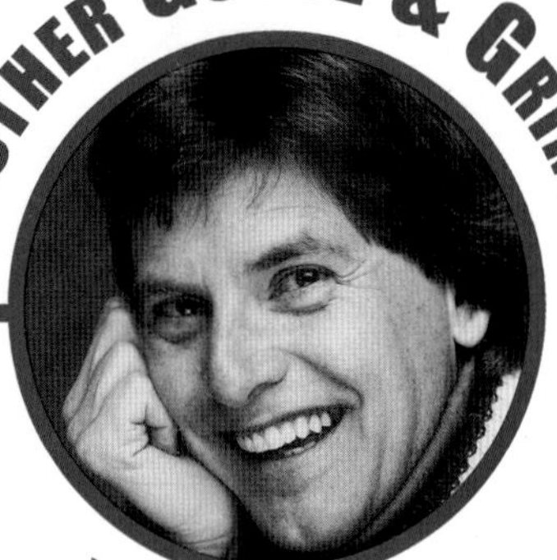

by Mike Peters

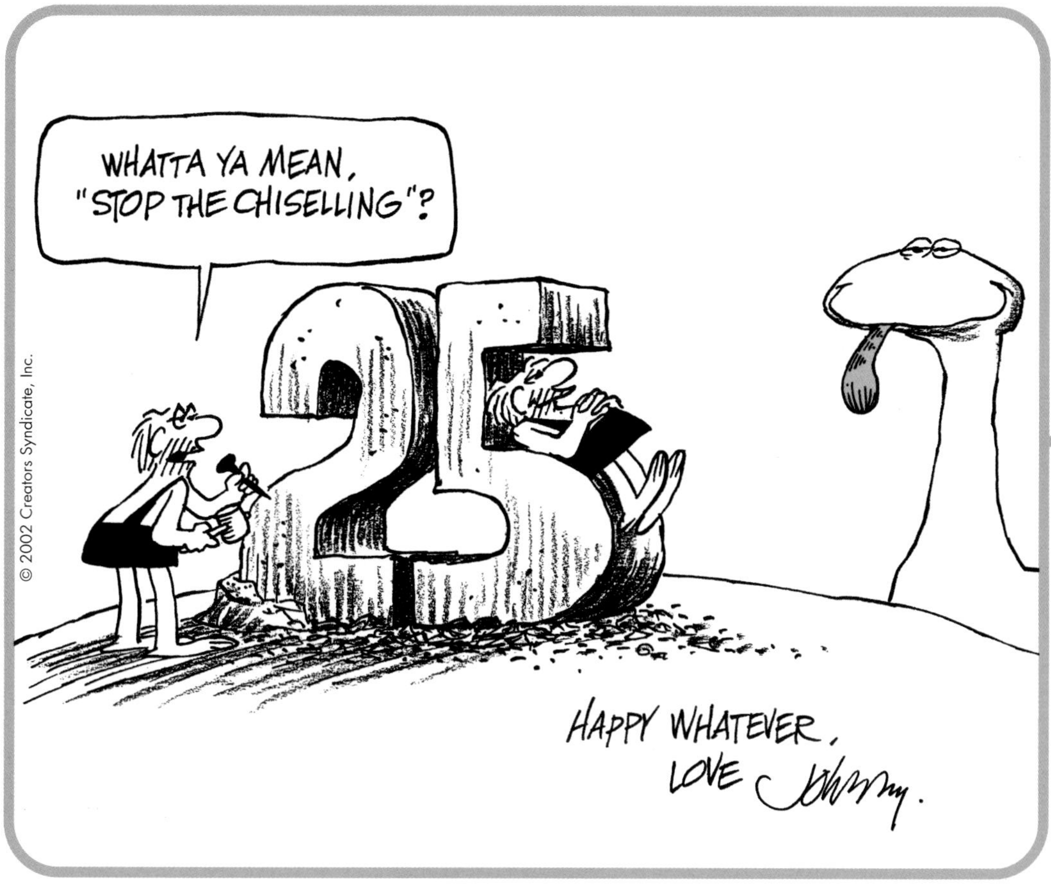
WHATTA YA MEAN, "STOP THE CHISELLING"?
HAPPY WHATEVER, LOVE Johnny.

B.C.

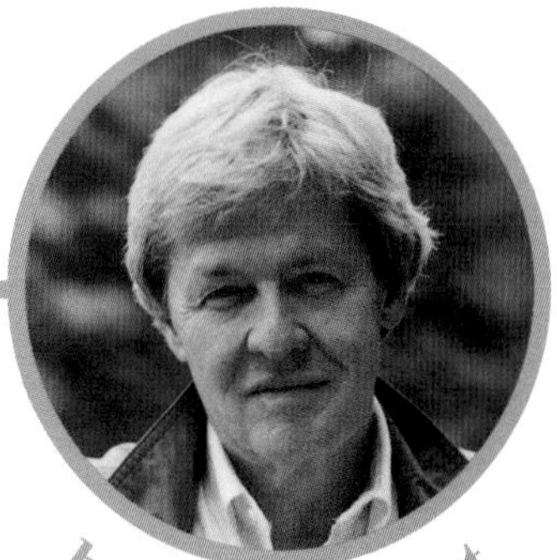

by Johnny Hart

Blondie

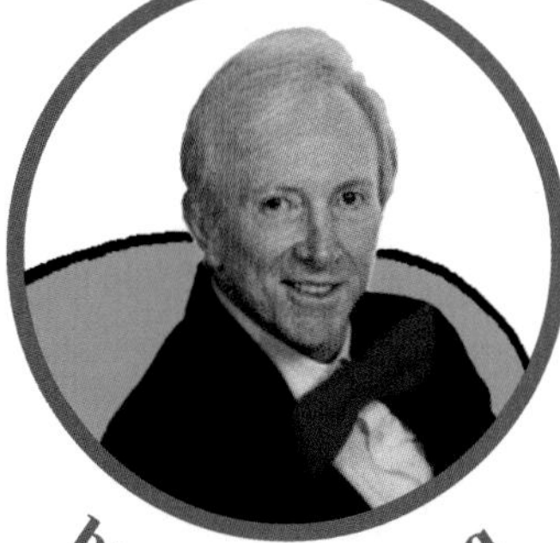

by Dean Young

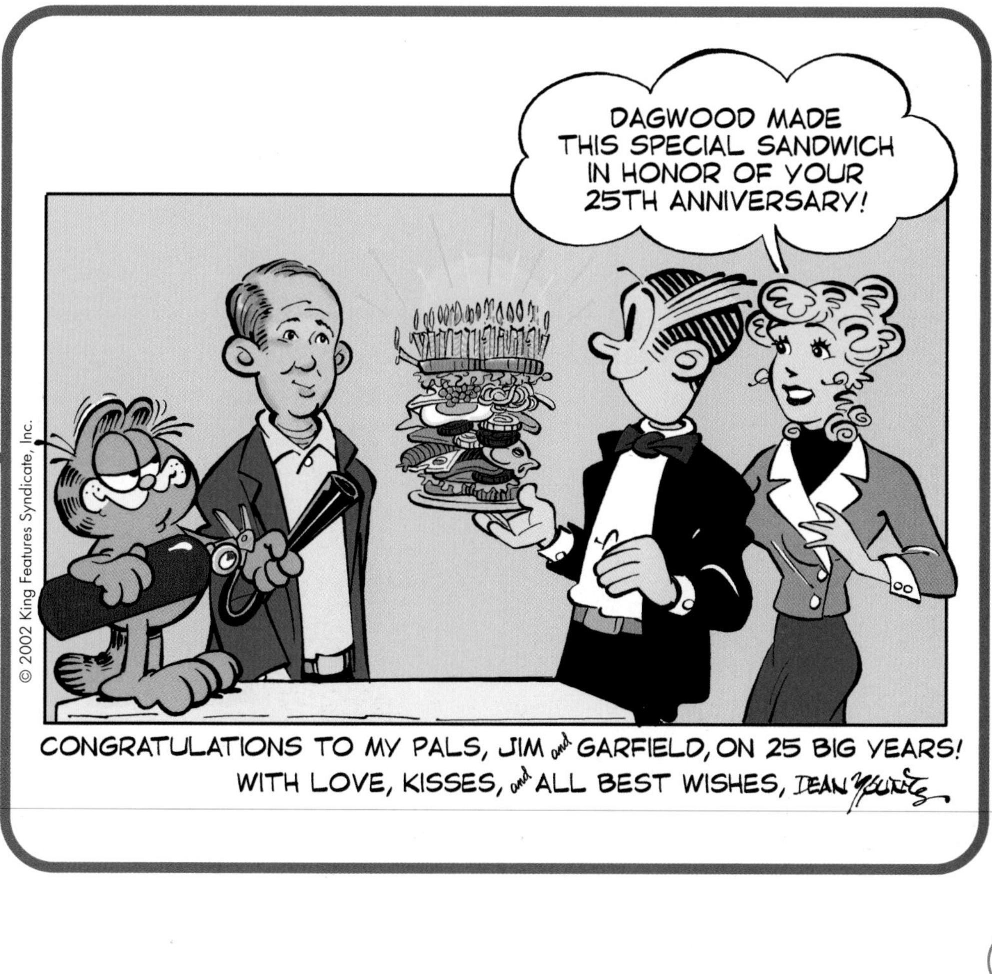
DAGWOOD MADE THIS SPECIAL SANDWICH IN HONOR OF YOUR 25TH ANNIVERSARY!
CONGRATULATIONS TO MY PALS, JIM and GARFIELD, ON 25 BIG YEARS!
WITH LOVE, KISSES, and ALL BEST WISHES, DEAN YOUNG

For Better or For Worse

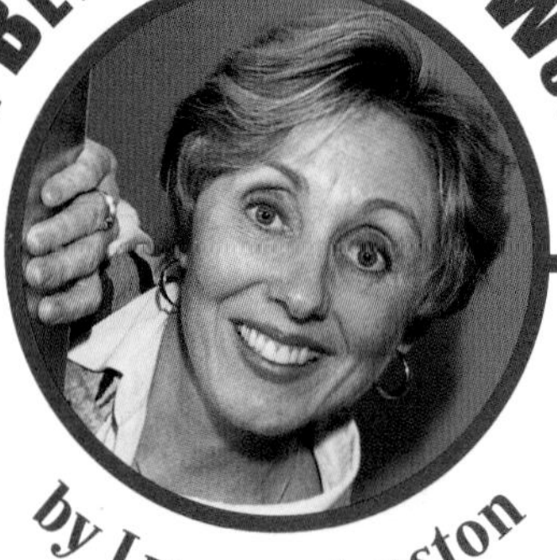

by Lynn Johnston

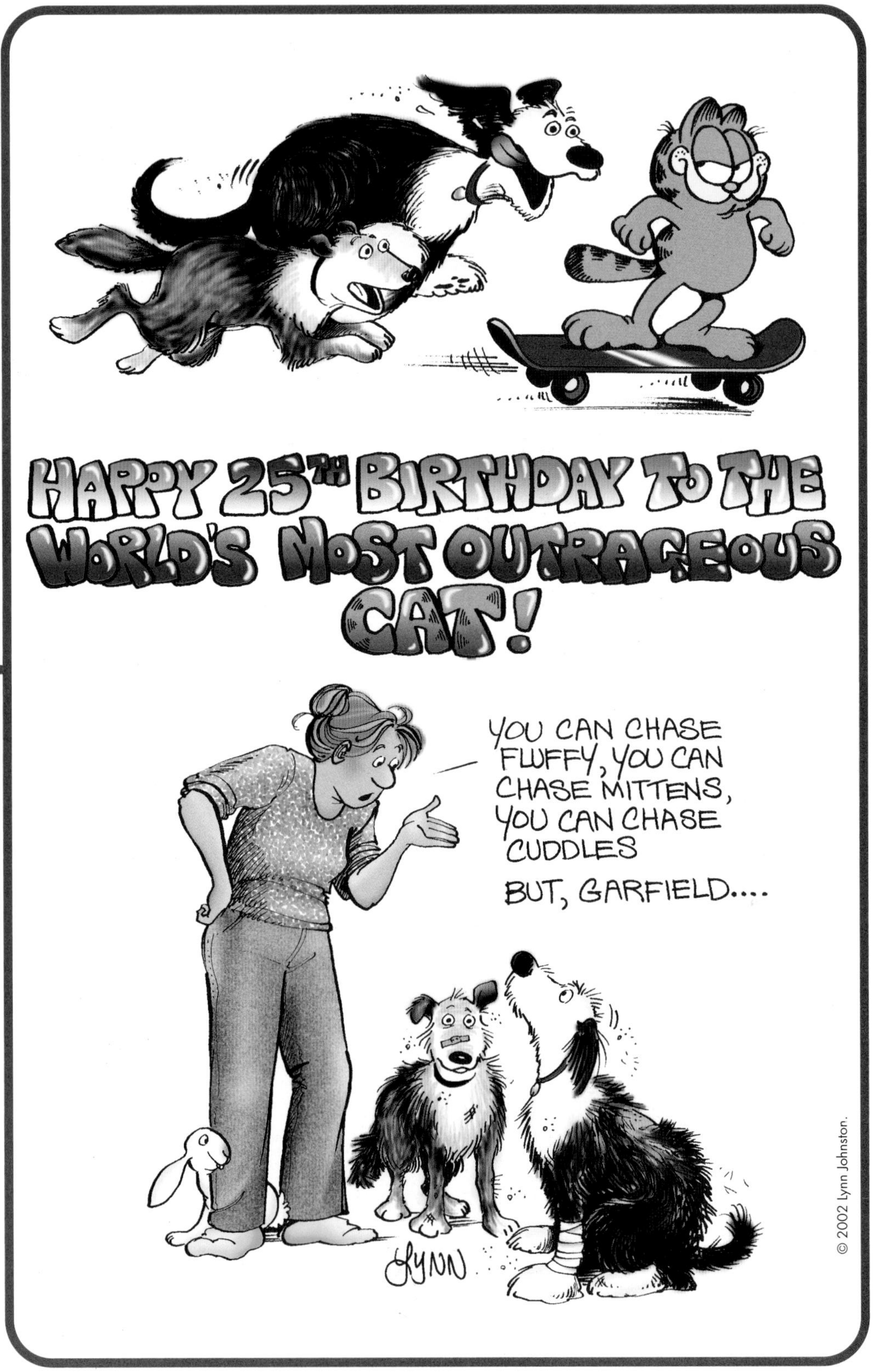
HAPPY 25TH BIRTHDAY TO THE WORLD'S MOST OUTRAGEOUS CAT!
YOU CAN CHASE FLUFFY, YOU CAN CHASE MITTENS, YOU CAN CHASE CUDDLES
BUT, GARFIELD....
LYNN

JIM— congratulations on 25 BIG YEARS!
JIMBORGMAN and JERRY SCOTT
MAN, HOW DID THIS BACKPACK GET SO HEAVY?

ZITS

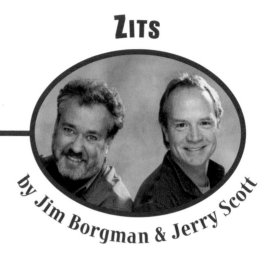

by Jim Borgman & Jerry Scott

BRAD ANDERSON
CONGRATULATIONS TO GARFIELD FROM MARMADUKE. 25 YEARS OF FUN AND GARFIELD IS EVERYWHERE!

MARMADUKE

by Brad Anderson

CURTIS

by Ray Billingsley

HERE YA GO, GARFIELD! TWENTY-FIVE PANS OF LASAGNA! ONE FOR EACH **YEAR**!

I THOUGHT IT WAS ONE FOR EACH **HOUR** OF THE DAY!

HAPPY **25**TH TO MY FAVORITE FAT, LAZY, CRANKY OL' TOMCAT!

*AND GARFIELD!

HERE'S TO TWENTY-FIVE MORE!
YOUR BUDDY,
Ray Billingsley

© 2002 King Features Syndicate, Inc.

HAPPY 25TH, GARFIELD!

THAT'S 175 IN CAT YEARS

© 2001 United Feature Syndicate, Inc.

FAGAN

DRABBLE

by Kevin Fagan

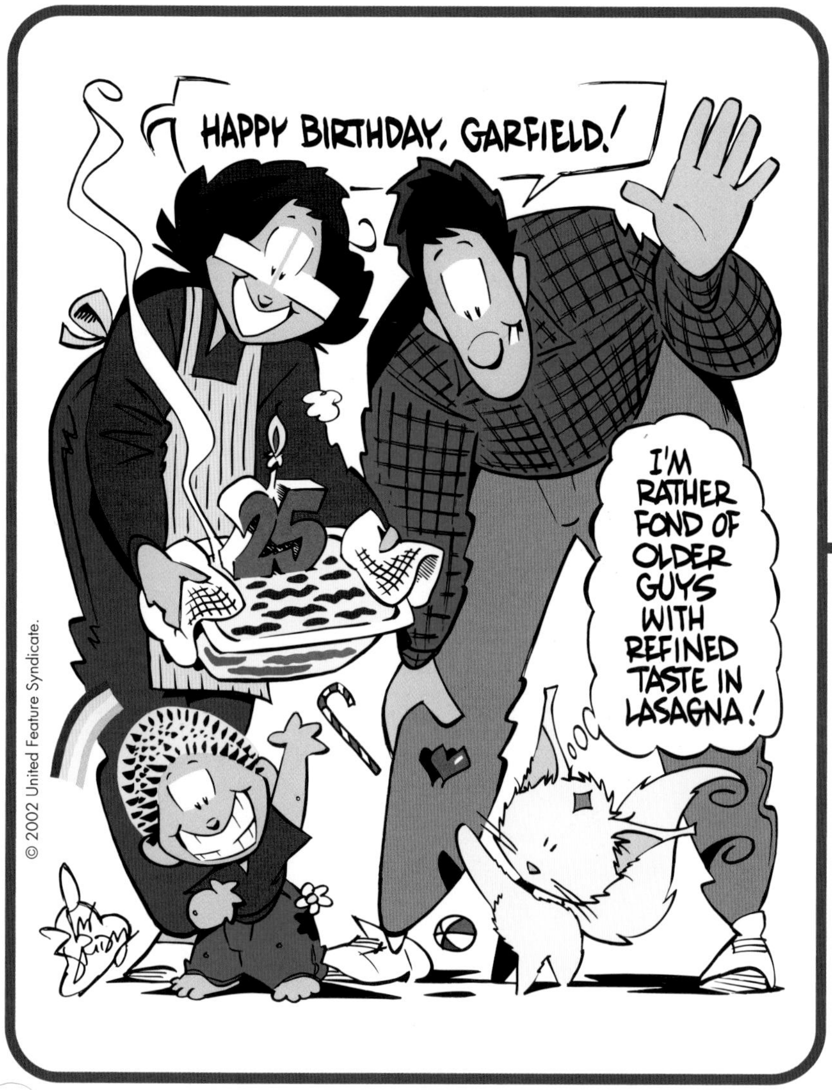
HAPPY BIRTHDAY, GARFIELD!
I'M RATHER FOND OF OLDER GUYS WITH REFINED TASTE IN LASAGNA!
25

Rose Is Rose

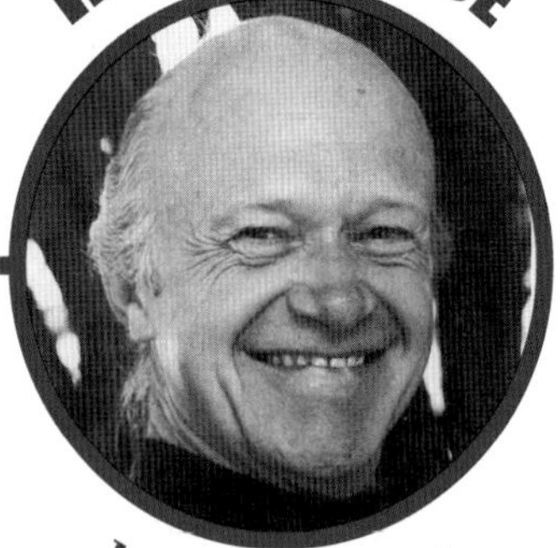

by Pat Brady

Hagar the Horrible

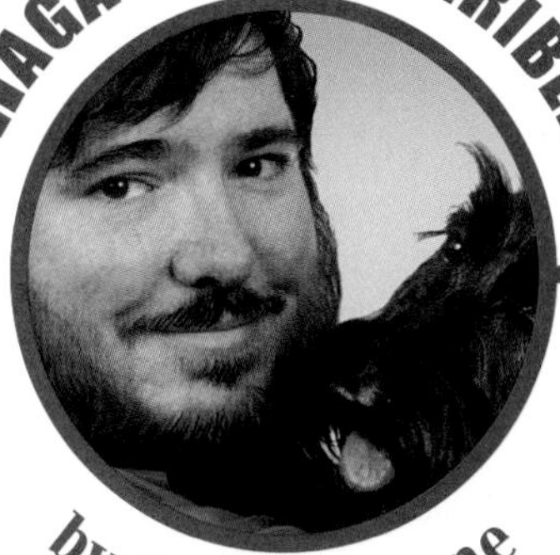

by Chris Browne

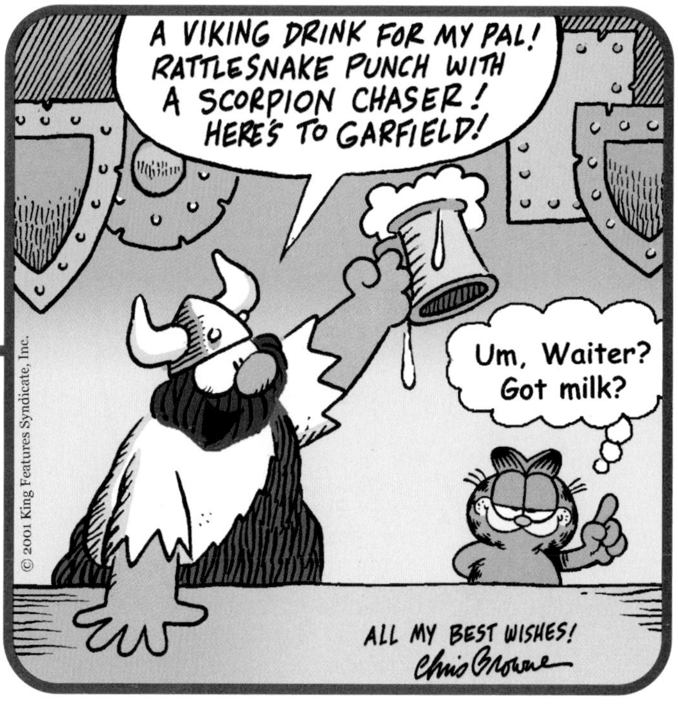
A VIKING DRINK FOR MY PAL! RATTLESNAKE PUNCH WITH A SCORPION CHASER! HERE'S TO GARFIELD!
Um, Waiter? Got milk?
ALL MY BEST WISHES!
Chris Browne

WOW, PUDDLES, CAN YOU BELIEVE GARFIELD IS 25?!
IS THAT HIS I.Q. OR HIS WAIST LINE?
GREG
©GEC Inc 2002
HAPPY BIRTHDAY, JIM & GARFIELD!
GREG EVANS • "LUANN"

LUANN

by Greg Evans

MARVIN

by Tom Armstrong

HAPPY 25th BIRTHDAY, GARFIELD!!
from MARVIN, BITSY...
©2001 by North America Syndicate, Inc. World rights reserved.
... and TOM ARMSTRONG

THE FAMILY CIRCUS®
By Bil Keane
© 2002 BKI
BIL KEANE

"I wish Kittycat was like Garfield so we could know what she's thinking."

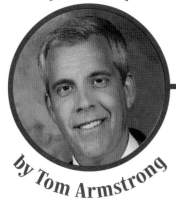

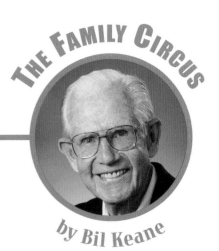

THE FAMILY CIRCUS

by Bil Keane

CHAPTER FOUR

Publishing Powerhouse

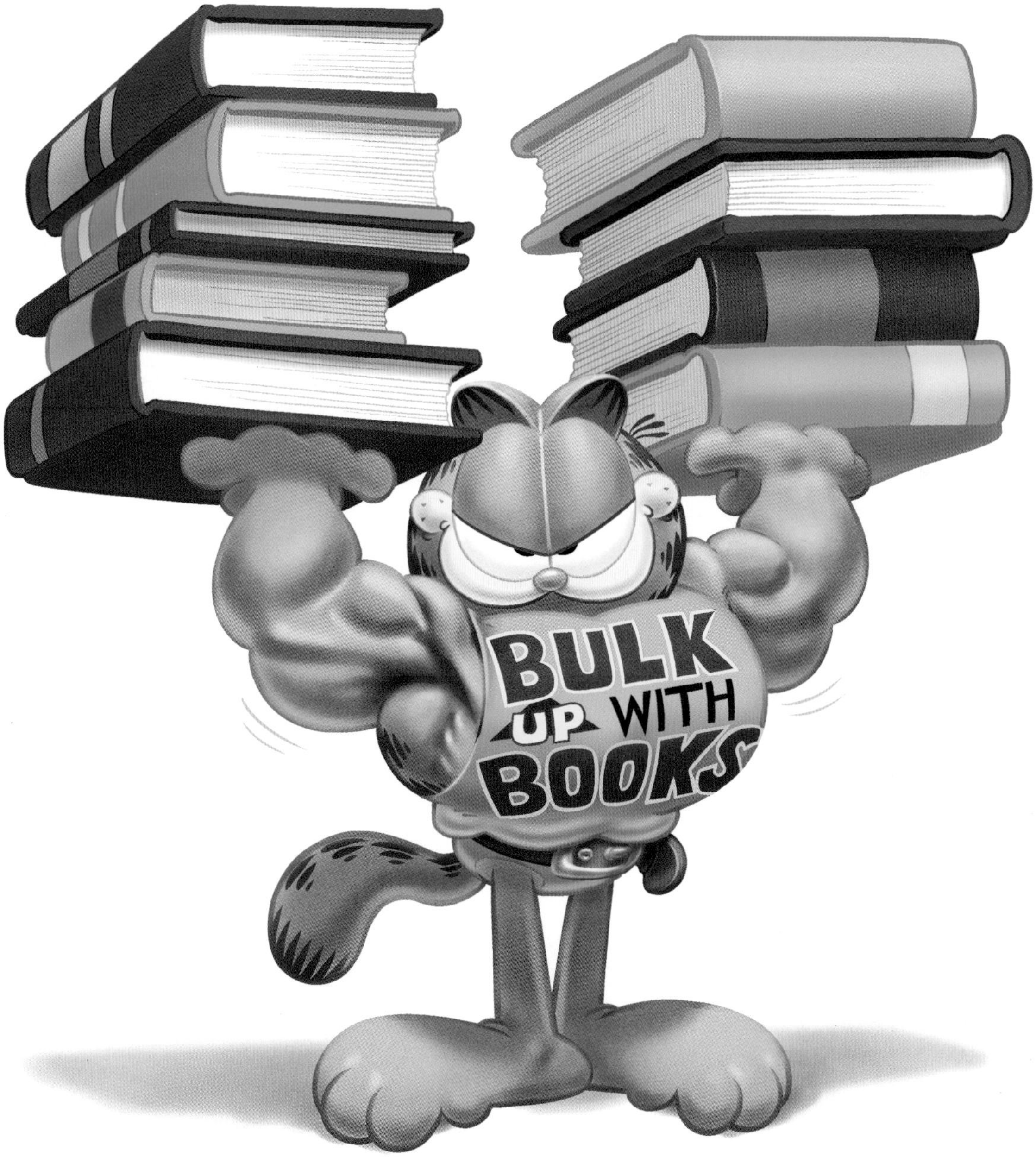
BULK
UP WITH
BOOKS

Once upon a time there was a lasagna-loving fat cat named Garfield who burst onto the literary scene and began clawing his way to the top of bestseller lists everywhere. As his popularity (and his waistline) spread, so did his publishing empire, which soon spanned the globe. And all his publishers bought big yachts and sailed happily ever after!

Fat Cat Comics

The comic-strip compilation books, featuring the strips that appear in newspapers around the world, are the foundation of Garfield's publishing program. Eleven of these books have hit the number-one spot on the *New York Times* bestseller list, and seven titles once appeared simultaneously—a never-before-seen feat that has yet to be matched. The first book, *Garfield at Large*, published in 1980, immediately hit #1 and stayed there for nearly two years.

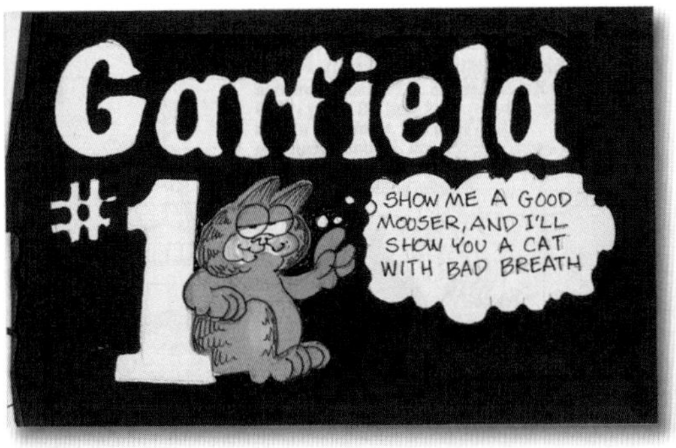

Garfield
#1
SHOW ME A GOOD MOUSER, AND I'LL SHOW YOU A CAT WITH BAD BREATH

Right and below: Actual mock-up Jim Davis created for Garfield's first comic-strip compilation book, and the finished product published by Ballantine.

Far right: Ballantine ran this full-page newspaper ad to celebrate Jim and Garfield's publishing prowess.

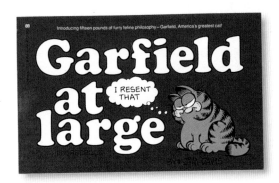

Jim never liked the pocket-sized paperbacks of the day, which were vertical, thus requiring the panels of a comic strip to be stacked one on top of another. Jim's idea of presenting the strips *horizontally* enabled the strip to retain its original flow. This eventually became known as the Garfield format, and it set the standard for the industry.

Introducing fifteen pounds of furry feline philosophy—Garfield, America's greatest cat!
Garfield at large
I RESENT THAT

Ballantine Books
congratulates
Jim Davis
on
Garfield's
seven bestsellers!
Garfield Treasury
Garfield at large
Garfield gains weight
Garfield bigger than life
Garfield weighs in
Garfield takes the cake
GARFIELD: © 1978 United Feature Syndicate, Inc.
All appeared on the New York Times bestseller list, November 21, 1982.

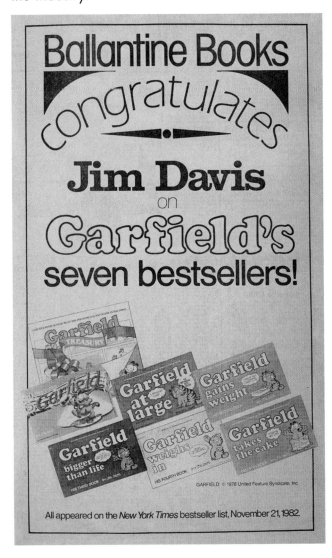

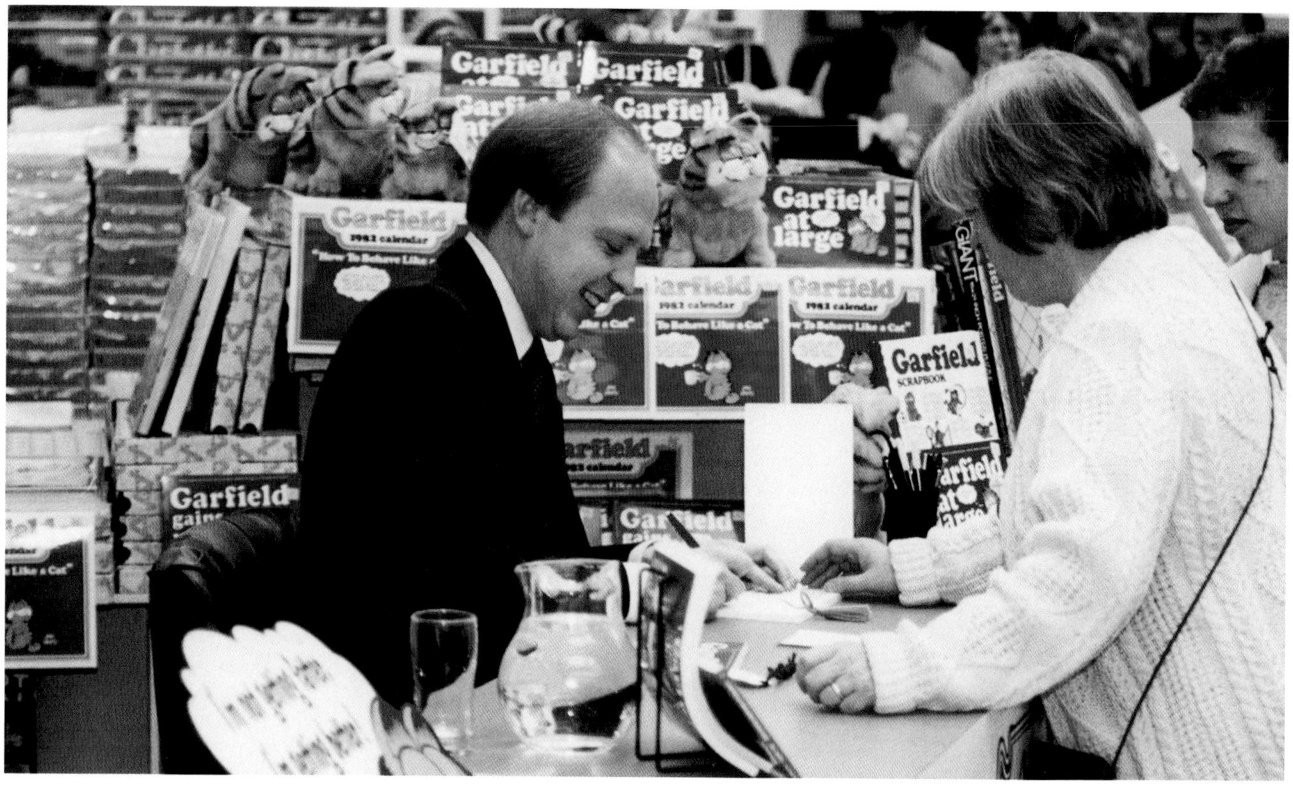
Garfield
Garfield at large
Garfield 1983 calendar
Garfield Scrapbook

Jim went on several extended book tours in the early 1980s, meeting fans, signing autographs, and spreading the word about Garfield. Here, in 1983, Jim signs a book for a Canadian fan at World's Biggest Bookstore, located in Toronto.

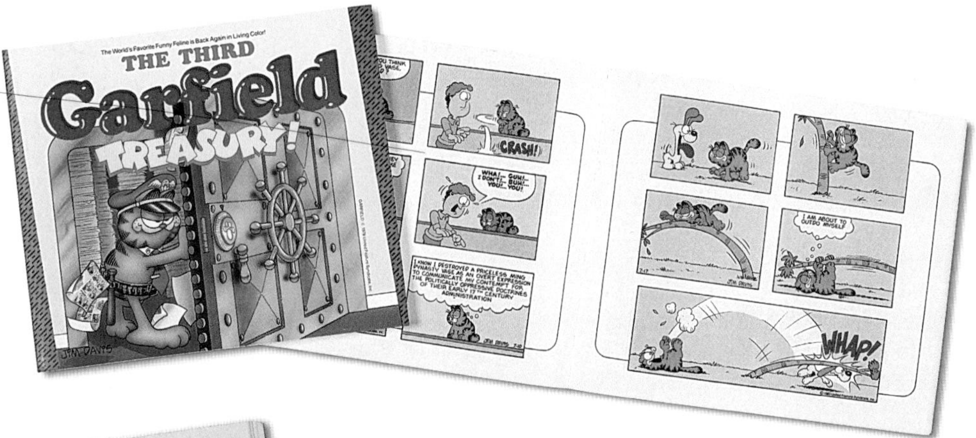
The World's Favorite Funny Feline is Back Again in Living Color!
THE THIRD
Garfield
TREASURY!
JIM DAVIS
CRASH!
WHAP!

The "treasuries" (ten in all) are collections of Sunday strips, presented in color, as they originally appeared in newspapers.

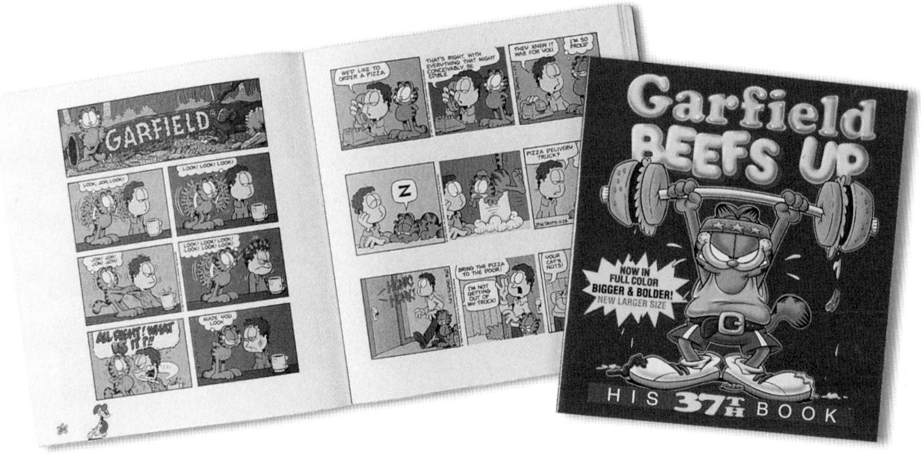
GARFIELD
Garfield
BEEFS UP
NOW IN FULL COLOR
BIGGER & BOLDER!
NEW LARGER SIZE
HIS 37TH BOOK

A new millennium brought a new supersized Garfield compilation book. Starting with #37, *Garfield Beefs Up*, both daily and Sunday strips appear in full color together in a new bigger, bolder format.

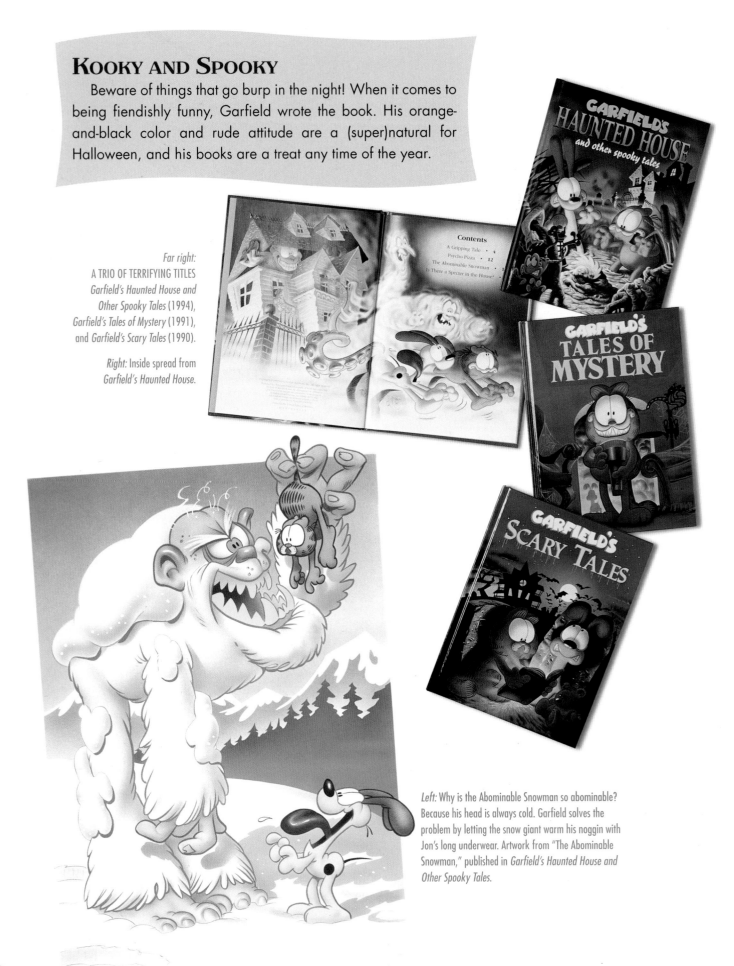

Kooky and Spooky

Beware of things that go burp in the night! When it comes to being fiendishly funny, Garfield wrote the book. His orange-and-black color and rude attitude are a (super)natural for Halloween, and his books are a treat any time of the year.

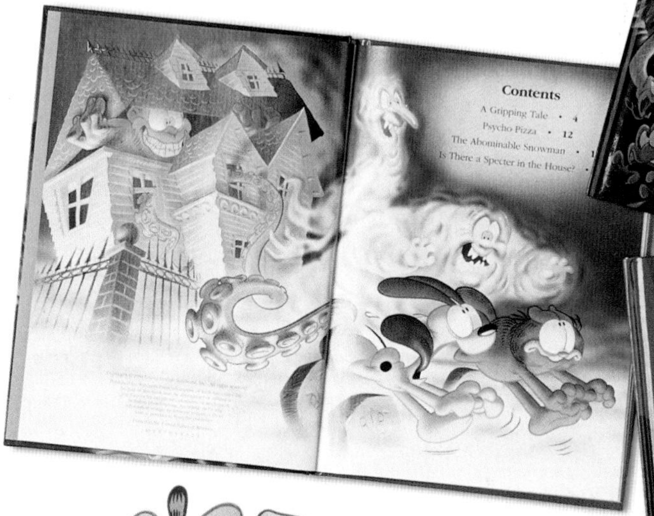
Contents
A Gripping Tale • 4
Psycho Pizza • 12
The Abominable Snowman •
Is There a Specter in the House?

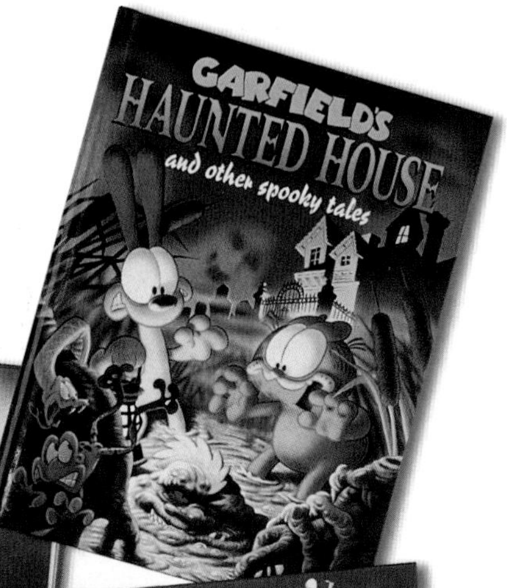
GARFIELD'S
HAUNTED HOUSE
and other spooky tales

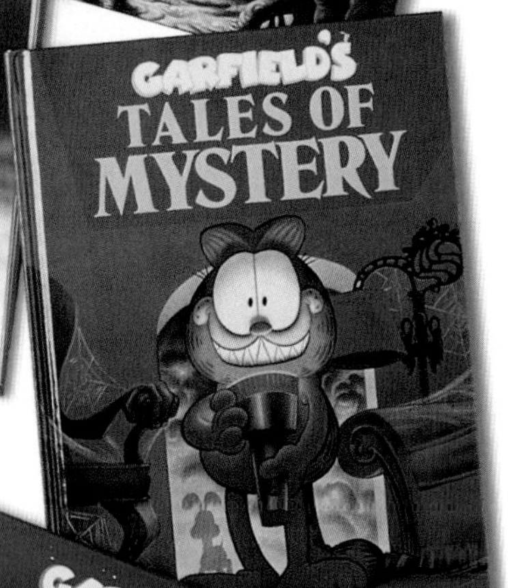
GARFIELD'S
TALES OF
MYSTERY

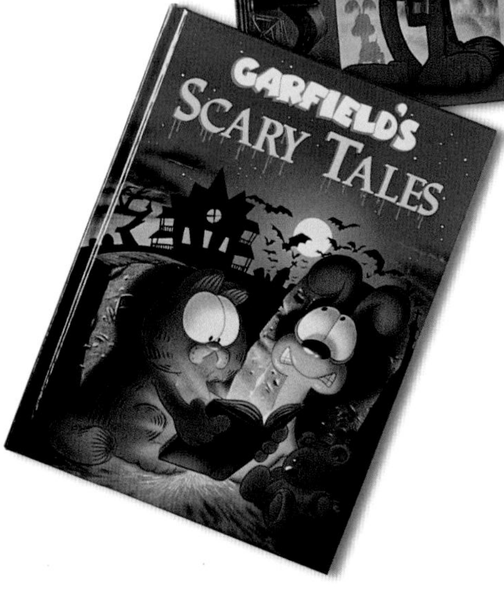
GARFIELD'S
SCARY TALES

Far right:
A TRIO OF TERRIFYING TITLES
Garfield's Haunted House and Other Spooky Tales (1994), *Garfield's Tales of Mystery* (1991), and *Garfield's Scary Tales* (1990).

Right: Inside spread from *Garfield's Haunted House.*

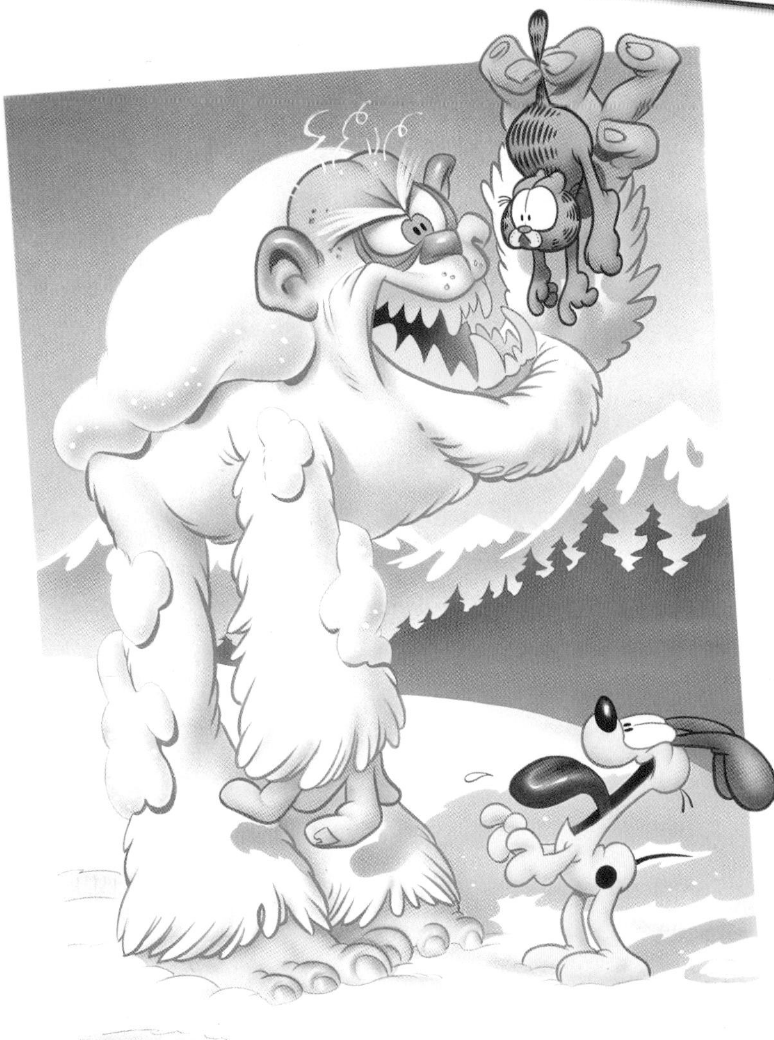

Left: Why is the Abominable Snowman so abominable? Because his head is always cold. Garfield solves the problem by letting the snow giant warm his noggin with Jon's long underwear. Artwork from "The Abominable Snowman," published in *Garfield's Haunted House and Other Spooky Tales.*

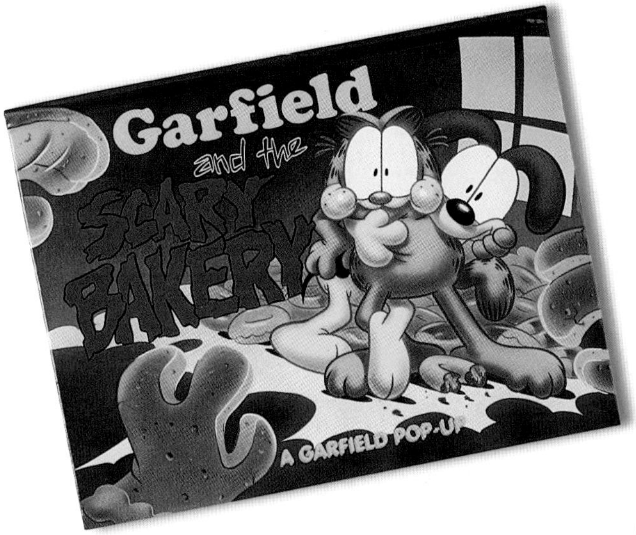
Garfield
and the
SCARY
BAKERY
A GARFIELD POP-UP

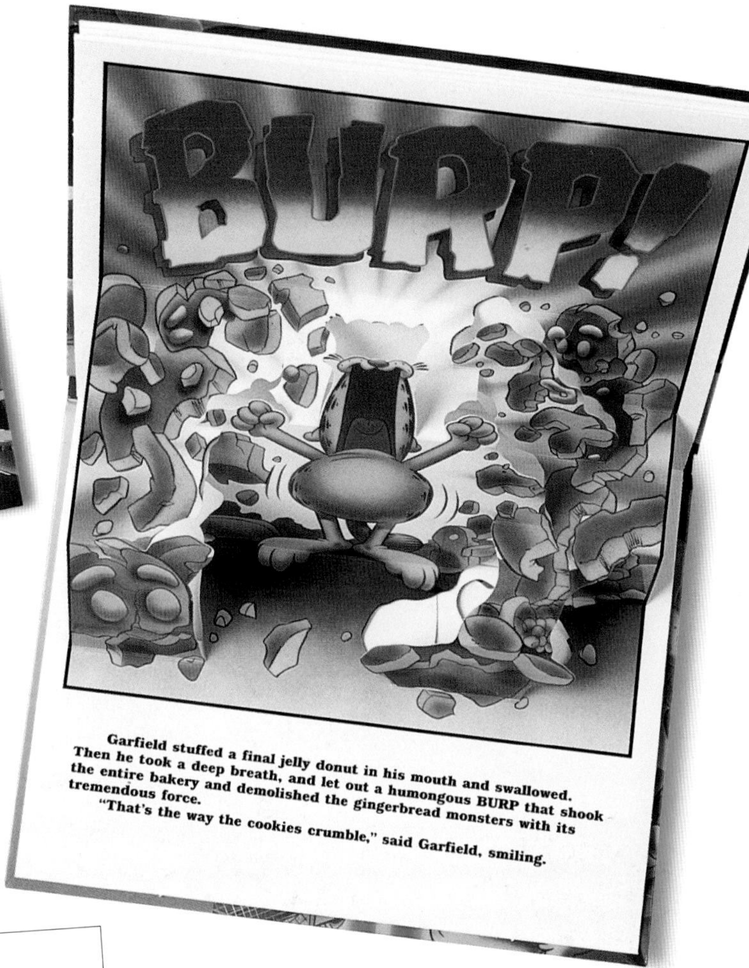
BURP!
Garfield stuffed a final jelly donut in his mouth and swallowed. Then he took a deep breath, and let out a humongous BURP that shook the entire bakery and demolished the gingerbread monsters with its tremendous force.
"That's the way the cookies crumble," said Garfield, smiling.

Right: A burp so real, you can almost taste it! Climactic scene from the pop-up book, *Garfield and the Scary Bakery*, 1997.

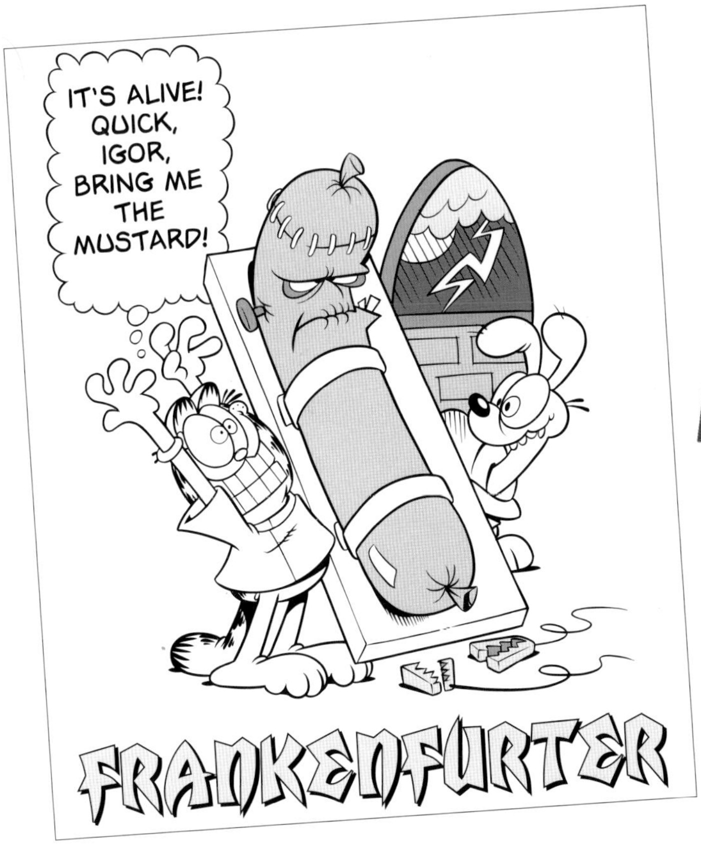
IT'S ALIVE! QUICK, IGOR, BRING ME THE MUSTARD!
FRANKENFURTER

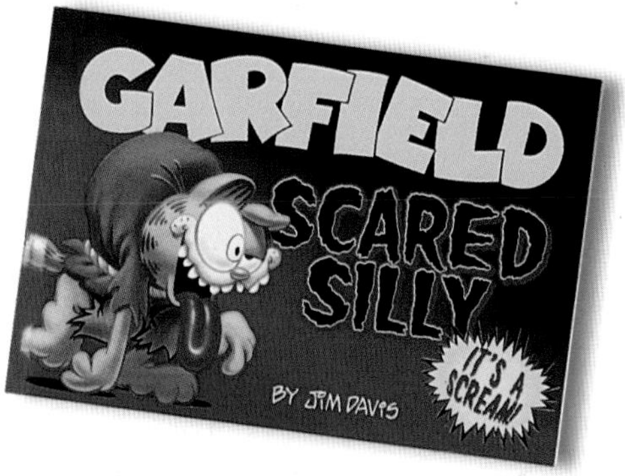
GARFIELD
SCARED
SILLY
IT'S A SCREAM!
BY JIM DAVIS

Above: A comedy of terrors, *Garfield Scared Silly* (2001) offers a monstrous mix of horror-themed comic strips, jokes, and riddles.

Left: "Frankenfurter" from *Garfield Scared Silly*.

Kiddy Kat

All kidding aside, Garfield's appeal stretches from toddlers to teens and to everyone in between. Whether it's silly storybooks or books of jokes, insults, or excuses, the flabby tabby sometimes educates but always entertains.

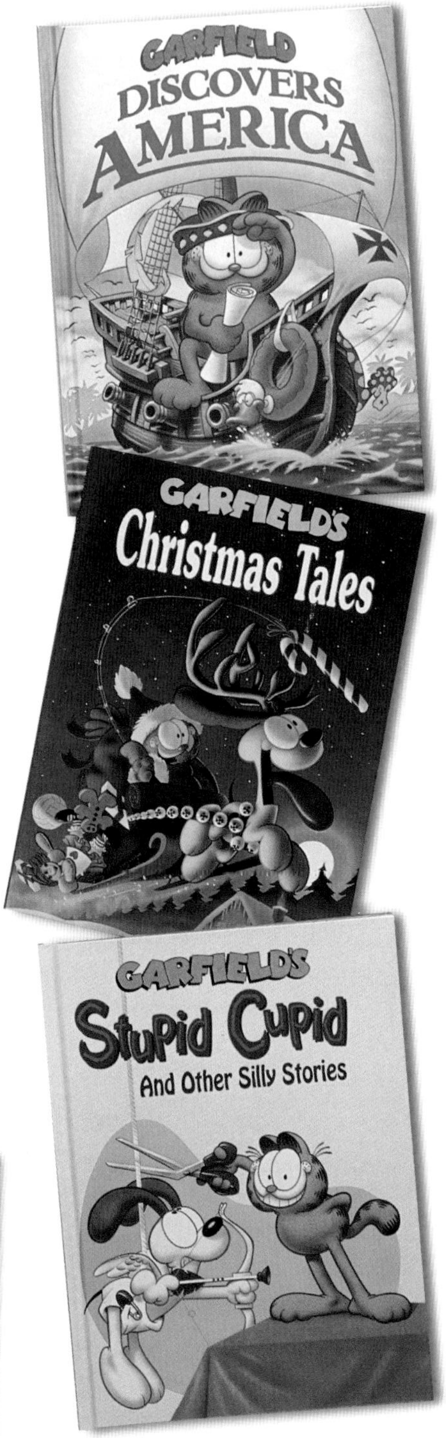
Garfield Discovers America
Garfield's Christmas Tales
Garfield's Stupid Cupid
And Other Silly Stories

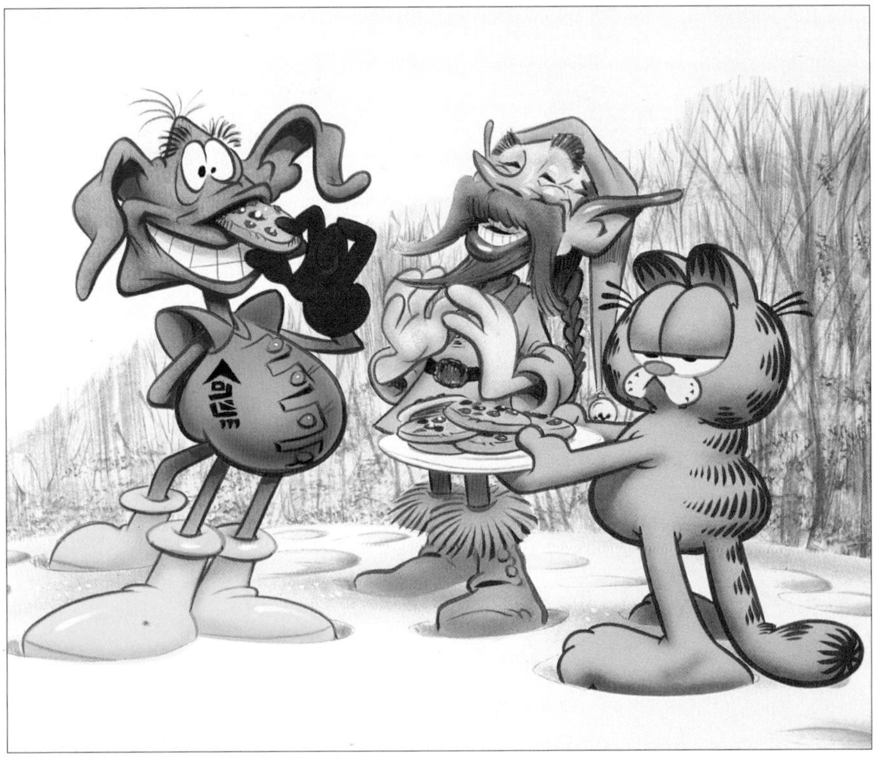

Right: Scene from "Garfield's Sweet Deal," published in *Garfield's Christmas Tales.* In this humorous holiday story, Garfield rescues Santa, who has been kidnapped by space aliens.

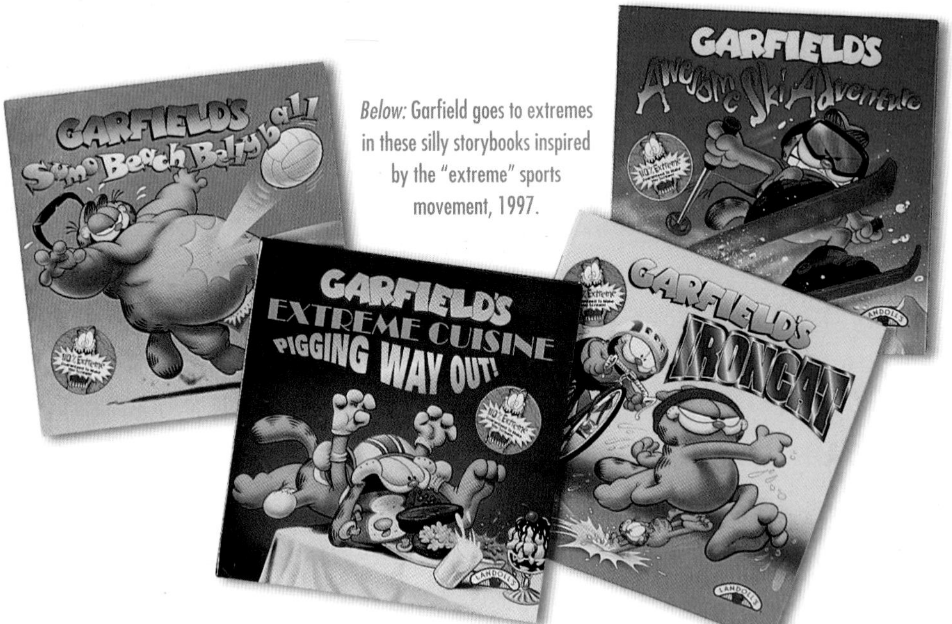
Garfield's
Sumo Beach Bellyball
Garfield's
Awesome Ski Adventure
Garfield's
Extreme Cuisine
Pigging Way Out!
Garfield's
Ironcat

Below: Garfield goes to extremes in these silly storybooks inspired by the "extreme" sports movement, 1997.

Above: CAT TALES
Garfield Discovers America (1992), *Garfield's Christmas Tales* (1995), and *Garfield's Stupid Cupid* (1995).

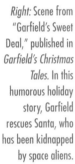

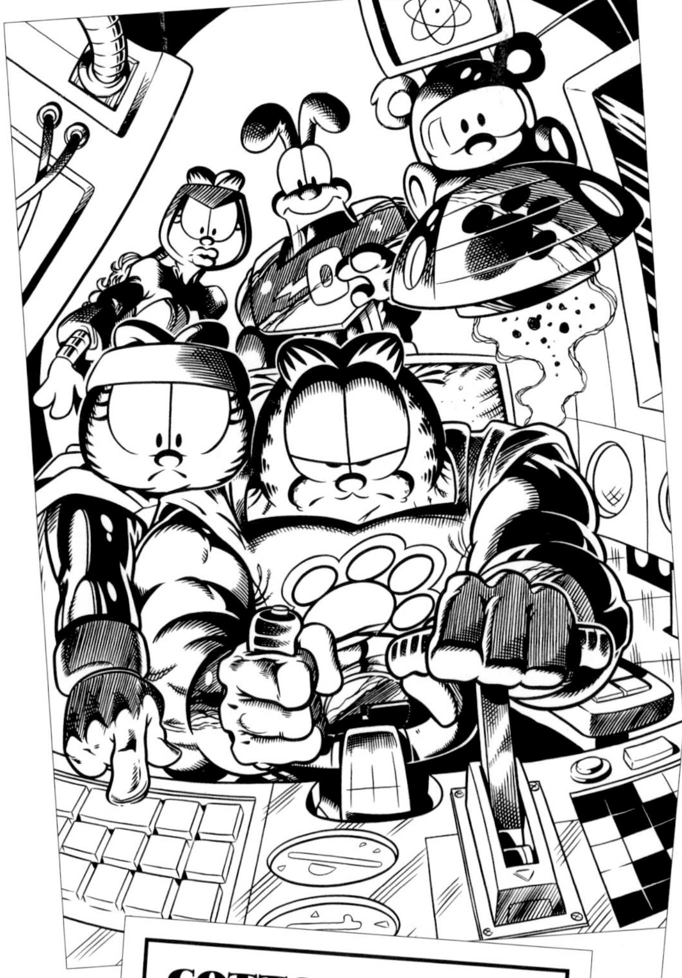

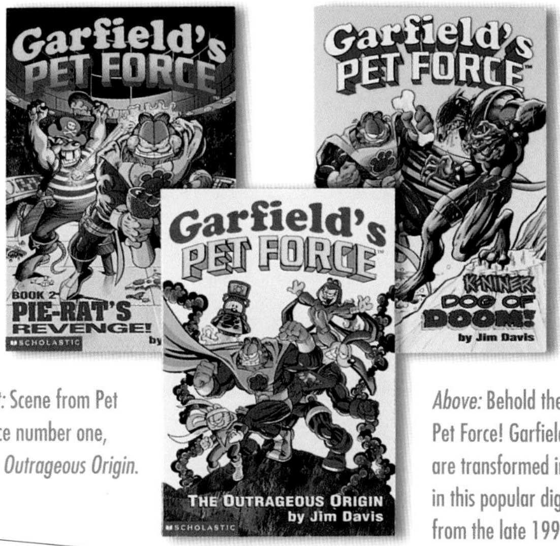
Garfield's
PET FORCE
BOOK 2
PIE-RAT'S
REVENGE!
SCHOLASTIC
Garfield's
PET FORCE
KANINE
DOG OF
DOOM!
by Jim Davis
Garfield's
PET FORCE
THE OUTRAGEOUS ORIGIN
by Jim Davis
SCHOLASTIC

Left: Scene from Pet Force number one, *The Outrageous Origin.*

Above: Behold the mighty Pet Force! Garfield and friends are transformed into superheroes in this popular digest-book series from the late 1990s.

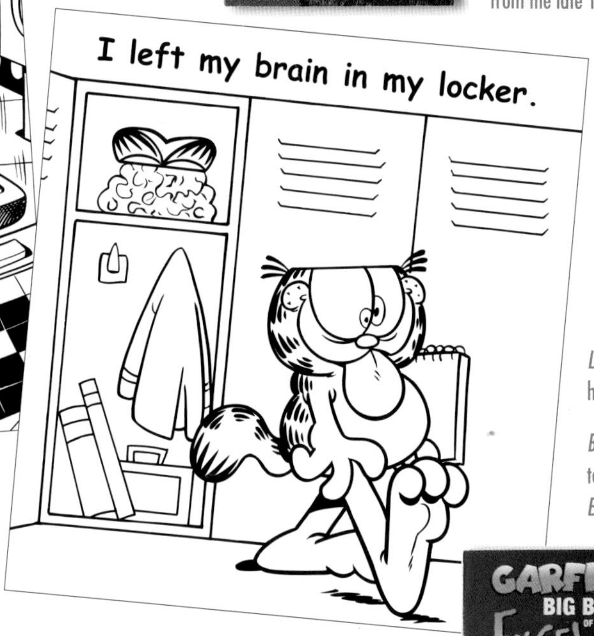
I left my brain in my locker.

Left: A ridiculous reason for not having your homework.

Below: There's no excuse not to like *Garfield's Big Book of Excellent Excuses*, 1999.

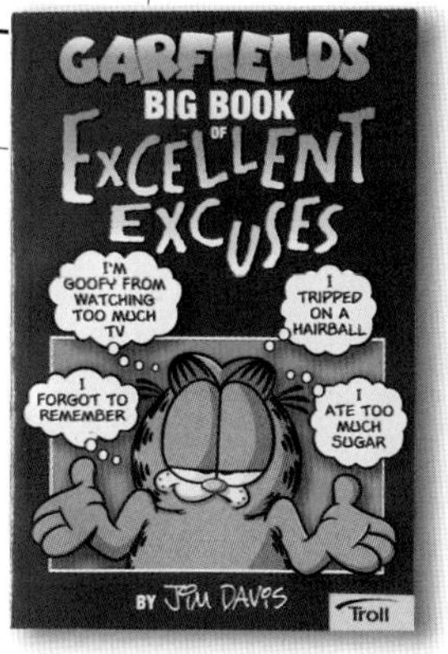
GARFIELD'S
BIG BOOK
OF
EXCELLENT
EXCUSES
I'M GOOFY FROM WATCHING TOO MUCH TV
I TRIPPED ON A HAIRBALL
I FORGOT TO REMEMBER
I ATE TOO MUCH SUGAR
BY JIM DAVIS
Troll

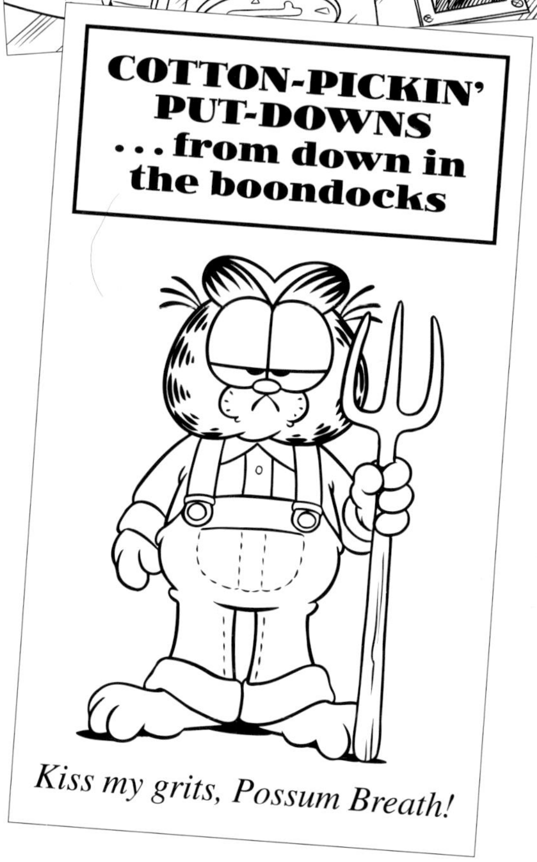
COTTON-PICKIN'
PUT-DOWNS
. . . from down in
the boondocks
Kiss my grits, Possum Breath!

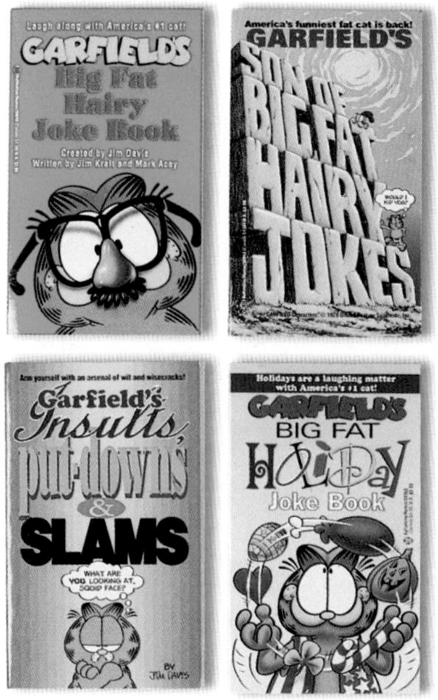
GARFIELD'S
Big Fat
Hairy
Joke Book
America's funniest fat cat is back!
GARFIELD'S
SON OF
BIG FAT
HAIRY
JOKES
Garfield's
Insults,
Put-downs
&
SLAMS
WHAT ARE YOU LOOKING AT, SQUID FACE?
GARFIELD'S
BIG FAT
HOLIDAY
Joke Book

Left: MORE YUK FOR THE BUCK
Garfield's mass-market-sized joke and insult books from 1994. Each joke book contained more than six hundred jokes.

Far left: A page from *Garfield's Insults, Put-Downs & Slams*, 1994.

Fun for Everyone

Garfield's brand of humor transcends age. Whether you're young or young at heart, or someone named Young with a transplanted pig heart . . . Garfield has a book for you!

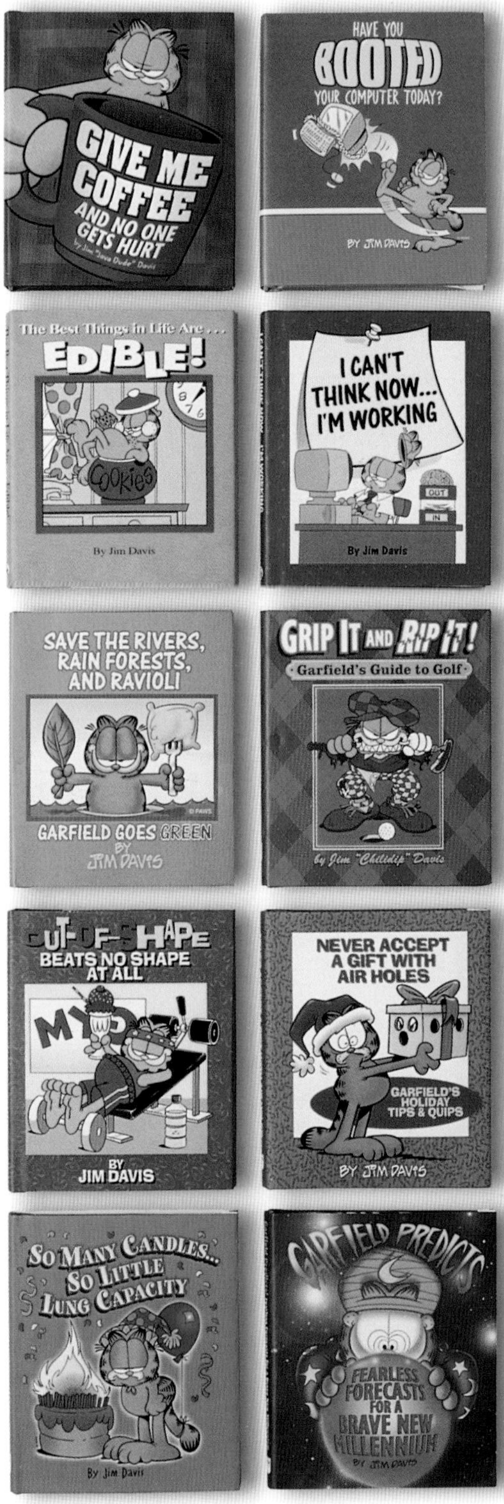
GIVE ME COFFEE AND NO ONE GETS HURT
BOOTED YOUR COMPUTER TODAY?
The Best Things In Life Are . . . EDIBLE!
I CAN'T THINK NOW... I'M WORKING
SAVE THE RIVERS, RAIN FORESTS, AND RAVIOLI
GARFIELD GOES GREEN
GRIP IT AND RIP IT!
Garfield's Guide to Golf
OUT-OF-SHAPE BEATS NO SHAPE AT ALL
NEVER ACCEPT A GIFT WITH AIR HOLES
GARFIELD'S HOLIDAY TIPS & QUIPS
SO MANY CANDLES... SO LITTLE LUNG CAPACITY
GARFIELD PREDICTS
FEARLESS FORECASTS FOR A BRAVE NEW MILLENNIUM

Right: These minibooks may be small in size, but they generate some big laughs. The series (1995–1999) covered such contemporary topics as computers, the environment, work, exercise, and the new millennium—all with a unique Garfield twist.

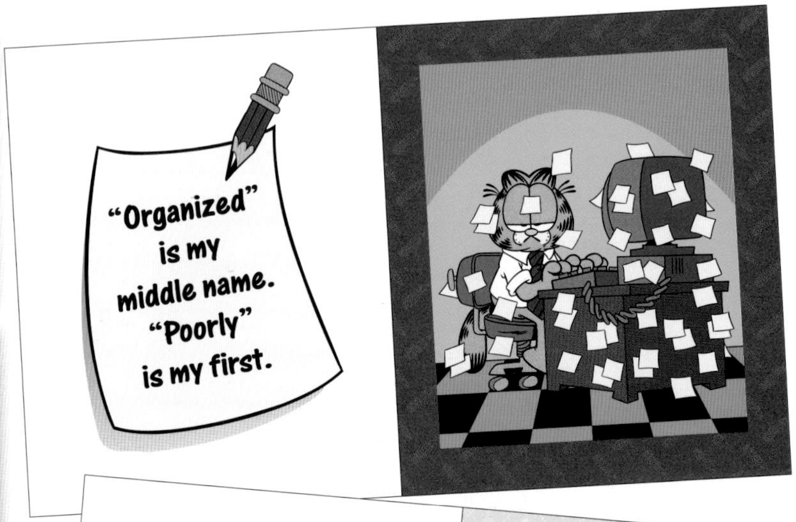
"Organized" is my middle name. "Poorly" is my first.

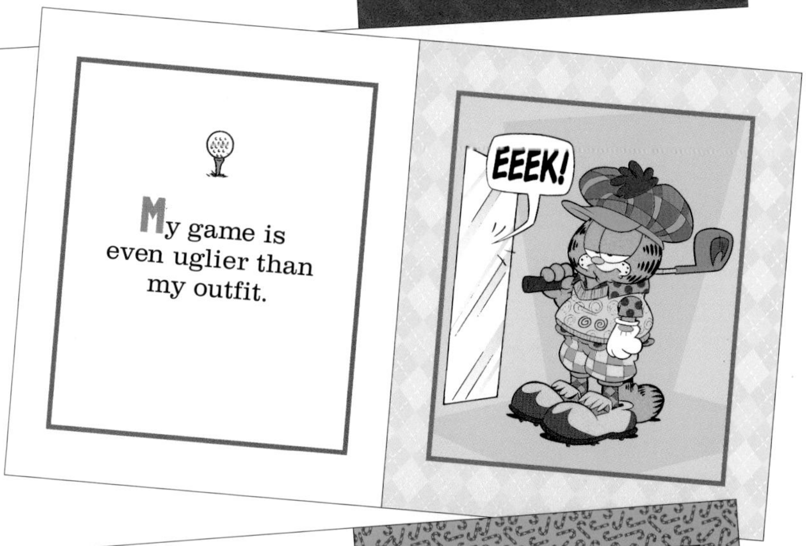
My game is even uglier than my outfit.
EEEK!

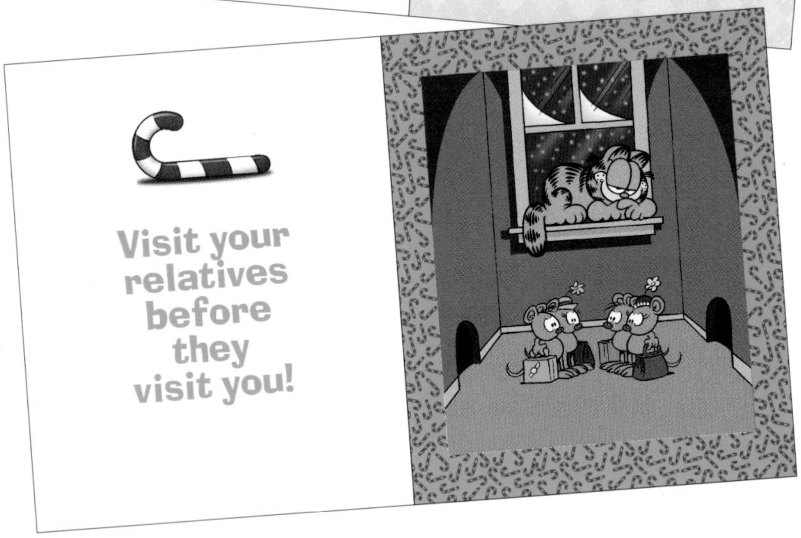
Visit your relatives before they visit you!

Far right: Excerpts from *I Can't Think Now . . . I'm Working, Grip It and Rip It!* and *Never Accept a Gift with Air Holes.*

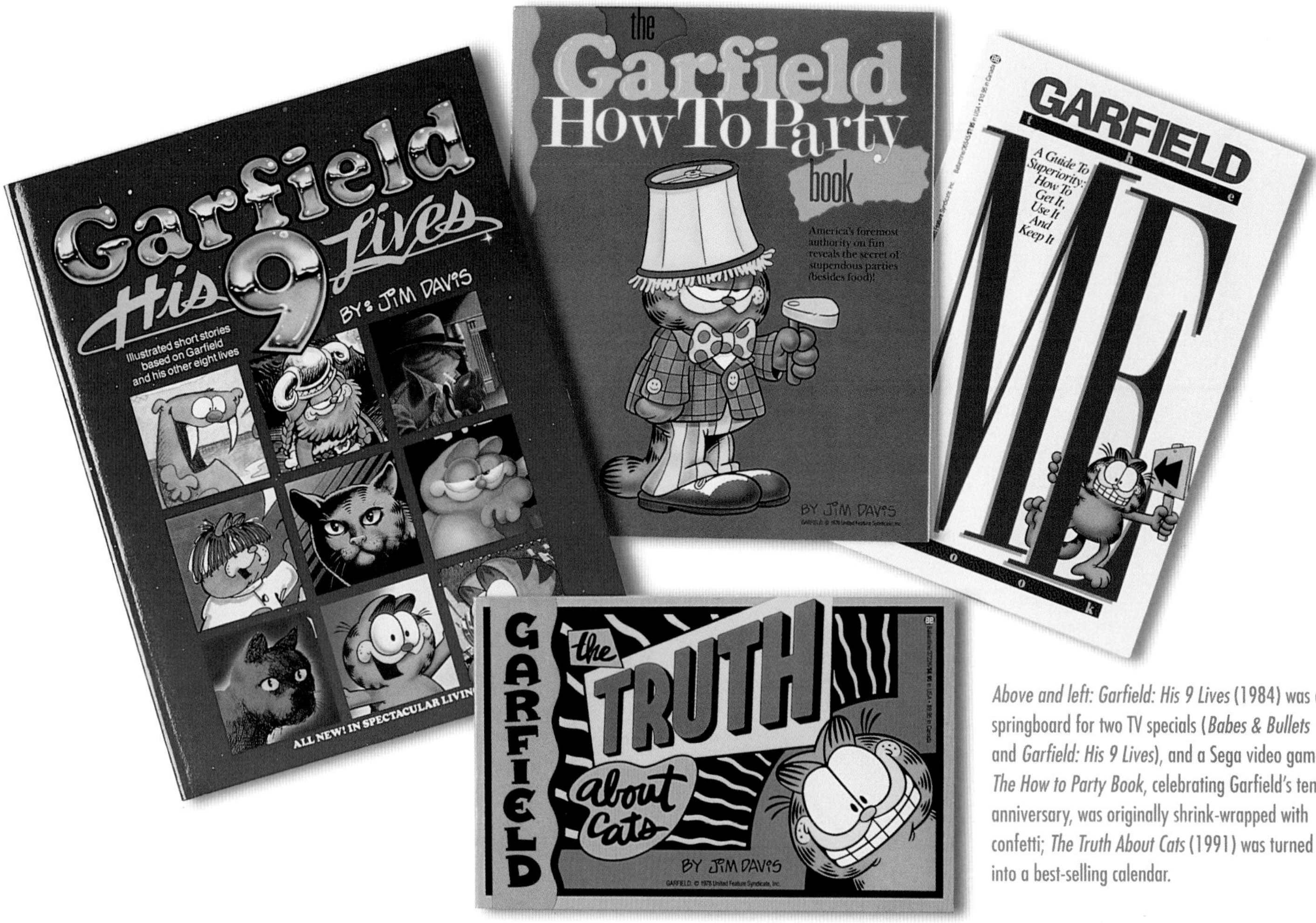
Garfield His 9 Lives
BY: JIM DAVIS
Illustrated short stories based on Garfield and his other eight lives
ALL NEW! IN SPECTACULAR LIVING
the Garfield How To Party book
America's foremost authority on fun reveals the secret of stupendous parties (besides food)!
BY JIM DAVIS
GARFIELD the ME book
A Guide To Superiority: How To Get It, Use It And Keep It
GARFIELD the TRUTH about Cats
BY JIM DAVIS

Above and left: Garfield: His 9 Lives (1984) was a springboard for two TV specials (*Babes & Bullets* and *Garfield: His 9 Lives*), and a Sega video game; *The How to Party Book*, celebrating Garfield's tenth anniversary, was originally shrink-wrapped with confetti; *The Truth About Cats* (1991) was turned into a best-selling calendar.

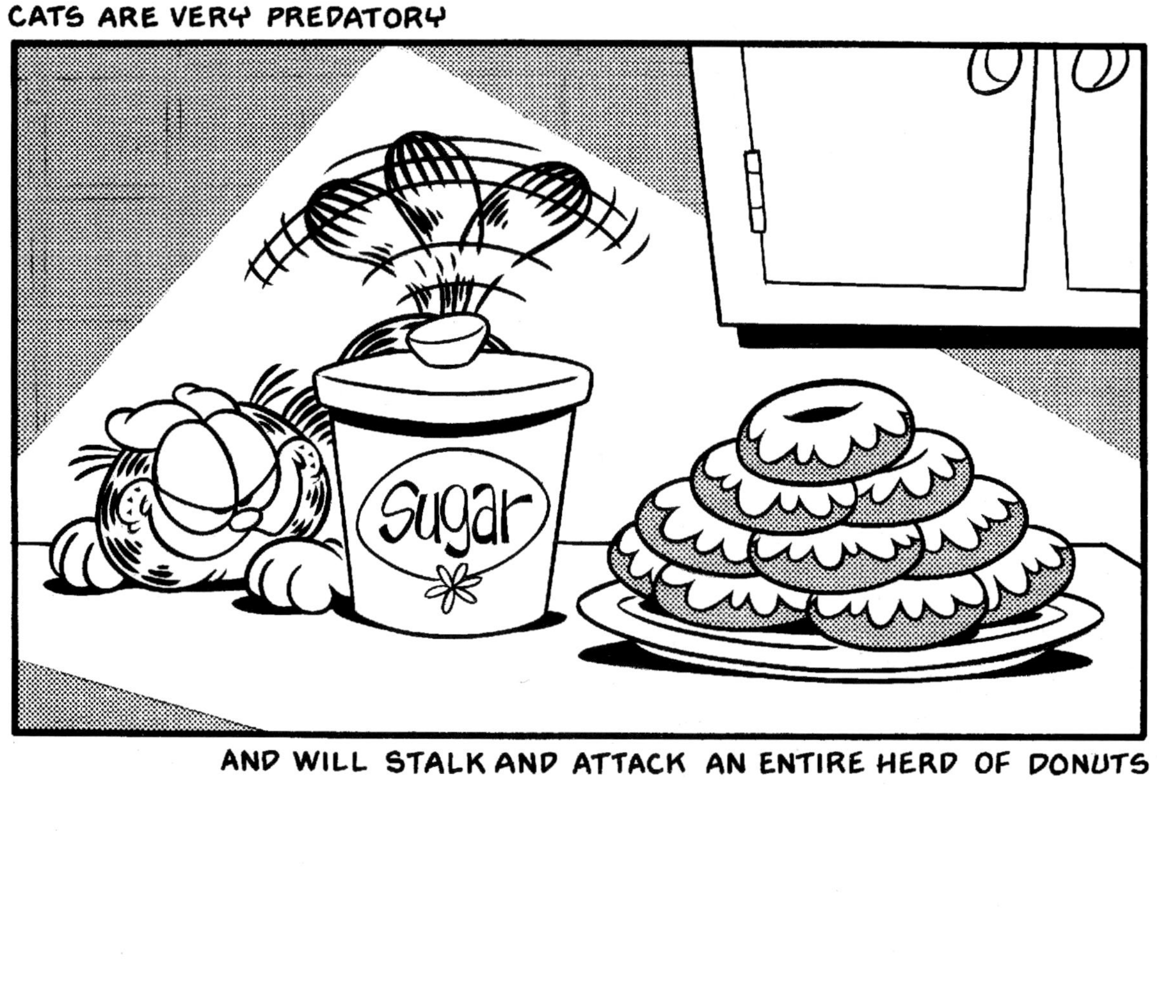
CATS ARE VERY PREDATORY
sugar
AND WILL STALK AND ATTACK AN ENTIRE HERD OF DONUTS

Left: A page from *The Truth About Cats* book.

COVER CAT

Garfield doesn't just appear in his own books. Check out the cover shots of this glamorous puss!

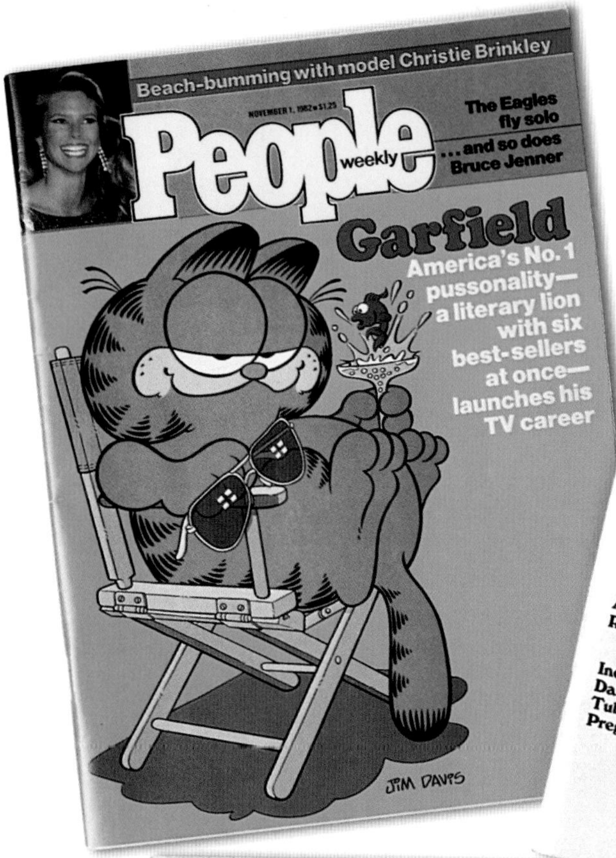
Beach-bumming with model Christie Brinkley
People weekly
The Eagles fly solo
...and so does Bruce Jenner
Garfield
America's No. 1 pussonality—a literary lion with six best-sellers at once—launches his TV career
JIM DAVIS

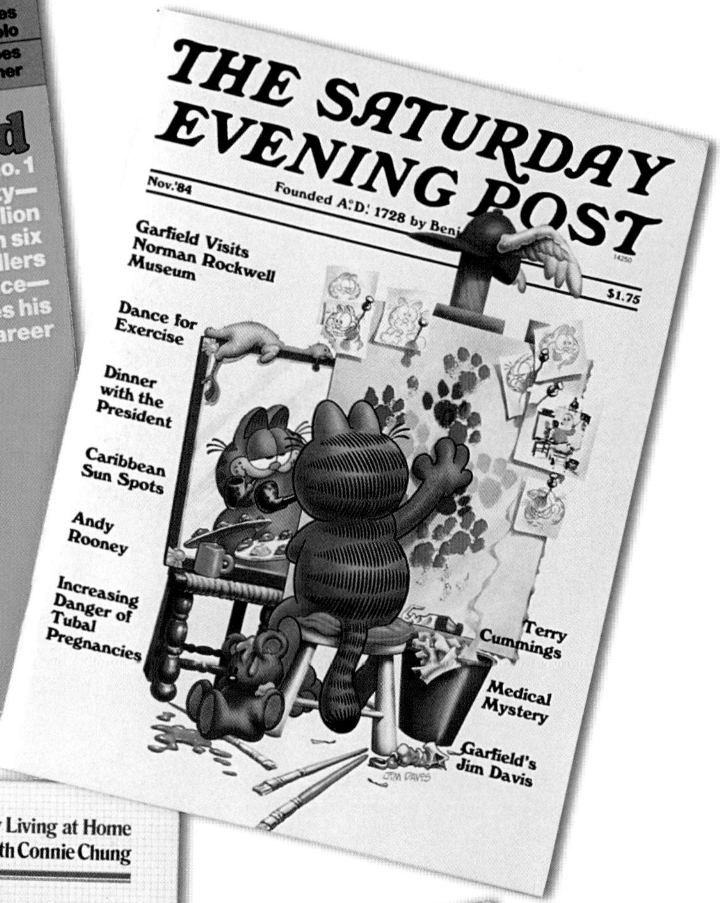
THE SATURDAY EVENING POST
Nov.'84
$1.75
Garfield Visits Norman Rockwell Museum
Dance for Exercise
Dinner with the President
Caribbean Sun Spots
Andy Rooney
Increasing Danger of Tubal Pregnancies
Terry Cummings
Medical Mystery
Garfield's Jim Davis

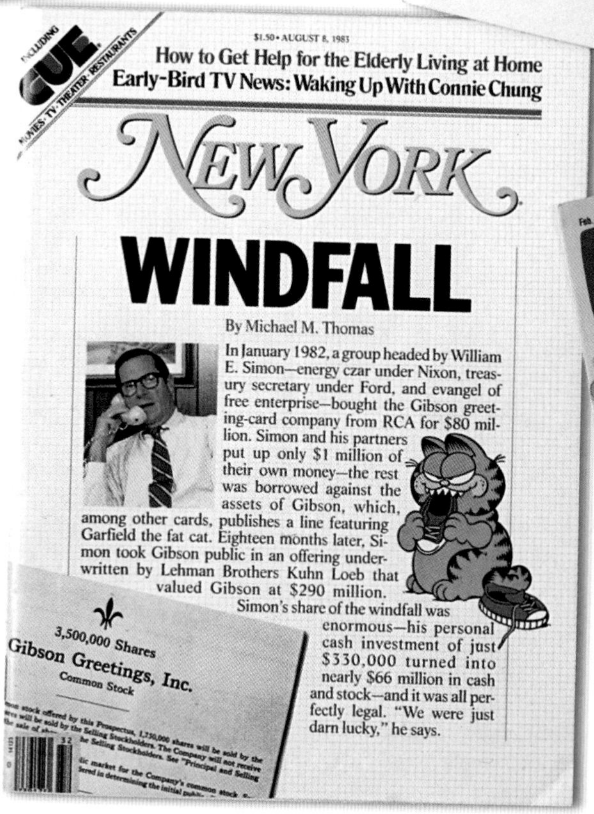
INCLUDING CUE
MOVIES · TV · THEATER · RESTAURANTS
$1.50 • AUGUST 8, 1983
How to Get Help for the Elderly Living at Home
Early-Bird TV News: Waking Up With Connie Chung
NEW YORK
WINDFALL
By Michael M. Thomas
In January 1982, a group headed by William E. Simon—energy czar under Nixon, treasury secretary under Ford, and evangel of free enterprise—bought the Gibson greeting-card company from RCA for $80 million. Simon and his partners put up only $1 million of their own money—the rest was borrowed against the assets of Gibson, which, among other cards, publishes a line featuring Garfield the fat cat. Eighteen months later, Simon took Gibson public in an offering underwritten by Lehman Brothers Kuhn Loeb that valued Gibson at $290 million.
Simon's share of the windfall was enormous—his personal cash investment of just $330,000 turned into nearly $66 million in cash and stock—and it was all perfectly legal. "We were just darn lucky," he says.
3,500,000 Shares
Gibson Greetings, Inc.
Common Stock

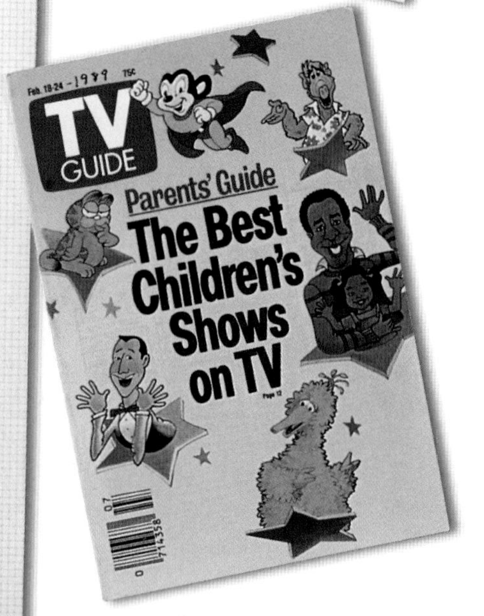
TV GUIDE
Parents' Guide
The Best Children's Shows on TV

Clockwise from top: People, 1982; The Saturday Evening Post, 1984; TV Guide, 1989; New York, 1983.

CHAPTER FIVE

Say It with Garfield!

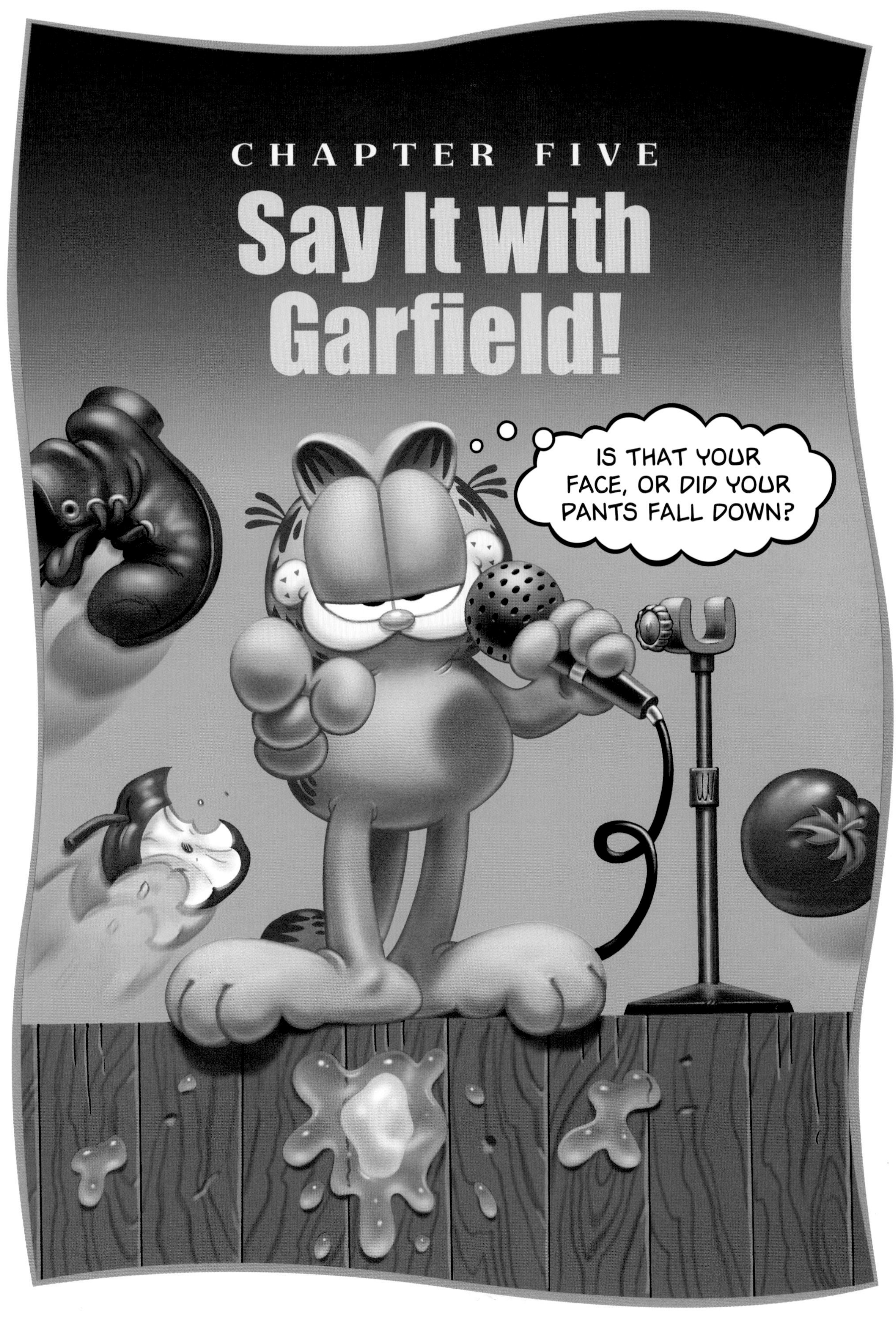
IS THAT YOUR FACE, OR DID YOUR PANTS FALL DOWN?

For Garfield, attitude is everything: He's made a career out of being catty. The witty kitty has put his distinctive paw print on posters, notebooks, T-shirts, mugs, rugs (no, not toupees—yet!), greeting cards galore, and much, much more. Whether it's "I Hate Mondays" or "Annoy Me at Your Own Risk," Garfield helps millions of people say what's on their minds. Check out this collection of classic "Garfisms." They speak for themselves . . . .

POSTERMANIA!

Posters are a vital part of the Garfield business. They not only entertain in their own right, but their crazy quips and images also feed other parts of the program.

Garfield and his biting humor debuted on Argus posters in 1980, and he's been appearing on them ever since. Through the years, Garfield has changed with the times, but he's never stopped saying it like it is.

Below: Argus poster introducing Garfield, circa 1980.

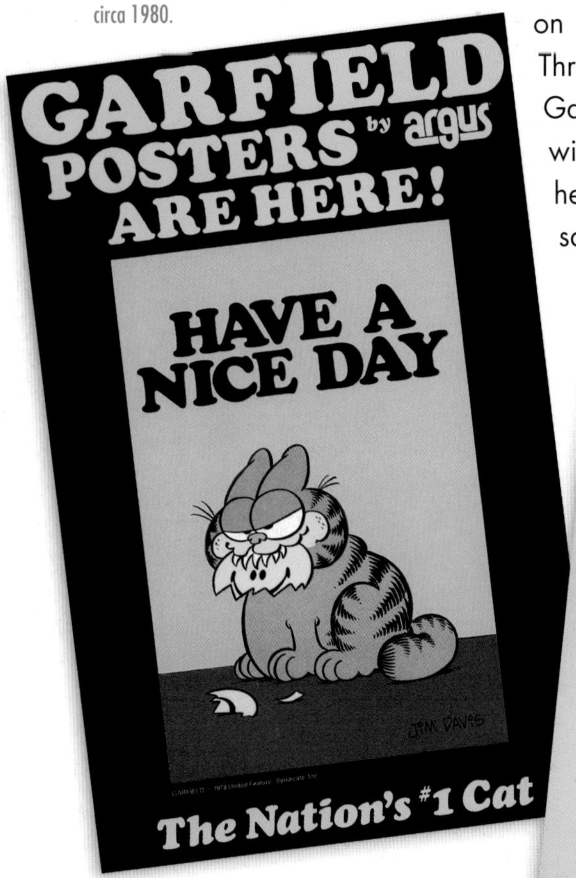
GARFIELD POSTERS by argus ARE HERE!
HAVE A NICE DAY
JIM DAVIS
The Nation's #1 Cat

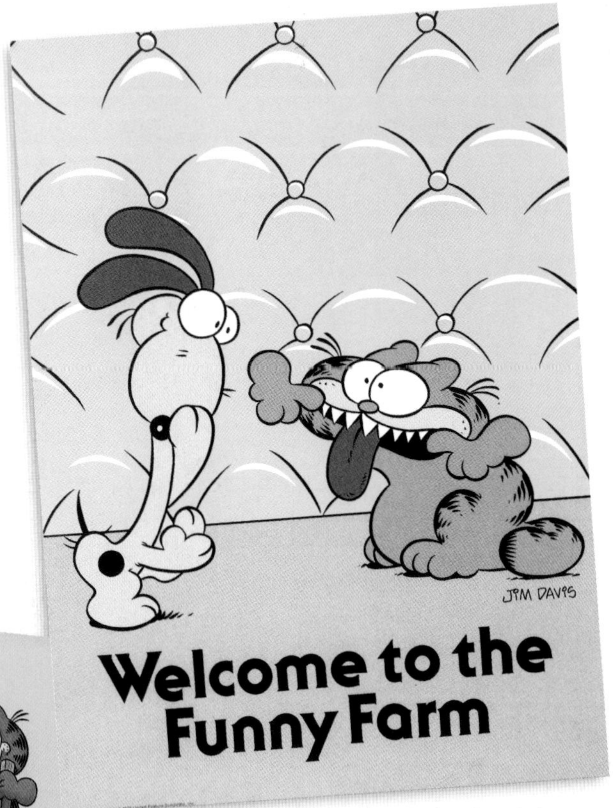
JIM DAVIS
Welcome to the Funny Farm

Above: Bonkers from the beginning: early poster, circa 1981.

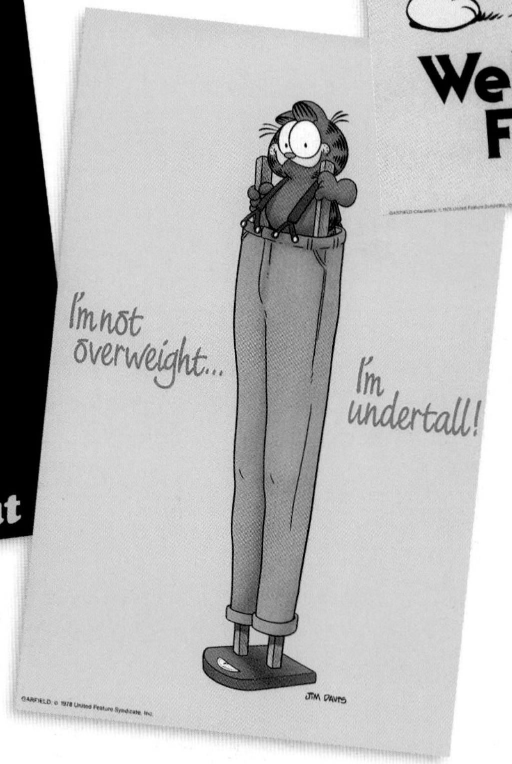
I'm not overweight...
I'm undertall!
JIM DAVIS

Right: A Garfield "quotable quote," based on a 1979 comic strip.

"Posters are right at the top of my list of favorite Garfield products. They provide a good opportunity to do one-panel gags."

—Jim Davis

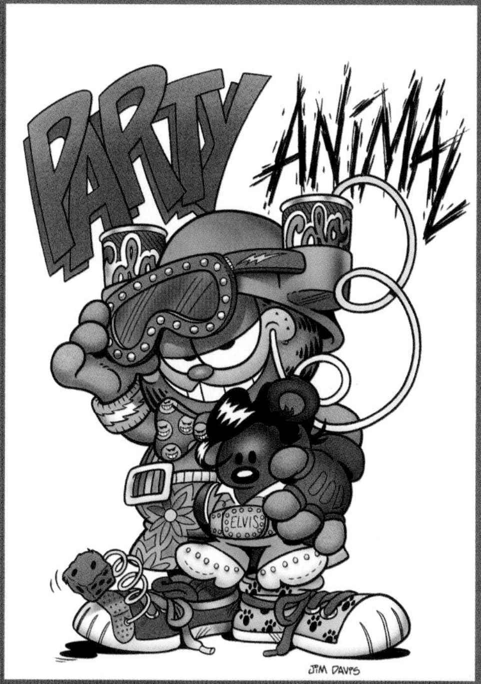
PARTY ANIMAL
ELVIS
JIM DAVIS

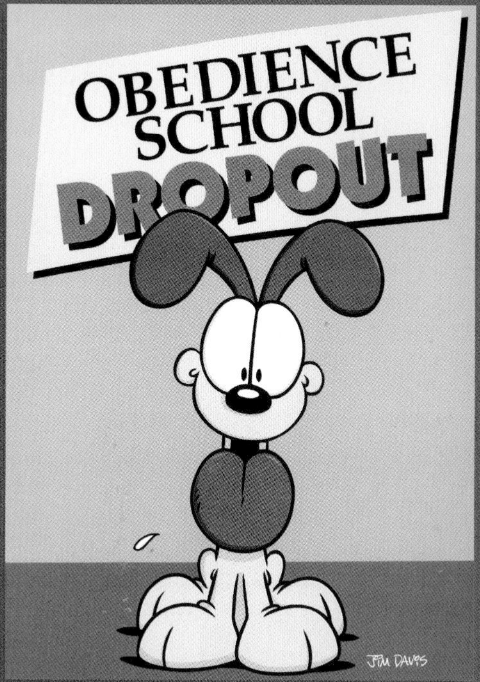
OBEDIENCE SCHOOL DROPOUT
JIM DAVIS

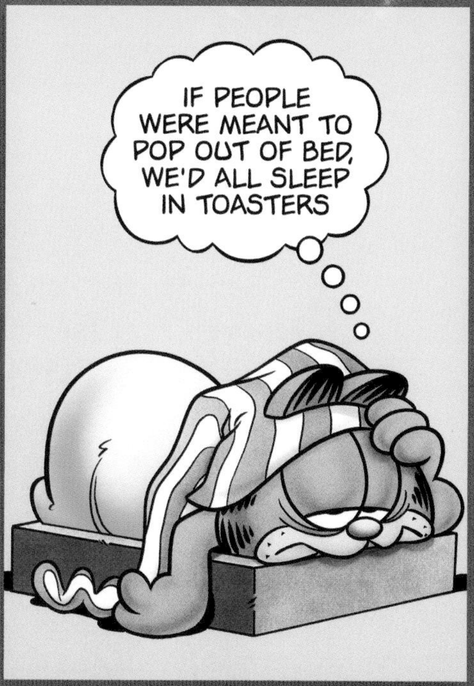
IF PEOPLE WERE MEANT TO POP OUT OF BED, WE'D ALL SLEEP IN TOASTERS

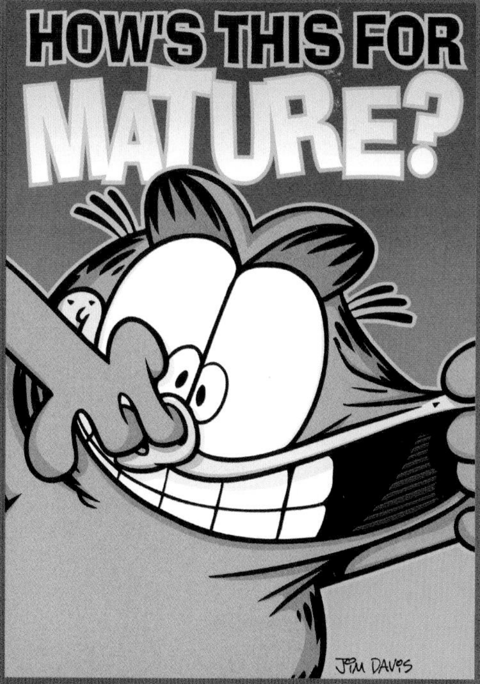
HOW'S THIS FOR MATURE?
JIM DAVIS

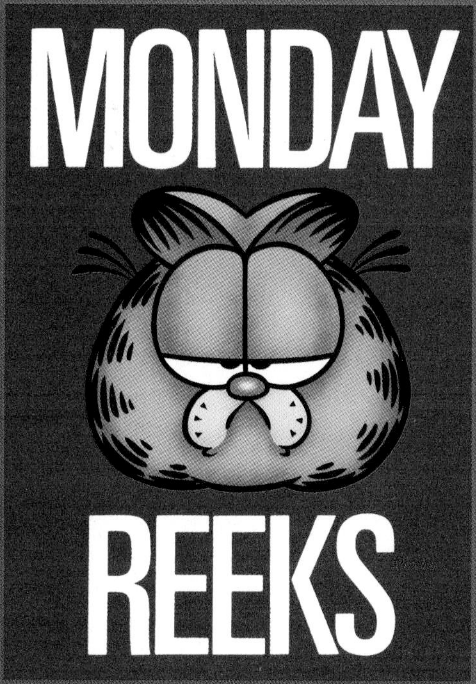
MONDAY
REEKS

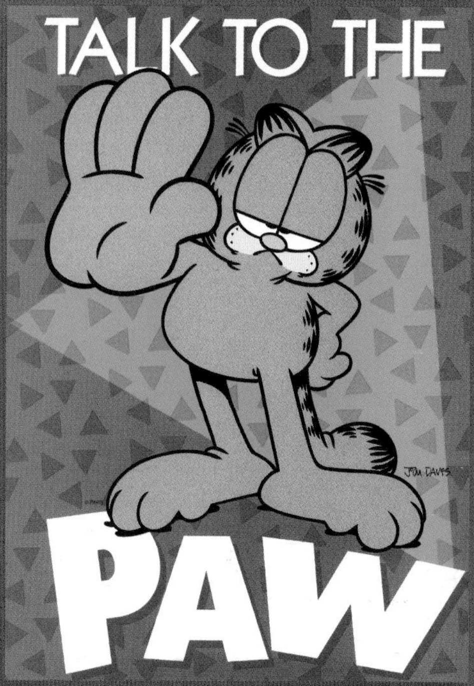
TALK TO THE
PAW
JIM DAVIS

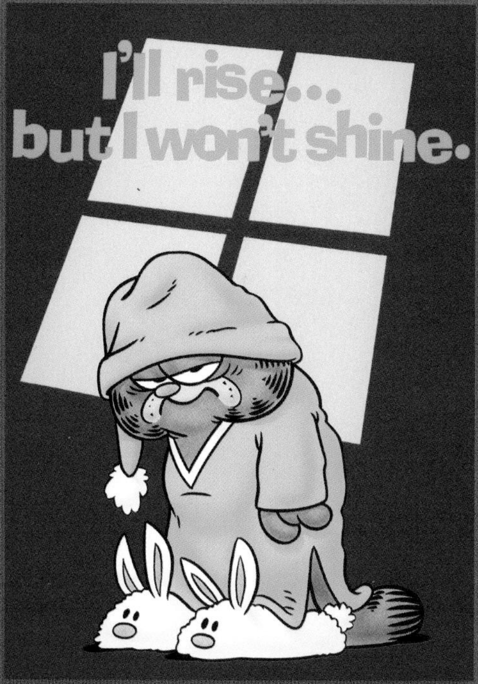
I'll rise...
but I won't shine.

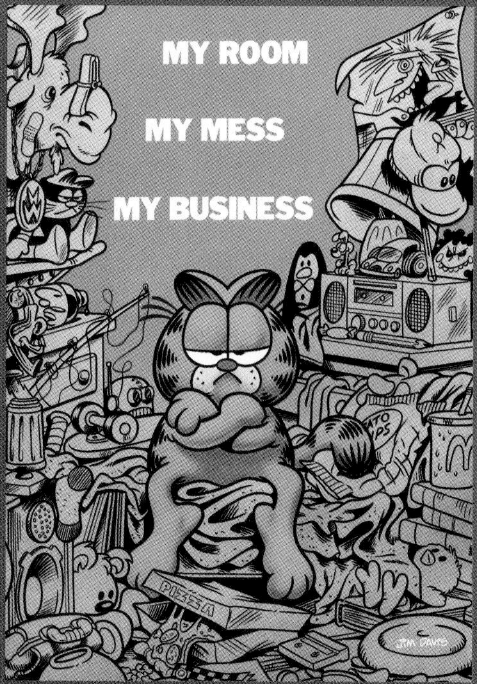
MY ROOM
MY MESS
MY BUSINESS
JIM DAVIS

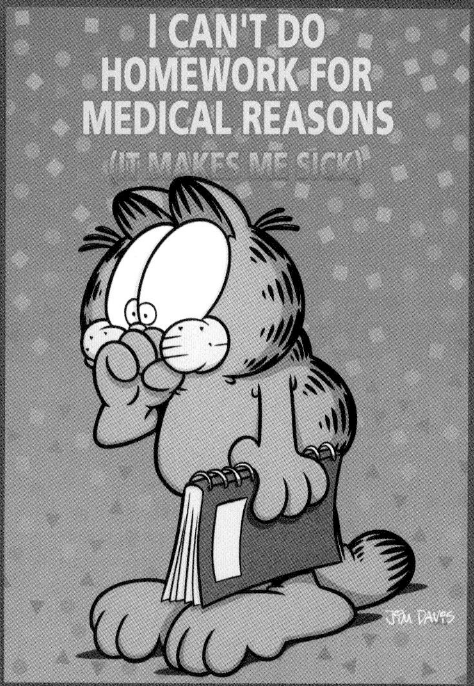
I CAN'T DO HOMEWORK FOR MEDICAL REASONS
(IT MAKES ME SICK)
JIM DAVIS

Garfield often lampoons popular culture, as seen here with these two '80s icons, Bruce Springsteen and *Miami Vice*, circa 1984.

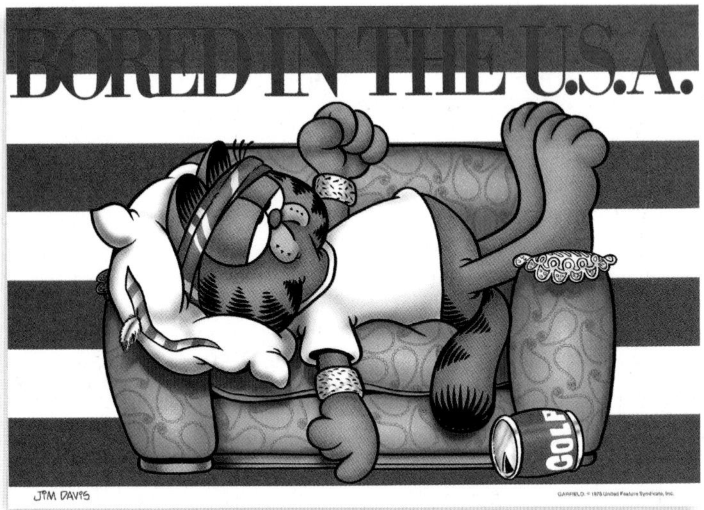
BORED IN THE U.S.A.
GOLF
JIM DAVIS

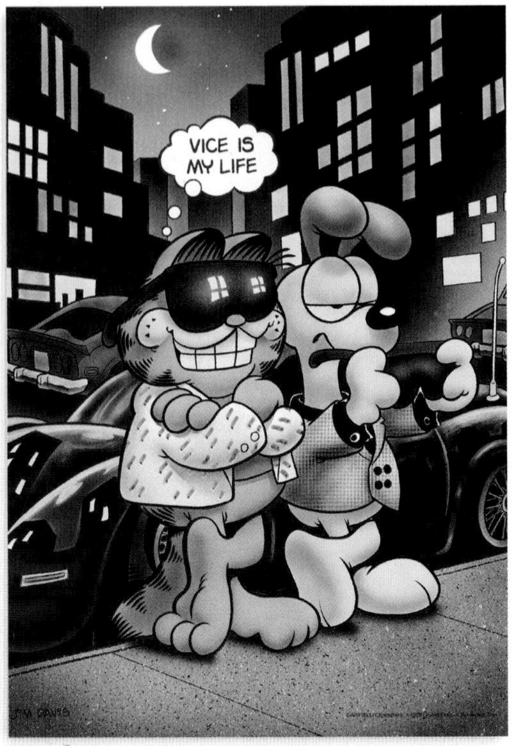
VICE IS MY LIFE
JIM DAVIS

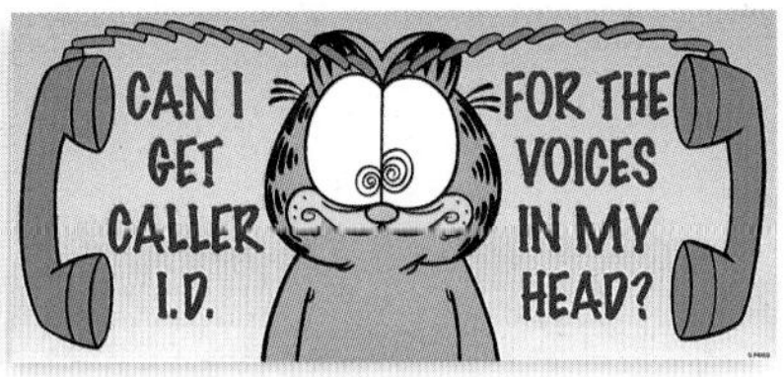
CAN I GET CALLER I.D.
FOR THE VOICES IN MY HEAD?

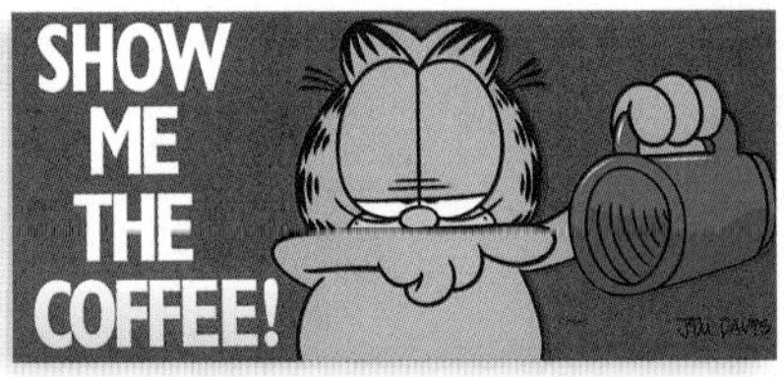
SHOW ME THE COFFEE!
JIM DAVIS

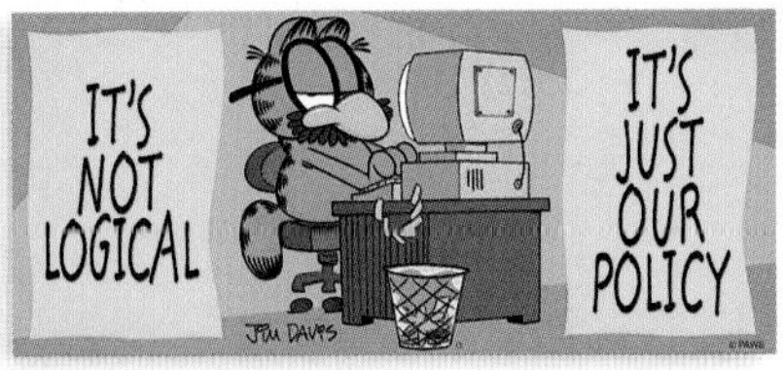
IT'S NOT LOGICAL
IT'S JUST OUR POLICY
JIM DAVIS

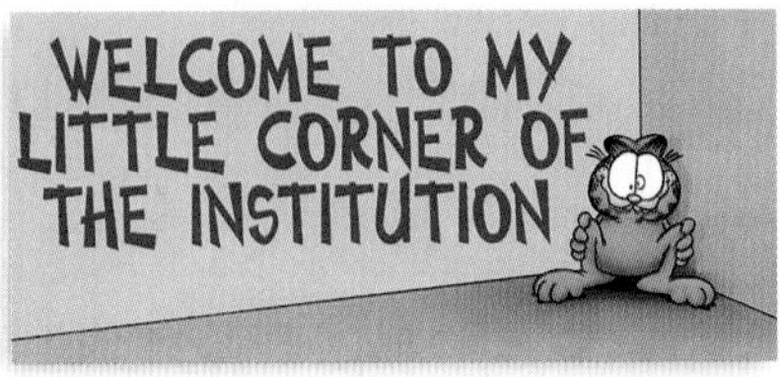
WELCOME TO MY LITTLE CORNER OF THE INSTITUTION

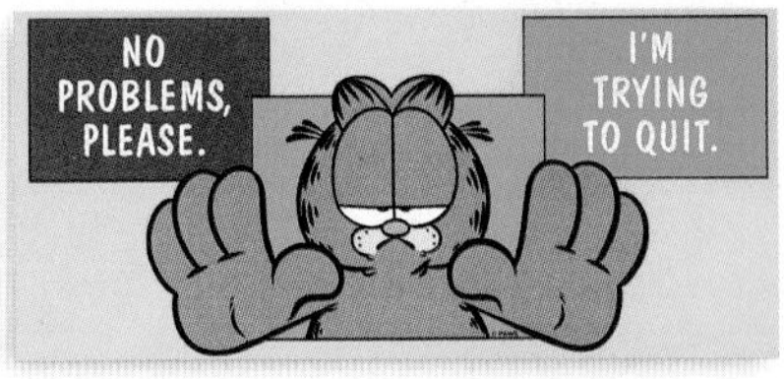
NO PROBLEMS, PLEASE.
I'M TRYING TO QUIT.

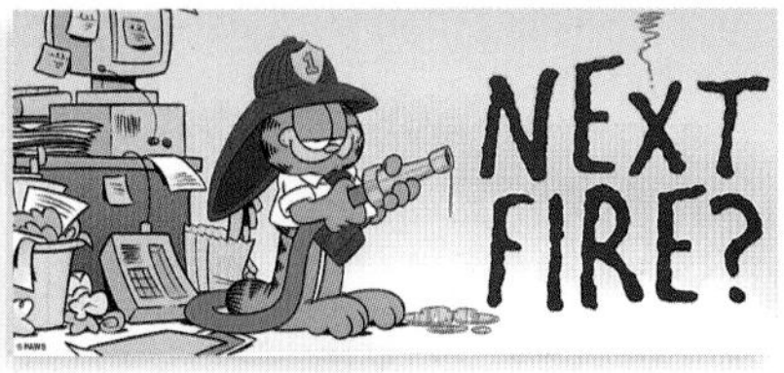
NEXT FIRE?

Above:
BEST IN THE BUSINESS
Garfield office-themed miniposters.

Right:
SIGNS OF THE TIMES
Posters playing off of pop-culture catchphrases.

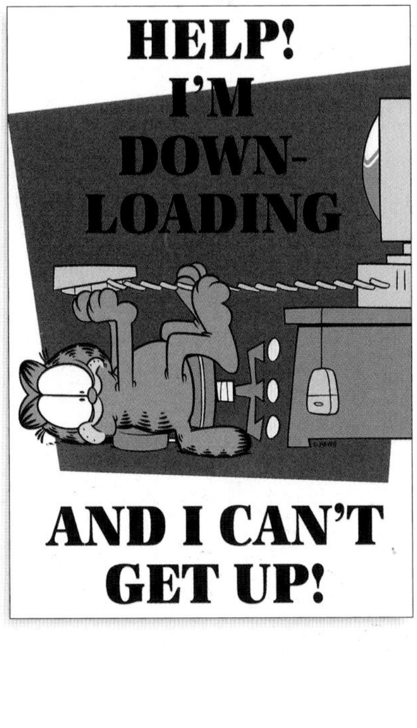
HELP! I'M DOWN-LOADING
AND I CAN'T GET UP!

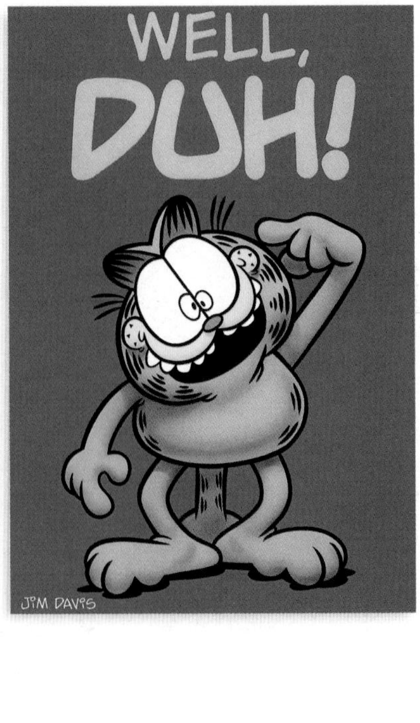
WELL, DUH!
JIM DAVIS

THE WRITE STUFF

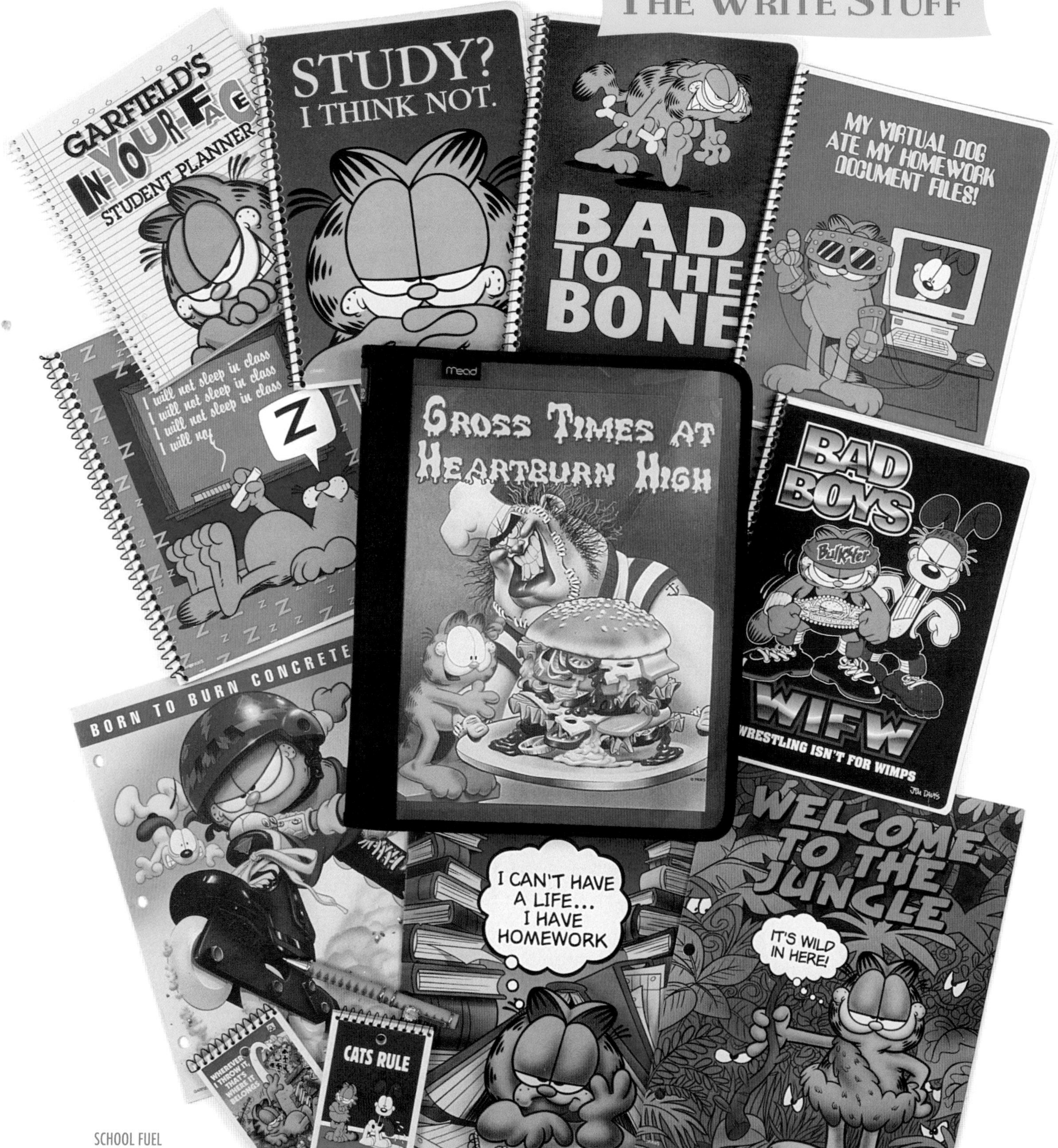
GARFIELD'S IN-YOUR-FACE STUDENT PLANNER
STUDY? I THINK NOT.
BAD TO THE BONE
MY VIRTUAL DOG ATE MY HOMEWORK DOCUMENT FILES!
I will not sleep in class
I will not sleep in class
I will not sleep in class
I will not
Z
mead
GROSS TIMES AT HEARTBURN HIGH
BAD BOYS
WIFW
WRESTLING ISN'T FOR WIMPS
BORN TO BURN CONCRETE
I CAN'T HAVE A LIFE... I HAVE HOMEWORK
WELCOME TO THE JUNGLE
IT'S WILD IN HERE!
CATS RULE
DOGS DROOL

SCHOOL FUEL
Notebooks, planners, and portfolios, 1996–2001.

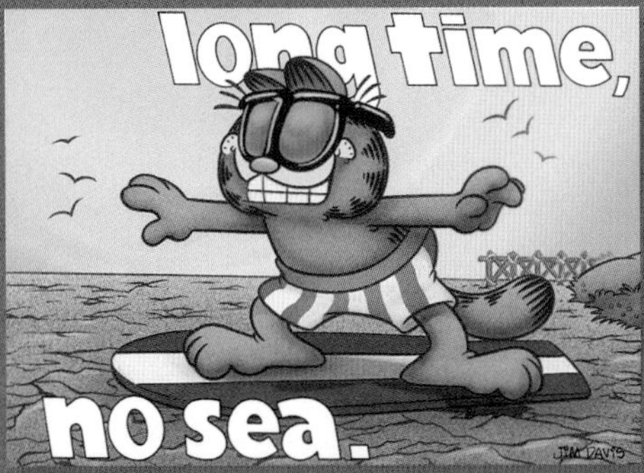
long time,
no sea.
JIM DAVIS

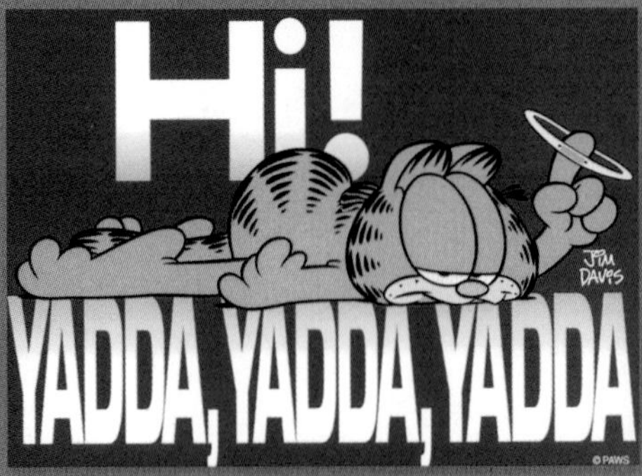
Hi!
YADDA, YADDA, YADDA
JIM DAVIS
© PAWS

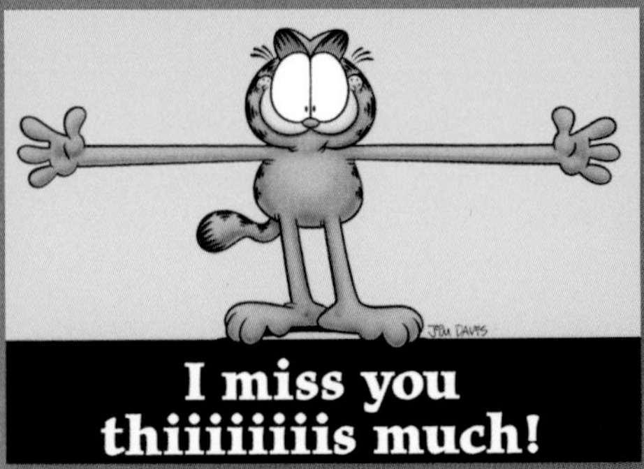
JIM DAVIS
I miss you
thiiiiiiiis much!

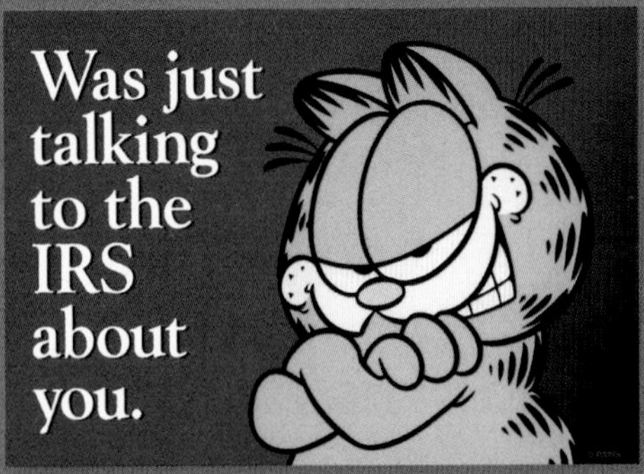
Was just
talking
to the
IRS
about
you.

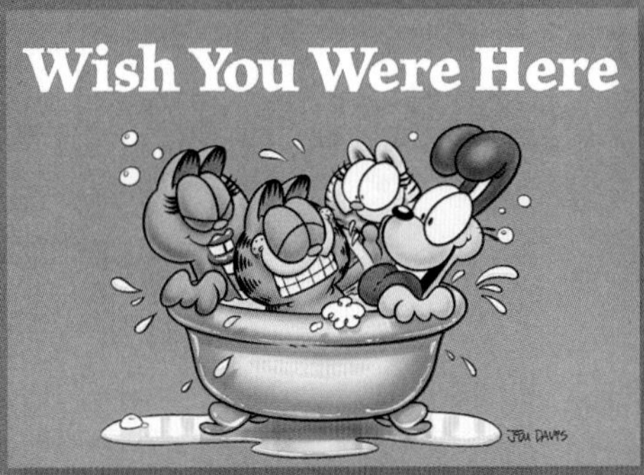
Wish You Were Here
JIM DAVIS

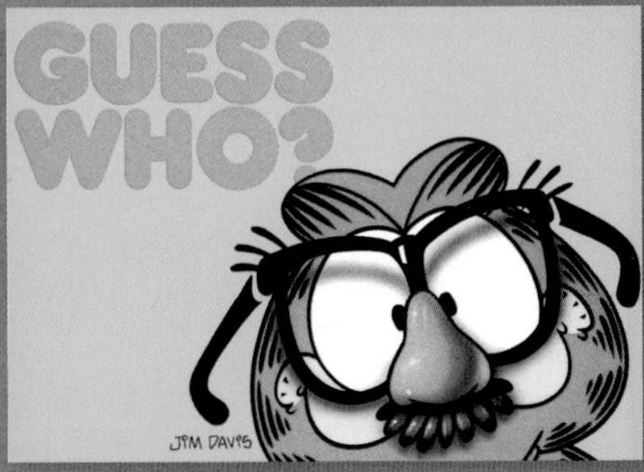
GUESS
WHO?
JIM DAVIS

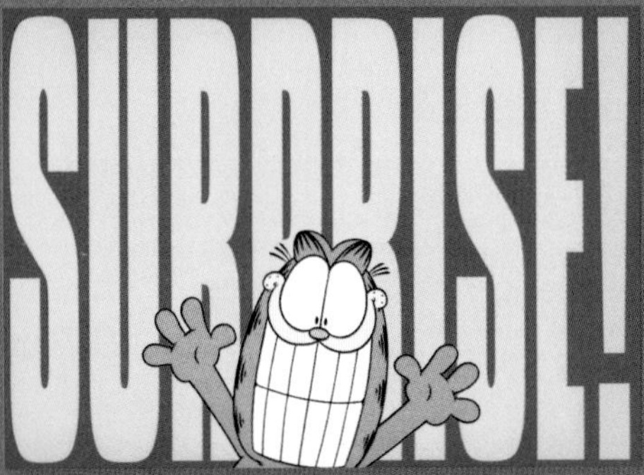
SURPRISE!

GARFIELD POSTCARD POTPOURRI

A mixture of festivity and frivolity, courtesy of the cat.

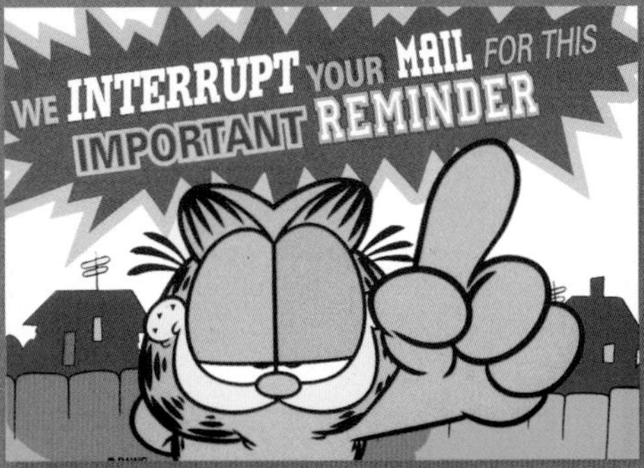
WE INTERRUPT YOUR MAIL FOR THIS
IMPORTANT REMINDER

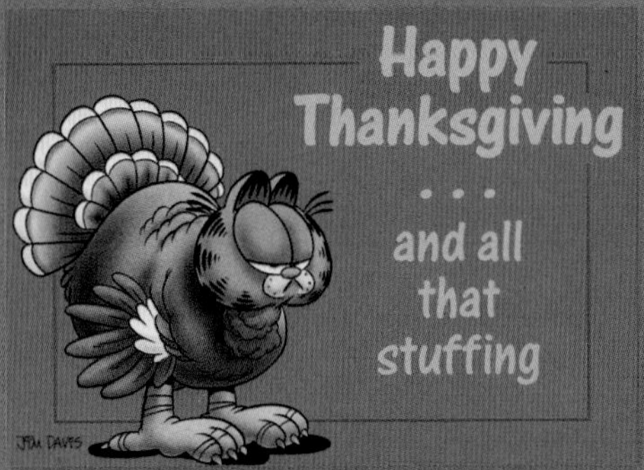
Happy
Thanksgiving
. . .
and all
that
stuffing
JIM DAVIS

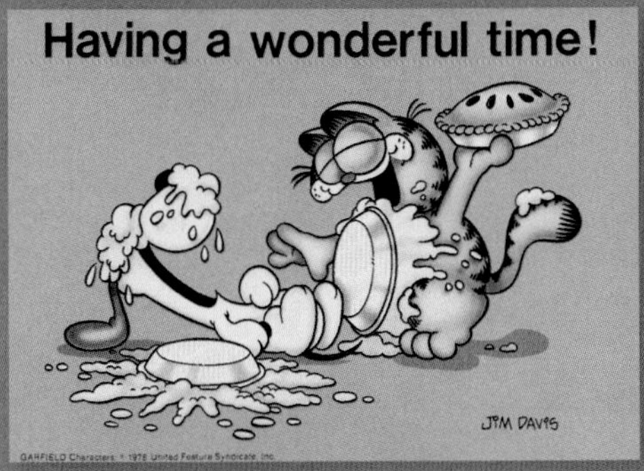
Having a wonderful time!
JIM DAVIS

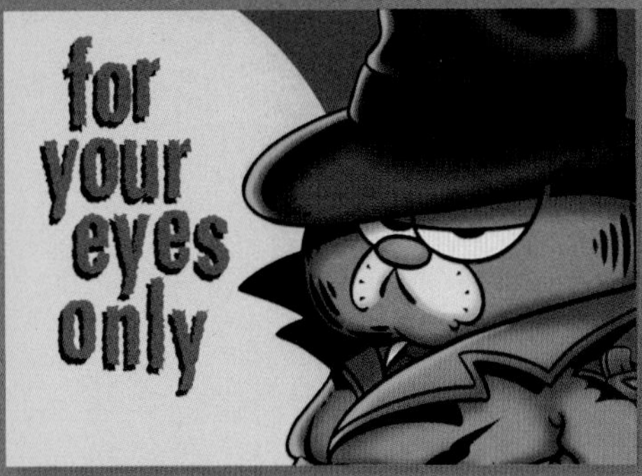
for
your
eyes
only

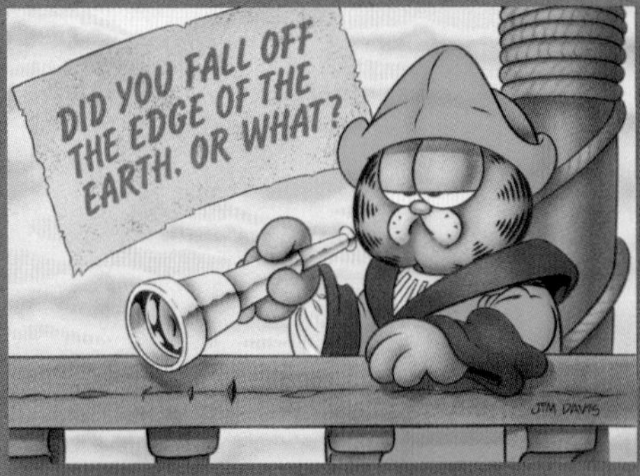
DID YOU FALL OFF
THE EDGE OF THE
EARTH, OR WHAT?
JIM DAVIS

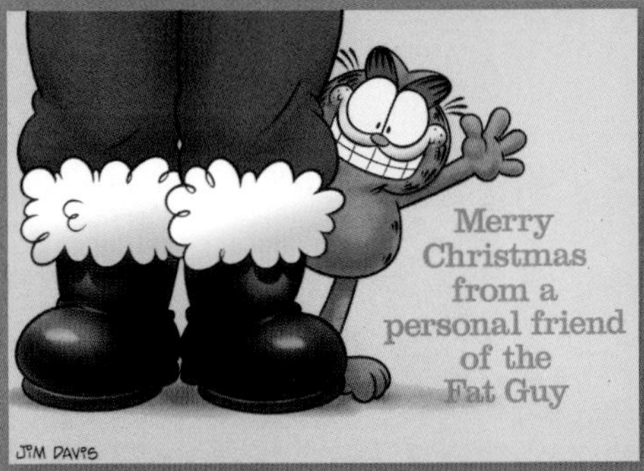
Merry
Christmas
from a
personal friend
of the
Fat Guy
JIM DAVIS

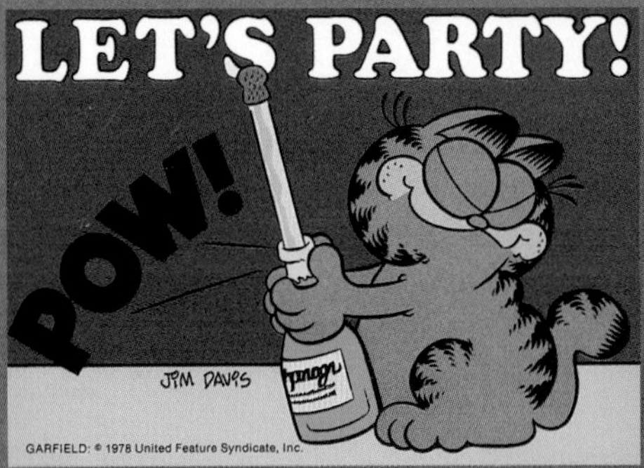
LET'S PARTY!
POW!
JIM DAVIS
GARFIELD: © 1978 United Feature Syndicate, Inc.

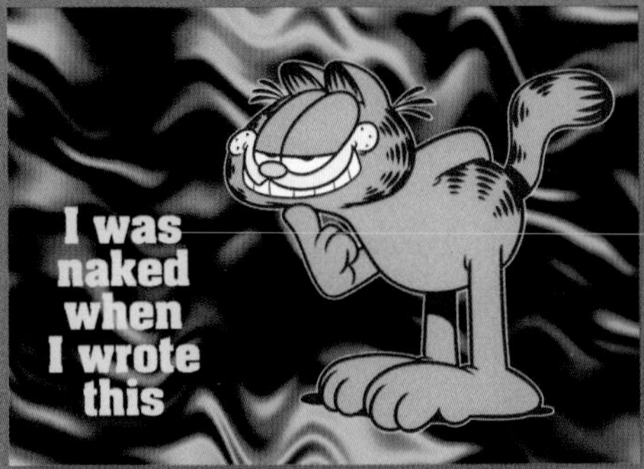
I was
naked
when
I wrote
this

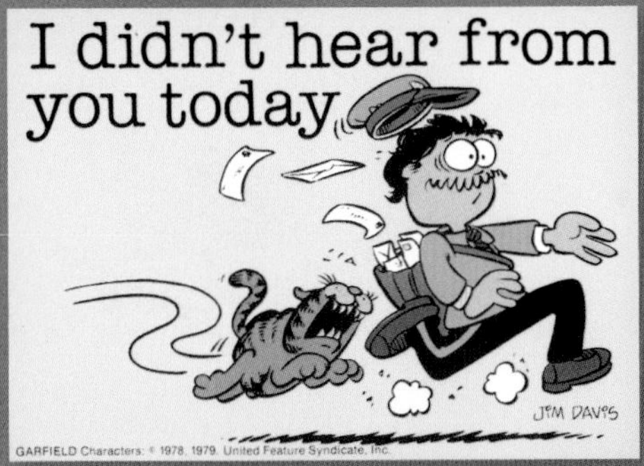
I didn't hear from
you today
JIM DAVIS
GARFIELD Characters: © 1978, 1979, United Feature Syndicate, Inc.

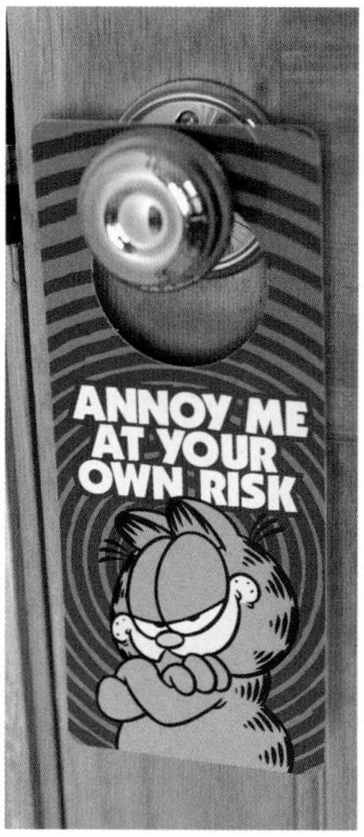
ANNOY ME
AT YOUR
OWN RISK

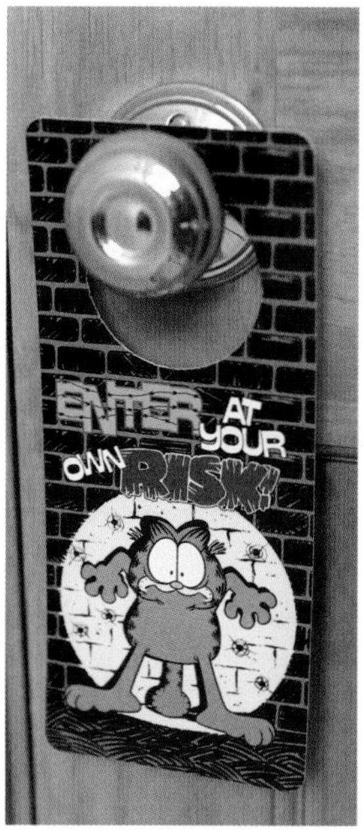
ENTER AT YOUR
OWN RISK!

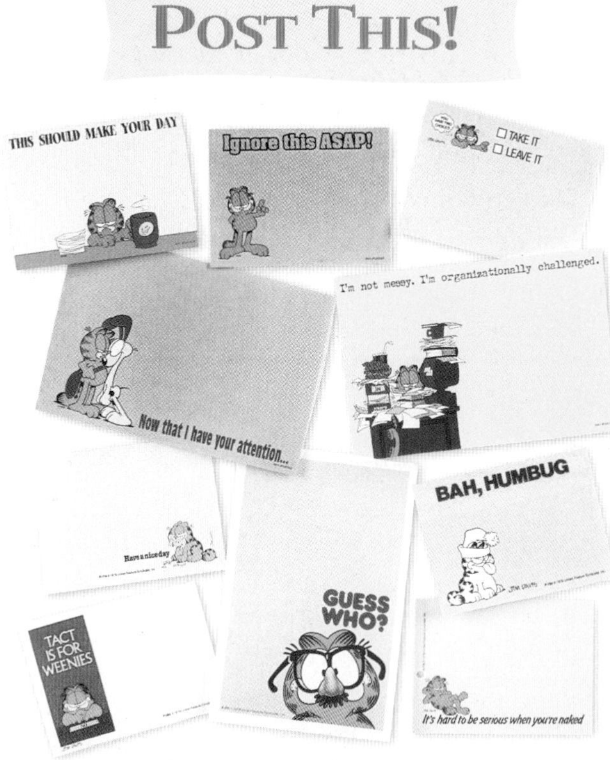
POST THIS!
THIS SHOULD MAKE YOUR DAY
Ignore this ASAP!
TAKE IT
LEAVE IT
I'm not messy. I'm organizationally challenged.
Now that I have your attention...
BAH, HUMBUG
GUESS WHO?
TACT IS FOR WEENIES
It's hard to be serious when you're naked

Far left, clockwise: "Posters" on products: doorhangers, self-stick notes, calendar and note cubes, magnets, bookmarks.

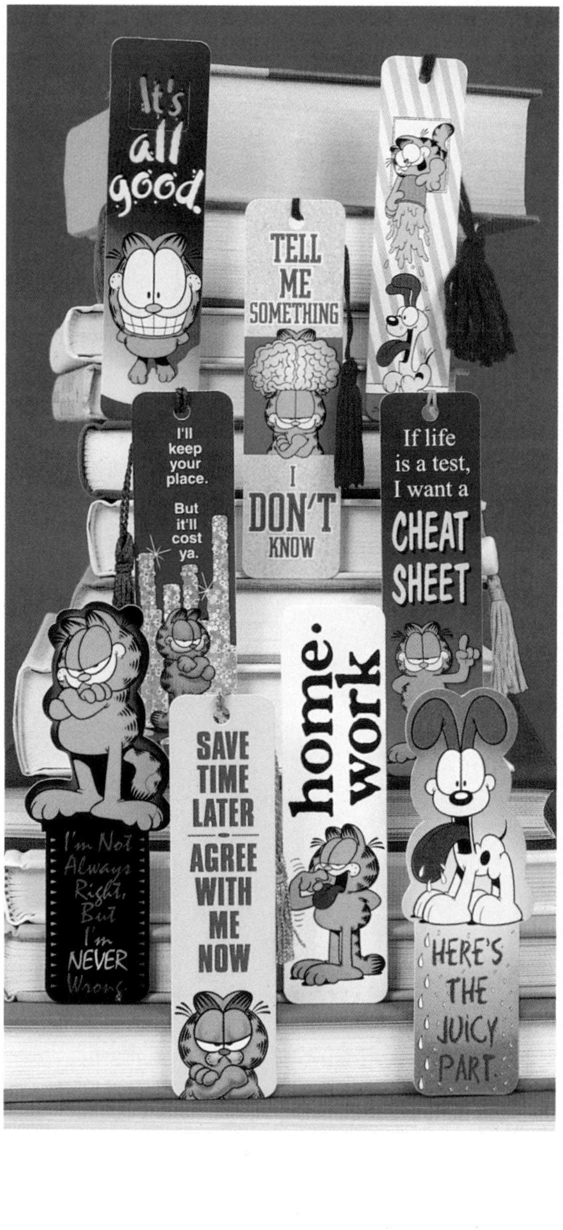
It's all good
TELL ME SOMETHING
I DON'T KNOW
I'll keep your place. But it'll cost ya.
If life is a test, I want a CHEAT SHEET
home. work
SAVE TIME LATER
AGREE WITH ME NOW
I'm Not Always Right, But I'm NEVER Wrong
HERE'S THE JUICY PART

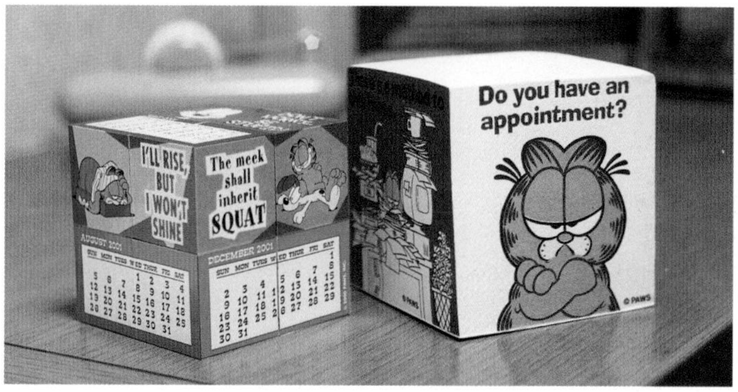
I'LL RISE, BUT I WON'T SHINE
The meek shall inherit SQUAT
Do you have an appointment?

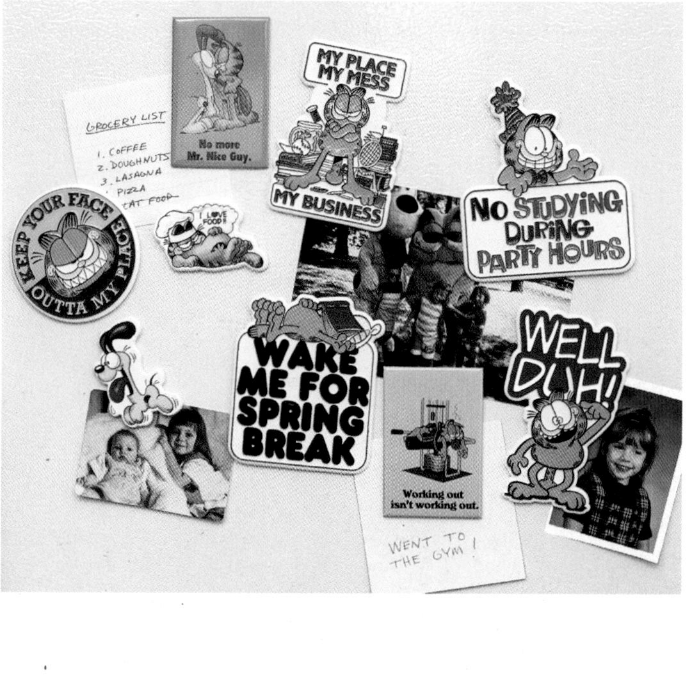
MY PLACE MY MESS MY BUSINESS
No more Mr. Nice Guy.
GROCERY LIST
1. COFFEE
2. DOUGHNUTS
3. LASAGNA
4. PIZZA
5. CAT FOOD
KEEP YOUR FACE OUTTA MY PLACE
NO STUDYING DURING PARTY HOURS
WAKE ME FOR SPRING BREAK
WELL DUH!
Working out isn't working out.
WENT TO THE GYM!

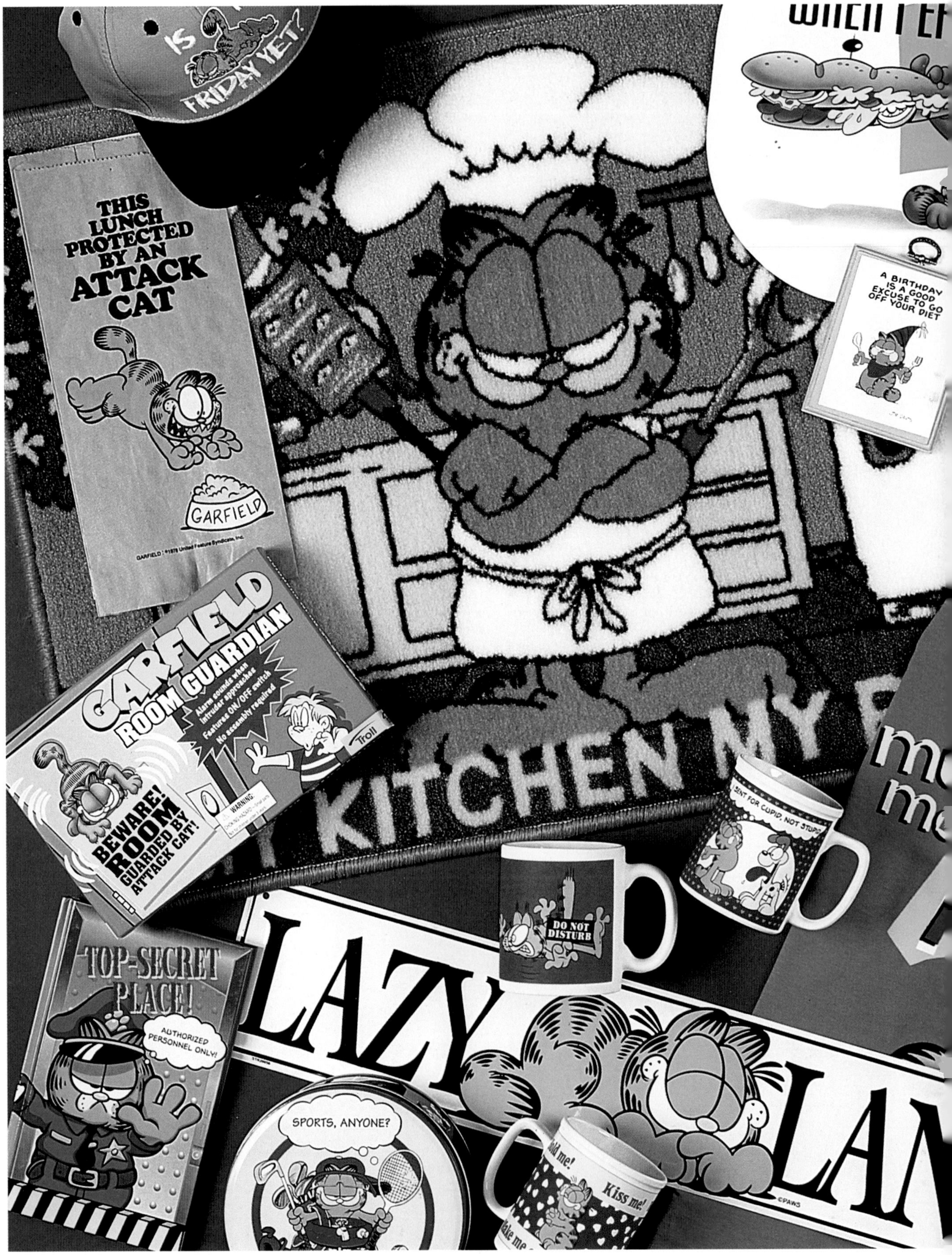
IS FRIDAY YET?
THIS LUNCH PROTECTED BY AN ATTACK CAT
GARFIELD
KITCHEN MY
A BIRTHDAY IS A GOOD EXCUSE TO GO OFF YOUR DIET
GARFIELD ROOM GUARDIAN
Alarm sounds when intruder approaches
Features ON/OFF switch
No assembly required
BEWARE! ROOM GUARDED BY ATTACK CAT!
Troll
I SENT FOR CUPID, NOT STUPID
DO NOT DISTURB
TOP-SECRET PLACE!
AUTHORIZED PERSONNEL ONLY!
LAZY
LAN
SPORTS, ANYONE?
Kiss me!

EXPRESS YOURSELF! A kaleidoscopic collection of Garfield goods.

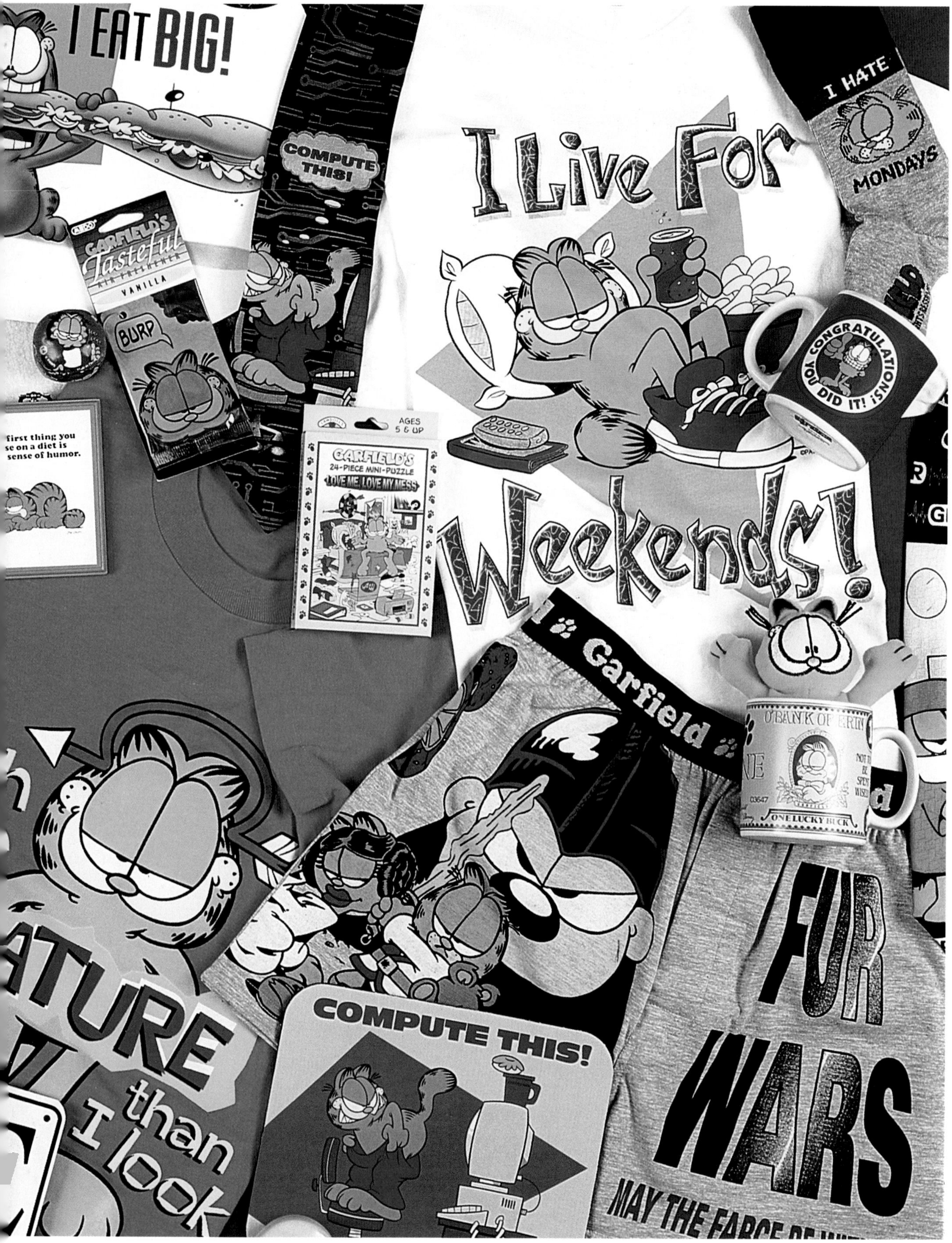
I EAT BIG!
COMPUTE THIS!
GARFIELD'S Tasteful AIR FRESHENER
VANILLA
BURP
I Live For Weekends!
I HATE MONDAYS
CONGRATULATIONS YOU DID IT!
first thing you se on a diet is sense of humor.
AGES 5 & UP
GARFIELD'S 24-PIECE MINI-PUZZLE
LOVE ME, LOVE MY MESS
Garfield
O'BANK OF ERIN
ONE LUCKY BUCK
COMPUTE THIS!
FUR WARS
than I look

Greetings Garfield Style!

Greeting cards have always been a big part of the Garfield business. From New Year's to Christmas and everything in between, card senders seem to find Garfield the right cat for all occasions. Whether people want to share a thought or a laugh, show their gratitude or just their attitude, Garfield makes sure they're never at a loss for words!

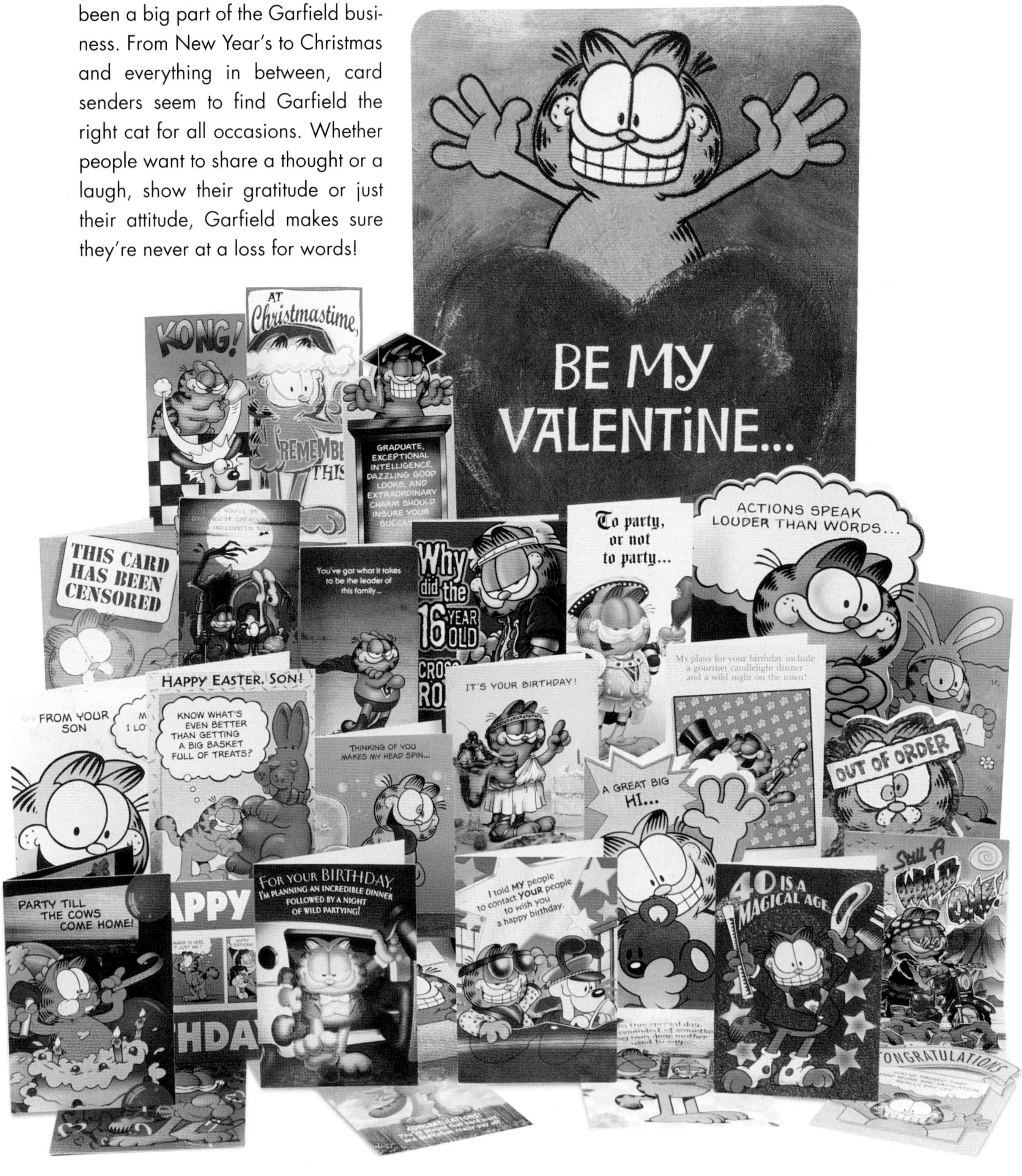
BE MY VALENTINE...
KONG!
AT Christmastime,
GRADUATE, EXCEPTIONAL INTELLIGENCE, DAZZLING GOOD LOOKS, AND EXTRAORDINARY CHARM SHOULD INSURE YOUR
THIS CARD HAS BEEN CENSORED
You've got what it takes to be the leader of this family...
Why did the 16 YEAR OLD
To party, or not to party...
ACTIONS SPEAK LOUDER THAN WORDS...
My plans for your birthday include a gourmet candlelight dinner and a wild night on the town!
HAPPY EASTER, SON!
FROM YOUR SON
KNOW WHAT'S EVEN BETTER THAN GETTING A BIG BASKET FULL OF TREATS?
IT'S YOUR BIRTHDAY!
THINKING OF YOU MAKES MY HEAD SPIN...
A GREAT BIG HI...
OUT OF ORDER
PARTY TILL THE COWS COME HOME!
FOR YOUR BIRTHDAY, I'M PLANNING AN INCREDIBLE DINNER FOLLOWED BY A NIGHT OF WILD PARTYING!
I told MY people to contact YOUR people to wish you a happy birthday.
40 IS A MAGICAL AGE

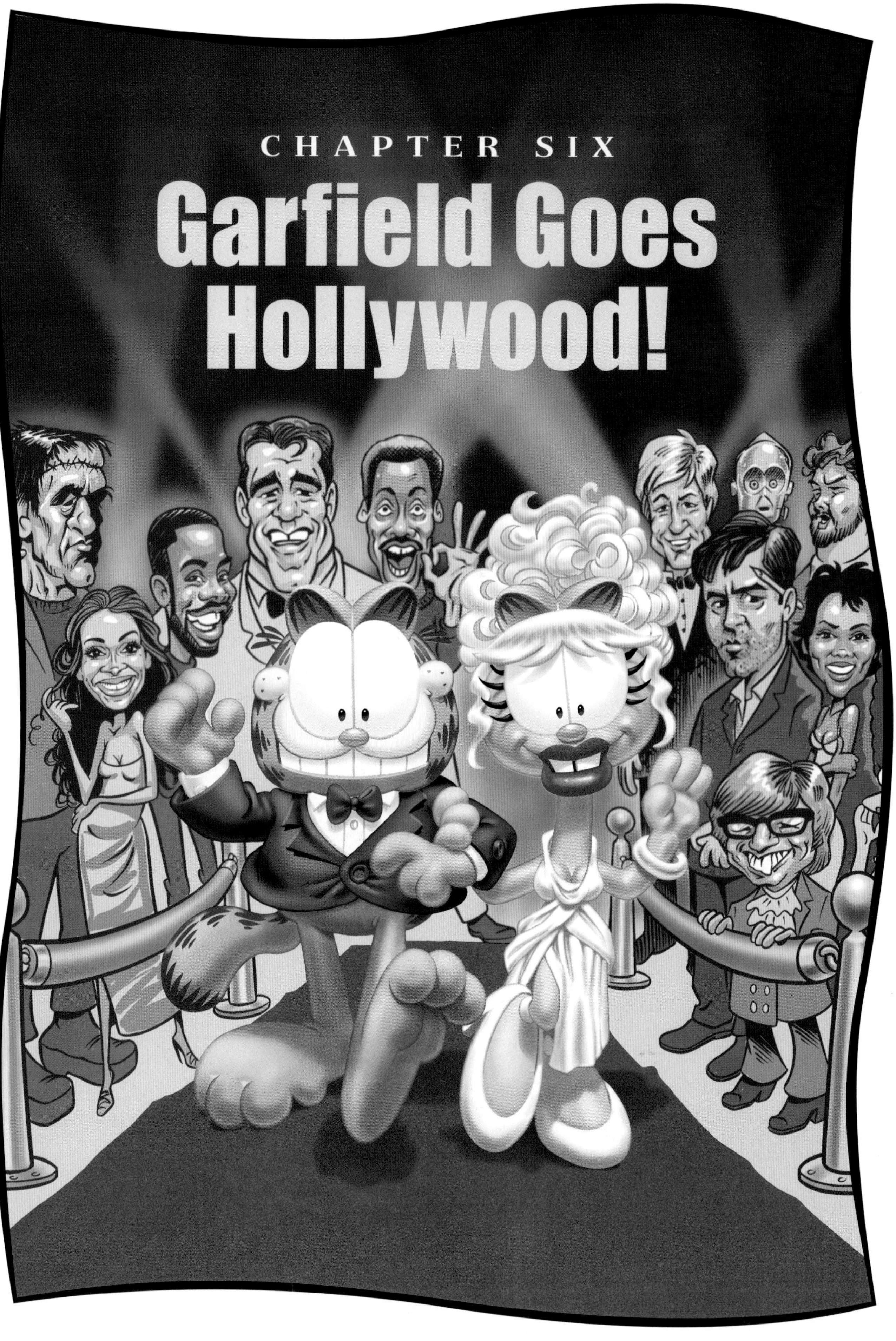
CHAPTER SIX
Garfield Goes Hollywood!

Garfield pounced from the comics pages onto the small screen on October 25, 1982, in his first prime-time television special, *Here Comes Garfield*. More than 40 million people tuned in to watch the comic-strip cat come to life, pushing the show into the top ten and catapulting Garfield into TV superstardom.

The corpulent cat with the oversized ego was happy to hog the spotlight, and twelve top-rated prime-time specials followed over the next ten years. The shows were honored by several Emmy nominations, with Garfield winning the coveted statuette four times.

An animated series, *Garfield and Friends*, joined the Saturday morning cartoon lineup in fall 1988, delighting fans with the weekly antics of Garfield, Jon, and Odie, and earning big ratings. The show also featured a regular segment starring the barnyard critters from *U.S.Acres*, Jim Davis's popular comic strip from the 1980s. *Garfield and Friends*—which boasted numerous celebrity guest stars—ran on Saturday mornings through 1995, and then went into syndication. It continues to be enjoyed by millions of viewers around the world.

Did all this success change Garfield? Oh, sure, he indulged in a little Hollywood excess—went to a few too many parties, did a little too much catnip—but the glitz and glamour never really went to his head.

Now on with the show. Lights! Camera! Laughter!

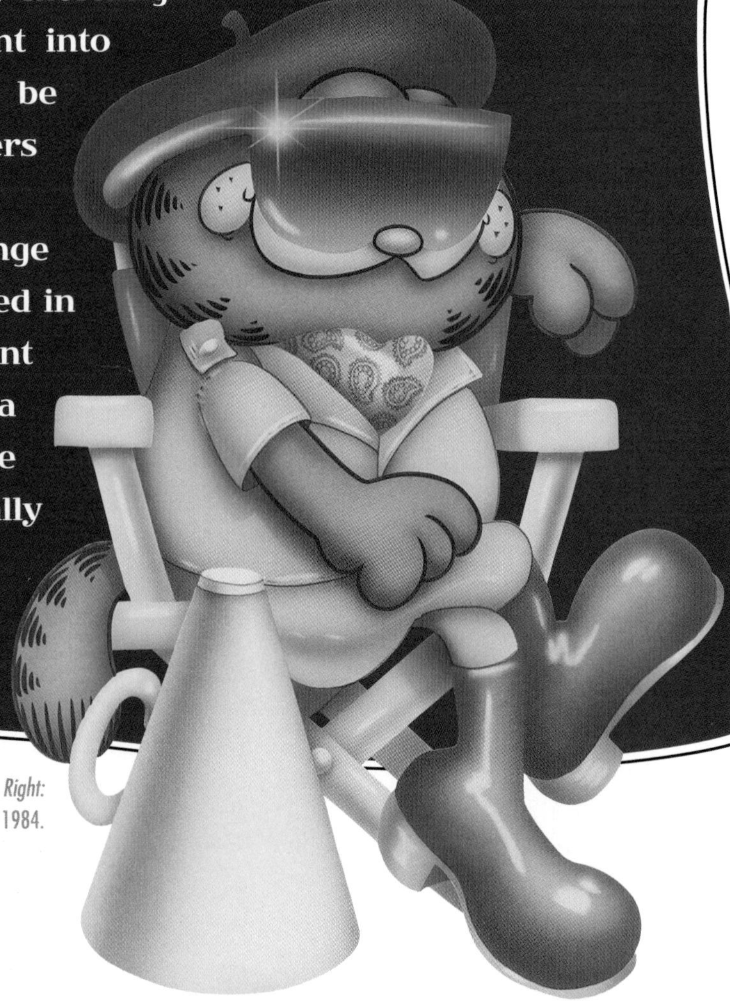

Right:
Airbrushed art, circa 1984.

THE SPECIALS

"In my wildest dreams, I hoped for a Garfield book, and maybe, if I was real lucky, a TV show."

—Jim Davis

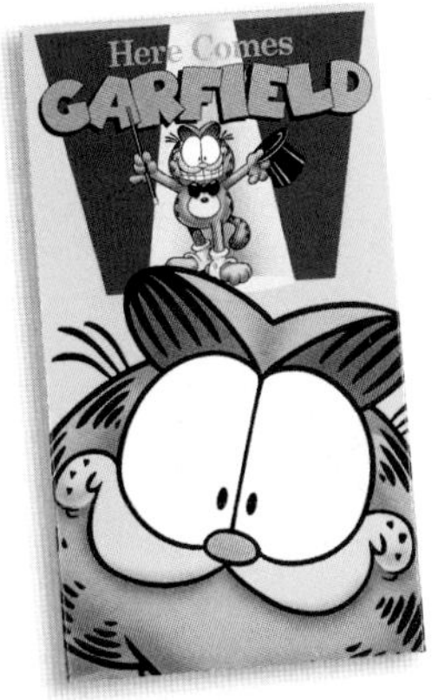
Here Comes
GARFIELD

Here Comes Garfield
Original airdate: October 25, 1982

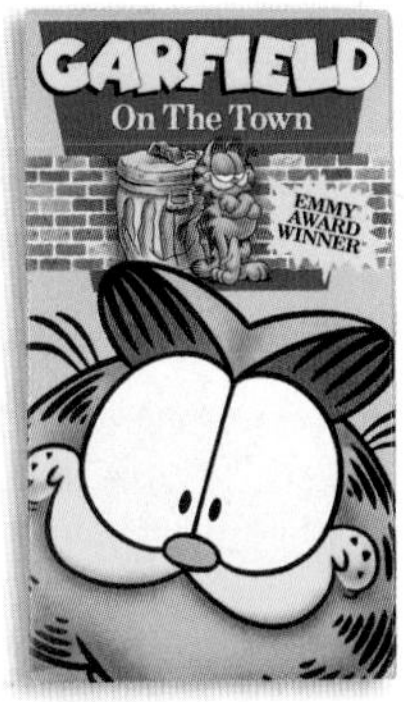
GARFIELD
On The Town
EMMY AWARD WINNER

Garfield on the Town
Original airdate: October 28,1983
Emmy award winner: Outstanding Animated Program

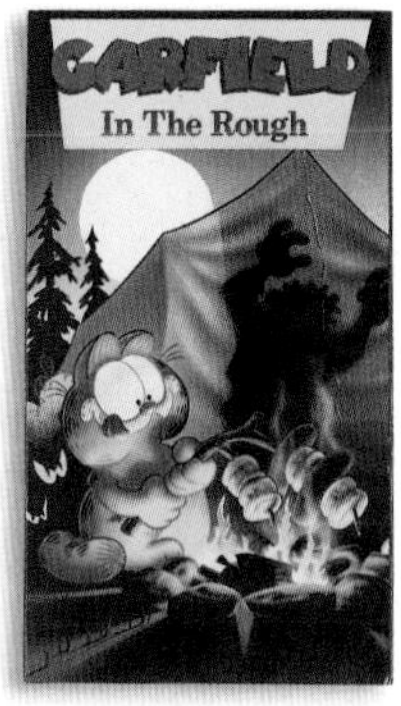
GARFIELD
In The Rough

Garfield in the Rough
Original airdate: October 26, 1984
Emmy award winner: Outstanding Animated Program

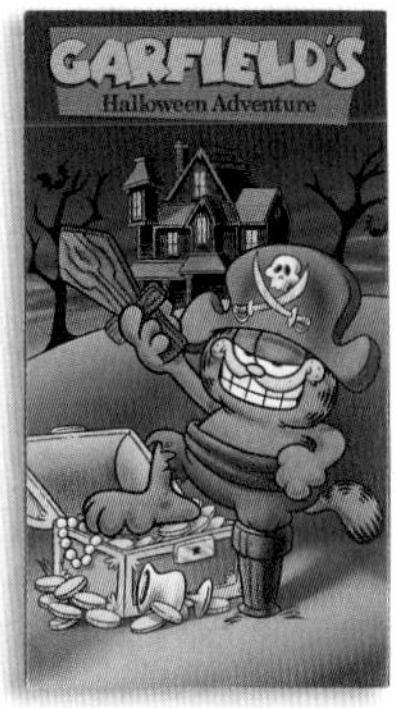
GARFIELD'S
Halloween Adventure

Garfield's Halloween Adventure
Original airdate: October 30,1985
Emmy award winner: Outstanding Animated Program

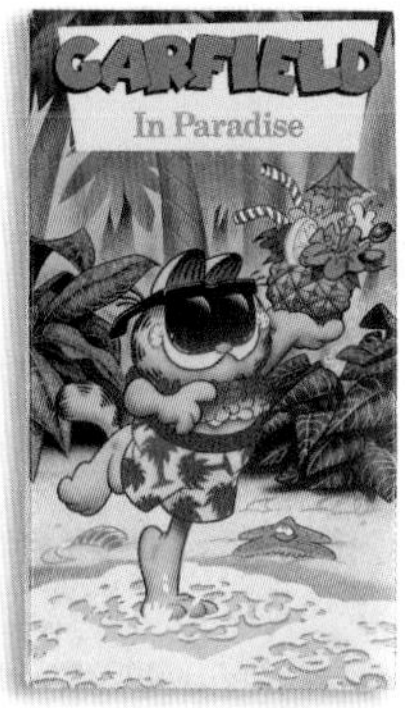
GARFIELD
In Paradise

Garfield in Paradise
Original airdate: May 27,1986

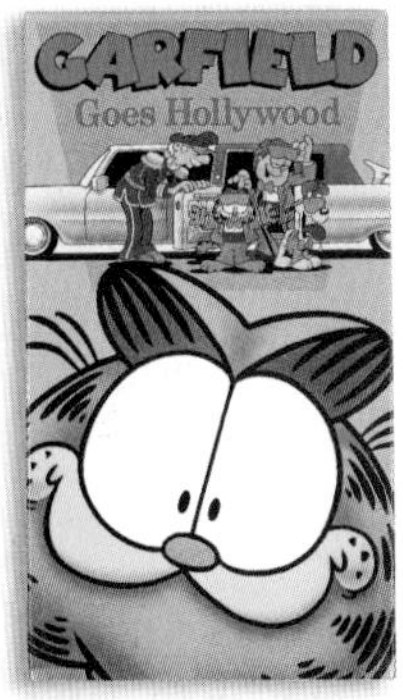
GARFIELD
Goes Hollywood

Garfield Goes Hollywood
Original airdate: May 8, 1987

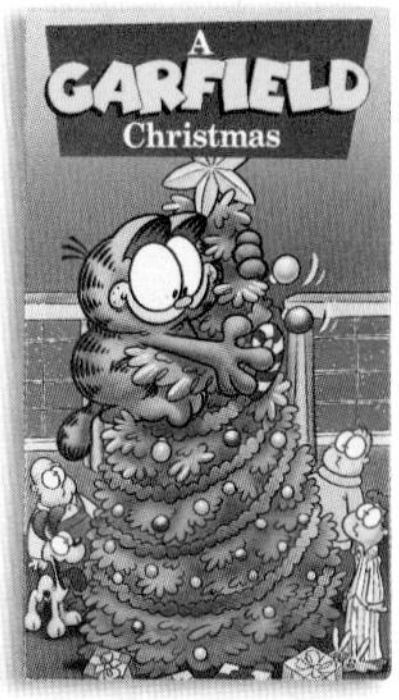
A
GARFIELD
Christmas

A Garfield Christmas
Original airdate: December 21, 1987

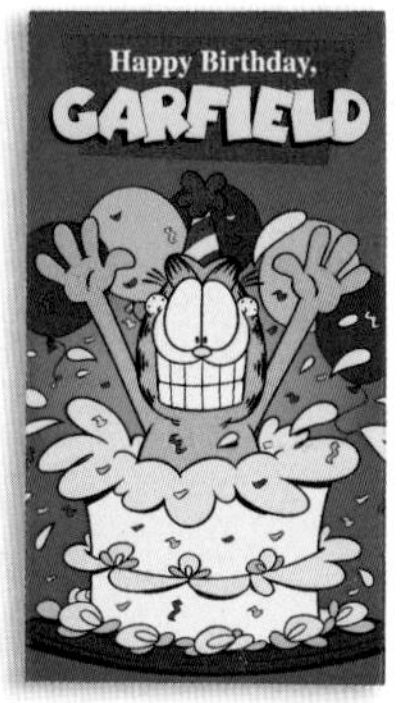
Happy Birthday,
GARFIELD

Happy Birthday, Garfield
Original airdate: May 17, 1988

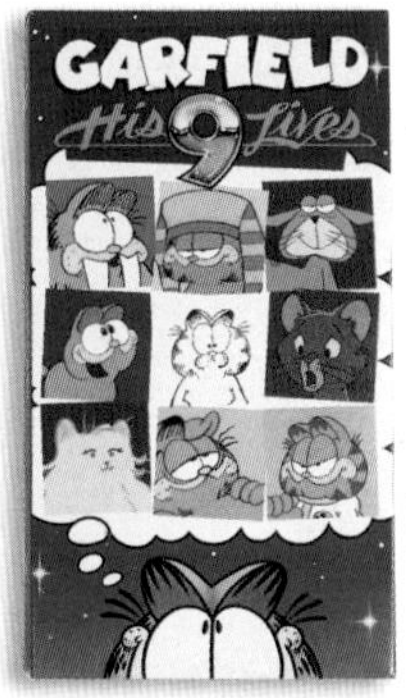
GARFIELD
His 9 Lives

Garfield: His 9 Lives
Original airdate: November 2, 1988

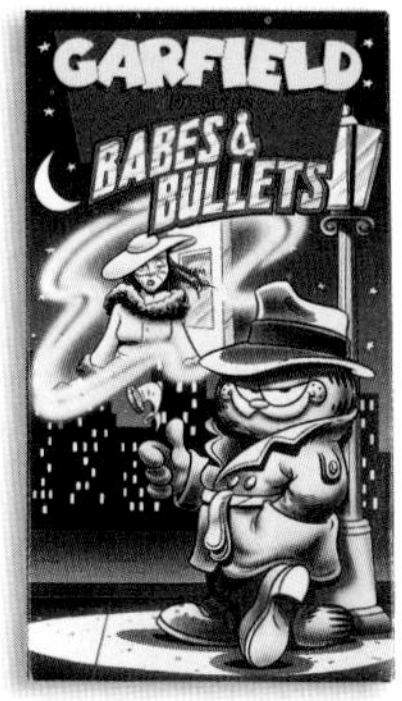
GARFIELD
BABES & BULLETS

Garfield Presents Babes & Bullets
Original airdate: May 23,1989
Emmy award winner: Outstanding Animated Program

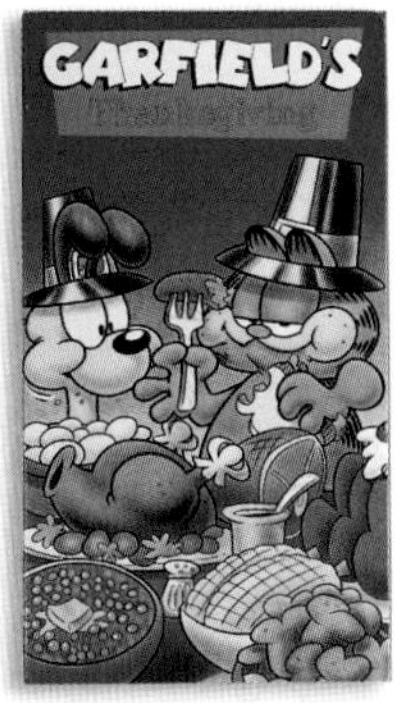
GARFIELD'S

Garfield's Thanksgiving
Original airdate: November 22, 1989

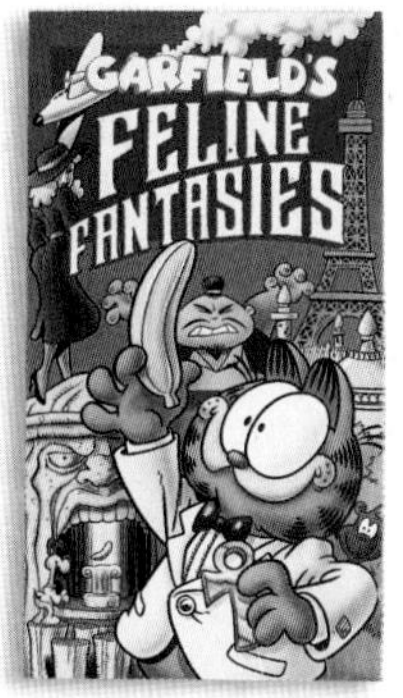
GARFIELD'S
FELINE
FANTASIES

Garfield's Feline Fantasies
Original airdate: May 18,1990

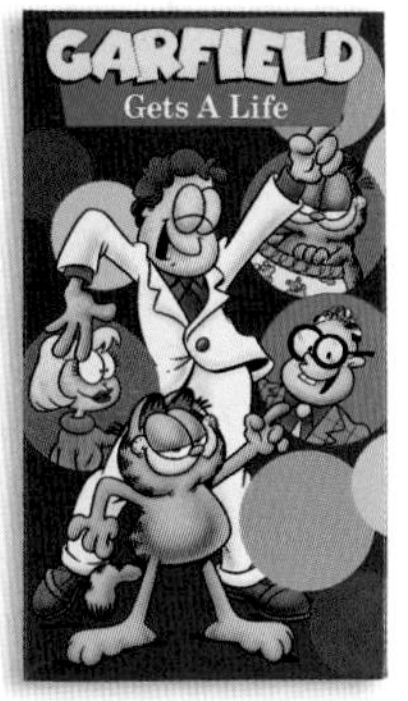
GARFIELD
Gets A Life

Garfield Gets a Life
Original airdate: May 8,1991

Jim Davis on the TV specials:

Here Comes Garfield

"In 1981 I was in a studio in California struggling with how to make Garfield stand up and dance in his first special. Charles Schulz happened to be working on a project at the same studio. He came by, and I explained my problem. Sparky (as he was known to friends) provided me with the solution on the spot. He started drawing over my drawing, saying, 'The problem is, you've made Garfield's feet too small—little tiny cat feet.' So he got Garfield, like Snoopy, up off all fours. I took Sparky's advice, and Garfield's been walking upright ever since."

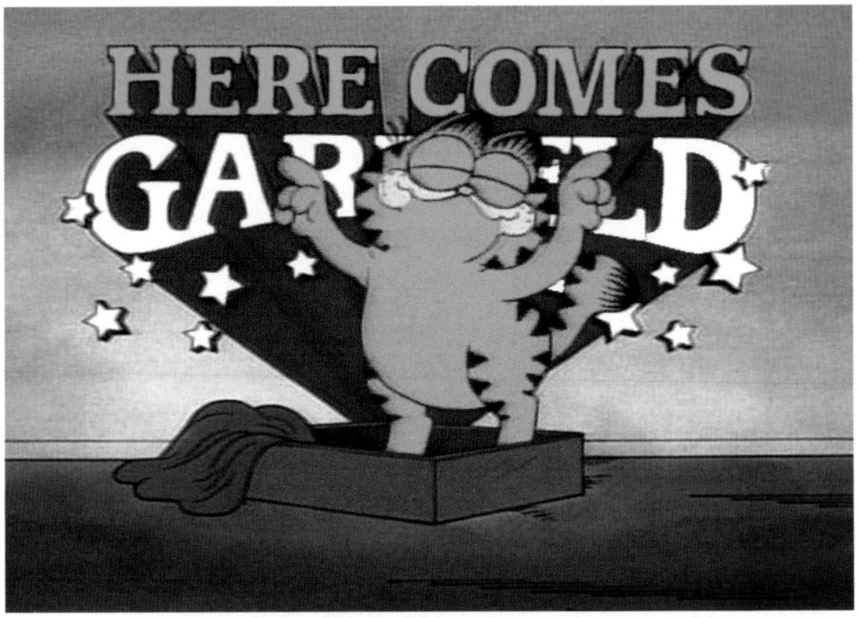
HERE COMES

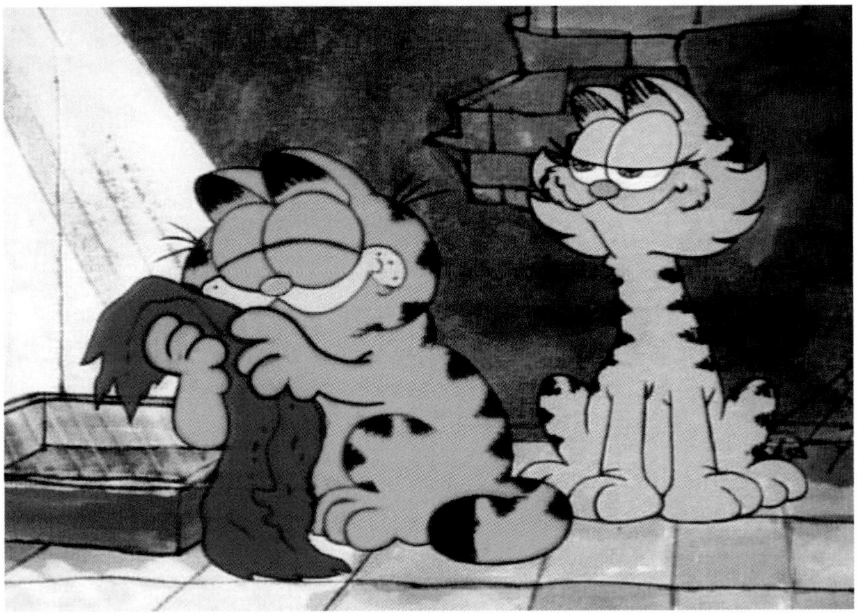

Garfield on the Town

"The second special was cowritten by Lorenzo Music and was the first Garfield special to win an Emmy. The show was also notable for reuniting Garfield with his long-lost mother and grandfather."

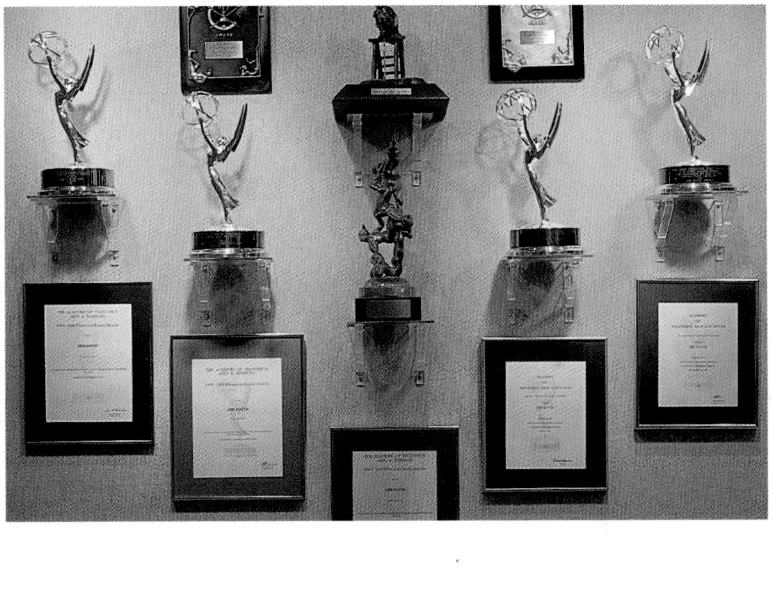

Right: Jim's Emmys are housed, along with many other awards, in the Paws studio.

Award-Winning Cat

"I remember when *Garfield in the Rough* received an Emmy. I took the stage with the producer and director and proceeded to make an acceptance speech. About midway through, I looked down and saw Farrah Fawcett and Linda Evans sitting in the front row. I was trying to thank the woman who had been writing music for the shows—a woman I had known for years! I couldn't remember her name!"

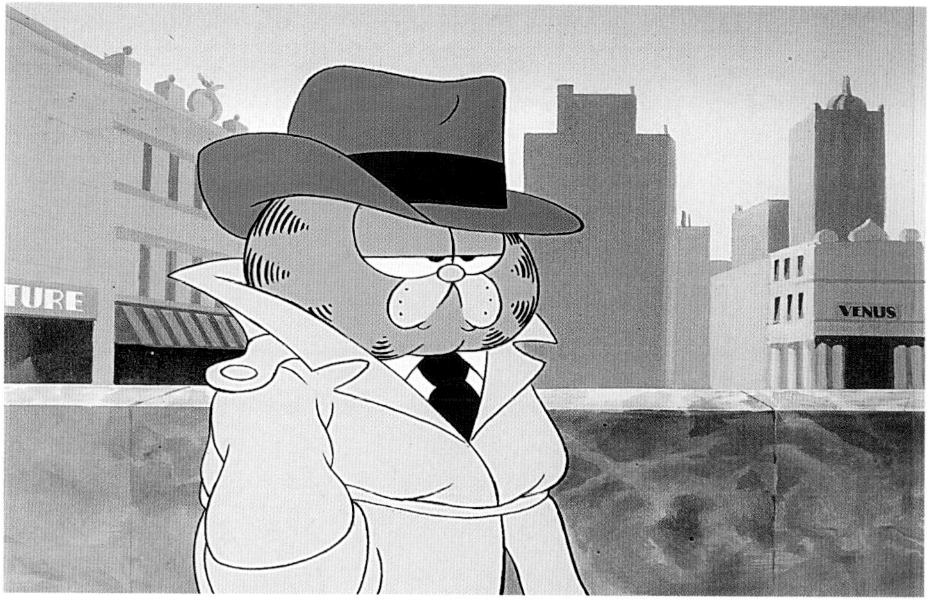
TURE
VENUS

Babes & Bullets

"We really tried something different with this special. Created in the style of classic film noir, *Babes & Bullets* featured Garfield as Sam Spayed, a tough-talking private eye beset by babes and bruisers as he tries to solve a murder case. It was great fun doing the animation in black-and-white."

A Garfield Christmas

"Christmas was definitely the big event of the year for our family. It was the time Dave, my younger brother, and I would get the 'big stuff' we'd been asking for all year. Of course, actually getting the 'big stuff' depended entirely on the success of Mom and Dad's crop that year. During a bad year, we'd probably get essentials like slippers, pajamas, and clothes. But during a good year, we received the essentials plus some great toys. I remember the year I got a red pedal-driven jeep and Dave got a rocking horse."

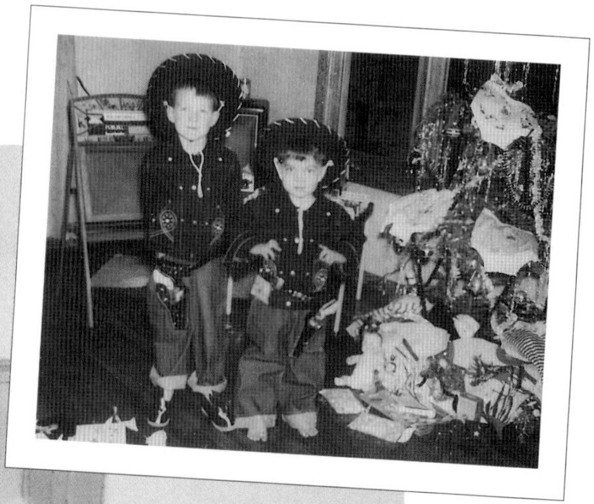

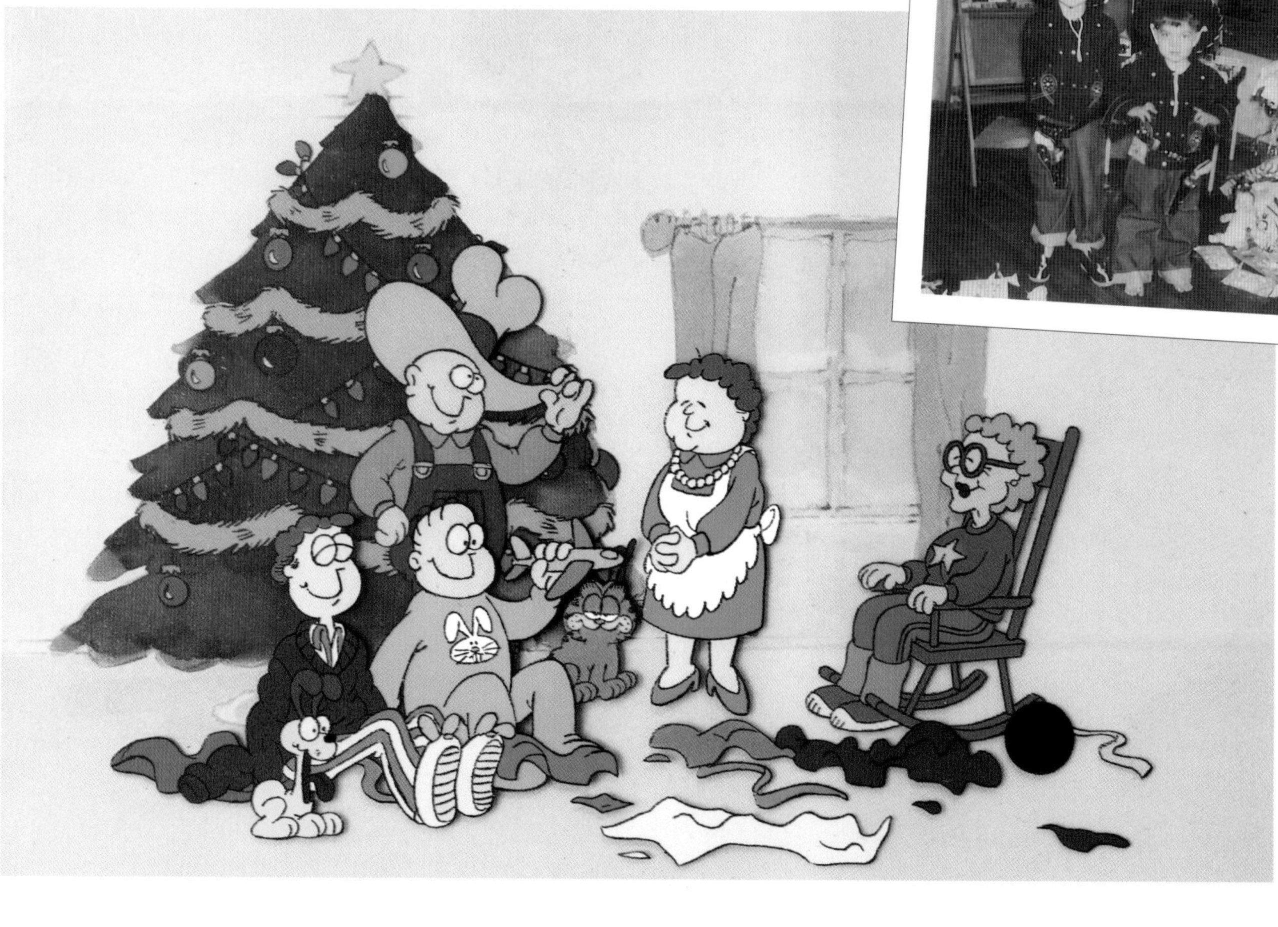

Above: Jim and Dave Davis, Christmas 1951.

Left: Scene from *A Garfield Christmas.* Jim used his family's holiday traditions as inspiration.

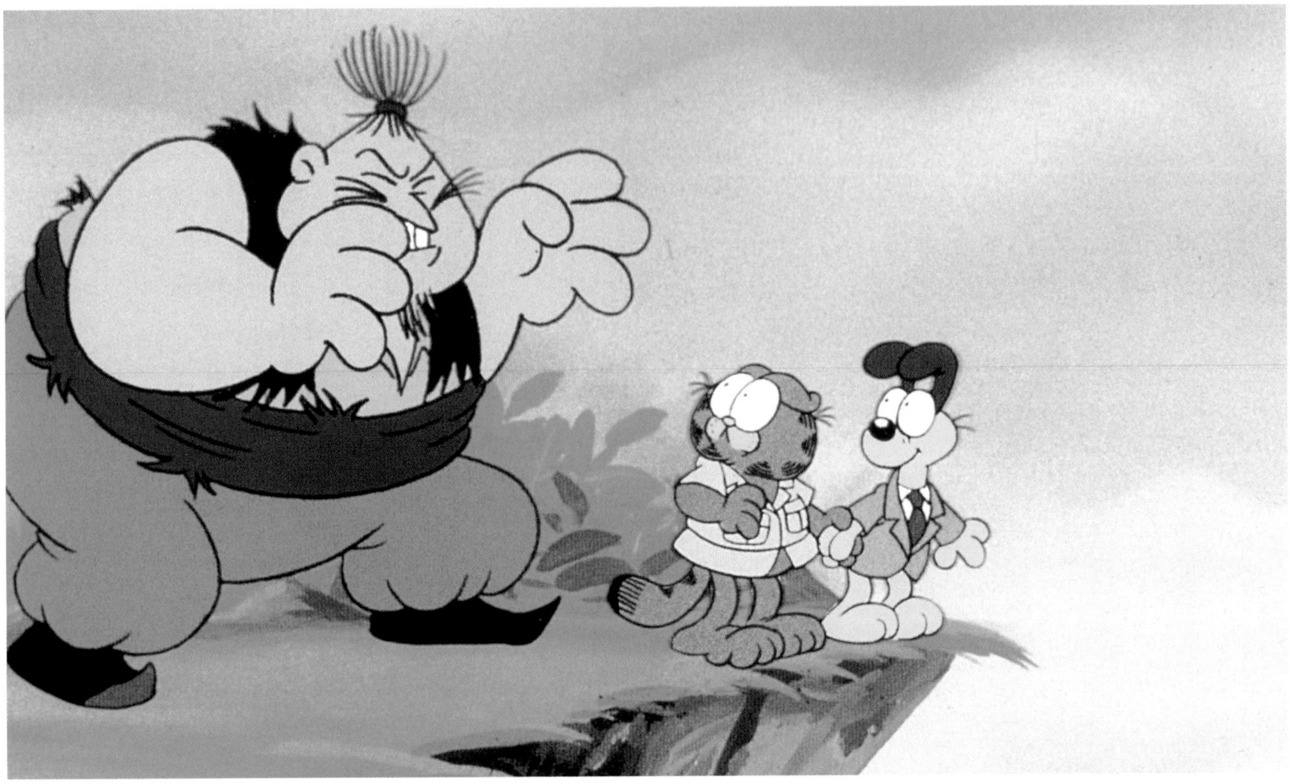

Garfield's Feline Fantasies

"It was a lot of fun turning the lazy cat into an action hero."

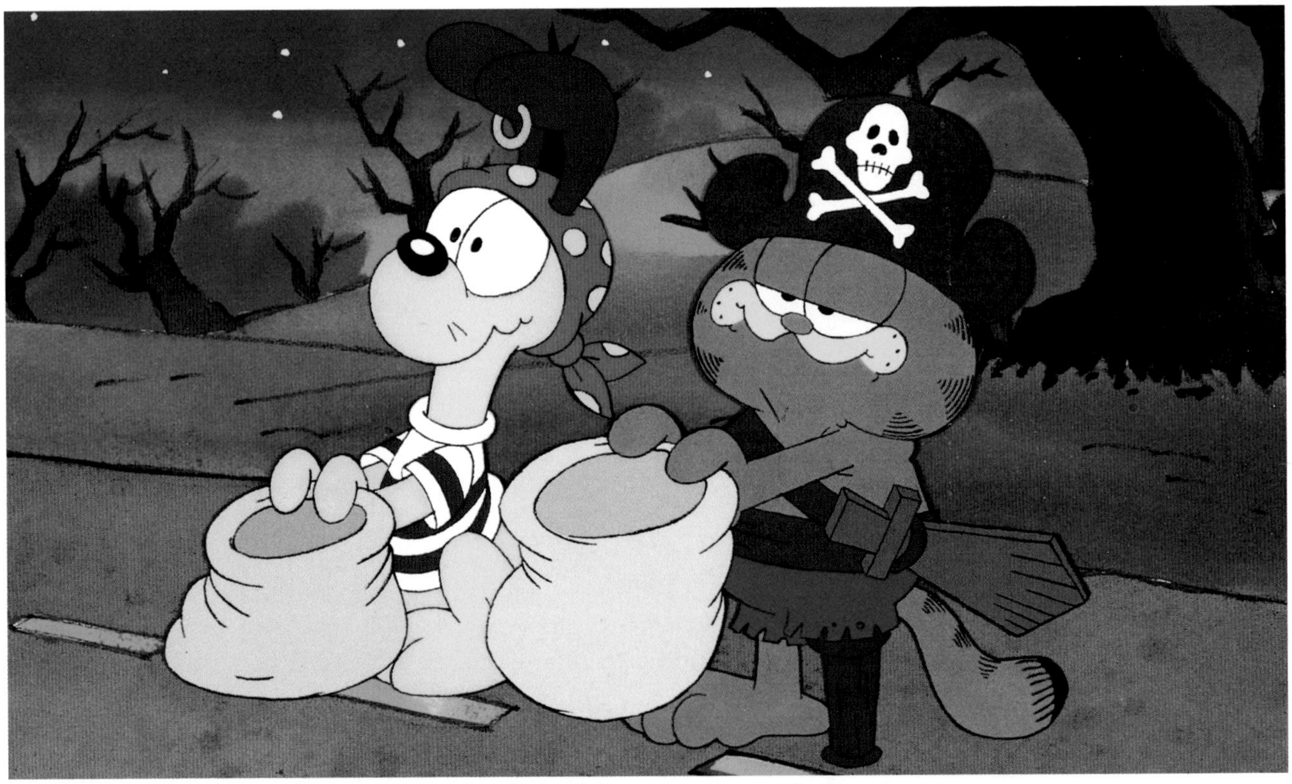

Garfield's Halloween Adventure

"I loved how Lorenzo Music read Garfield's line, 'Candy, candy, candy!'"

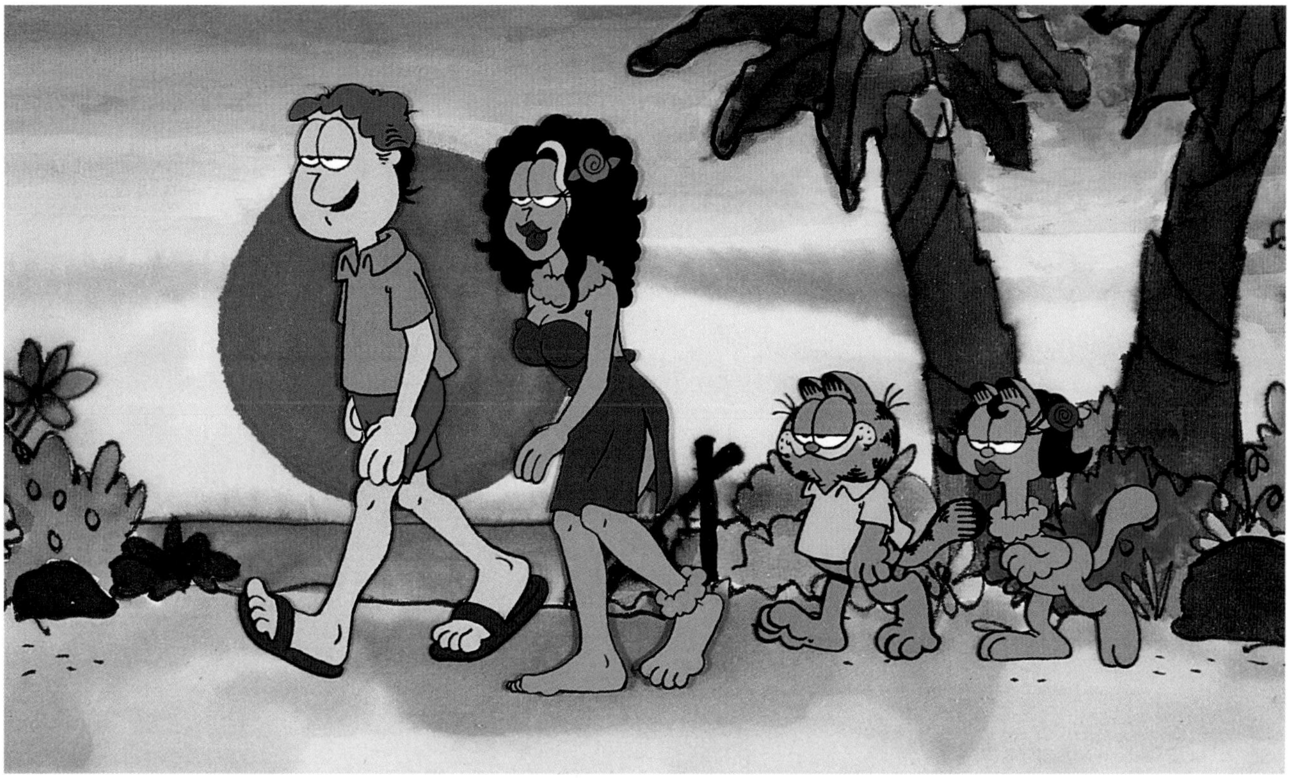

Garfield in Paradise

"This is my favorite Garfield special."

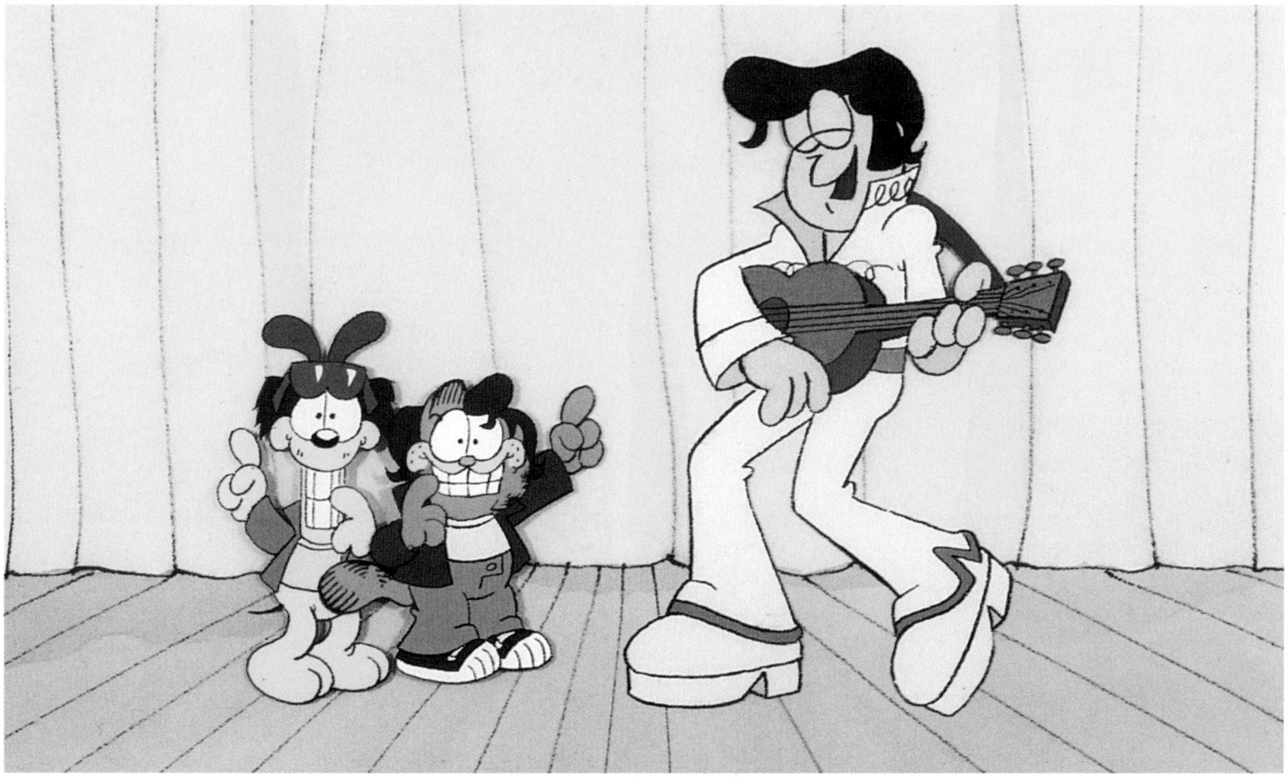

Garfield Goes Hollywood

"I had to fly out to California to do research for this special.
The sun, the surf, the supermodels . . . it was murder."

the VOICE behind the Cat

Few knew his face, but his voice was heard—and loved—by millions. Lorenzo Music portrayed Garfield from 1982 to 2001, using his unique vocal talents to create the fat cat's signature sound in television specials, the animated series, and countless promotions, products, and ads.

"He was a huge talent, a dear man, and a friend," Jim Davis says, remembering his former collaborator. "When we first auditioned actors for the voice of Garfield, I wasn't exactly sure what we were looking for. I just knew I'd know it when I heard it. After a dozen or more auditions, I began to wonder if anyone could deliver the sardonic, lazy voice

I was hearing in my head. Then Lorenzo sat down to the mike. He helped define Garfield."

Lorenzo worked right up to the end of his life, recording a Garfield spot just a month before his death on August 4, 2001, from bone cancer. And although he was known primarily for his vocal talents, he had an impressive Hollywood résumé that included writing and producing credits for *The Smothers Brothers Comedy Hour*, *The Mary Tyler Moore Show*, *Rhoda*, and *The Bob Newhart Show*. Lorenzo and his wife, Henrietta, even wrote the theme song for Newhart's show.

Born Gerald David Music on May 2, 1937, in Brooklyn, New York, Lorenzo grew up in Duluth, Minnesota, and eventually attended the University of Minnesota, where, according to his official bio, he "majored in English Literature, and minored in Banjo Playing,

Janitorial Works, and Being in a Lot of Plays." It was in one of these plays that Lorenzo met his future wife.

He performed in a comedy act with Henrietta for several years, and later brought their offbeat routine to television in a short-lived 1976 syndicated program, *The Lorenzo and Henrietta Music Show*.

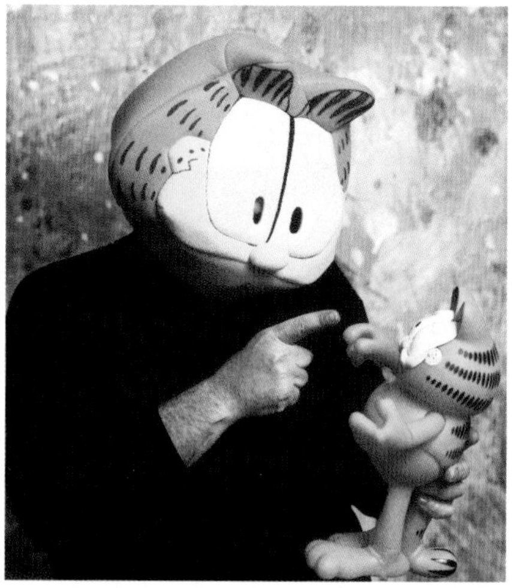

Moving from performing to writing, Lorenzo got his first big break in 1967 when he joined the staff of Tom and Dick Smothers's variety hour. A few years later, Lorenzo and his partner, David Davis, accepted positions on the fledgling *Mary Tyler Moore Show*. The program soon became a hit and Music and Davis were made story editors. Next the pair created *The Bob Newhart Show*, featuring the comedian as psychiatrist Dr. Robert Hartley.

Then came the *Mary Tyler Moore Show* spin-off, *Rhoda*, which Lorenzo cocreated and produced. He also returned to performing, supplying the voice for the never-seen, never-sober Carlton the doorman.

Lorenzo became a voice-over performer almost by accident. After a chance audition won him a role in the 1982 *Pac Man* animated show, Lorenzo began getting offers for voice work. He went on to record several TV shows (like the animated *Real Ghostbusters* and *Gummi Bears*) and hundreds of radio and TV commercials. Lorenzo's voice was instantly recognizable, whether he was playing a cartoon cat or a crash test dummy.

Lorenzo enjoyed the public curiosity that had surrounded his portrayal of Carlton, and he decided to cultivate an image of mystery by keeping his face hidden. Publicity photos showed him in silhouette—or, in the case of the Garfield show, wearing a big cat mask—and he relished being one of the most famous stars that people had never seen.

According to Mark Evanier, *Garfield and Friends* writer and coproducer, "Lorenzo was a performer who would instantly grasp what had been written and, as often as not, come up with a way to maximize the humor. His suggestions were nearly always good and contributed to making Garfield a truly memorable personality."

Like Garfield, Lorenzo was an original. And he'll be missed.

LORENZO MUSIC

May 2, 1937–August 4, 2001

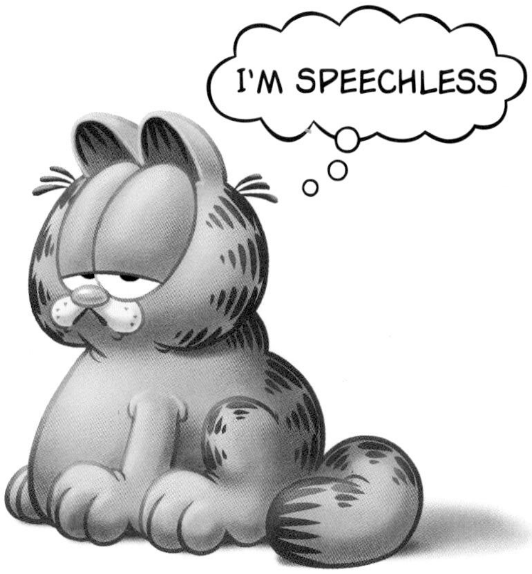
I'M SPEECHLESS

The TV Series

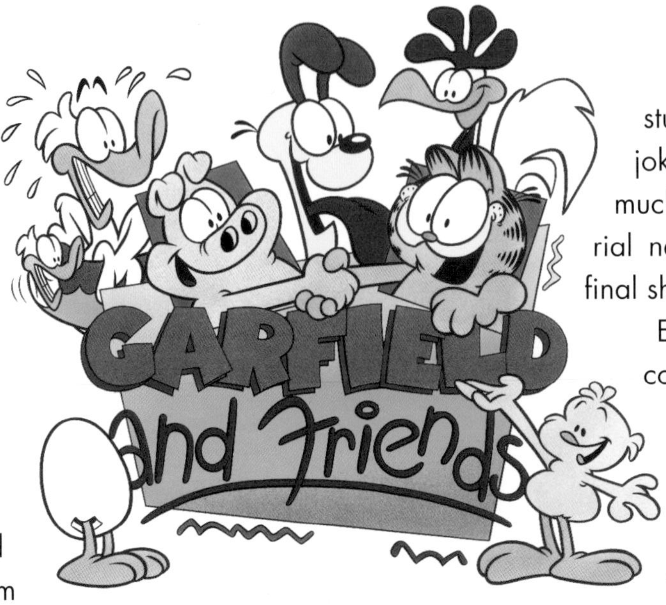
GARFIELD
and Friends

Garfield and Friends began its first season on CBS on October 15, 1988. The half-hour program was so popular it was expanded to one hour for its second season. The series was primarily written by Mark Evanier, a prolific L.A.–based TV and comic-book writer, and executive-produced by Jim Davis, Lee Mendelson, and Phil Roman. Jim also helped direct the voice talent, flying out to California for recording sessions, which often turned into zany improvisational free-for-alls (especially when Jonathan Winters or Buddy Hackett was in the studio). The ad-libs and jokes flowed freely, with much of the funniest material never making it to the final show.

Each half-hour episode contained two Garfield cartoons and one *U.S.Acres* cartoon. Most shows also featured a number of "Garfield Quickies"—super-short comedy vignettes that acted as bumpers between the stories. Lorenzo Music was once again the voice of Garfield, and many celebrities lent their voices to the show throughout its seven-year, 121-episode run.

Right: The Garfield and Friends gang *(left to right):* Jim Davis, Gregg Berger, Thom Huge, Frank Welker, Howie Morris, Julie Payne, Gary Owens, Lorenzo Music *(behind cup)*, and Mark Evanier.

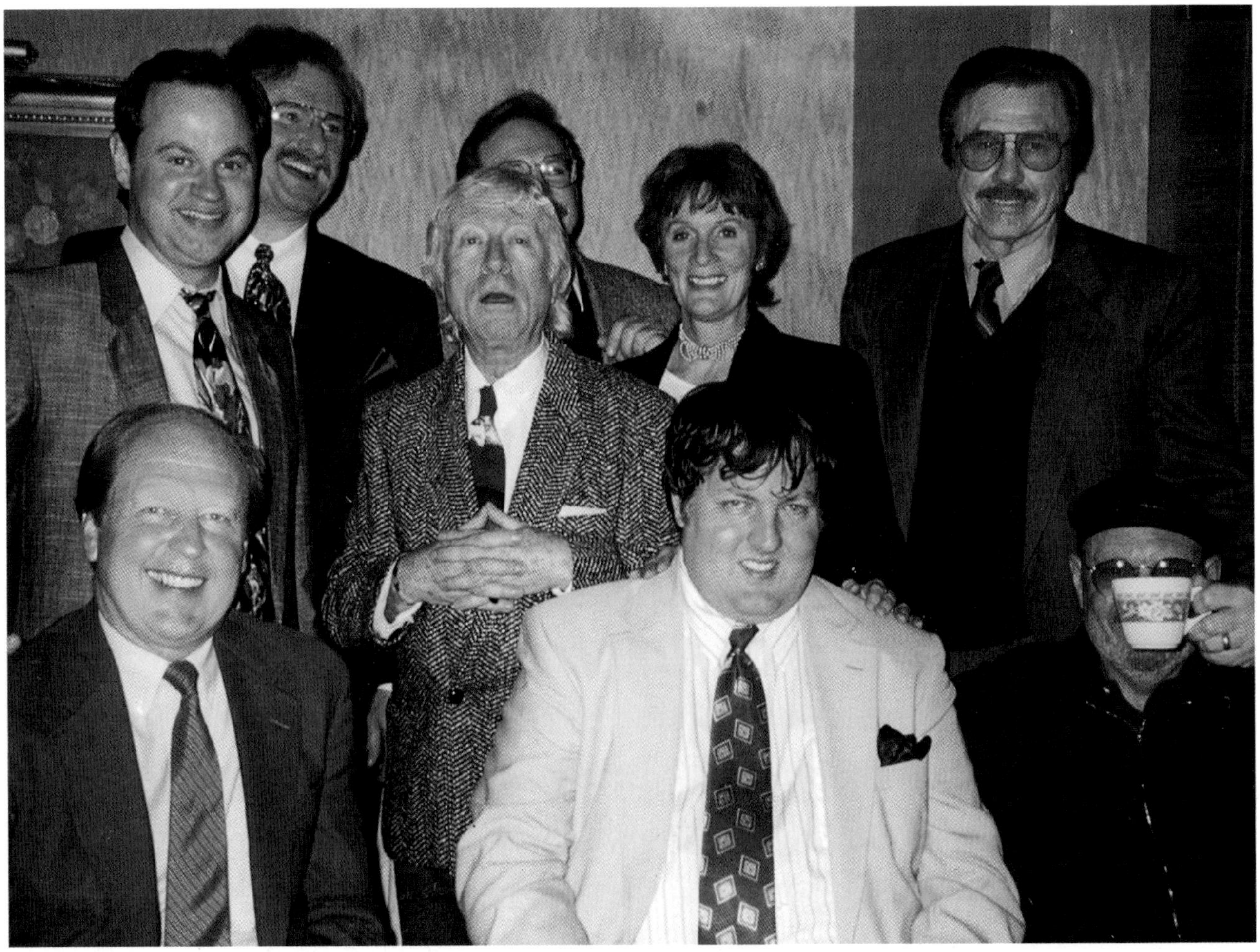

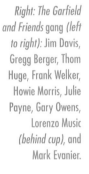

Binky   Penelope   Nermal   Garfield   Odie   Jon   Liz

THE REGULARS:
LORENZO MUSIC • GARFIELD
THOM HUGE • JON & BINKY THE CLOWN
GREGG BERGER • ODIE
DESIREE GOYETTE • NERMAL
JULIE PAYNE • LIZ
VICTORIA JACKSON • PENELOPE
GARY OWENS • ANNOUNCER

VOICE TALENT

Left:
GARFIELD MAKES
THE SCENE
A collection of shots
from the animated
TV series.

U.S. ACRES

Wade   Lanolin   Sheldon   Orson   Booker   Bo   Roy

THE REGULARS:

GREGG BERGER • **Orson**

THOM HUGE • **Roy**

HOWIE MORRIS • **Wade**

JULIE PAYNE • **Lanolin**

FRANK WELKER • **Bo, Booker, Sheldon**

Right:
FARM FOLLIES
Shots from various
U.S. Acres episodes.
Check out Lanolin
the punk!

The *U.S.Acres* characters also appeared in a comic strip that ran from 1986 to 1989. It debuted in an unprecedented 505 newspapers! Jim created the strip specifically for younger fans (and farm aficionados). The barnyard buddies were quite popular and, like Garfield, made the leap from the comics page to books, calendars, plush toys, and other assorted products.

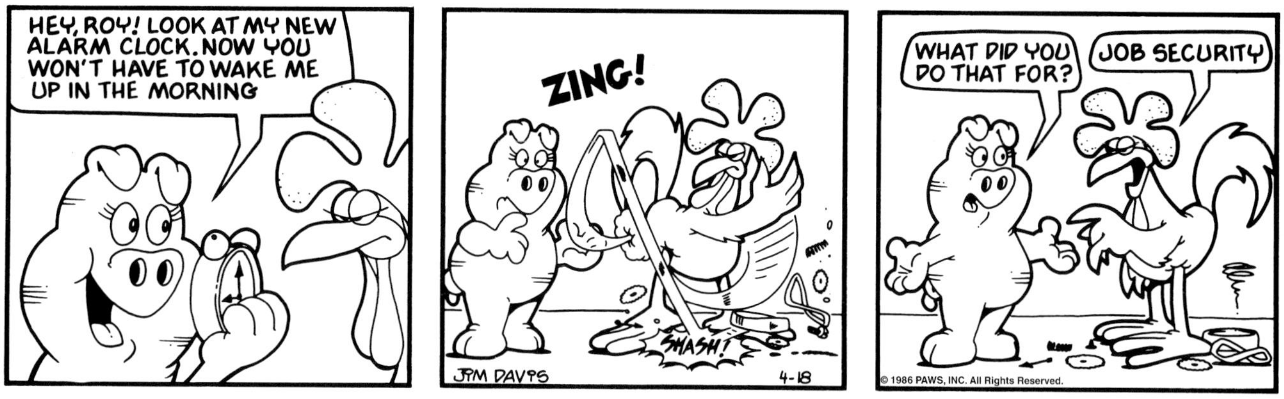
HEY, ROY! LOOK AT MY NEW ALARM CLOCK. NOW YOU WON'T HAVE TO WAKE ME UP IN THE MORNING
ZING!
SMASH!
JIM DAVIS
4-18
WHAT DID YOU DO THAT FOR?
JOB SECURITY
© 1986 PAWS, INC. All Rights Reserved.

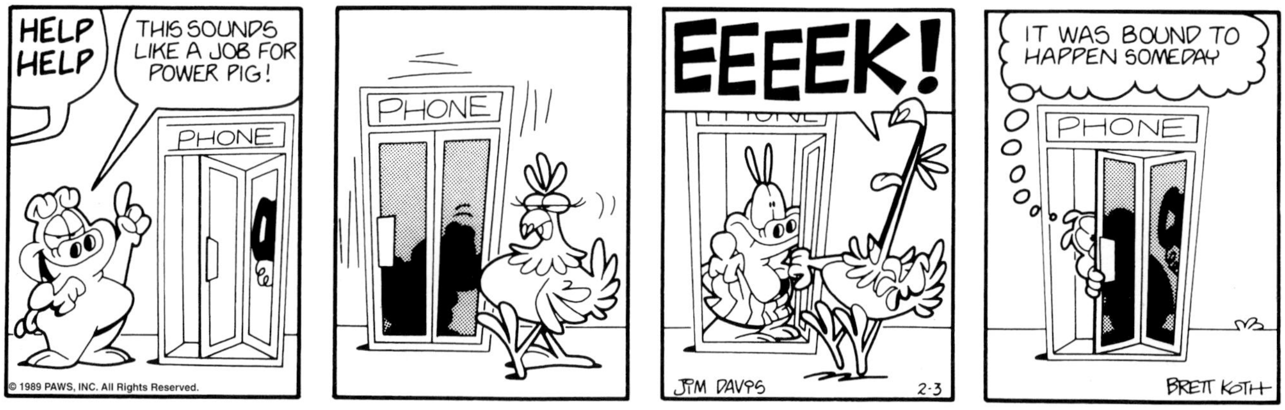
HELP HELP
THIS SOUNDS LIKE A JOB FOR POWER PIG!
PHONE
© 1989 PAWS, INC. All Rights Reserved.
PHONE
EEEEK!
JIM DAVIS
2-3
IT WAS BOUND TO HAPPEN SOMEDAY
PHONE
BRETT KOTH

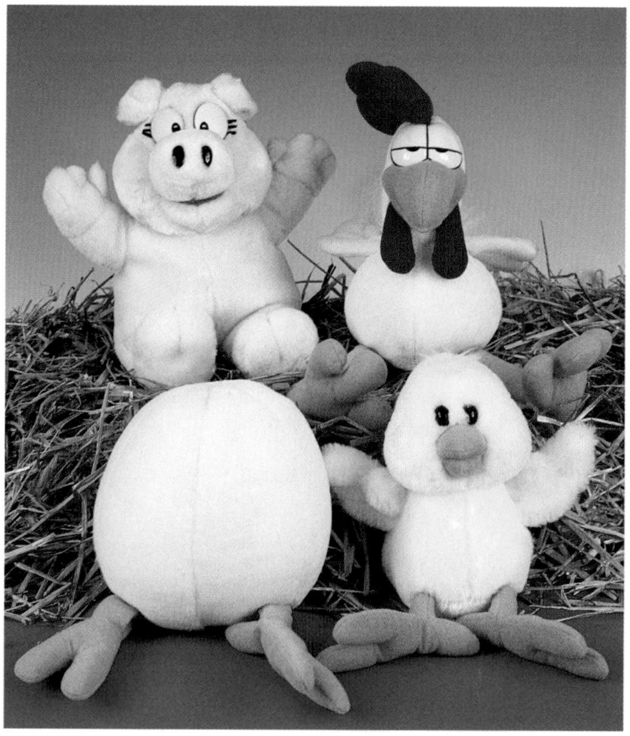

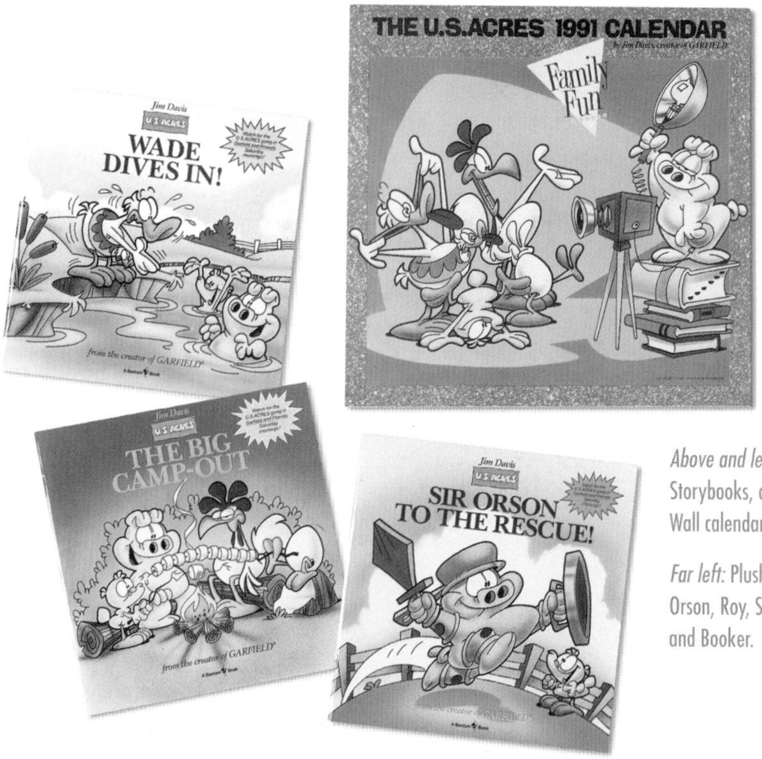
WADE DIVES IN!
THE BIG CAMP-OUT
SIR ORSON TO THE RESCUE!
THE U.S.ACRES 1991 CALENDAR
Family Fun

Above and left: Storybooks, circa 1989. Wall calendar, 1991.

Far left: Plush critters Orson, Roy, Sheldon, and Booker.

Right: Jim with veteran voice-over actress June Foray. June's work is legendary, and she's best known for her portrayal of Bullwinkle's sidekick, Rocky the Flying Squirrel.

Below: MAY THE FARCE BE WITH YOU Actor James Earl Jones, star of stage, screen, and TV.

THE GUEST STARS

Carl Ballantine	James Earl Jones
Pat Buttram	Don Knotts
John Byner	Harvey Korman
Pat Carroll	David L. Lander
Imogene Coca	Robin Leach
June Foray	Howie Mandel
George Foreman	Kenneth Mars
Stan Freberg	Chuck McCann
Dick Gautier	Howard Morris
Buddy Hackett	Arnold Stang
Mark Hamill	Larry Storch
Pat Harrington	Rip Taylor
Wolfman Jack	Jesse White
Victoria Jackson	Paul Winchell
Jonathan Winters	

"Meeting and working with some of TV's greats has been thrilling. I'll never forget the time Jonathan Winters was booked to do a voice for the show. He showed up about an hour before the session and entertained us with a brilliant but rambling monologue. He had us on the floor. No one could finish their tuna melts that day. Another time, we were doing a parody of *Lifestyles of the Rich and Famous*, and we had planned to mimic Robin Leach's voice. Turns out he was in the next recording room and we were able to get him to play himself."

—Jim Davis

Far left: Little-known fact: Mark Evanier wrote an entire episode of *Garfield and Friends* while unconscious!

Left: To play Jon Arbuckle, Thom Huge (rhymes with loogey) must get in touch with his inner dweeb.

Below: Guest-star Buddy Hackett, in the middle of telling a really dirty joke. Also pictured are Lorenzo Music, Thom Huge, Gregg Berger, and Jim Davis.

COMMERCIAL CAT
We interrupt this program for a brief word from our sponsors.

Do You Know This Cat?
Garfield and Jim Davis appear in a 1984 American Express commercial.

Room Service
Garfield gets the full fat-cat treatment in this 1986 Embassy Suites ad.

Stuck on Garfield!
The plush puss travels in style. Plymouth Voyager commercial, 1996.

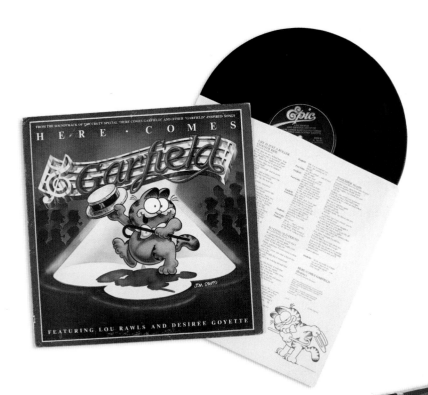

Songs in the Key of G

HERE · COMES
Garfield
FEATURING LOU RAWLS AND DESIREE GOYETTE

Show Tunes

Garfield's just a song-and-dance cat at heart, and each of his prime-time specials featured musical numbers. Garfield's theme song, "Here Comes Garfield," was sung by legendary soul man Lou Rawls. Pictured here is a rare soundtrack LP.

GARFIELD
"AM I COOL OR WHAT?"
THE POINTER SISTERS
PATTI LABELLE
NATALIE COLE
THE TEMPTATIONS
DIANE SCHUUR
B.B. KING
LOU RAWLS
CARL ANDERSON
DESIREE GOYETTE
DAVID BENOIT
DIGITAL MASTER

Left and below: The CD cover folded out to show all the contributing performers.

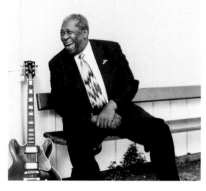

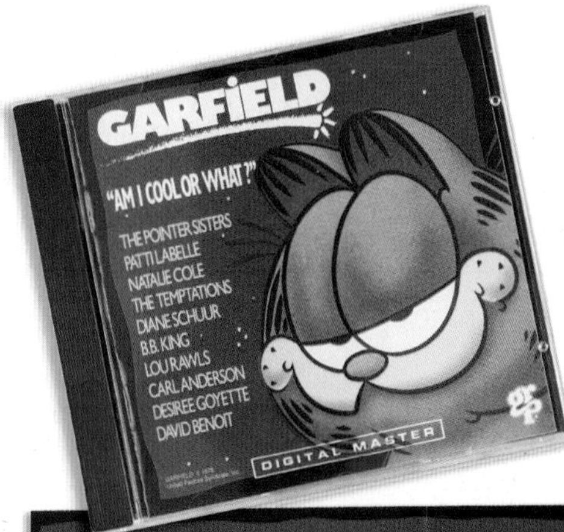

"I'm a big fan of Garfield, and when I was offered the chance to record a song for his CD, I grabbed it!"
—B. B. King

The Pointer Sisters
Carl Anderson
Patti LaBelle
Lou Rawls
Diane Schuur
The Temptations
Natalie Cole
B.B. King
Desiree Goyette
David Benoit

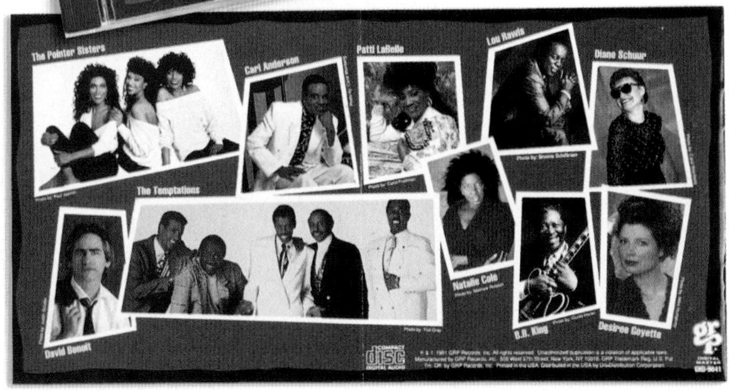

Get Down, Get Chunky!

Some of the music industry's biggest stars weighed in on Garfield's 1991 album, *Am I Cool or What?* The record included performances by the Pointer Sisters, Patti LaBelle, B. B. King, Lou Rawls, Natalie Cole, and the Temptations.

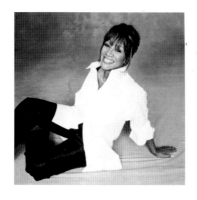

"I love Garfield because he's always getting in trouble. But the best part is, he always ends up on top!"
—Patti LaBelle

THE TEMPTATIONS
"SHAKE YOUR PAW"
DIGITAL MASTER

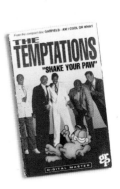

Perfect Harmony

"Shake Your Paw," performed by the Temptations, became an international hit in 1991.

MAKING THE SCENE

1

It all starts with the story. The script includes character dialogue and action along with notes on direction.

GARFIELD AND FRIENDS
GARFIELD
"KNIGHTS AND DAZE"
- SCRIPT -
WIPE TO:
INT. — ARBUCKLE HOUSE - DAY
Jon, dressed in old clothes, is on the phone.
WIDER SHOT
GARFIELD
Just leave food for the cat.

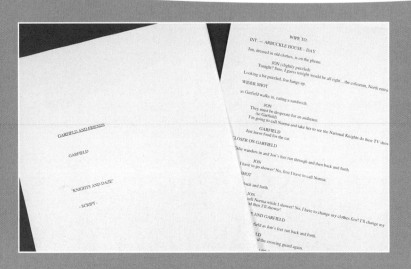

2

Next the script is broken down into a series of pictures. This helps the director visualize the scenes and choreograph the action and camera shots.

PROD. # 7412/G-204
SC. 51 A
START PAN
FILM ROMAN
SC. 51 A CONT
PAN 3G.
SC.
CUT TO GARFIELD LEAVING THE KITCHEN WITH HIS FOOD DISH. PAN WITH GARFIELD.
CONTINUE PANNING WITH GARFIELD AS HE TOSSES DISH OUT OF FRAME.
GARFIELD: DON'T FORGET TO LEAVE FOOD...
GARFIELD (CONT): FOR THE CAT.

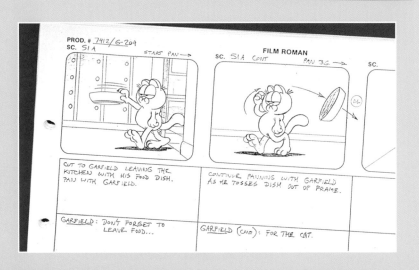

3

The dialogue is actually recorded before the animation. This way the show's timing is worked out, and the artists can create drawings based on the actors' performances.

Creating a cartoon requires lots of separate steps—and lots of talented people.

Background paintings are created for various locations in the script. The animated characters are filmed on top of the background paintings.

Talented artists, called animators, draw the characters for the cartoon. Each cartoon can have literally thousands of drawings. A key animator draws the basic poses for a sequence. Then an artist called an "in-betweener" makes the drawings to "fill in" the action between the key poses.

Traditional animation is produced with art created on clear acetate sheets called "cels." The cels are painted on the reverse side with special vinyl paints. Today's animators use computers to scan and color the individual drawings, thus speeding up the process significantly.

GARFIELD TV TRIVIA QUIZ

Test your GQ (Garfield Quotient) with our brain-crunching quiz!
Answers are at the bottom of the page. (No cheating!)

1. In the Christmas special, what gift did Garfield give Grandma?

A. A hairball shaped like a reindeer
B. Old love letters from her husband
C. Cash
D. Risqué photos of Wilford Brimley

2. Which of these celebrities did NOT guest-star on *Garfield and Friends*?

A. James Earl "Darth Vader" Jones
B. Mark "Luke Skywalker" Hamill
C. Don "Mr. Furley" Knotts
D. Tom "Billy Jack" Laughlin

3. What danger lurks in the woods in *Garfield in the Rough*?

A. Poison ivy mistaken for toilet paper
B. AWOL army ants toting AK-47s
C. Bloodthirsty panther that has escaped from the zoo
D. Garfield's bean-fueled flatulence

4. In the Halloween special, what is Garfield's famous food line?

A. "Curry, curry, curry!"
B. "Gravy, gravy, gravy!"
C. "Chutney, chutney, chutney!"
D. "Candy, candy, candy!"

5. What is Binky's job?

A. Clown
B. Brain surgeon
C. Female impersonator
D. Stunt double for Jackie Chan

6. In the Garfield Thanksgiving special, how did Jon greet Liz at the door?

A. Dressed as Dr. Zaius from *The Planet of the Apes*
B. In his polka-dot boxer shorts
C. In a stunning chiffon evening gown with matching pearls
D. With the words "It's clobberin' time!"

7. In the *U.S. Acres* cartoons, what are the names of Orson's troublemaking siblings, the Grunt Brothers?

A. Huey, Dewey, and Louie
B. Lenin, Stalin, and Trotsky
C. Mort, Wart, and Gort
D. Shaft, Superfly, and Blacula

8. In *Garfield: His 9 Lives*, which of the following was one of Garfield's lives?

A. Nick Neutered, Private Investigator
B. Chin So Fat, Kung-Fu Kitty
C. Sir Lunchalot, Knight of the Dinner Table
D. Cave Cat

9. Complete this lyric, repeatedly sung by those annoying dancing bears: "Oh, we are the Buddy Bears, we always get _____."

A. soused
B. naked
C. along
D. jiggy wit' it

10. In *Garfield Gets a Life*, Jon seeks help at which of the following establishments:

A. The Clinic for Chronic Bedwetters
B. Clarence's Tattoo and Chili Parlor
C. Lorenzo's School for the Personality Impaired
D. International House of Prayer and Pancakes

11. In *Garfield in Paradise*, what was the name of Jon and Garfield's hotel room?

A. The Jack Benny Suite
B. Suite: Judy Blue Eyes
C. The Bowery Boys Bungalow
D. Stalag 13

12. In *Garfield's Feline Fantasies*, Garfield and Odie appear as secret agents:

A. Wood Nickel and Spitball
B. Lance Sterling and Slobber Job
C. Deuce Acey and Drool Bucket
D. Hairy Palmer and Phlegm Face

ANSWERS: 1. B, 2. D, 3. C, 4. D, 5. A, 6. B, 7. C, 8. D, 9. C, 10. C, 11. A, 12. B

CHAPTER SEVEN

Stuck on You: The Phenomenon

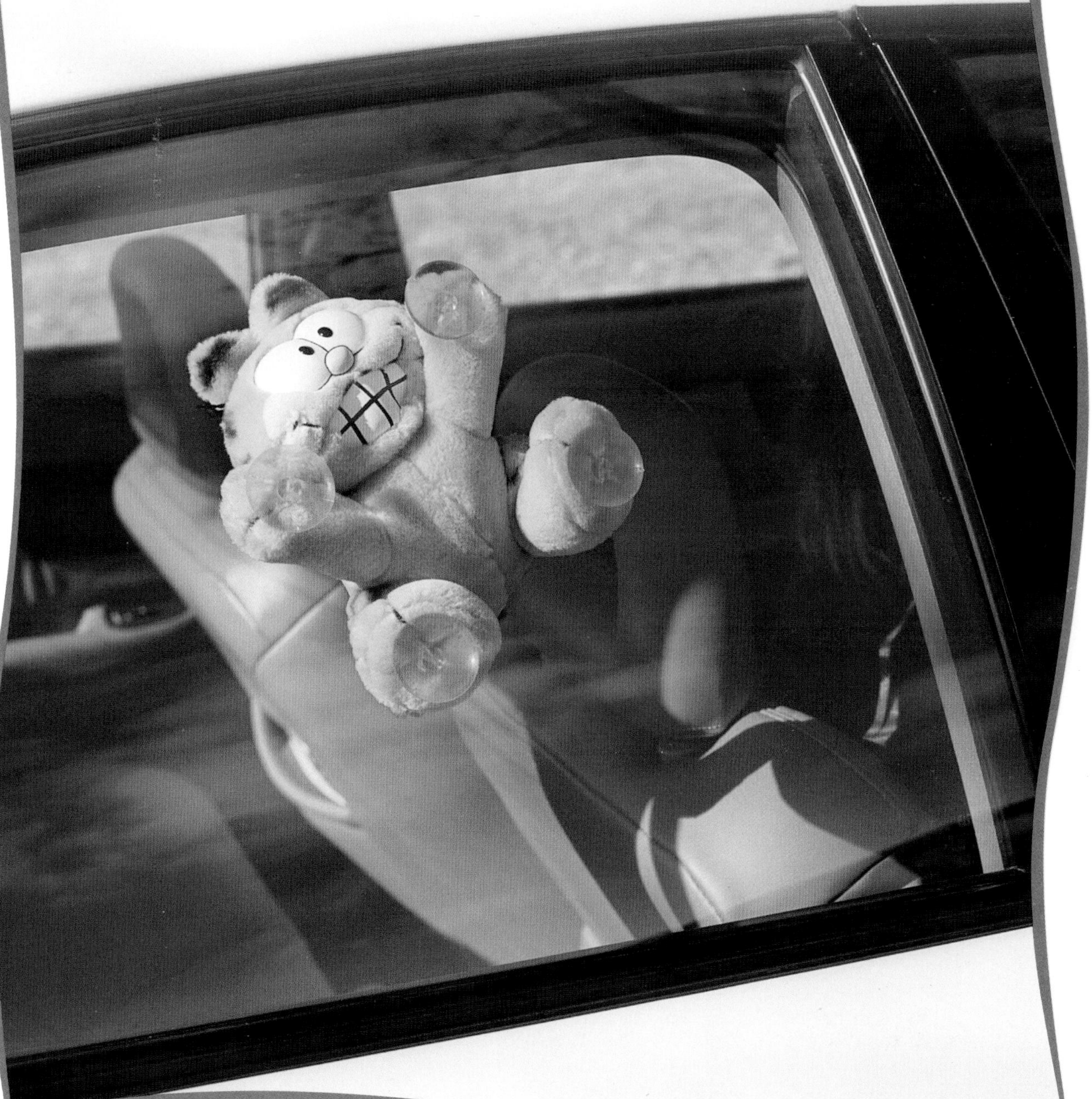

A grinning orange cat suction-cupped to a car window. It was an image that captivated the public's imagination and turned Garfield into a pop culture icon. In the mid-to-late 1980s the "Stuck on You" Garfield was everywhere: on cars, buses, trains, planes—even the space shuttle (or was that just a rumor?). The stuffed Garfields became so popular that a rash of "cat burglaries" swept the country, with overzealous fans breaking into cars and stealing the plush pussycat.

More than just a fad, the "Stuck on You" Garfield craze (which the *New York Times* called "Cat Chic") was a full-blown phenomenon, and tens of millions were sold between 1987 and 1989.

Fearing overexposure, Jim Davis retired the item in 1992, and only recently allowed it to be manufactured again. With the rerelease of the suction-cupped kitty, a whole new generation is now stuck on Garfield.

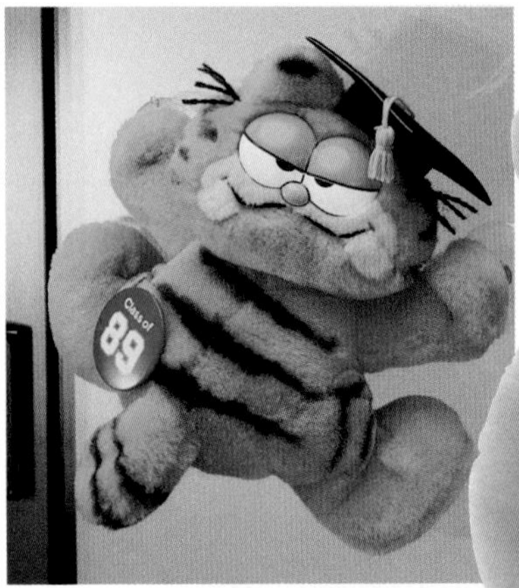
89

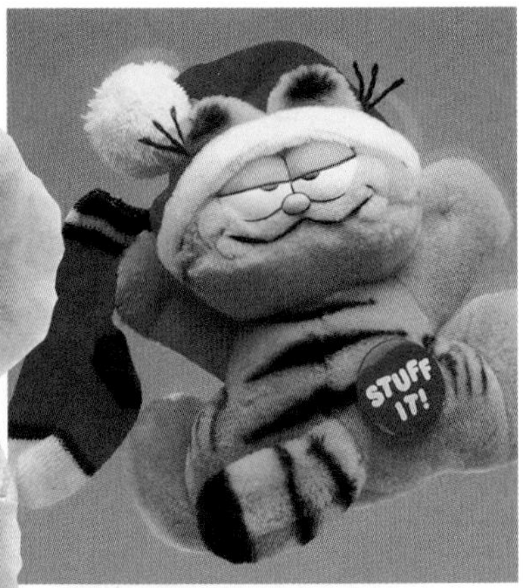
STUFF IT!

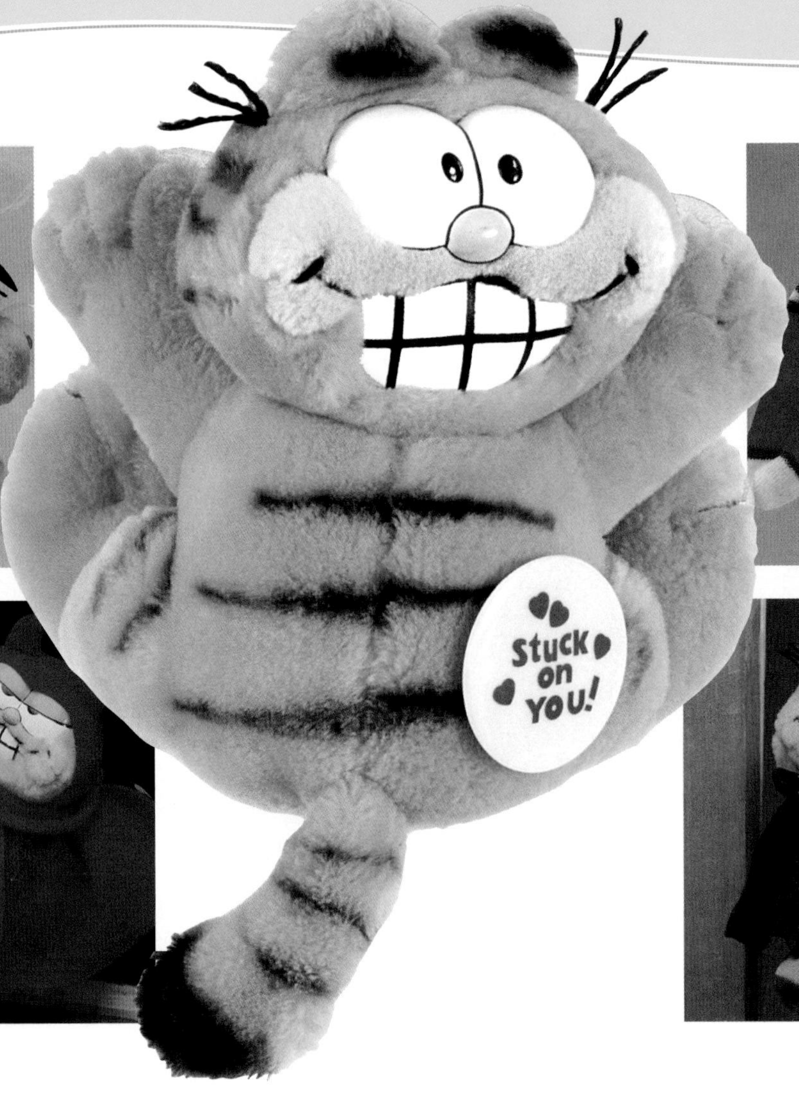
Stuck on YOU!

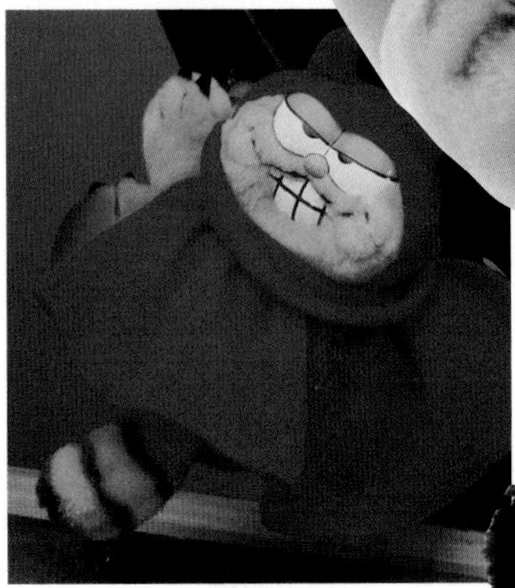

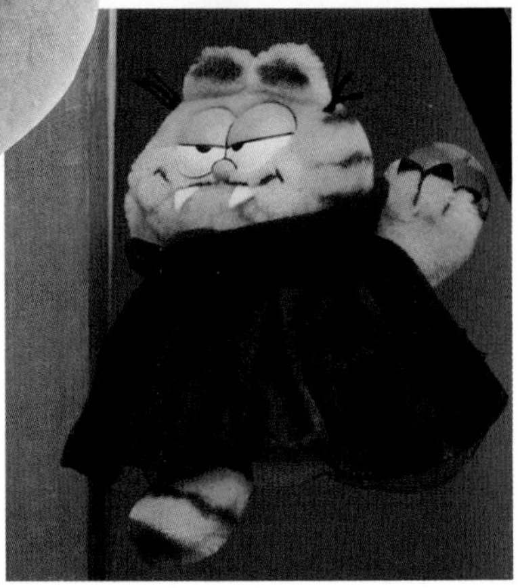

Center: Original "Stuck on You" plush doll by Dakin.

Above and right: Other incarnations of the cat from the 1980s.

Jim Davis on the origin of the "Stuck on You"

"Originally, we had an idea for a Garfield with Velcro on his paws that would stick to the fabric of sofas and chairs. Dakin, our plush licensee at the time, sent back a Garfield stuffed doll with suction cups sewed to his paws, but no specific instructions for its use. It wasn't quite what we had in mind, but we were intrigued by the idea. I stuck the doll to a window and said, 'If this doesn't fall off in the next two days, go ahead and approve it.' Well, it stuck and we approved it. It wasn't our idea—or Dakin's—to place Garfield in car windows. It just sort of happened. In California, people started putting the 'Stuck on You' plush in their cars—kind of like those 'Baby on Board' signs. Fans in other states started putting Garfield in their cars, too. Suddenly, everyone wants one, and stores can't keep the thing in stock. Then people started breaking into cars and taking the Garfields. They'd leave other valuables—radios, briefcases—they just wanted the plush. It was incredible. People ask me if I ever had a Garfield 'Stuck on You.' I never had one. I didn't want my car window to get broken."

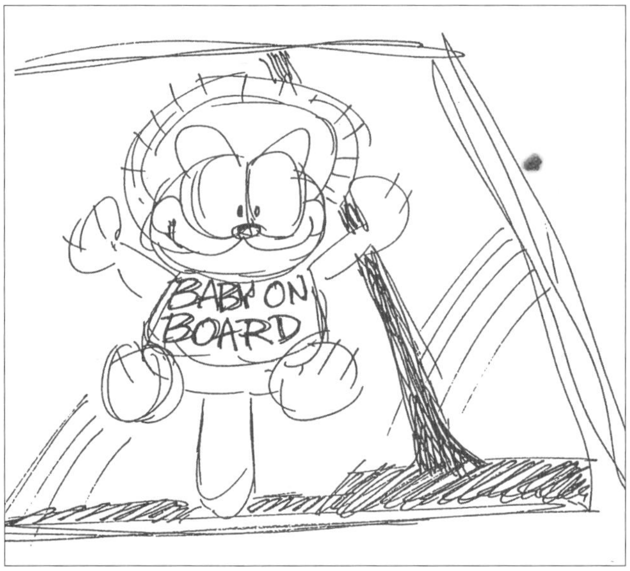
BABY ON
BOARD

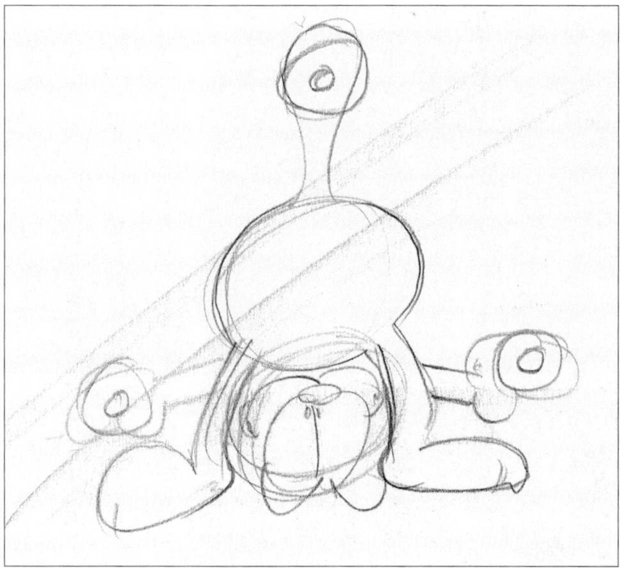

Left: After the initial success of the suction-cupped plush, Jim played around with a lot of different ideas, as shown in these rough concept sketches.

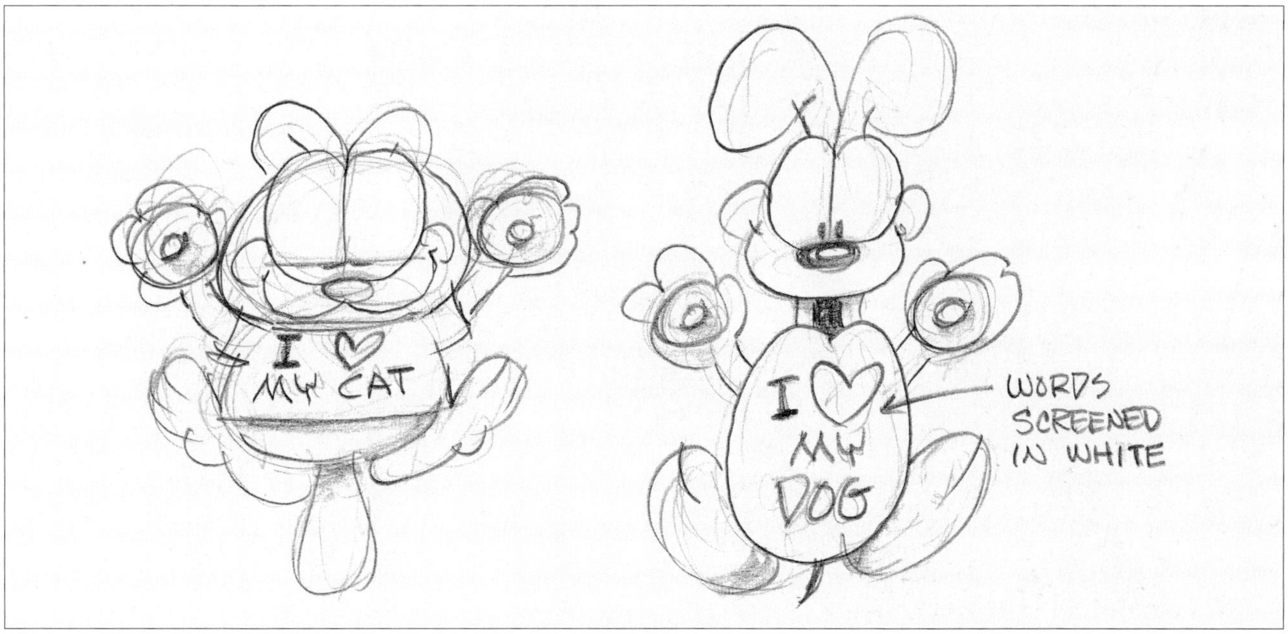
I ♥
MY CAT
I ♥
MY
DOG
WORDS
SCREENED
IN WHITE

Sellout

Dakin test-marketed ten thousand plush Garfields in stores in the San Francisco area. Within forty-eight hours, *all* the Garfield dolls had been sold. This unprecedented success story was soon duplicated throughout the U.S., and it eventually spread to parts of Europe and even Australia.

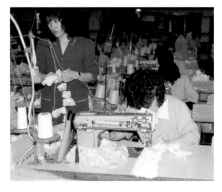

Frisky Business

Dakin began producing the dolls at four additional plants, but it took more than a year for supply to catch up with demand. At one Korean plant, there were nearly two hundred workers whose sole task was spray-painting stripes on Garfield.

Copycat

The "Stuck on You" craze spawned the inevitable backlash (albeit a humorous one). The answer to Garfield in the window of a car was this funny (though completely unauthorized) "Krushed Kitty" plush doll. Apparently the joke was lost on the syndicate's lawyers, who issued an immediate cease-and-desist order.

Comeback Kitty

The renamed Garfield "Stuck-Up" was released in 1995, and it included some delightfully different variations.

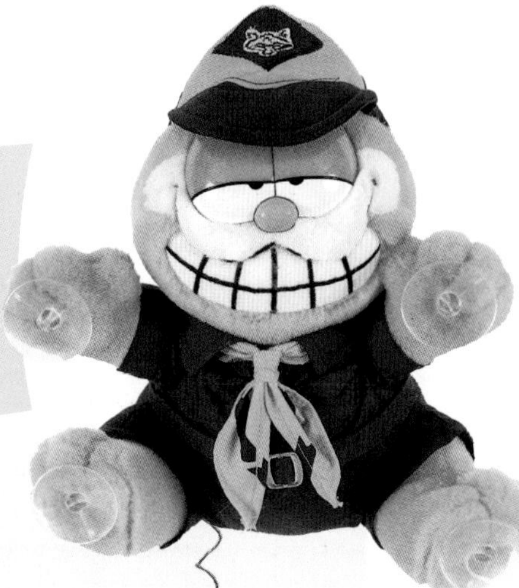

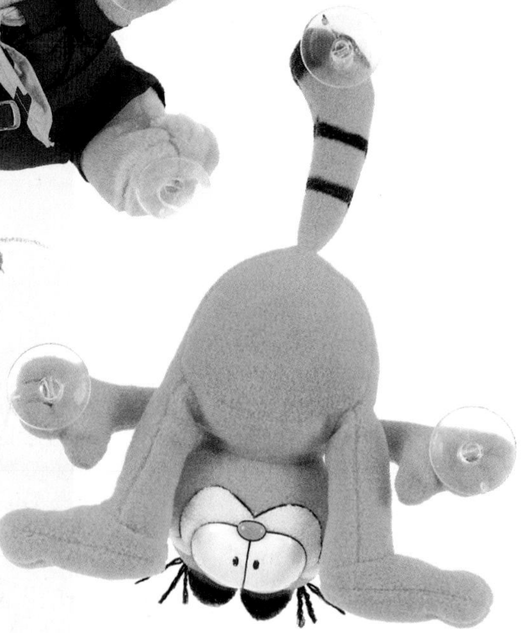

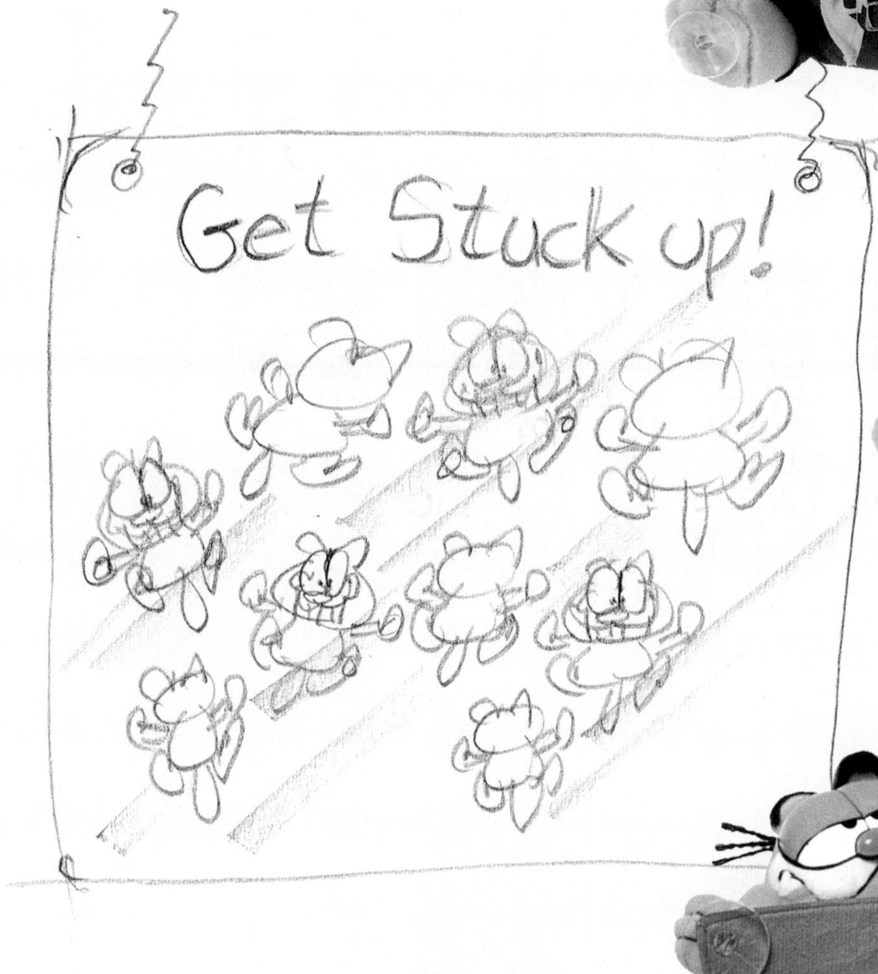
Get Stuck up!

"My favorite new plush is the 'Mooning Stuck-Up.' Some say it's Garfield's best side!"
—Jim Davis

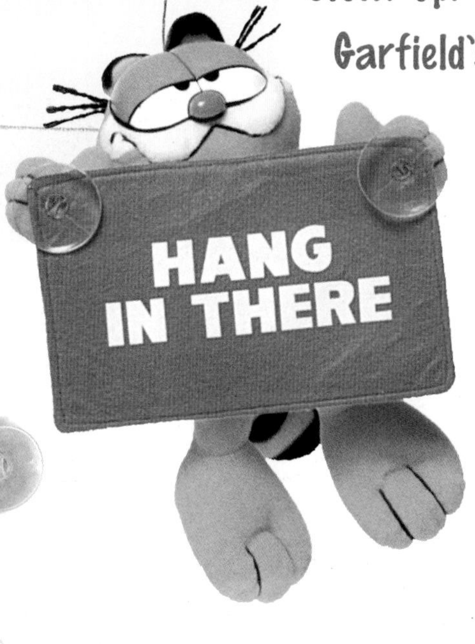
HANG
IN THERE

Above: Original Jim Davis sketch for hanging plush display made of clear plastic.

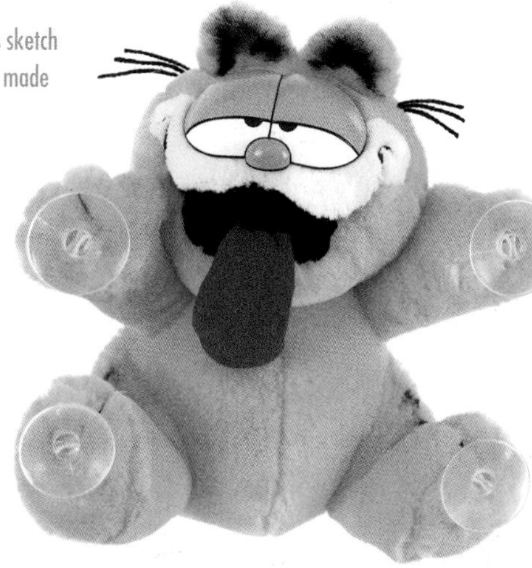

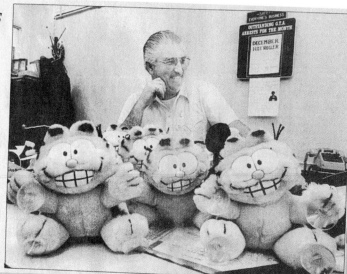

Cat Burglars Tripped Up by Long Paw of the Law

By BOB POOL, *Times Staff Writer*

Police say they have broken up an unusual gang of San Fernando Valley cat burglars who were driven by puppy love.

Four teen-age North Hollywood boys were arrested on suspicion of breaking into 30 cars to steal popular Garfield the Cat dolls for their girlfriends, Los Angeles police said Friday.

The boys, whose ages ranged from 13 and 15, prowled shopping center parking lots in North Hollywood and Burbank on bicycles looking for the stuffed animals to impress the girls, Detective Charlie Vaughn said.

They smashed windows to snatch the $20 dolls, which feature grin-and-bear-it smiles and suction-cup paws that stick to car windows, he said.

"All they wanted were the Garfields," Vaughn said. "They left behind stereos, briefcases and, in one case, even a wallet."

The outbreak of stuffed cat-nappings began in late November. The most recent theft occurred just hours before

OUTSTANDING G.T.A. ARRESTS FOR THE MONTH
DECEMBER
HOT ROLLER

Hot Property

Garfield was so popular in the '80s that some people even broke the law *(right and below)* to get their paws on him.

THE HUDSON DISPATCH

25 CENTS

TUESDAY, JUNE 14, 1988

VOL. 62 NO. 142

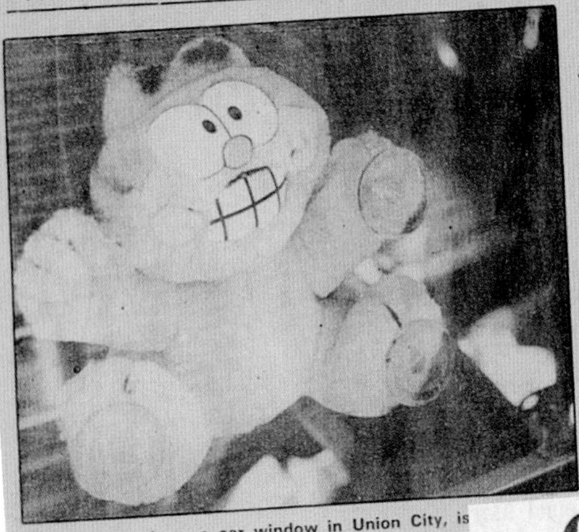

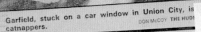

Garfield, stuck on a car window in Union City, is ... catnappers. DON McCOY THE HUD...

A NATIONAL TREND

Catnappers hit Hudson!

Thugs smash car windows, grab Garfield dolls

By JUDY TEMES and NINA SHAPIRO
Staff Writers

Garfield, the famous comic strip cat, is so popular in these parts that people are breaking car windows to get their hands on stuffed animals that look like the sarcastic, but lovable creature.

Police in Hudson and Bergen counties said yesterday that the furry animals, attached to car windows by suction cups, have fallen prey to catnappers during the past few months. Most communities have missing.

About 10 stuffed cats have been stolen from cars in Hoboken, according to police. Several cats have been stolen from cars in Fairview and Secaucus, and one Ridgefield police officer had his Garfield removed recently.

The catnappings locally are part of a national phenomenon that started six months ago in Southern California, according to a spokesman for Dakin Inc., a San Francisco company that makes the stuffed animals. About 200 animals, adorned with a pin say- ... n reported sto- ... id C... spokesman for Dakin.

Catnapping has been reported in other states, including Kansas, Connecticut, Florida and New York. Catnappers started surfacing in New Jersey two or three months ago, say authorities.

Local police said they do not know the identities of the thieves. No catnapper has been arrested to date here. But teenagers pulling pranks have been identified and arrested in other states, said Susan Chan McCarthy, general counsel for Dakin.

Some police officers believe thieves are

Please see GARFIELD Page 22

Garfield Saves Girl

CORPUS CHRISTI, Texas (AP) — A stuffed animal attached to the window of a family's pickup truck deflected a mysterious gunshot and saved a 5-year-old girl from serious injury, police said.

Cynthia Guerrero suffered some facial cuts Sunday night when the window was shattered by the .22-caliber bullet. Police don't know who fired the shot.

"While passing through the window the bullet apparently struck the lower body of the stuffed animal, causing the bullet to change direction and minimize the injury to the child," Sgt. John Priest said in his report on the incident.

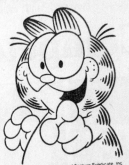

GARFIELD © 1978 United Feature Syndicate, Inc

GARFIELD — OUR HERO

The doll of the cartoon a... comic strip cat Garfield w... attached to the window w... suction cups.

Feline Intervention

In 1989, a little girl from Texas was saved when the plush pussycat deflected a stray bullet.

SWAT
PTWING!
KIRKMAN
The Associated Press
CORPUS CHRISTI, Texas—The Corpus Christi Police Department's SWAT Team unveiled its newly designed bullet-proof vests today.

Far right: Illustration by Rick Kirkman, artist of the *Baby Blues* comic strip.

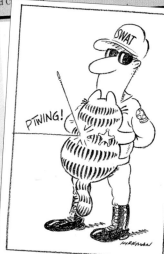

Sticking Power

What made Garfield so popular in the 1980s? Was it luck? Timing? Mass hysteria? Whatever the reasons, Hollywood cashed in on the craze and included Garfield in several productions. The suction-cupped cat appeared in *Falling Down*, *L.A. Story*, *Hot Shots*, *Naked Gun 33 1/3*, and TV's *The Tonight Show* with both Johnny Carson and Jay Leno. And the furry phenom continues to stick around, with guest shots on such popular shows as *Home Improvement*, *Just Shoot Me*, and *Charmed.* Despite having rubbed paws with show biz's elite, Garfield has never gotten stuck-up.

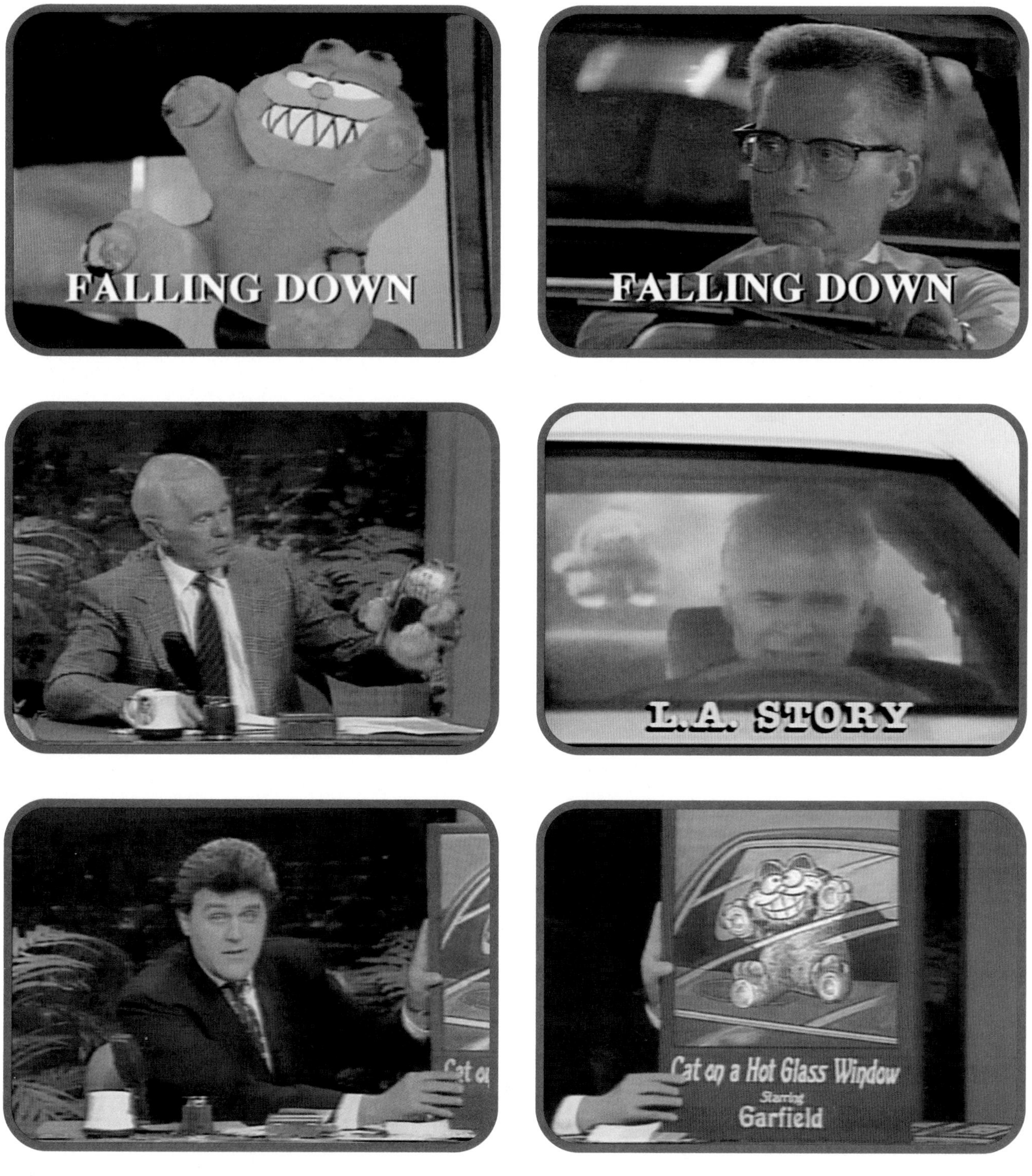
FALLING DOWN
FALLING DOWN
L.A. STORY
Cat on a Hot Glass Window
Starring
Garfield

Video captures of *Falling Down* starring Michael Douglas (1993), a 1990 appearance on *The Tonight Show* with Johnny Carson, *L. A. Story* with Steve Martin (1991), and a 1989 Jay Leno *Tonight Show* routine.

Famous Feline

The Garfield fad did not go unnoticed by cartoonists, and the renowned cat popped up in several comic strips and single-panel cartoons. Jim himself was even given the "Stuck on You" treatment.

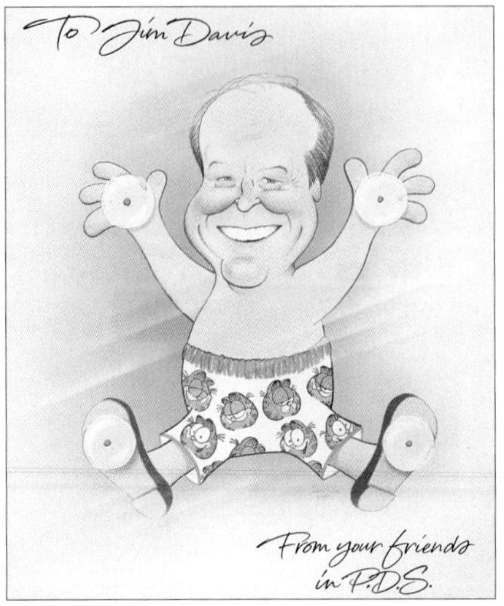
To Jim Davis
From your friends in P.D.S.

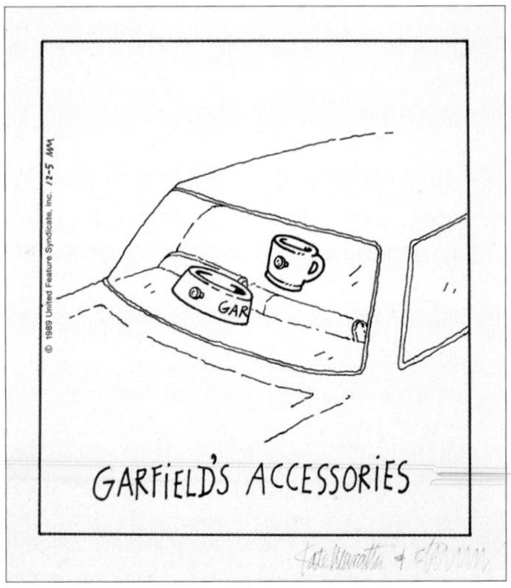
GAR
GARFIELD'S ACCESSORIES

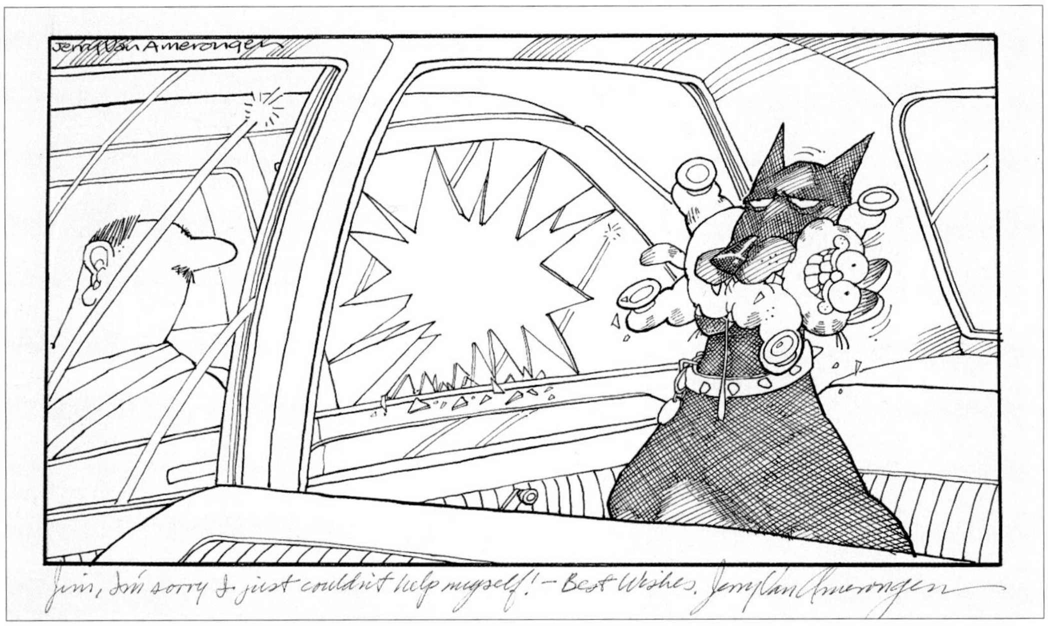
Jerry Van Amerongen
Jim, I'm sorry I just couldn't help myself! — Best Wishes, Jerry Van Amerongen

Above left: Jim Davis becomes a suction-cupped cartoonist in this caricature from the late 1980s.

Above right: A gag cartoon from the late 1980s.

Right: The Neighborhood by Jerry Van Amerongen. This is one of Jim's favorite cartoons dealing with the "Stuck on You" craze.

Below: The Duplex by Glenn McCoy.

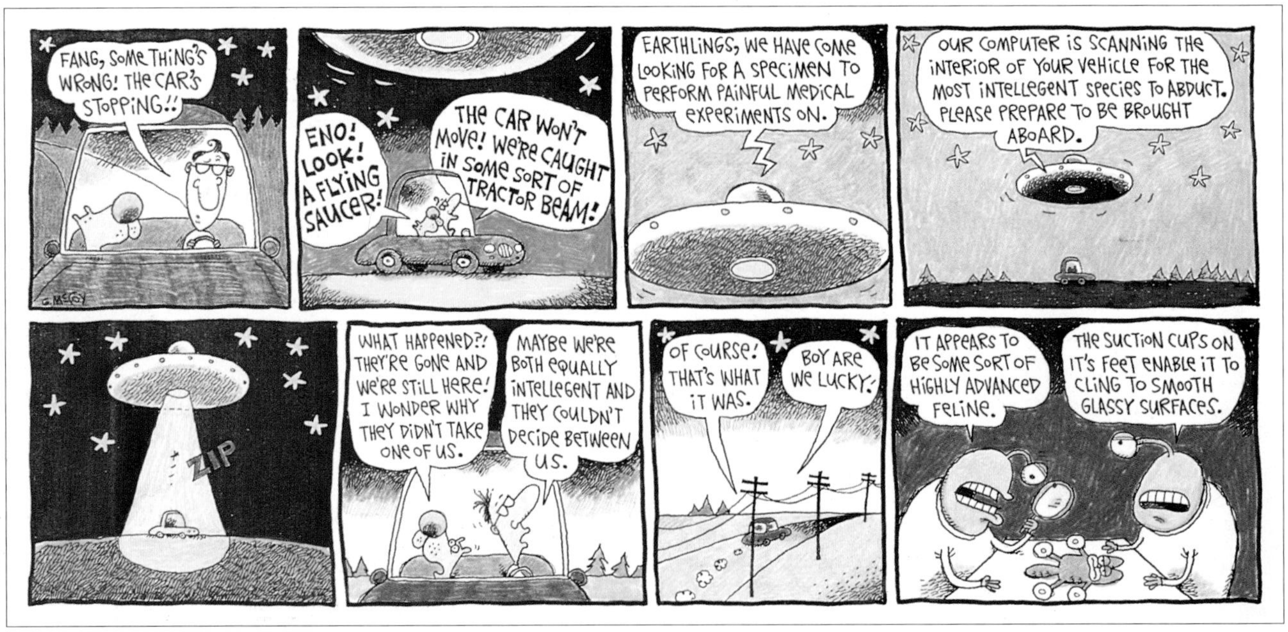
FANG, SOMETHING'S WRONG! THE CAR'S STOPPING!!
ENO! LOOK! A FLYING SAUCER!
THE CAR WON'T MOVE! WE'RE CAUGHT IN SOME SORT OF TRACTOR BEAM!
EARTHLINGS, WE HAVE COME LOOKING FOR A SPECIMEN TO PERFORM PAINFUL MEDICAL EXPERIMENTS ON.
OUR COMPUTER IS SCANNING THE INTERIOR OF YOUR VEHICLE FOR THE MOST INTELLEGENT SPECIES TO ABDUCT. PLEASE PREPARE TO BE BROUGHT ABOARD.
ZIP
WHAT HAPPENED?! THEY'RE GONE AND WE'RE STILL HERE! I WONDER WHY THEY DIDN'T TAKE ONE OF US.
MAYBE WE'RE BOTH EQUALLY INTELLEGENT AND THEY COULDN'T DECIDE BETWEEN US.
OF COURSE! THAT'S WHAT IT WAS.
BOY ARE WE LUCKY.
IT APPEARS TO BE SOME SORT OF HIGHLY ADVANCED FELINE.
THE SUCTION CUPS ON IT'S FEET ENABLE IT TO CLING TO SMOOTH GLASSY SURFACES.

CHAPTER EIGHT

Garfield Stuff from A to Z

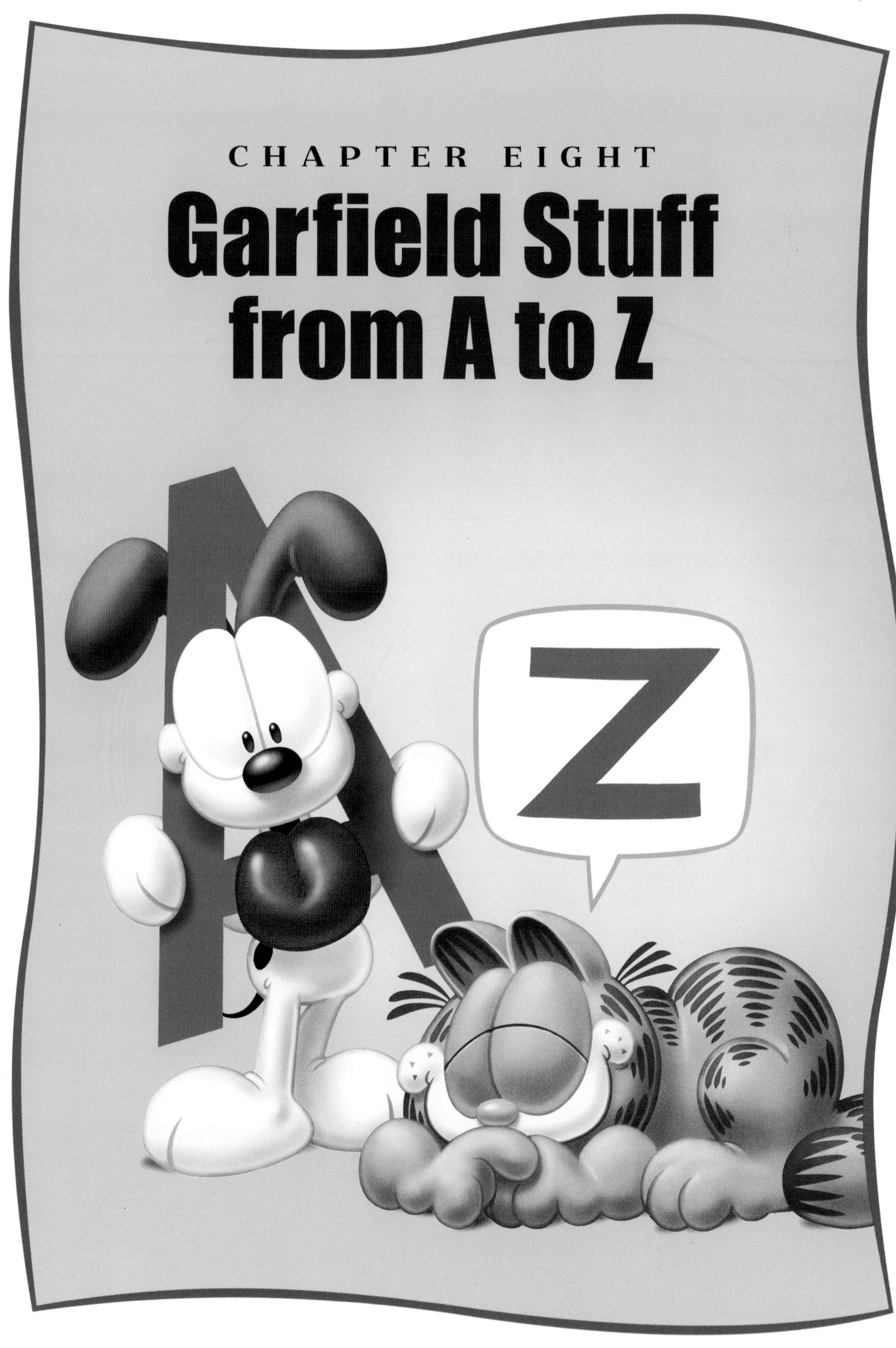
Z

When it comes to Garfield, too much stuff is never enough! The iconic cat comes in a wide array of products, including pet beds, pasta, puppets, pooper-scoopers . . . and that's just the *p*'s! These are a few of our favorite things from A to Z:

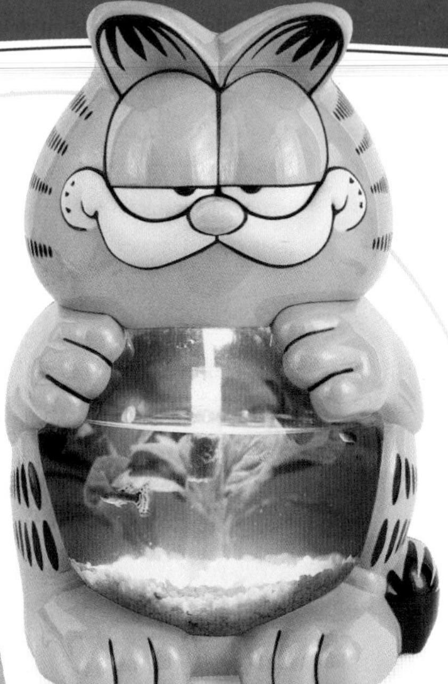

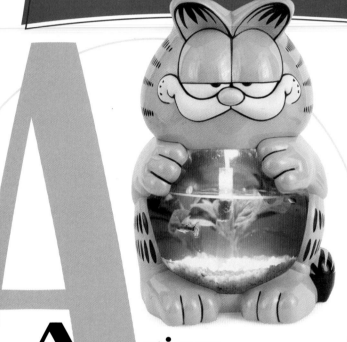

Aquarium

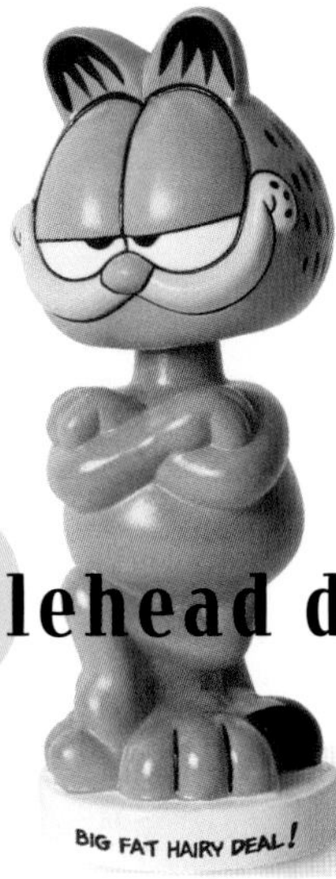
BIG FAT HAIRY DEAL!

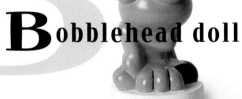

Bobblehead doll

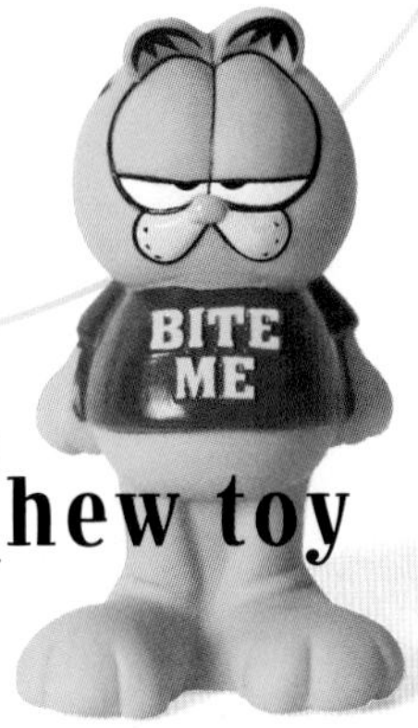
BITE ME

Chew toy

Draft eliminator

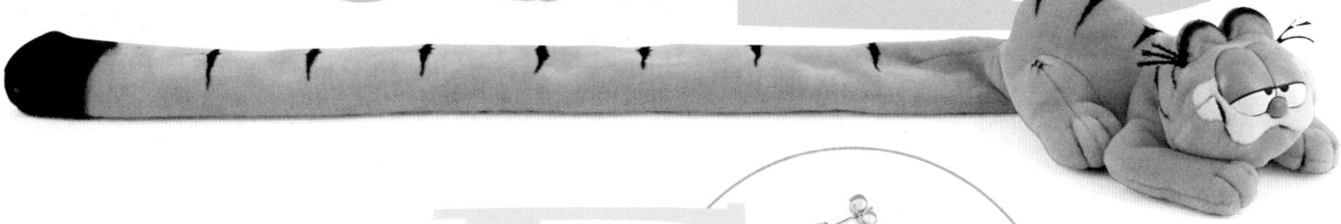

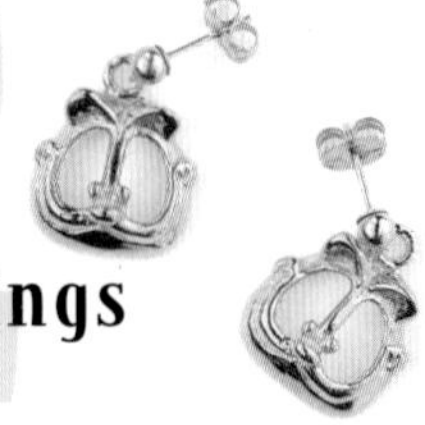

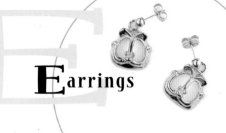

Earrings

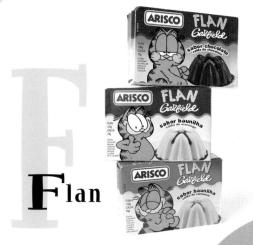

Flan

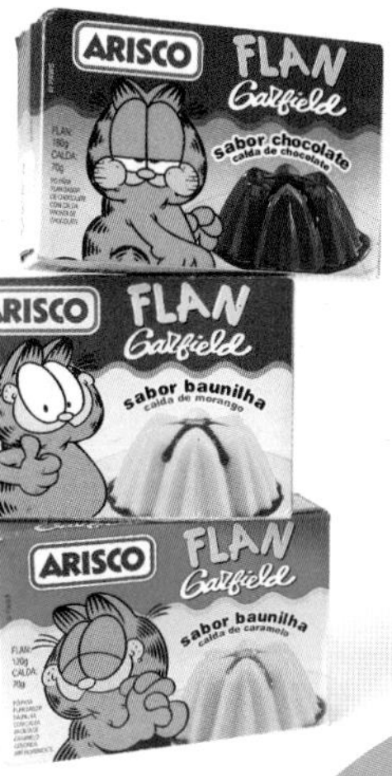
ARISCO
FLAN
Garfield
sabor chocolate
ARISCO
FLAN
Garfield
sabor baunilha
ARISCO
FLAN
Garfield
sabor baunilha

Globe

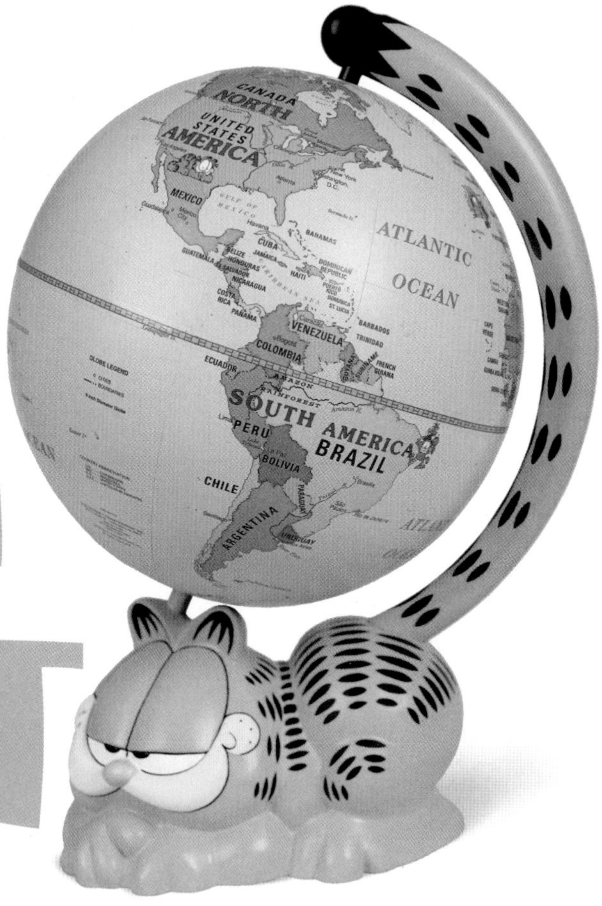
CANADA
UNITED STATES
AMERICA
MEXICO
CUBA
ATLANTIC
OCEAN
VENEZUELA
COLOMBIA
ECUADOR
SOUTH AMERICA
PERU
BRAZIL
BOLIVIA
CHILE
ARGENTINA

Hangers

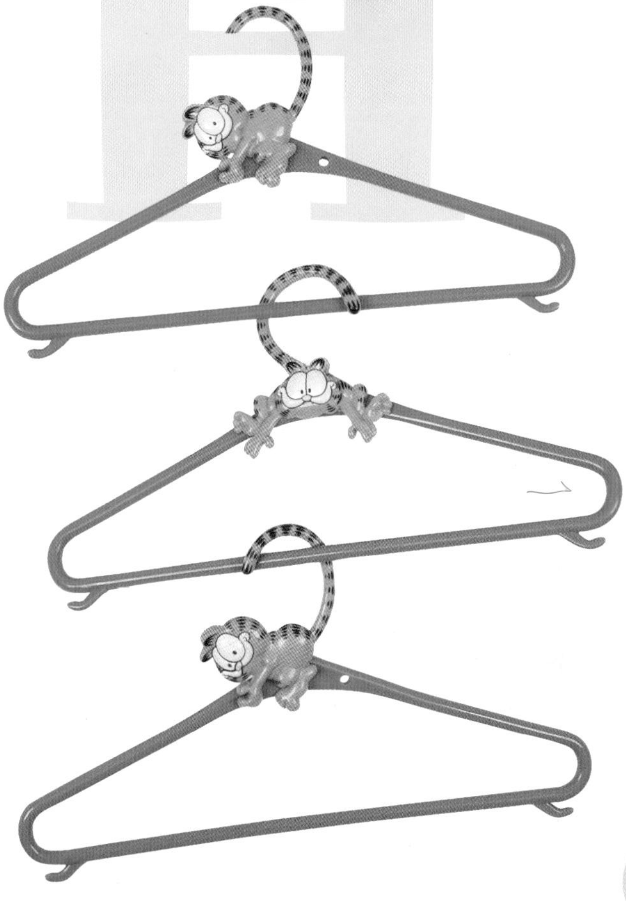

Indiana license plate

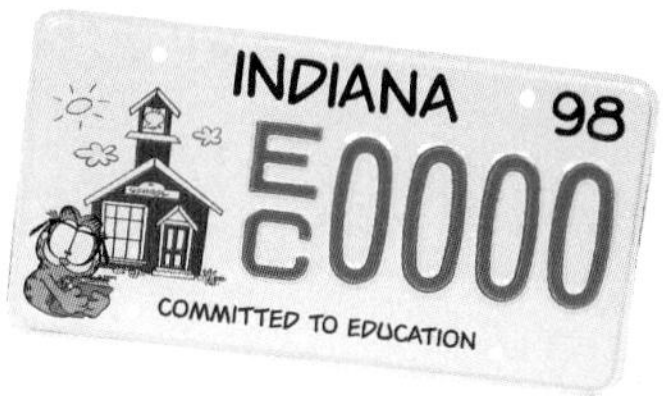
INDIANA
98
EC0000
COMMITTED TO EDUCATION

Jacket

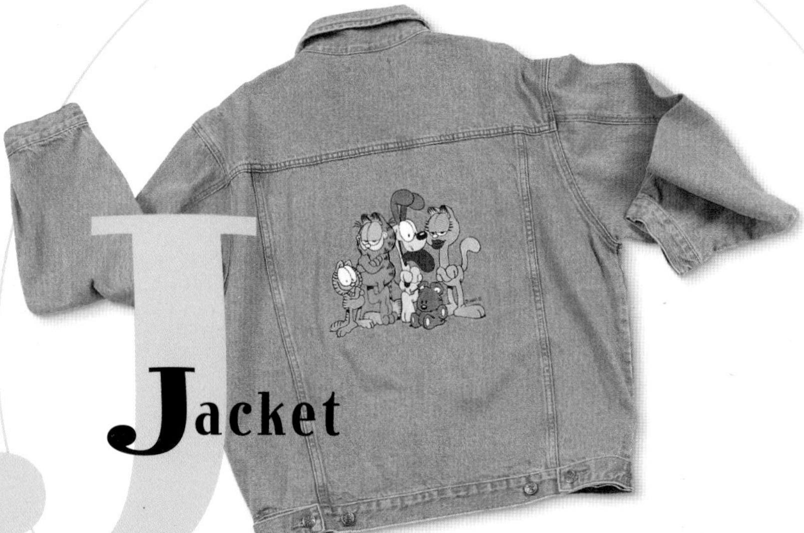

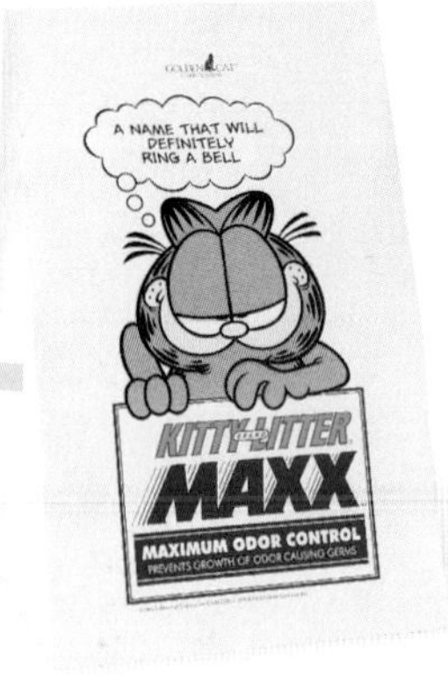
A NAME THAT WILL DEFINITELY RING A BELL
KITTY LITTER
MAXX
MAXIMUM ODOR CONTROL

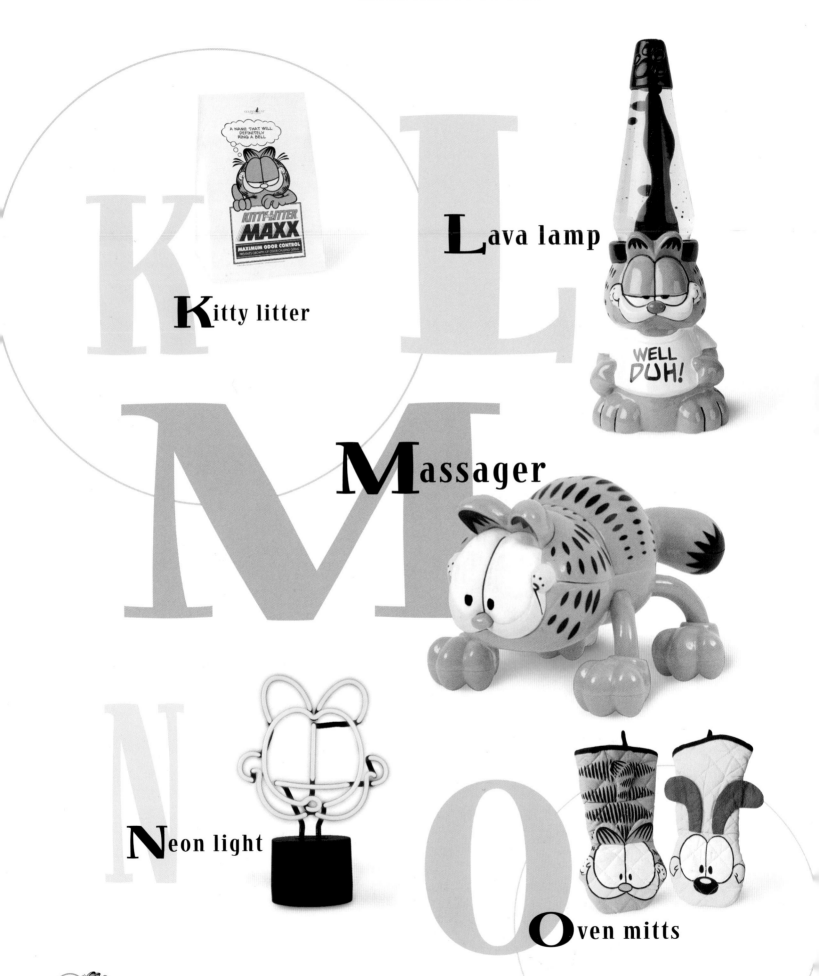

Kitty litter

Lava lamp

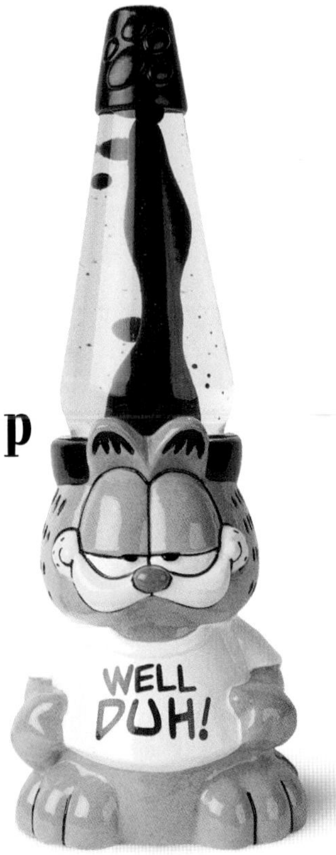
WELL
DUH!

Massager

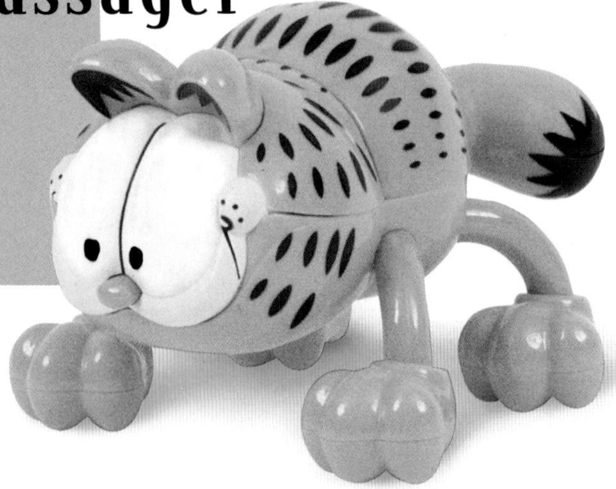

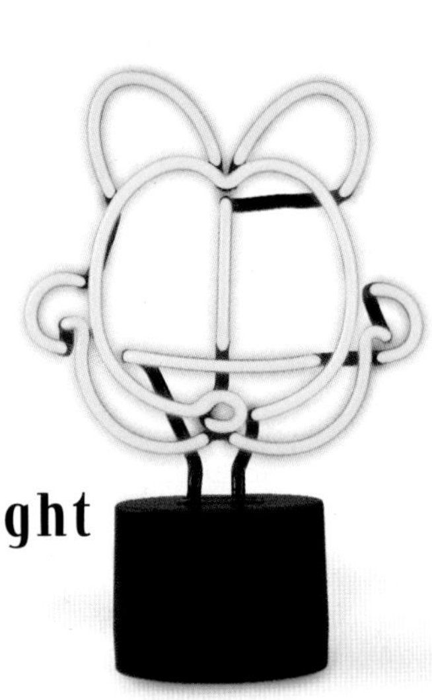

Neon light

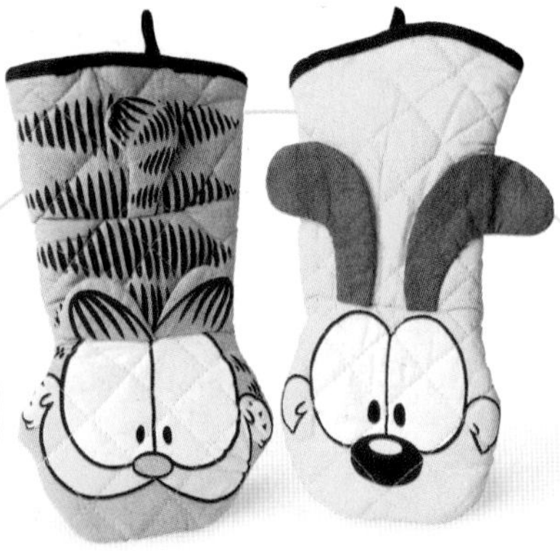

Oven mitts

Porcelain dolls

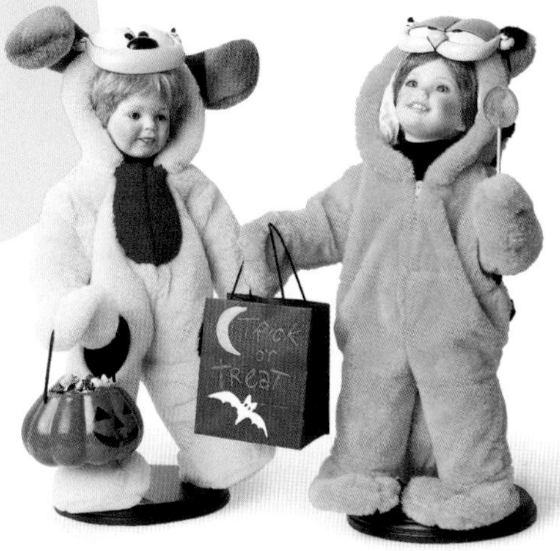
TRICK or TREAT

"Queen of Caffeine" mug

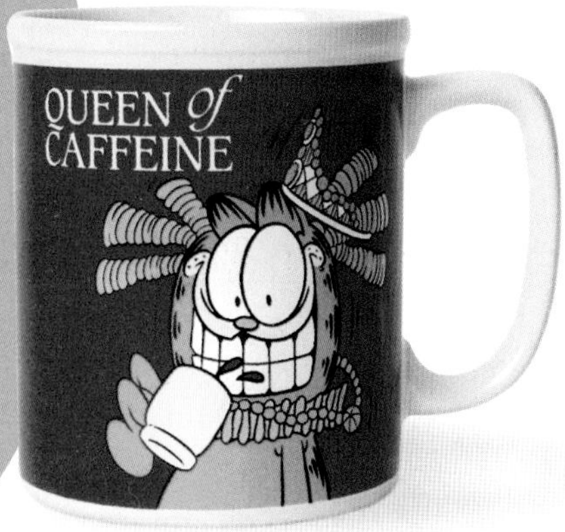
QUEEN of
CAFFEINE

Rock

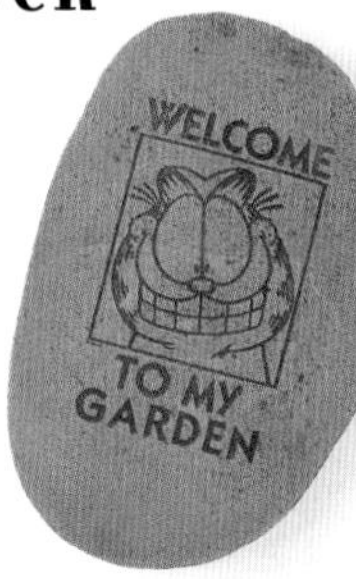
WELCOME
TO MY GARDEN

Soup

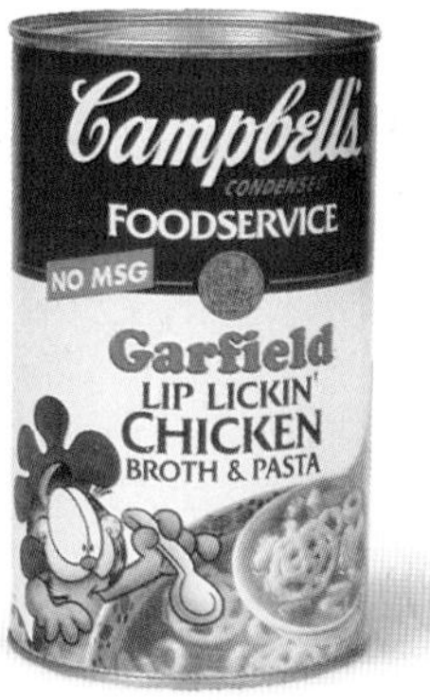
Campbell's
FOODSERVICE
NO MSG
Garfield
LIP LICKIN'
CHICKEN
BROTH & PASTA

Toilet seat

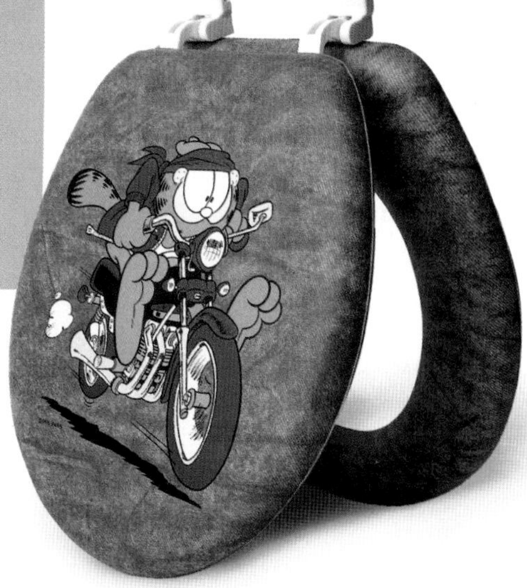

Underwear

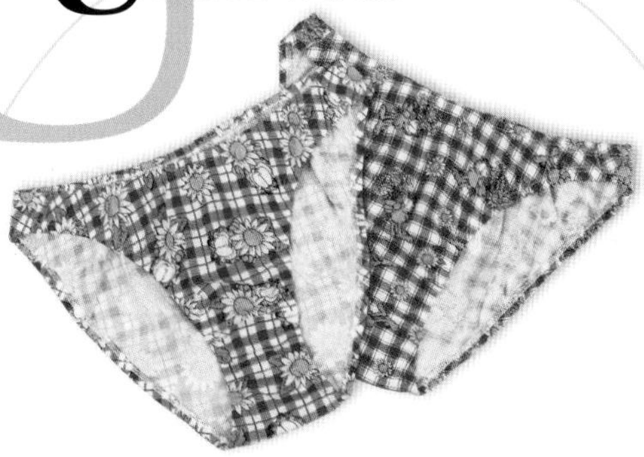

Vitamins

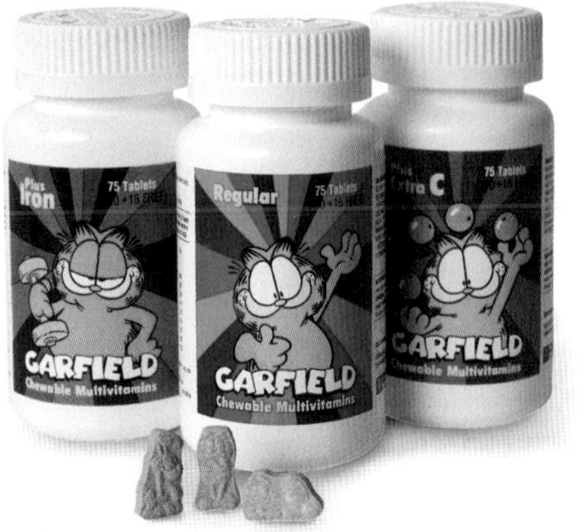
Regular
75 Tablets
Plus Iron
Plus Extra C
GARFIELD
Chewable Multivitamins

Whirligig

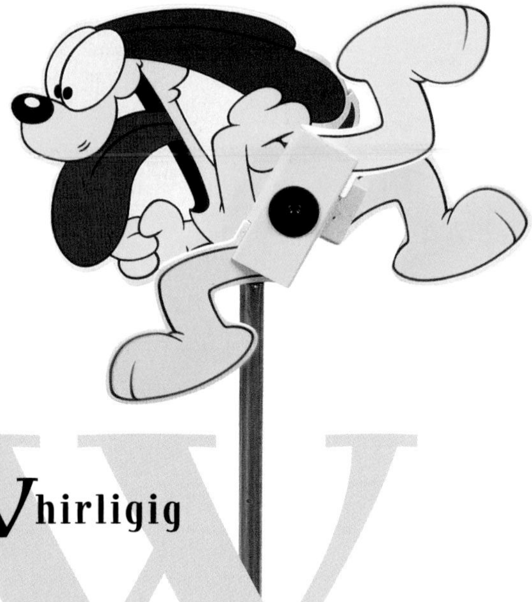

X-treme books

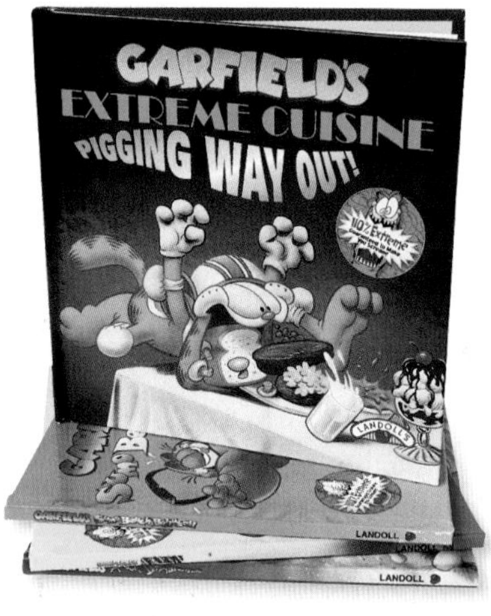
GARFIELD'S
EXTREME CUISINE
PIGGING WAY OUT!
LANDOLL

Yo-yo

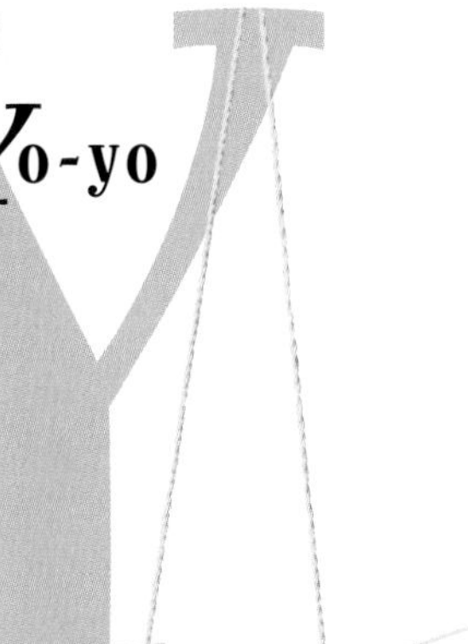

Zodiac

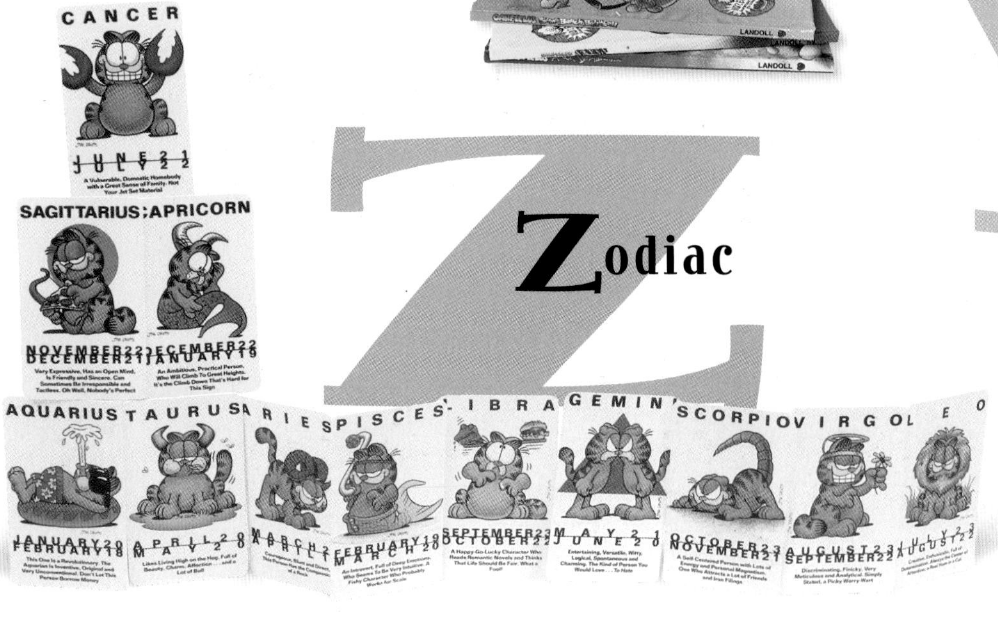
CANCER
SAGITTARIUS
CAPRICORN
AQUARIUS
TAURUS
ARIES
PISCES
LIBRA
GEMINI
SCORPIO
VIRGO
LEO

CHAPTER NINE

'Toon Talk: An Interview with Jim Davis

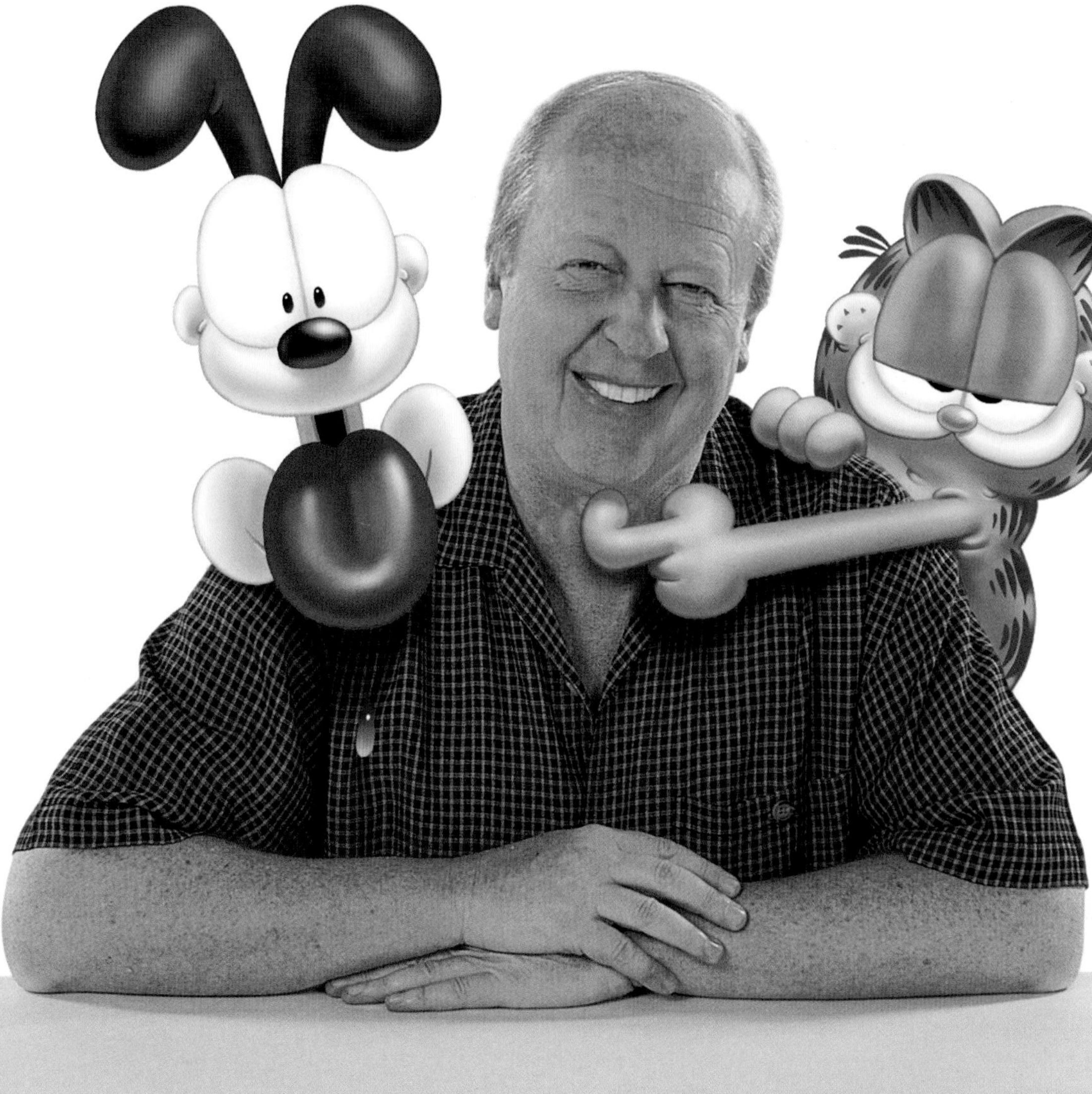

Did you know Garfield would be such a big success?

Never in my wildest dreams. Like every cartoonist, I wanted a successful strip, maybe a book or two. Nothing prepared me for the phenomenal reaction to Garfield. Luckily, I wasn't in completely uncharted territory. *Peanuts* had been very successful with licensing, and I learned a lot by studying that program. By examining how each area was handled (TV, products, books, promotions), I was able to create a template that I could apply to Garfield. We always made sure we weren't just rubber-stamping the character on a product. There had to be a real fit between Garfield and the product, and it had to be entertaining. We tried to bring fans the very best, and I think they appreciated it.

How did you think up Garfield?

I had tried a comic strip based on a bug, Gnorm Gnat. Comics editors at the syndicates thought there was something there, but bugs? Who can relate to bugs? So I took a long look at the comics pages and noticed there were a lot of dogs doing quite well. There was Snoopy, Marmaduke, and Belvedere, but no cats. So I took my memories of all the cats from my childhood home—on a country farm it's not unusual to have dozens of cats—and I combined those traits with those of my grandfather, James A. Garfield Davis. He was a curmudgeon with a dry wit and, deep down, a warm heart. Voilà! Garfield was born.

Has success spoiled you?

Duh. I was a farm kid who grew up doing lots of chores, milking cows, baling hay, plowing fields. Once I was successful, I made someone else milk the cows.

DOWN ON THE FARM: Jim and little brother, Dave, circa 1955.

Nothing prepared me for the phenomenal reaction to Garfield.

Where do you get ideas?

Schenectady. I think that's an old vaudeville line. Actually, I get ideas from everywhere—people, pets, books, movies, music . . . the usual places.

How far ahead do you work?

I'm supposed to work six weeks ahead on dailies and eight weeks ahead on Sundays. I'm usually on the ragged edge of disaster.

How do you explain Garfield's enormous appeal?

I've been giving the same answer for a long time. A publicist told me I should get a fresh answer, but I can't because it's the truth and my only explanation. Number one, there are a lot of cat lovers who can relate to Garfield because their cats are big fat slobs, too. Number two, Garfield is an antihero. He defends our right to pig out, sleep in, and be selfish. He says and does the stuff we'd all like to say and do if we thought we could get away with it. In short, people identify with him. Like I always say, he's a human in a cat suit.

Is there one feature of Garfield you think accounts for his seemingly universal appeal?

Garfield is funny—pure and simple. He's a smart aleck and a lazy glutton. He's also a cat who has the upper hand; he knows it and so does everyone around him. The relationship between pets and humans is funny. Look at what humans put up with—shredded furniture, broken lamps, chewed-up shoes—it's a comical situation. I also think people, both adults and children, can relate to Garfield's sense of humor because he deals with two things that all people can relate to—eating and sleeping.

Aren't you a bit bothered by the commercialization of Garfield?

No, I'm glad people want to have Garfield on their coffee cups, T-shirts, or posters. He's really a character with many expressions and attitudes, and I think it's neat if someone can relate to the character enough to want to demonstrate that by owning something "Garfield." It's flattering. Garfield's success has opened up many doors for me, allowed me to live a comfortable life, to travel and see things I might never have seen otherwise. It also allows me to wear different hats on the job. I can be an artist and cartoonist

one minute, a designer the next minute, an advertising executive the next. I also happen to like the people I work with. If Garfield weren't a commercial success, I would never have had the opportunity to meet and work with so many nice, creative, talented, funny people.

What's a typical day like for you?

Every day is different with the exception of "writing week" (a month's worth of gags can be generated in a week). The day starts between three to five a.m.; that's my quiet time to catch up, doodle, write, and generally put the day in order before the phone starts ringing. Most days, I hit the art department by nine to fiddle with concepts for new products. Licensees visit a couple of days a week to brainstorm new programs. There are always business decisions that have to be made since *Garfield* is now read around the world, and

BACK TO THE DRAWING BOARD: Jim reworks a sketch.

there are licensing, publishing, and TV syndication deals in almost every country. Part of the day is always devoted to figuring out what's next and how to approach it. On a normal day, I'd say I work twelve to fourteen hours—thank goodness I love what I'm doing.

What does it take to be a cartoonist?

Al Capp (*Li'l Abner*) said, "It helps to have been dropped on your head as a baby." He may be right. It also takes writing and drawing skills, and the ability to find humor in the mundanity of life. Try not to take everything so seriously. It helps to have a point of view, something to say. It also helps to be organized and dependable. Syndicates don't like it when you miss deadlines.

What is your advice for a cartoonist who wants to become syndicated?

Have a unique look or point of view—a style or statement that's all your own. Don't try to be the next Bill Watterson or Gary Larson. Do your homework on the syndicate and make sure you're sending the right stuff to the right person. Be patient.

Do you have any tips for young comics artists?

Yes—read, read, and read. To be a good comic-strip artist you must be a good writer. Art's important, but writing will make or break you. Learn all you can. Watch movies and TV. Socialize. Have friends and activities. Study people and their behavior. Draw. Try different drawing tools and styles. Above all, have something to say that's unique or different—something that's especially "you." Oh, yes, and have fun with your feature. If you have fun doing it, people will have fun reading it. Something translates through . . .

To be a good comic-strip artist you must be a good writer.

How did you get your start in cartooning?

I was asthmatic when I was a kid. On a farm, that's not a good thing, especially since almost everything on the farm threw me into an asthmatic fit. I used to have to spend a lot of time in bed. My mom shoved a pencil and a pad of paper in front of me and told me to entertain myself.

I started off drawing cows, dogs, and horses. They were so bad I had to label everything. But in time, I got better. Pretty soon I started writing little captions with the characters. Lo and behold, I was cartooning.

Years later I lucked into a position assisting Tom Ryan (*Tumbleweeds*) on his strip. I saw the discipline and long hours it took to be a success. I started trying to get my own strip syndicated. It took years of trying, but finally I found a comics editor who saw something in my work.

Who were your inspirations career-wise?

Charles Schulz (*Peanuts*) and Johnny Hart (*B.C.*). Sparky (Schulz) showed me how powerful humor can be when based on simple situations and honest relationships. Johnny gave me the courage to simply be silly at times with the comic strip.

What are your favorite comics?

Zits, by Jerry Scott and Jim Borgman, is wonderfully drawn and always makes me smile. I loved Bill Watterson's *Calvin and Hobbes*. Beautiful, brilliant, and funny. Gary Larson (*The Far Side*) is nuts, a true genius. I love *For Better or For Worse* by Lynn Johnston because her art is charming, her characters engaging, and she provides some touching personal insights. Mike Peters (*Mother Goose & Grimm*) is pure electricity, a lovably demented dynamo, and all that comes through in his work. I grew up on *Blondie*, and now Chic Young's son, Dean, has taken over the strip and has just done a fabulous job of bringing Blondie and Dagwood into the twenty-first century while still staying true to his characters. I enjoy *Cathy* by Cathy Guisewite; it's sort of a woman's point of view of the world, and I think the world's better for it. I also love Mort Walker's *Beetle Bailey*. Mort knows how to do the old one-two-three punch line like a stand-up comedian. And, of course, we all owe a debt to Sparky.

Come to think of it, I love just about all the comics. Classics like *Pogo* (Walt Kelly) and *Krazy Kat* (George Herriman), *Prince Valiant* (John Cullen Murphy) and *Steve Canyon* (Milton Caniff). The editorial cartoons of Jim Borgman and Mike Peters, Garry Trudeau's work . . . it's all special. I guess when you do it for a living you can really appreciate what it takes to make someone laugh, or smile, or think, for that matter.

What makes a strip funny?

Timing is everything. There's nothing better than a well-timed gag. I like slapstick, but I also like the element of surprise. I also think there are funny words and funny combinations of words. I liked the words "sick monkey" and "leaf weasels." Don't ask me why or how they got put together, but the words alone made me laugh, and I had to somehow put them in a strip. I also think there are funny numbers. Forty-two is funny. Fifteen is funny. Twelve isn't. Three is hysterical!

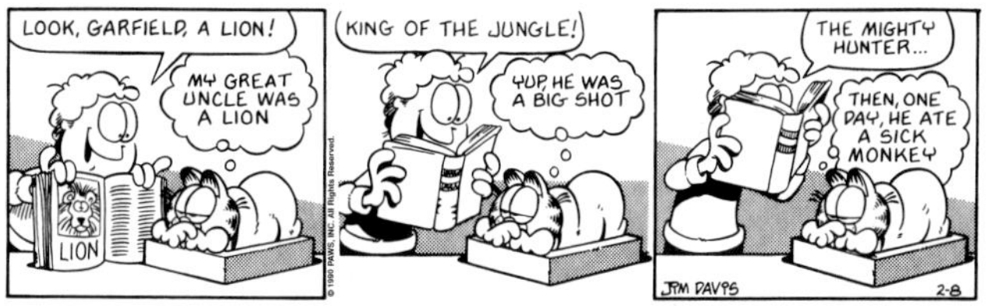
LOOK, GARFIELD, A LION!
MY GREAT UNCLE WAS A LION
LION
KING OF THE JUNGLE!
YUP, HE WAS A BIG SHOT
THE MIGHTY HUNTER...
THEN, ONE DAY, HE ATE A SICK MONKEY
JIM DAVIS
2-8
© 1990 PAWS, INC. All Rights Reserved.

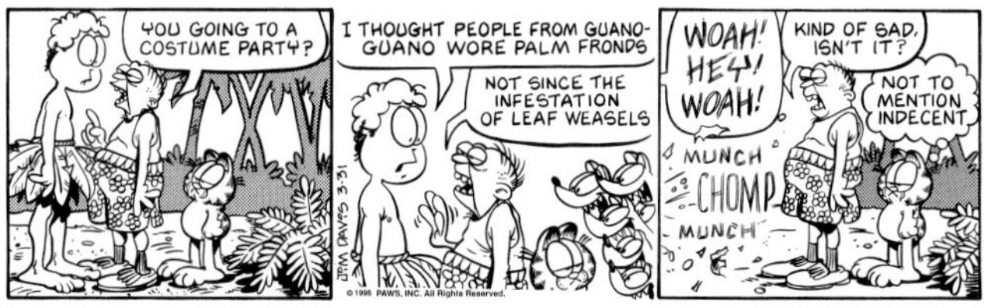
YOU GOING TO A COSTUME PARTY?
I THOUGHT PEOPLE FROM GUANO-GUANO WORE PALM FRONDS
NOT SINCE THE INFESTATION OF LEAF WEASELS
WOAH! HEY! WOAH!
MUNCH
CHOMP
MUNCH
KIND OF SAD, ISN'T IT?
NOT TO MENTION INDECENT
JIM DAVIS 3-31
© 1995 PAWS, INC. All Rights Reserved.

I'd like to think Garfield is funny every day, but more often than not I think he hits the nail on the head when it comes to the truth.

How do you know what will amuse the readers?

It's true that everyone has a different idea of what's funny. I figure if I laugh at a gag, someone else will, too. You just have to trust your gut instinct in that area. I try not to cross the line of good taste, although I've been close a few times. I also try to stick with themes that are universal.

Have you always been funny?

Except for the time I had back surgery.

Are you in the strip? Who are you? Garfield or Jon?

Both. I can be like Garfield—I love to eat (yes, lasagna) and take catnaps, and I can be sarcastic. And I hate "cute." But unlike Garfield, I'm basically an optimist. I love to work, and I don't hate Mondays. Like Jon, I can be laid-back. I also had dating disasters similar to Jon's. But, egad, I hope I'm never that nerdy.

Has Garfield changed over the years? How?

Well, his looks have changed quite a bit since the early days. He's friendlier-looking now than he was in 1978. Back then his body was more of a big blob, his eyes were smaller, and he had more stripes. He also had shorter legs. Over the years, he's become more proportionally round, has bigger eyes, fewer stripes, and longer limbs. It was a natural evolution.

Personality-wise, though, Garfield really hasn't changed much over the years. He's basically the same self-centered, lazy, egotistical, lasagna-loving, coffee-drinking, dog-hating cat he's always been. But he does seem to be catching on to new technologies: VCRs, TVs, computers . . . and, of course, he loves the remote control. So in a way I guess he's gotten smarter.

Has technology changed your craft?

Oh, definitely. With the advent of computers, I can now surf zillions of Web sites when I should be working. Seriously, technology has had a big impact on Garfield. We have an art bank of Garfield poses that can be accessed by computer for licensing. We also color the comic strip in the computer, and transmit it to the syndicate electronically. No more mailing of original art. But while technology is a great tool, we still create the strip the old-fashioned way: brush and ink on bristol

TECHNO-WIZARD: Jim interviewed after "test-driving" the new Sony Vaio in 2001.

board. Everything is hand lettered, too. We want to preserve the original comic strips, and you can't frame and hang a computer file.

Why is Garfield orange?

I never considered anything but orange. In my head, the sky is blue, the grass is green, and cats are orange.

Why does Garfield always pick on Odie?

Odie is just so "pick-on-able." But Odie doesn't mind; Garfield would never really hurt him. It's just a cat-eat-dog world.

Which do you think is smarter? Humans or cats?

Cats. Absolutely. We're off slaving away at our desks, stressing ourselves out trying to make a living, and our cats are home taking naps in the sun waiting for us to rush home and feed them their next meals. Cats. Most definitely cats.

Do you own any cats?

Three, but, being cats, *they* actually own *me*.

Why did you choose to stay in a small town in Indiana?

Ask John Mellencamp. I love the people, the seasons, the trees, the quiet and lack of traffic . . . . Staying in Indiana has been good for my work. I'm happy here, and, for me, being happy is very conducive to doing humor.

Garfield has done a plethora of things in the last twenty-five years. Should we expect anything special or different in the future?

Garfield says he'd like to do a centerfold, as soon as they make one that's big enough. Really though, the cat will just keep on entertaining. That's what the strip and the TV shows have been all about. That's Garfield's raison d'être.

> ## In my head, the sky is blue, the grass is green, and cats are orange.

What do you consider the highlight of your career?

There have been so many wonderful things; it's hard to pick just one. Getting Garfield on TV would certainly be up there; having the strip in 2,000 newspapers was also a thrill, and something I was very proud of; meeting so many of my childhood heroes—Charles Schulz, Mort Walker—was another high point. To me, my entire career has been a gift. I feel very fortunate.

When do you plan to retire?

When they pry the pencil from my cold, dead fingers. Actually, I don't plan on ever retiring. I'm having way too much fun.

CHAPTER TEN
The Art of Garfield

Garfield started out as black lines on paper, but he's become so much more. Take a stroll through the Garfield Gallery and feast your eyes on this masterpiece of mirth . . . .

Right:
Watercolor dyes on illustration board. Created for *World* magazine, 1985.

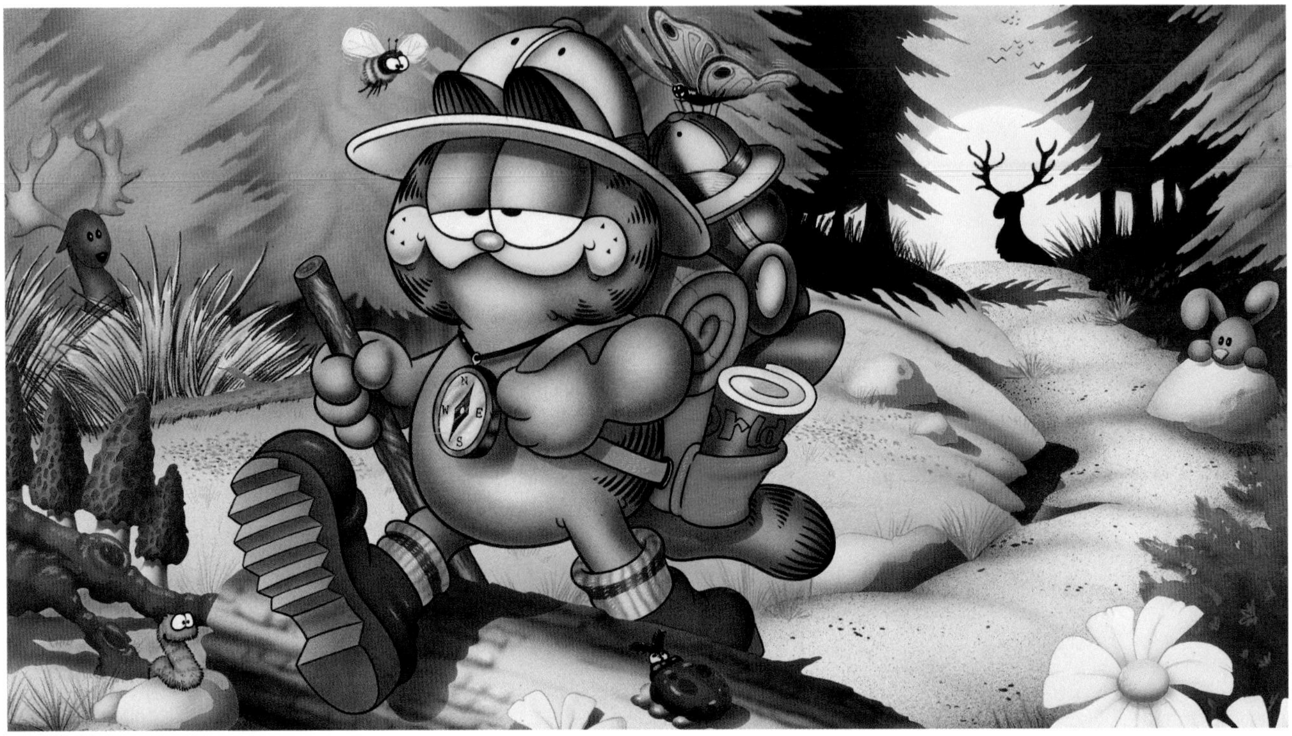

Right:
Gouache airbrushed on bristol board. Illustration created for *Garfield's 1998–1999 Extreme Student Planner.*

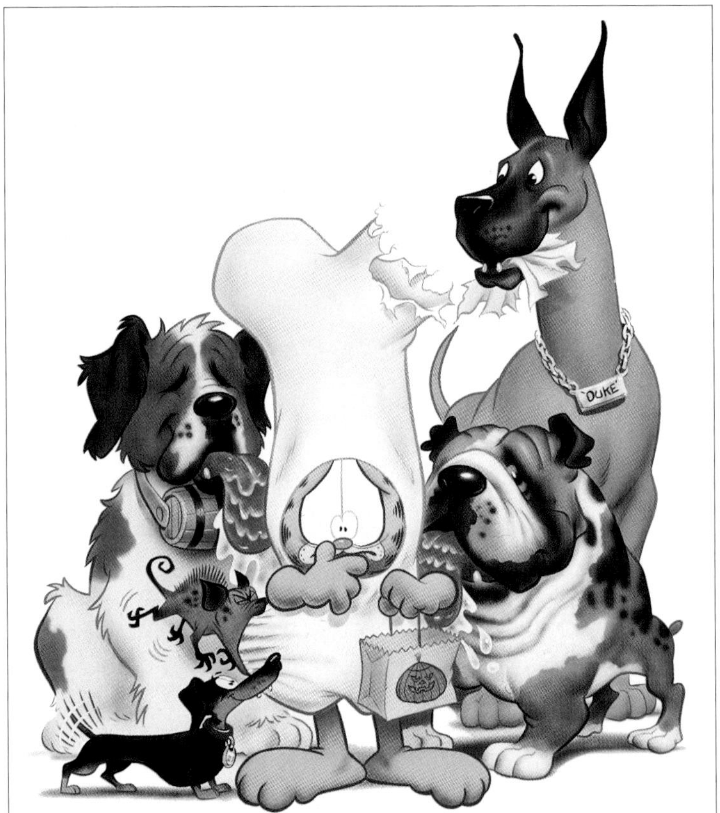
DUKE

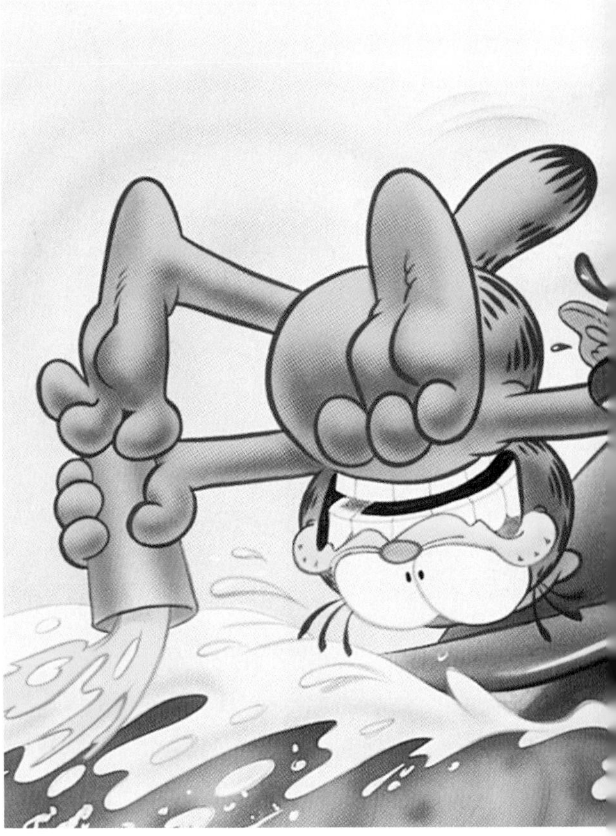

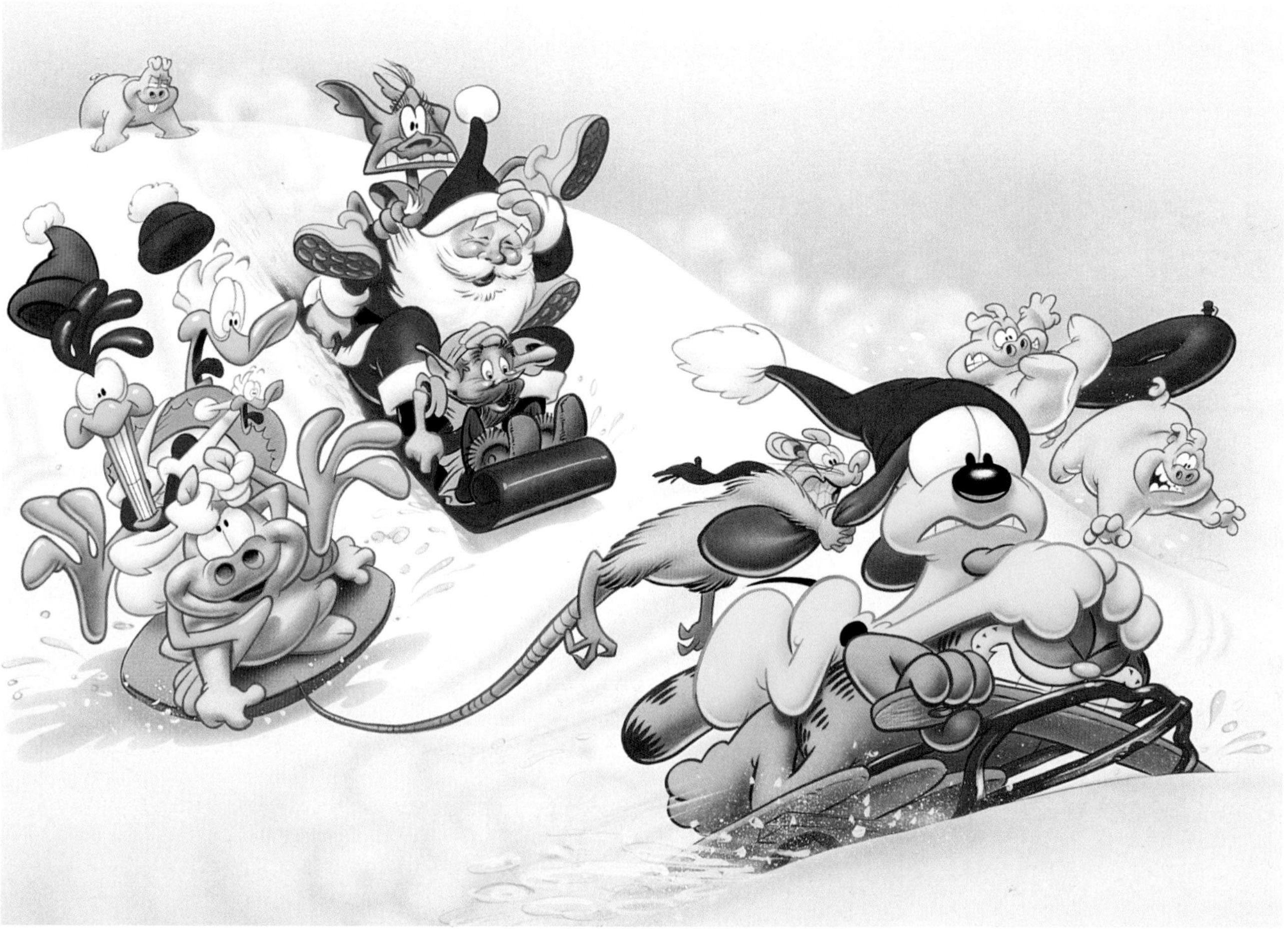

Left:
Gouache airbrushed on bristol board. Illustration created for the table of contents of *Garfield's Christmas Tales*, 1995.

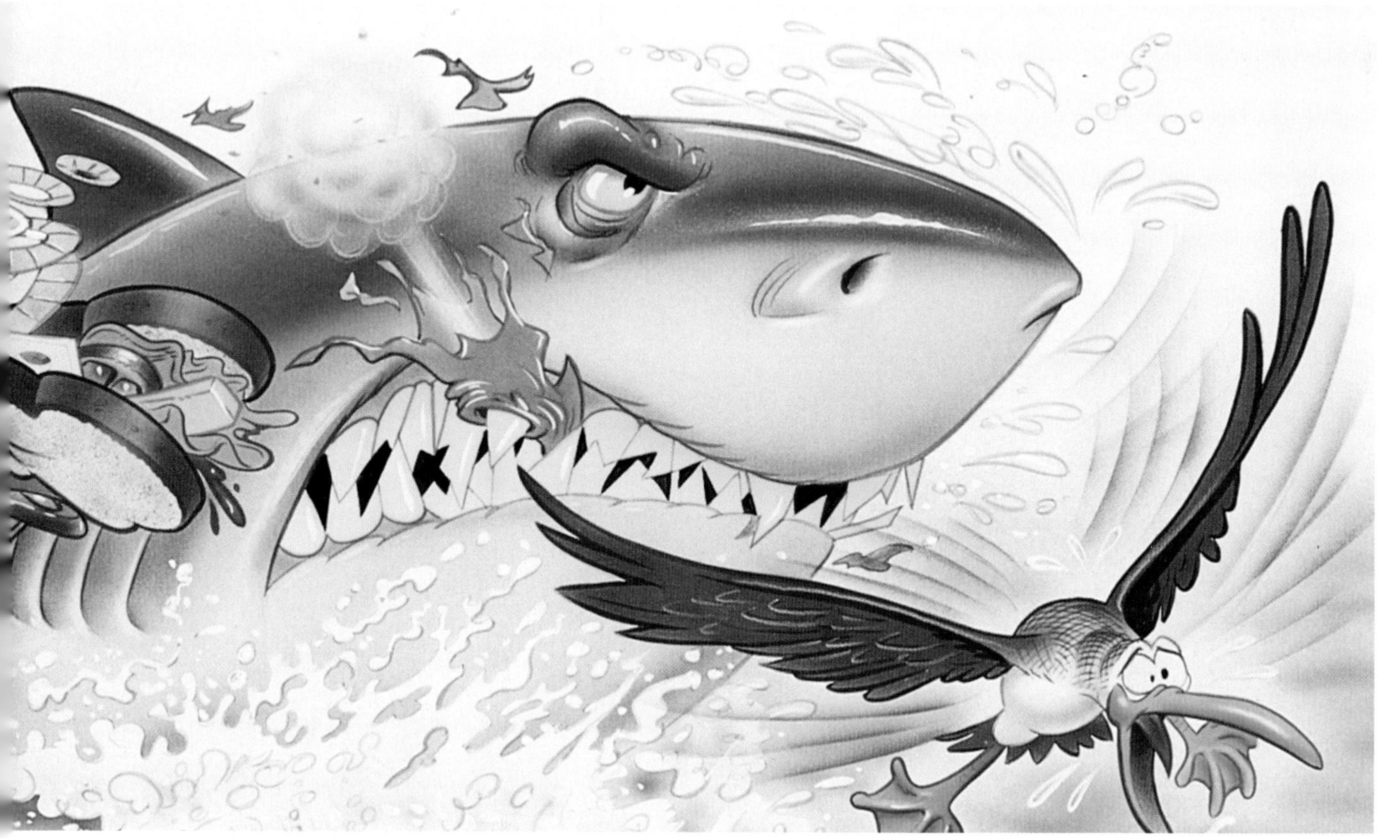

Left:
Gouache airbrushed on bristol board. Illustration created for the storybook *Garfield's Ironcat*, 1997.

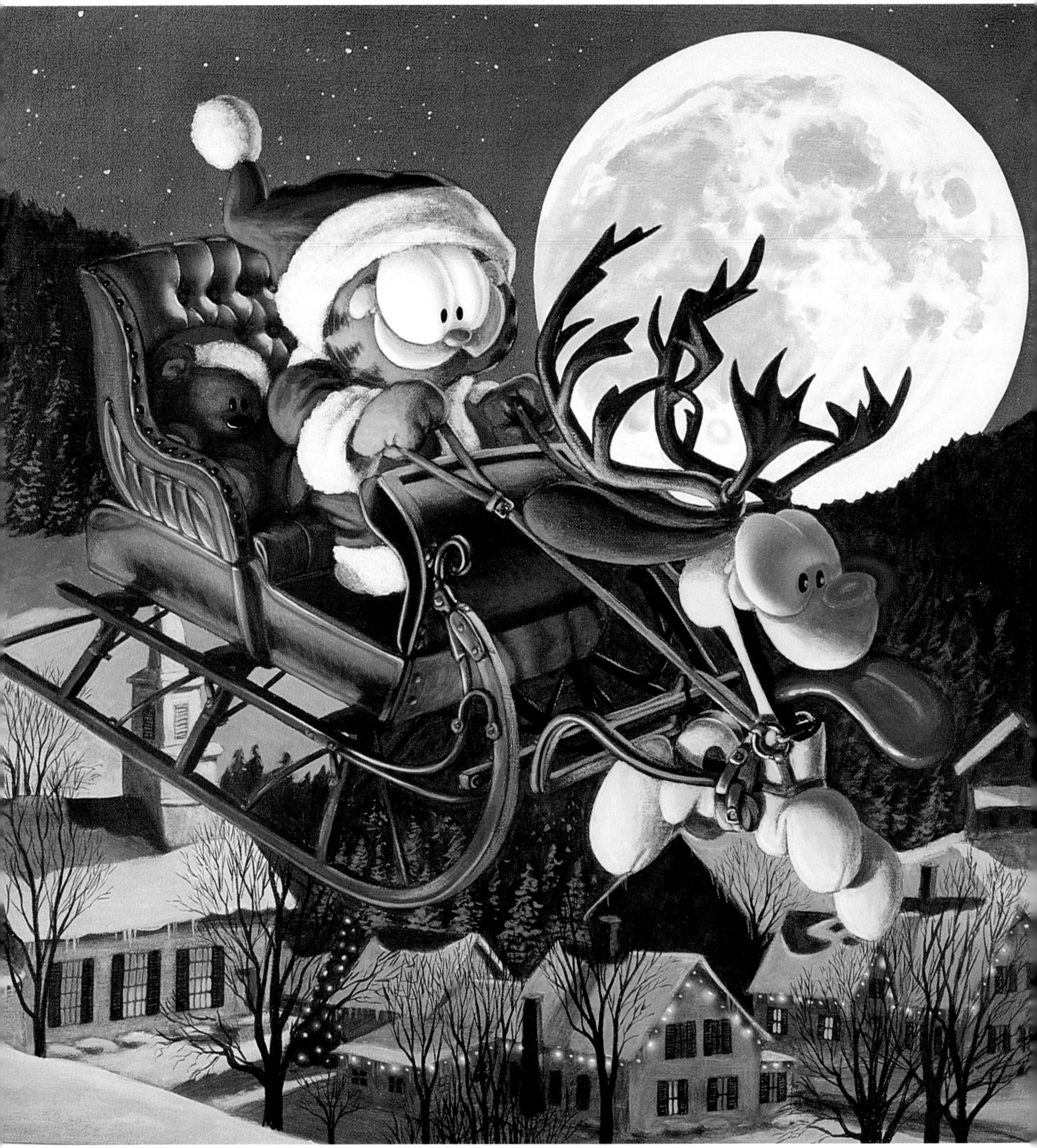

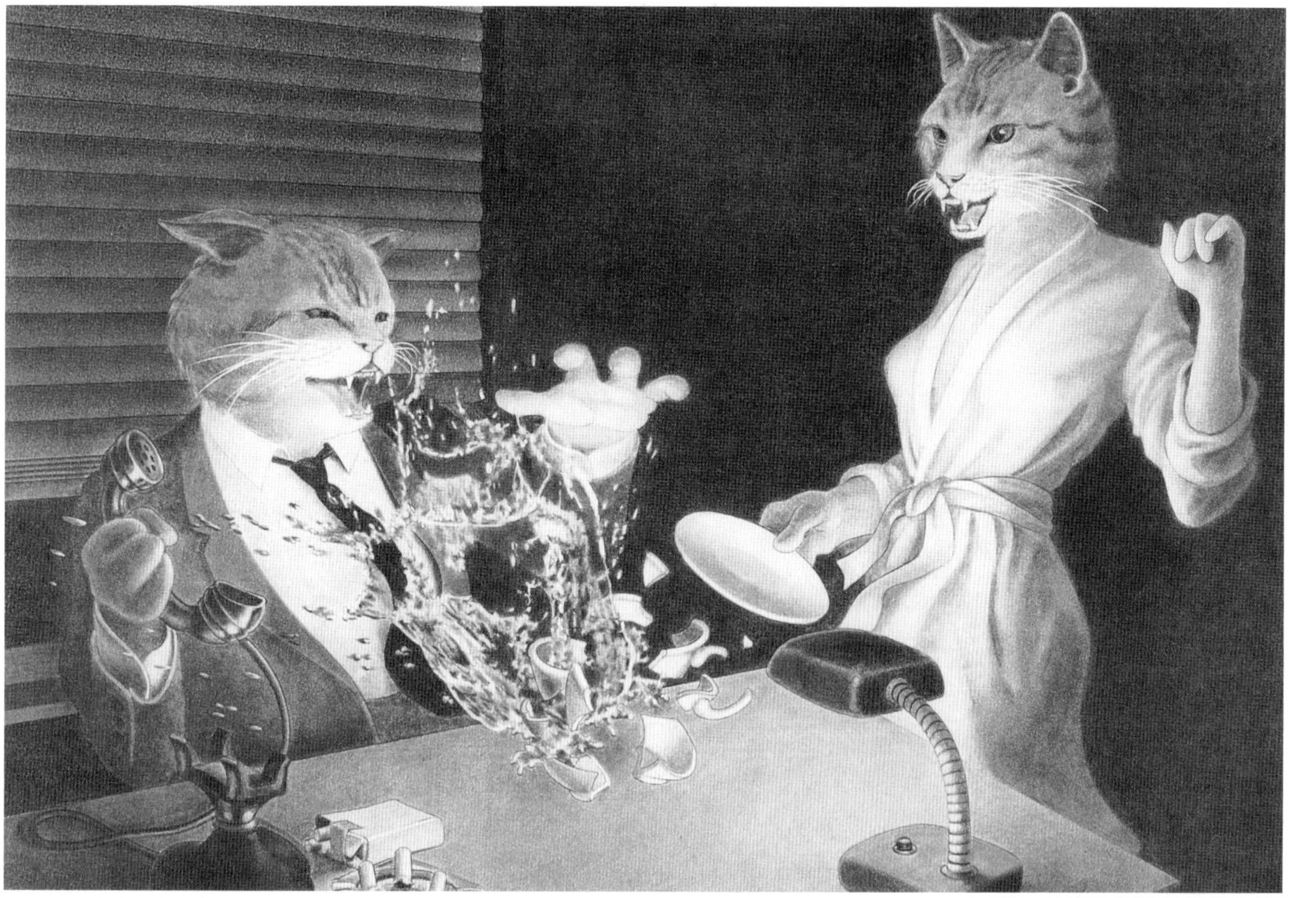

Opposite page:
Acrylic on canvas. Illustration created for The Danbury Mint, 1994.

Left:
Graphite on bristol board. Illustration created for the "Babes & Bullets" story in the book *Garfield: His 9 Lives,* 1984.

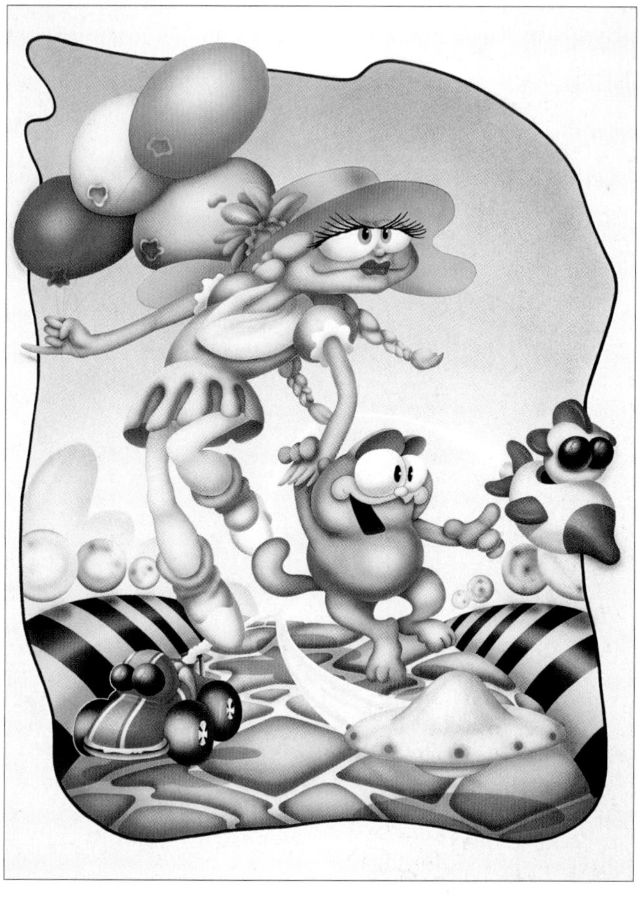

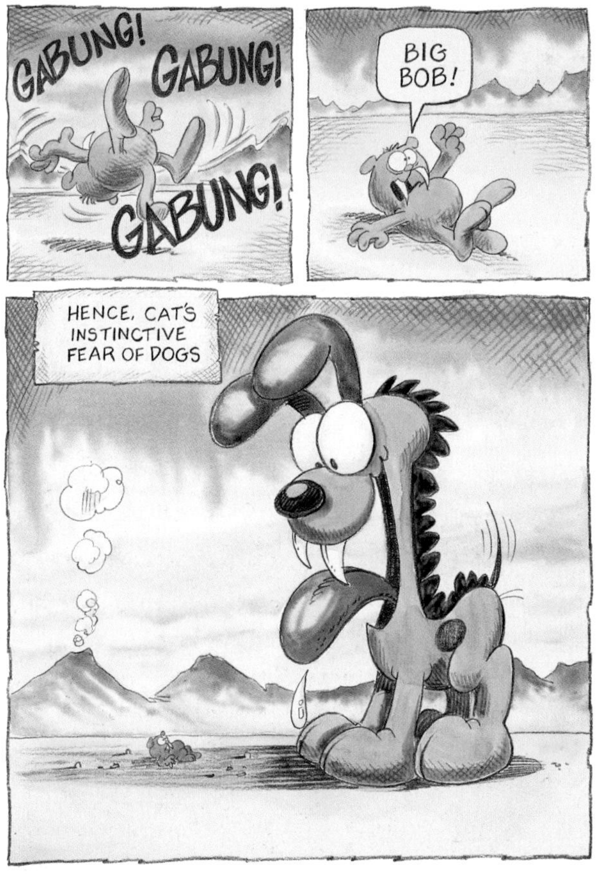
GABUNG! GABUNG! GABUNG!
BIG BOB!
HENCE, CAT'S INSTINCTIVE FEAR OF DOGS

Far left:
Gouache airbrushed on board. Illustration created for "The Garden" story in the book *Garfield: His 9 Lives,* 1984.

Left:
Marker and colored pencil on bristol board. Illustration created for the "Cave Cat" story in the book *Garfield: His 9 Lives,* 1984.

Right: Watercolor and gouache on board. Inspired by the art of Maxfield Parrish. Garfield as "Garcissus," created for the *Myths, Legends, & Heroes* calendar, 1994.

Below: Acrylic on canvas. Inspired by the paintings of Chuck Close. Used on the cover of *The Tenth Garfield Treasury*, 1999.

Opposite page: Garfield painted in oil on canvas, then digitally incorporated into a Norman Rockwell illustration. Created for the *Garfield Visits Rockwell* calendar, 1997.

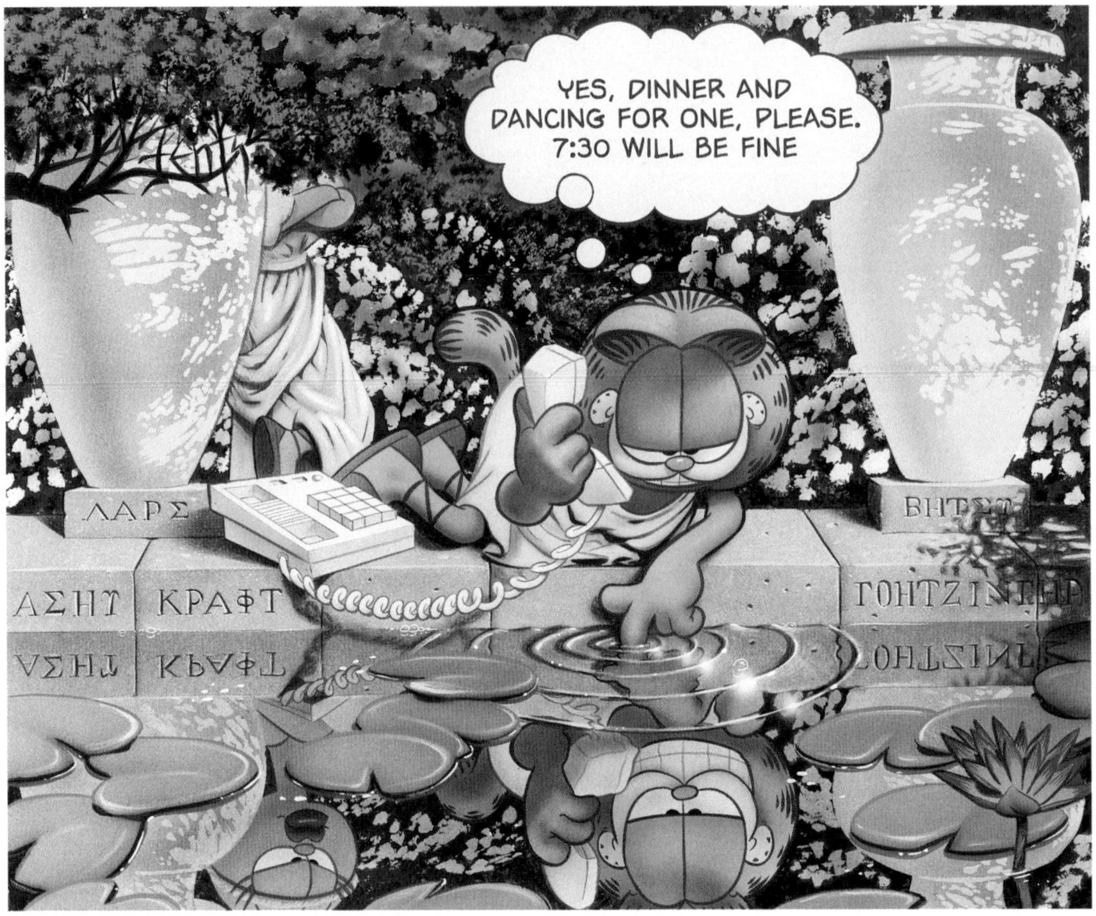
YES, DINNER AND DANCING FOR ONE, PLEASE. 7:30 WILL BE FINE
ΛΑΡΣ
ΑΣΗΥ
ΚΡΑΦΤ
ΓΟΗΤΖΙΝ

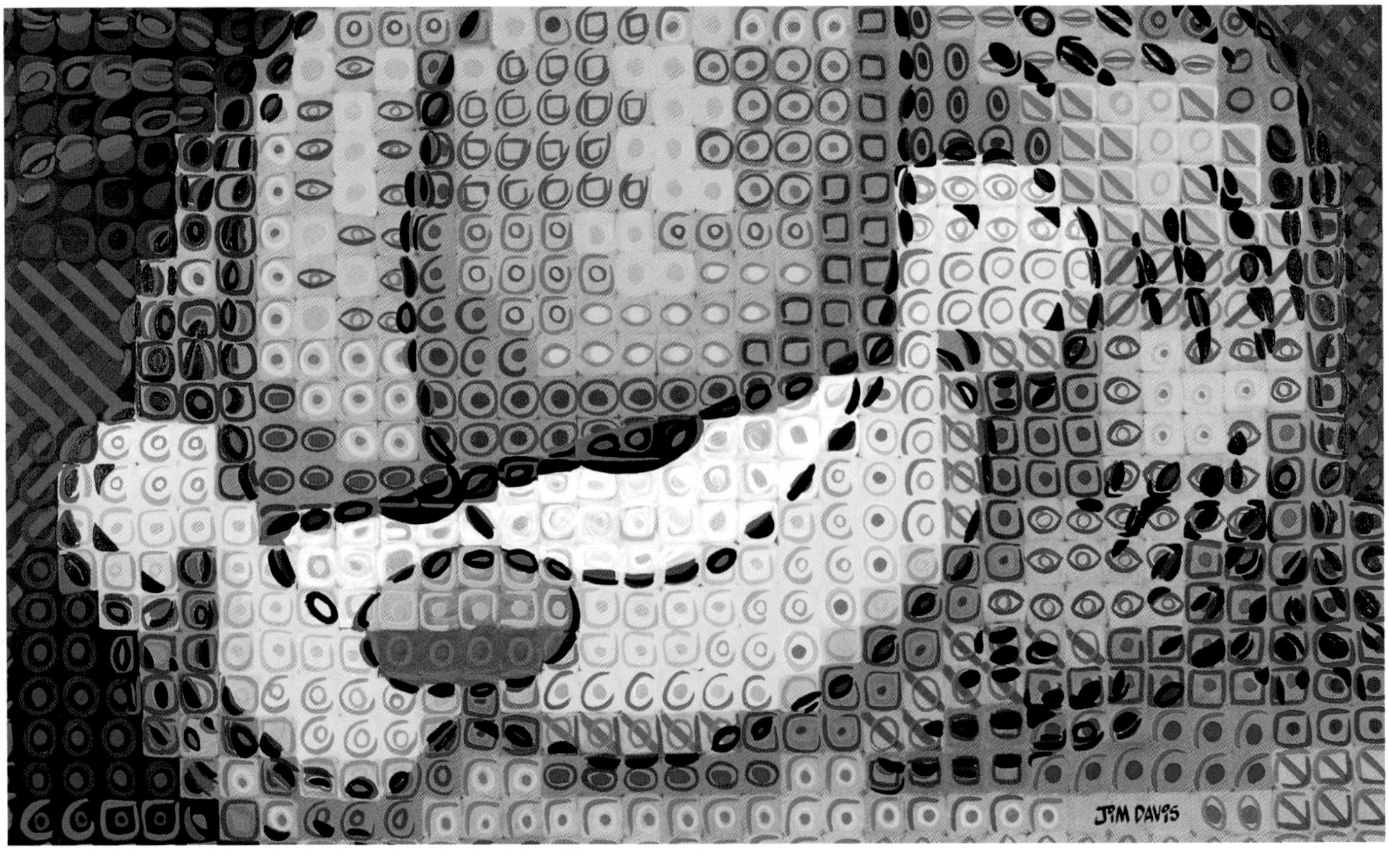
JIM DAVIS

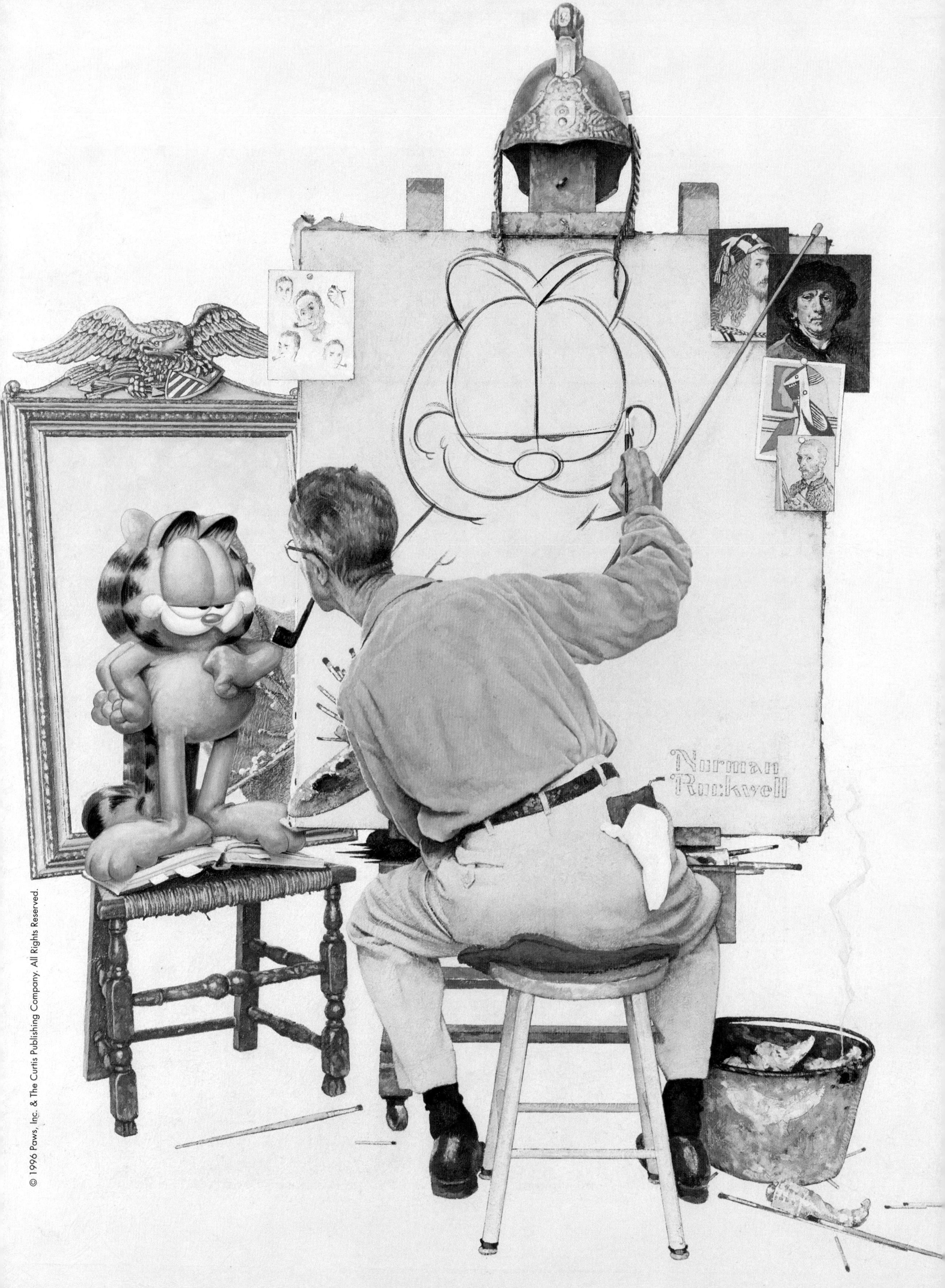
Norman
Rockwell

Right:
Watercolor dyes on illustration board. Designed to look like a Garfield cake, this piece was created as part of a greeting card line, 1985.

Far right:
Graphite on bristol board drawing, scanned into the computer and digitally colored, 2000.

Below:
Acrylic on canvas, 1998.

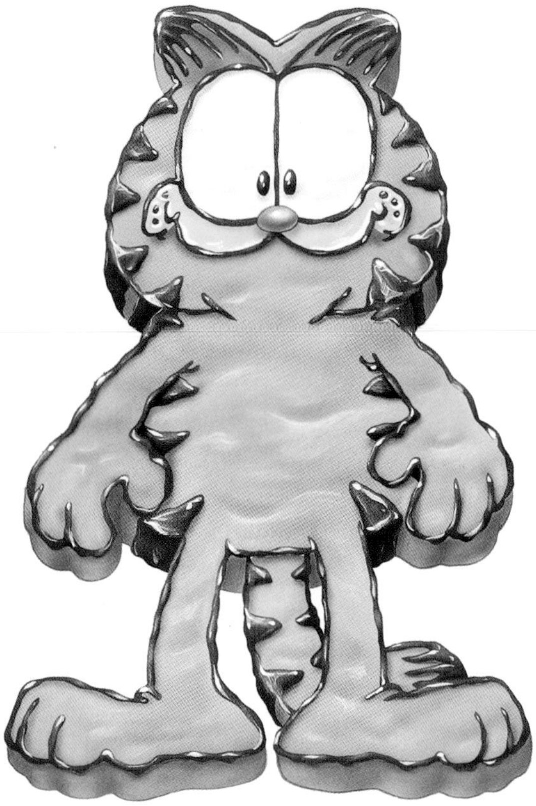

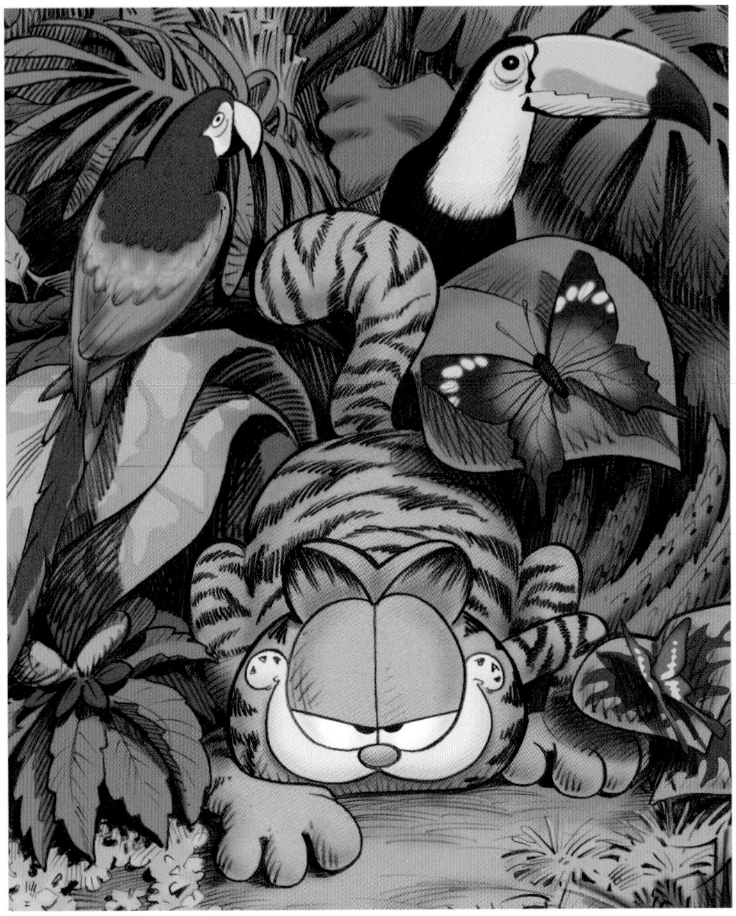

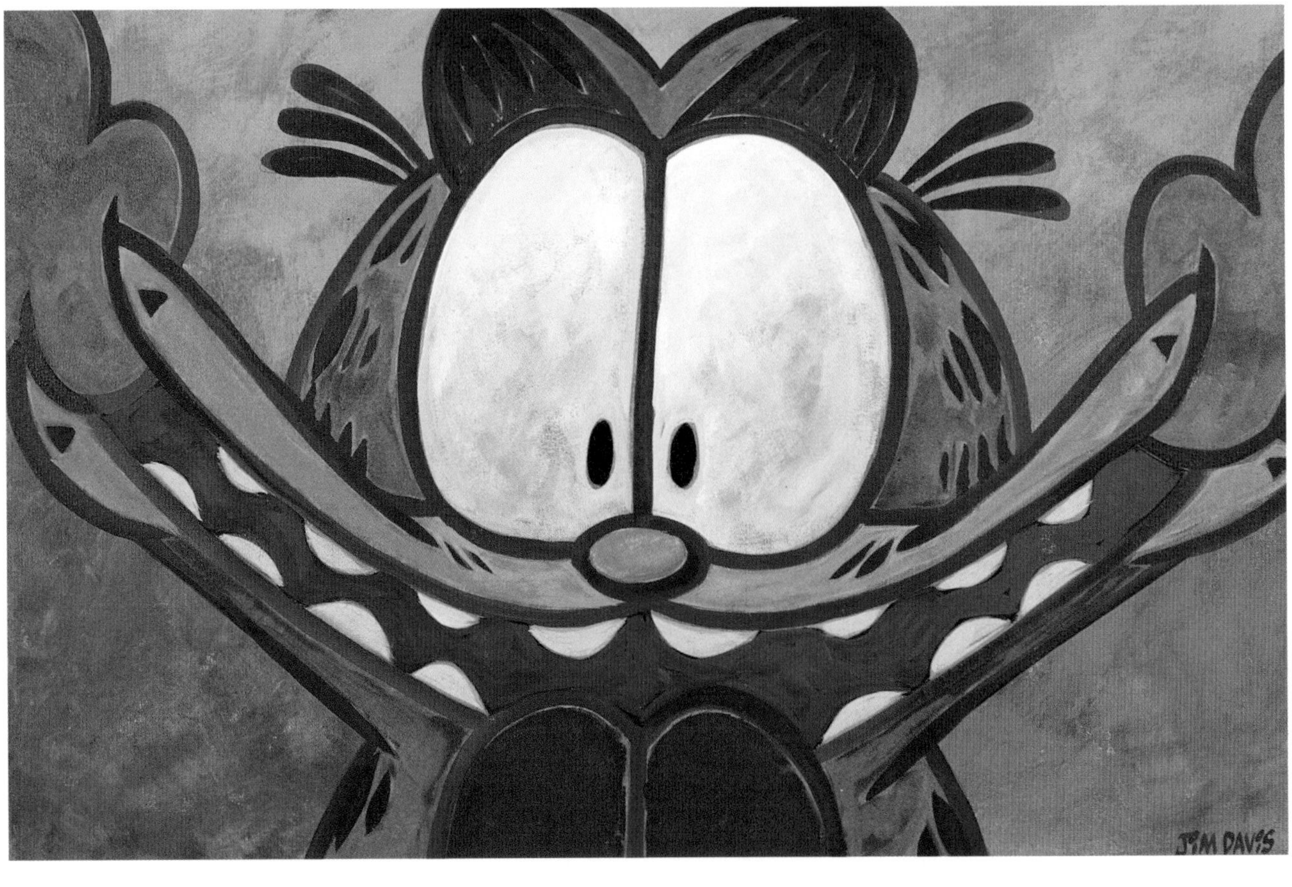
JIM DAVIS

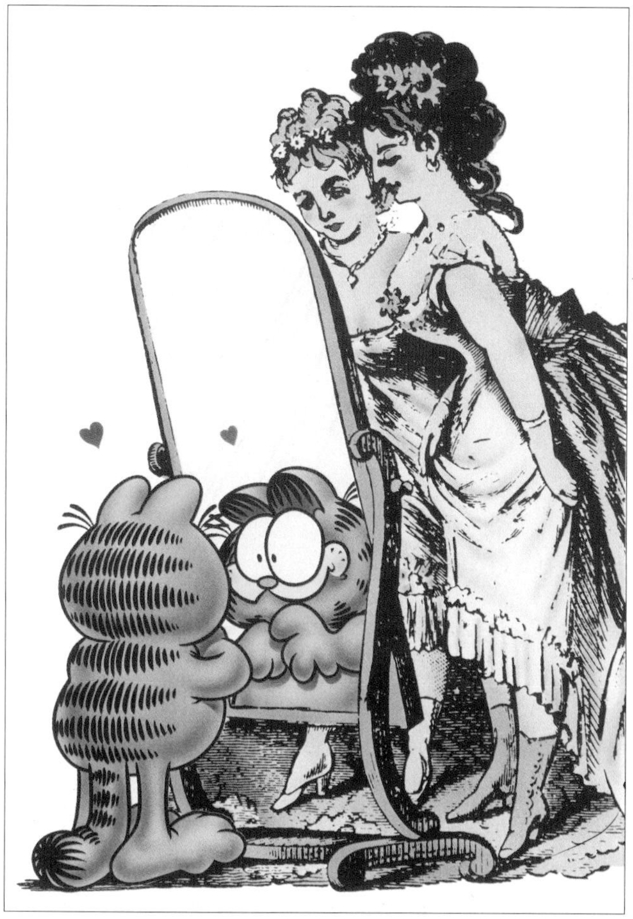

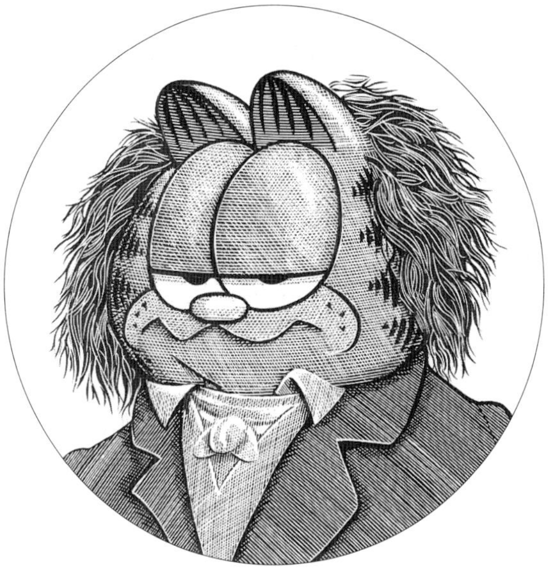

Far left:
Watercolor airbrushed on photostat of Victorian-era clip art. Illustration created for use in a line of international greeting cards, 1989.

Left:
Garfield as Beethoven. Pen and ink, 1989.

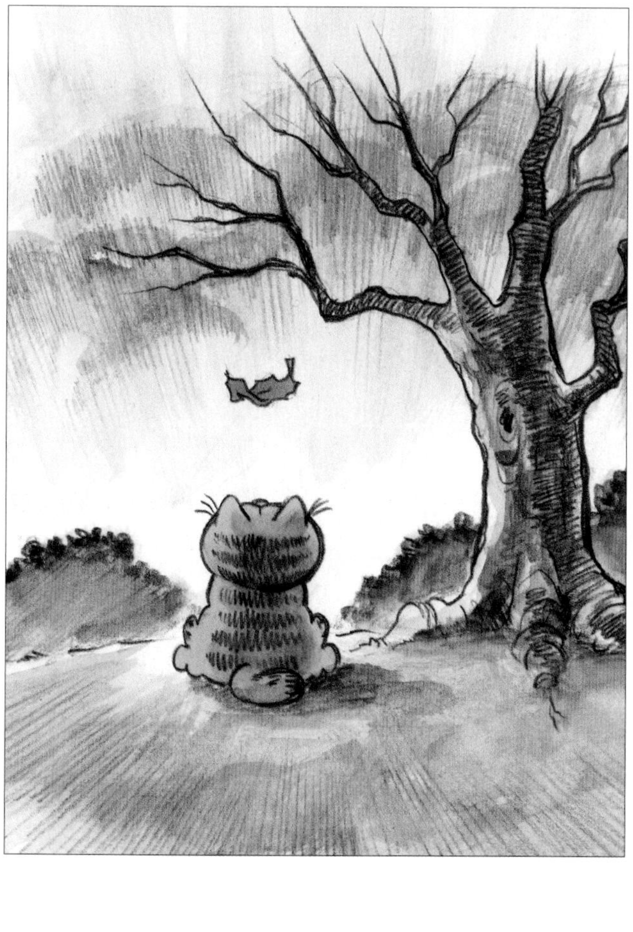

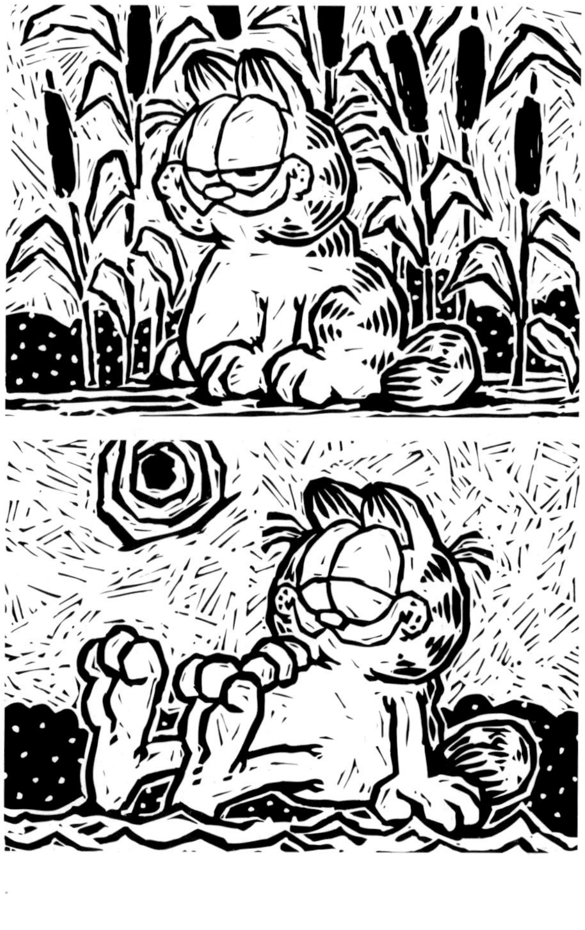

Far left:
Graphite and watercolor on art board, early 1980s.

Left and below:
Woodcut, 1990.

Right:
Black marker on paper with digital coloring. Used as part of the "Garfield Baby" promotional campaign, 1999.

Far right:
Ink on bristol board with digital coloring. Created for the Pet Force digest-book series, 1997.

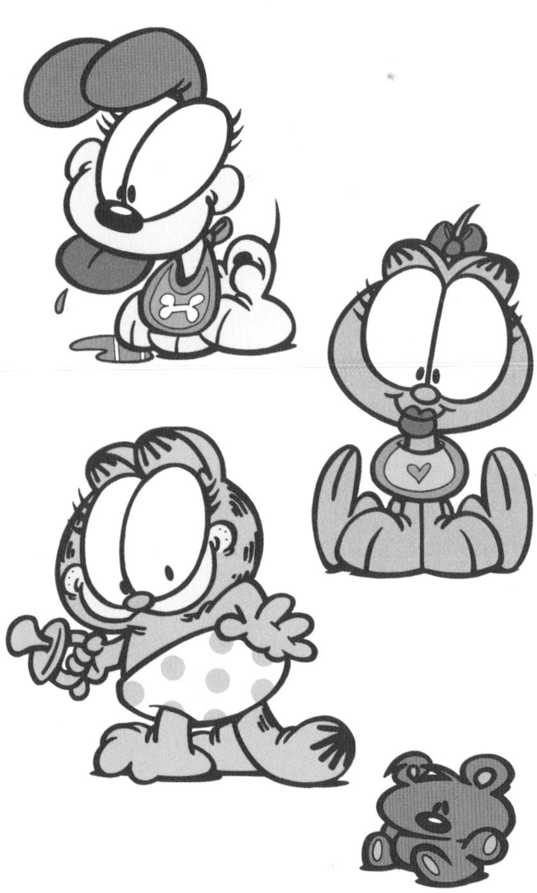

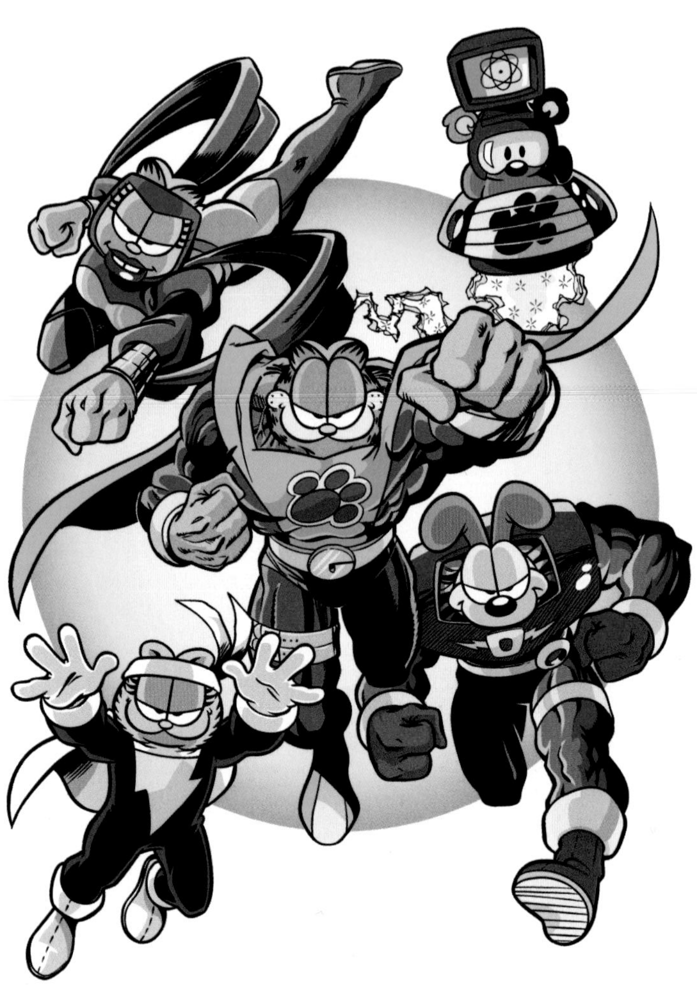

Right and far right:
Gouache on board. Created as front-and-back designs for a Mead school portfolio, 1991.

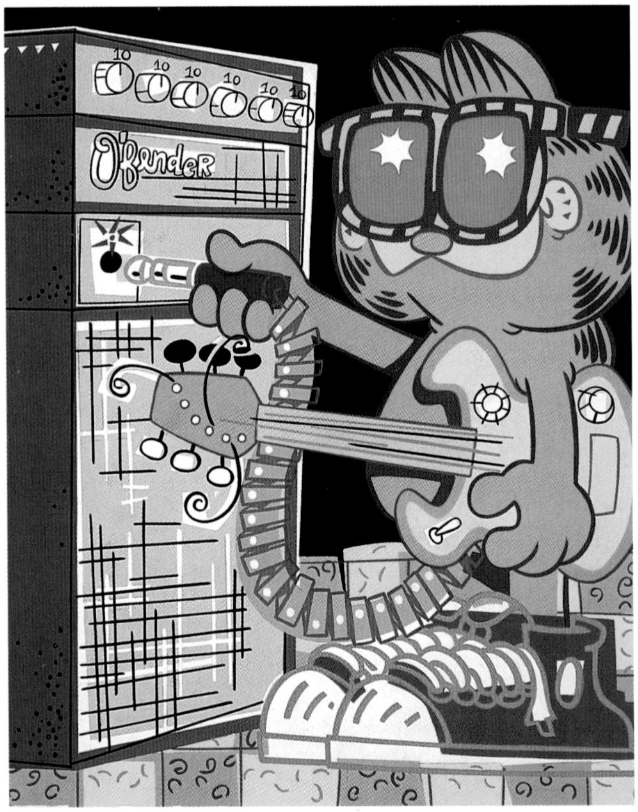

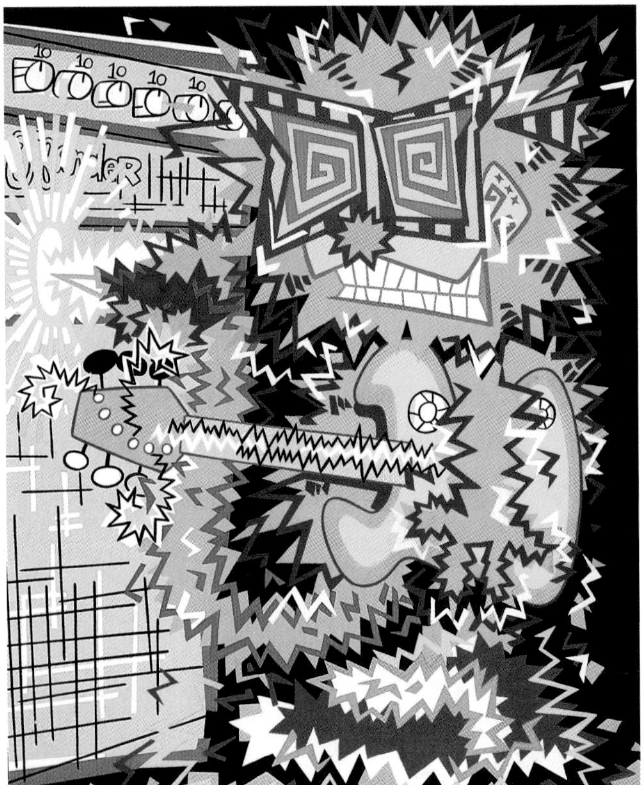

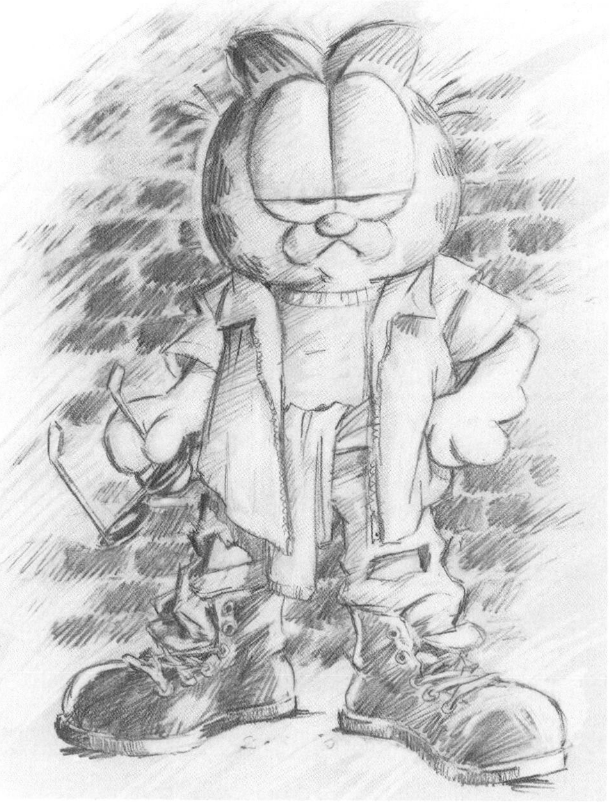

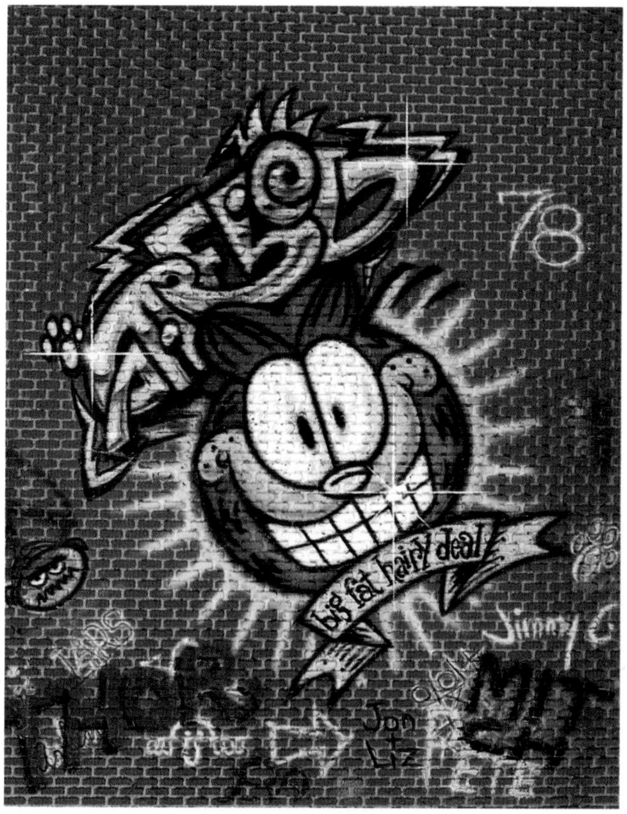
78
big fat hairy deal

Far left:
Grunge-look Garfield. Graphite on bristol board, 1992.

Left:
Mixed-media application of airbrush on miniature sculpted "brick" wall, 1993.

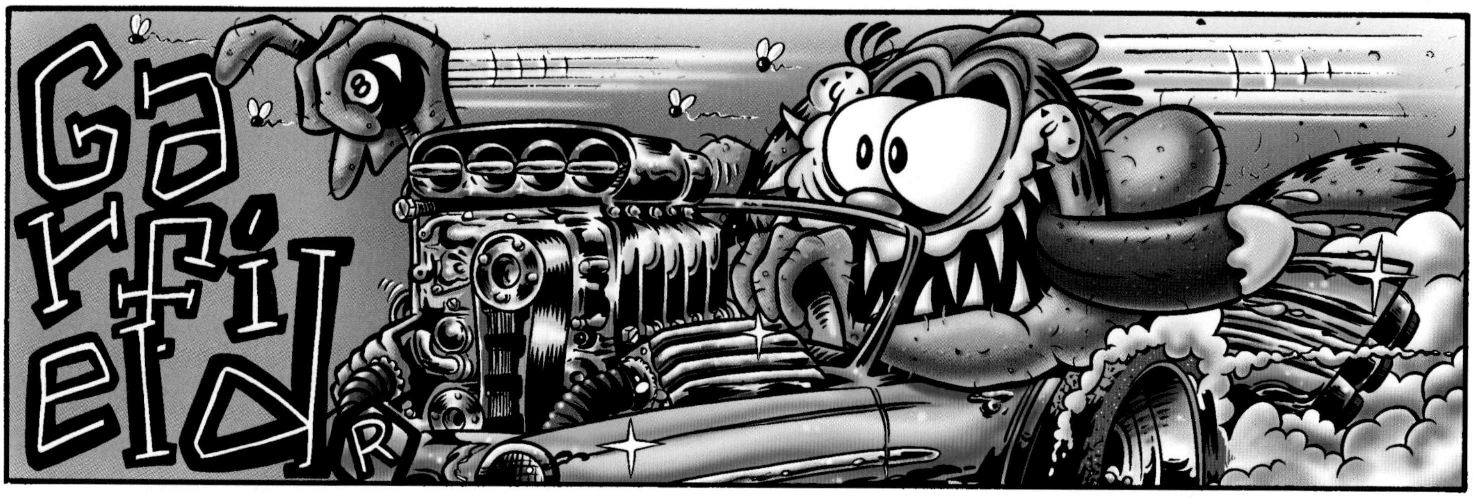

Below:
Ink on bristol board with digital coloring. Inspired by Ed "Big Daddy" Roth's Rat Fink artwork. Created as a logo box for the October 14, 2001, Sunday *Garfield* comic.

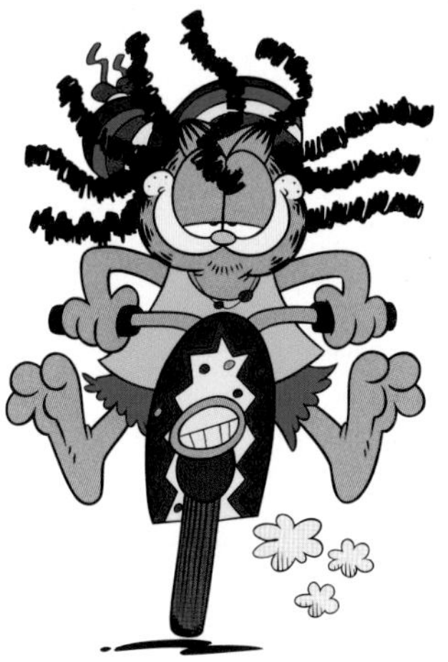

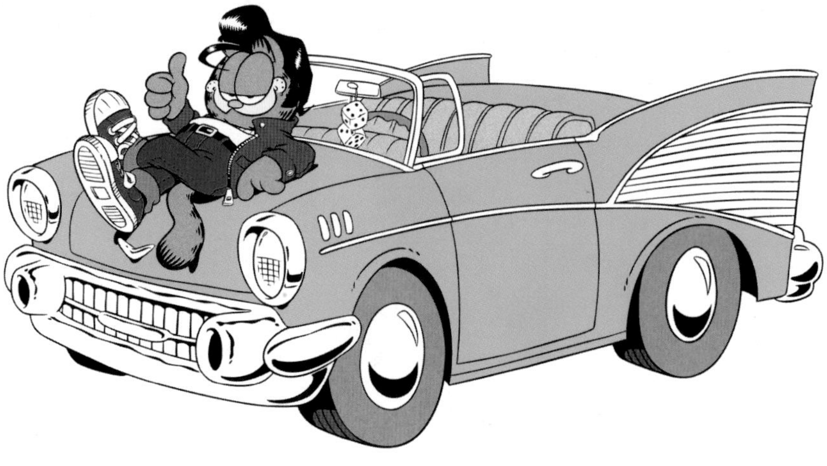

Far left:
Rasta-look Garfield. Ink on bristol board with digital coloring, 1997.

Left:
Ink on bristol board with digital coloring, 1995.

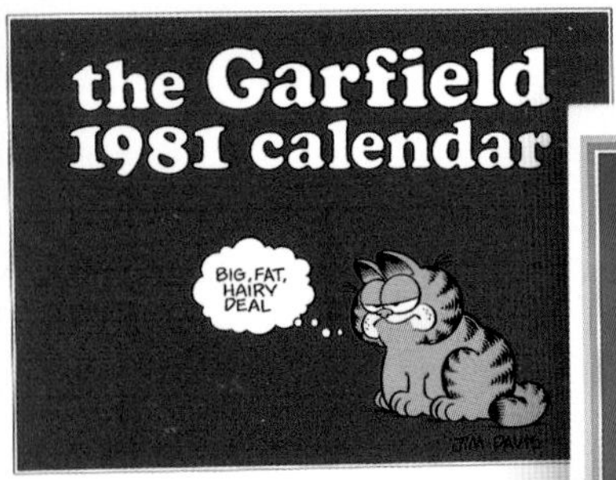
the Garfield
1981 calendar
BIG, FAT, HAIRY DEAL
JIM DAVIS

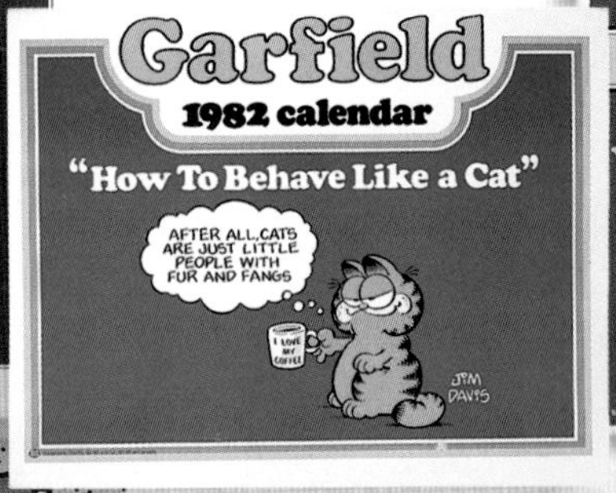
Garfield
1982 calendar
"How To Behave Like a Cat"
AFTER ALL, CATS ARE JUST LITTLE PEOPLE WITH FUR AND FANGS
JIM DAVIS

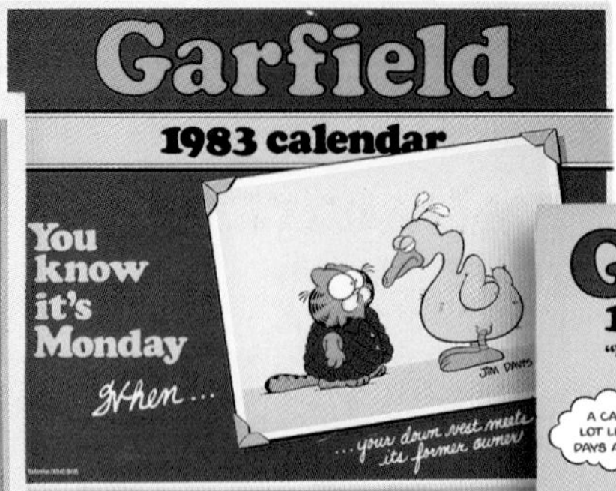
Garfield
1983 calendar
You know it's Monday
When...
...your down vest meets its former owner

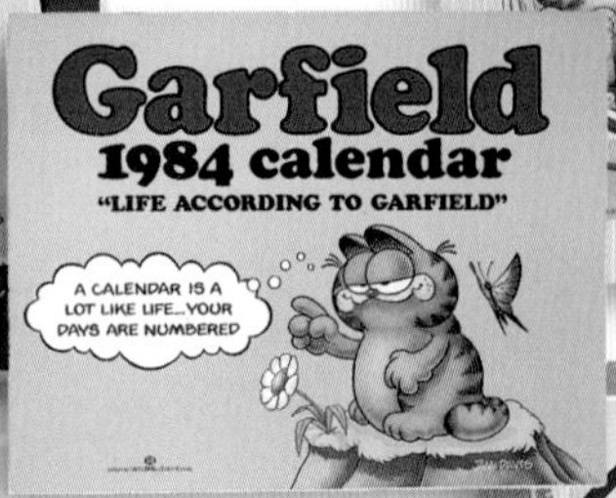
Garfield
1984 calendar
"LIFE ACCORDING TO GARFIELD"
A CALENDAR IS A LOT LIKE LIFE... YOUR DAYS ARE NUMBERED

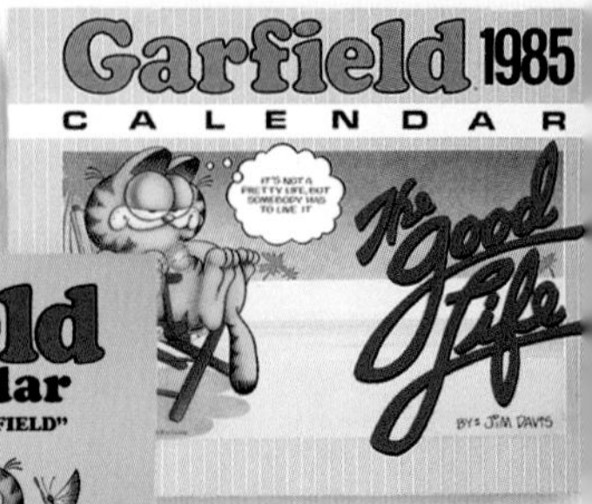
Garfield 1985
CALENDAR
The Good Life

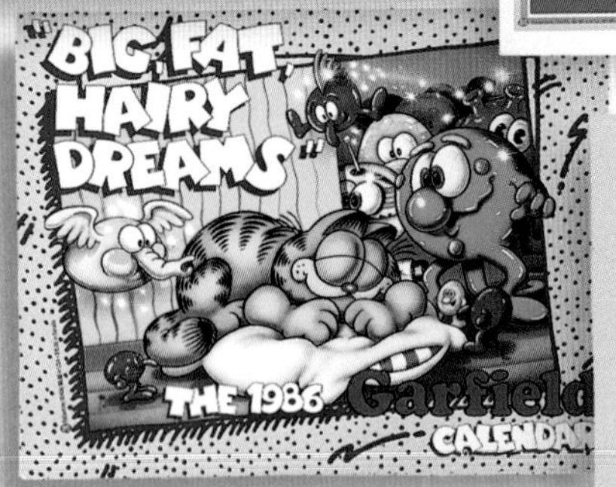
"BIG, FAT, HAIRY DREAMS"
THE 1986 Garfield CALENDAR

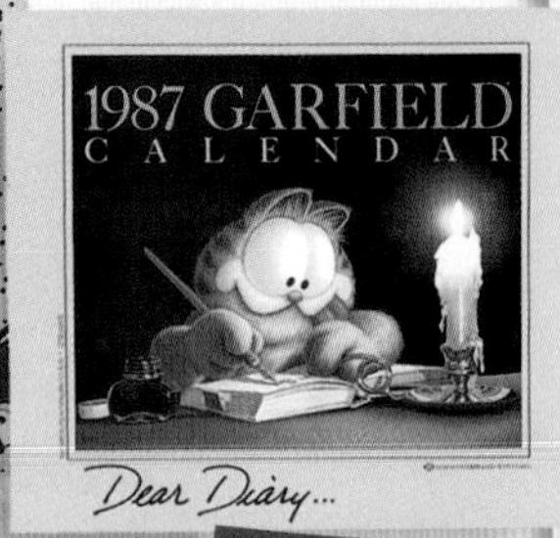
1987 GARFIELD
CALENDAR
Dear Diary...

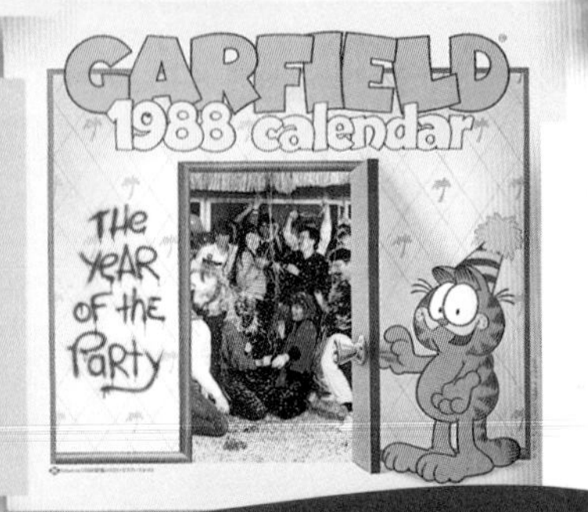
GARFIELD
1988 calendar
The Year of the Party

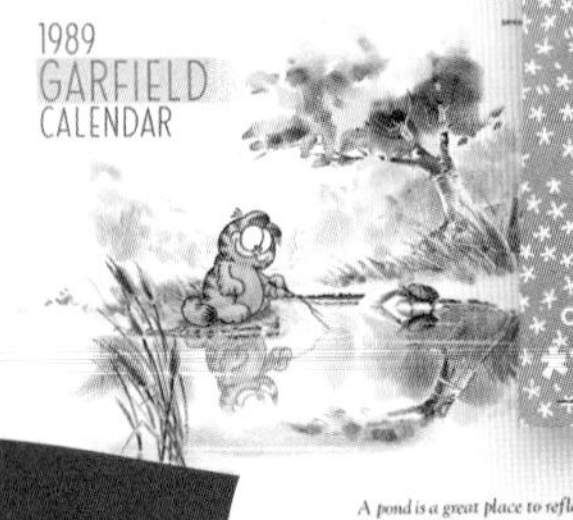
1989
GARFIELD
CALENDAR
A pond is a great place to reflect.

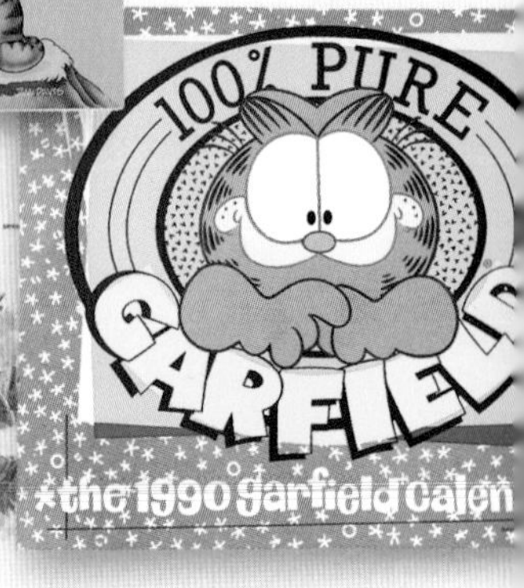
100% PURE
GARFIELD
the 1990 garfield calen

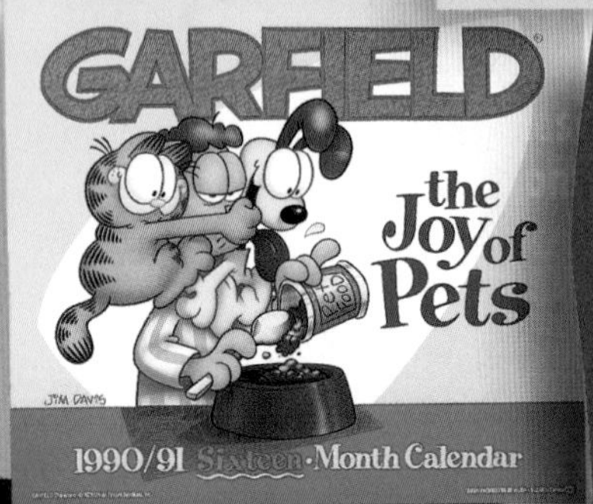
GARFIELD
the Joy of Pets
JIM DAVIS
1990/91 Sixteen-Month Calendar

CALENDAR CAT

Some of the most interesting art treatments have been showcased in the annual Garfield wall calendar. From the very beginning, the calendar was one of Jim's pet projects. "People look at each page for a whole month. I want to make sure the illustrations are strong enough to hold their interest." To achieve this, Jim and his artists have constantly pushed the envelope, turning each year's offering into a lasting work of art.

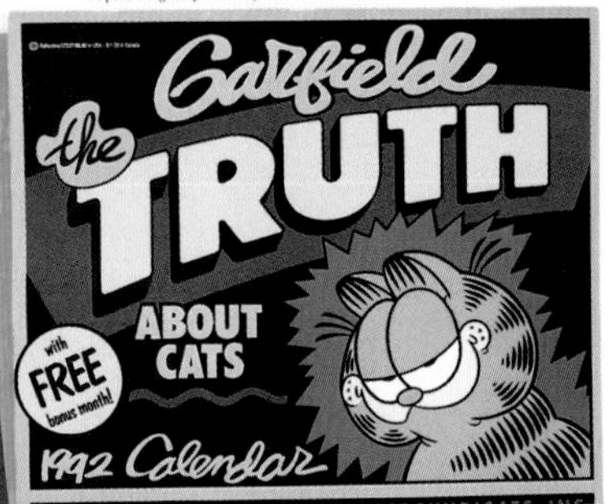
Garfield
the TRUTH
ABOUT CATS
with FREE bonus month!
1992 Calendar

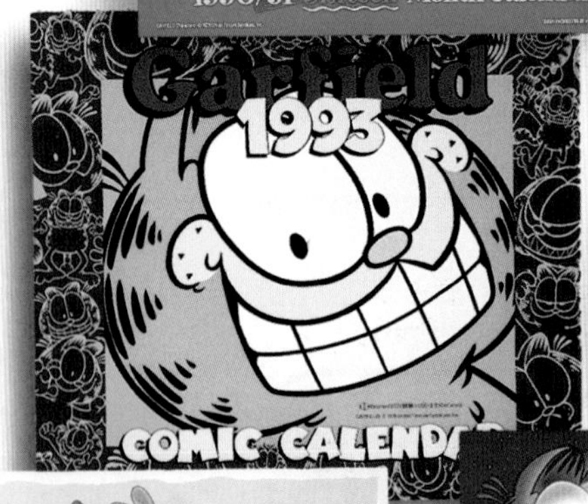
Garfield
1993
COMIC CALENDAR

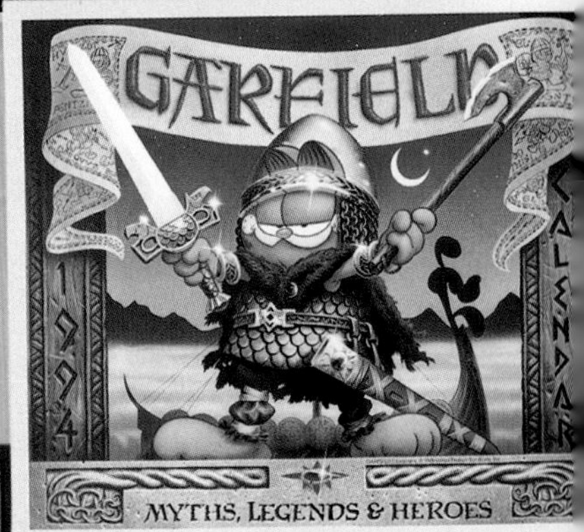
GARFIELD
1994
CALENDAR
MYTHS, LEGENDS & HEROES

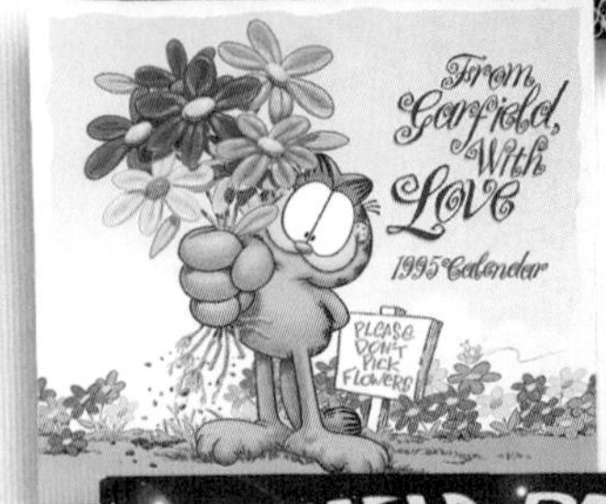
From Garfield With Love
1995 Calendar
PLEASE DON'T PICK FLOWERS

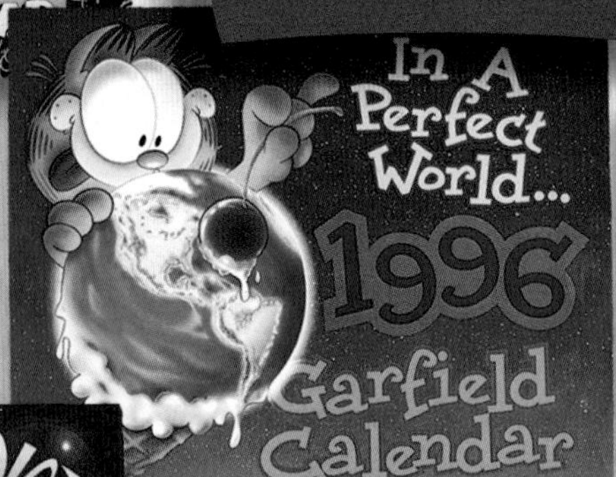
In A Perfect World...
1996
Garfield Calendar

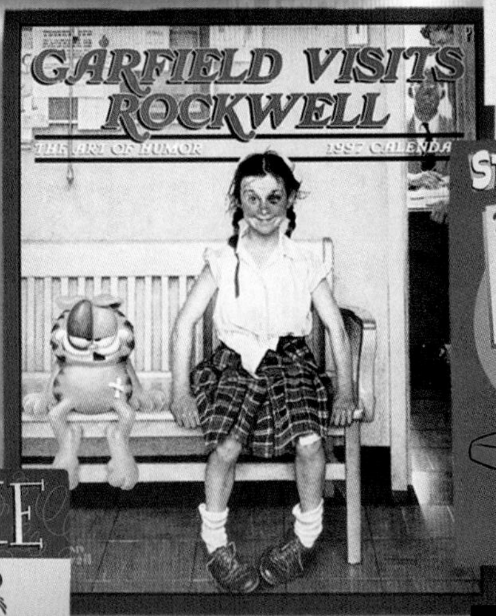
GARFIELD VISITS ROCKWELL
THE ART OF HUMOR
1997 CALENDAR

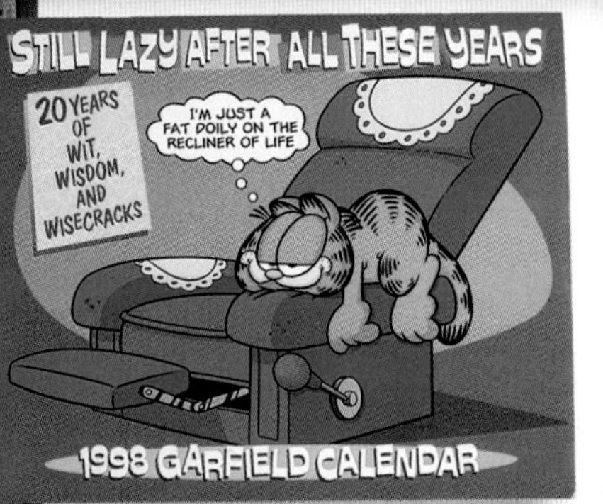
STILL LAZY AFTER ALL THESE YEARS
20 YEARS OF WIT, WISDOM, AND WISECRACKS
I'M JUST A FAT DOILY ON THE RECLINER OF LIFE
1998 GARFIELD CALENDAR

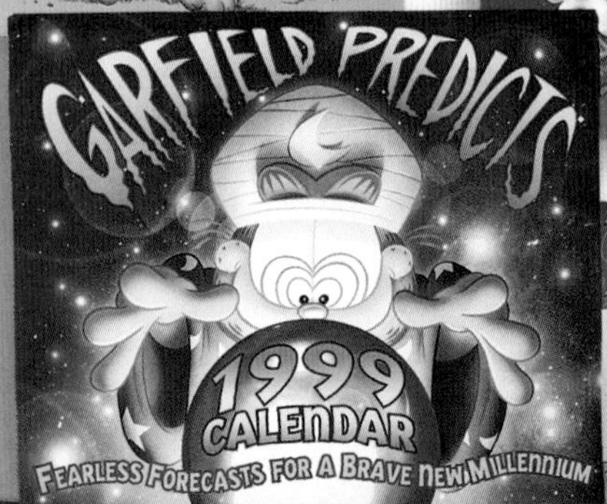
GARFIELD PREDICTS
1999
CALENDAR
FEARLESS FORECASTS FOR A BRAVE NEW MILLENNIUM

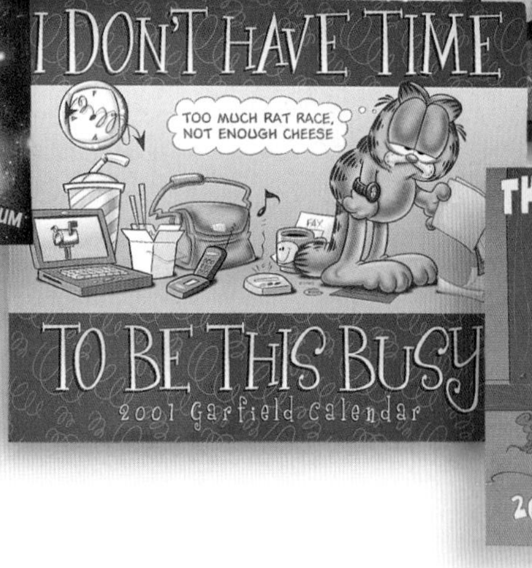
I DON'T HAVE TIME
TOO MUCH RAT RACE, NOT ENOUGH CHEESE
TO BE THIS BUSY
2001 Garfield Calendar

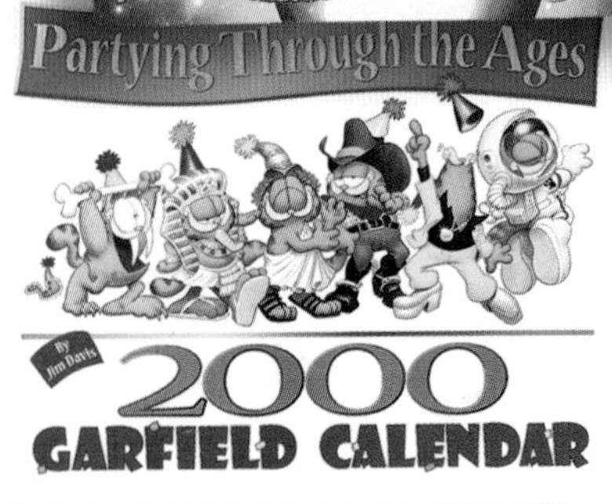
Partying Through the Ages
By Jim Davis
2000
GARFIELD CALENDAR

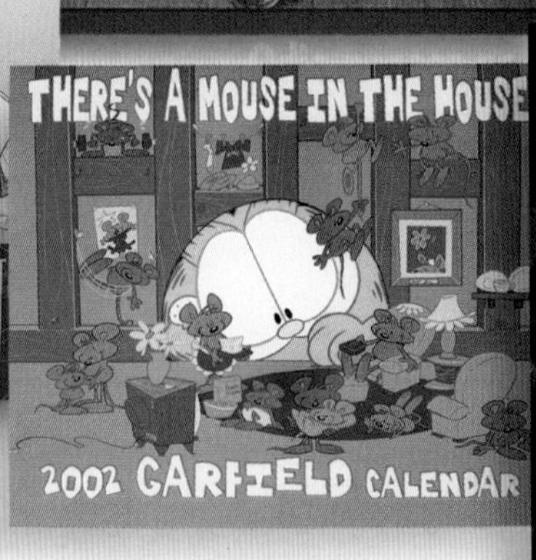
THERE'S A MOUSE IN THE HOUSE
2002 GARFIELD CALENDAR

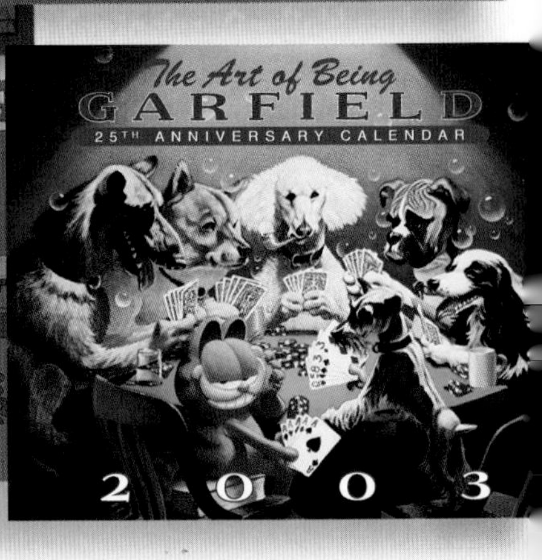
The Art of Being
GARFIELD
25TH ANNIVERSARY CALENDAR
2 0 0 3

...AND SOME LASAGNA FOR GARFIELD
JIM DAVIS
the Garfield 1981 calendar
BIG, FAT, HAIRY DEAL
JIM DAVIS
Sunday
Monday
6
7
13
14
20
21
27
28
29
30
31

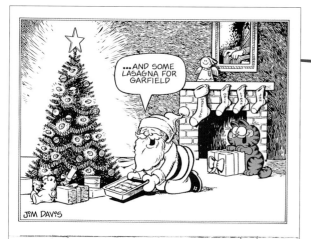

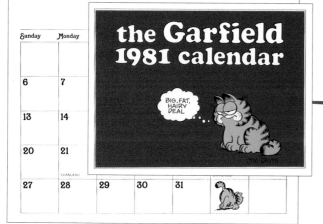

THE GARFIELD 1981 CALENDAR

Garfield's very first calendar was executed in brush and India ink and printed in two colors. The cover echoed the design of Garfield's first compilation book and featured a simple image of the character on a bright red background. Jim remembers "sitting for hours doing the crosshatching marks on these pieces."

EAT AND SLEEP, EAT AND SLEEP, EAT AND SLEEP. THERE MUST BE MORE TO A CAT'S LIFE THAN THAT. BUT I HOPE NOT
GARFIELD
JIM DAVIS

SPRING IS HERE... BIG, FAT, HAIRY DEAL
JIM DAVIS

Dear Diary... What a night! I had to do six encores at the club.
1987 GARFIELD CALENDAR
Dear Diary...
Fri.
Sat.
4
5
11
12
18
19
25
26

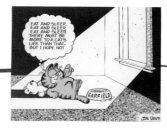

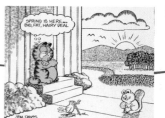

THE GARFIELD 1987 CALENDAR

DEAR DIARY

A typical Garfield day is captured in lush detail in thirteen meticulously rendered acrylic paintings. Jim was fascinated by the style of photo-realism, and wanted to apply this technique to Garfield. Jim and the Paws artists spent months on the project, working up ideas, finding props, and laboring over each canvas. The result is some of the richest artwork ever created for the cat.

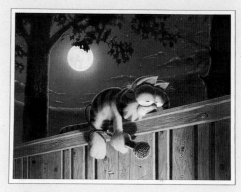

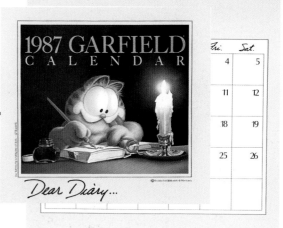

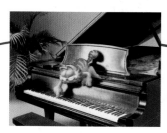

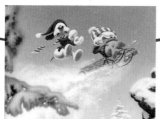

THE GARFIELD 1989 CALENDAR

A POND IS A GREAT PLACE TO REFLECT

Painted in transparent watercolors, the 1989 calendar presented a quieter, gentler Garfield. Eschewing humor, this softer approach depicted the character in a series of tranquil landscapes. It was a Garfield that fans hadn't seen before and a further indication of how far the character could stretch.

All the world's a stage, and all the cats merely players.

GARFIELD © 1978 United Feature Syndicate, Inc.

1989 GARFIELD CALENDAR

A pond is a great place to reflect.

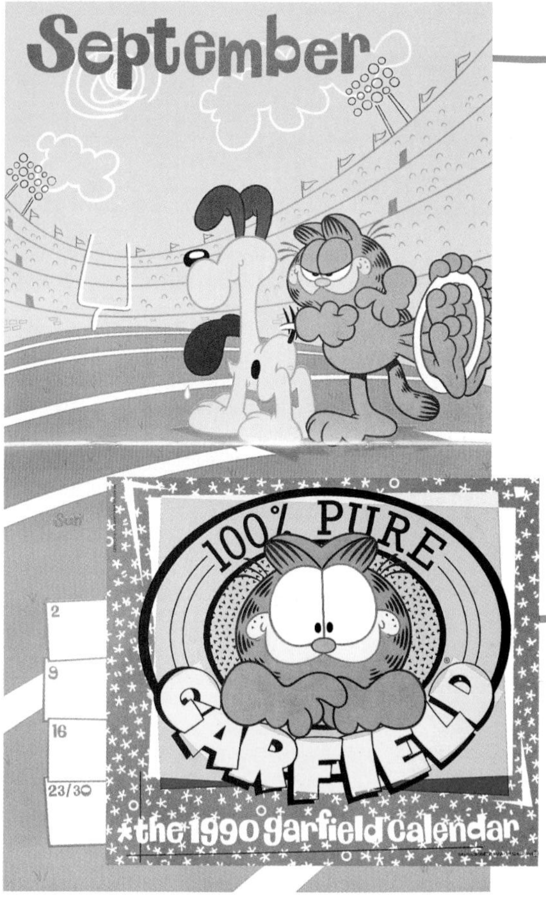
September
2
9
16
23/30
100% PURE
GARFIELD
the 1990 garfield calendar

The Garfield 1990 Calendar

100% PURE GARFIELD

The tubby tabby's larger-than-life personality was back on display in bold, colorful gouache illustrations that emphasized merriment over mood. The finished calendar was 100% pure fun.

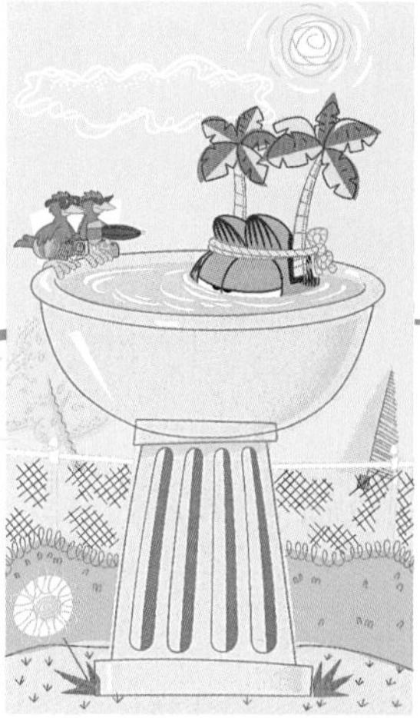

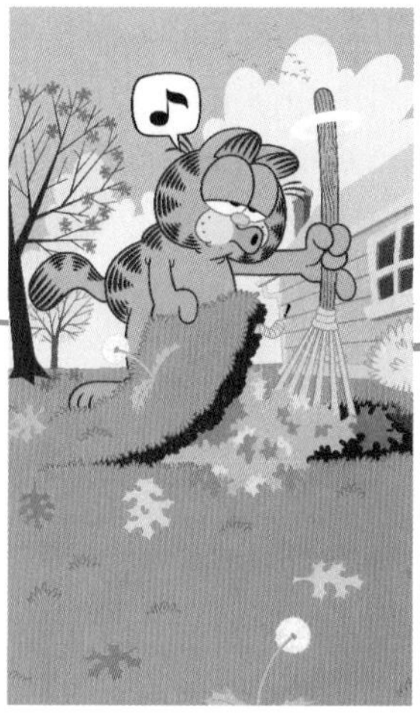

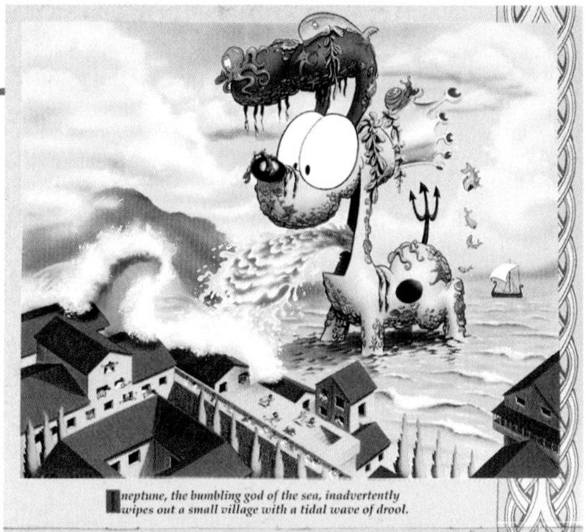
neptune, the bumbling god of the sea, inadvertently wipes out a small village with a tidal wave of drool.

The Garfield 1994 Calendar

MYTHS, LEGENDS, & HEROES

Jim toyed with several different ideas for the 1994 calendar. He finally settled on the somewhat unlikely theme of mythology, instructing his writers and artist to "Garfieldize" various mythological characters. With its references to Roman, Norse, and Greek gods and Arthurian legend, the calendar remains one of the most sophisticated pieces in the Garfield oeuvre. (Highbrow, ain't we?)

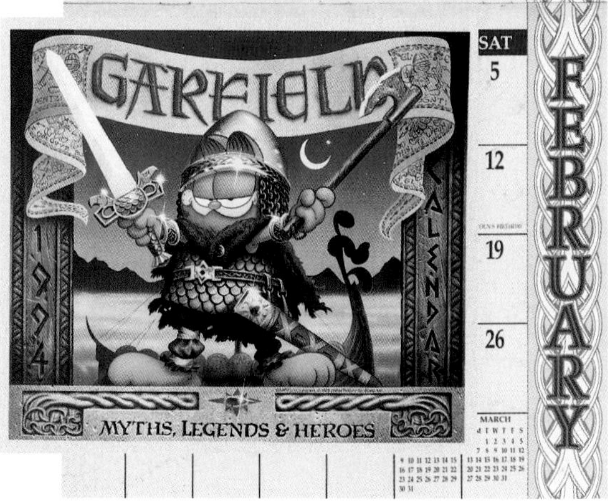
GARFIELD
1994
CALENDAR
MYTHS, LEGENDS & HEROES
SAT
5
12
19
26
FEBRUARY

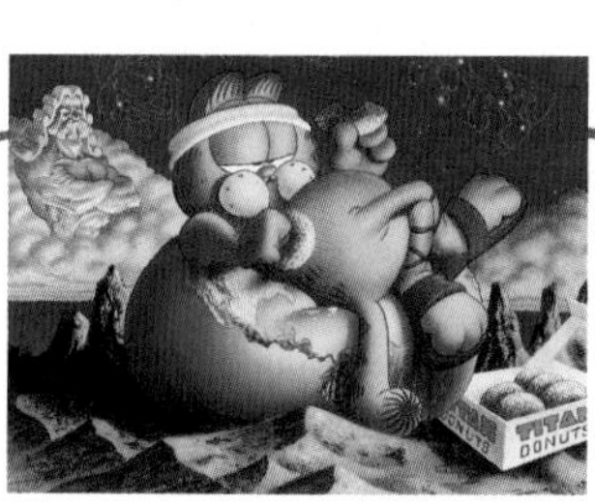

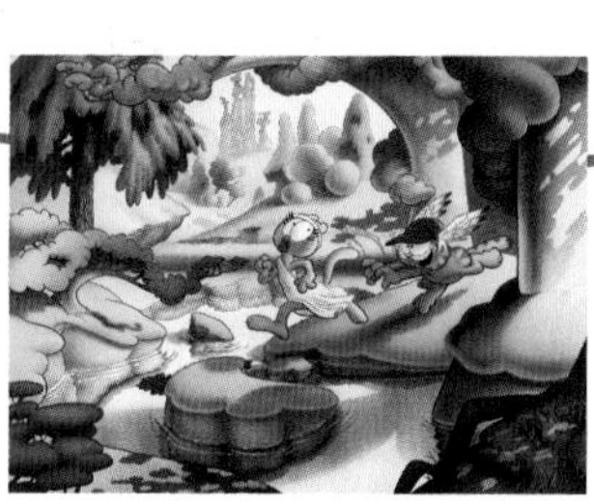

The Garfield 1997 Calendar

GARFIELD VISITS ROCKWELL

This very special project featured Garfield literally "inside" the paintings of American icon Norman Rockwell. How did it work? High-quality prints of Rockwell art were scanned into a computer. Garfield art was painted separately and also scanned. The two images were merged to create a single digital image. The actual Rockwell originals were never altered during this process.

Norman Rockwell
NOVEMBER
Sunday
Monday
Tuesday
Wednesday
Thursday
Friday
Saturday
1
2
3
4
5
6
7
8
15
22
29

GARFIELD IS A GOOD BOY!
Christmas

54 53

GARFIELD VISITS ROCKWELL
THE ART OF HUMOR
1997 CALENDAR
Norman Rockwell

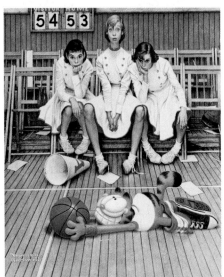

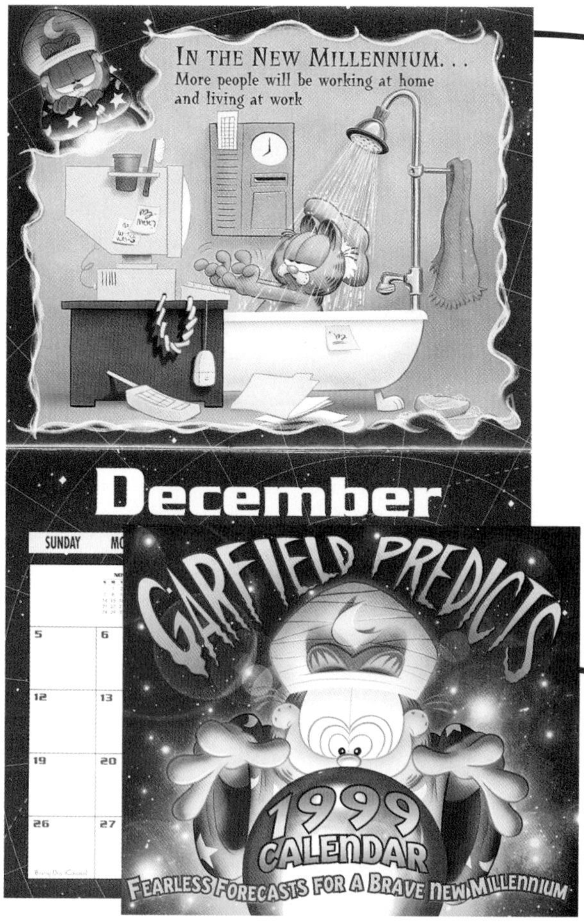
IN THE NEW MILLENNIUM. . .
More people will be working at home and living at work
December
SUNDAY
GARFIELD PREDICTS
1999
CALENDAR
FEARLESS FORECASTS FOR A BRAVE NEW MILLENNIUM

THE GARFIELD 1999 CALENDAR

GARFIELD PREDICTS: FEARLESS FORECASTS FOR A BRAVE NEW MILLENNIUM

What will the new millennium hold? Will Mondays be eliminated? Will hairball hacking become an Olympic event? This calendar, rendered in airbrushed gouache, offered pithy predictions for the twenty-first century (and beyond). It spawned a minibook of the same name and was a good example of how the calendars were sometimes driven by editorial content, and not art treatment.

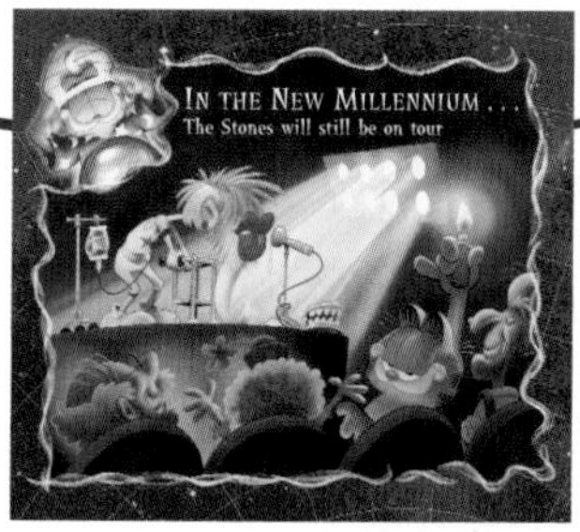
IN THE NEW MILLENNIUM . . .
The Stones will still be on tour

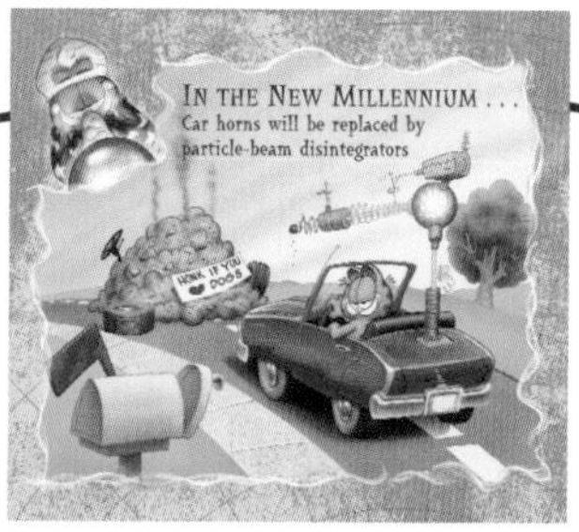
IN THE NEW MILLENNIUM . . .
Car horns will be replaced by particle-beam disintegrators

THE GARFIELD 2003 CALENDAR

THE ART OF BEING GARFIELD

Commemorating Garfield's twenty-fifth anniversary, this calendar marks the return of the realistic painting style popularized in 1987's *Dear Diary*. Jim and his writers worked up the twelve concepts during several lengthy creative sessions, and then turned them over to the artist to illustrate. Eagle-eyed fans will notice the number 25 hidden in each picture.

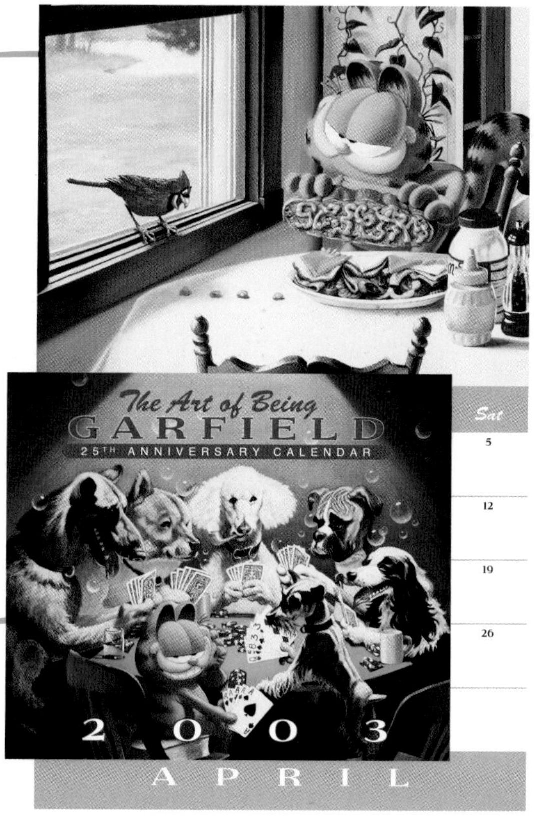
The Art of Being
GARFIELD
25TH ANNIVERSARY CALENDAR
2003
APRIL
Sat

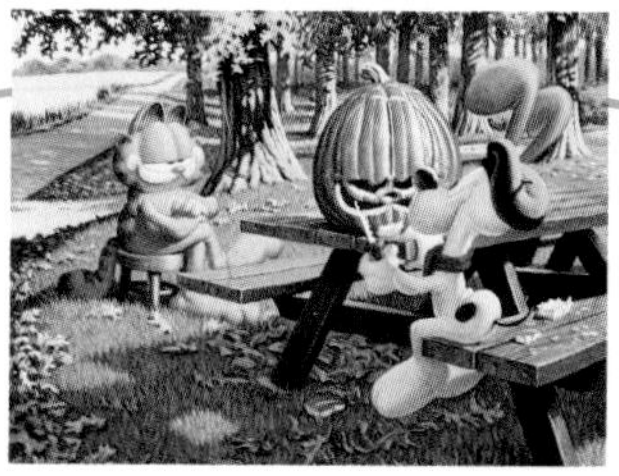

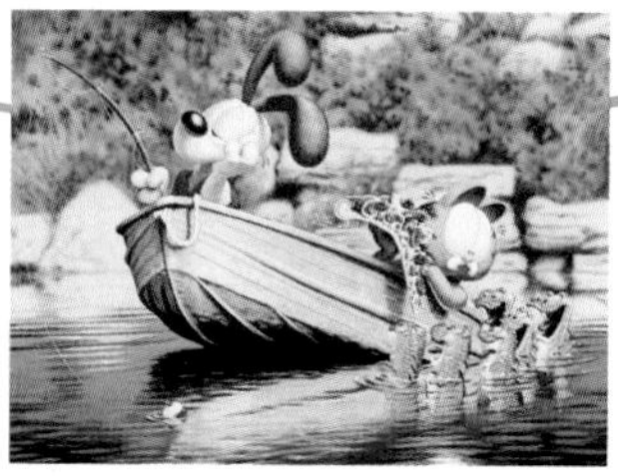

Full-Figured Feline

It all starts with a lump of clay. Using tools that seem more at home in a dentist's office than an art studio, Paws sculptors carve, mold, and scrape, transforming a big shapeless blob into a big *shapely* blob: Garfield the cat. Over the past twenty-odd years, he's been immortalized in ceramic, resin, plastic, bronze, and stone. Who would have thought this portly pussycat could ever be a hardbody?

Below: "The Spirit of '76"; original clay sculpture and decorated cold-cast porcelain casting, 1998.

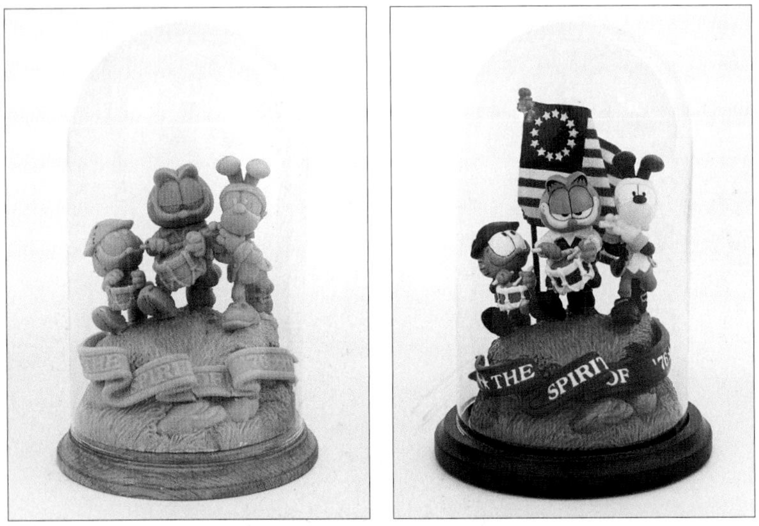
THE SPIRIT OF '76

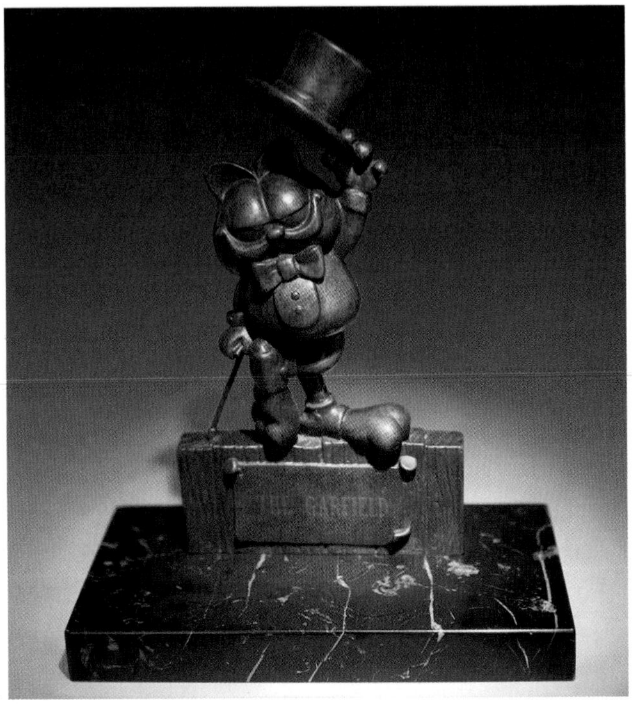

Above: Created as an award for very special licensees, "The Garfield" was cast in bronze and weighed more than twenty-three pounds. Only ten of these pieces were ever made; six were given to licensees, with the first awarded in 1991.

Right: "Attack cat" Garfield was sculpted in clay and cast in resin, 2000.

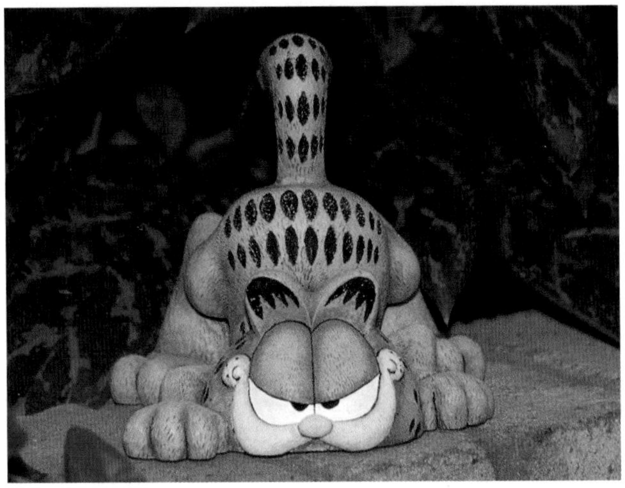

Far right: Created exclusively for the Garfield Stuff® catalog, this garden plaque was sculpted in clay (on top of a carved wooden base) and cast in a special weather-resistant, polyester-filled urethane, 2001.

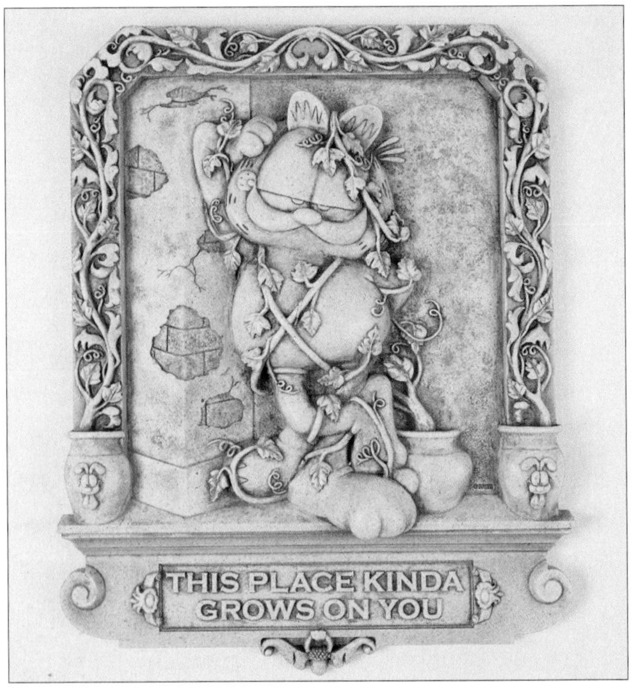
THIS PLACE KINDA
GROWS ON YOU

Bottom: Bigger isn't always better, as these miniature PVC figurines for Russell Stover illustrate. Originals sculpted in wax; each is approximately two inches tall, 2000–2002.

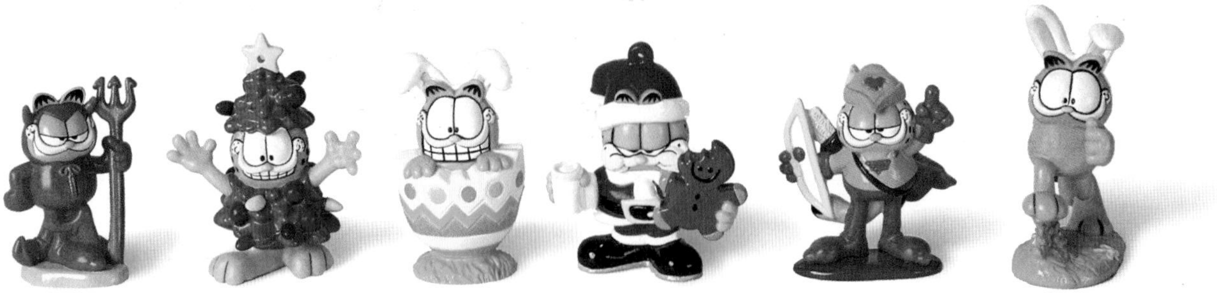

CHAPTER ELEVEN

Garfield for President

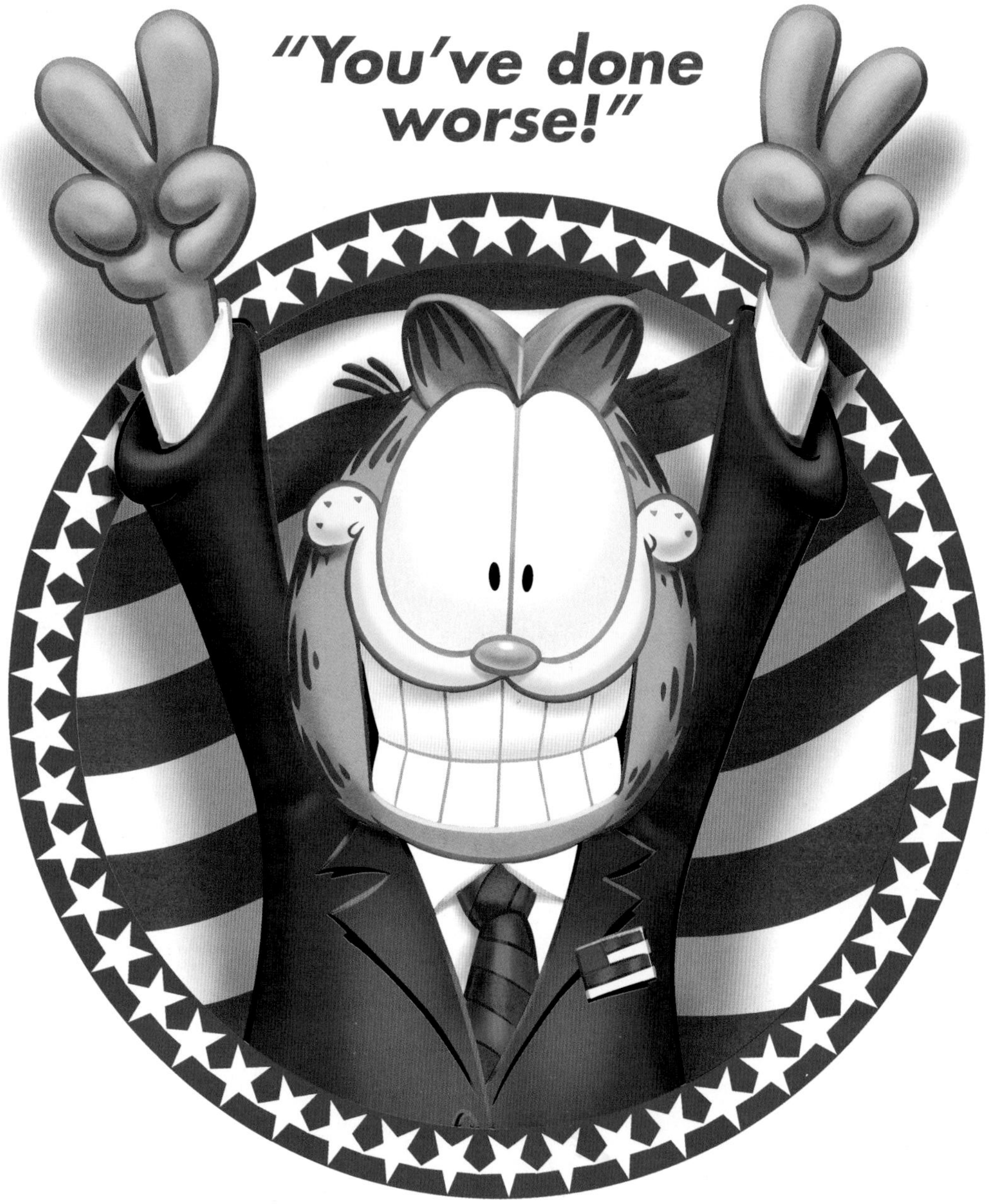
"You've done worse!"

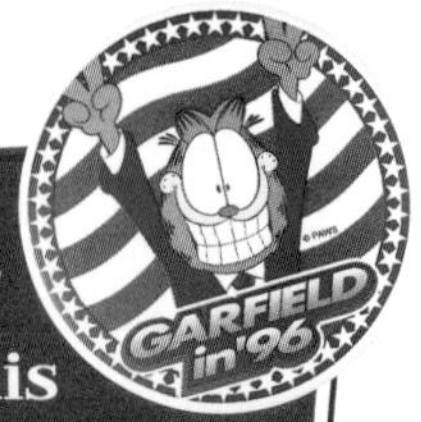
GARFIELD
in '96

"Eaters of the world, unite!" With that rallying cry, Garfield threw his fat into the ring and launched his campaign for the U.S. presidency in 1996. Though his bid was ultimately unsuccessful (losing to incumbent Bill Clinton), Garfield proved more potent than Bob Dole and less cartoonish than Ross Perot.

A Garfield victory would have dramatically changed American life and the course of history. Imagine, if you will . . .

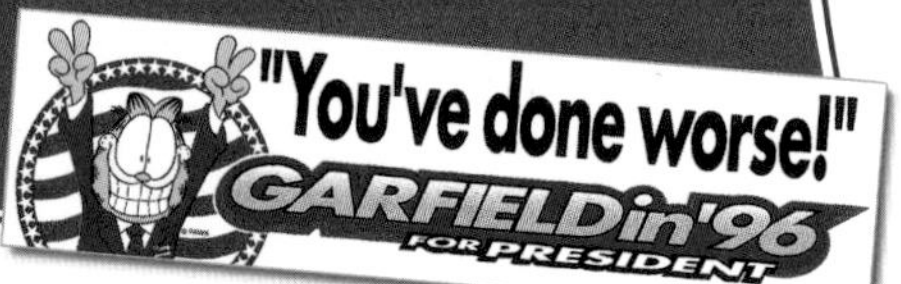
"You've done worse!"
GARFIELD in '96
FOR PRESIDENT

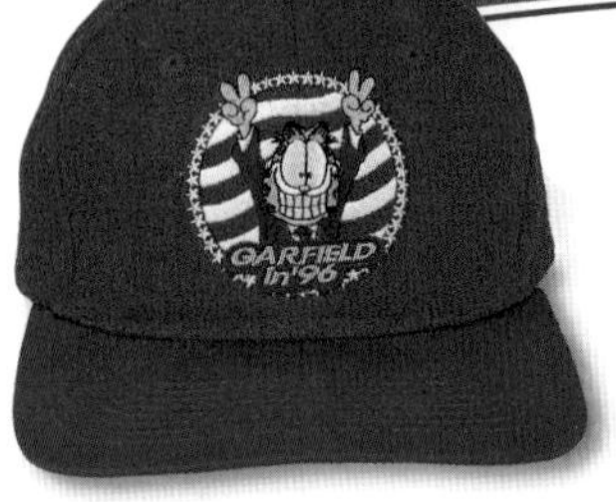
GARFIELD
in '96

IF I WERE PRESIDENT GARFIELD

Everyone's favorite fat cat would usher in a kinder, gentler, and lazier America

If I were president, the first thing I'd do is take a nap. After a long campaign, I'd be exhausted. (Actually, after a walk from the couch to the refrigerator, I'd be exhausted.)

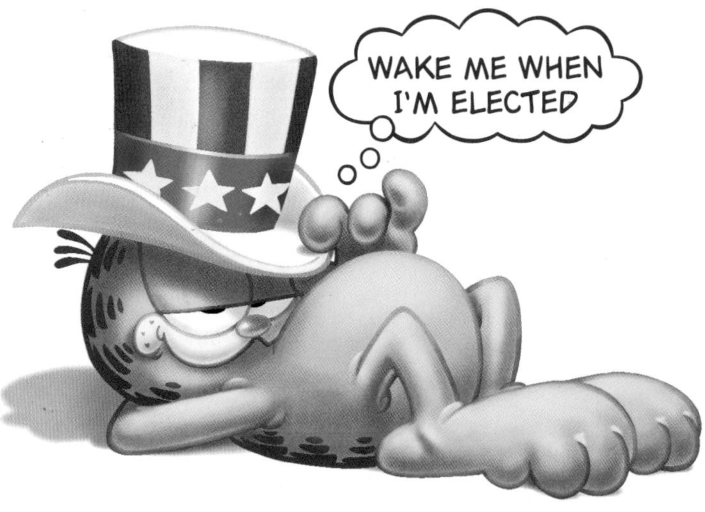
WAKE ME WHEN I'M ELECTED

Next, I'd have the White House kitchen fix me a truly presidential snack: a fifty-pound pepperoni pizza shaped like a map of the United States.

Properly rested and fed, I'd get right down to business. My first hundred days in office would see sweeping changes in government. Then I could spend the rest of my term dealing with the really important issues: eating and sleeping.

If I were president, here's what I'd do . . .

TAXES
Less tax, more snacks. 'Nuff said.

HEALTH CARE
I'm for universal health care for pets! However, I would abolish all shots, needles, flea dips, and other forms of medical torture. (Needless to say, no cat will be "fixed" under my administration.)

THE ENVIRONMENT
Plant a tree. Plant two; then make a hammock!

EDUCATION
I will be the education president. But I'll make school fun. Pop quizzes will be eliminated. Lunch will be the most important subject. And I promise that under my administration all cafeterias will be equipped with dessert bars!

SOCIAL SECURITY

Concerned citizens, I feel your pain. I'd rather pass a kidney Stonehenge than tap into these sacred funds.

NUTRITION

When it comes to food, I say, "Feed my lips!"

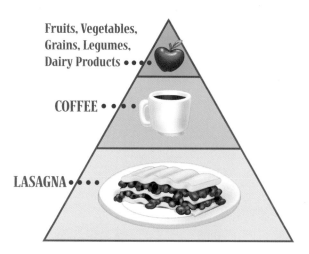

Fruits, Vegetables, Grains, Legumes, Dairy Products
COFFEE
LASAGNA

GOBBLE
NARF NARF
CHOMP
GULP
GARFIEL

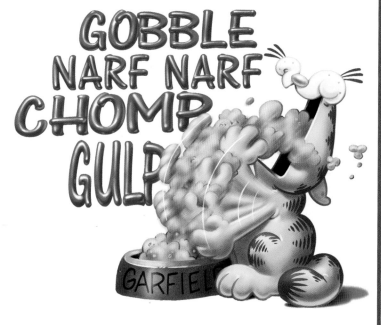

FOREIGN POLICY

I propose we do away with all weapons of war, and unilaterally agree to settle any disputes with food fights.

★★★

Rest assured, I would serve only one term. Four years is all I'd need to change America forever. Besides, running the country is work. And if there's one thing I avoid like the vet, it's work.

Which reminds me—as president, there is one thing that I, Garfield, would never, ever do: jog. Well, I'm outta here. Remember my motto: "Life, Liberty, and the Pursuit of Pasta!"

TOP TEN REASONS WHY GARFIELD WOULD MAKE A GOOD PRESIDENT

10. Can't talk on the phone, so no embarrassing calls to Super Bowl winners

9. No problem napping during boring Cabinet briefings

8. Would appoint Speedy Gonzalez Postmaster General

7. Congressmen's cats would give him the dirt on their owners

6. Wouldn't waste Secret Service men by dragging them around some jogging trail

5. Lincoln Memorial would become "Abe's Memorial Munch 'n' Go"

4. Would beef up border patrols to halt illegal flow of dogs

3. Would end federal funding of diet clinics

2. Deranged despots often allergic to cat hair

1. Let's face it—we've done worse!

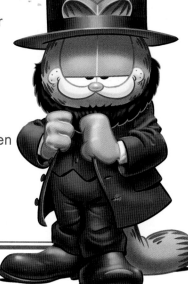

And what if Odie made it a real dogfight by running against

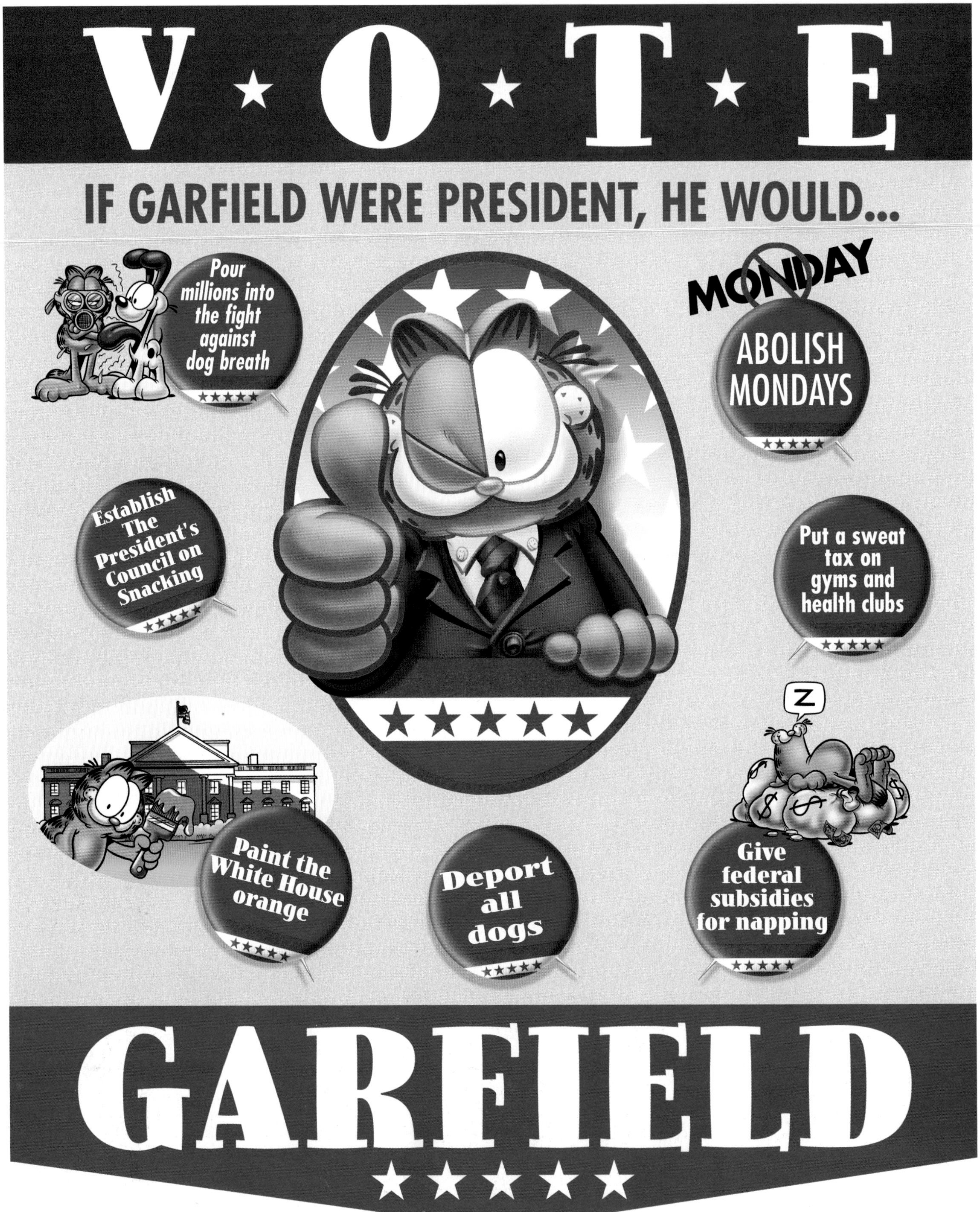

V ★ O ★ T ★ E
IF GARFIELD WERE PRESIDENT, HE WOULD...
Pour millions into the fight against dog breath
MONDAY
ABOLISH MONDAYS
Establish The President's Council on Snacking
Put a sweat tax on gyms and health clubs
Z
Paint the White House orange
Deport all dogs
Give federal subsidies for napping
GARFIELD

Garfield? Here's a look at their competing platforms:

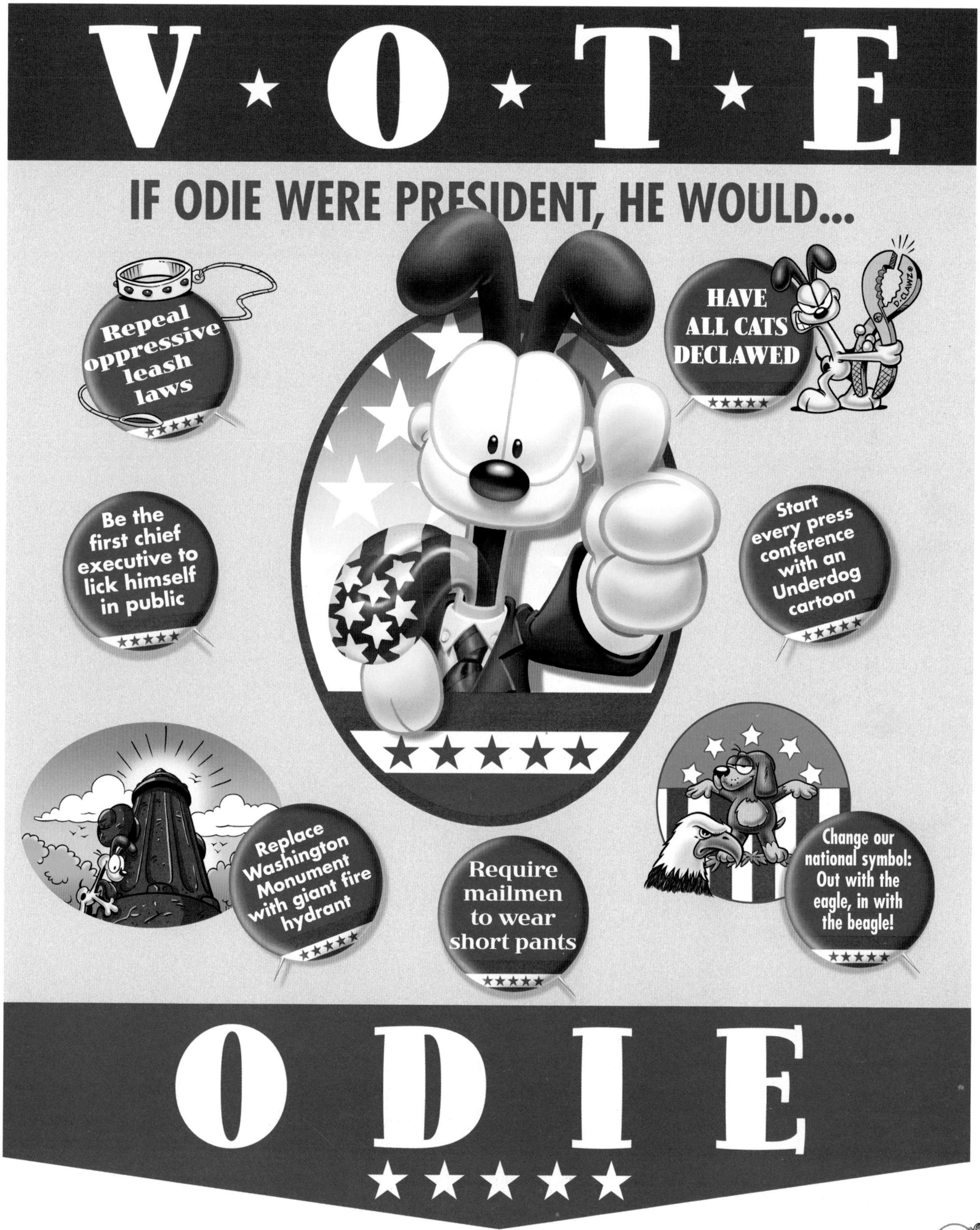
V • O • T • E
IF ODIE WERE PRESIDENT, HE WOULD...
Repeal oppressive leash laws
HAVE ALL CATS DECLAWED
D-CLAWZ
Be the first chief executive to lick himself in public
Start every press conference with an Underdog cartoon
Replace Washington Monument with giant fire hydrant
Require mailmen to wear short pants
Change our national symbol: Out with the eagle, in with the beagle!
O D I E

☆☆☆ Presidential Potpourri

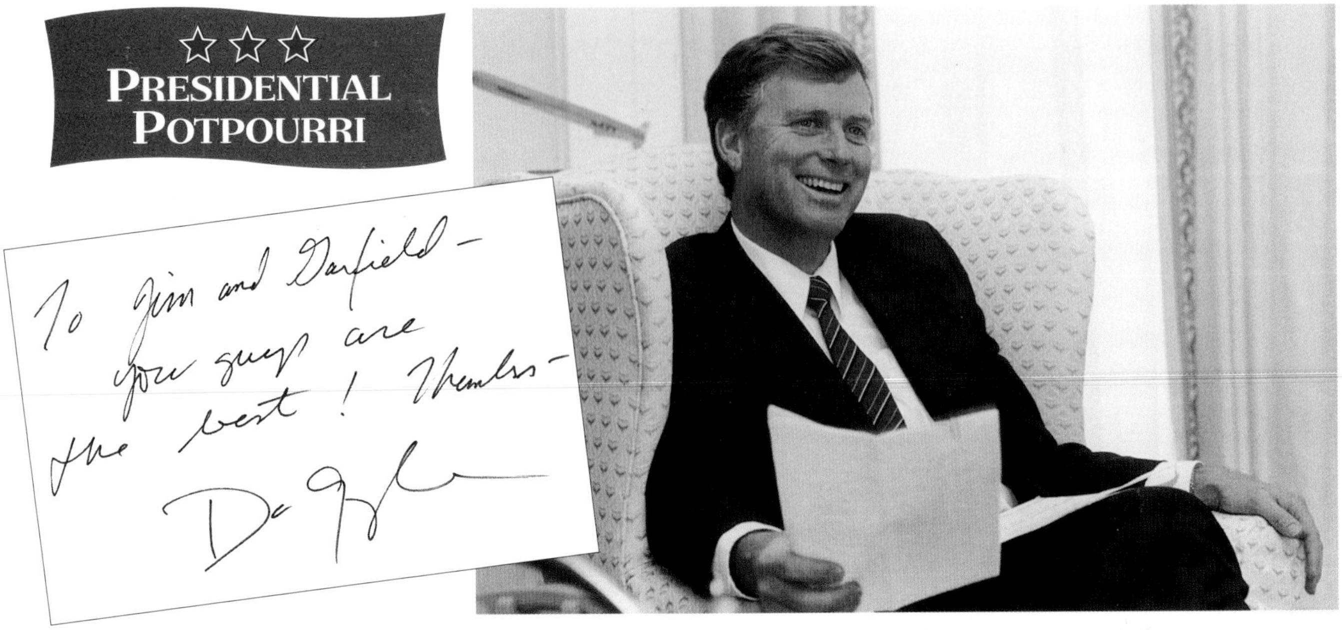
To Jim and Garfield –
you guys are
the best! Thanks –

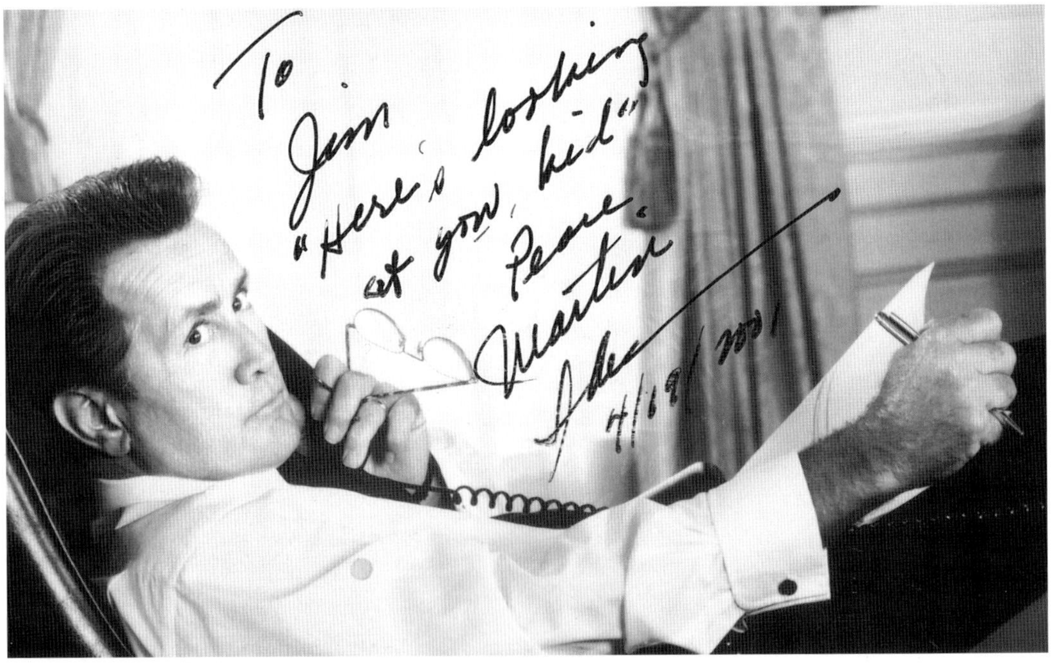
To
Jim
"Here's looking
at you, kid"
Peace
Martin

Above: A note from former U.S. vice president and fellow Hoosier Dan Quayle.

Right: Greetings from *The West Wing*: Actor Martin Sheen, aka President Josiah Bartlet, sends a wish to Paws chief executive Jim Davis.

Below left: Forget Millie and Socks! Snoopy and Garfield look for a house worthy of their status.

Below right: Presidential portrait by Pulitzer Prize–winning editorial cartoonist Mike Peters.

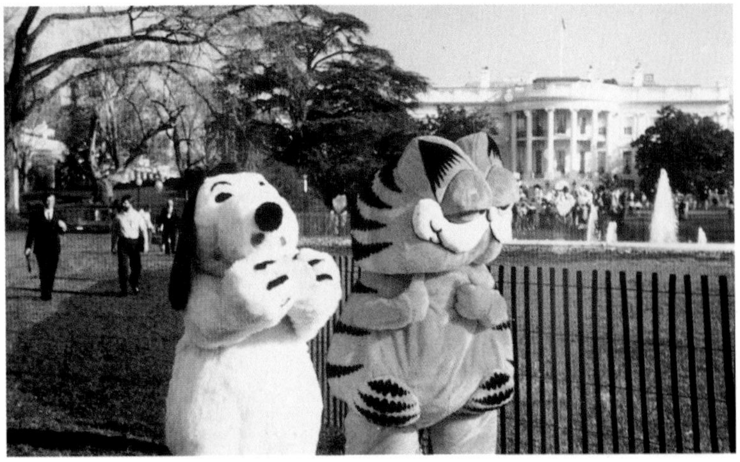

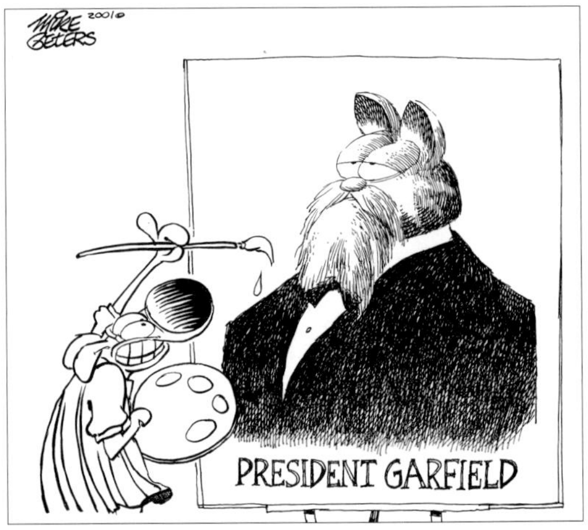
MIKE PETERS
PRESIDENT GARFIELD

CHAPTER TWELVE

Education Sensation

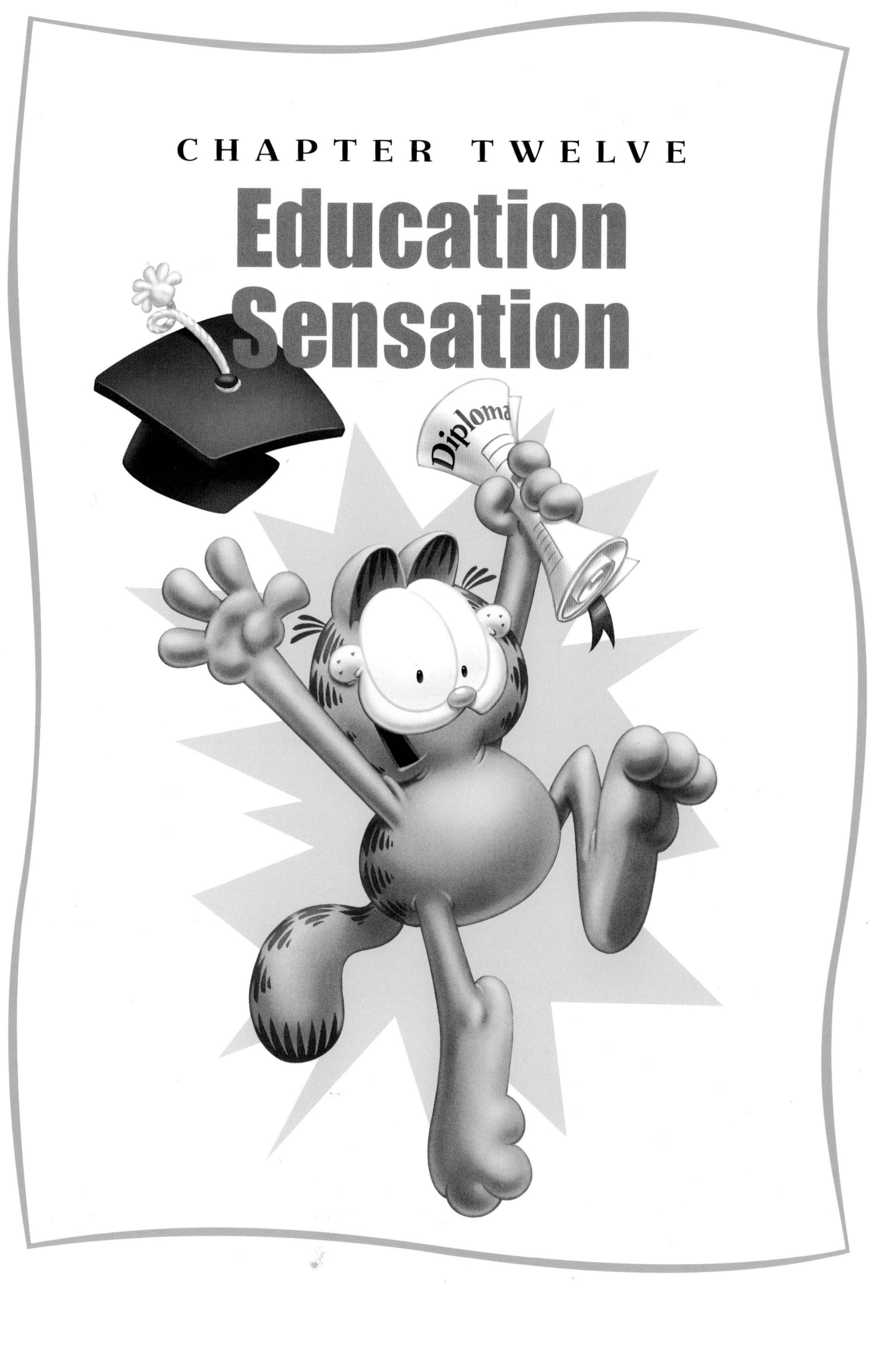
Diploma

See Garfield. See Garfield educate. Educate, Garfield, educate! **Throughout his career, Garfield's been the spokescat for numerous literacy and reading programs. He's on posters, bookmobiles, and public service announcements. He even has his own dictionary. The smart-alecky cat promoting homework and reading? Has Garfield changed his stripes? Don't count on it. Sure, he educates—but he's always entertaining.**

Since the early days of the *Garfield* comic, Jim has received letters from fans telling him how the strip helped their kids learn to read. Something about combining a picture with the words helped jump-start the reading process. With that in mind, Jim formulated the idea of using the comic strips with an actual dictionary. After a few false starts, Jim presented the concept to Merriam-Webster, the leader in dictionaries and reference books. The publisher immediately saw the merits of the project, and Jim's twenty-year dream of helping young readers was fulfilled.

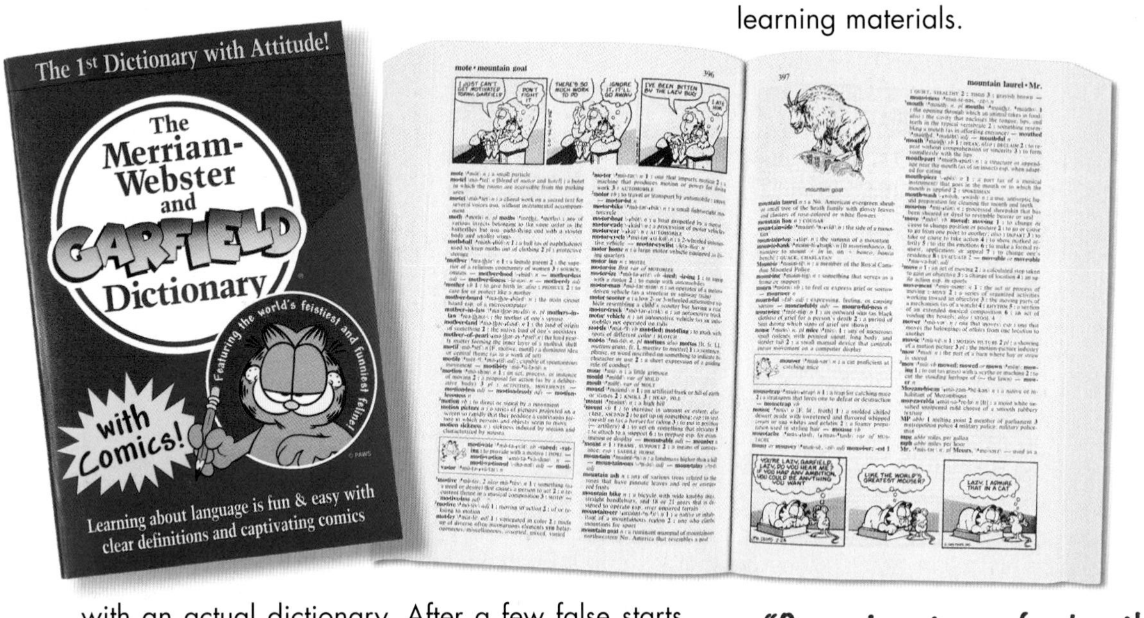
The 1st Dictionary with Attitude!
The Merriam-Webster and GARFIELD Dictionary
Featuring the world's feistiest and funniest feline!
with Comics!
Learning about language is fun & easy with clear definitions and captivating comics

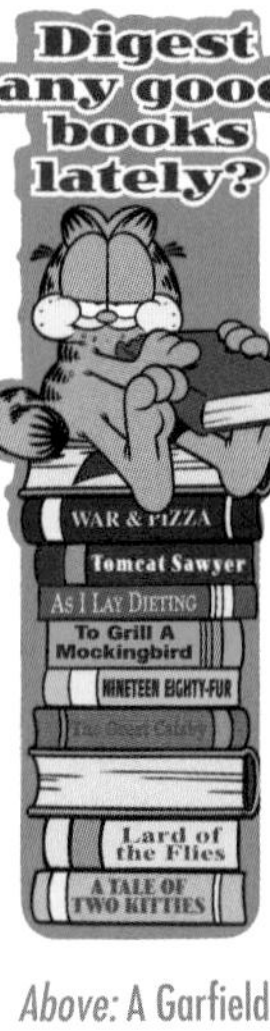
Digest any good books lately?
WAR & PIZZA
Tomcat Sawyer
As I Lay Dieting
To Grill A Mockingbird
NINETEEN EIGHTY-FUR
Lard of the Flies
A TALE OF TWO KITTIES

Above: A Garfield bookmark of "Kooky Classics."

A Dictionary with Cattitude!

The Merriam-Webster and Garfield Dictionary (1999) contains more than 65,000 definitions and highlights a word on nearly every spread with a corresponding comic strip.

The dictionary received the Parents' Choice Award in the category of Best Reference Books. The Parents' Choice Award is the country's most distinguished not-for-profit evaluator of children's learning materials.

"One advantage of using the comic strip to build vocabulary is that the words are utilized squarely within the American vernacular, and not in a dry way. An educator once told me that first you have to get a student's attention. With that accomplished, teaching is easy."

—Jim Davis

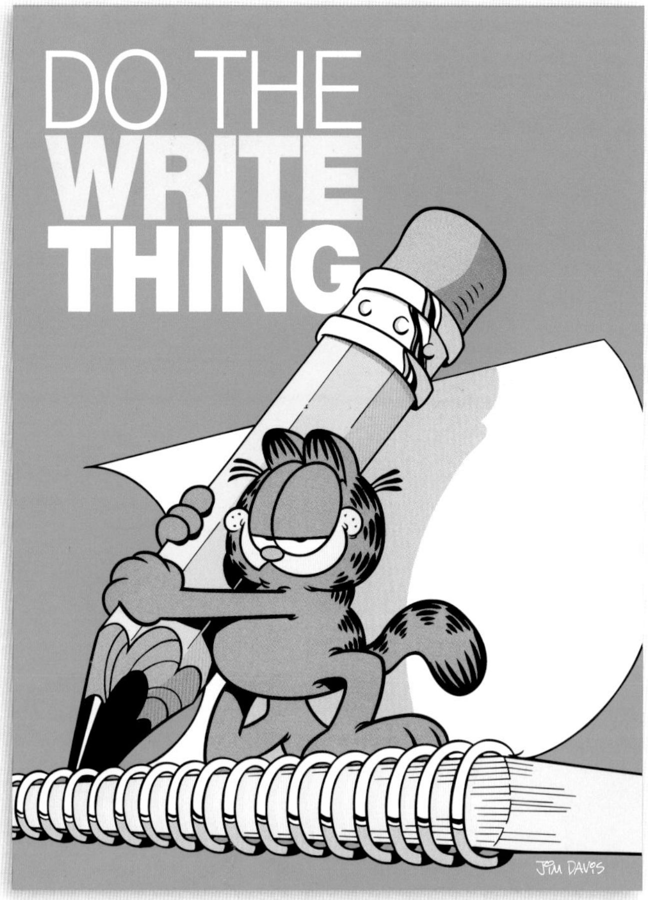
DO THE
WRITE
THING

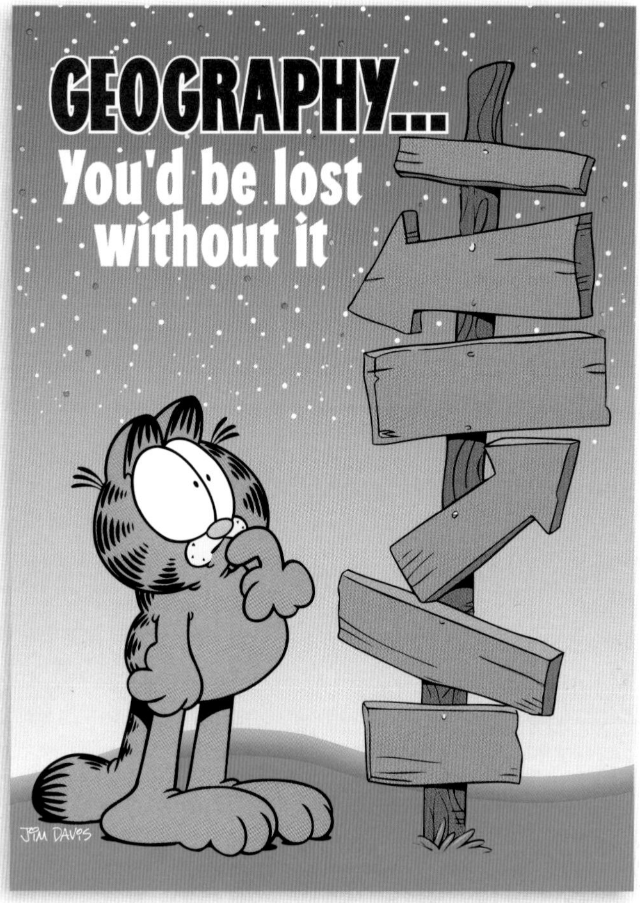
GEOGRAPHY...
You'd be lost
without it

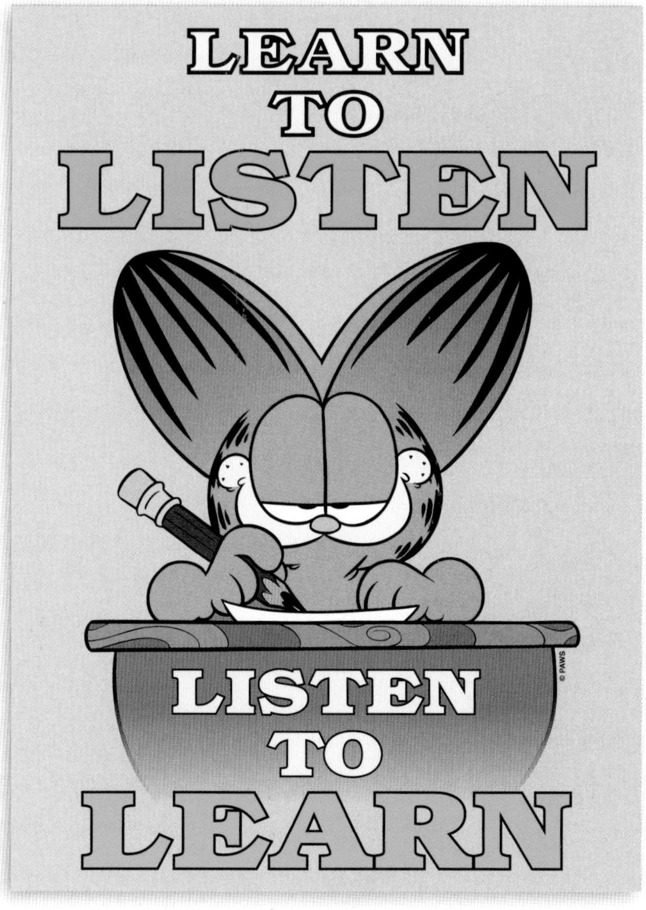
LEARN
TO
LISTEN
LISTEN
TO
LEARN

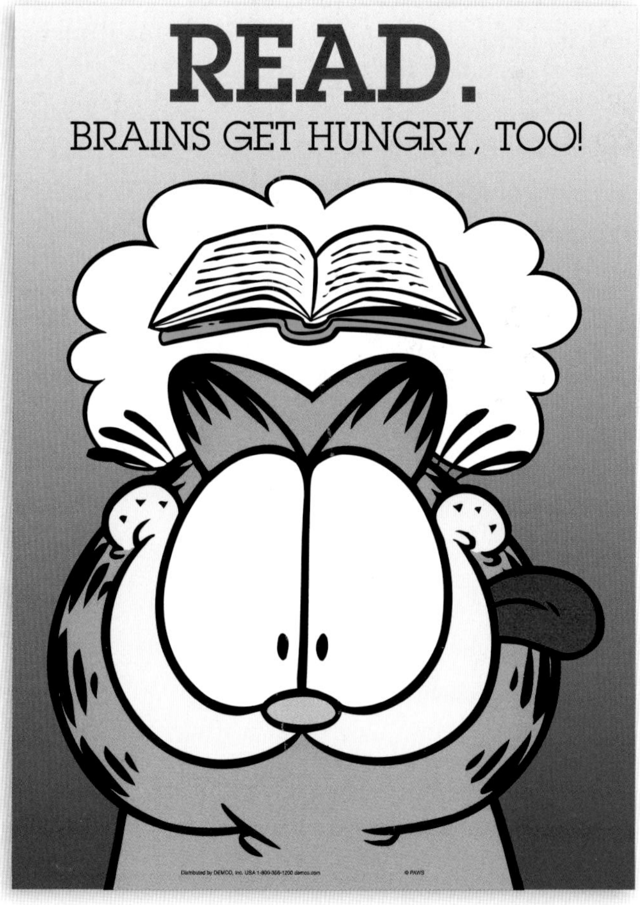
READ.
BRAINS GET HUNGRY, TOO!

Showcasing just a few of the many educational posters on which Garfield has appeared.

Furry Tales

Garfield books were used in several reading programs, most notably Ravenous Reader, the Literacy Volunteers of America, and *Mrs. Bush's Story Time*, a syndicated radio show the former First Lady hosted in the early 1990s. Garfield also garnered his share of educational accolades, including the LVA's Stars in Literacy award, which the well-read (and well-fed) cat and his creator received in 1995.

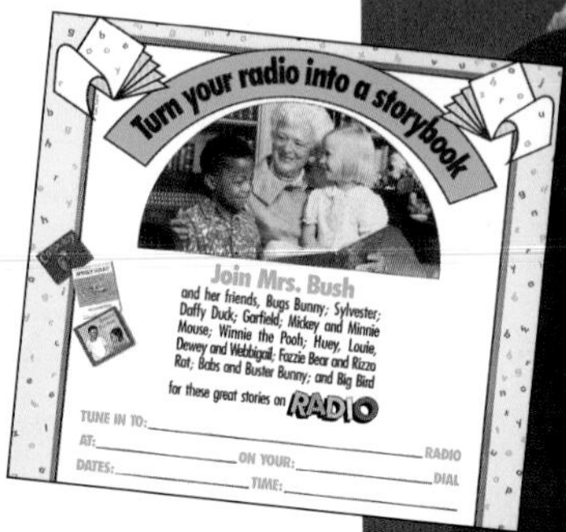
Turn your radio into a storybook
Join Mrs. Bush
and her friends, Bugs Bunny; Sylvester; Daffy Duck; Garfield; Mickey and Minnie Mouse; Winnie the Pooh; Huey, Louie, Dewey and Webbigail; Fozzie Bear and Rizzo Rat; Babs and Buster Bunny; and Big Bird
for these great stories on RADIO
TUNE IN TO:
AT:
ON YOUR:
RADIO
DATES:
TIME:
DIAL

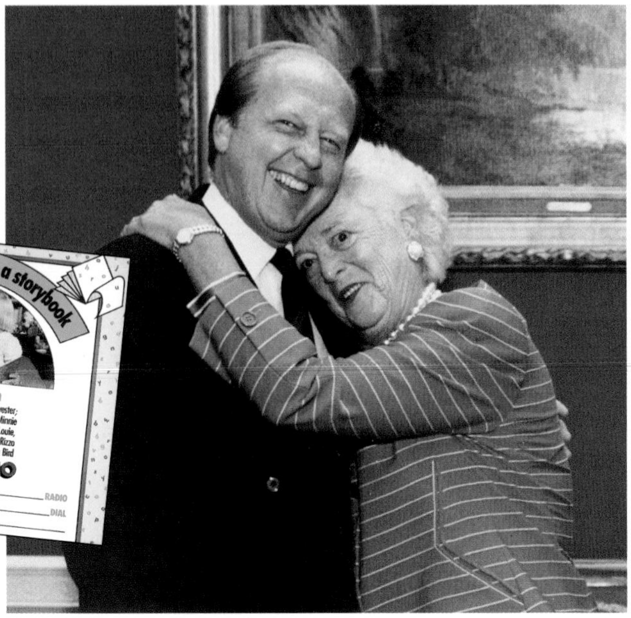

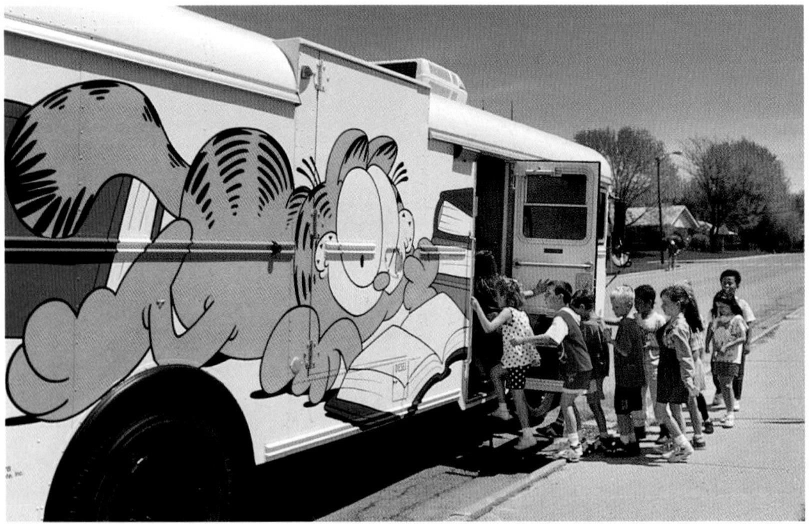

Take Me to Your Reader!

The Garfield bookmobile began hitting the streets in 1994, bringing books and other educational materials to kids in such areas as Indiana, Florida, Kentucky, Maryland, and Canada.

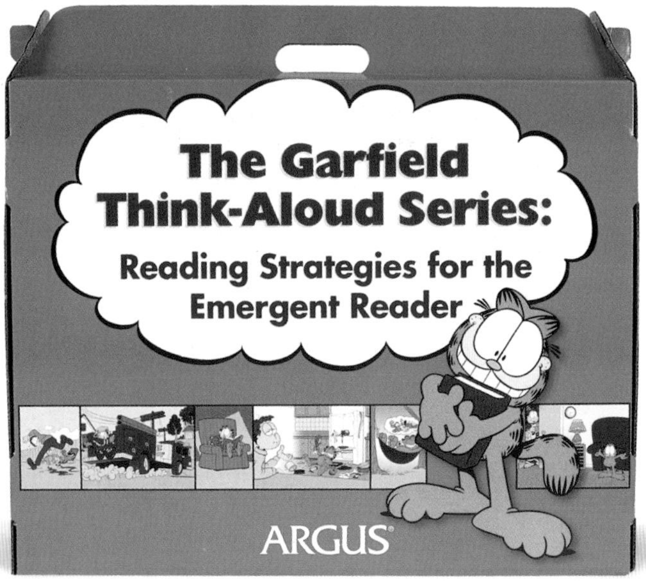
The Garfield Think-Aloud Series:
Reading Strategies for the Emergent Reader
ARGUS

Big Books

The titanic tabby went to the head of the class with the 2001 Garfield Think-Aloud Series, designed for use in school curriculums. Garfield's personality and humor were once again utilized, this time in a series of large-sized books that helped children in kindergarten and first grade learn to read.

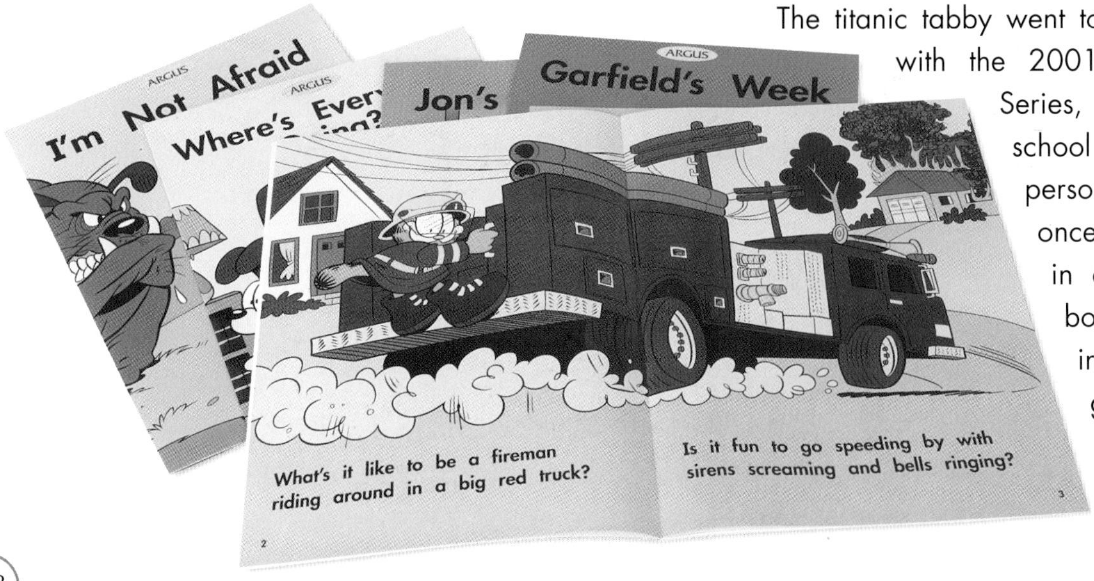
ARGUS
I'm Not Afraid
ARGUS
Jon's
ARGUS
Garfield's Week
What's it like to be a fireman riding around in a big red truck?
Is it fun to go speeding by with sirens screaming and bells ringing?
2
3

Garfield Goes to China

In 1996 Jim and Garfield undertook a bold mission: teaching English to Chinese children in China. With the cooperation of China's officially sanctioned school textbook publisher—People's Education Press (PEP)—storybooks, activity books, audiotapes, and learning materials were created. Jim sent a writer and an artist to China for a week to work with educators on the project. The resulting four-volume series, created in the United States and translated and printed in China, featured a unique story line, in which Garfield and Odie travel from America to China and meet a young boy, Ai-Lun, and his friends and family.

Launched in China on June 1, 1997, on the national holiday Children's Day, the program marked the first time the Chinese government has partnered with an American licensed character to teach English.

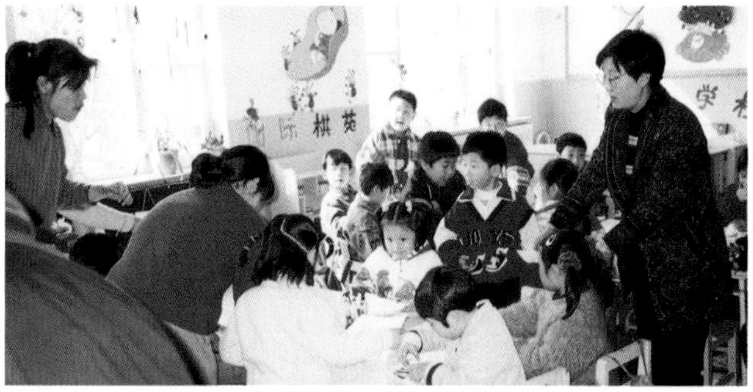

Left and below: A kindergarten in Beijing.

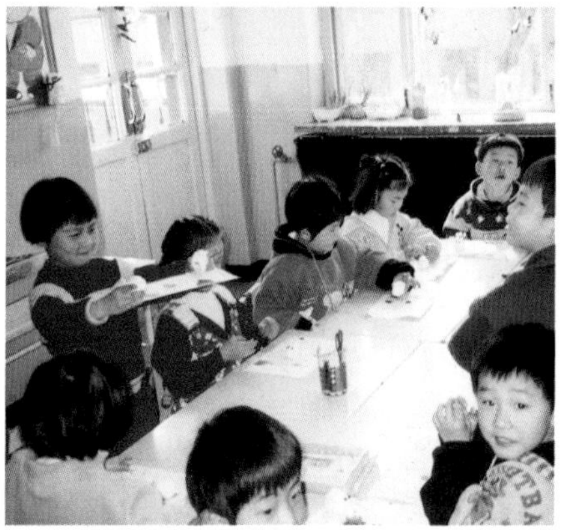

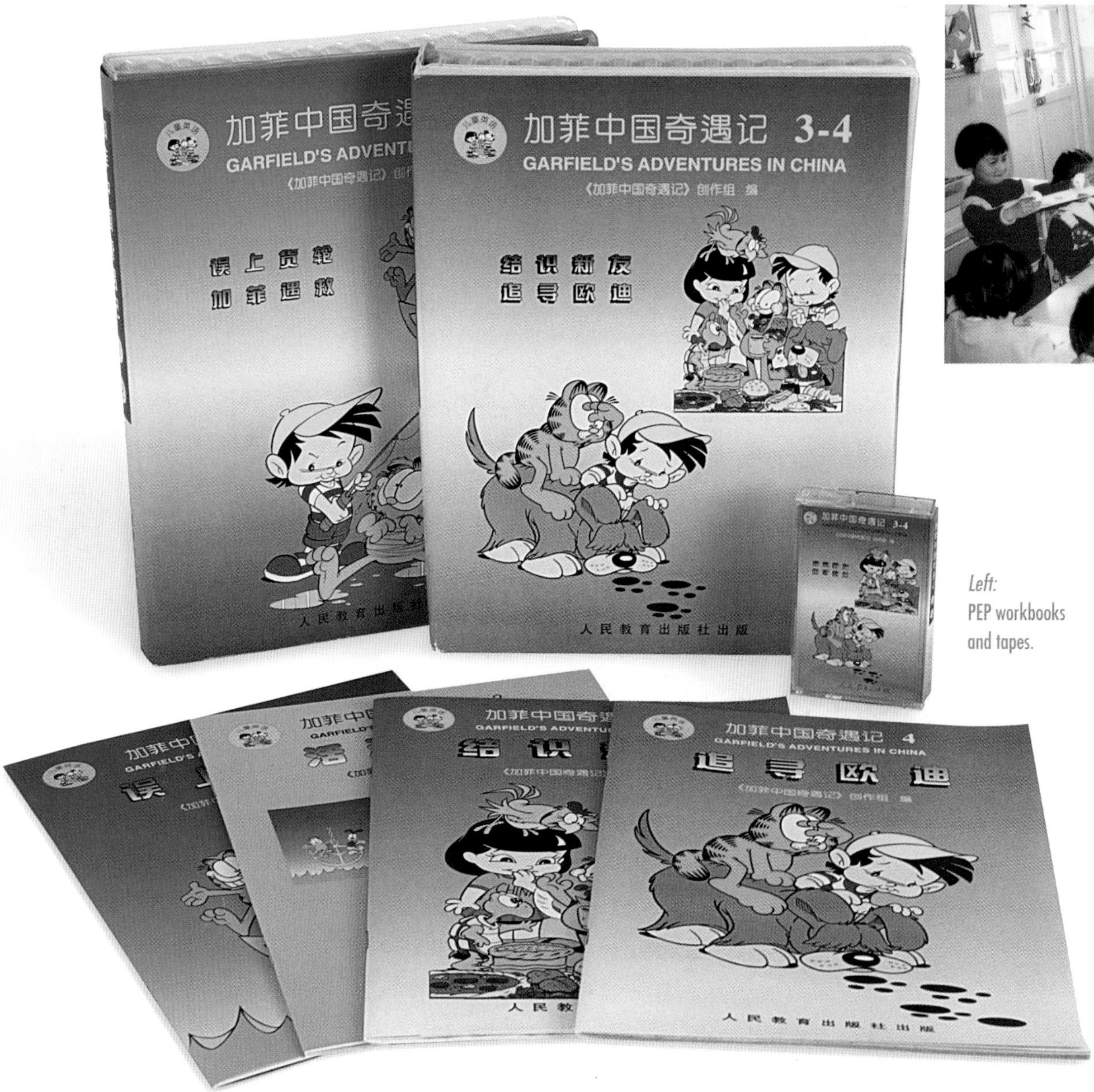
加菲中国奇遇记 3-4
GARFIELD'S ADVENTURES IN CHINA
《加菲中国奇遇记》创作组 编
结识新友
追寻欧迪
人民教育出版社出版
加菲中国奇遇记 4
GARFIELD'S ADVENTURES IN CHINA
追寻欧迪

Left: PEP workbooks and tapes.

Born to Snooze!

Garfield was the perfect choice for the National Institute of Health's Star Sleeper project, a nation-wide campaign to help teach youngsters about the importance of getting a good night's sleep. The 2001 program included publicity, contests, and free goodies for kids, like the activity pad and plush shown here.

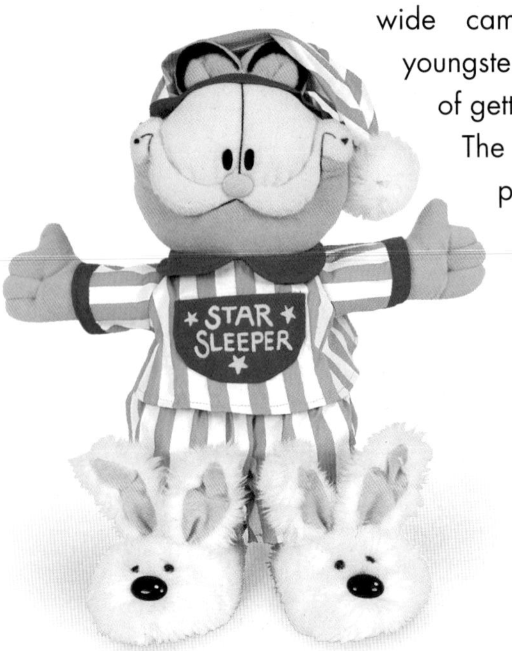
STAR SLEEPER

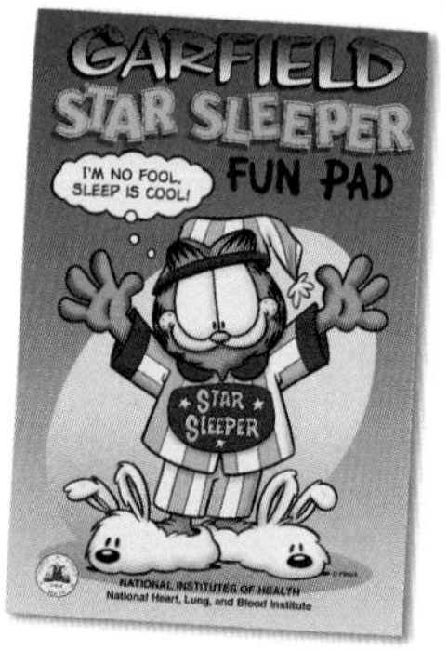
GARFIELD
STAR SLEEPER
FUN PAD
I'M NO FOOL. SLEEP IS COOL!
STAR SLEEPER
NATIONAL INSTITUTES OF HEALTH
National Heart, Lung, and Blood Institute

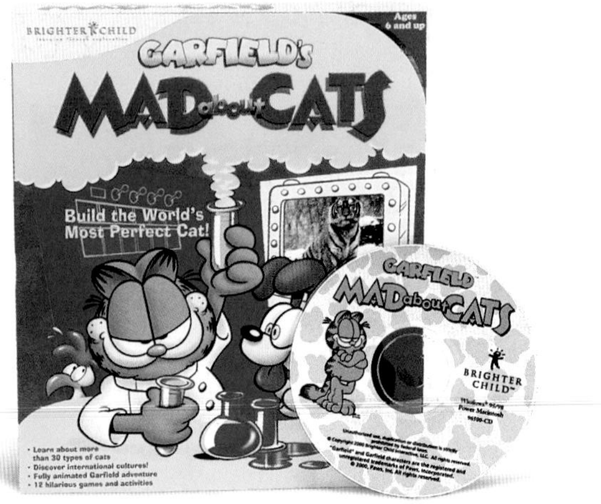
BRIGHTER CHILD
Ages 6 and up
GARFIELD's
MAD about CATS
Build the World's Most Perfect Cat!

Mad About Cats

With Odie as his silly assistant, Garfield (aka Dr. Frankencat) helped kids build the world's perfect cat, while learning about geography and international cultures in this 1999 CD-ROM. The disk featured animation, audio/video clips about more than thirty species of cats, and lots of crazy games.

Color Him Cool

Garfield lent a helping paw to this series of instructional coloring and activity books that stressed laughter as much as learning. Whether the subject is pet care or eye care, auto safety or moving, the witty kitty always makes learning about it fun.

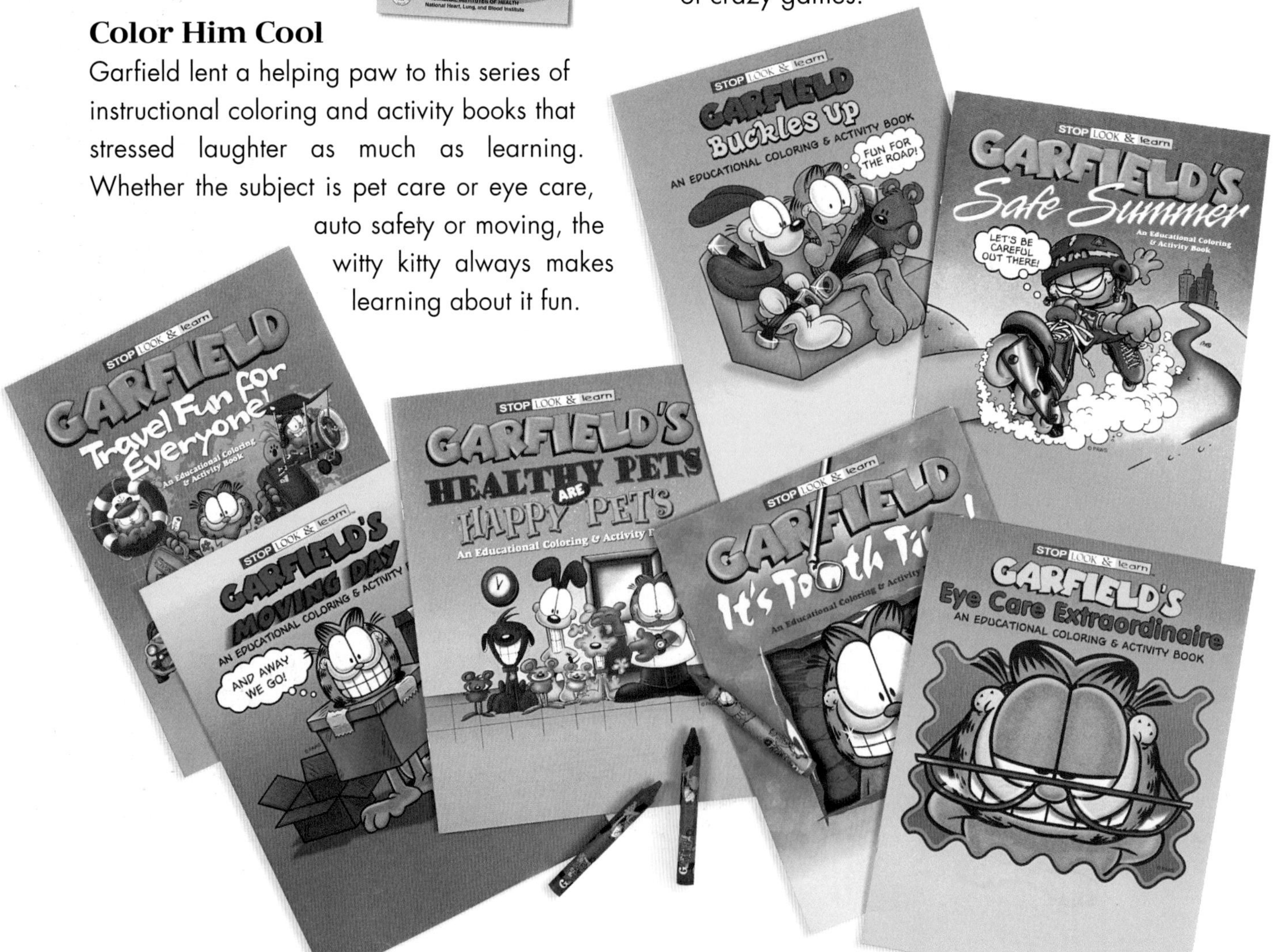
STOP LOOK & learn
GARFIELD
Buckles Up
AN EDUCATIONAL COLORING & ACTIVITY BOOK
FUN FOR THE ROAD!
GARFIELD'S
Safe Summer
An Educational Coloring & Activity Book
LET'S BE CAREFUL OUT THERE!
GARFIELD
Travel Fun for Everyone!
An Educational Coloring & Activity Book
GARFIELD'S
HEALTHY PETS ARE HAPPY PETS
GARFIELD'S
MOVING DAY
AN EDUCATIONAL COLORING & ACTIVITY BOOK
AND AWAY WE GO!
GARFIELD'S
Eye Care Extraordinaire
AN EDUCATIONAL COLORING & ACTIVITY BOOK

CHAPTER THIRTEEN

Around the World in 25 Years

I'VE GONE GLOBAL!

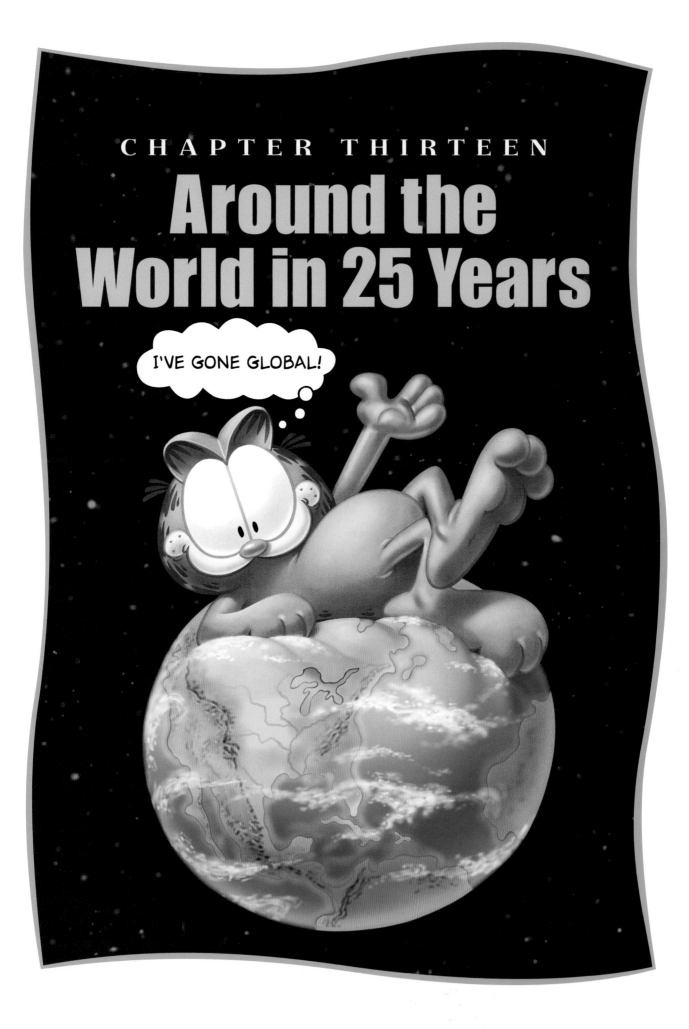

Garfield speaks the international language of laughter, and spreads his mirth—and girth—all over the world. The comic strip appears in more than a hundred countries—locations as far-flung as Istanbul and Pago Pago—and in languages as diverse as Afrikaans and Hindi. Likewise, his syndicated TV show, *Garfield and Friends*, is seen by millions of fans around the globe. A cat for all countries, he's known as Gustaf in Sweden, Pusur in Norway, and Karvinen in Finland. Europeans love the feisty feline, but he's particularly popular in Asia and Latin America (perhaps for his love of food and siestas).

Here's your chance to go globe-trotting with Garfield. It's just like a vacation around the world—without the lost luggage and dysentery.

Below: A sampling of Garfield books from around the world.

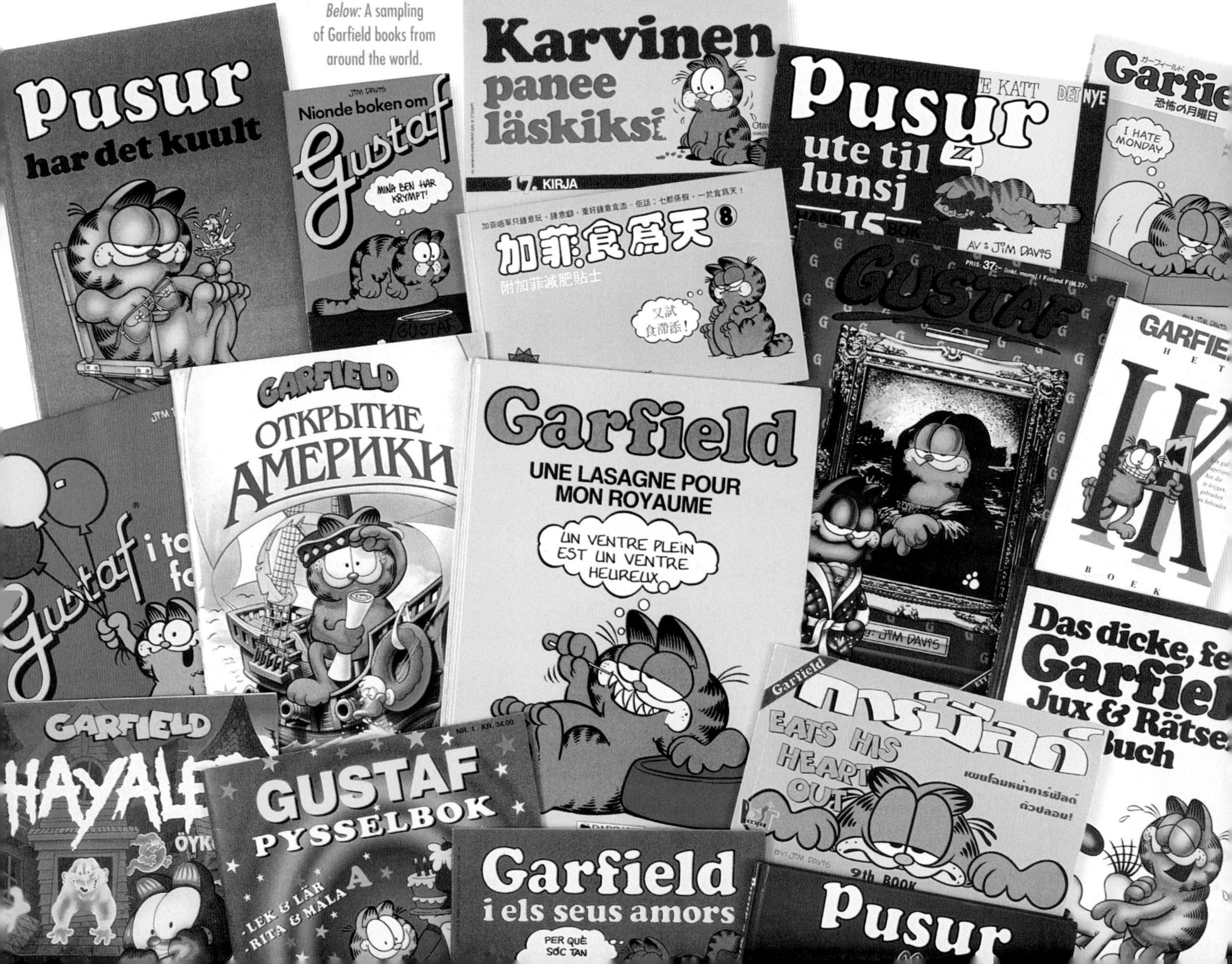
pusur
har det kuult
JIM DAVIS
Nionde boken om
Gustaf
MINA BEN HAR KRYMPT!
Karvinen
panee
läskiksi
17. KIRJA
pusur
ute til
lunsj
AV: JIM DAVIS
加菲食為天 8
附加菲減肥貼士
I HATE MONDAY
GUSTAF
GARFIELD
ОТКРЫТИЕ
АМЕРИКИ
Garfield
UNE LASAGNE POUR
MON ROYAUME
UN VENTRE PLEIN
EST UN VENTRE
HEUREUX
BY: JIM DAVIS
Das dicke, fe
Garfie
Jux & Rätse
Buch
GARFIELD
GUSTAF
PYSSELBOK
LEK & LÄR
RITA & MÅLA
EATS HIS
HEART
OUT
9th BOOK
Garfield
i els seus amors
Pusur

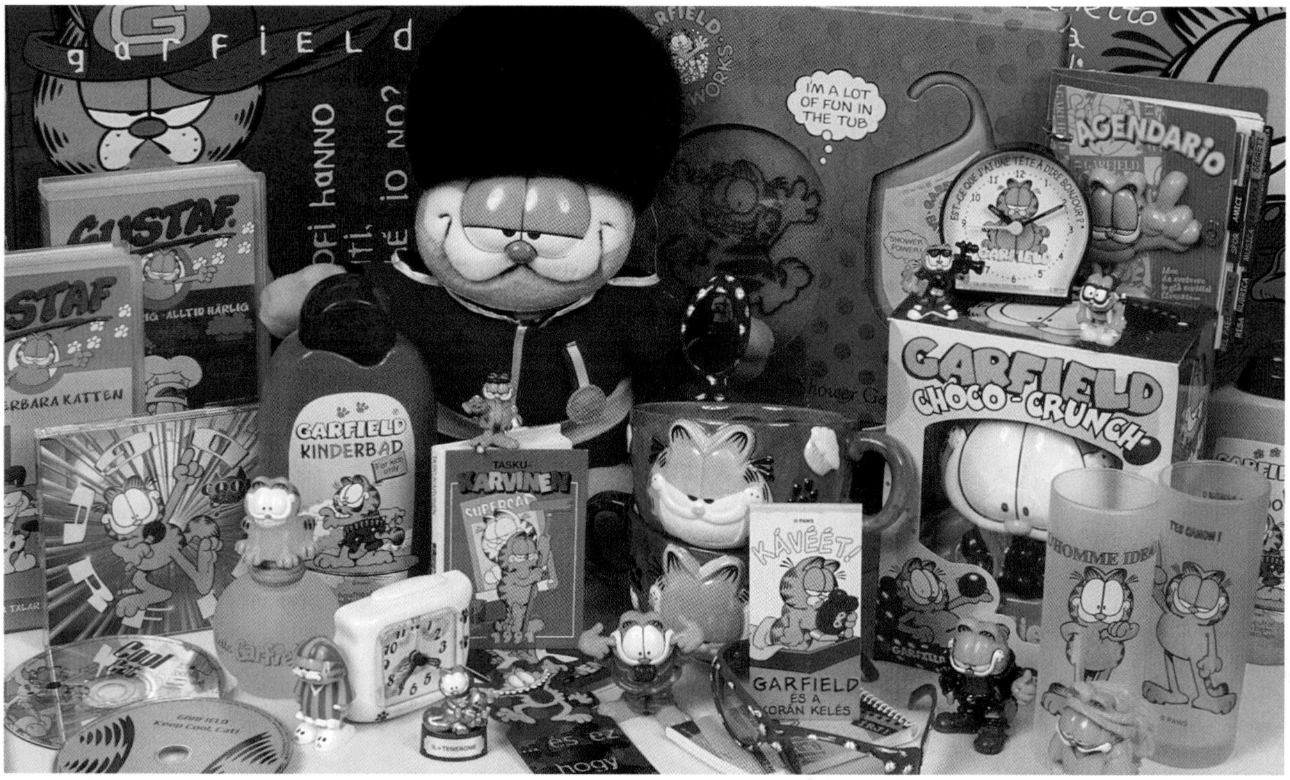
garfield
I'M A LOT OF FUN IN THE TUB
AGENDARIO
GUSTAF
GARFIELD KINDERBAD
TASKU-KARVINEN
KÁVÉÉT!
GARFIELD CHOCO-CRUNCH
GARFIELD ÉS A KORÁN KELÉS
L'HOMME IDÉAL

Left: European products include a CD and bubble bath from Germany, and chocolate and a palace guard plush from the UK.

Continental Cat

Garfield's unique personality translates well in Europe, and the famous feline is loved from London to Lisbon.

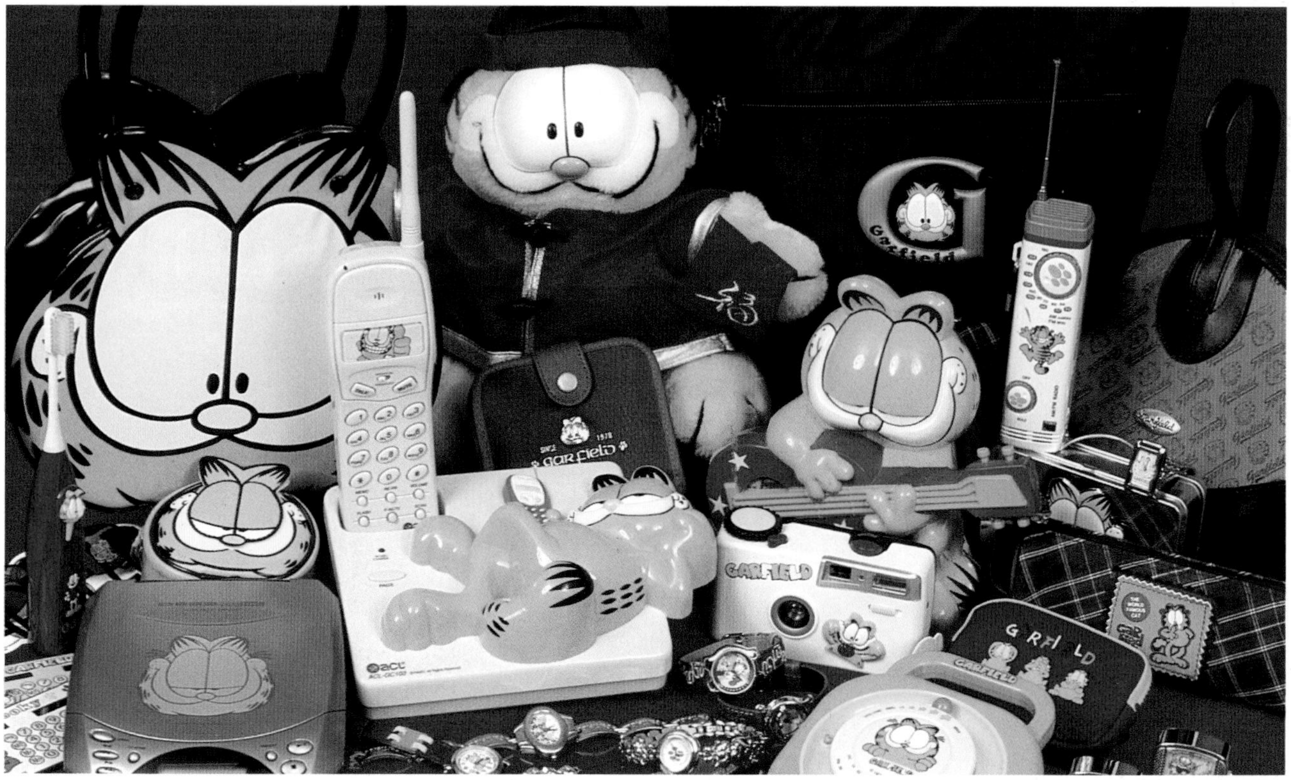
GARFIELD

Left: Phones, CD players, watches, and clocks from the Pac Rim.

Asian Invasion

Garfield has taken the Far East by storm. The cat's made his mark on electronics and high-end fashion accessories like watches, wallets, and purses.

Dutch Treat

The Royal Delft Company is famous for its blue dinnerware. This handcrafted plate is a one-of-a-kind creation made as a gift for Jim Davis in honor of Garfield's twentieth anniversary.

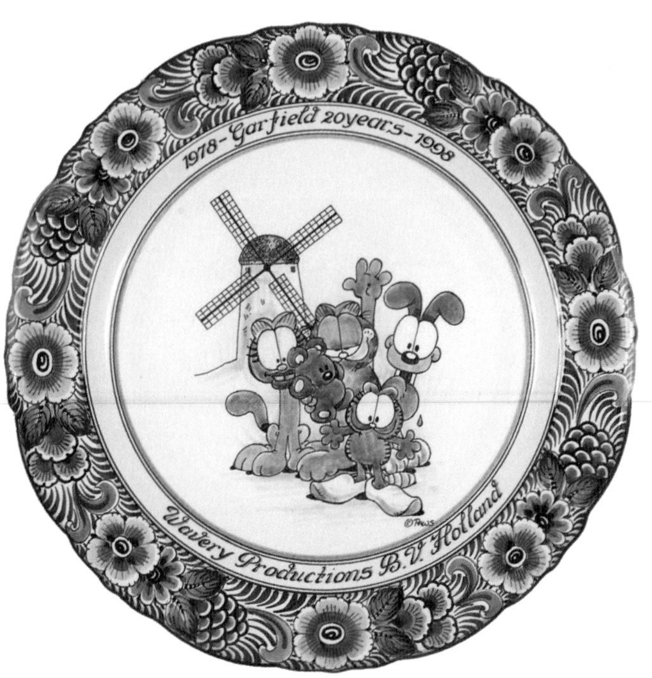
1978 - Garfield 20years - 1998
Wavery Productions B.V. Holland

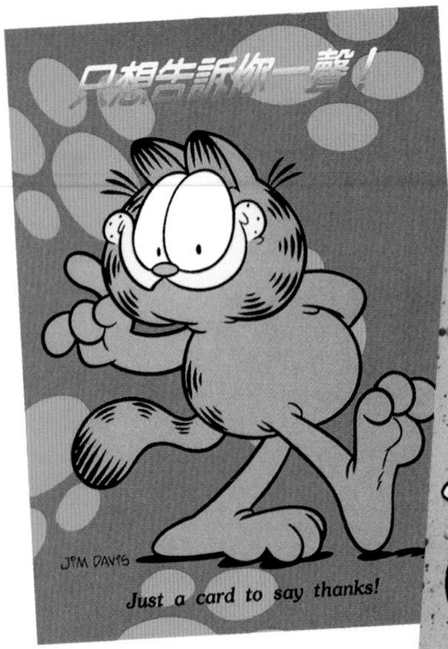
只想告訴你一聲!
JIM DAVIS
Just a card to say thanks!

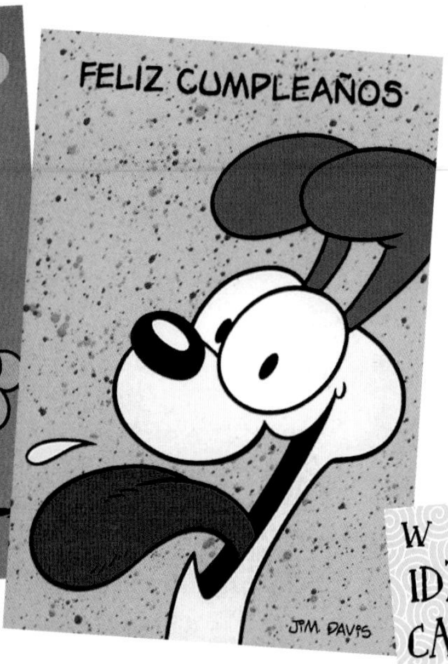
FELIZ CUMPLEAÑOS
JIM DAVIS

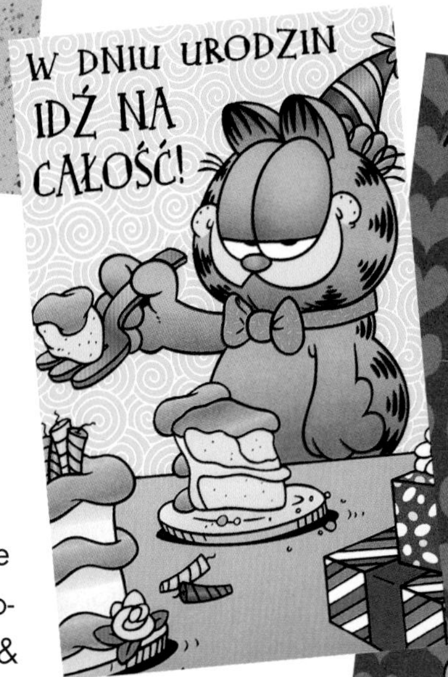
W DNIU URODZIN
IDŹ NA CAŁOŚĆ!

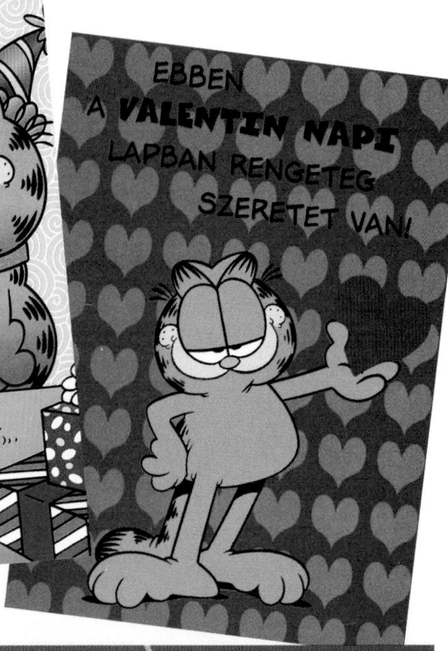
EBBEN A VALENTIN NAPI LAPBAN RENGETEG SZERETET VAN!

Se Habla Garfield?

In any language, Garfield means "fun." His greeting cards are created in several languages and are sold in countries as diverse as Mexico and China.

Historical Figures

Some of the world's most important people are given the Garfield treatment in this promotional figurine set created by Procter & Gamble for the Asian market.

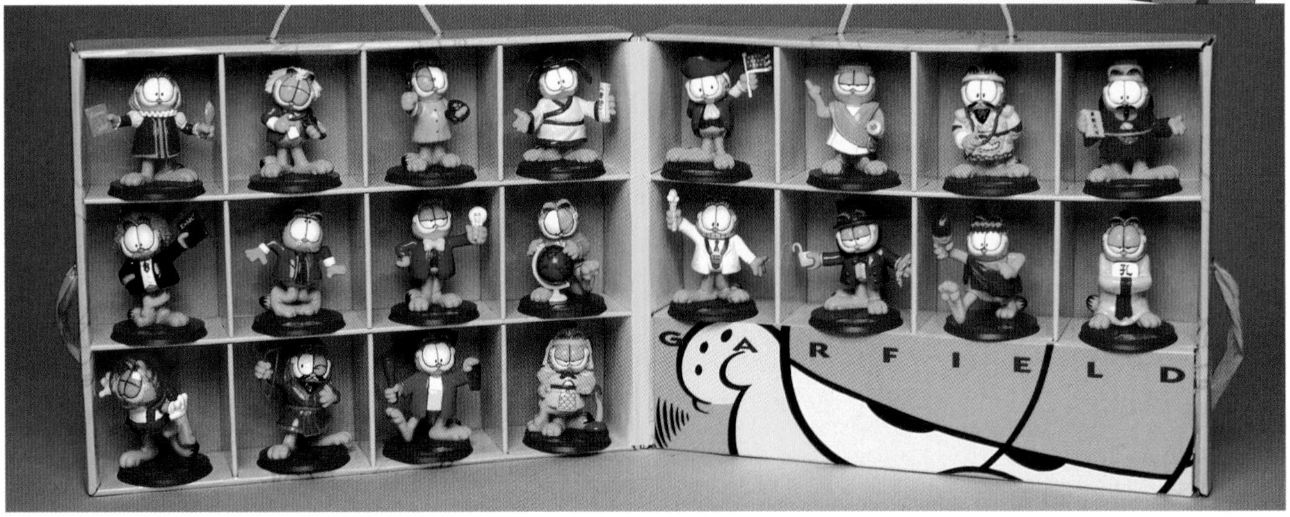
GARFIELD

Right: Garfield is depicted as Confucius, Genghis Khan, William Shakespeare, Isaac Newton, George Washington, Abraham Lincoln, Albert Einstein, and other historical characters.

Say What?

Because the comic strip is translated into so many different languages, Jim avoids topical humor and colloquialisms and sticks to humor about eating and sleeping—something familiar to any person in any culture.

"The strip is hard to translate into Japanese. Garfield says, 'I hate mornings,' and the translation is, 'It is quite early, and I wish it weren't so.' Apparently, one-liners aren't done in Japan. The strip also looks very strange in Arabic. It's backwards, with the third panel appearing first and the first panel appearing last."

—Jim Davis

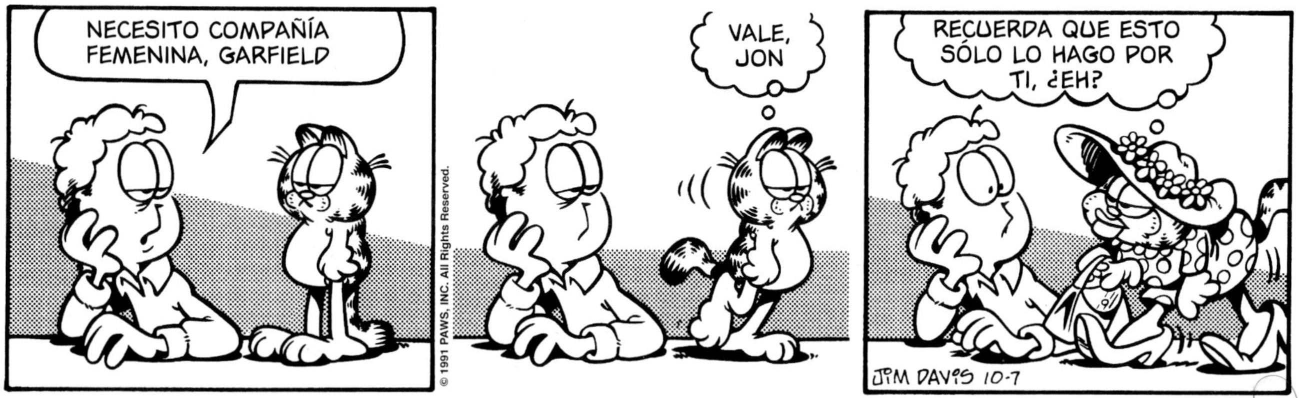
NECESITO COMPAÑÍA FEMENINA, GARFIELD
VALE, JON
RECUERDA QUE ESTO SÓLO LO HAGO POR TI, ¿EH?
JIM DAVIS 10-7
© 1991 PAWS, INC. All Rights Reserved.

"Garfield, I need some female companionship." "Okay, Jon." "You realize I'd only do this for you."

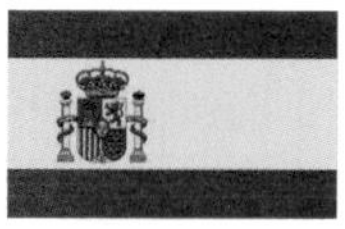

SPAIN

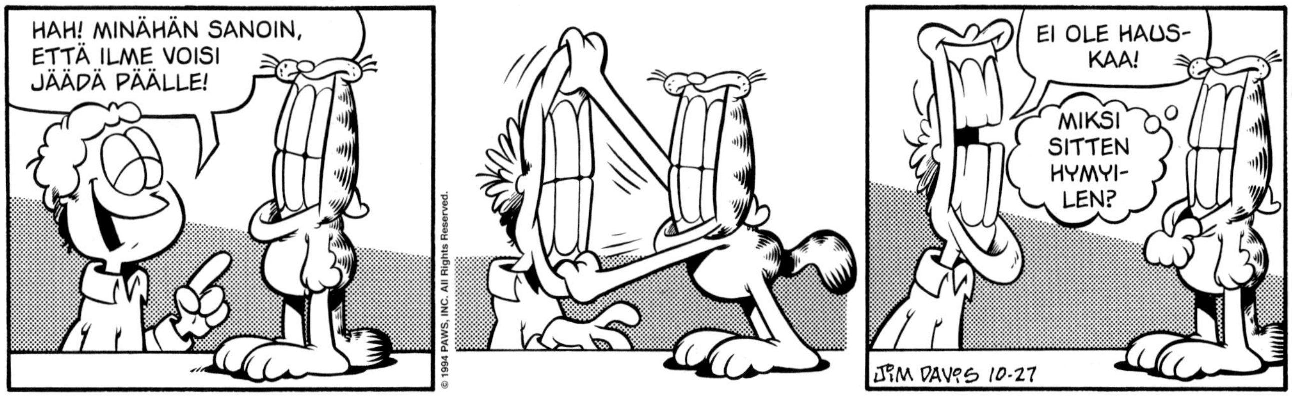
HAH! MINÄHÄN SANOIN, ETTÄ ILME VOISI JÄÄDÄ PÄÄLLE!
EI OLE HAUSKAA!
MIKSI SITTEN HYMYILEN?
JIM DAVIS 10-27
© 1994 PAWS, INC. All Rights Reserved.

"Ha! Ha! I told you if you made a face, it would stick!" "That's not funny!" "Then why am I smiling?"

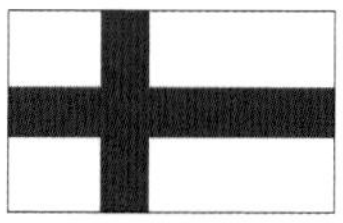

FINLAND

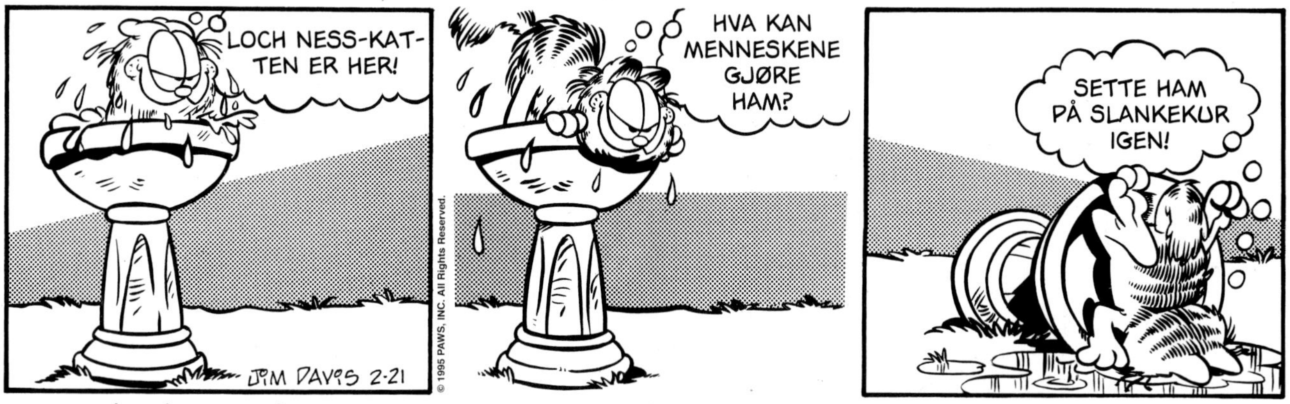
LOCH NESS-KATTEN ER HER!
HVA KAN MENNESKENE GJØRE HAM?
SETTE HAM PÅ SLANKEKUR IGEN!
JIM DAVIS 2-21
© 1995 PAWS, INC. All Rights Reserved.

"The Loch Ness cat surfaces." "He surveys his territory." "And spies a diet on the horizon."

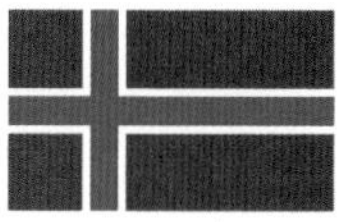

NORWAY

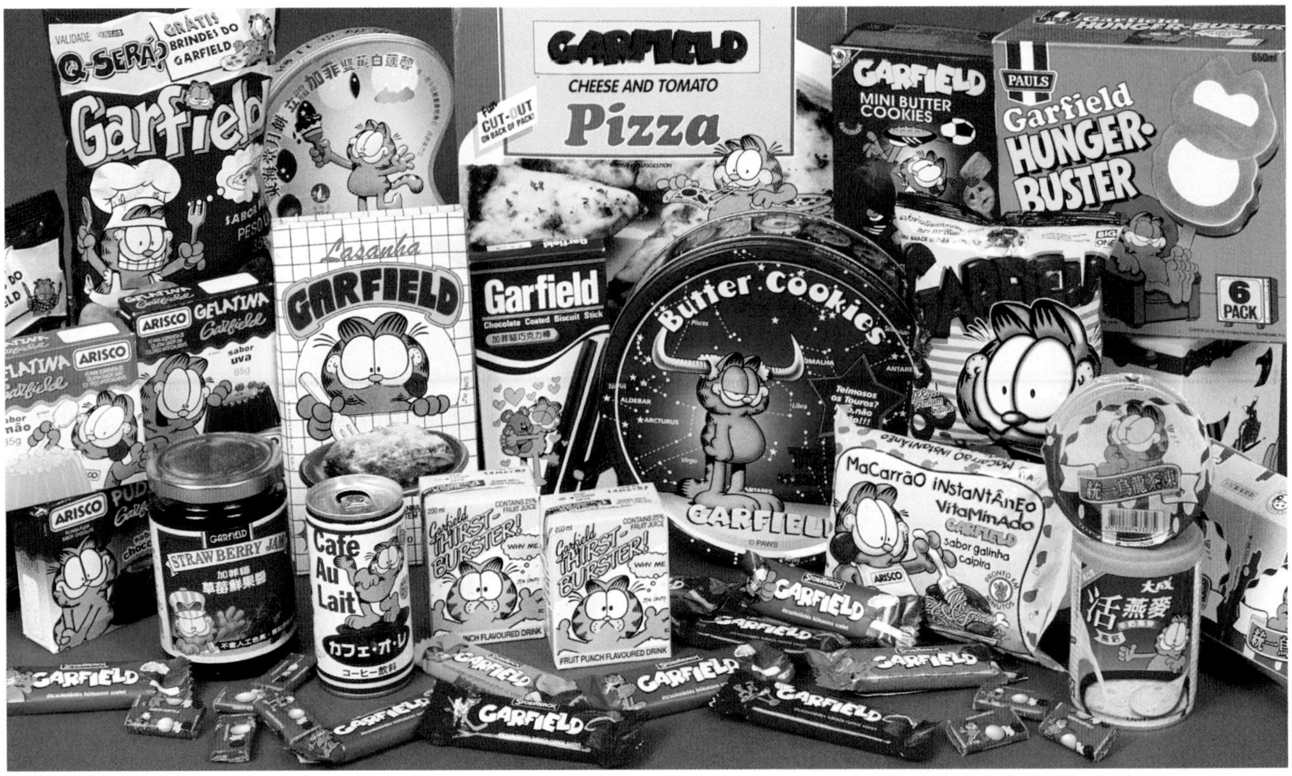
Garfield
CHEESE AND TOMATO
Pizza
CUT-OUT ON BACK OF PACK!
MINI BUTTER COOKIES
PAULS
Garfield HUNGER-BUSTER
Q-SERÁ?
GRÁTIS BRINDES DO GARFIELD
Lasanha
Garfield
Chocolate Coated Biscuit Stick
Butter Cookies
6 PACK
ARISCO
GELATINA
STRAWBERRY JAM
Café Au Lait
カフェ・オ・レ
Garfield THIRST-BURSTER!
MaCarrão INStaNtÂNEo VitaMiNado
Sabor galinha caipira

Right: Garfield taste treats from around the world.

Hungry for Fun

International fans get a steady diet of Garfield snacks. You can indulge in pasta from Brazil, cookies from Portugal, candy bars from Hungary, strawberry jam from Taiwan, and fruit punch from Australia. There's even café au lait from (of all places) Japan!

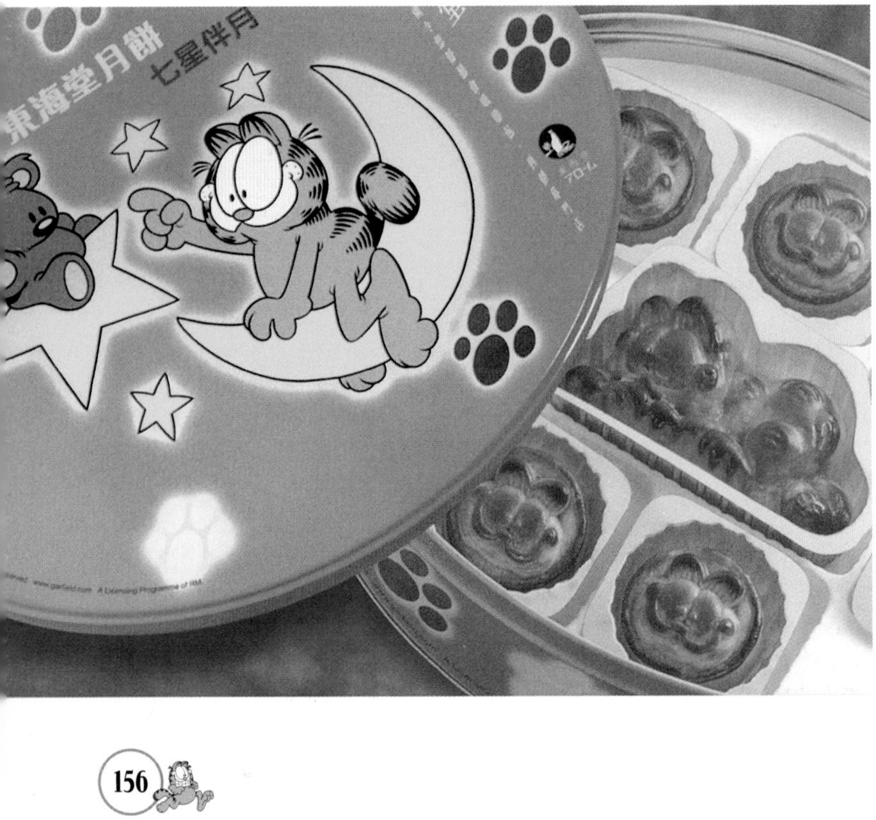
東海堂月餅
七星伴月

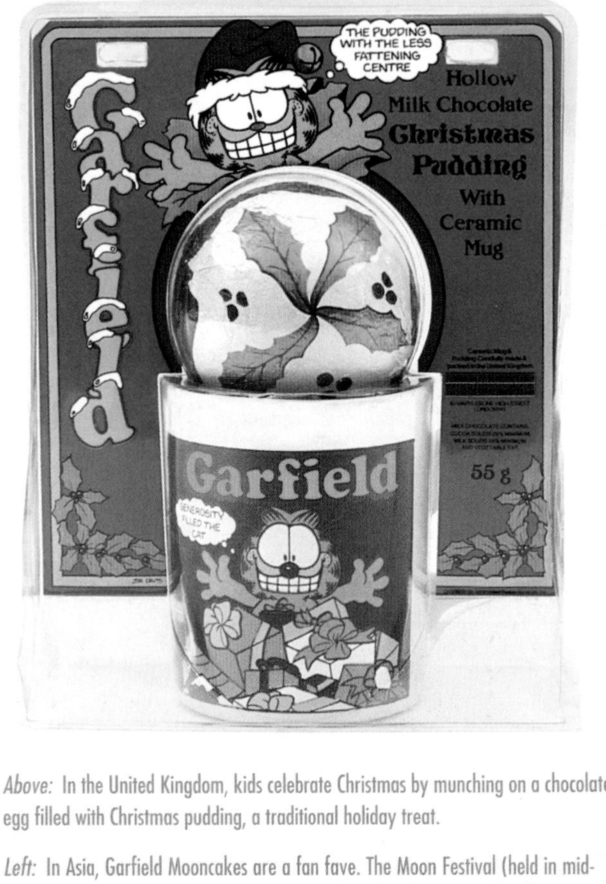
THE PUDDING WITH THE LESS FATTENING CENTRE
Hollow Milk Chocolate Christmas Pudding With Ceramic Mug
Garfield
55 g
GENEROSITY FILLED THE CAT

Above: In the United Kingdom, kids celebrate Christmas by munching on a chocolate egg filled with Christmas pudding, a traditional holiday treat.

Left: In Asia, Garfield Mooncakes are a fan fave. The Moon Festival (held in mid-autumn) is part of a long-standing tradition where the Chinese people offer special round cakes to the mystical moon goddess during the full moon in the eighth month of the Chinese lunar calendar. Usually, thirteen mooncakes are stacked in offering. As the cakes are offered, everyone makes a wish.

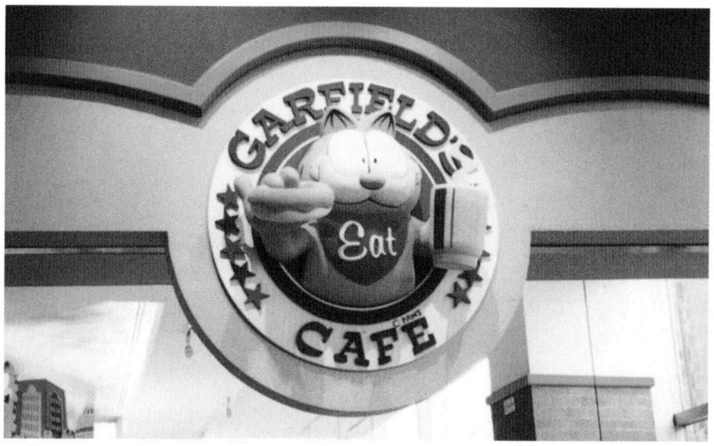
GARFIELD'S
Eat
CAFE

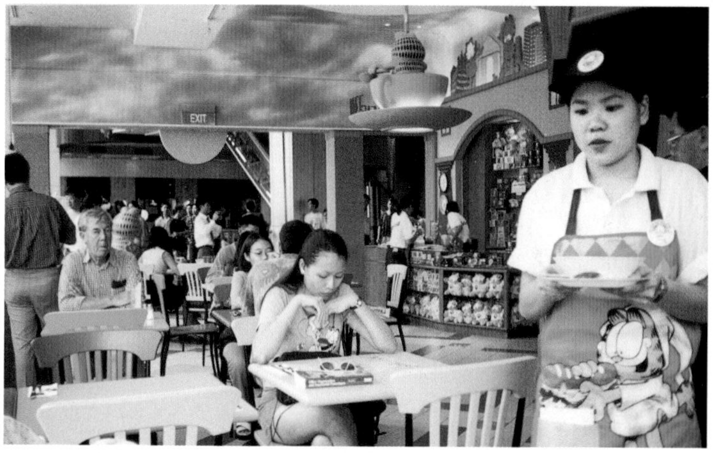

CAT CUISINE

Where would you expect to find Garfield's Café—a fine eatery that specializes in Italian cooking? If you guessed Malaysia, you win a free lunch! Yes, believe it or not, Singapore, Malaysia, is home to Garfield's Italian-themed eatery. Hungry fans at Garfield's Café feast on pizza, spaghetti, sandwiches, and, of course, lasagna.

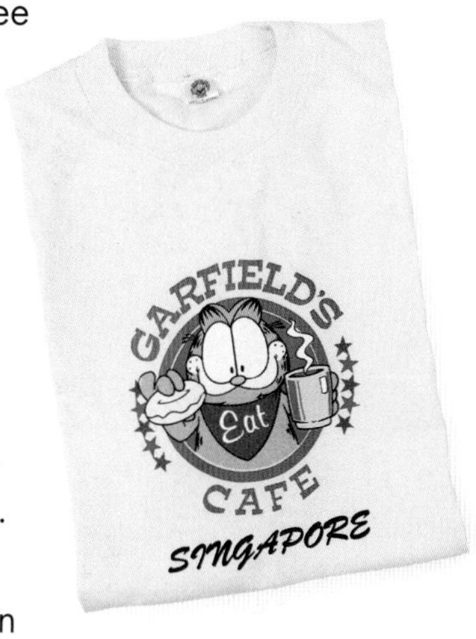
GARFIELD'S
Eat
CAFE
SINGAPORE

Not to be outdone, a German pizza chain *(below)* invited Jim Davis himself to help serve up a Garfield pie in 1998. The evening was a great success. Fans got to meet and eat with Garfield's creator, and Jim made a bundle in tips.

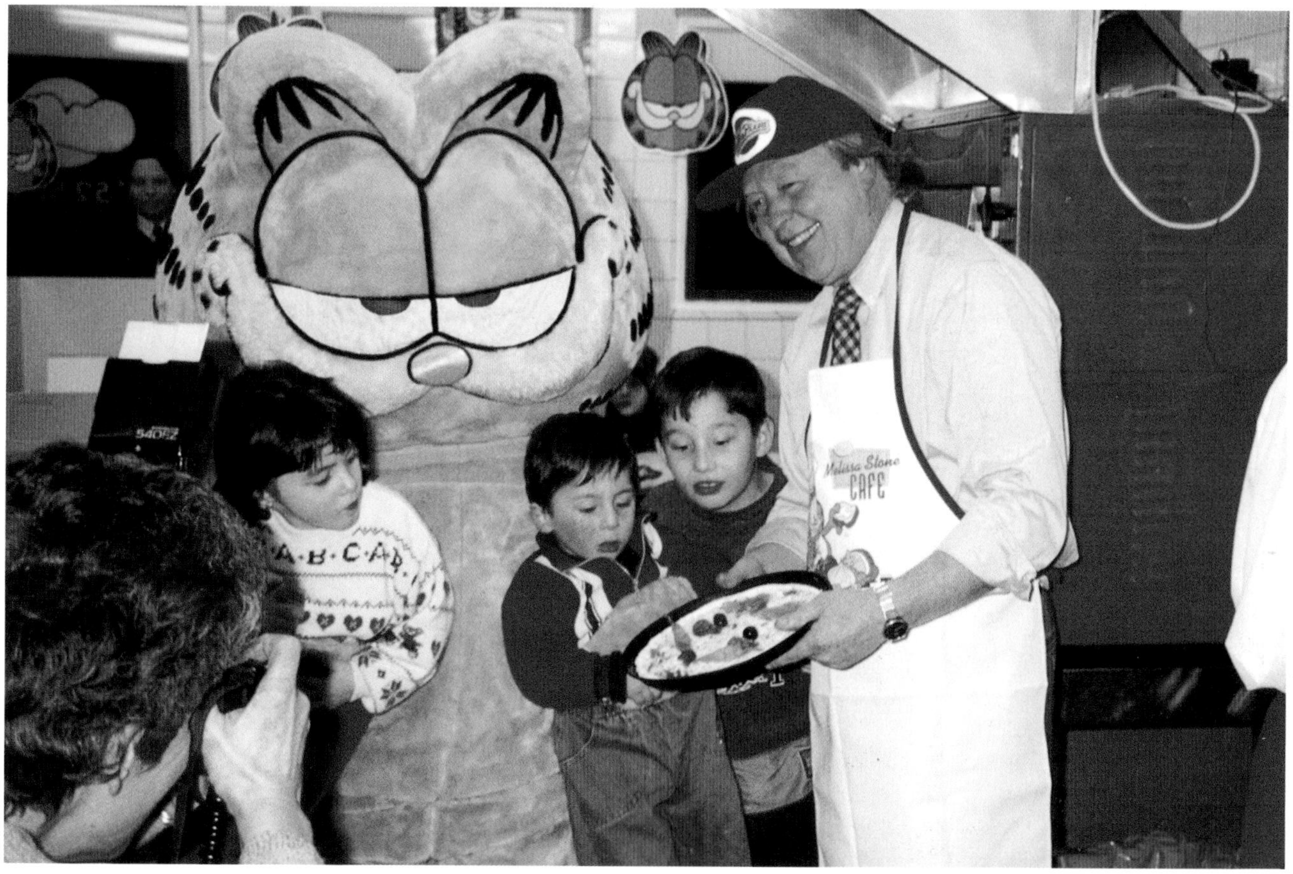

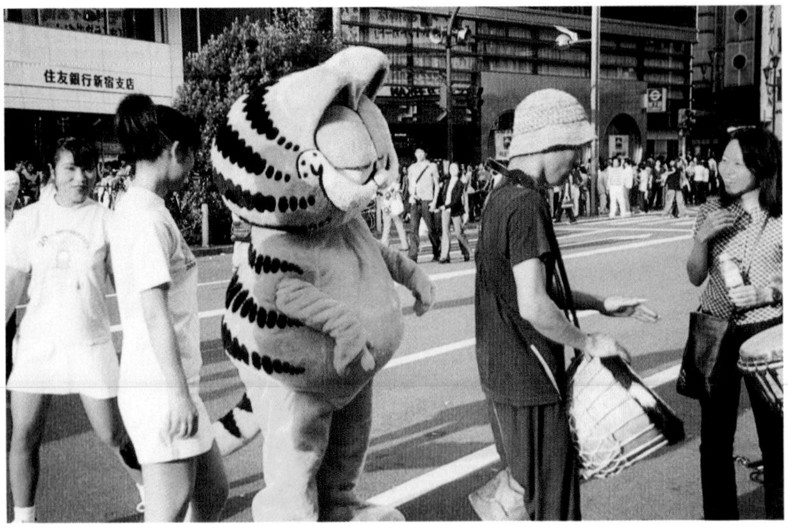

Above: Takin' it to the streets!

Far right: Advertising at the Sudnade center, 1998.

Tokyo Tabby

The cat struts his stuff at a special twentieth-anniversary celebration in Japan.

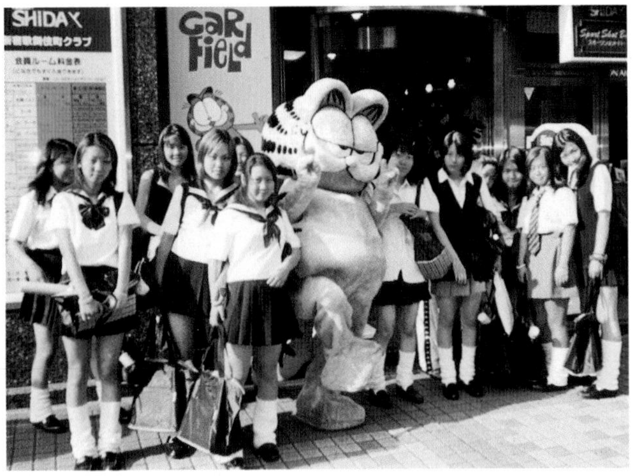
SHIDAX

Schoolgirl Crush

Garfield makes the teen scene during a late-1990s karaoke promotion in Tokyo.

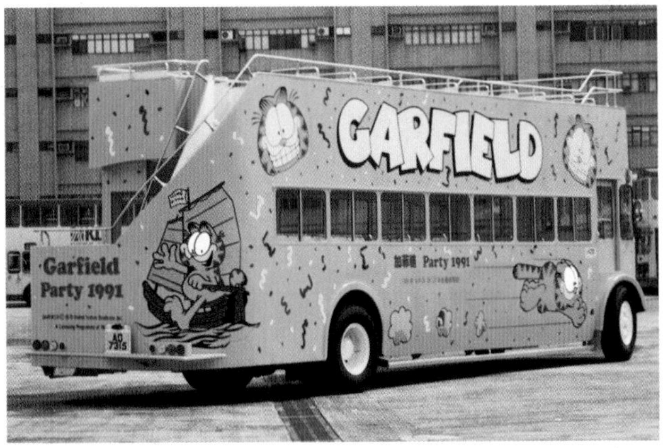
GARFIELD
Garfield Party 1991

Magic Bus

The Garfield Party Bus rolls through Asia in 1991.

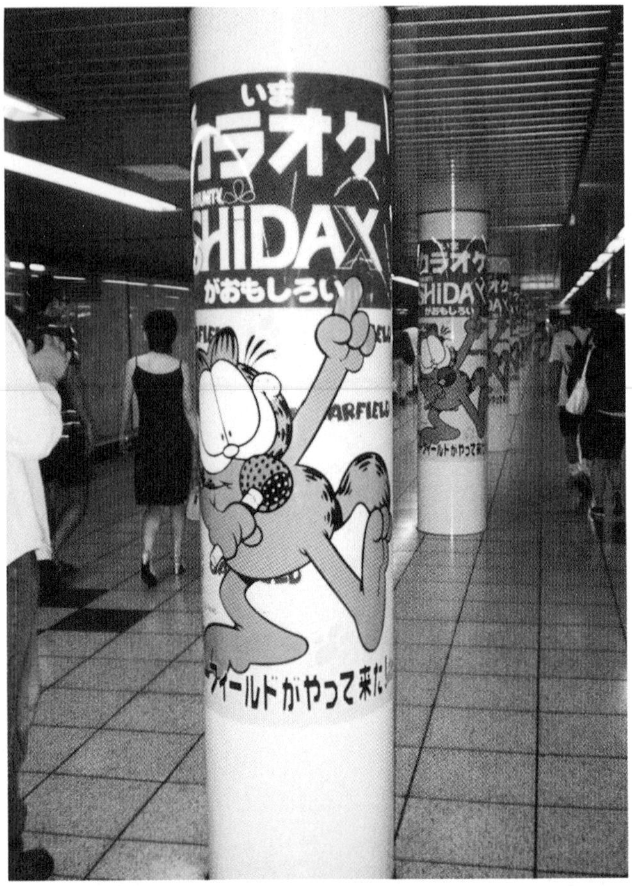
カラオケ
SHIDAX
がおもしろい

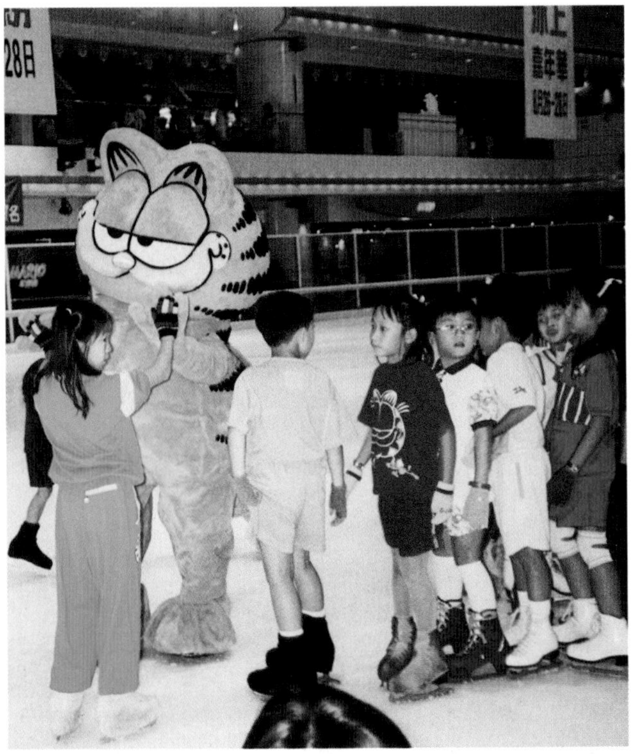

Ice, Ice Baby!

The cool cat skates with young fans in the *Garfield on Ice* show in Hong Kong, 1995.

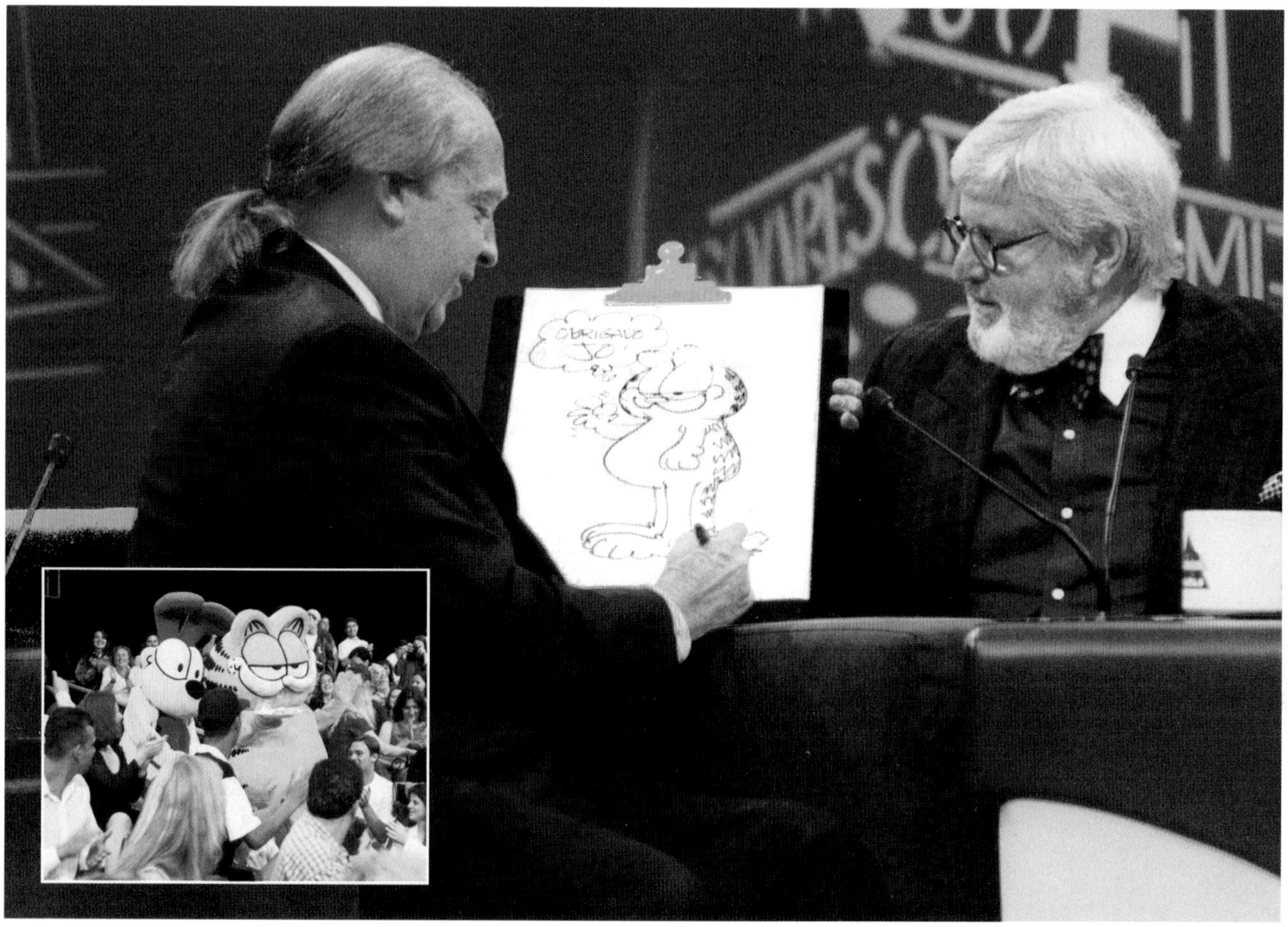

Left: Jim does a sketch for TV host Jo Soares.

Inset: Garfield and Odie party hardy with the studio audience.

As Seen on TV

Jim Davis, Garfield, and Odie burn up the airwaves on Brazilian television in this 1997 appearance.

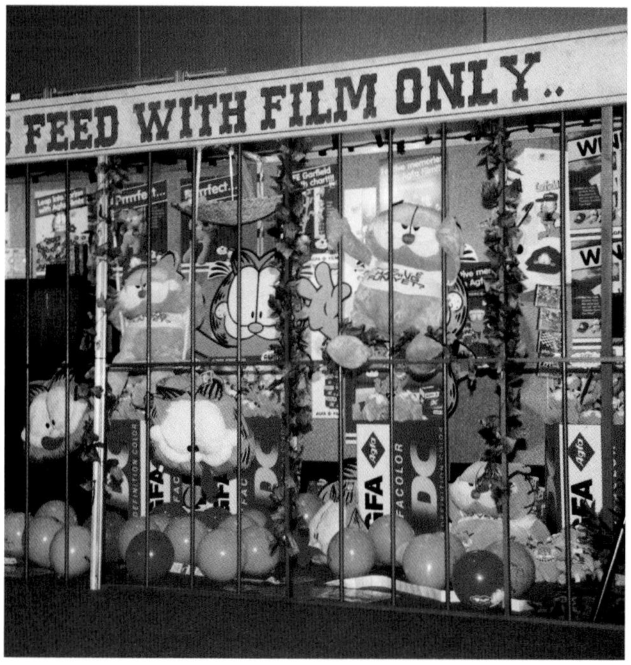
FEED WITH FILM ONLY..

Thunder Down Under

An Agfa film promotion in Australia gets wild.

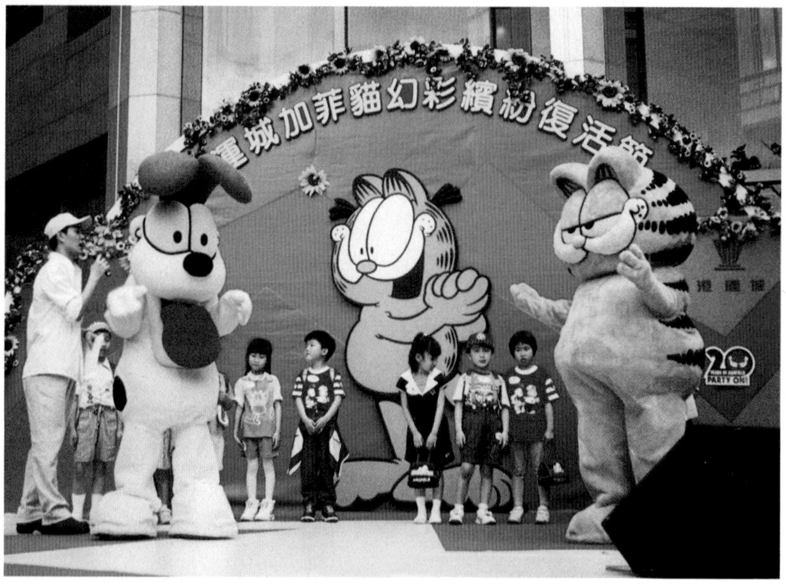

Good Show!

Garfield and Odie bring fans onstage during a 1998 performance at Hong Kong's City Plaza Shopping Mall.

COUNTERFEIT CAT

They say imitation is the sincerest form of flattery, but these pirated products are an insult. Unauthorized knockoffs are a big problem in the international market and keep the Paws legal eagles very busy.

JEEPERS CREEPERS
Where'd he get those goofy peepers?
Plastic mug from Turkey.

BARF BAG
This bootleg backpack from Taiwan is
sickeningly substandard.

WHAZZUUUUP?
Bootleg plush from Turkey. Check out that tongue!

Putting his foot down

An elephant stomps counterfeit Garfield stuffed cats outside the Thai police's economic crime division office in Bangkok yesterday. Thailand is a center for many counterfeit and bootleg products, and the police routinely hold public displays to destroy confiscated items.

AP

CAT ON THE FLYING TRAPEZE
Knockoff plush from India.

Above: Associated Press photo, December 2001.

HALL OF SHAME
This hand puppet makes Garfield look like a Muppet
gone bad. Country of origin unknown.

PHONE SCAM
Telephone from China. Should we call our lawyers?

DISFIGURED FIGURINE
Unauthorized porcelain figure from
Venezuela, lovingly hand painted.

CHAPTER FOURTEEN

Fat Cat Fanatics

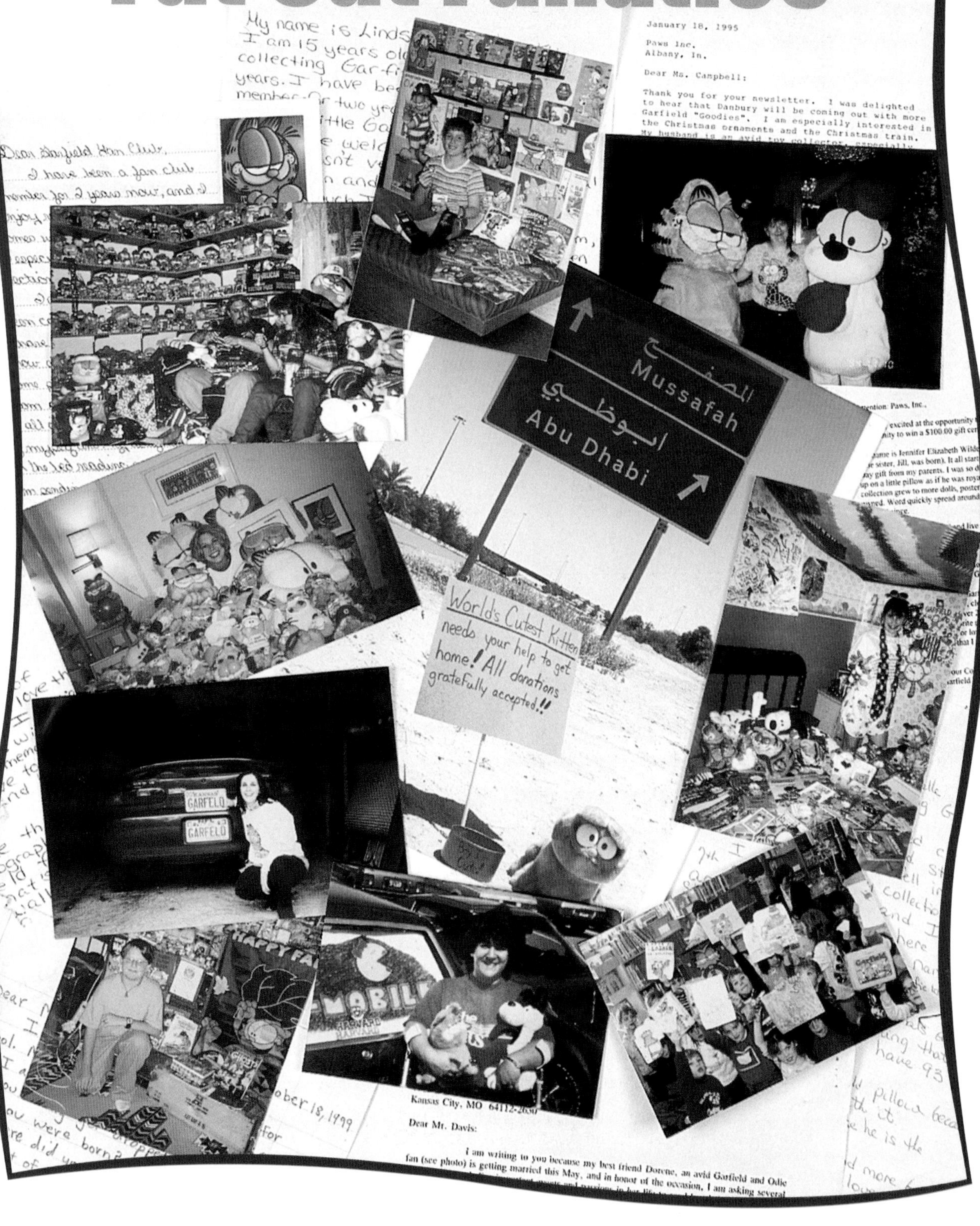
January 18, 1995
Paws Inc.
Dear Ms. Campbell:
Mussafah
Abu Dhabi
World's Cutest Kitten needs your help to get home! All donations gratefully accepted!!
GARFELD
Kansas City, MO
Dear Mr. Davis:

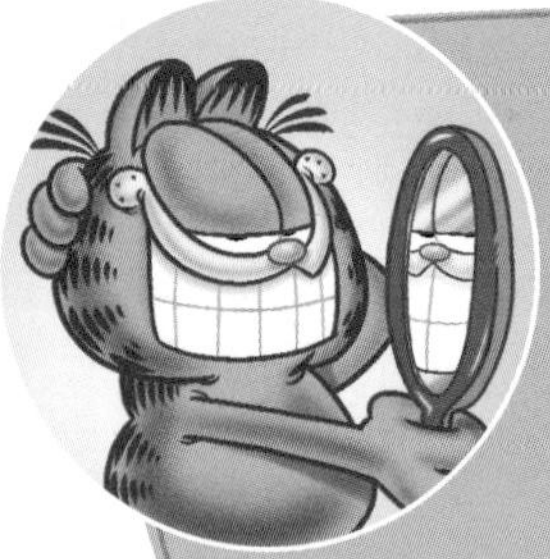

Sure, everyone loves Garfield . . . but some people really *love* Garfield. It is to these fiercely loyal and uncommonly dedicated fans that we pay tribute.

Below: Robert and Gretchen Gipson.

Far right: Garfield fan and organizer extraordinaire Tony Capuano Jr.

Gaga Over Garfield

Robert and Gretchen Gipson of Pennsylvania are Garfield uberfans—amassing a super collection of more than ten thousand items, publishing a collectibles guide, and arranging special events for fellow collectors.

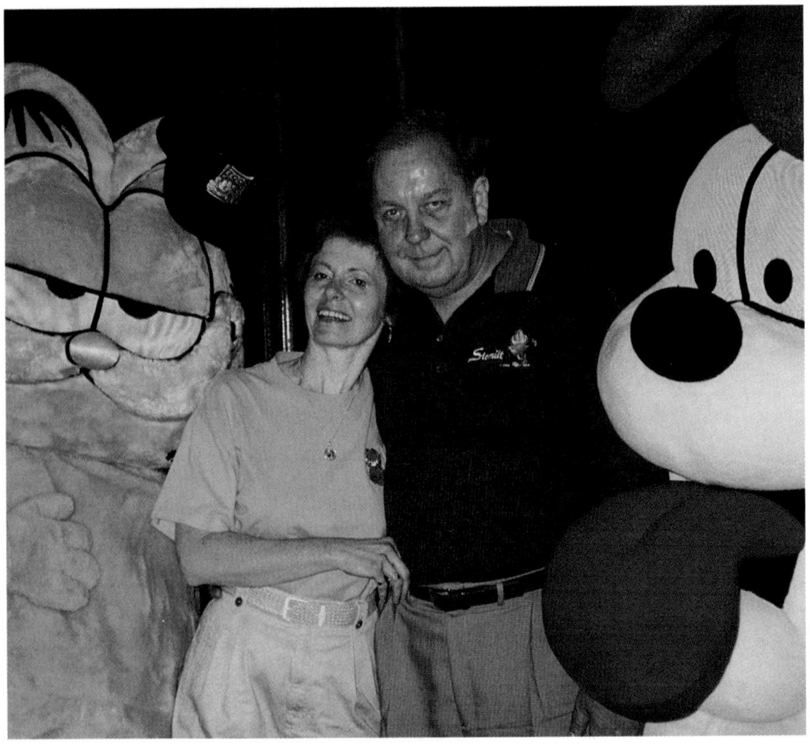

Collectors' Convention

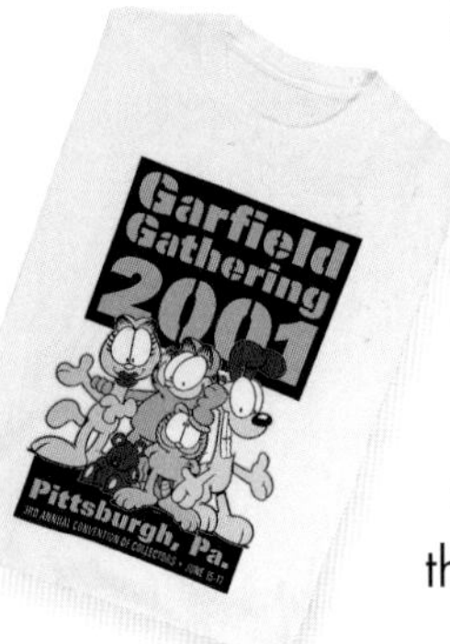
Garfield Gathering 2001
Pittsburgh, Pa.

Fans held informal get-togethers for years, but it wasn't until 1999 that the Garfield Gathering became an official annual event. Organized by the Gipsons and fan Tony Capuano Jr., these shows are indeed big fat hairy deals, and each year fans come from all over the country to buy and sell Garfield stuff. The first Garfield Gathering was convened from August 27 to 29 in Denver, Pennsylvania. Since then, it's been held in such cities as St. Louis, Pittsburgh, and Muncie, Indiana (Garfield's hometown!).

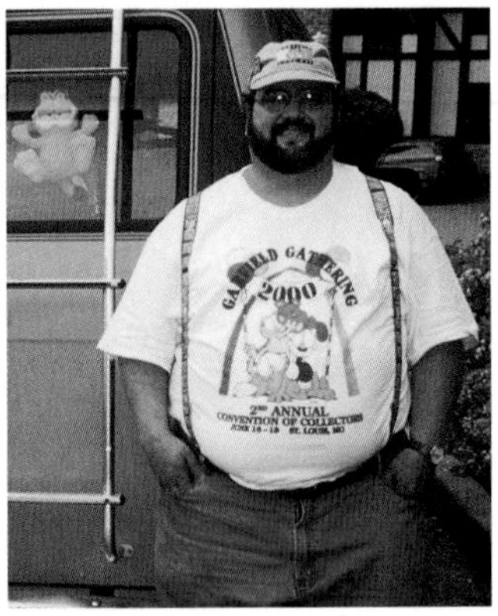

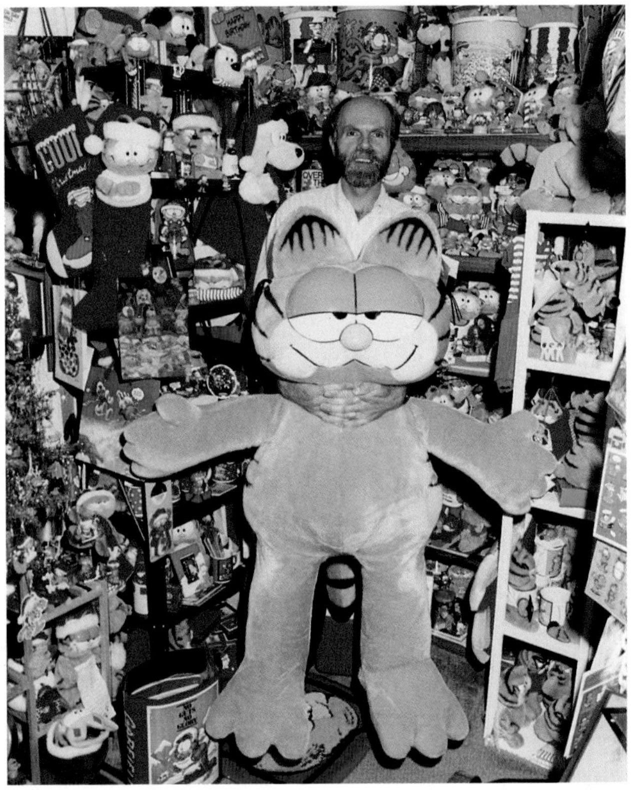

Fan Man

Indiana's Gary Skinner shows he's behind Garfield all the way. Skinner has acquired more than eight thousand Garfield items since the early 1980s.

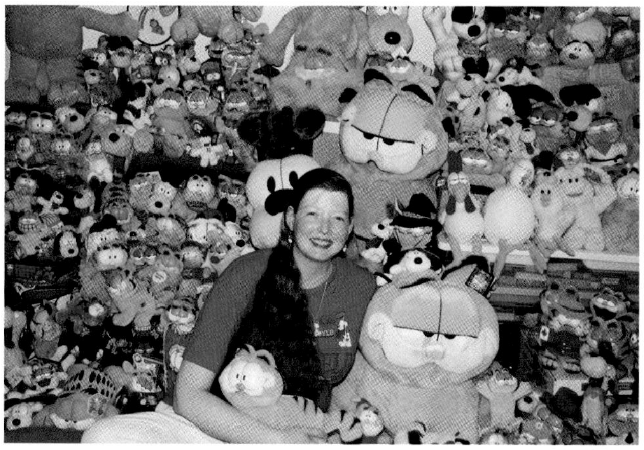

Crazy for the Cat

Sheila Dawn Gebauer of Canada: "It doesn't matter what it is. If Garfield's on it, I buy it."

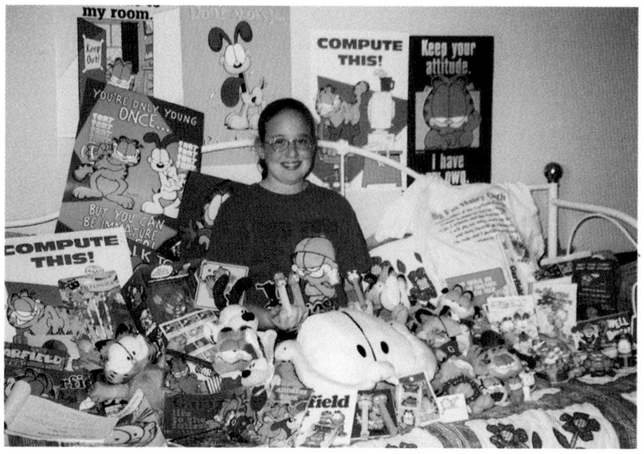
my room.
COMPUTE THIS!
Keep your attitude.
YOU'RE ONLY YOUNG ONCE
COMPUTE THIS!

Room with a Mew

Ohio fan Michelle Steingesser adds a touch of sass to her décor.

"This barely scratches the surface. There are millions of Garfield fans all over the world with their own cool collections. I'd like to thank everyone for all the years of support. As Garfield would say—consider yourself appreciated!"

—Jim Davis

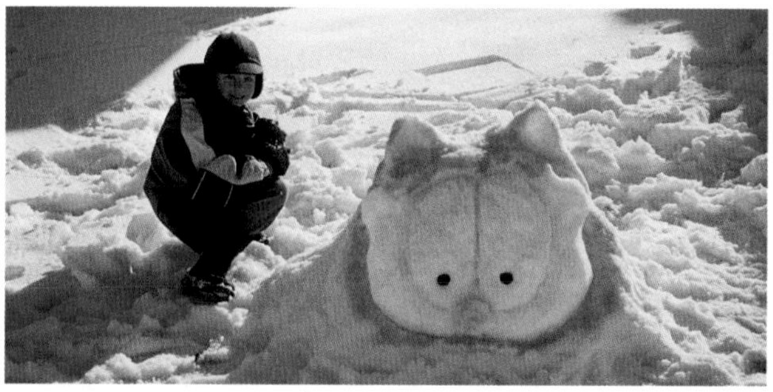

Winter Wondercat

David Nickel of Indiana chills out with his Garfield snow sculpture.

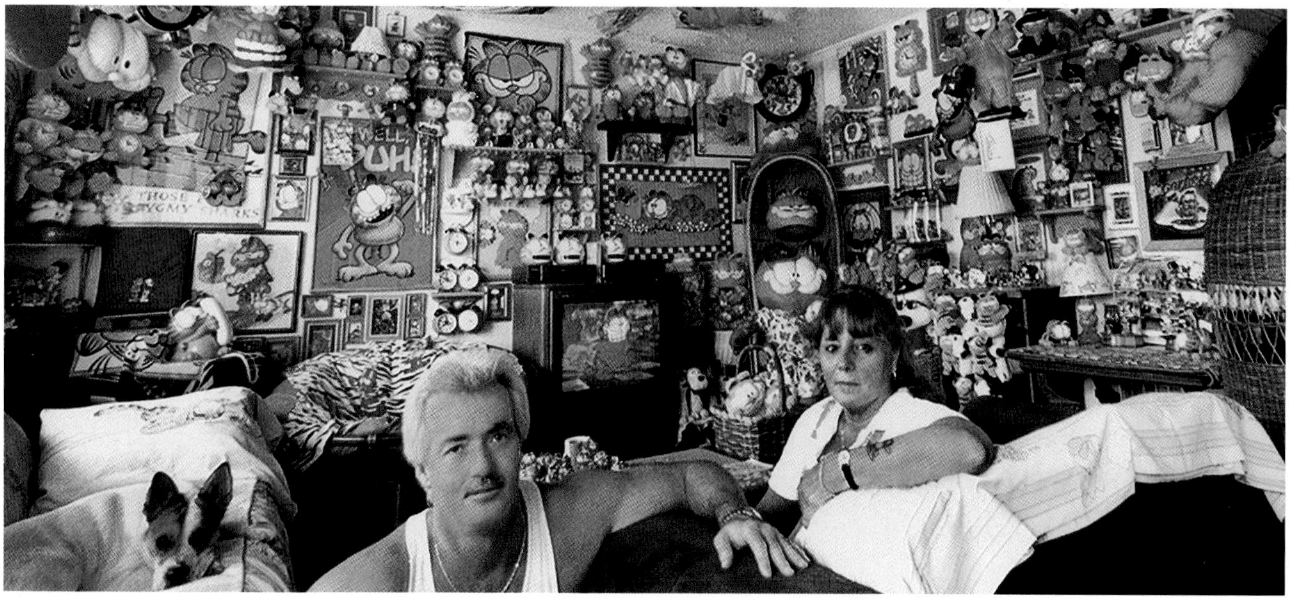

Fat Cat Funhouse

California collectors Mike Drysdale and Gayle Brennen made it into the 2000 edition of the *Guinness Book of World Records* with their awesome assortment of Garfield goodies.

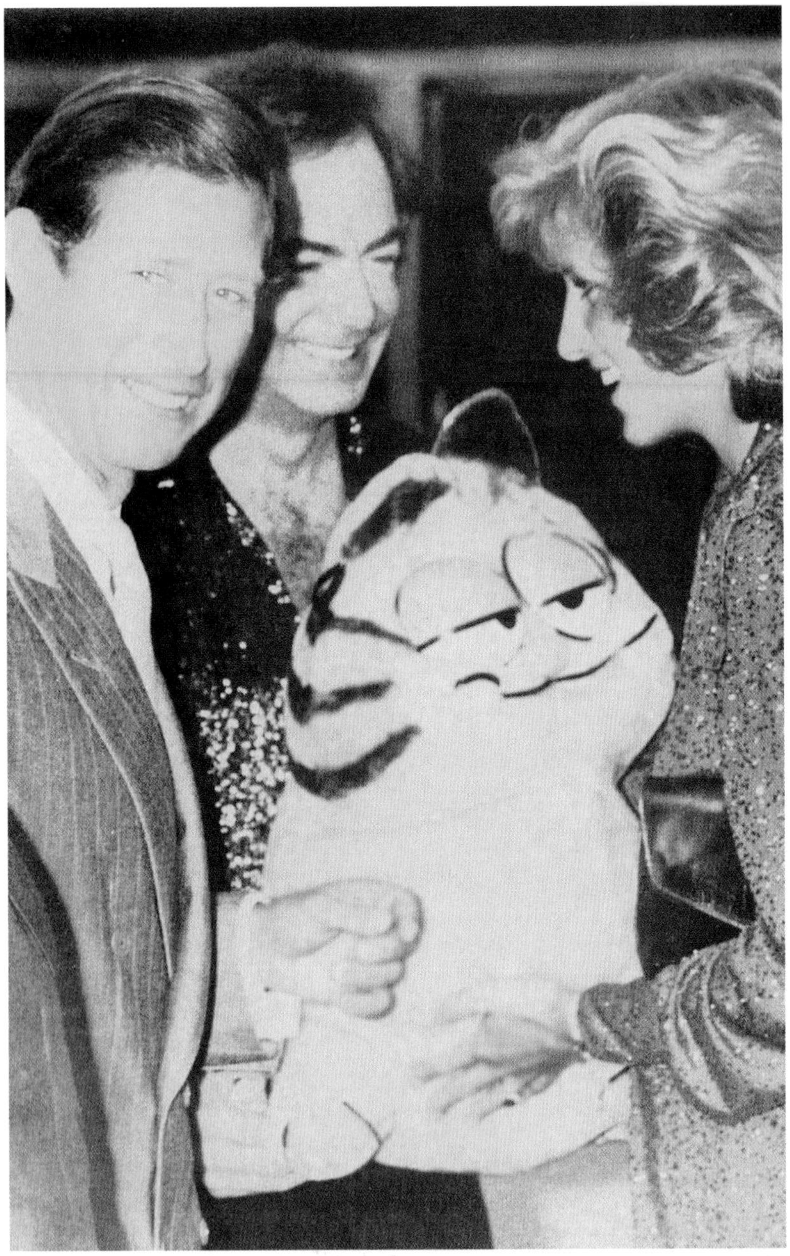

Photo: Press Association

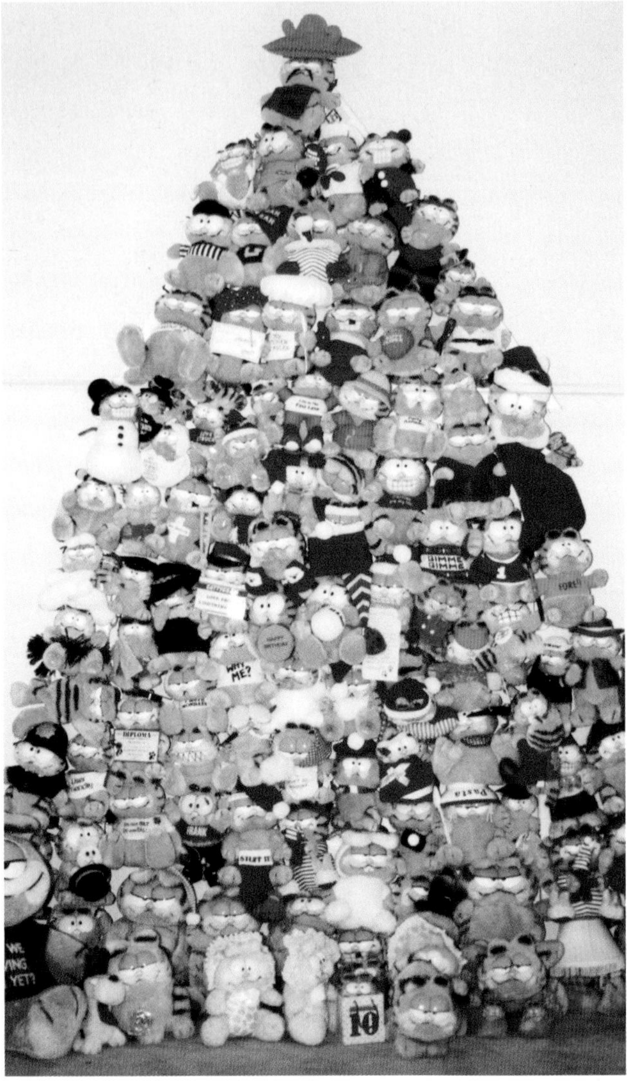

Meowy Christmas!
Florida fan John Vocell created this unique Christmas "tree" from more than a hundred Garfield plush dolls.

Royal Treatment
Pop crooner Neil Diamond delivers a Garfield plush to Princess Di backstage at a 1984 benefit concert. Diana's then-husband Prince Charles arranged the meeting as part of her twenty-third birthday celebration (photo from *People* magazine, July 23, 1984).

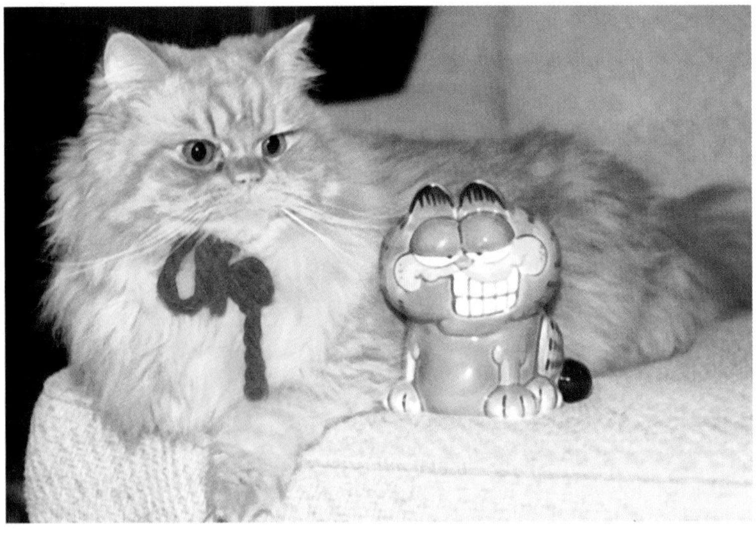

Getting Catty
An unidentified feline fan checks out the competition.

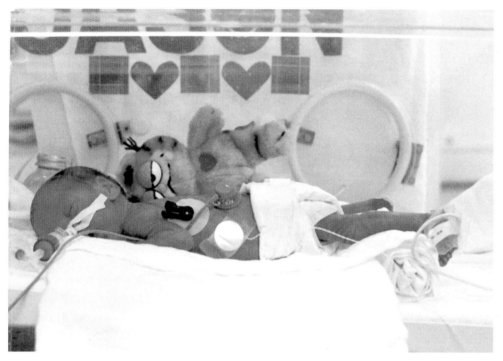

Security Kitty
Garfield watches over one of his itty bitty fans in this 1985 snapshot.

Painting for Peanuts
With brush in trunk, Ivory the elephant created this "portrait" of Garfield at a special Indianapolis Zoo festival in 1986.

Leader of the Pack
Garfield's been a part of Scouting since 1998. Like every Cub Scout, he's loyal, true, and loves to eat s'mores. Pictured here are fans from Den 1, Pack 11 in Muncie, Indiana.

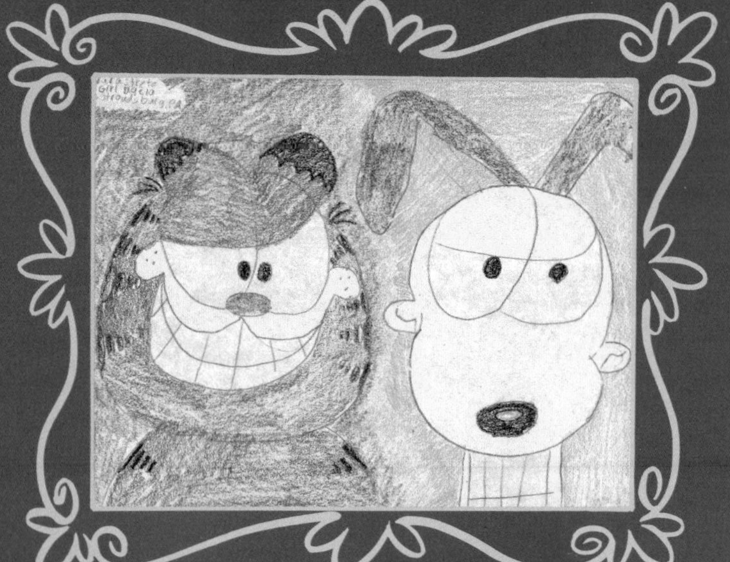

FAN TASTIC ART

Kids draw the darndest things! We reached into our mailbags and selected these mini-masterpieces for your viewing pleasure.

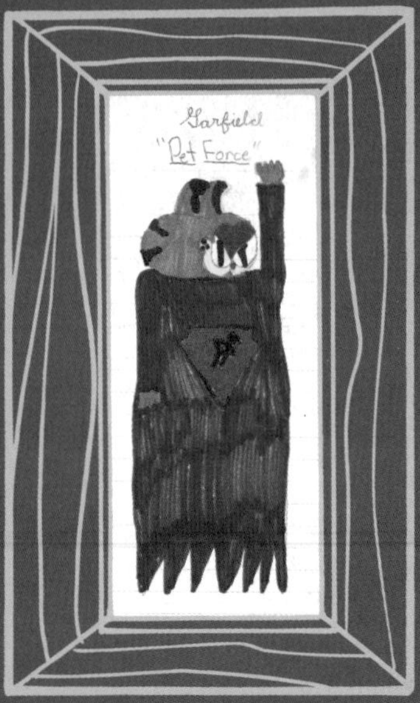
Garfield
"Pet Force"

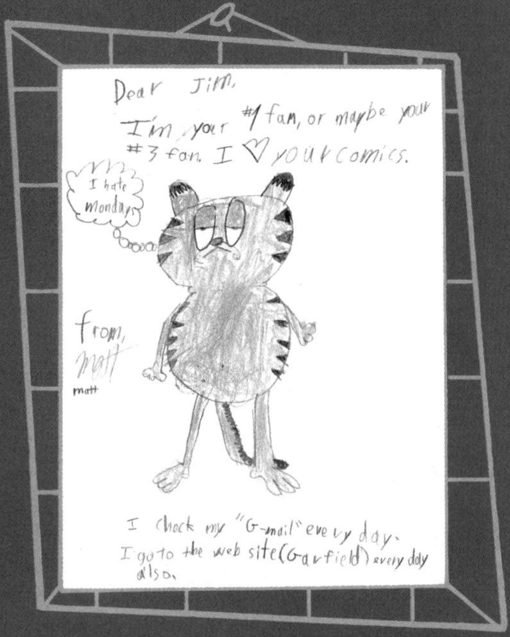
Dear Jim,
I'm your #1 fan, or maybe your #3 fan. I ♥ your comics.
I hate mondays
From, Matt
matt
I check my "G-mail" every day.
I go to the web site (Garfield) every day also.

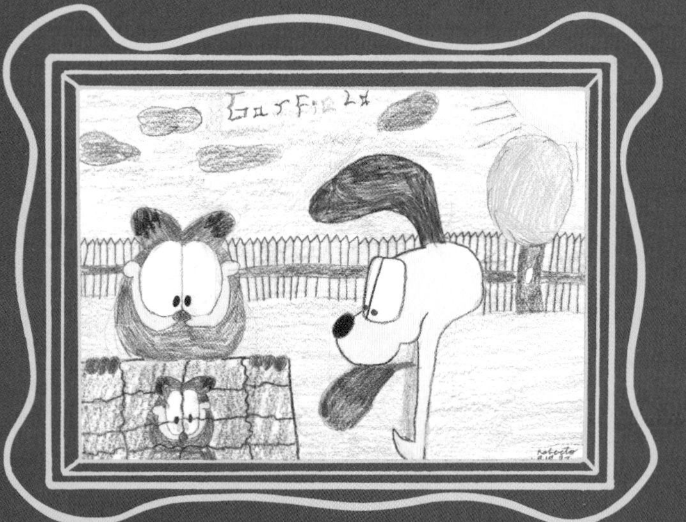
GARFIELD

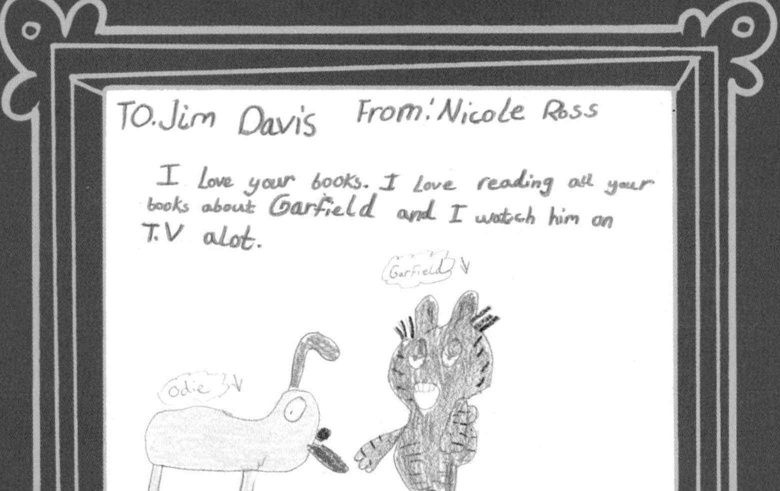
TO. Jim Davis From: Nicole Ross
I love your books. I love reading all your books about Garfield and I watch him on T.V alot.
Garfield
odie

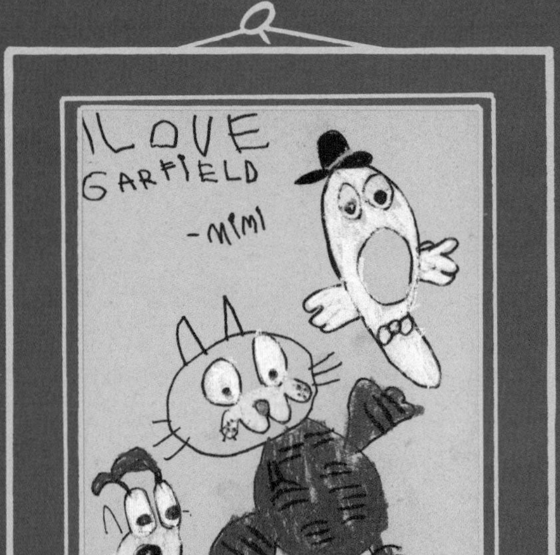
I LOVE GARFIELD
-mimi

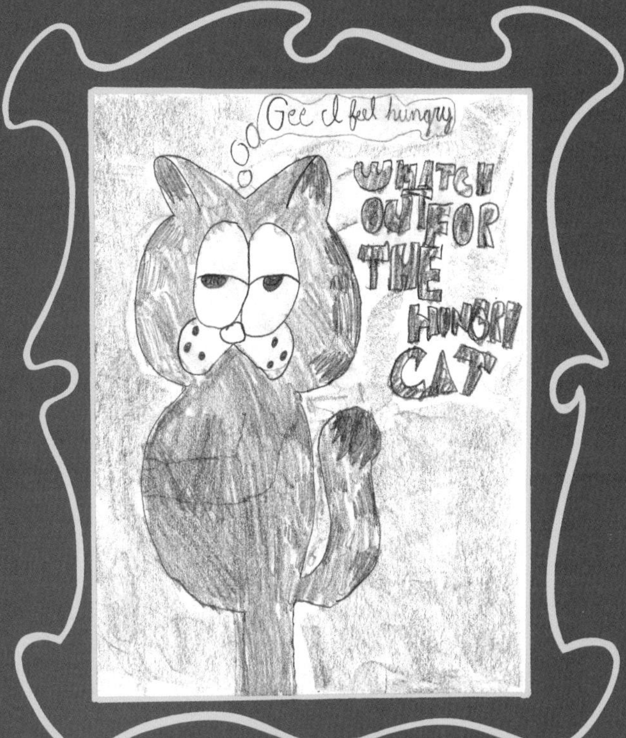
Gee I feel hungry
WHATCH OUT FOR THE HUNGRY CAT

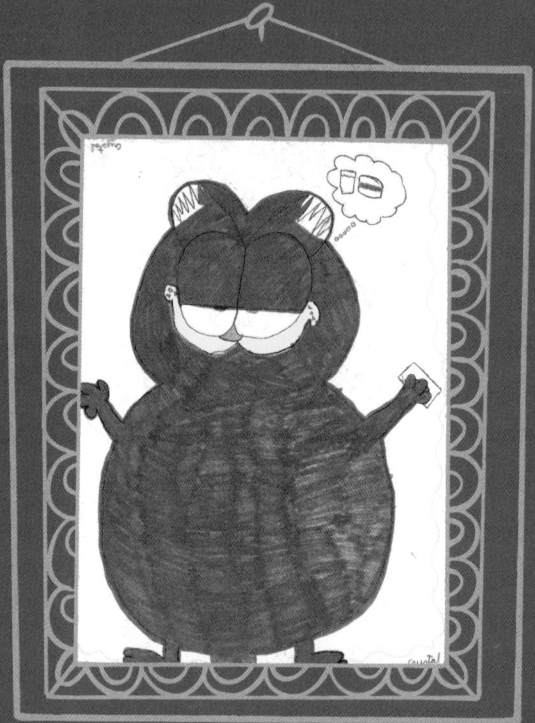

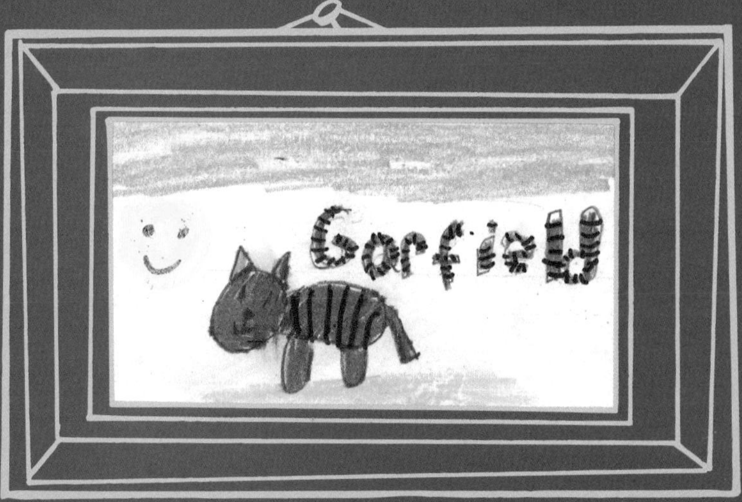
Garfield

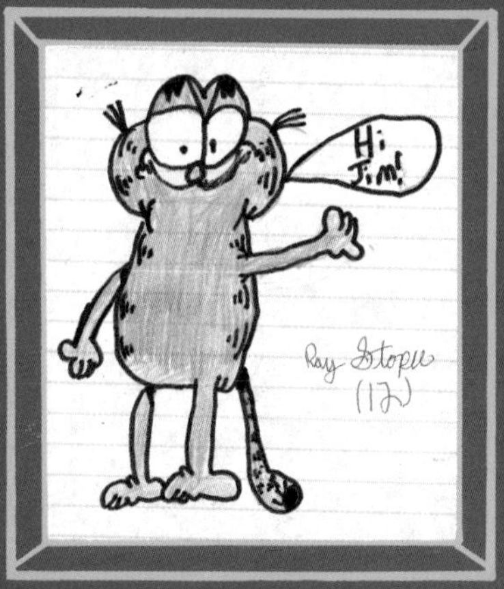
Hi Jim!

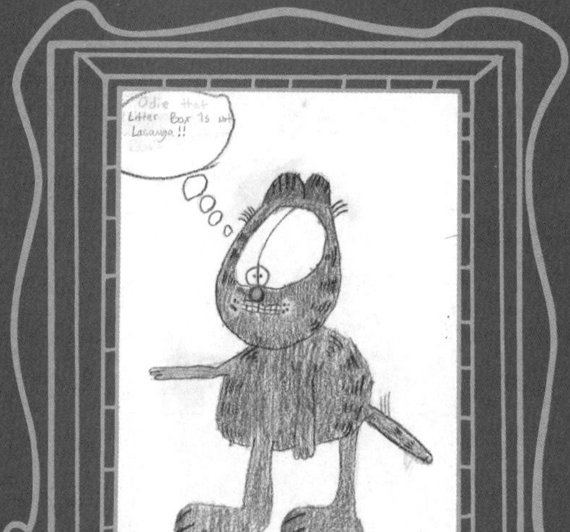
Odie that Litter Box Is not Lasanga!!

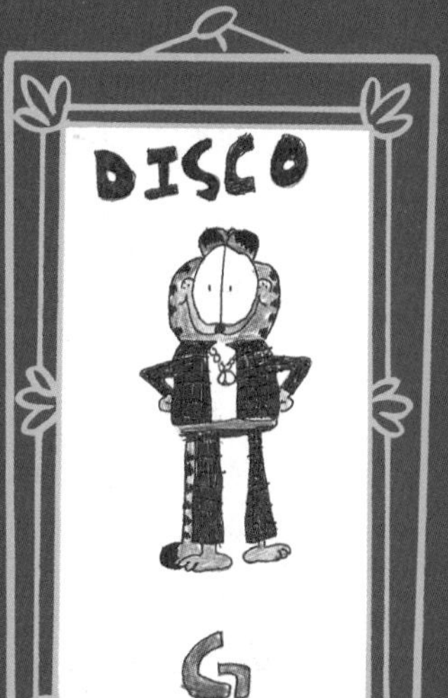
DISCO
G

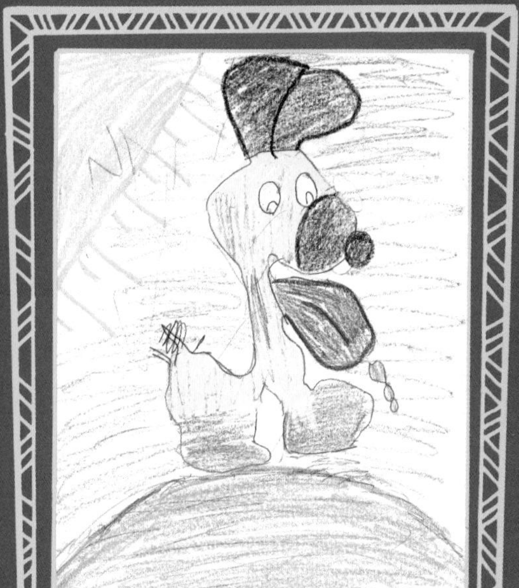

Collectible Kitty

Some Garfield collectors specialize in plush; others buy only ceramic figurines; but most just have a huge appetite for anything Garfield. To help feed this need, several independent collectors' guides have been published, and online auction sites have tons of Garfield items listed for sale.

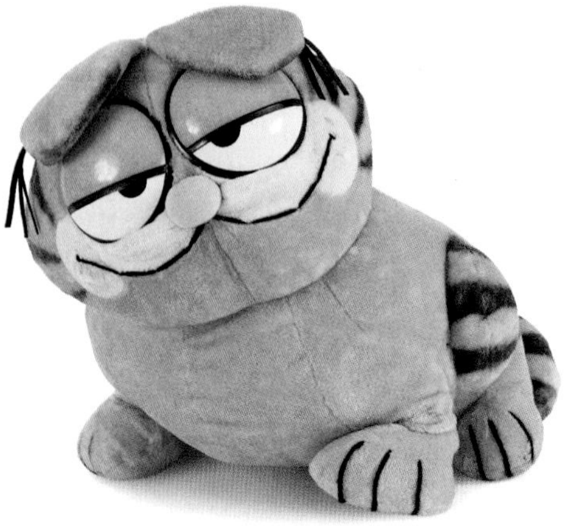

Above: One of the first large-size plush dolls from Dakin, this tubby tabby is over 30" tall.

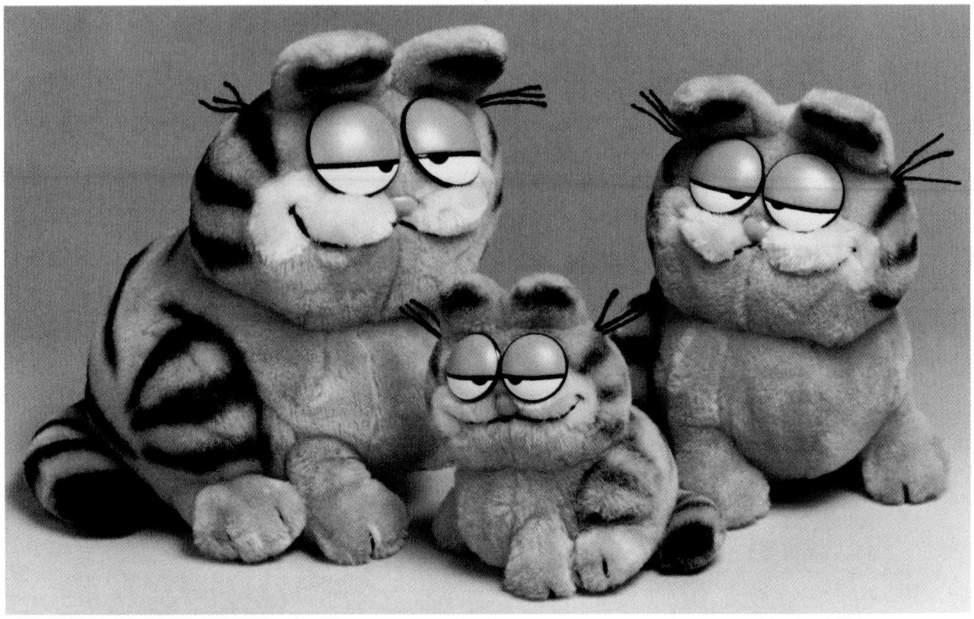

These plush dolls capture Garfield's distinctive (and relatively primitive) early '80s look.

Handy handbooks provide full-color photos and comprehensive price guides for collectors.

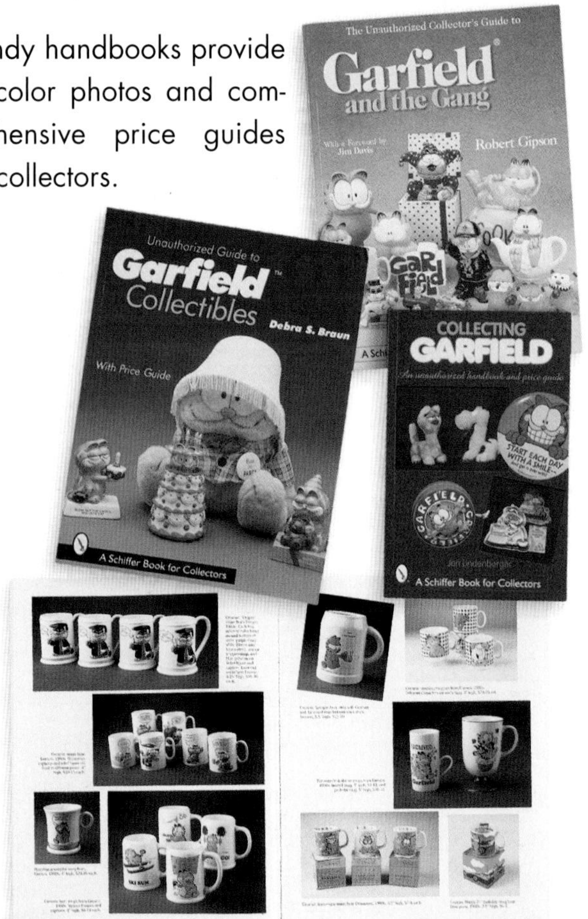
The Unauthorized Collector's Guide to
Garfield and the Gang
Robert Gipson
Unauthorized Guide to
Garfield Collectibles
Debra S. Braun
With Price Guide
A Schiffer Book for Collectors
COLLECTING GARFIELD
A Schiffer Book for Collectors

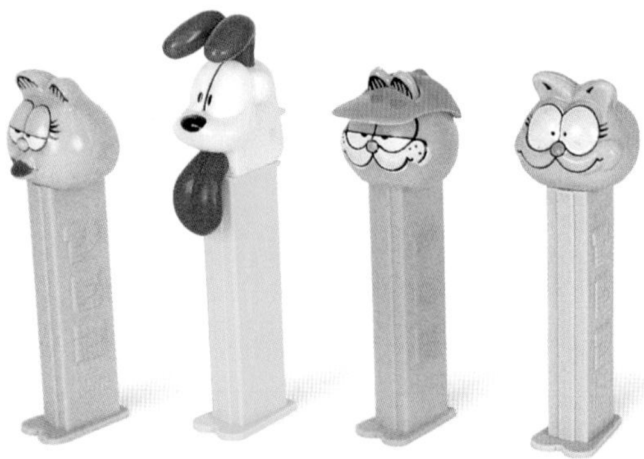

Pez collectors gobbled up these candy dispensers.

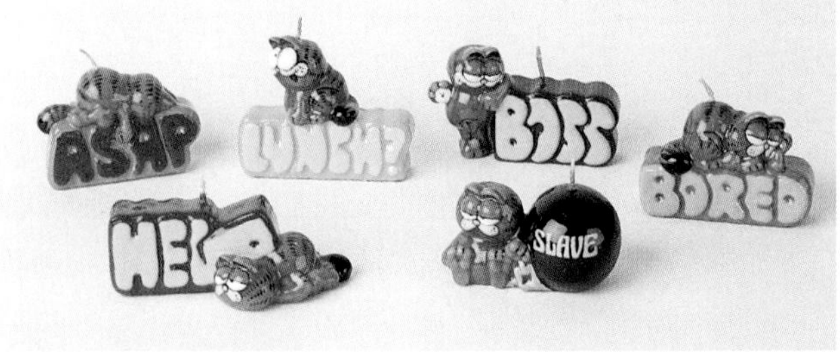
ASAP
LUNCH?
BOSS
BORED
HELP
SLAVE

Sculpted candles from the early 1980s illuminated Garfield's inimitable attitude.

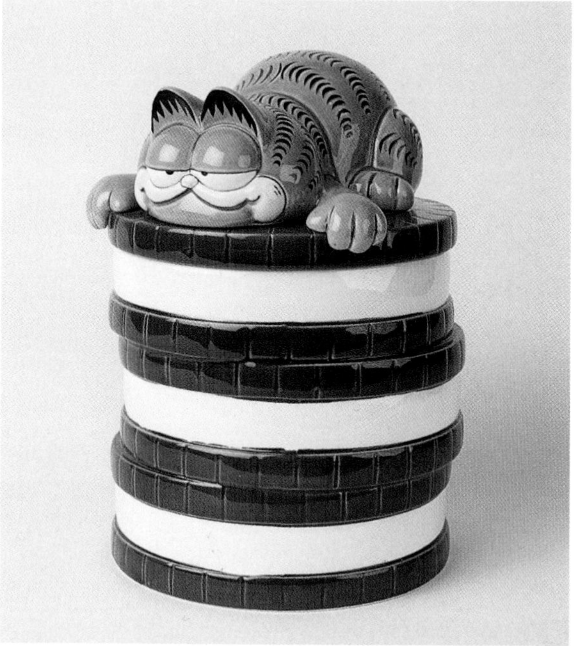

Cookie jar

Ceramics manufacturer Enesco launched a huge Garfield program in the 1980s that included figurines, tea sets, cookie jars, and more.

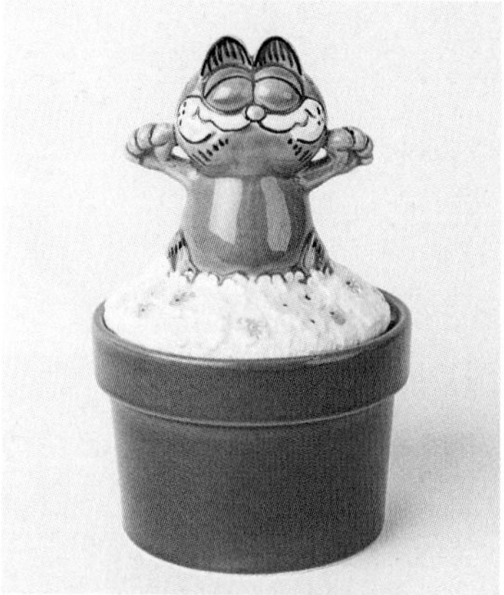

Keepsake container

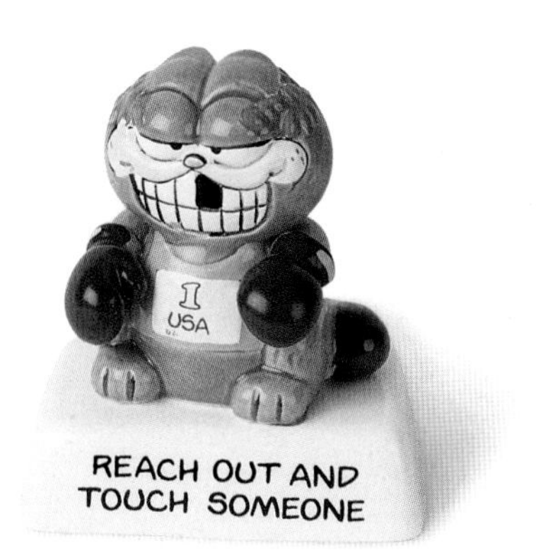
REACH OUT AND
TOUCH SOMEONE

Figurine

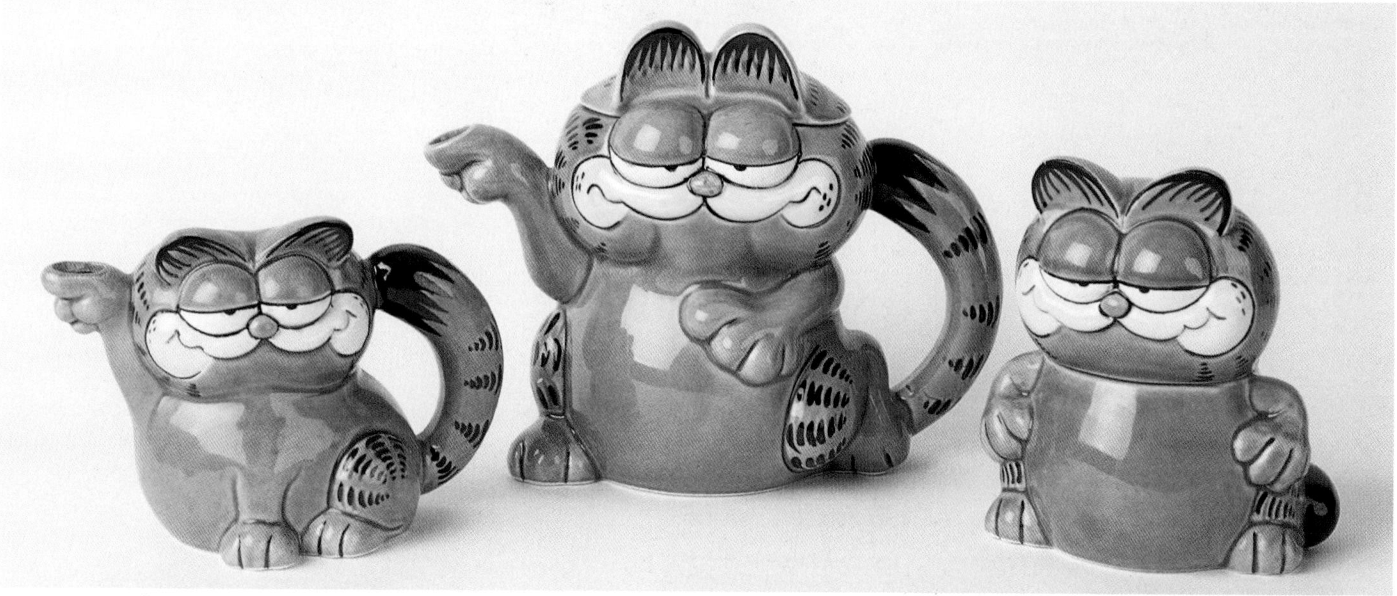

Teapot, creamer, and sugar set

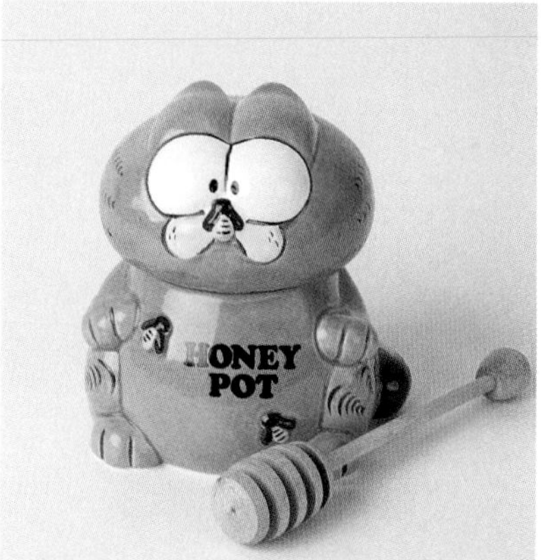
HONEY
POT

Honey pot

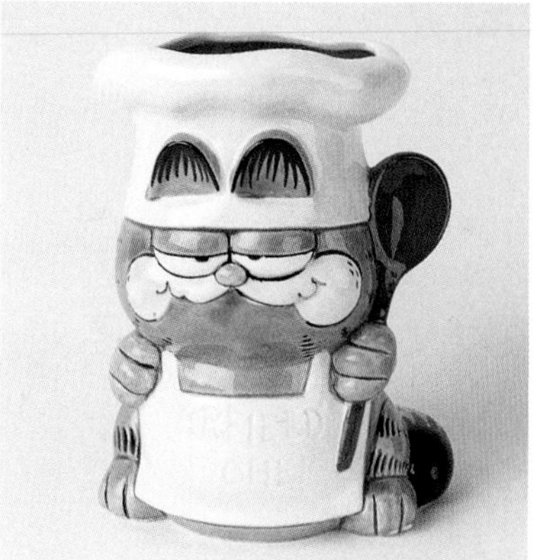

Kitchen utensil holder

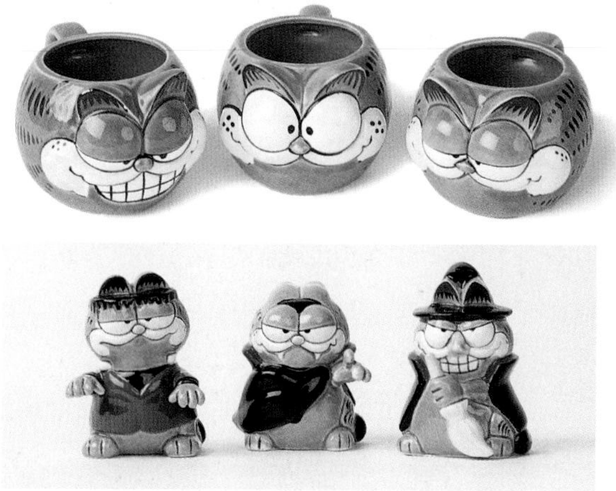

Garfield mugs *(above)* and Halloween figurines

No fishin'
Sittin' on the Dock of the Bay

The Danbury Mint has been serving the collectibles market for years, producing limited-edition figurines, plates, and high-end plush characters.

McDonald's
McDonald's

McDonald's Happy Meal featuring
GARFIELD

McDonald's Happy Meal featuring
GARFIELD
CAUTION: May contain small parts.
Not intended for children under 3.
ASK ABOUT SPECIAL TOYS FOR KIDS UNDER 3!

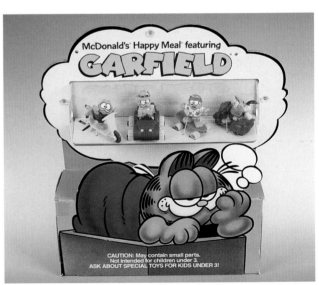

Premiums from fast-food restaurants have long been a fan favorite. Over the years, Garfield has done successful promotions with KFC, Dairy Queen, Wendy's, Pizza Hut, and McDonald's. The McDonald's premiums were especially popular and included Happy Meal boxes and toys, collector glasses and mugs, and a special limited-edition Garfield crew member plush doll.

"To those who would say collecting Garfield stuff is a bad habit, I'd say there are a lot worse habits to have."

—Jim Davis

CHAPTER FIFTEEN

Q & A with

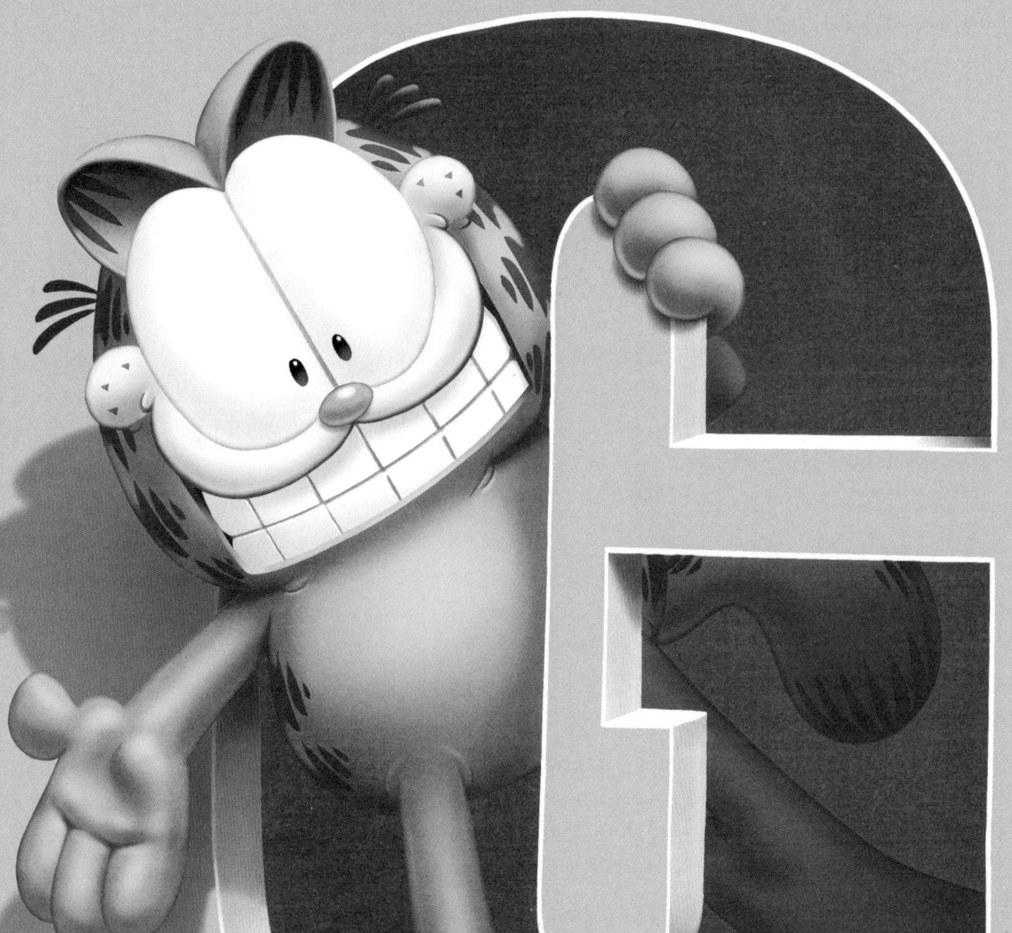
G

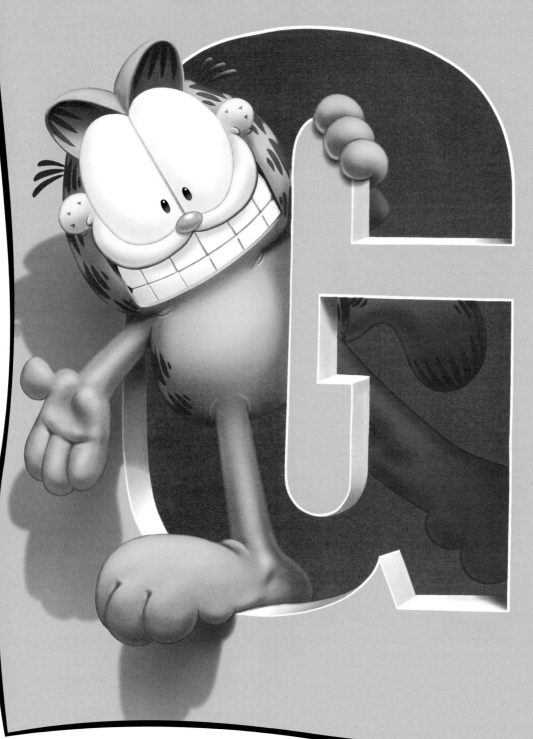

1 **Now that you've hit the landmark age of twenty-five, do you feel older and wiser?**

Older, yes. Wiser, maybe. Hungrier, definitely!

2 **Are there any advantages to being twenty-five?**

Now I can get the seniors' discount at all-you-can-eat restaurants.

3 **Do you have any advice for someone as old as you?**

Eat lots of junk food. You need all the preservatives you can get.

4 **Well, you still look great. How do you stay so young? Surely it can't be diet or exercise.**

It's mirrors and formaldehyde.

5 **Do you have any birthday tips?**

Yeah—a cake in your mouth is worth two in the fridge.

6 **Anything special you want for your twenty-fifth birthday? What do you give a cat who has everything?**

How 'bout a sponge bath from Buffy the Vampire Slayer! But seriously, I'd just settle for a lifetime supply of canned hams.

7 **Let's talk for a moment about your creator, Jim Davis. How old is he now?**

Let's just say he's chronologically challenged. His first pet was a brontosaurus.

8 **How are you and Jim alike, and how are you different?**

He's a farm boy at heart, and I'm a big-city kitty. He wakes up at the crack of dawn; I wake up at the crack of noon. But we both enjoy life's simple pleasures: eating, sleeping, and scratching ourselves.

9 **What do you like best about your owner, Jon Arbuckle?**

His mindless obedience.

25 Years . . .

13 **Do you consider yourself a role model?**

Yeah, for couch potatoes everywhere who love a big meal followed by a big burp and a long nap.

10 **What about Odie? Are you guys better friends than you sometimes like to show?**

Actually, I love Odie. It's his breath I hate.

14 **Do you consider yourself a sex symbol?**

Is Jon Arbuckle a nerd? Is Mr. Magoo nearsighted? Is Yogi smarter than the average bear?

11 **Now that you're getting a little more mature, are you planning a serious relationship with Arlene?**

I doubt it. She's a fine feline, but I'm already deeply in love with someone else . . . me.

15 **What was the greatest moment in your career?**

Hmm, that's a toughie. Maybe when I reached the career milestone of 3,000 hits —upside Odie's head. That pretty much punched my ticket to the Hall of Fame.

12 **Did you have a hero growing up?**

Meat Loaf . . . the singer *and* the food.

25 Questions

16 **If you could be in another comic strip, which one would it be and why?**

Maybe *Marmaduke*. I could use a new dog to torment.

17 **How would you describe yourself?**

Funky, chunky, hunky, spunky . . . and that's just the "unky" words.

18 | **Why are you so lazy?**
It's a talent I was born with, and I've worked hard to develop it.

19 | **What's your sign?**
"Wide Load." Actually, it's Gemini. That's why I'm double trouble.

20 | **If you were a tree, what kind would you be?**
A pantry.

21 | **Have you ever cried?**
Once, when my food dish was empty.

22 | **Have you ever done time?**
No. Officer McGruff once nabbed me for stealing cookies, but the Girl Scouts dropped the charges.

23 | **What three things would you take to a desert island?**
A big-screen TV, a pepperoni pizza, and a six-pack of slave dogs!

24 | **Now that you're older, do you ever get nostalgic?**
It's hard to be nostalgic when you can't remember anything.

**Well, it's certainly been an eventful twenty-five years.
What do you see in your future?**
25 Incontinence, arthritis, dementia . . . you know, the usual geezer stuff. Actually, I'm just gonna keep doing my thing: eating, sleeping, and kicking some major dog butt!

CHAPTER SIXTEEN

Paws: The House That Garfield Built

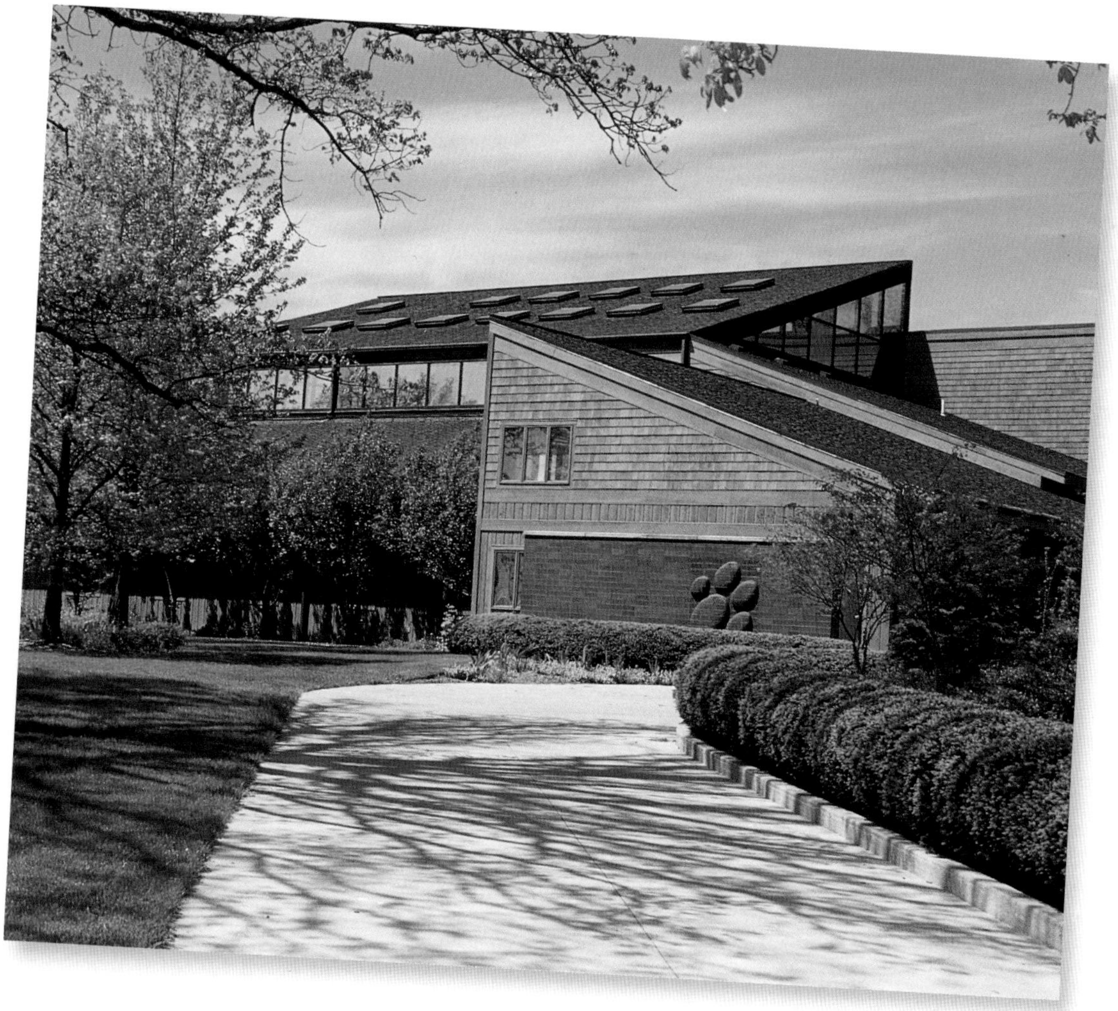

Garfield is a very special cat. And he deserves to live in a very special place. Paws Incorporated is the house that Garfield built. Jim started Paws, Inc. in 1981 as a creative studio to handle the writing, drawing, and design for all Garfield products.

Nestled in the Indiana countryside, Paws is a state-of-the-art studio and business facility. This "country contemporary" complex boasts a three-story, glass-enclosed atrium (so you can stop and smell the African violets) and houses an art department, showroom/conference room, exercise room, cafeteria (Garfield's favorite), animation studio, the Big Guy's office (Jim Davis, not Garfield), and

Above: The Paws studio in 1981 was a simple ranch house.

enough computer hardware and software to run the space program. Paws also operates its own solar aquatic system water treatment plant, because a clean planet is a happy planet!

The staff has grown from three in 1981 to nearly sixty (as of this writing). And the whole crazy crew of creative and business people all do their part to keep the cat purring. (Hey, it beats working for a living!)

In 1990, Jim was able to build his "dream studio"—thanks in large part to the revenue generated by the "Stuck on You" craze. Jim personally

Above: Garfield's Hoosier headquarters under construction, 1990. The building sits on 121 acres of farmland, surrounded by corn and soybean fields.

supervised the design of the massive 36,000-square-foot facility, and added several unique touches. Each office has a window, allowing the staff to enjoy the beautiful Indiana countryside while they work. Jim also covered the walls of each office in fabric, so that artwork could be easily displayed during creative sessions.

Crack(ed) Staff

The Paws staff includes artists, writers, sculptors, accountants, salespeople, computer guys, account managers, clerical support, licensing coordinators, landscapers, kitchen workers, a maintenance crew, and a lawyer.

Art Work

It's the art department's job to make Garfield look good (and to eat all the donuts at the monthly staff meeting). These talented artisans handle the design, illustration, and production for Garfield merchandise. Pictured: *(back row, left to right)* Larry Fentz, Dave Kuhn, Brad Hill, Tom Howard, Eric Reaves, Jeff Wesley, Betsy Knotts, and Mike Fentz, *(front row, left to right)* Linda Duell, Lynette Nuding, Kenny Goetzinger, *(seated, left to right)* Lori Barker, Gary Barker, and Sheila Bolduc.

Do the Write Thing!

Jim with his gargantuanly gifted, incredibly intelligent, and extremely modest writers, Mark Acey and Scott Nickel. (Can you guess who wrote this caption?)

Carving Out Their Niche

Paws's resident sculptors Marvin Porter and Jamie Crawford keep Garfield well rounded.

Laughter Is What They're After

Jim and cartoonist Brett Koth get together regularly and brainstorm ideas for the Garfield comic strip. Here, the two review a new batch of concepts.

The Show Must Go On

Paws Productions brings Garfield to life with animation, music, and sound. Irreverent producer/director Jon Barnard wears a lot of different hats (as well as a few dresses), and animator Glenn Zimmerman makes working on Garfield a very moving experience.

Left: Jim Davis and his wife Jill, senior vice president of licensing.

All in the Family

"Jill's been with Paws for more than twenty years, and handles product, promotions, and marketing for the cat," says husband Jim Davis. "Jill can't draw, but I can read her flailing hand movements when she's trying to communicate a product idea. We live on the Paws complex and have about a hundred-yard commute to work each morning. Our family includes three kids, James, Ashley, and Chris, and a granddaughter, Chloe. In the pet department, there are three cats (Link, Spunky, and Spritzy), our Labrador retriever, Molly, and the occasional deer, squirrel, or raccoon that wanders onto the property. When we're not working on Garfield, Jill and I like to golf, garden, attend school activities with the kids, and go out for dinner and a movie once a week. Jill's like me; we both enjoy the simple pleasures of country living."

Far left: Jim and Jill with art director Betsy Knotts.

Left: Staff dog, Molly, watches over the empire.

Taking Care of Business

Each day starts with the morning meeting in the art department. Jim and Jill look over concepts, review artwork and copy, and approve (or reject) products from licensees.

Let's Get Physical

The staff can keep fit in the company workout room, which comes equipped with weights, treadmills, stair machines, and that most essential piece of exercise equipment, a TV!

Garfield-a-palooza!

One showroom houses domestic products; the other showcases international items. Licensee meetings are also held in these areas.

Glass Act

The centerpiece of the studio is this three-story, glass-enclosed atrium, featuring a meeting and dining area, jukebox (stocked with Jim's favorite songs from the '50s and '60s), and lush tropical foliage.

What's Cookin'?

The Paws cafeteria specializes in down-home country cooking. The daily menu includes soups, salads, entrees, desserts, and the occasional possum (just kidding!). Garfield's (and Jim's) love of Italian food is also indulged. Lasagna is served on Garfield's birthday, and every Monday is "Spaghetti Day."

Natural Selection

When the new studio was built, Jim faced a dilemma about how to handle the building's wastewater. Given the size of the studio, a traditional septic system wasn't really feasible, and connecting to the city's sewer would require installing more than three miles of pipe. Then Jim heard about the solar aquatic system (SAS), a process that treats water using natural purifiers such as plants, minnows, snails, and ultraviolet light. The system is highly efficient, and the treated water is returned to the ground 95% free of impurities. An avid environmentalist, Jim was instantly sold on this eco-friendly solution.

The Paws SAS plant is the first permanent, licensed water treatment plant of its kind in the world and has been featured in newspapers, in magazines, and on the Discovery Channel.

Top Cat

The Paws complex consists of three buildings: the main studio, the Paws production facility, and Jim's studio. Jim's office has all the comforts of home, including a fireplace and kitchen.

Going Green

Connected to Jim's studio is his own private greenhouse, stocked with a variety of exotic plants (but no *dog*wood, per Garfield's orders).

Staff Gifts

Each year, Paws employees get together and select a very special gift for Jim. But what do you get a guy who has everything? Some past presents include gourmet cooking lessons, a specially designed fountain, an original *Henry* comic strip, a DVD player with DVDs of his favorite films, a telescope, and a putting green.

TO JIM WITH LOVE
JUNE 19, 1989
FROM YOUR STAFF

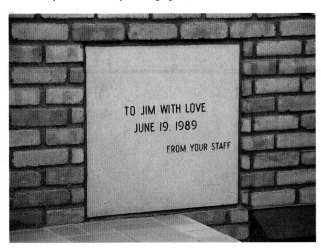

Wall of Fame

When the new studio was being constructed, the staff put together a special twenty-five-year time capsule. Items placed inside included letters and audiotapes from employees, pop culture objects of the day, and several bottles of vintage Bordeaux. The time capsule—and the wine—are slated to be opened in 2014.

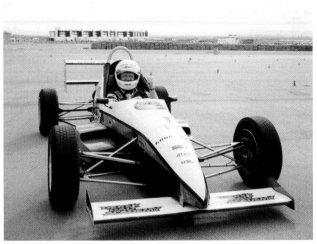

Speed Demon

One year, Paws sent Jim to racing school in Las Vegas. Jim got behind the wheel of an actual race car and tore up the track!

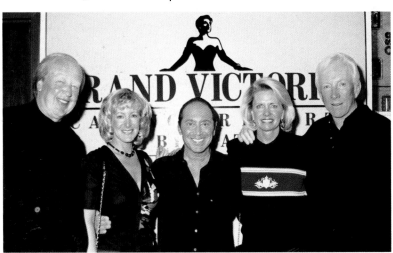

Hitting the Jackpot!

Jim and Jill spent a VIP weekend at the Grand Victoria and met singer Paul Anka! Joining the Davises were *Blondie* cartoonist Dean Young and his wife, Charlotte.

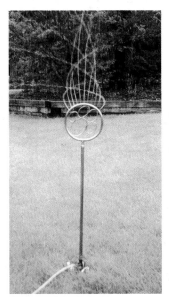

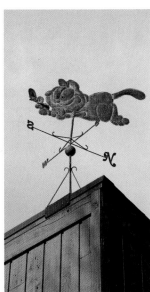

The Great Outdoors

Two unique staff birthday gifts: a specially designed copper lawn sprinkler shaped like a paw print, and this one-of-a-kind weathervane, which sits atop Jim's studio.

CHAPTER SEVENTEEN

Photo Fun Fest

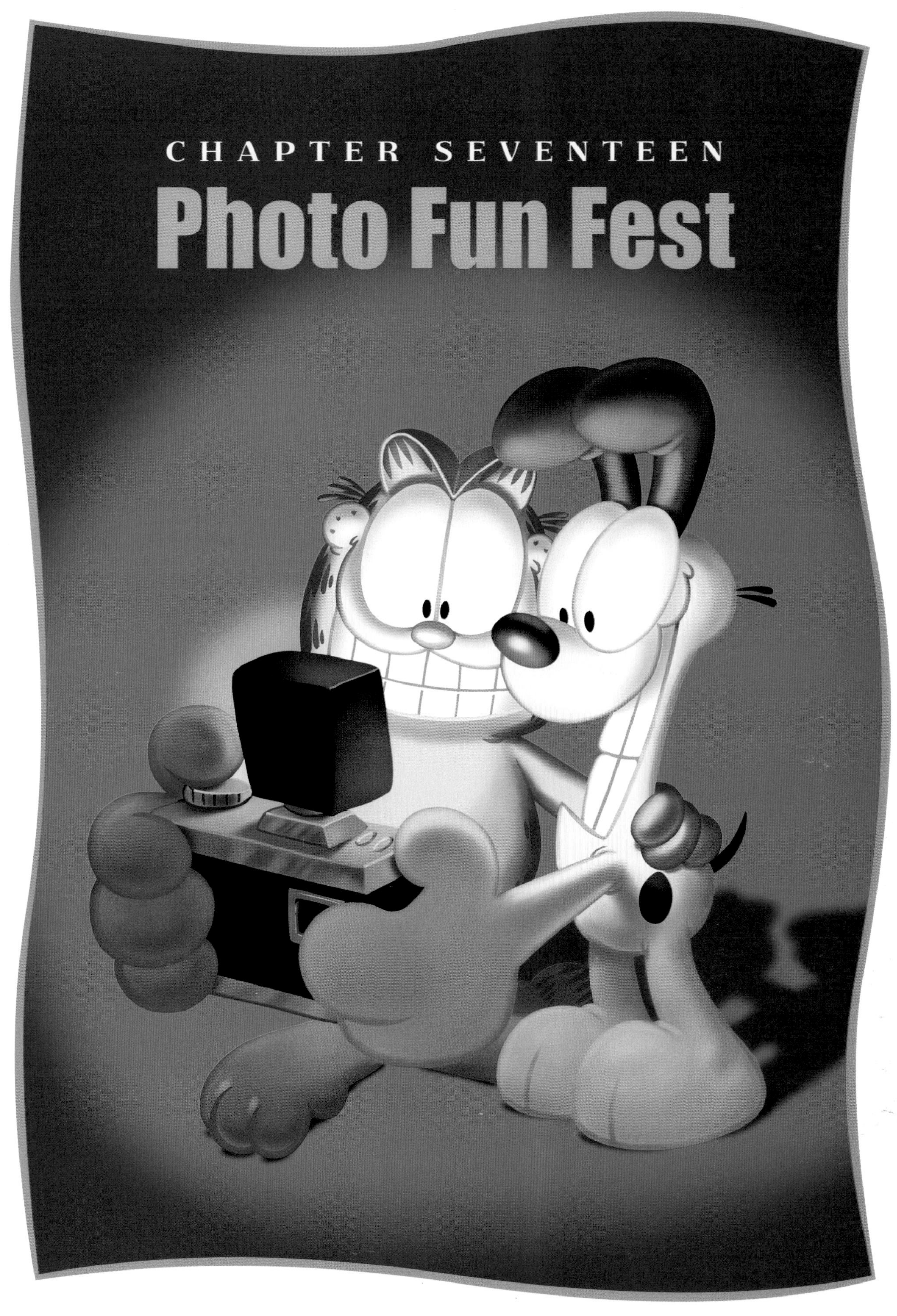

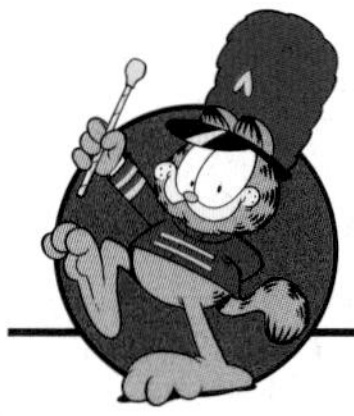

Garfield on Parade

1
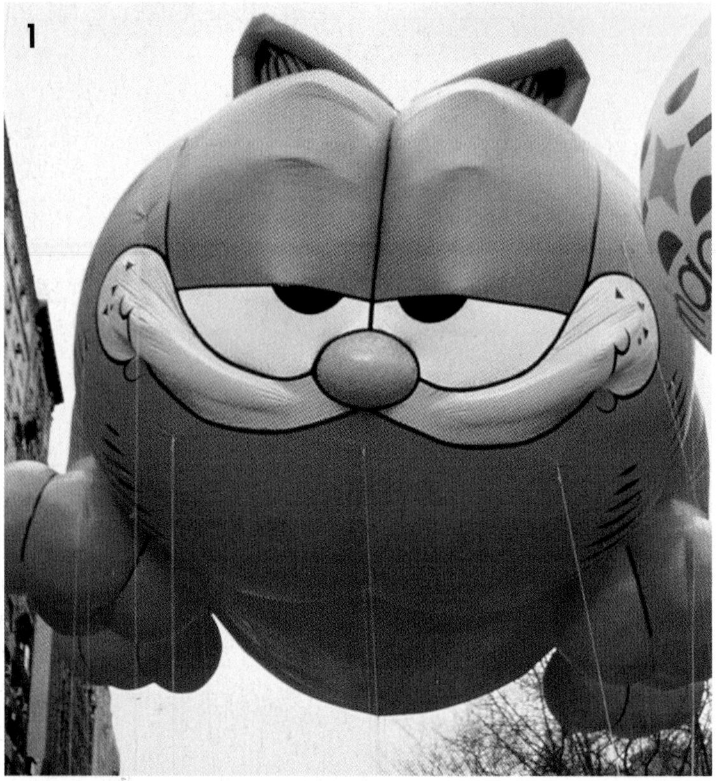

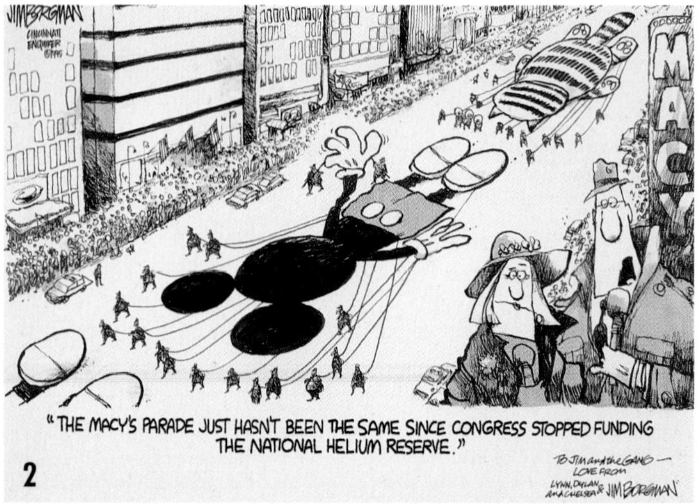
JIM BORGMAN
MACY
"THE MACY'S PARADE JUST HASN'T BEEN THE SAME SINCE CONGRESS STOPPED FUNDING THE NATIONAL HELIUM RESERVE."

2

1. IT'S A BIRD . . . IT'S A PLANE . . . IT'S GARFIELD?! The fat cat flies high above the streets of New York in the Macy's Thanksgiving Day Parade. Garfield first appeared in the parade in 1984, and he's in very good company: Fellow cartoon characters Snoopy, Bart Simpson, Spider-Man, and Big Bird have all been given the big-balloon treatment.

2. Editorial cartoon by Jim Borgman, the *Cincinnati Enquirer*, 1995.

3. FUN IN BLOOM! This whimsical Garfield float appeared in the 1986 Rose Parade in Pasadena, California. Thousands of flowers, leaves, and seeds were used in the decoration process.

Facing page: UP, UP, AND AWAY! The Garfield hot-air balloon by day and by night.

3
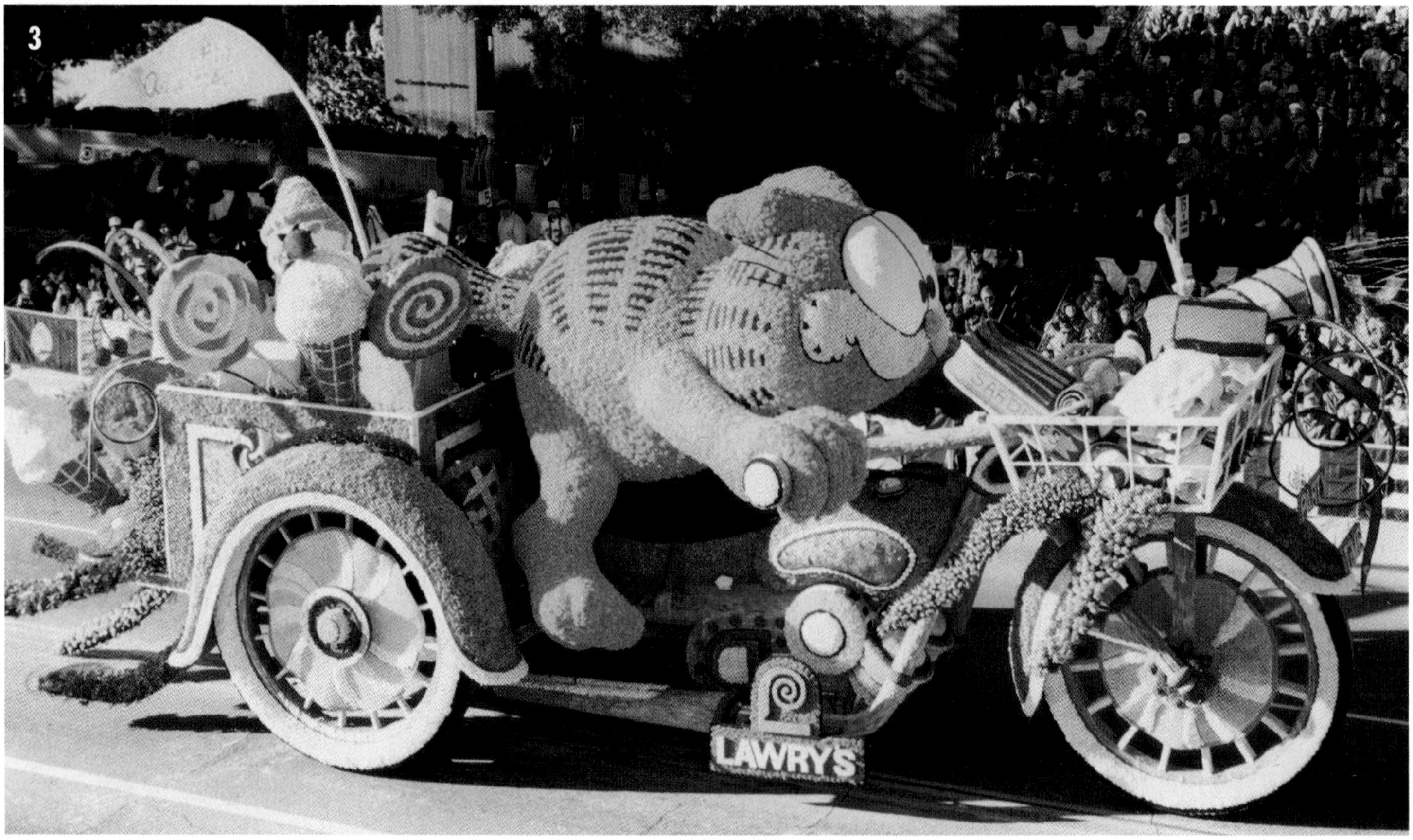
LAWRY'S

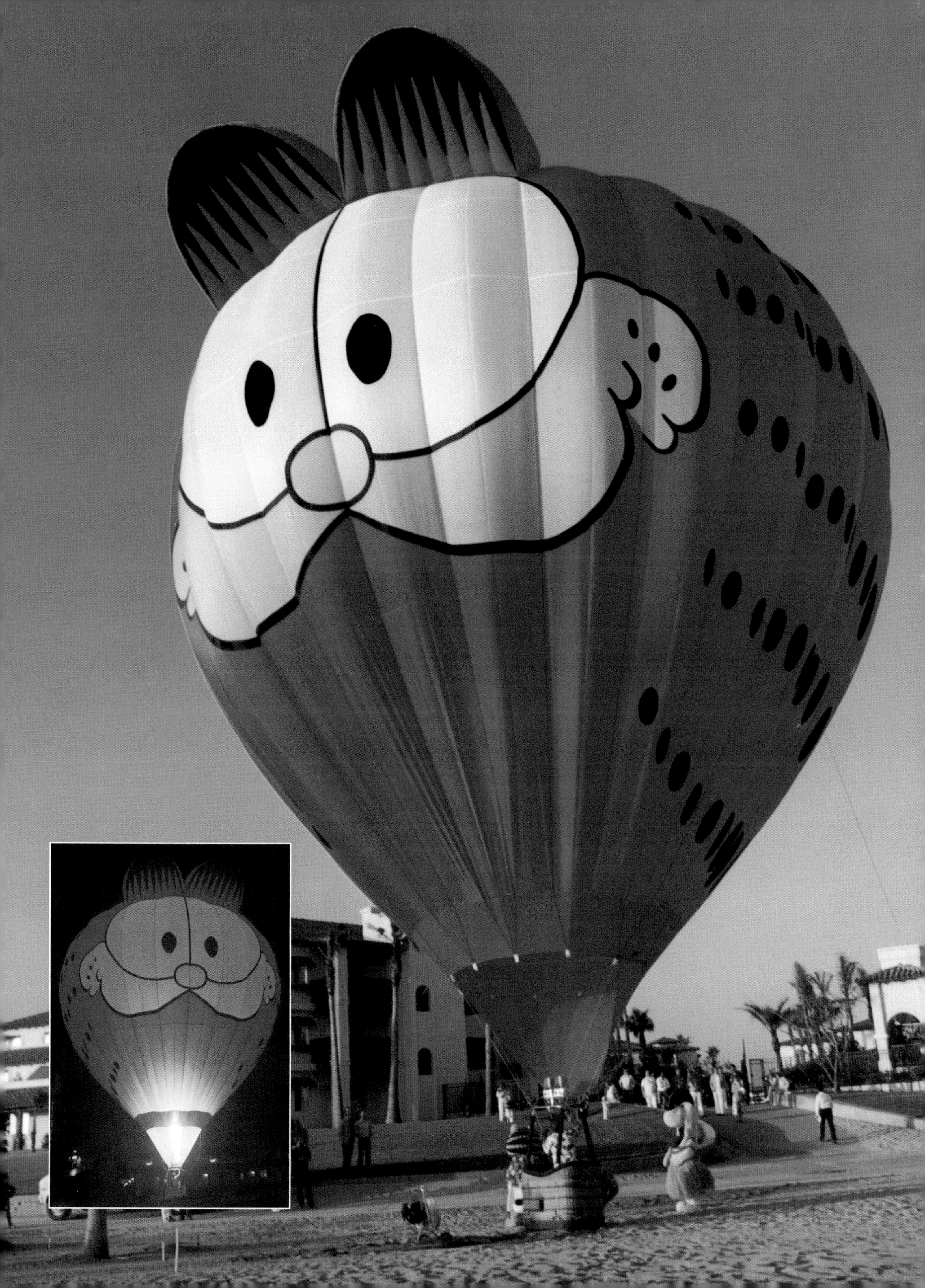

It's Tee Time!

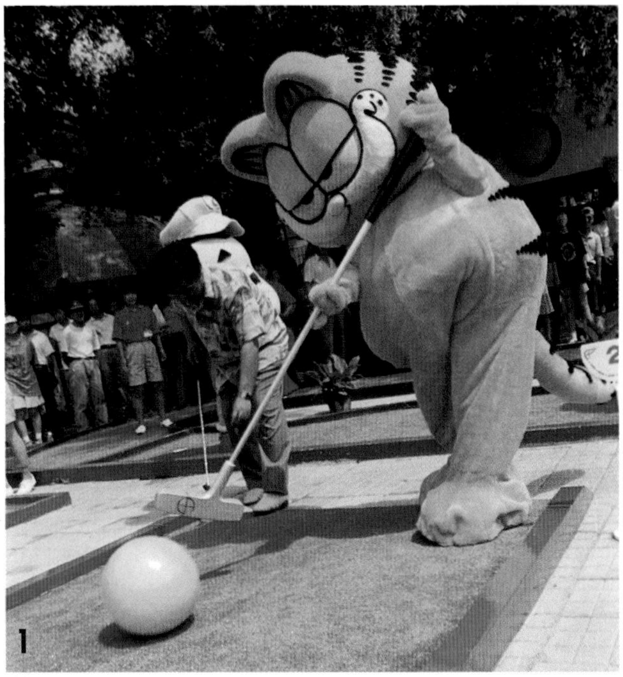

1. NO PUTTS, NO GLORY! Garfield golfing during a promotional event in Asia.

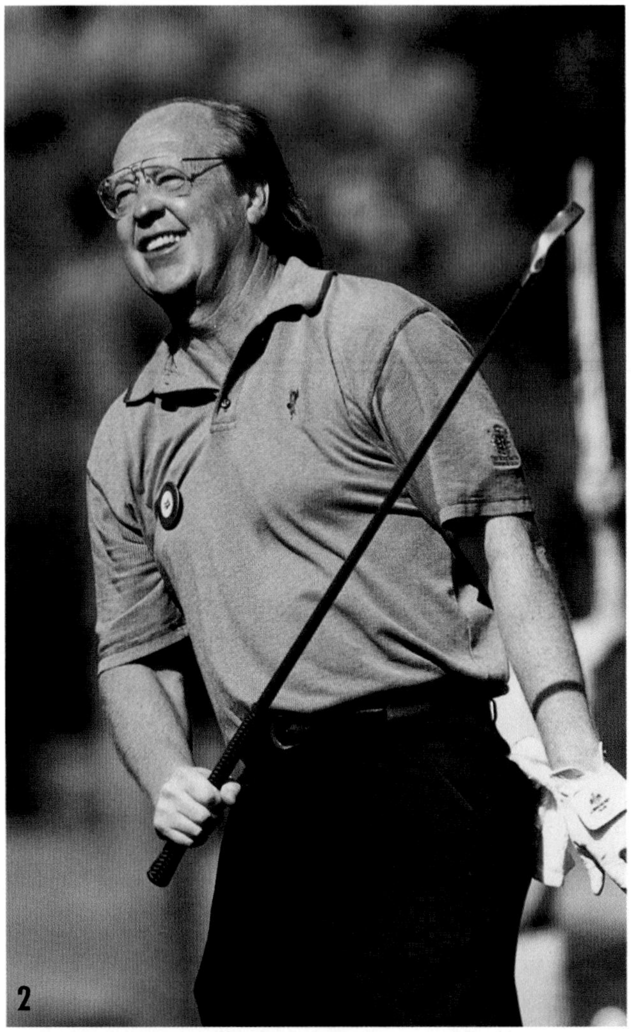

2. Jim stays the course.

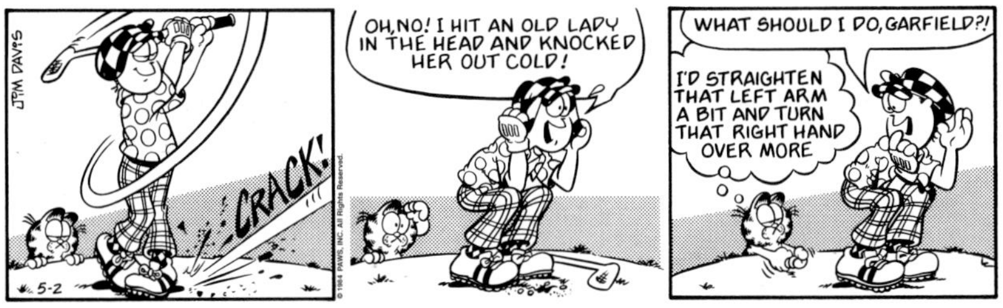
JIM DAVIS
5-2
CRACK!
OH, NO! I HIT AN OLD LADY IN THE HEAD AND KNOCKED HER OUT COLD!
WHAT SHOULD I DO, GARFIELD?!
I'D STRAIGHTEN THAT LEFT ARM A BIT AND TURN THAT RIGHT HAND OVER MORE

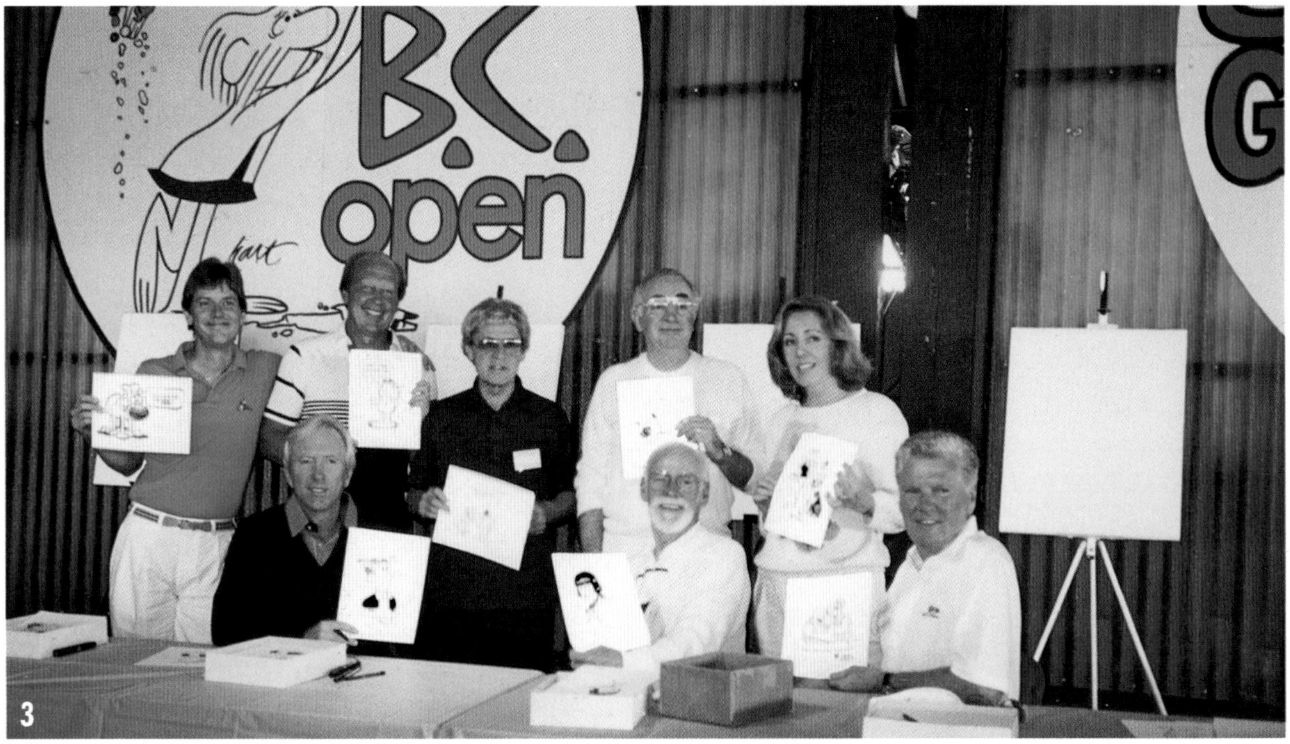
B.C.
open
hart

3. At Johnny Hart's B.C. Open, a golf tournament for cartoonists. Pictured standing *(left to right)*: Mike Peters, Jim Davis, Johnny Hart, Brant Parker, Lynn Johnston. Seated: Dean Young, John Cullen Murphy, Frank Johnson.

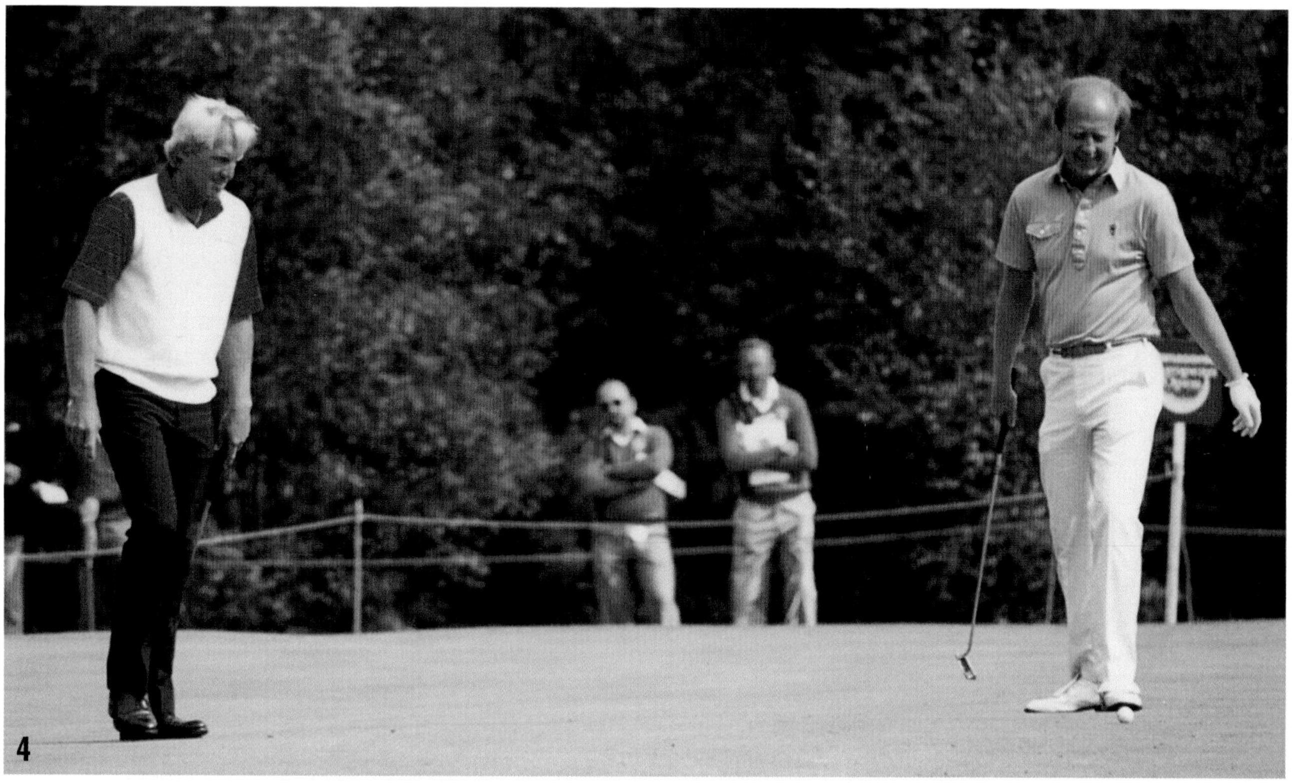

4 & 5.
"SHARK" ATTACK!
Jim plays a round with Greg "The Great White Shark" Norman at the European Open in the '80s.

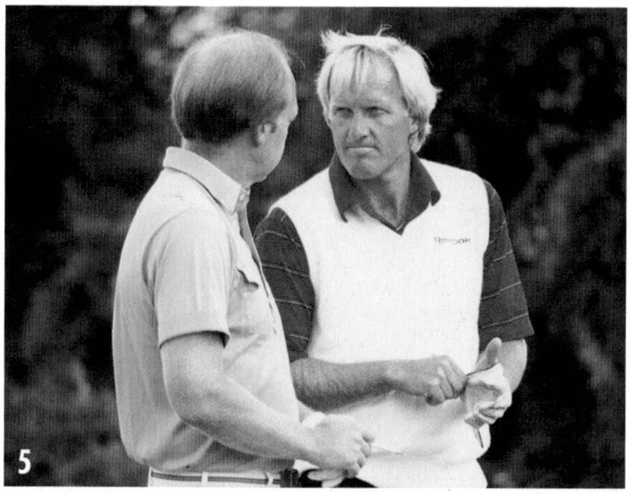

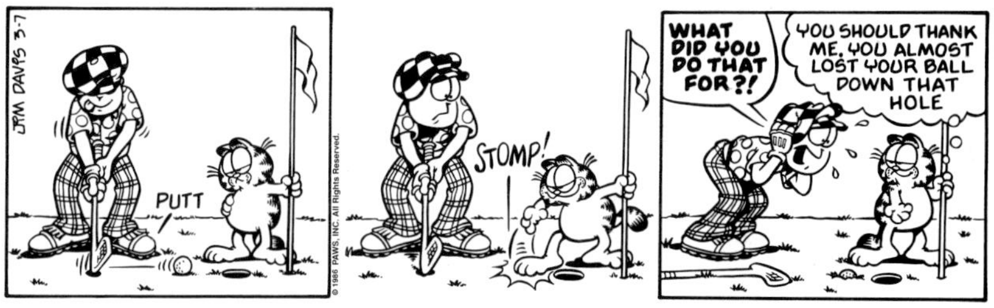
JIM DAVIS 3-7
PUTT
© 1986 PAWS, INC. All Rights Reserved.
STOMP!
WHAT DID YOU DO THAT FOR?!
YOU SHOULD THANK ME. YOU ALMOST LOST YOUR BALL DOWN THAT HOLE

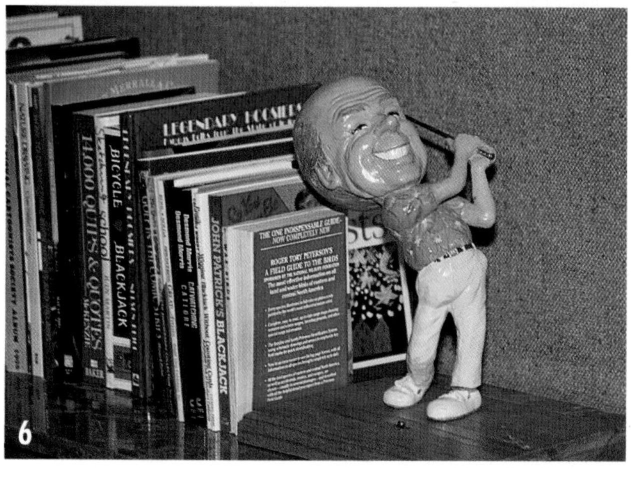

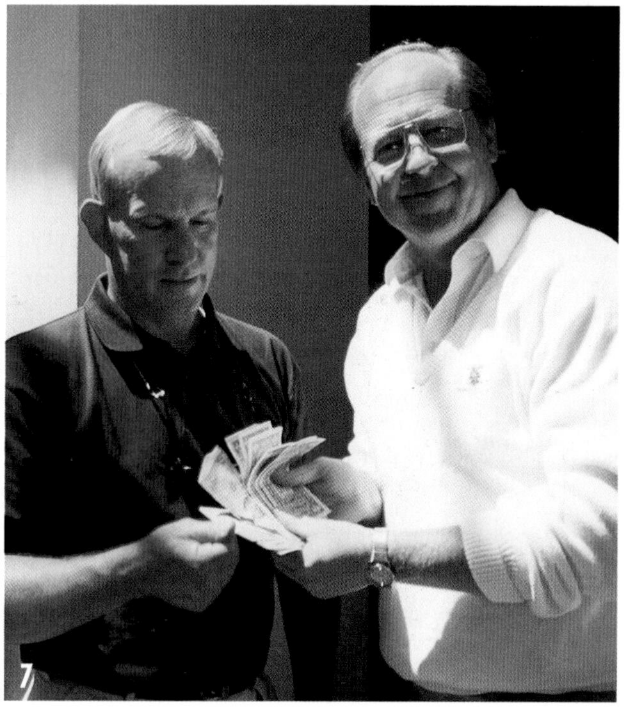

6. KING OF SWING
Handmade sculpture of Jim given to him by the Paws staff.

7. NEVER LET 'EM SEE YOU CHEAT!
Jim settles up with Tom Smothers.

Polka! Polka! Polka!

CAT FIGHT

It all started innocently enough. Who knew it was going to become such a big fat hairy deal? In March of 1999, Jim wrote a week's worth of strips poking fun at polka music and the inventor of the accordion. But the gags struck a sour note with a diehard accordion enthusiast from Pennsylvania, Joe Blazejewski (aka "Polka Joe"). Polka Joe assembled a small group of friends, dubbed "Polka People," and protested outside the offices of his local newspaper, which had published the *Garfield* strips. Enter Comedy Central's *The Daily Show*. The irreverent cable program heard about the odd little news story and interviewed both Jim and Polka Joe, who was shown onscreen battling a large Garfield plush. Said Polka Joe: "*Garfield* is an insult to accordion people and not funny at all!"

Oh well, guess that's show biz...

Mo Rocca
Correspondent

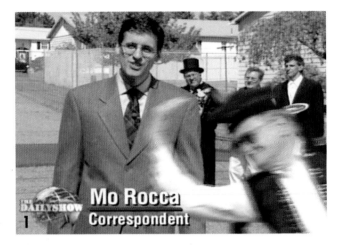

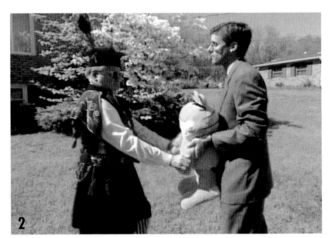

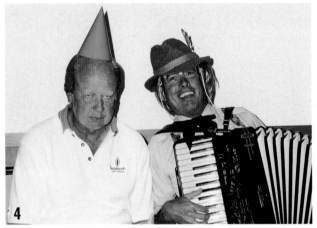

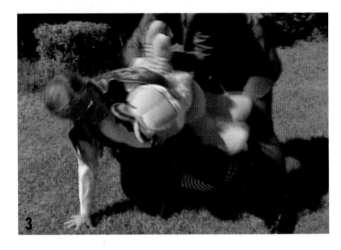

1–3. Screen captures of Polka Joe on *The Daily Show with Jon Stewart*, May 26, 1999.

4. Jim Davis being serenaded (or is that "serenerded"?) on Garfield's twenty-third birthday.

Below: One of the offending articles.

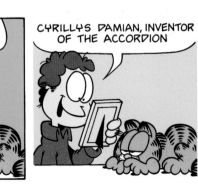

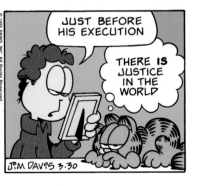

I FRAMED A PICTURE OF MY HERO
CYRILLYS DAMIAN, INVENTOR OF THE ACCORDION
© 1999 PAWS, INC. All Rights Reserved.
JUST BEFORE HIS EXECUTION
THERE **IS** JUSTICE IN THE WORLD
JIM DAVIS 3-30

Fun Fact:
Jim Davis and polka legend Frankie Yankovic share the same birthday. (And the same taste in lederhosen!)

Costume Capers

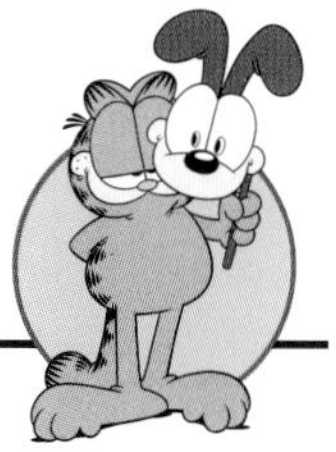

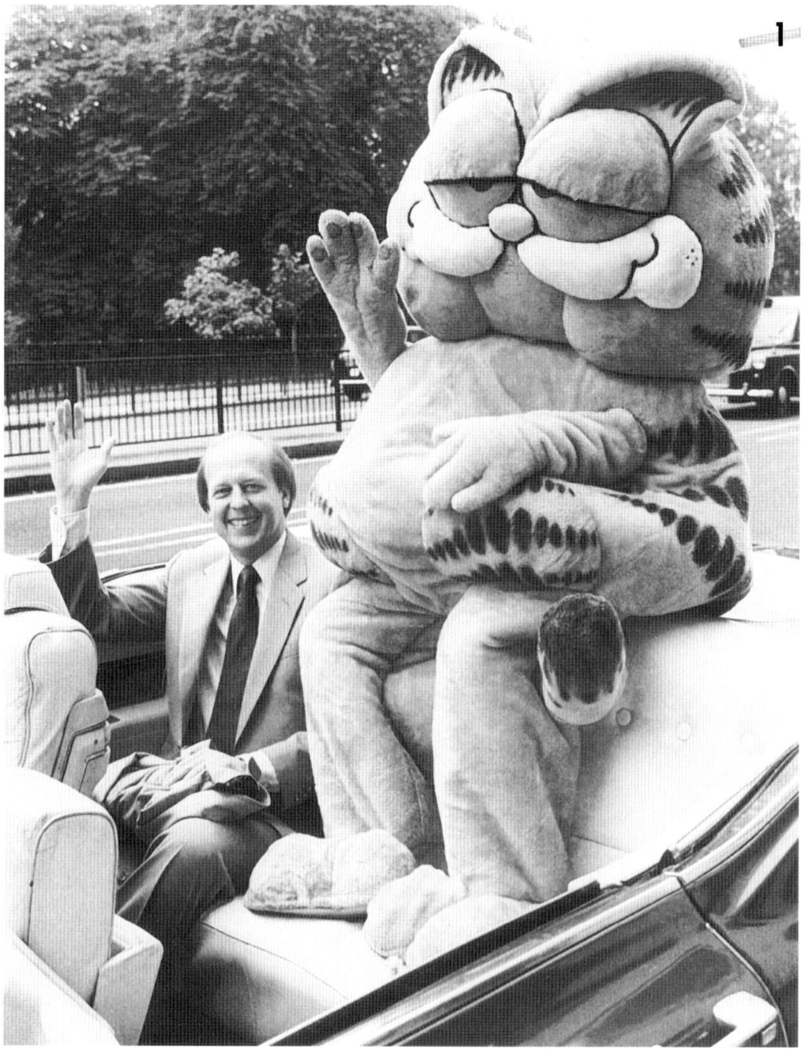

1. ON HOLIDAY! Jim Davis and Garfield tour England. (Next stop: Ye Olde Fish and Chips Shoppe!)

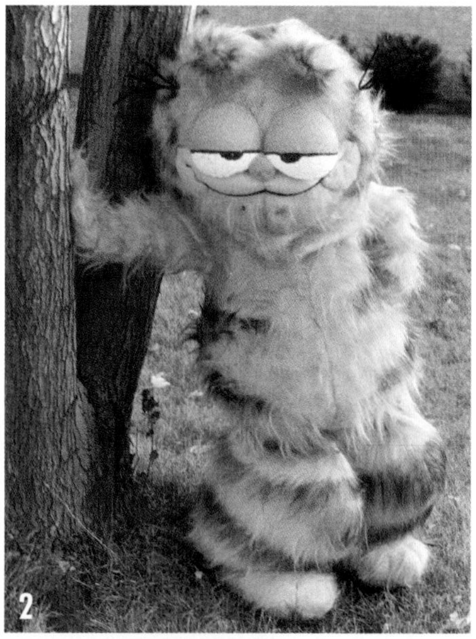

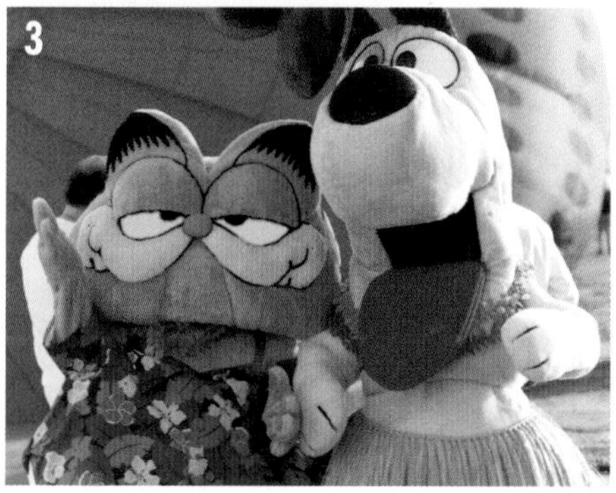

2. BAD FUR DAY
This fan-made costume shows what happens when you try to give a cat a bath.

3. BEACH BOYS
Which way to the luau?

4. THRILLER!
Garfield gets down with "The Gloved One." Is it the King of Pop or an incredible simulation?

5. PAS DE CHAT
Garfield toured the country in "Music Is My Life," which featured local symphony orchestras performing a variety of classical and contemporary songs. In this 1989 concert, the larger-than-life cat dons a tutu and dances ballet (*Swine Lake*, no doubt).

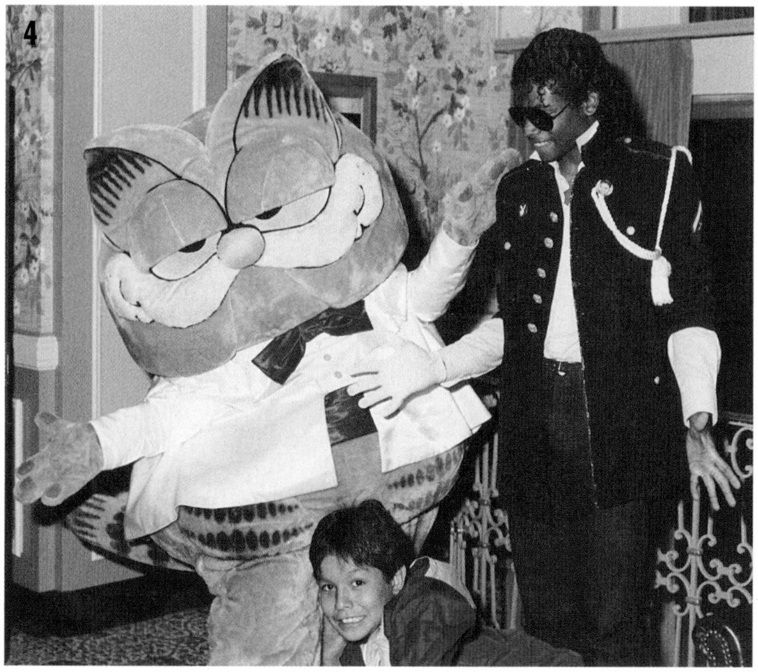

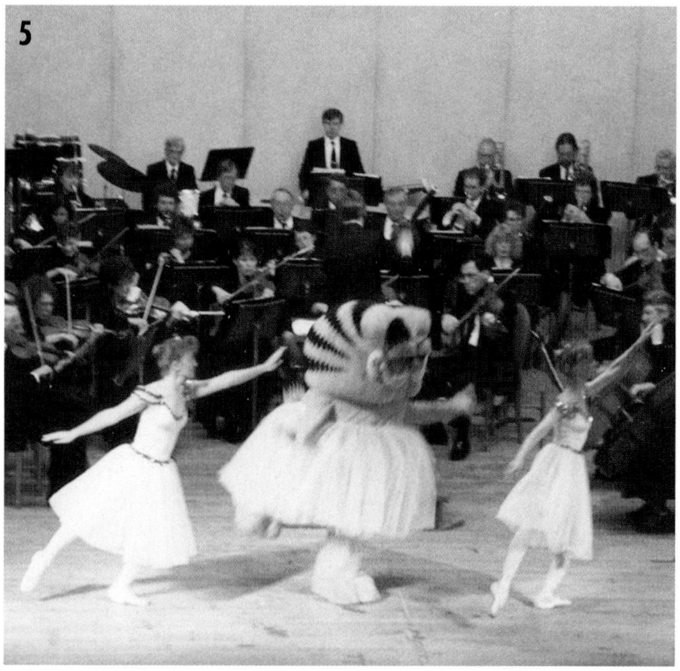

Just Plain Silly

1. I DID IT MY WAY!

2. BLUSHING BRIDE
At a costume party in the mid-1980s. (That's Jim's story, and he's sticking to it.)

3. THANK YOU. THANK YOU VERY MUCH.
Jim at a Paws Christmas party with "The King," circa 1994.

4. YEAH, BABY!
Jim (experiencing some sort of hippie flashback) rocks out with Paws' groovy chick Madelyn Ferris, circa 1988.

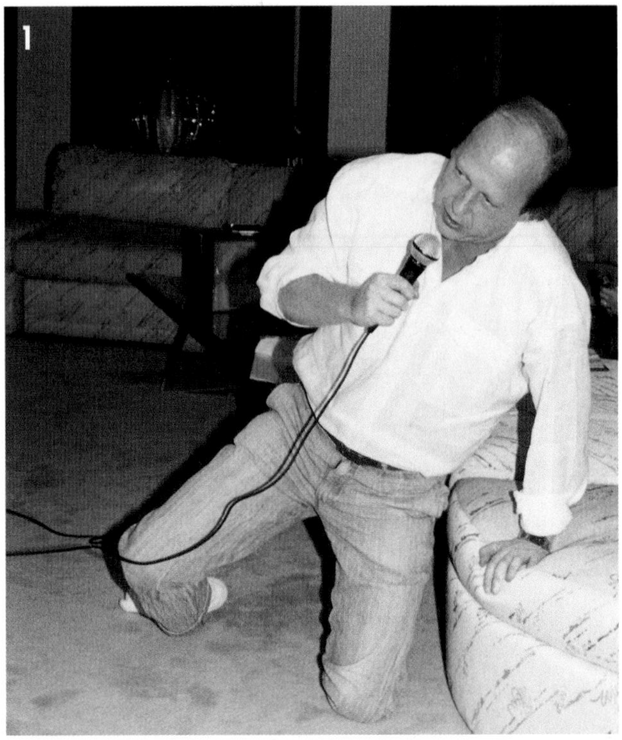

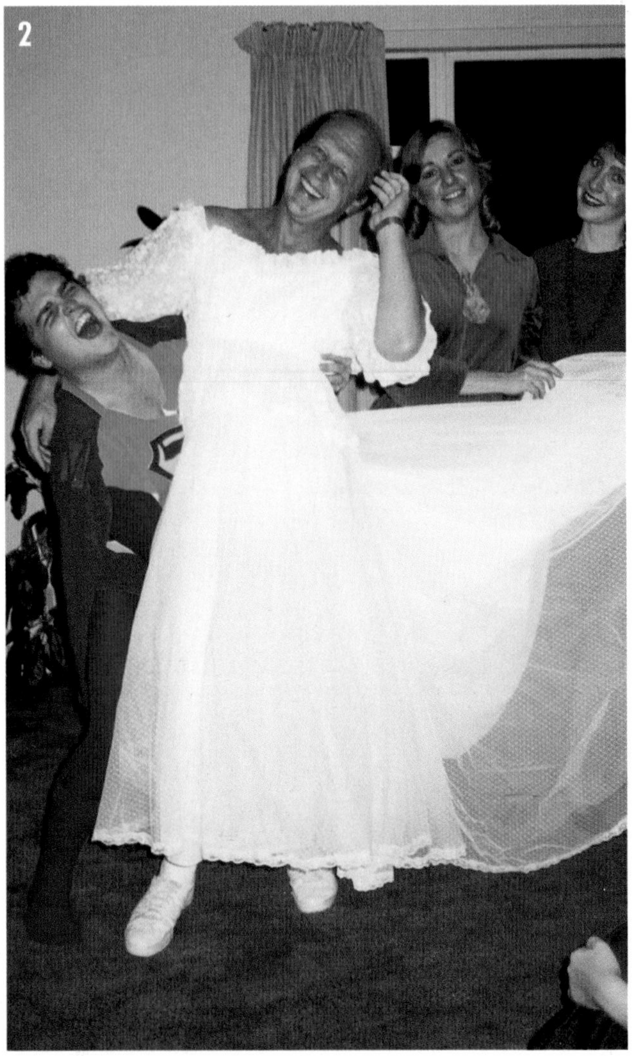

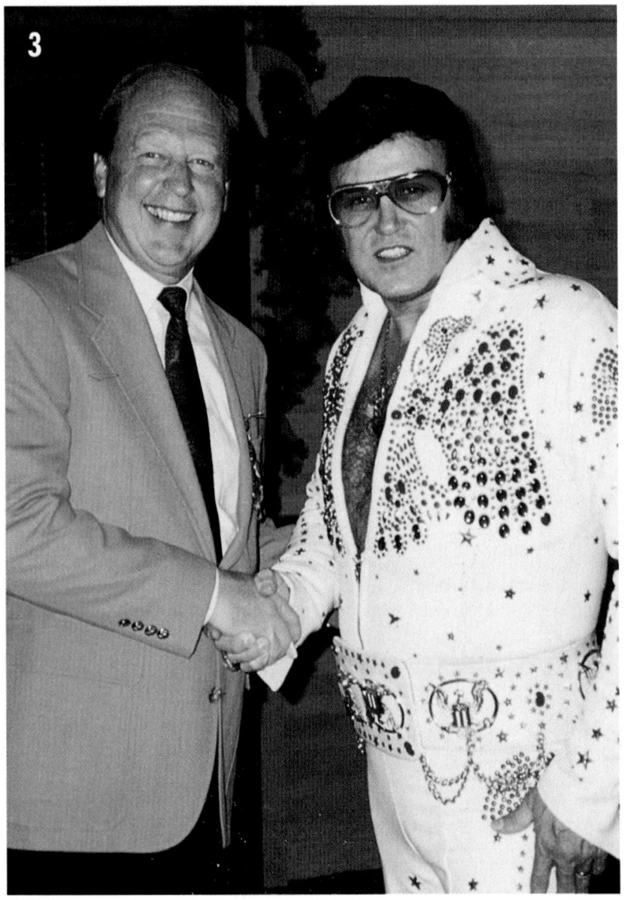

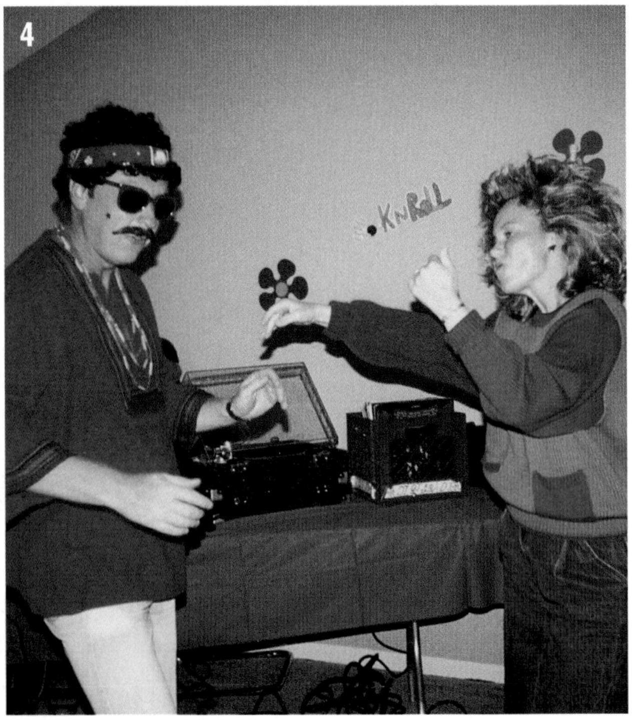

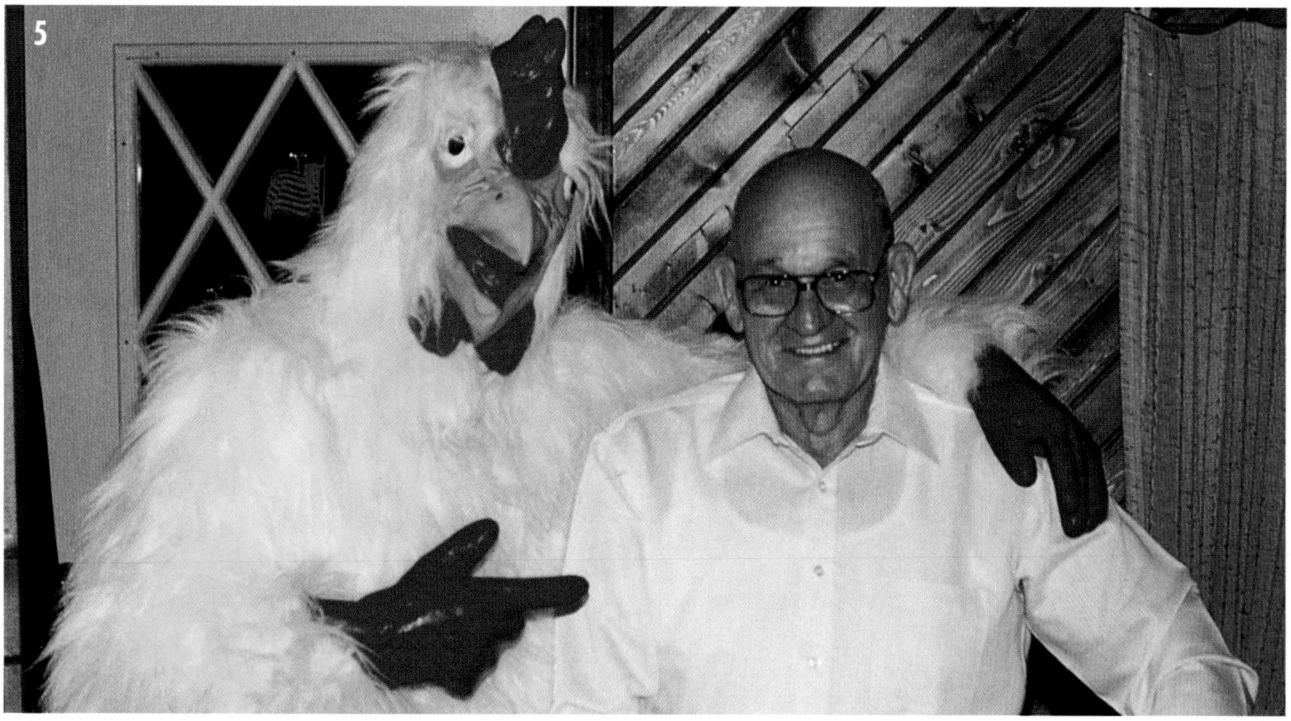

5

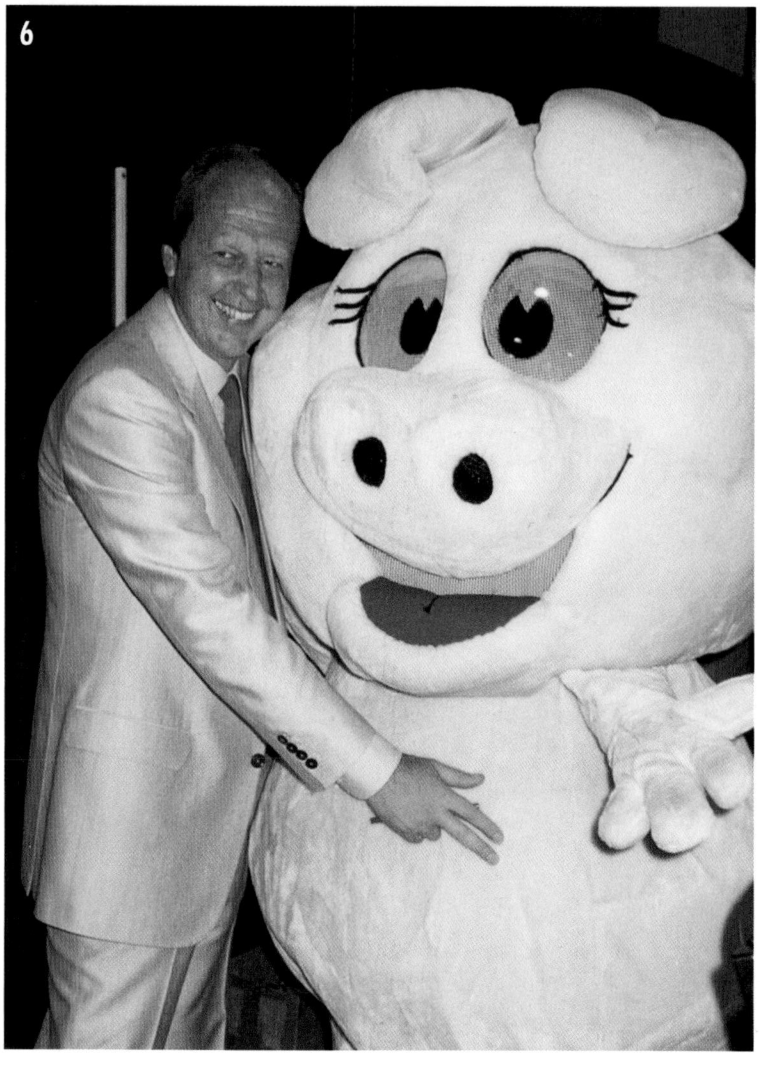

6

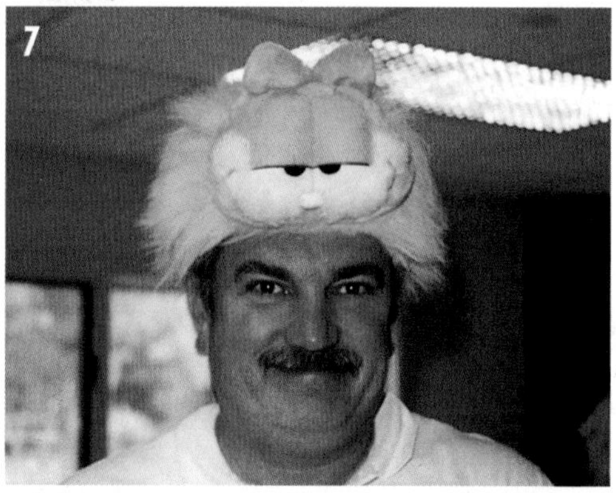

7

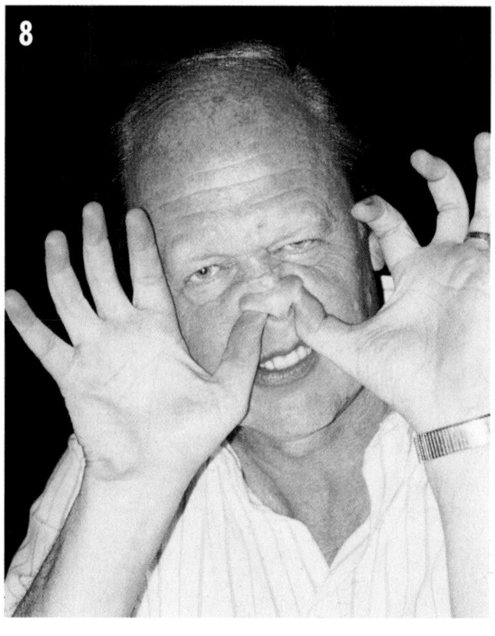

8

5. FOWL PLAY
Jim's dad with a giant chicken. Don't ask.

6. WHOLE HOG
Jim with a giant pig. Really, don't ask.

7. HAIRBALL CLUB FOR MEN
Doc Davis: He's not just the president... he's also a member!

8. MATURITY IS OVERRATED
Who says cartoonists aren't dignified?

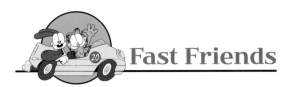

Fast Friends

1. MAKING TRACKS
The Garfield-and-Odie float rumbles along at the 1996 Indianapolis 500 Festival Parade.

2. KINGS OF THE ROAD
Garfield and Jim were Grand Marshals of the Indianapolis 500 Festival Parade in 1988 and 1996. Garfield was also the official mascot for the Indianapolis 500 Festival in '96.

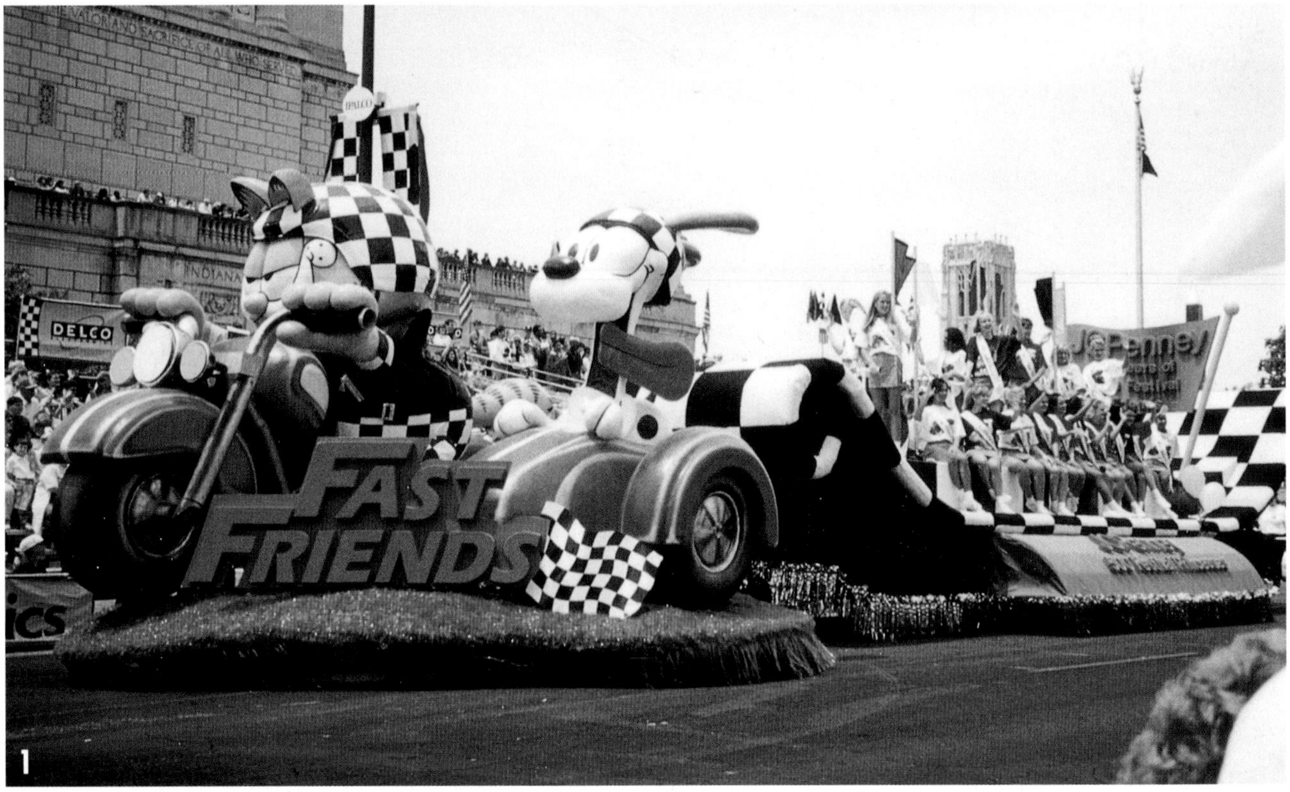
FAST FRIENDS
DELCO
1

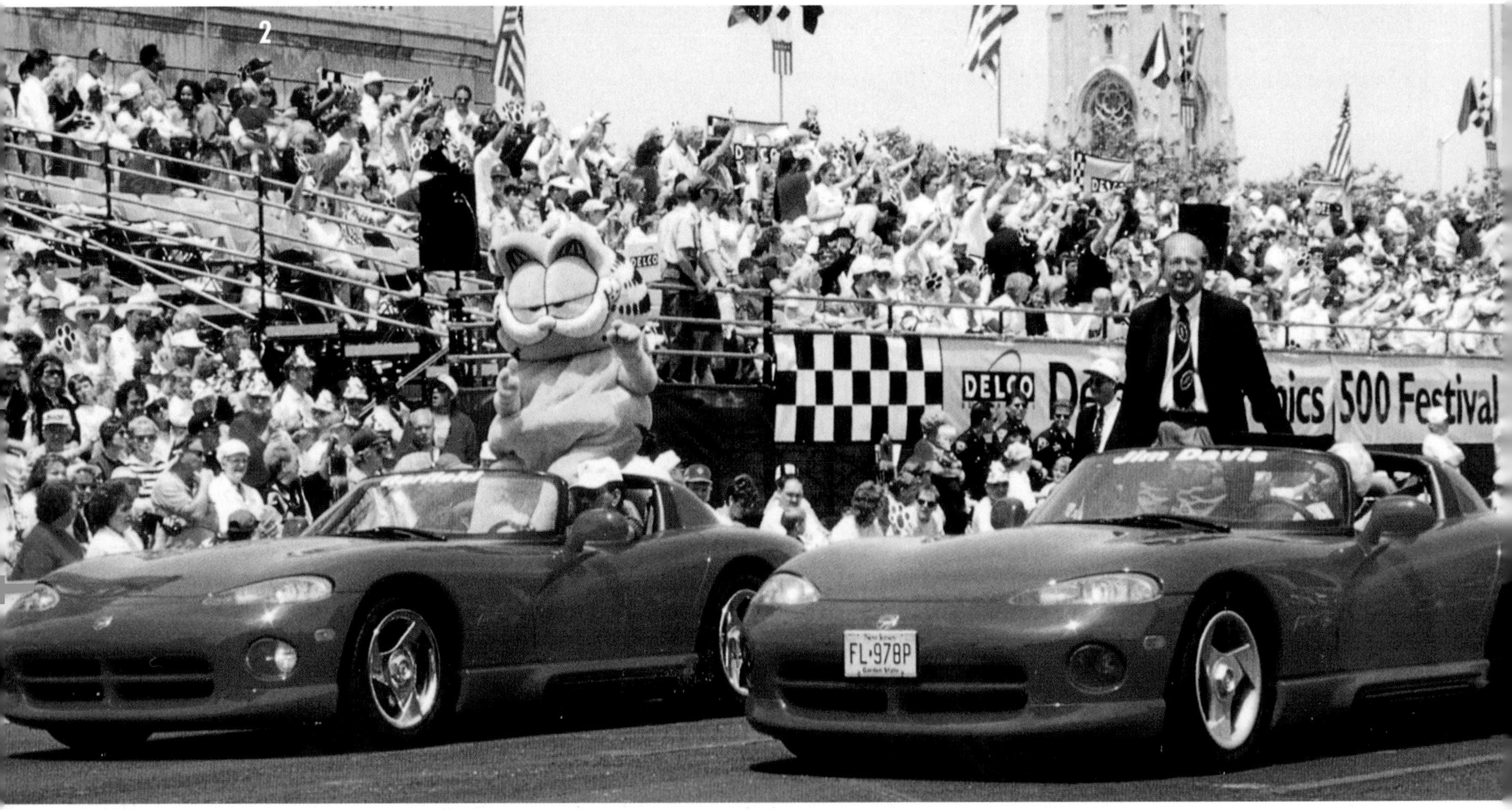
2
DELCO
500 Festival
Jim Davis
FL·978P

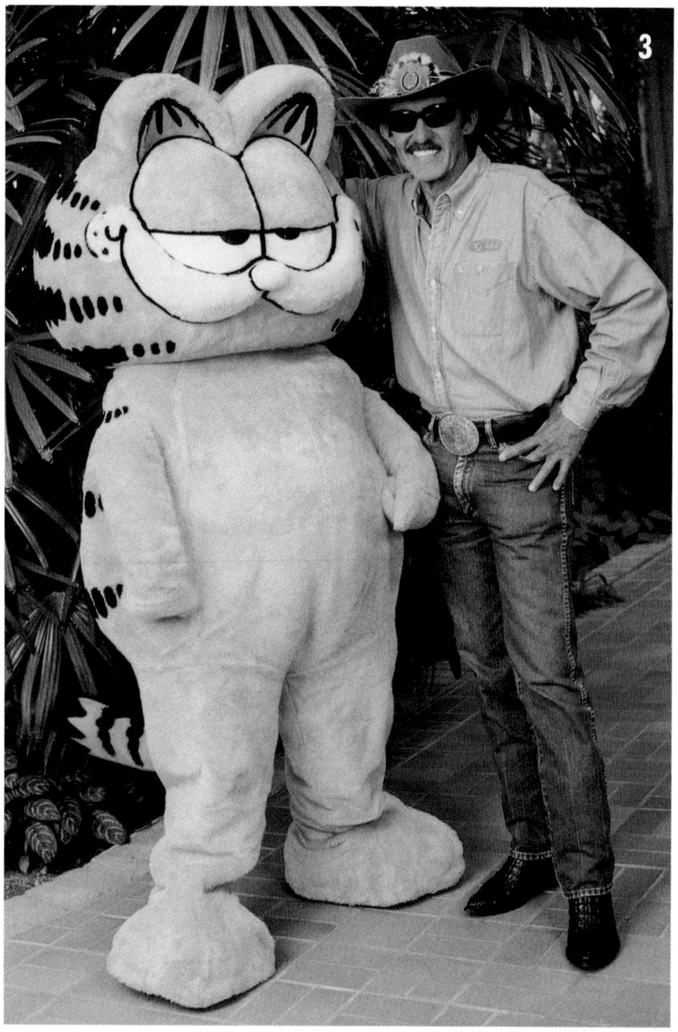
3

GRINNIN' AND WINNIN'!

In 2002, Garfield and race-car legend Richard Petty joined forces for a special licensing partnership, with much of the proceeds generated during the two-year affiliation going to the Victory Junction Gang Camp for chronically ill children and the Kyle Petty Charity Ride. The big announcement was made at the Daytona International Speedway, where Jim also unveiled the Garfield fantasy car.

Photo: Paul D. Coleman

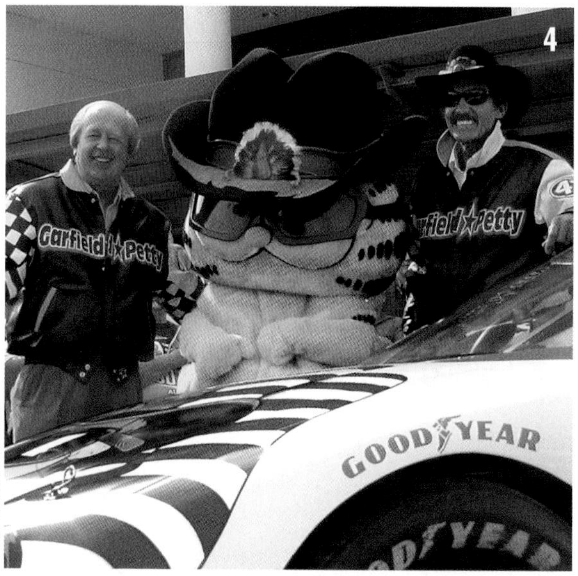
4
Garfield Petty
GOODYEAR

3. COOL CATS
Garfield meets Richard Petty at Paws, Inc., 2001.

4. SPEED RACERS
Jim, Garfield, and Richard Petty at the Daytona International Speedway, February 2002.

5. CAR-TOON
Publicity shot of Richard and Garfield.

6. HOT WHEELS
Garfield all revved up over his special fantasy car, which was created in conjunction with Petty Enterprises.

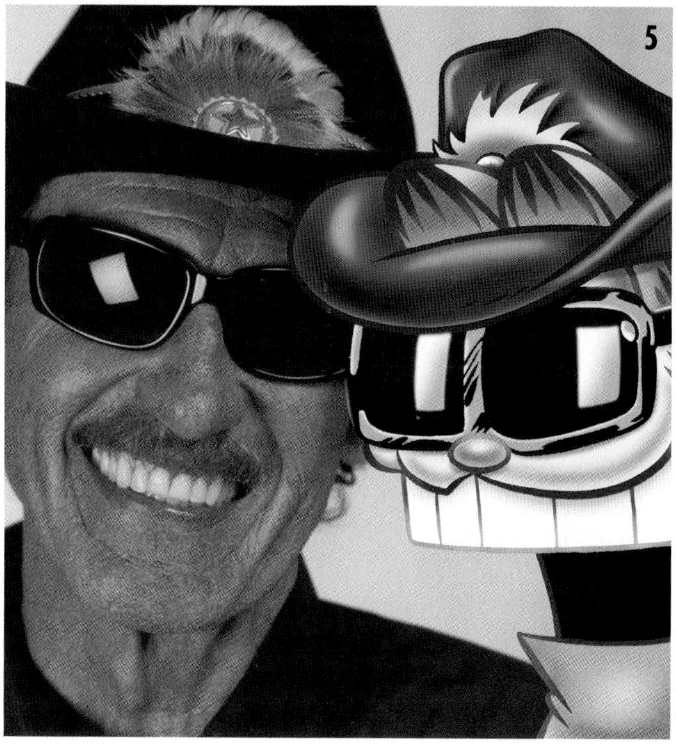
5

Photo: Paul D. Coleman

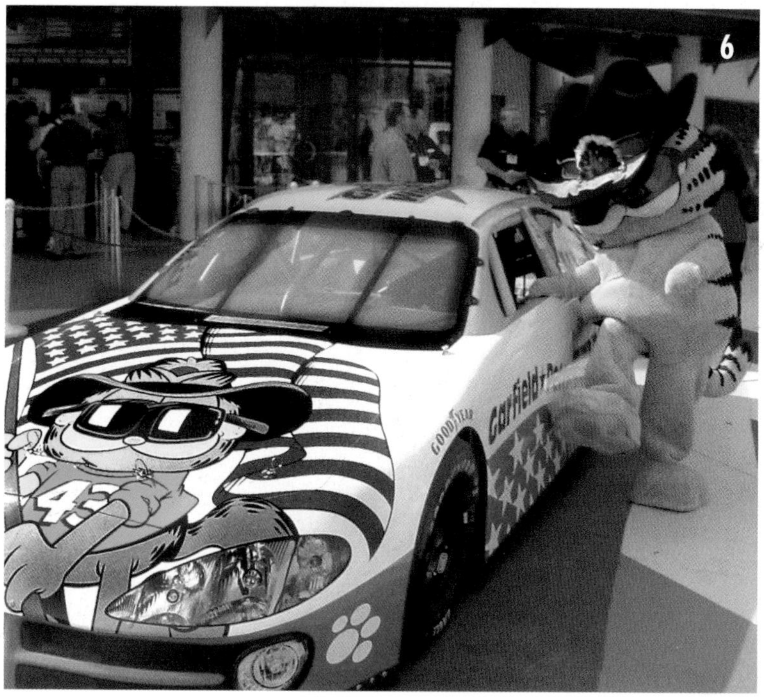
6

Cartoonist Cronies

1. Over the years several of Jim's fellow cartoonists have visited the Paws studio to give informal "chalk talks." Jim Borgman, Jeff MacNelly, Dean Young, and Mort Walker have all come to the studio to speak and draw before Jim's staff. In this snapshot, Jeff MacNelly, Pulitzer Prize–winning editorial cartoonist and the creator of the daily comic strip *Shoe*, does a quick sketch during a mid-1990s presentation. Sadly, MacNelly passed away in 2000 after battling cancer.

2. Jim at the B.C. Open golf tournament with Lynn Johnston, creator of the long-running comic strip *For Better or For Worse.*

3. Each year the National Cartoonist Society awards the Reuben (not the sandwich, but a statuette designed by and named after the NCS's first president, Rube Goldberg) for Cartoonist of the Year. The Reuben is cartooning's crowning achievement. Jim was nominated several times for the award and won it in 1989 for his work on *Garfield*. In this photo, taken at the 1983 Reuben ceremony at the Beverly Hills Hotel in Los Angeles, Jim enjoys a toast with legendary *Peanuts* creator Charles Schulz *(far right)* and United Feature Syndicate president Bob Metz *(center)*. At the time, both creators called UFS home. In 1994 Jim purchased the worldwide rights to *Garfield* and moved the strip over to Universal Press Syndicate.

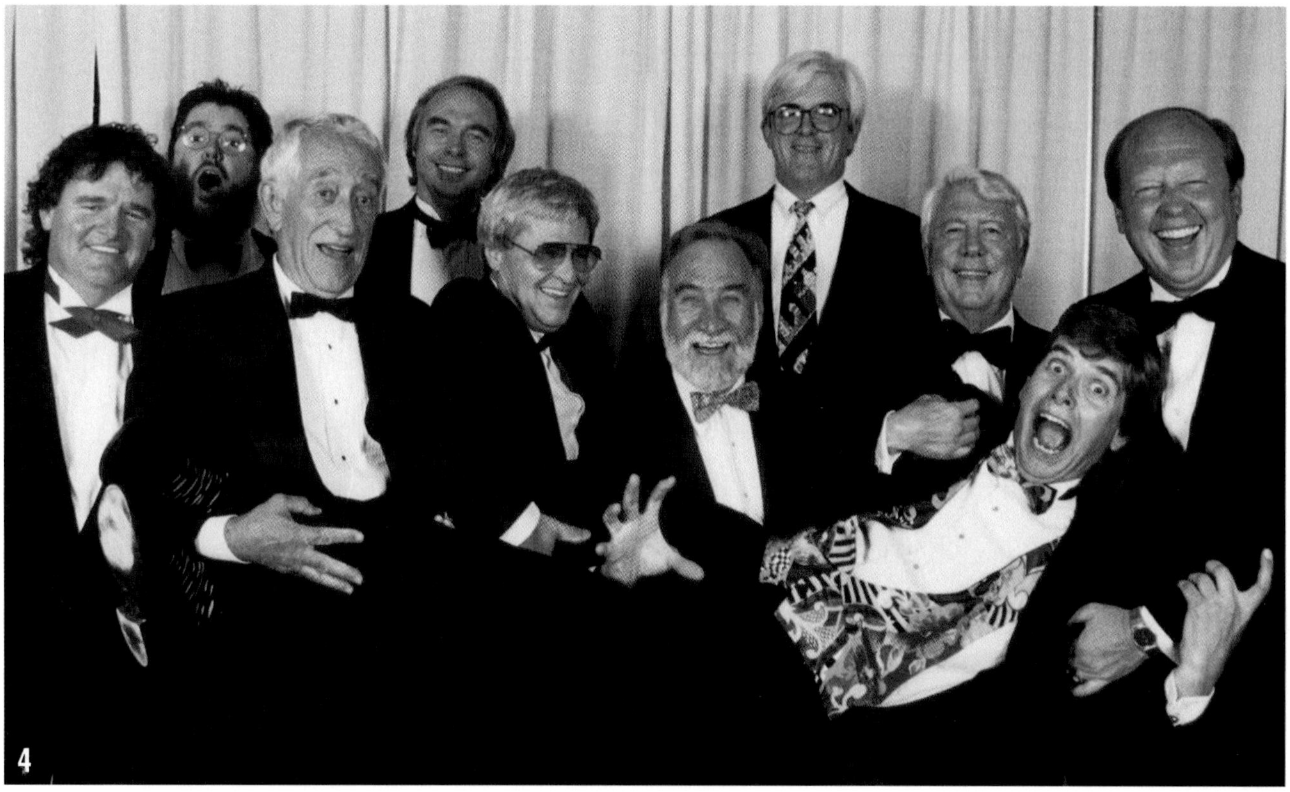

4. Funnymen in monkey suits at an NCS awards ceremony. Pictured: *(back row)* Chris Browne, Doug Marlette, Jeff MacNelly, *(front row)* Paul Szep, comedian Pat Paulsen, Johnny Hart, Tony Auth, Mort Walker, Jim Davis. Mike Peters *(being carried)*.

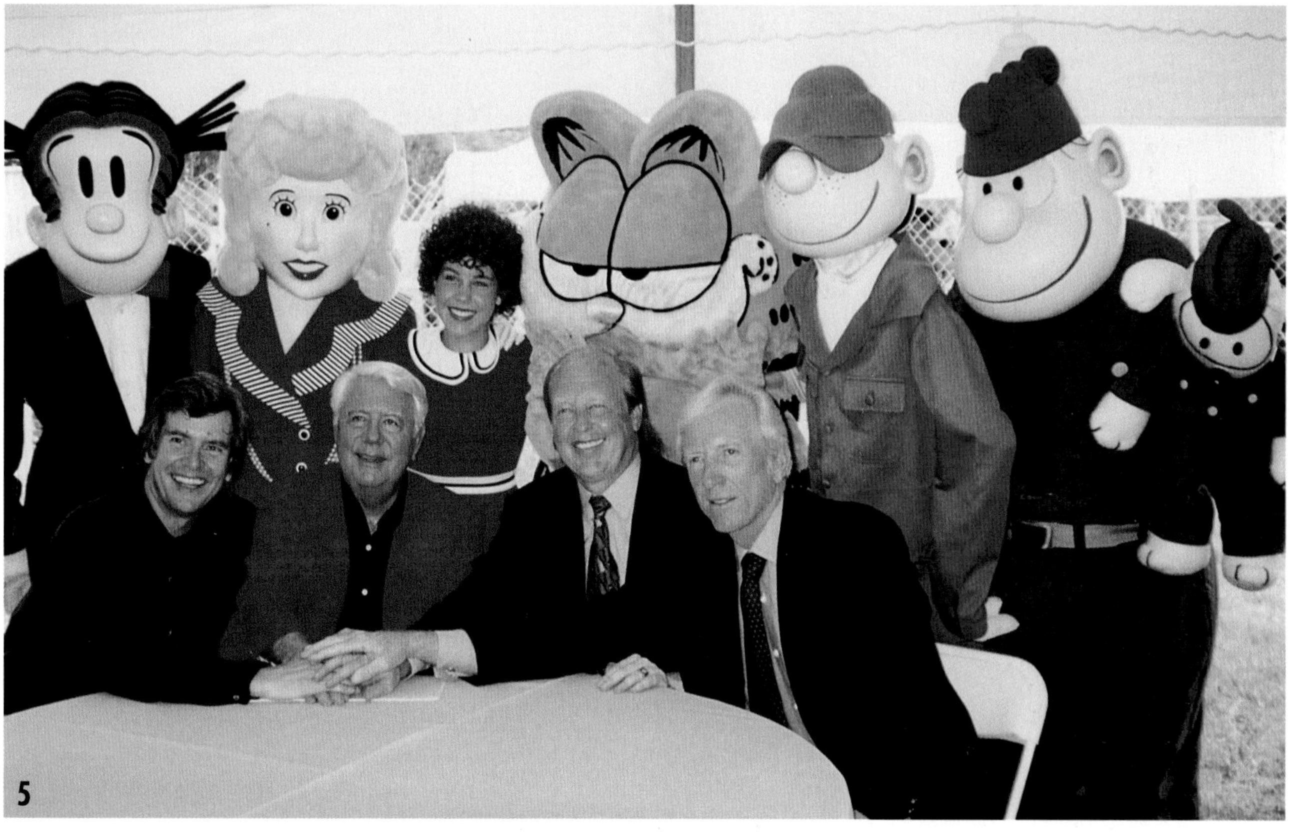

5. Jim and a few colorful characters celebrate the launch of the International Museum of Cartoon Art in Boca Raton, Florida, 1998. Pictured: *(back row)* Dagwood, Blondie, Annie, Garfield, Beetle Bailey, Sarge, Otto, *(seated)* Mike Peters, Mort Walker, Jim Davis, Dean Young.

Livin' Large

1. SIZE DOES MATTER
Holding fifteen liters of wine (the equivalent of twenty bottles), the "Nebuchadnezzar" (as it's known in the industry), stands over twenty-seven inches high and features beautifully engraved artwork of the cat. Jim Davis and Gary Hogue of The Hogue Cellars in Seattle, Washington, created several limited-edition wine bottles that were auctioned off for charity.

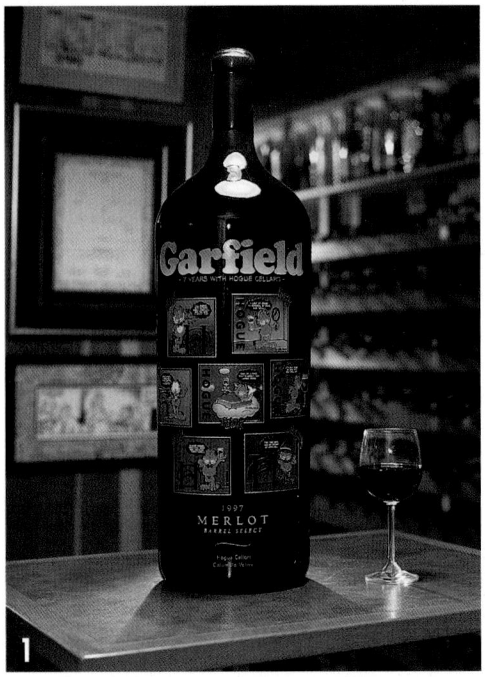
Garfield
1997
MERLOT

1

2. TOYS FOR BIG BOYS
Jim indulged his need for speed with a 1994 Viper.

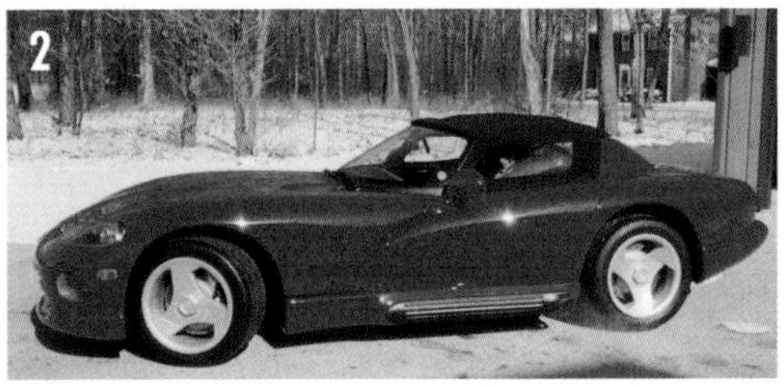

2

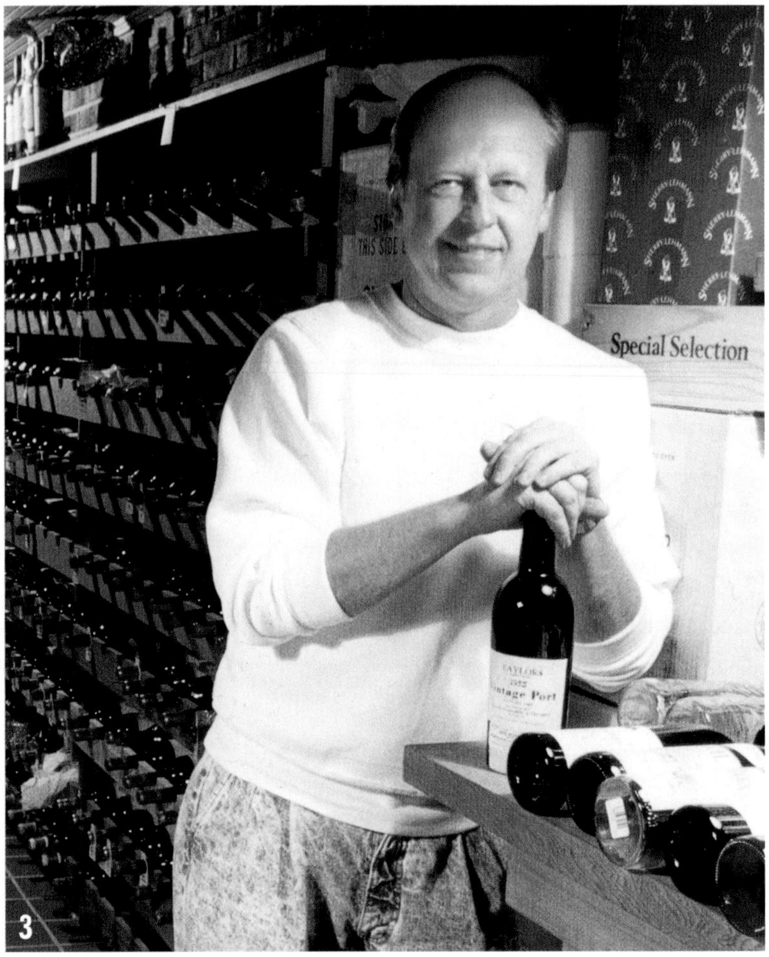
Special Selection

3

3. GRAPE EXPECTATIONS
An avid wine collector since the mid-1980s, Jim installed a temperature-controlled wine cellar in his basement that houses some 3,000 bottles. Jim's favorite wine? A 1947 Cheval Blanc.

4

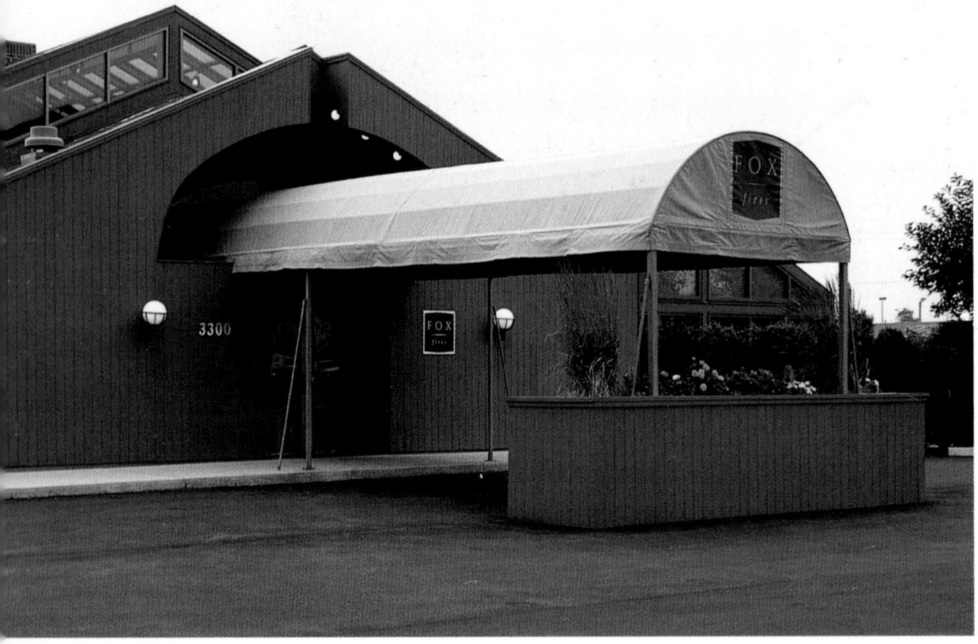
FOX
3300

5

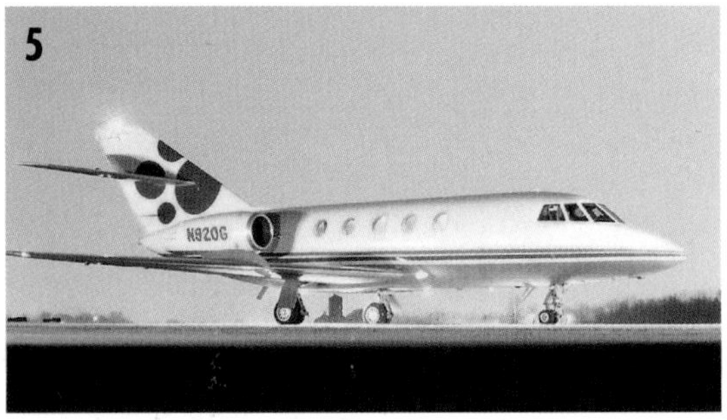
N920G

4. LE GRAND GOURMET
Where do you find chilled white gazpacho and ostrich tamales in Muncie, Indiana? At Foxfires, of course. Jim added restaurateur to his résumé with this fine-dining establishment that included one of the most impressive wine collections in the Midwest.

5. AN AIRCRAFT FIT FOR A FAT CAT
The Paws corporate plane, nicknamed "Junior" by Jim, is a 10-passenger Dassault Falcon 20F-5 and sports a burgundy paw print on the tail.

Momentous Moments

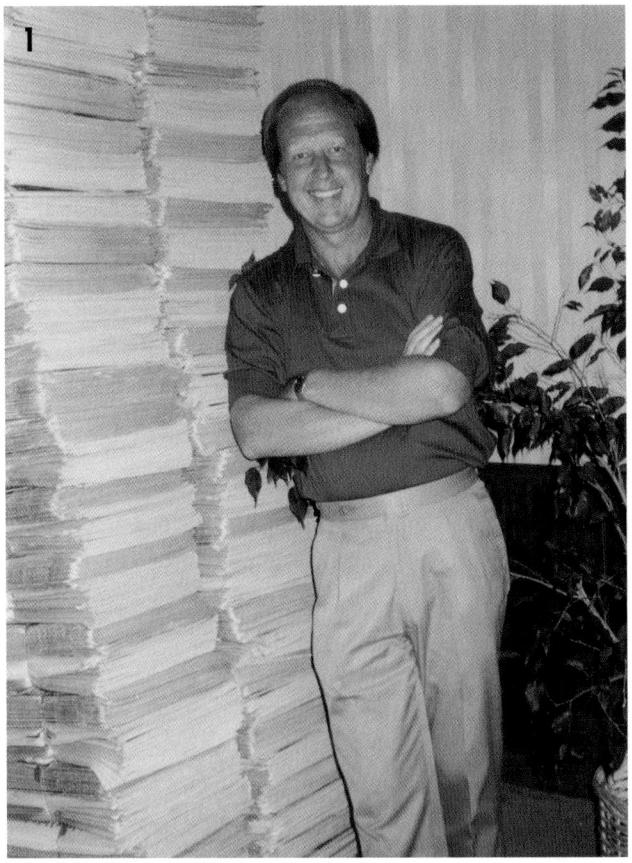

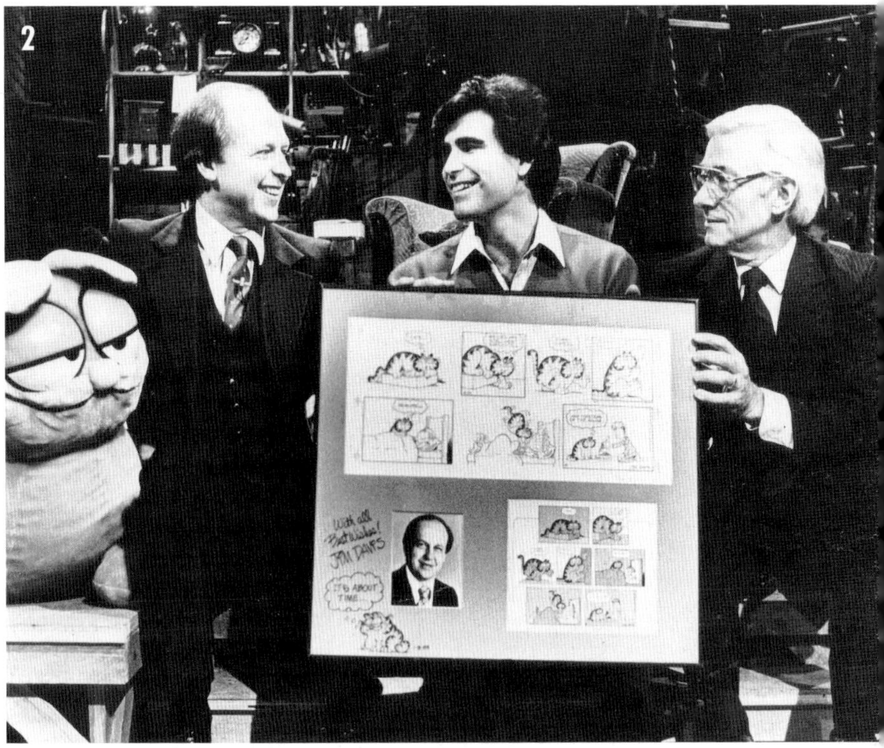

1. HOT OFF THE PRESS! *Garfield* reached the 2,000-newspaper mark on August 3, 1987. (The paper that put the cat over the top was the Danville, Illinois *Commercial-News.*) Here, Jim poses with a stack of—coincidentally enough—2,000 papers.

2. GARFIELD INSTITUTIONALIZED? It's true! The kooky cat became part of the Smithsonian Institution's Museum of American History on January 9, 1983. Jim Davis presented the Smithsonian with the original artwork for the first *Garfield* Sunday comic strip during a taping of a syndicated TV special. Seen here *(from left to right)* on the set are Jim Davis, host Michael Young, and James R. Morris Jr., director of the Smithsonian's Performing Arts division.

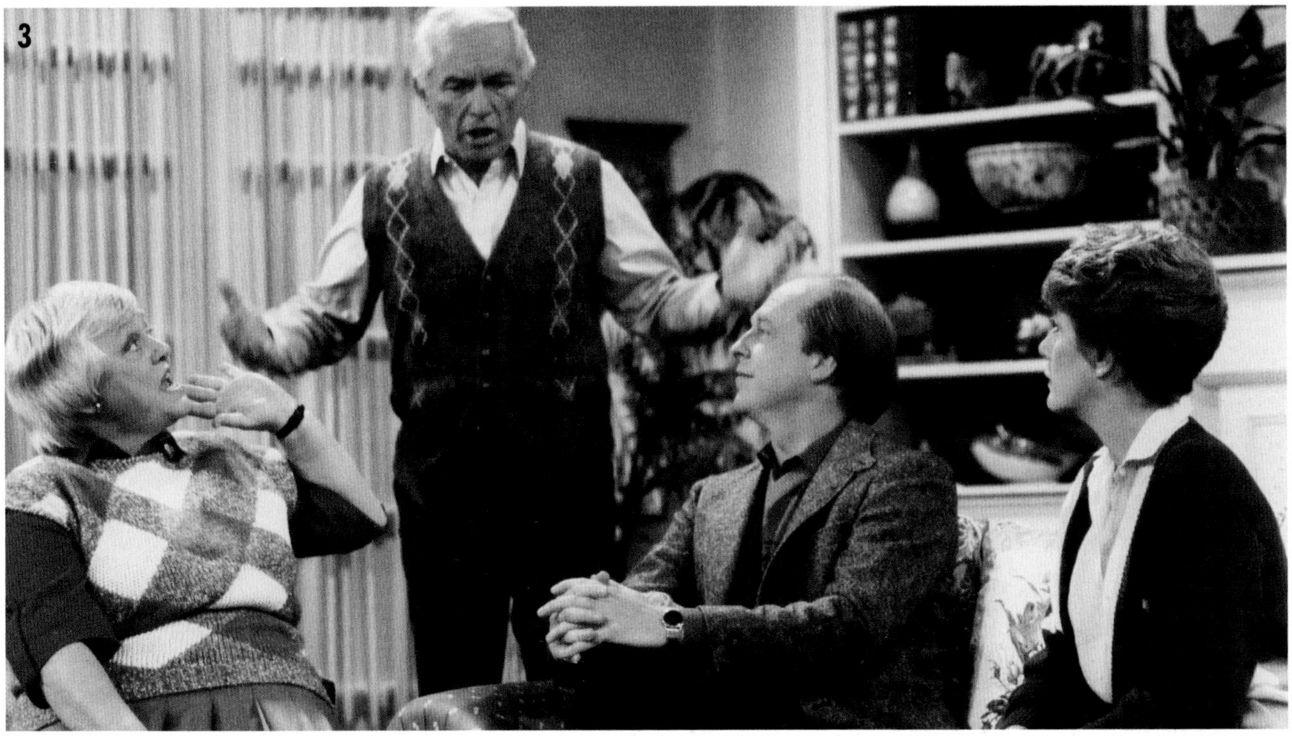

3. TOO CLOSE FOR COMFORT
In 1986, Jim made a cameo appearance (as himself, natch) in the Ted Knight series about a cartoonist. Pictured here are series stars Ted Knight, Nancy Dussault *(right)*, and Pat Carroll. Incidentally, Pat later provided the voice of Grandma in the Garfield Christmas special.

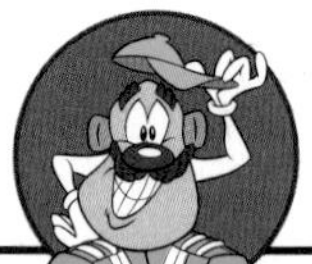

Mr. Potato Head

1. SPUD BUDS
Jim Davis and Brett Koth pose with their cartoon counterparts.

2. HOT POTATO
Mr. Potato Head turned fifty in 2002. Here, Jim Davis and Hasbro executives blow out the candles at a special birthday party for the illustrious tuber in New York.

3. TATER TIME
Jim holds the comic strip—dated March 5, 2002—celebrating Mr. Potato Head's fiftieth birthday.

4. YOU MAY NOW KISS THE SPUD
A wedding gift from Hasbro to Jim and Jill Davis, this whimsical piece depicts Garfield marrying a Potato Head couple . . . and they lived starchily ever after.

What does a fat orange cat have to do with America's most famous potato? In 2001, Jim Davis teamed with cartoonist Brett Koth to produce the Mr. Potato Head comic strip, chronicling the adventures of the potato patriarch, his wife, and kids Chip and Julienne. The result: a comic with real appeal.

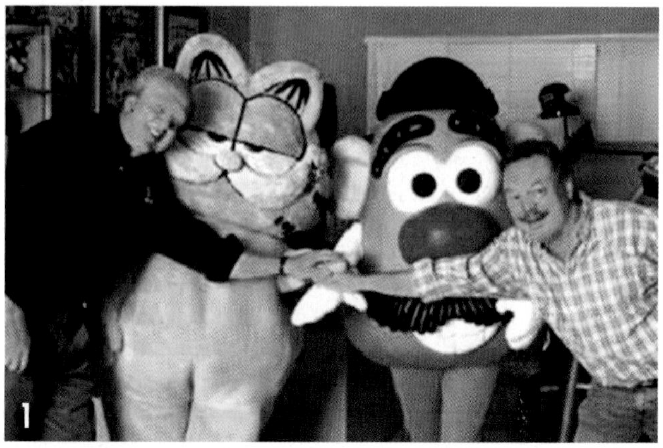
1

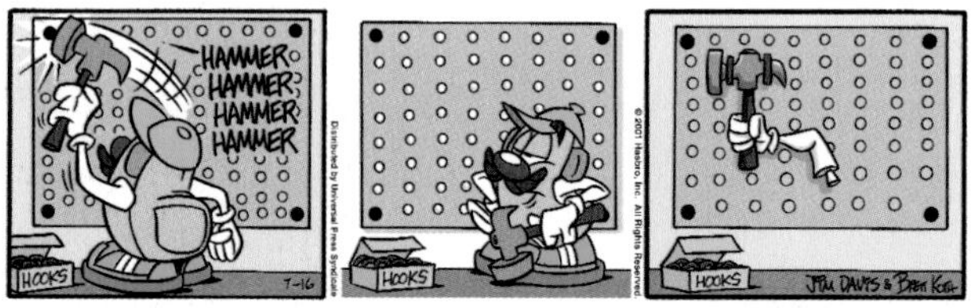
HAMMER
HAMMER?
HAMMER
HAMMER
HOOKS
HOOKS
HOOKS

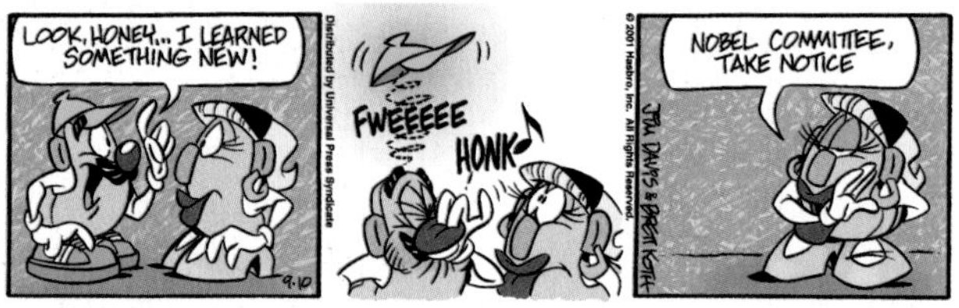
LOOK, HONEY... I LEARNED SOMETHING NEW!
FWEEEEE
HONK
NOBEL COMMITTEE, TAKE NOTICE

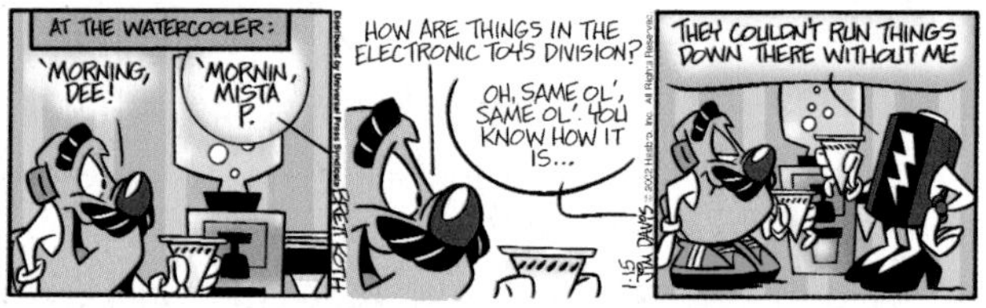
AT THE WATERCOOLER:
'MORNING, DEE!
'MORNIN, MISTA P.
HOW ARE THINGS IN THE ELECTRONIC TOYS DIVISION?
OH, SAME OL', SAME OL'. YOU KNOW HOW IT IS...
THEY COULDN'T RUN THINGS DOWN THERE WITHOUT ME

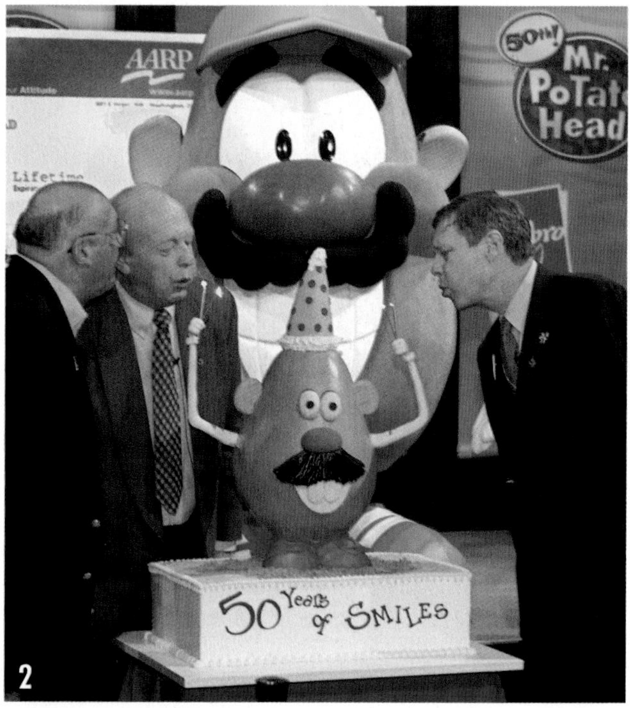
AARP
Mr. Potato Head
50 Years of SMILES
2

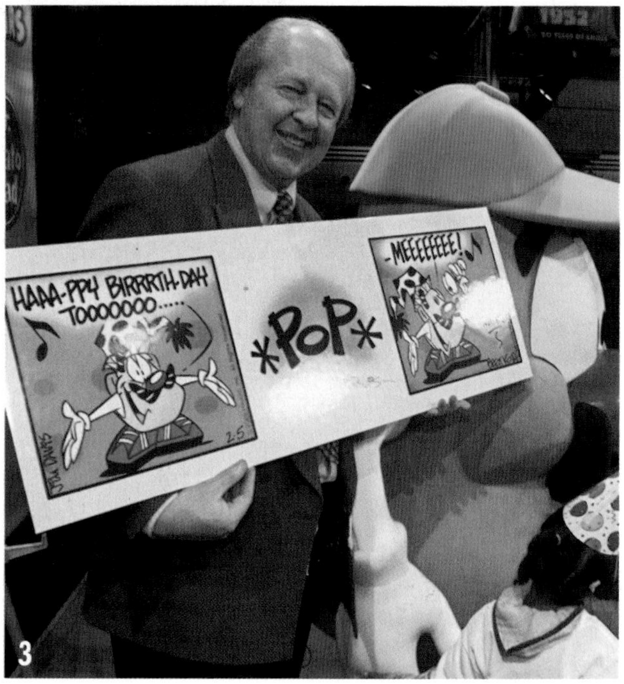
HAAA-PPY BIRRRTH-DAH TOOOOOOO.....
POP
MEEEEEEE!
3

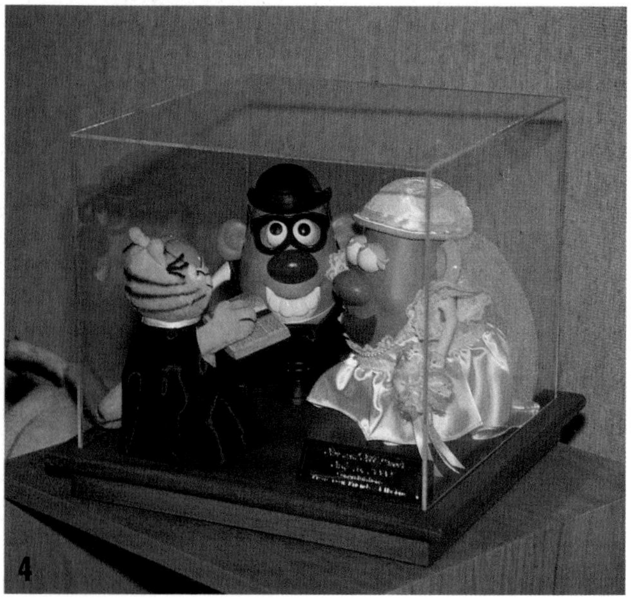
4

CHAPTER EIGHTEEN

Did You Know?

Fun Facts about Jim Davis and Garfield

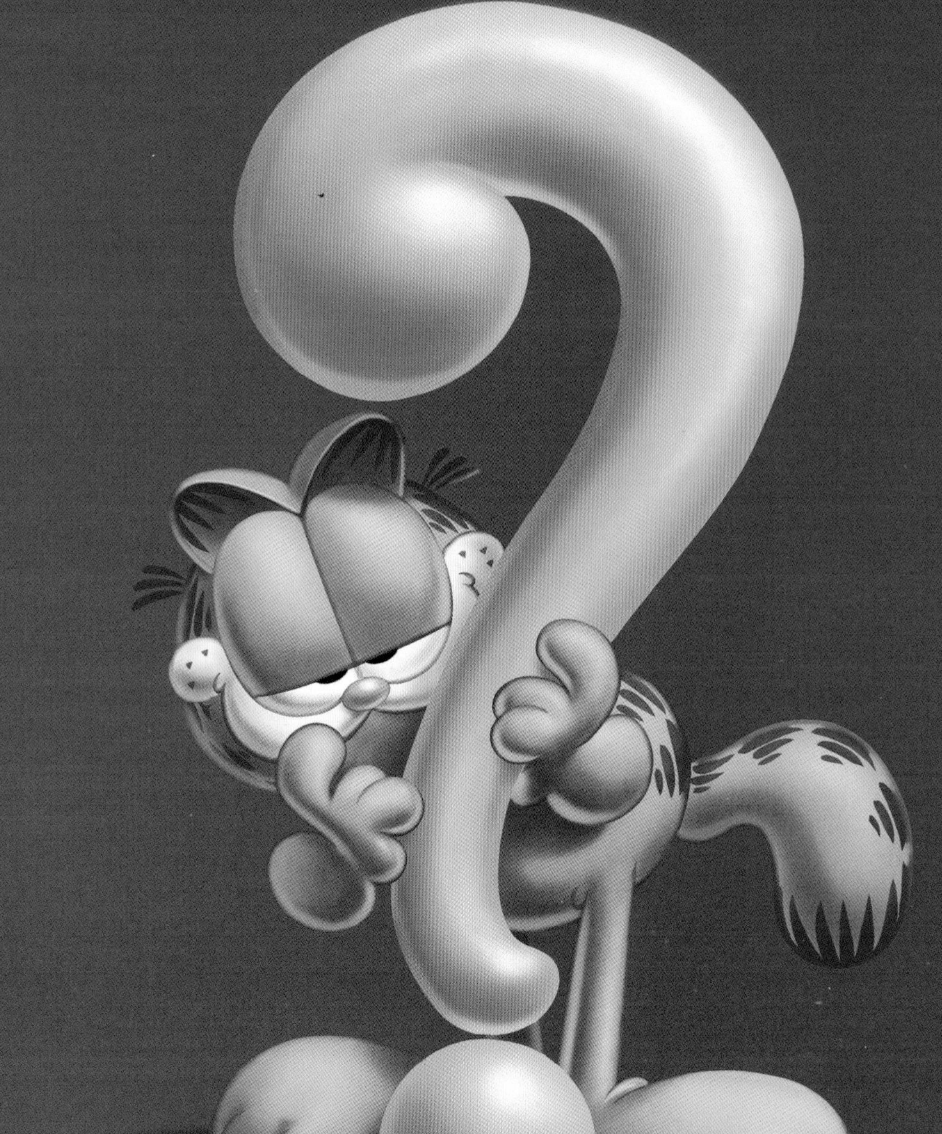

Did You Know?

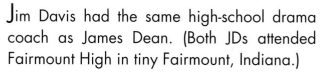

Jim Davis had the same high-school drama coach as James Dean. (Both JDs attended Fairmount High in tiny Fairmount, Indiana.)

Jim played lovable bumpkin Will Stockdale in the civic-theater production of *No Time for Sergeants*, winning the 1976 Indiana Theater League's Best Actor award. (Garfield was born soon after, dimming the lights on Jim's stage career.)

Get your butt outta bed!

As a kid, Jim's favorite book was *Call of the Wild*.

Jim really wanted to be a farmer, but suffered from asthma. (He still gets up with the chickens, though, often rising before 4 a.m.!)

Jim attended Ball State University (in Muncie, Indiana) at the same time as David Letterman. (The two funmeisters knew each other and were in rival fraternities.)

In college, Jim was a gymnast. During a routine, he ruptured a disk, resulting in two back surgeries. (A great excuse for that funky golf swing!)

Jim's first new car was a '68 Dodge Monaco convertible.

Garfield is recognized by Guinness World Records as the most widely syndicated cartoon strip in the world.

Stephen King, Steven Spielberg, and the Smothers Brothers are among the many celebrities who own original *Garfield* strips.

The little circles leading from the thought balloon to the character in the strip are called "doo-dahs."

The last sentence in a *Garfield* thought balloon never ends in a period.

Each month, Garfield receives over 1,600 pieces of fan mail.

The Garfield Macy's Thanksgiving Day Parade balloon is 61 feet long, 35 feet wide, and 35 feet high. It holds 18,907 cubic feet of helium.

The Paws Solar Aquatic System treats more than 620,000 gallons of wastewater a year. (Yuck!)

Garfield has his own catalog called Garfield Stuff®, which has featured more than 800 products.

Jim's all-time favorite Garfield product is the Garfield phone. (Makes a great conversation piece!)

Launched in 1996, the official Garfield Web site, www.garfield.com, is more than a thousand pages in size and has more than a million and a half visitors each month.

Garfield and Jon Arbuckle's favorite waitress is named Irma; her name—but not her personality—was borrowed from Jim's aunt Irma.

Jim likes his steaks so rare, he tells the server, "Bring me something a good doctor could save."

Jim is powerless to resist a jelly donut.

Jim's favorite condiment is Miracle Whip.

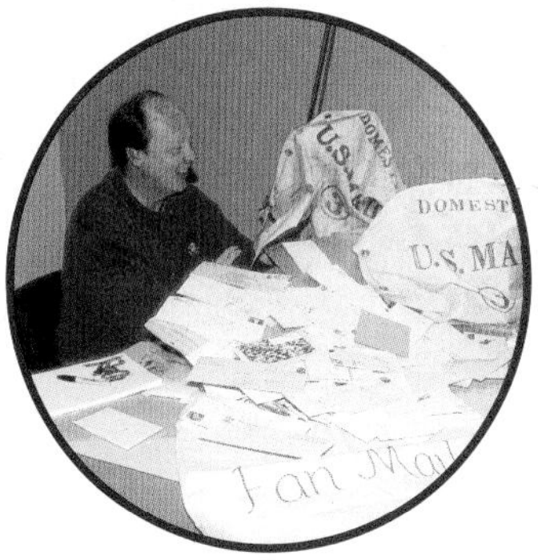

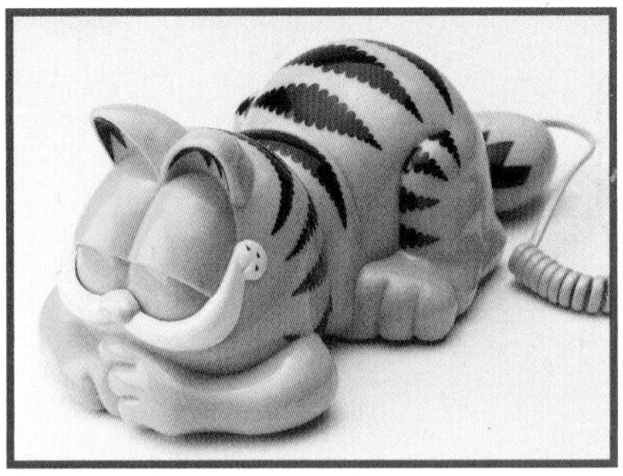

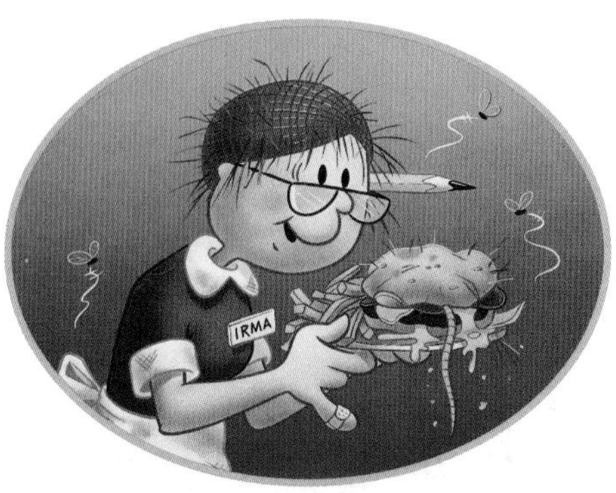
IRMA

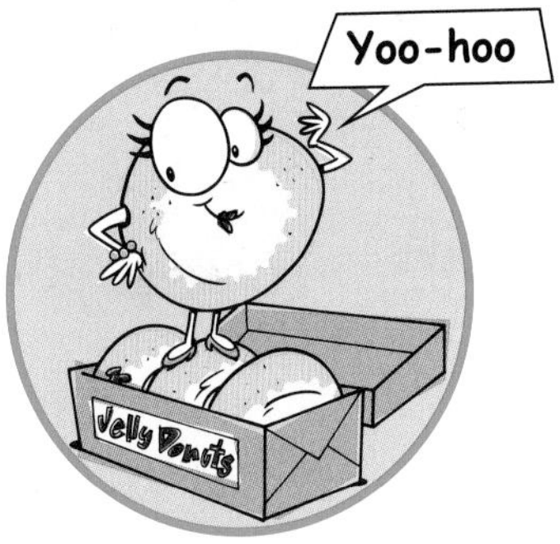
Yoo-hoo
Jelly Donuts

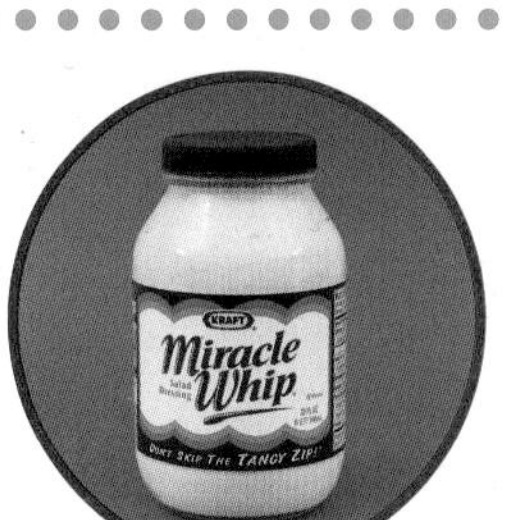
Miracle Whip

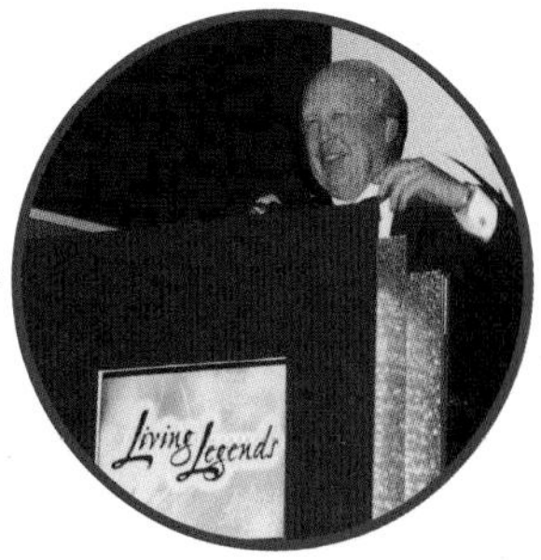
Living Legends

Jim was named an Indiana Living Legend by the Indiana Historical Society. (Other Living Legends include Larry Bird, David Letterman, Senator Richard Lugar, John Mellencamp, and Kurt Vonnegut.)

In Garfield's first TV appearance (a special on newspaper comics), San Francisco radio personality Scott Beach, not Lorenzo Music, provided the voice of the wisecracking cat.

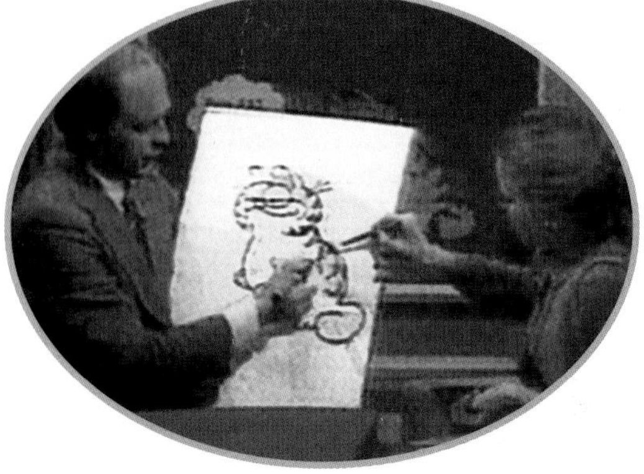

The first national TV show that Jim appeared on was *The Today Show*. He was interviewed by Jane Pauley (another Indiana Living Legend).

Odie, the clueless canine, was originally going to be named Spot.

Snoopy, Marmaduke, and Dagwood, three other popular comic-strip characters, have appeared in the *Garfield* strip.

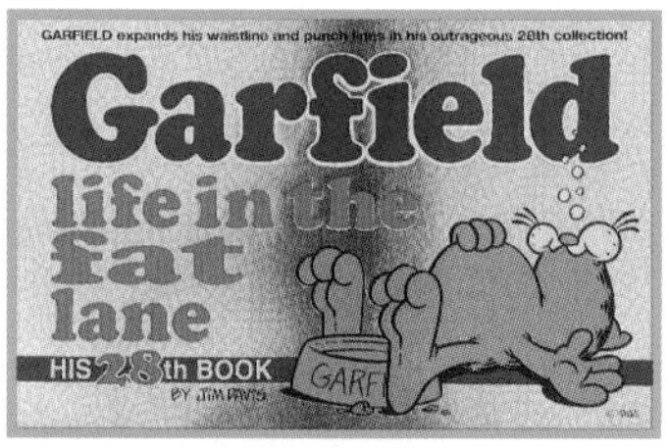
GARFIELD expands his waistline and punch lines in his outrageous 28th collection!
Garfield
life in the fat lane
HIS 28th BOOK
BY JIM DAVIS

Every comic-strip compilation book title has a food or weight theme.

Garfield and Jim both hate raisins. (And, as they approach geezerdom, prunes, too!)

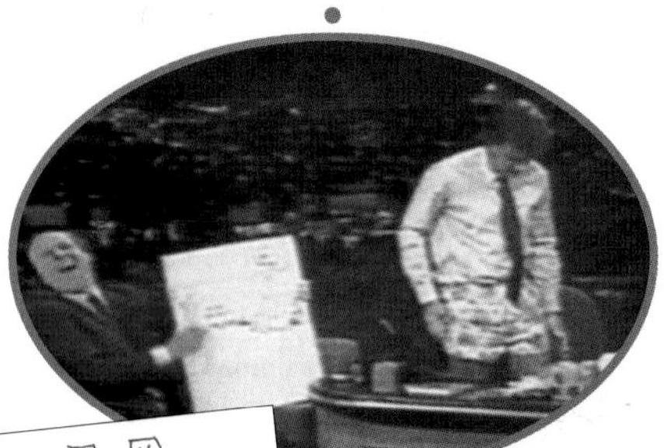

Jim made an appearance on *The Pat Sajak Show*.

Jim loves to play euchre, a card game popular in Indiana and Ohio.

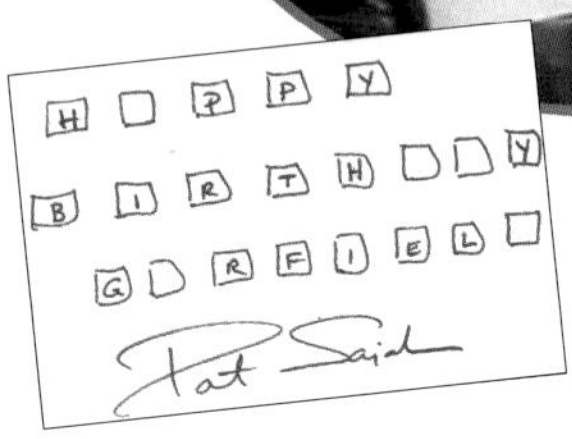

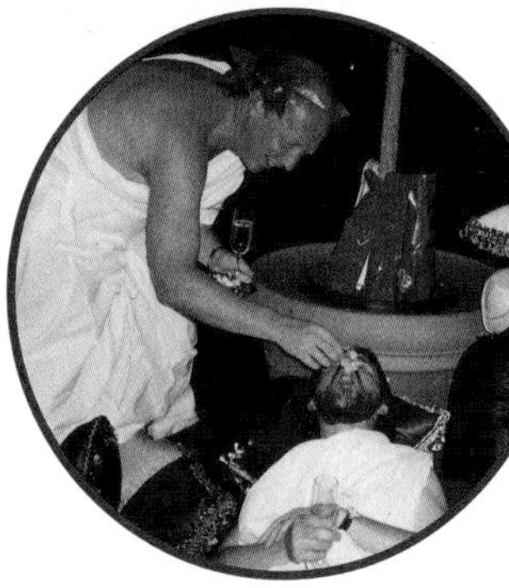

Jim celebrated his fiftieth birthday with a toga party!

Burt Reynolds and Loni Anderson battled over an autographed Garfield sketch during their much-publicized divorce proceedings.

On the *Late Show with David Letterman*, Halle Berry revealed that she has a Garfield tattoo on her tush. (Great way to end, huh?)

CHAPTER NINETEEN

Outtakes

Never-before-seen, funky cartoon clippings swept up from the editing room floor. Get down with your weird self!

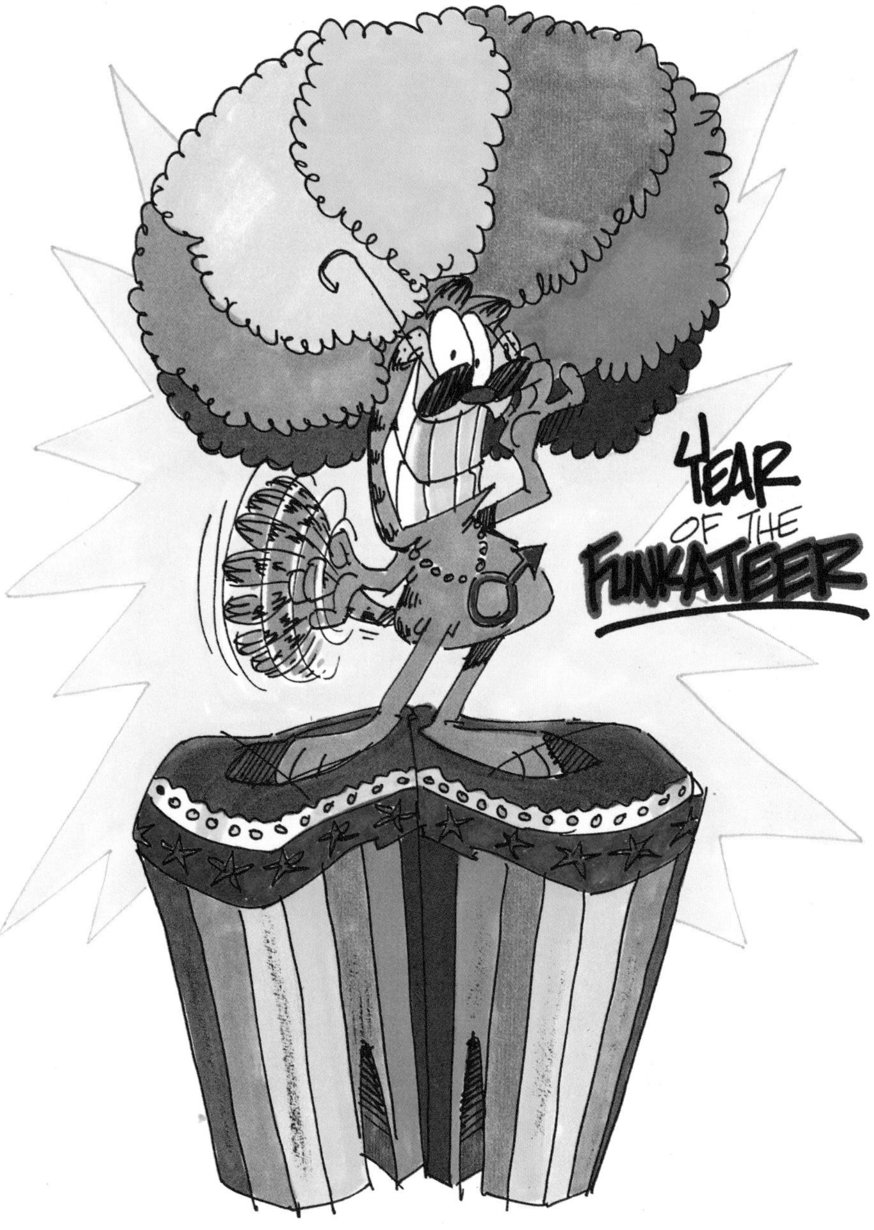
YEAR
OF THE
FUNKATEER

GONZO GARFIELD: Rejected comic strips

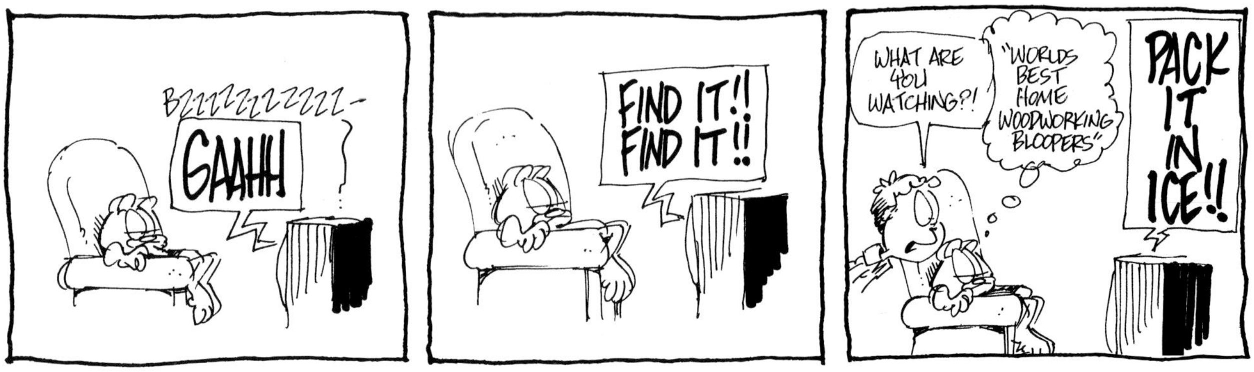
BZZZZZZZZZZZ-
GAAHH!
FIND IT!! FIND IT!!
WHAT ARE YOU WATCHING?!
"WORLDS BEST HOME WOODWORKING BLOOPERS"
PACK IT IN ICE!!

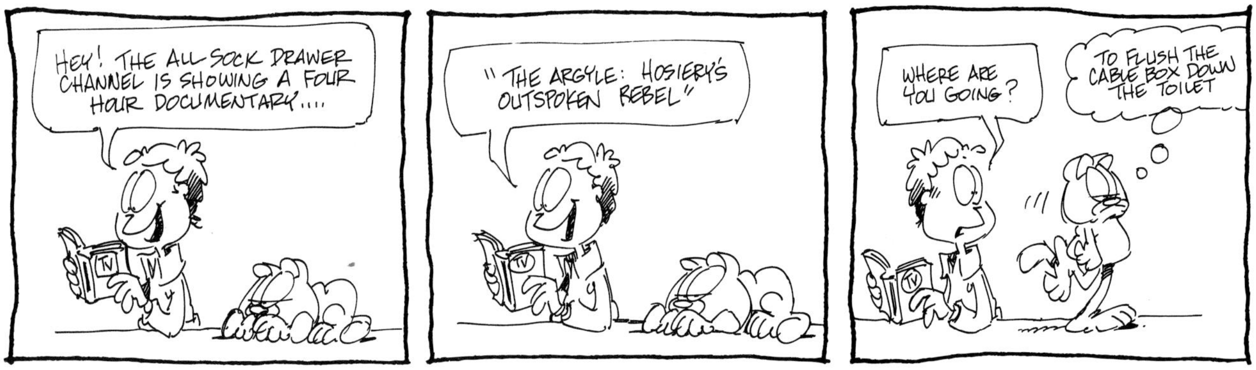
HEY! THE ALL-SOCK DRAWER CHANNEL IS SHOWING A FOUR HOUR DOCUMENTARY....
"THE ARGYLE: HOSIERY'S OUTSPOKEN REBEL"
WHERE ARE YOU GOING?
TO FLUSH THE CABLE BOX DOWN THE TOILET

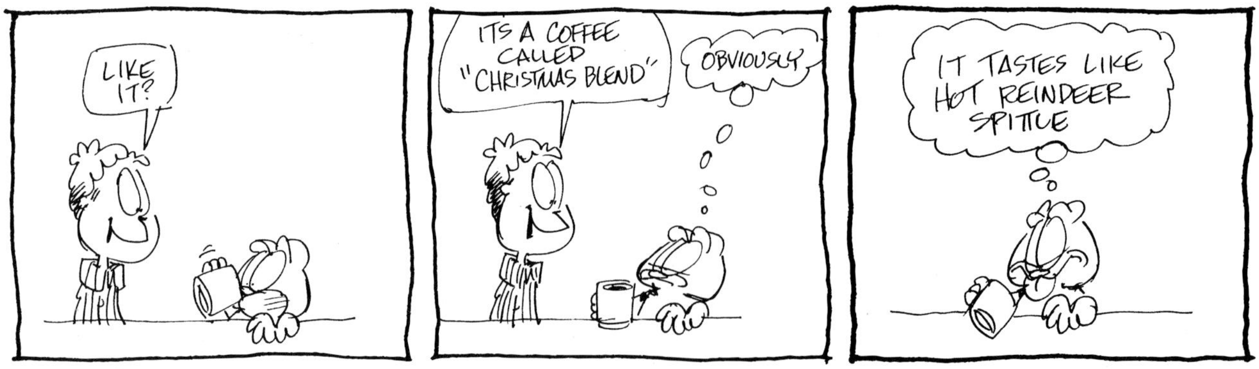
LIKE IT?
ITS A COFFEE CALLED "CHRISTMAS BLEND"
OBVIOUSLY
IT TASTES LIKE HOT REINDEER SPITTLE

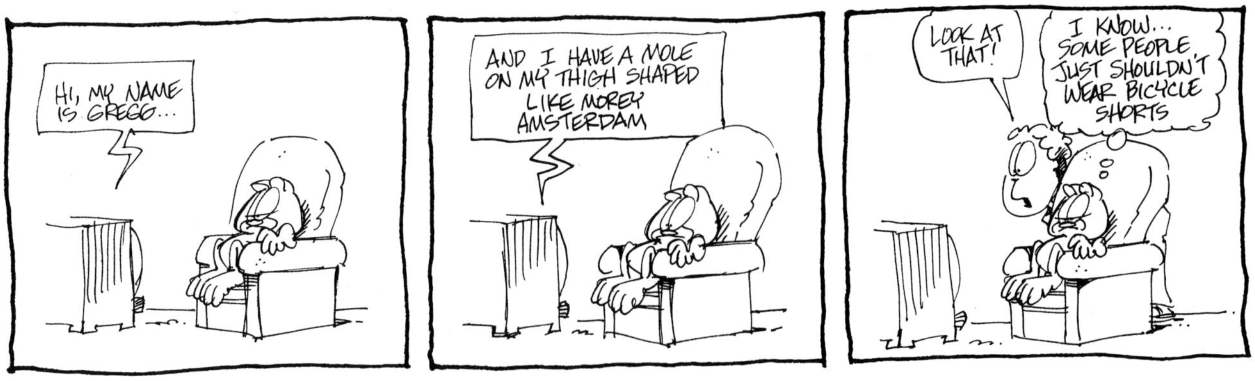
HI, MY NAME IS GREGG...
AND I HAVE A MOLE ON MY THIGH SHAPED LIKE MOREY AMSTERDAM
LOOK AT THAT!
I KNOW... SOME PEOPLE JUST SHOULDN'T WEAR BICYCLE SHORTS

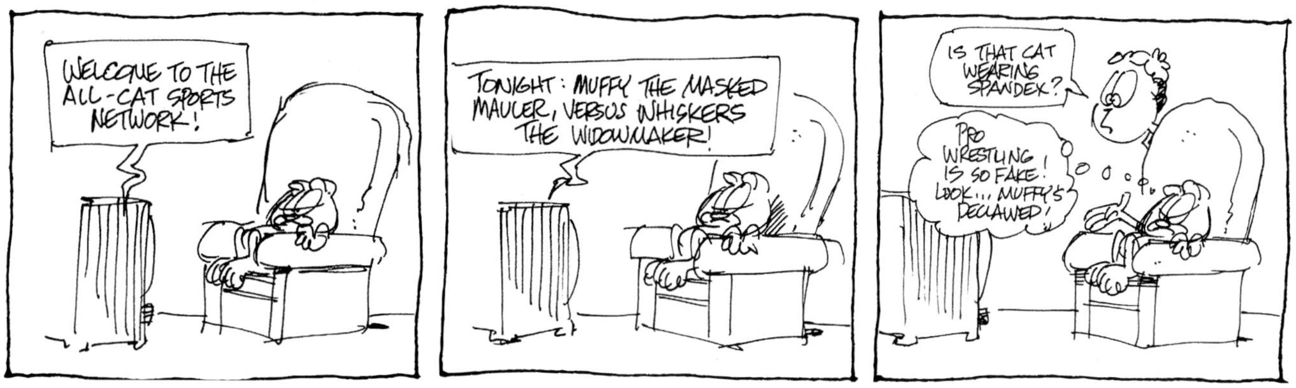
WELCOME TO THE ALL-CAT SPORTS NETWORK!
TONIGHT: MUFFY THE MASKED MAULER, VERSUS WHISKERS THE WIDOWMAKER!
IS THAT CAT WEARING SPANDEX?
PRO WRESTLING IS SO FAKE! LOOK... MUFFY'S DECLAWED!

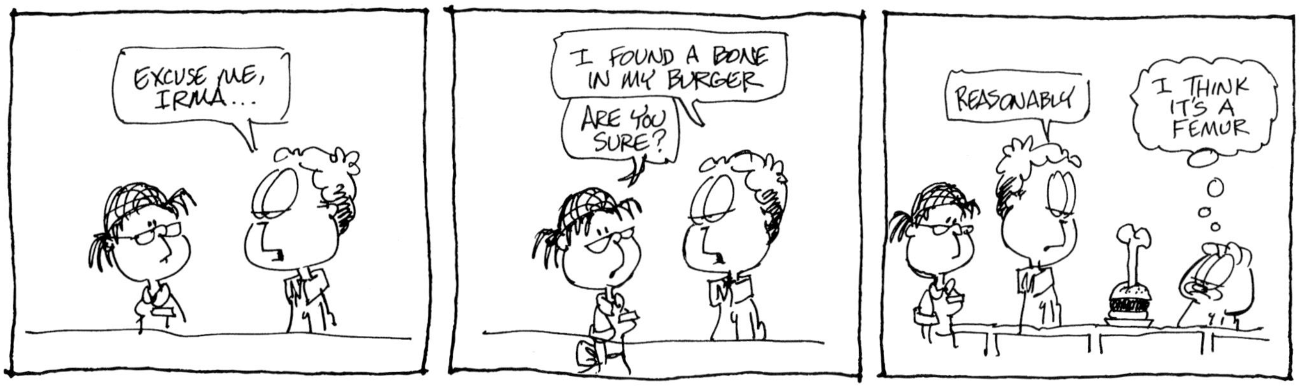
EXCUSE ME, IRMA...
I FOUND A BONE IN MY BURGER
ARE YOU SURE?
REASONABLY
I THINK IT'S A FEMUR

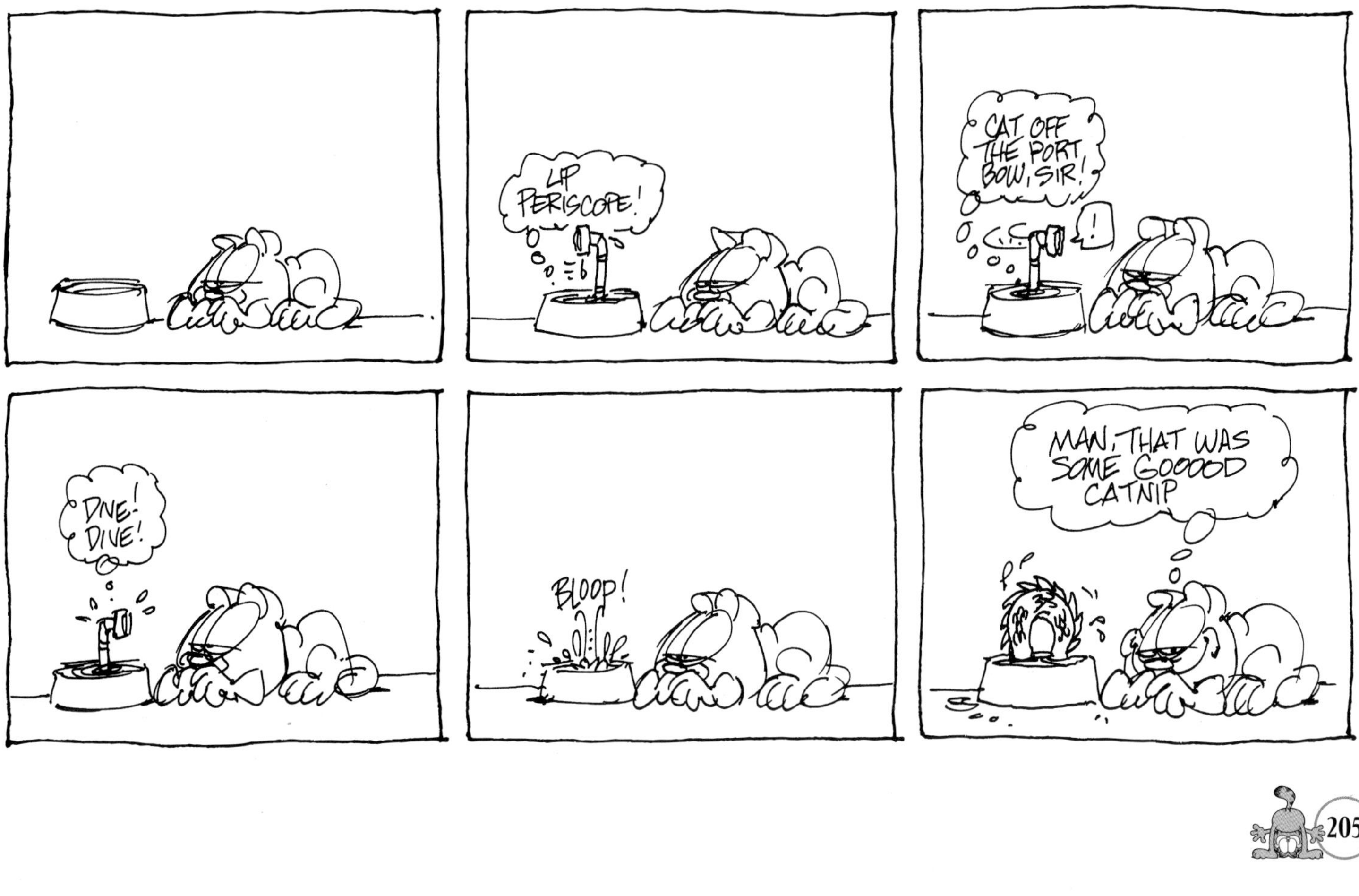
UP PERISCOPE!
CAT OFF THE PORT BOW, SIR!
!
DIVE! DIVE!
BLOOP!
MAN, THAT WAS SOME GOOOOD CATNIP

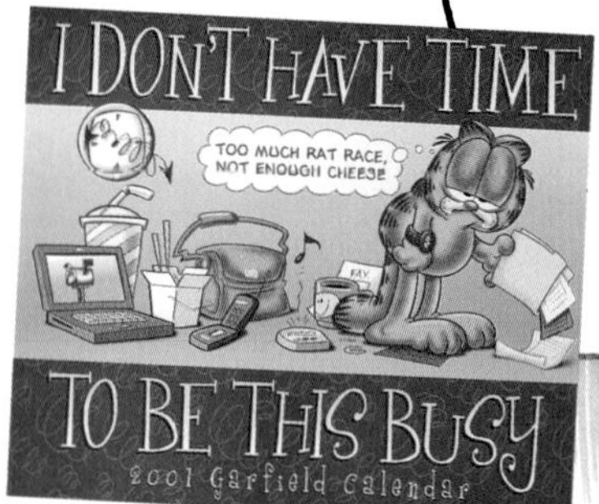
I DON'T HAVE TIME
TOO MUCH RAT RACE, NOT ENOUGH CHEESE
TO BE THIS BUSY
2001 Garfield Calendar

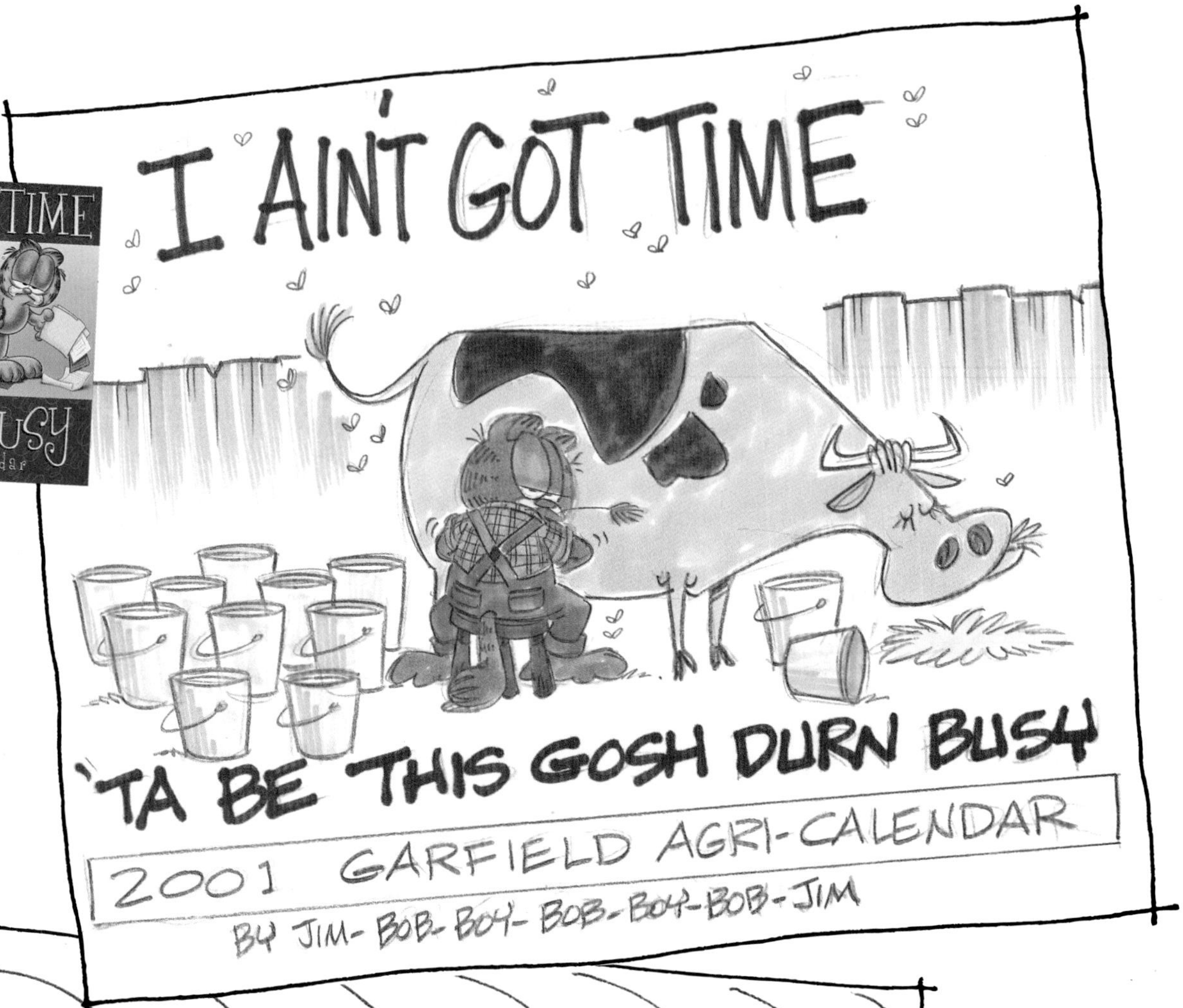
I AIN'T GOT TIME
'TA BE THIS GOSH DURN BUSY
2001 GARFIELD AGRI-CALENDAR
BY JIM-BOB-BOY-BOB-BOY-BOB-JIM

Right: HICK SCHTICK
Countrified version of the 2001 calendar, *I Don't Have Time to Be This Busy.*

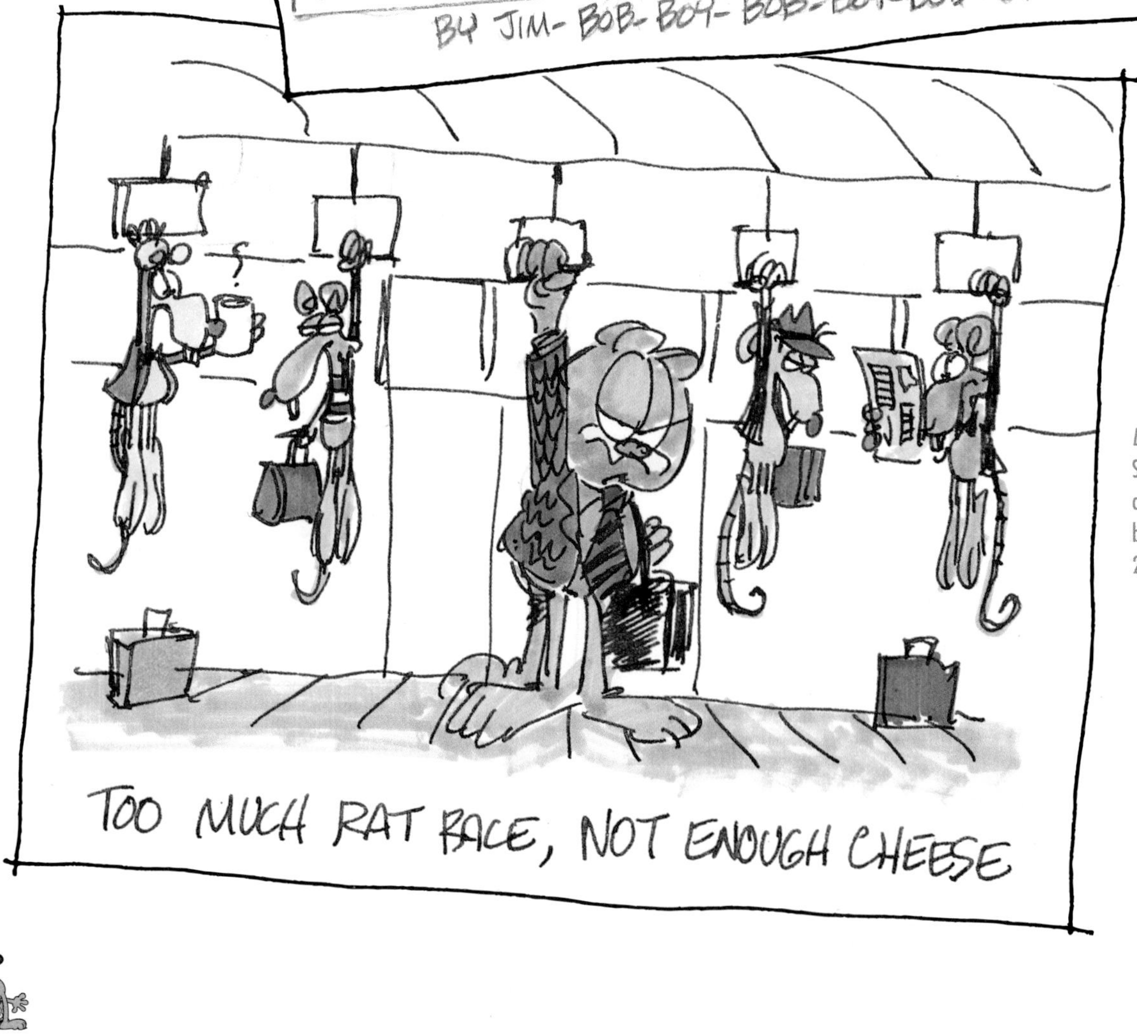
TOO MUCH RAT RACE, NOT ENOUGH CHEESE

Left: URBAN RAT RACE
Sketch never used, but copy appeared as thought balloon on cover of the 2001 calendar.

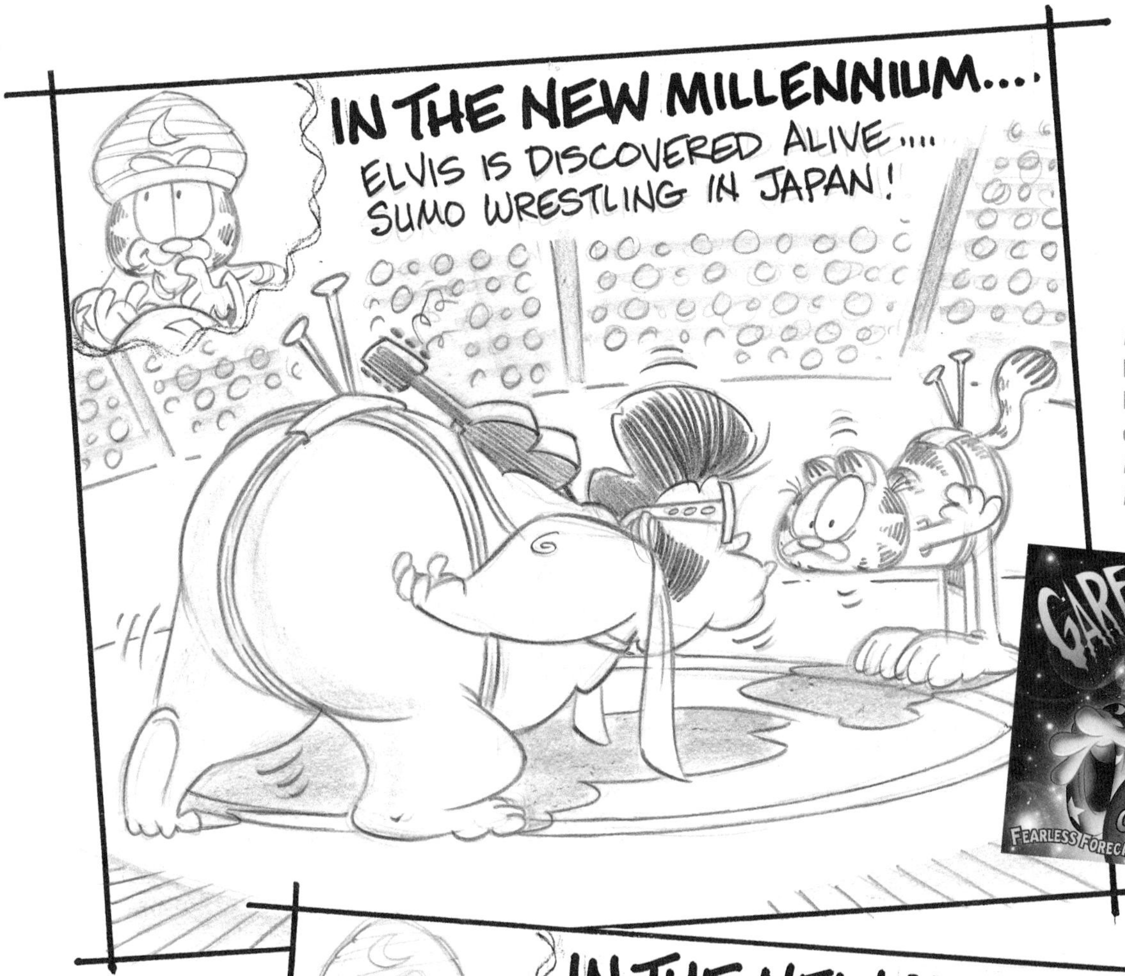
IN THE NEW MILLENNIUM....
ELVIS IS DISCOVERED ALIVE....
SUMO WRESTLING IN JAPAN!

Left and below:
PREPOSTEROUS PREDICTIONS
Rejected gags from the 1999 calendar, *Garfield Predicts: Fearless Forecasts for a Brave New Millennium.*

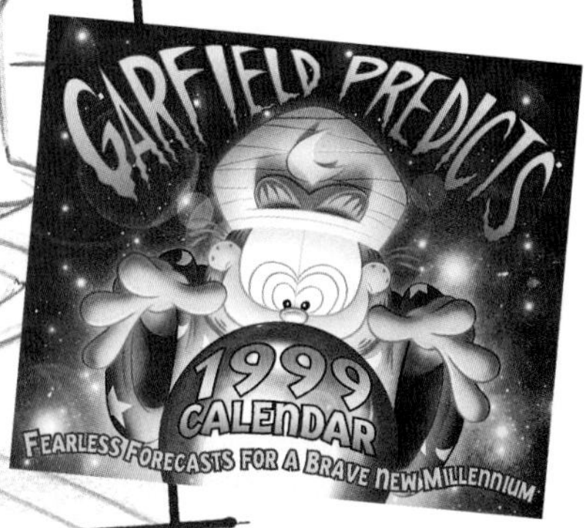
GARFIELD PREDICTS
1999
CALENDAR
FEARLESS FORECASTS FOR A BRAVE NEW MILLENNIUM

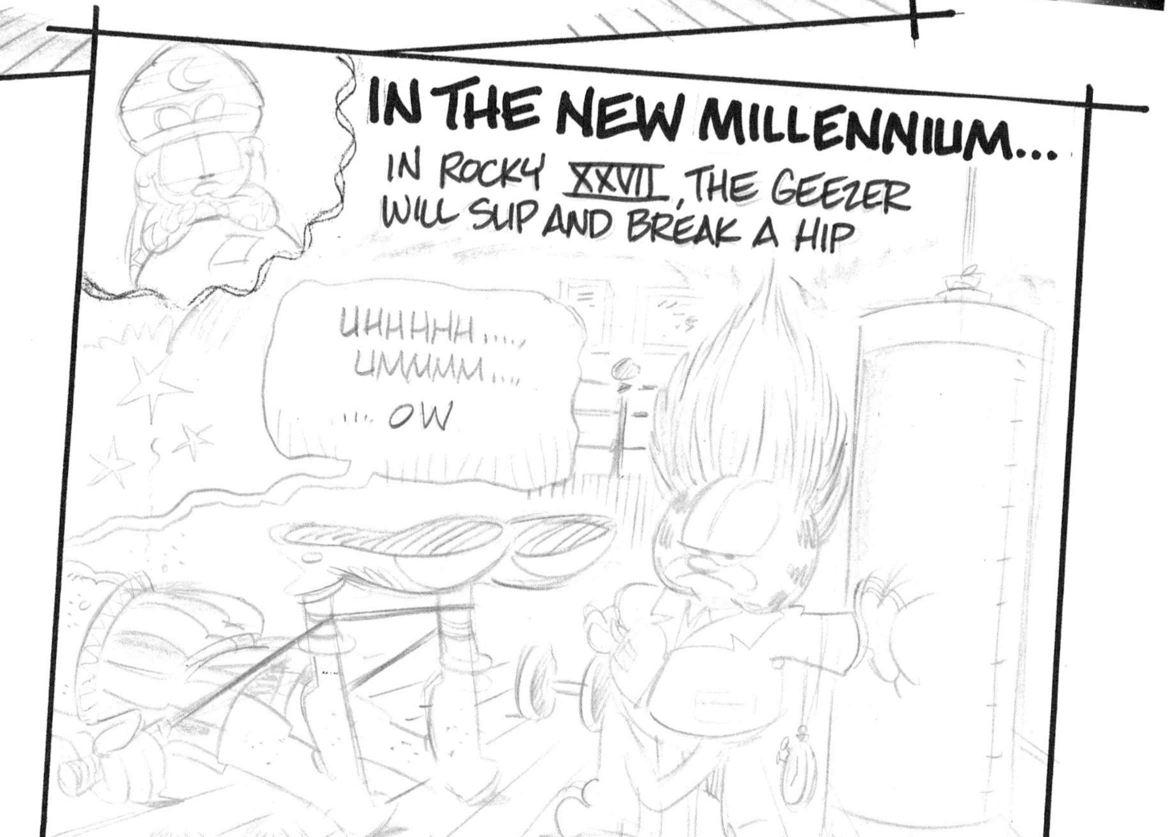
IN THE NEW MILLENNIUM...
IN ROCKY XXVII, THE GEEZER WILL SLIP AND BREAK A HIP
UHHHHH....,
UMMMM....
....OW

Petty Offenses
Rejected gags from Garfield "Little Books" series.

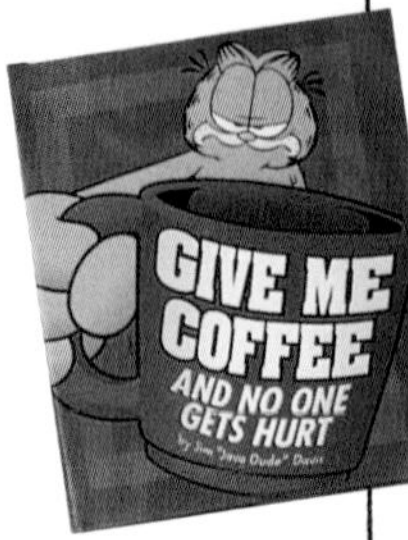
GIVE ME COFFEE
AND NO ONE GETS HURT

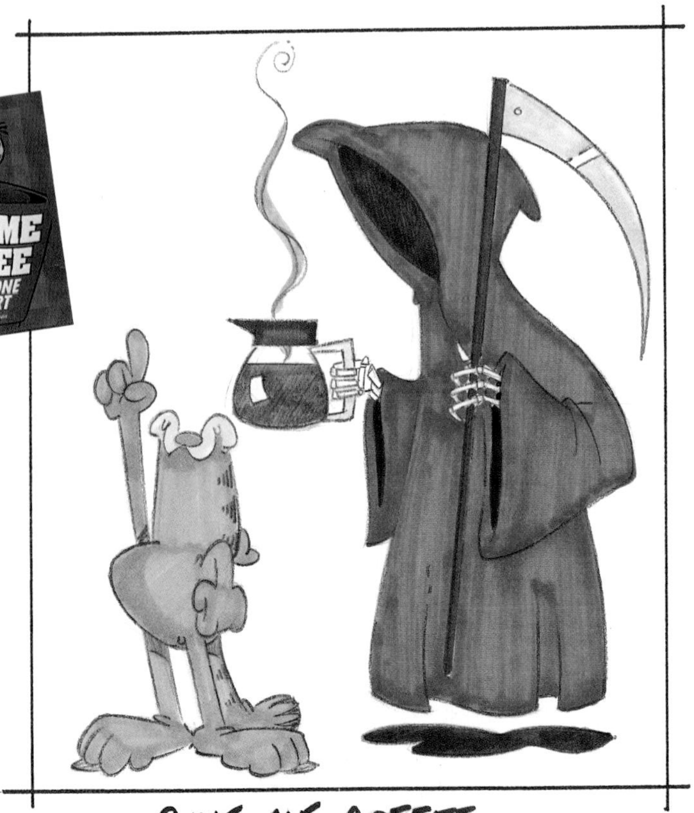

GIVE ME COFFEE, OR GIVE ME DEATH!

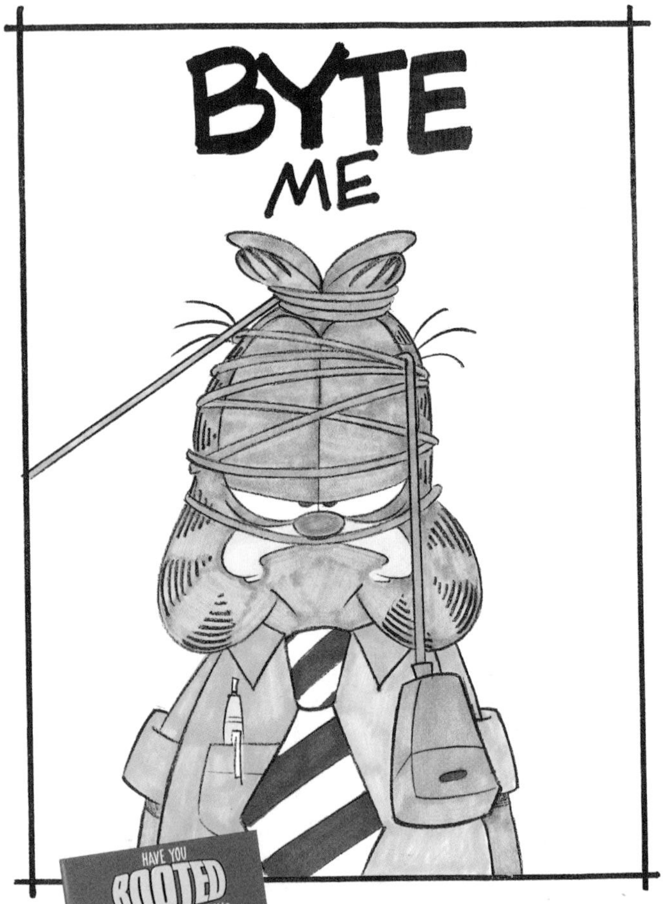
BYTE
ME

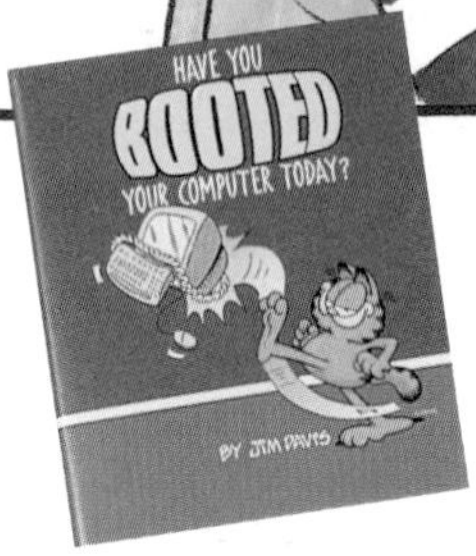
HAVE YOU
BOOTED
YOUR COMPUTER TODAY?
BY JIM DAVIS

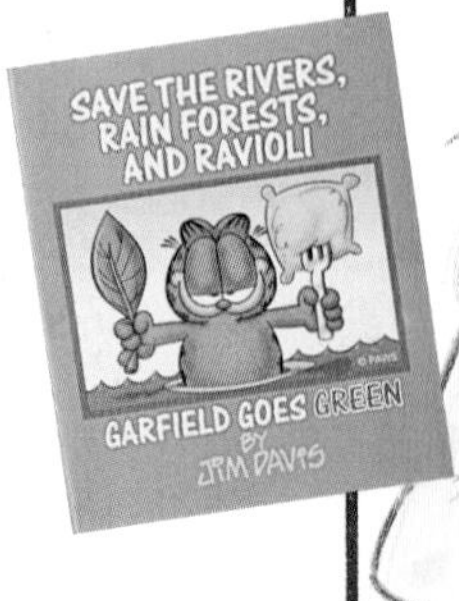
SAVE THE RIVERS, RAIN FORESTS, AND RAVIOLI
GARFIELD GOES GREEN
BY JIM DAVIS

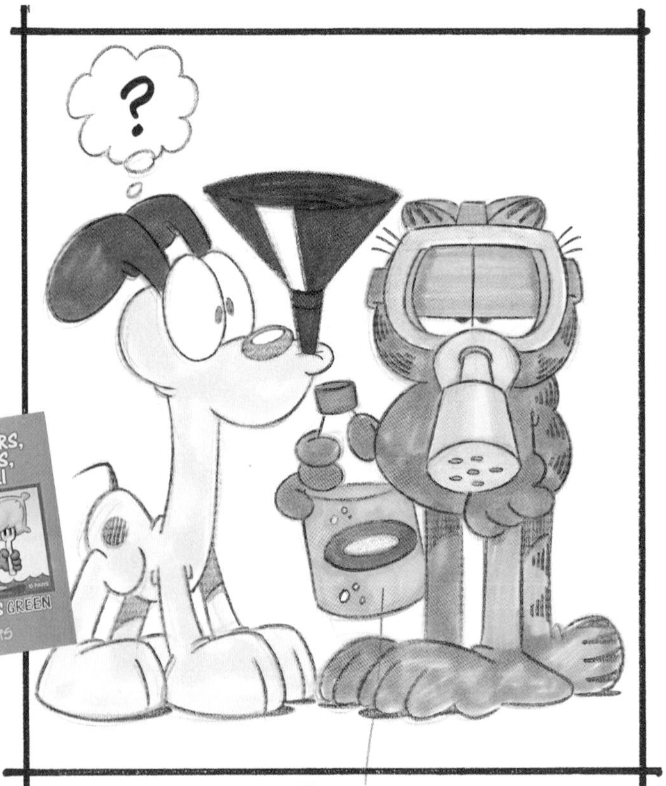

STOP AIR POLLUTION. MAKE YOUR DOG GARGLE.

ODE TO DAVE

Wacky and tacky top ten lists not published in *Garfield's Top Ten Tomcatfoolery*.

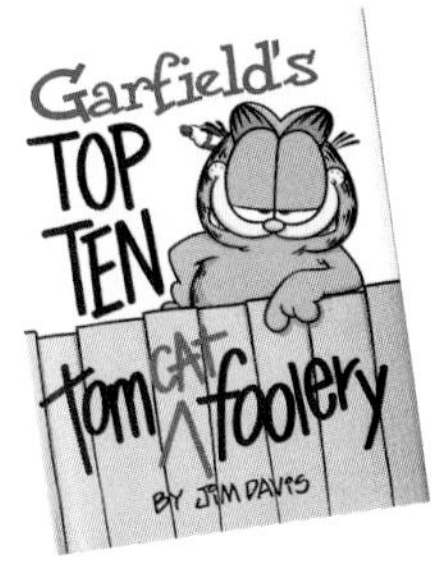
Garfield's
TOP
TEN
tom CAT foolery
BY JIM DAVIS

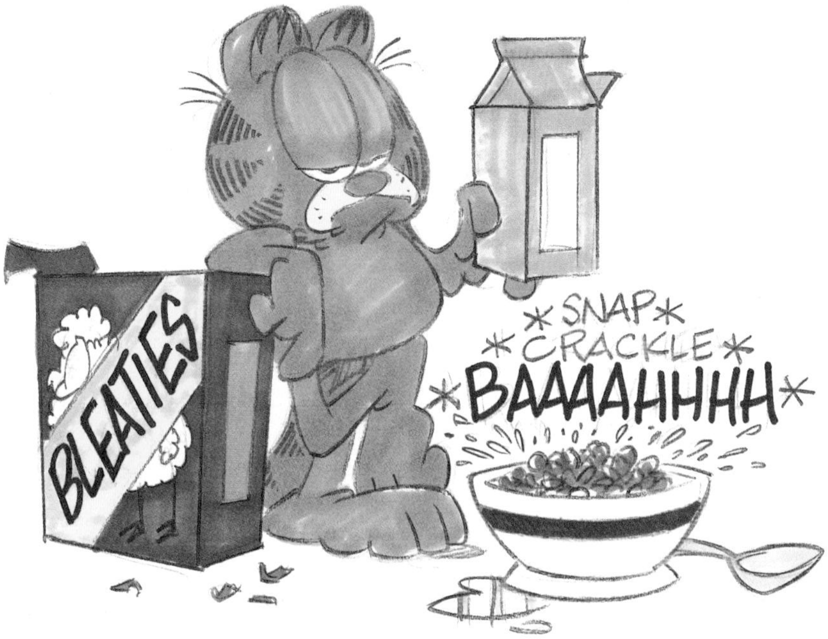
BLEATIES
SNAP
CRACKLE
BAAAAHHHH

GARFIELD'S TOP TEN LEAST FAVORITE CEREALS

10. Frosted Phlegm Flakes
9. Lice Krispies
8. Fruit 'n' Fur
7. Beet Chex
6. Puffed Rice and Hair Plugs
5. Resin Bran
4. Grape Lug Nuts
3. Honey Bunches of Goats
2. Lucky Germs
1. Cereal Killer

GARFIELD'S TOP TEN EPITAPHS FOR HIMSELF

10. "I came. I saw. I ate bad clams."
9. "This should only happen to a dog."
8. "I had the time of my lives."
7. "On the whole, I'd rather be in a deli."
6. "Big fat hereafter deal"
5. "I can use the rest."
4. "Hey! Watch your feet!"
3. "Just a fat doily on the recliner of life"
2. "I ate it my way."
1. "Get me out of here!"

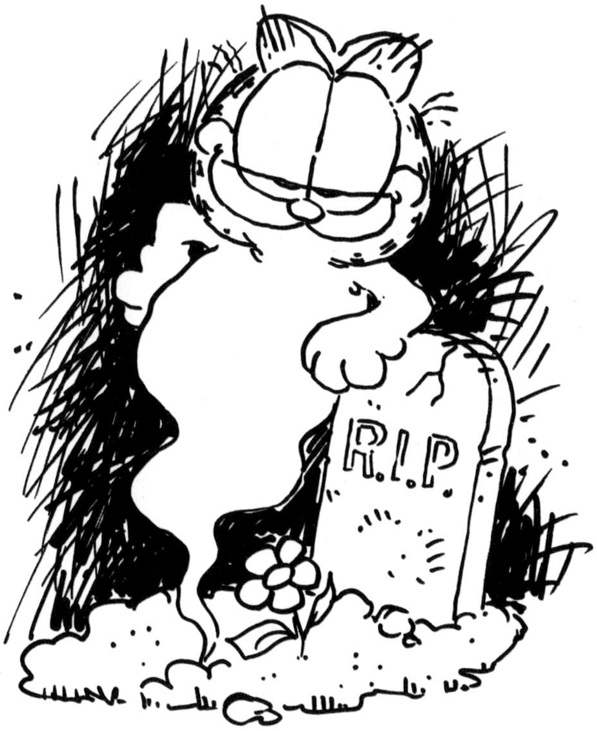
R.I.P.

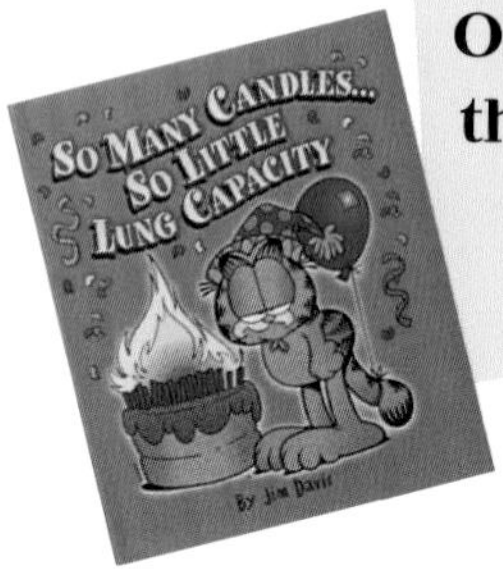
So Many Candles...
So Little
Lung Capacity
By Jim Davis

Age Happens
Old material not used in the minibook *So Many Candles . . . So Little Lung Capacity*.

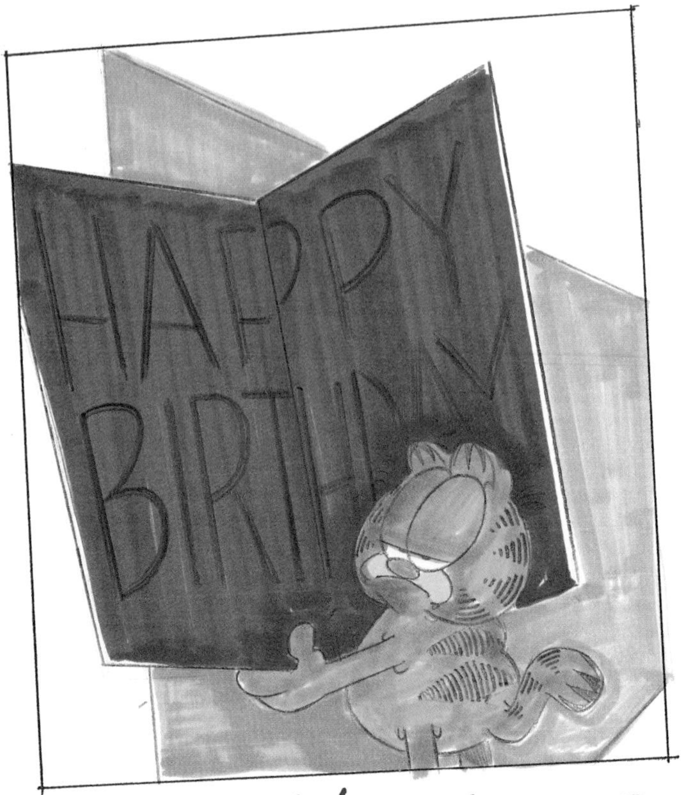
HAPPY
BIRTHDAY

AGE IS JUST A STATE OF MIND... ZZZZZzz

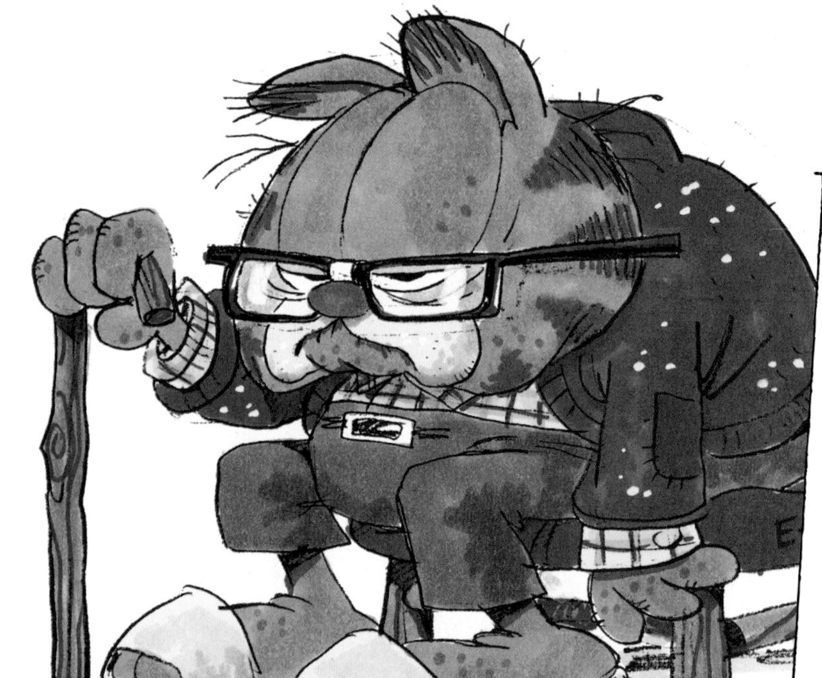

YOU KNOW YOU'RE GETTING OLDER WHEN:
YOU BEGIN RECEIVING "LARGE PRINT" BIRTHDAY CARDS

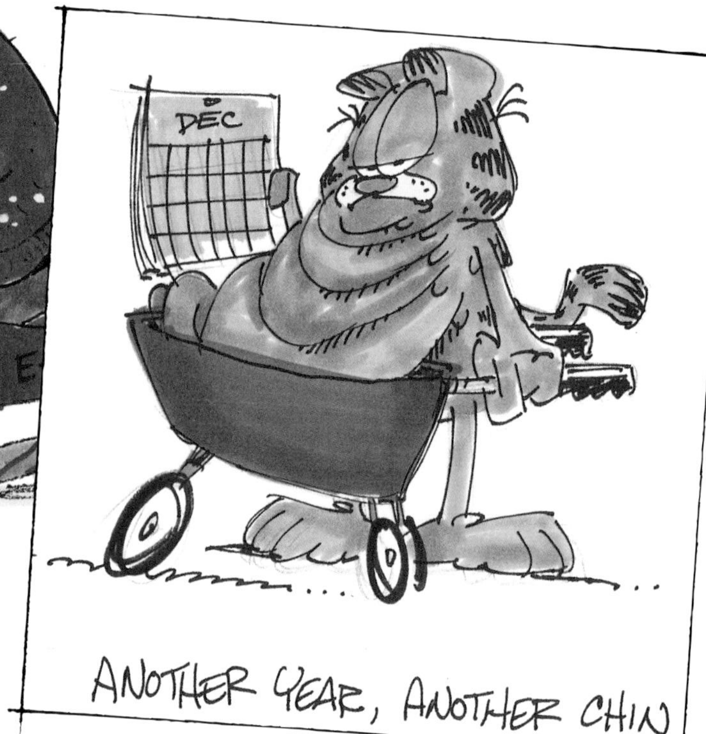
DEC
ANOTHER YEAR, ANOTHER CHIN

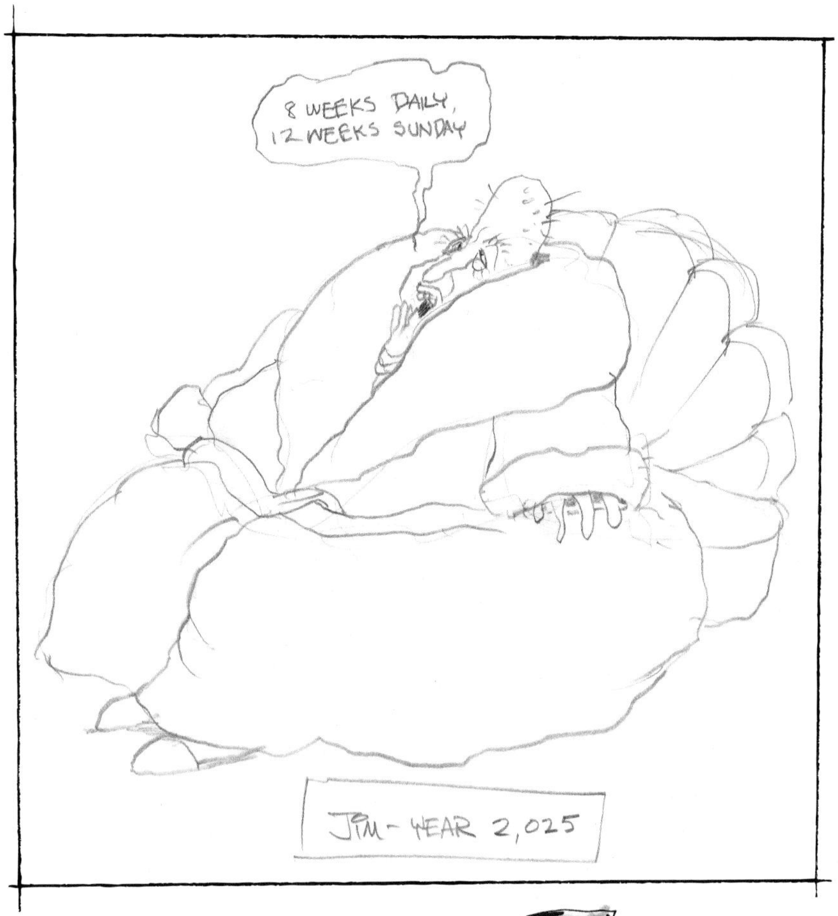
8 WEEKS DAILY,
12 WEEKS SUNDAY
JIM - YEAR 2,025

Left: OLDER AND WIDER
Jim Davis self-portrait in the style of noted cartoonist Gahan Wilson. An eighty-year-old Jim is responding—for the zillionth time—to the question "How far ahead do you work on the strip?"

Below: BIRTHDAY BASHING
Top ten list and caricature created by Paws staffers to commemorate and/or desecrate Jim's fiftieth birthday.

TOP TEN SIGNS
JIM DAVIS HAS TURNED 50

10. Sprinkles tenderizer on his gazpacho
9. Had his red Viper painted beige
8. Paws artists playing connect-the-dots on his liver spots
7. Used to put amaretto in his coffee; now puts formaldehyde
6. Went to antique auction . . . three people bid on him
5. Prostate now the size of a pumpkin
4. Always reminiscing about his first pet—a brontosaurus
3. When golfing, sometimes takes a nap during his back swing
2. Worries if he'll ever find a nursing home with a decent wine cellar
1. Still growing hair . . . but only in his nose!

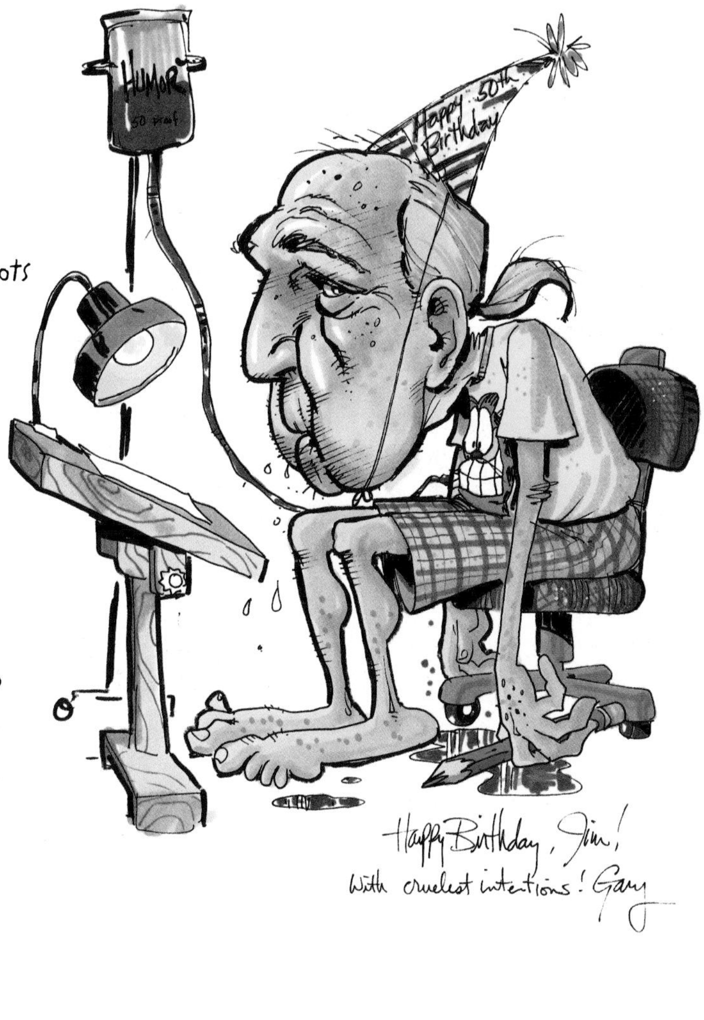
HUMOR
50 Proof
Happy 50th Birthday
Happy Birthday, Jim!
With cruelest intentions! Gary

BAD CAT!
Rejected comic-strip compilation-book covers.

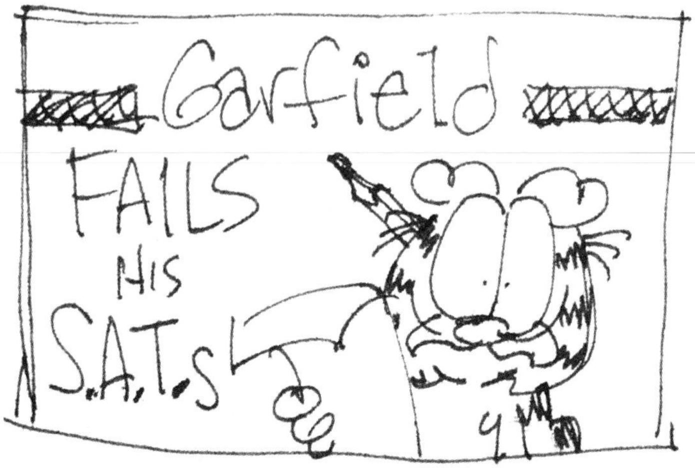
Garfield
FAILS HIS S.A.T.s

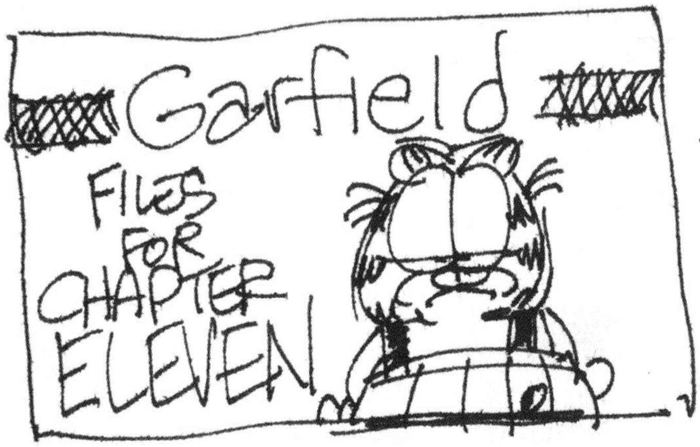
Garfield
FILES FOR CHAPTER ELEVEN

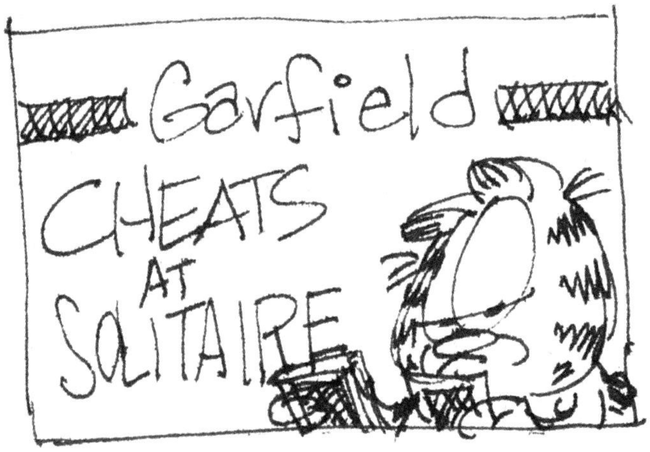
Garfield
CHEATS AT SOLITAIRE

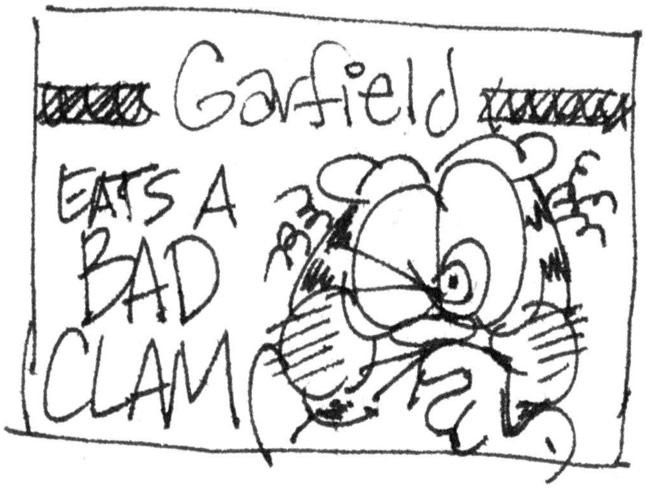
Garfield
EATS A BAD CLAM

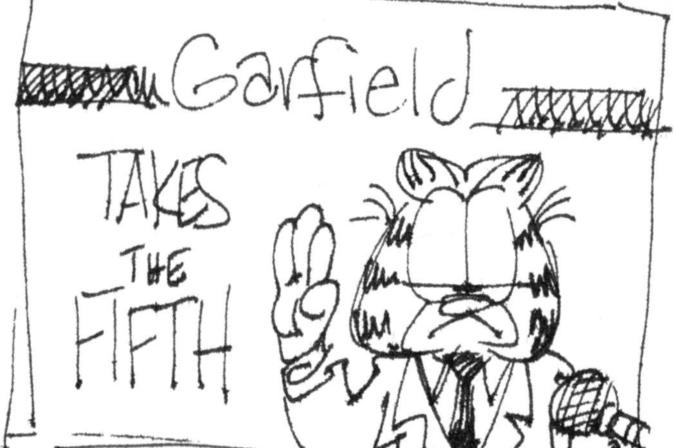
Garfield
TAKES THE FIFTH

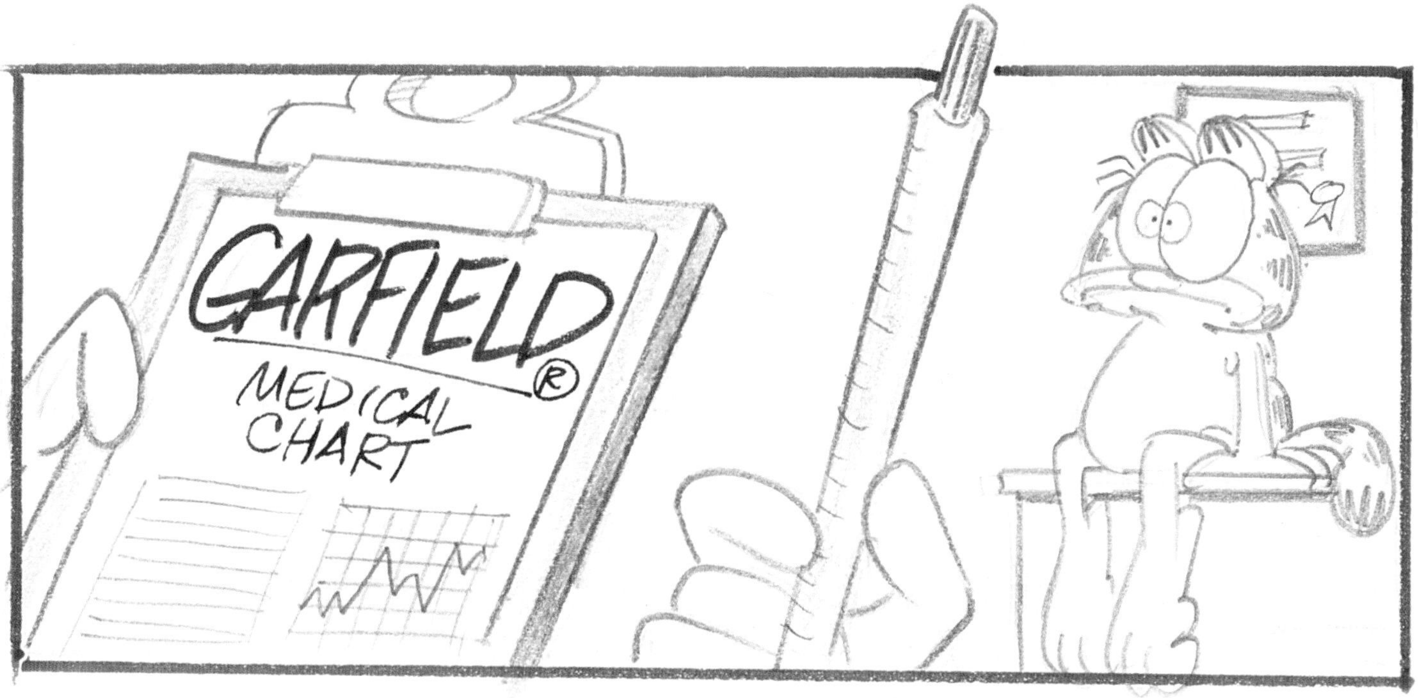
GARFIELD®
MEDICAL CHART

PRIVATE ARCHIVES
Rejected logo box *(above)* and comic strips *(below)*.

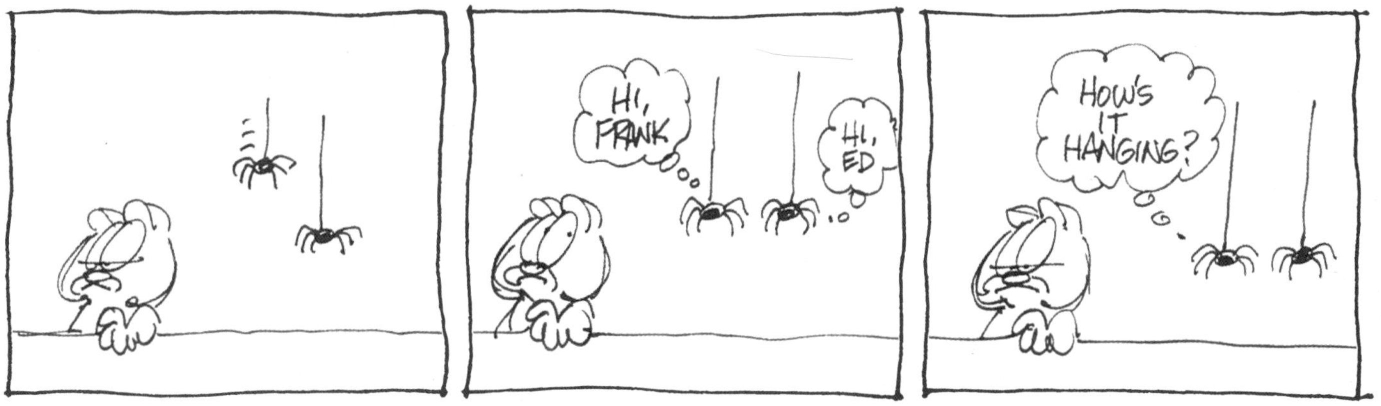
HI, FRANK
HI, ED
HOW'S IT HANGING?

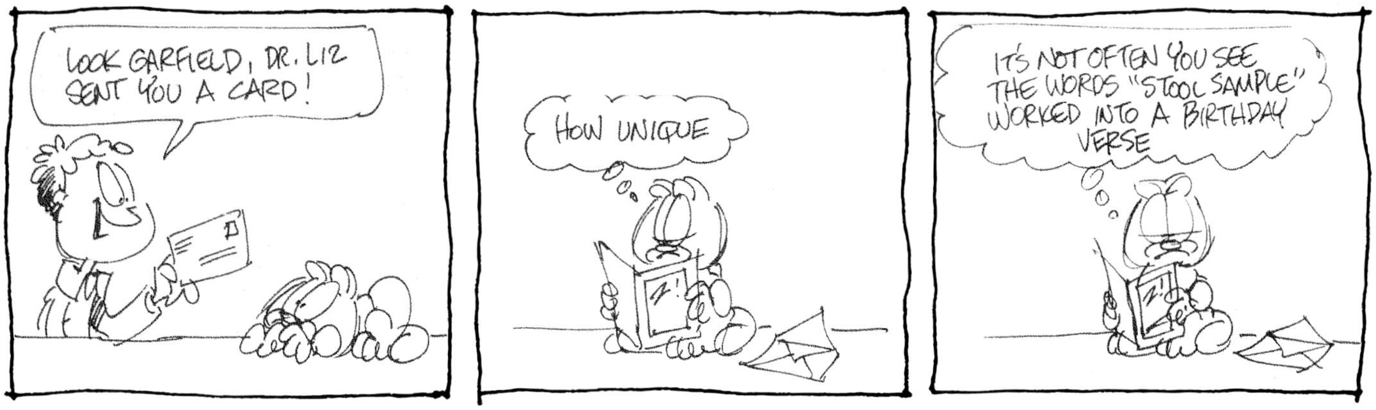
LOOK GARFIELD, DR. LIZ SENT YOU A CARD!
HOW UNIQUE
IT'S NOT OFTEN YOU SEE THE WORDS "STOOL SAMPLE" WORKED INTO A BIRTHDAY VERSE

Curiouser and Curiouser

Unedited—and (until now) unpublished—gags and poster concepts.

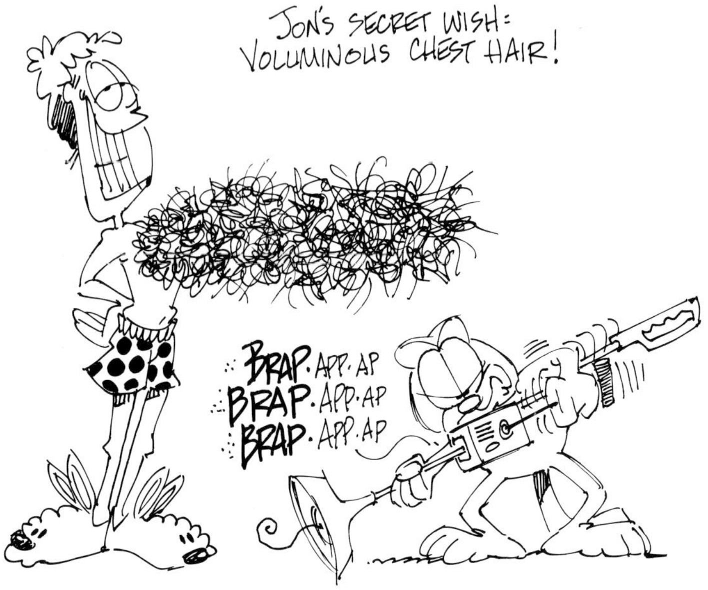
JON'S SECRET WISH: VOLUMINOUS CHEST HAIR!
BRAP·APP·AP
BRAP·APP·AP
BRAP·APP·AP

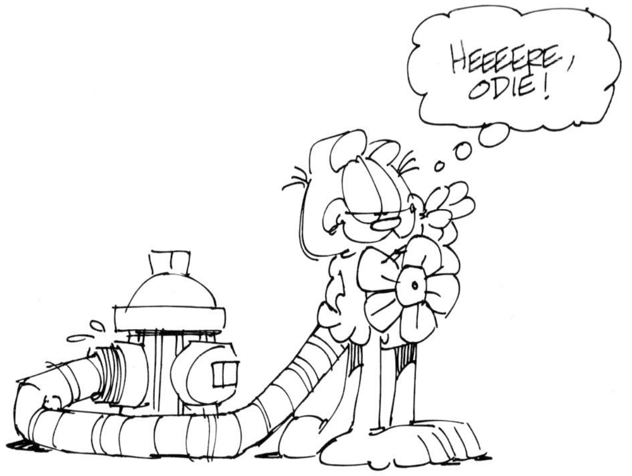
HEEEERE, ODIE!

WHY DO WE ALWAYS SQUIRT THE ONES WE LOVE?

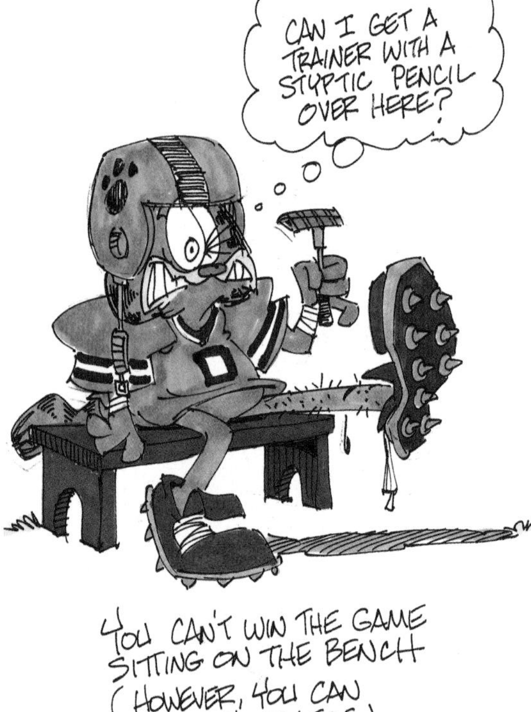
CAN I GET A TRAINER WITH A STYPTIC PENCIL OVER HERE?
D

YOU CAN'T WIN THE GAME SITTING ON THE BENCH (HOWEVER, YOU CAN SHAVE YOUR LEGS)

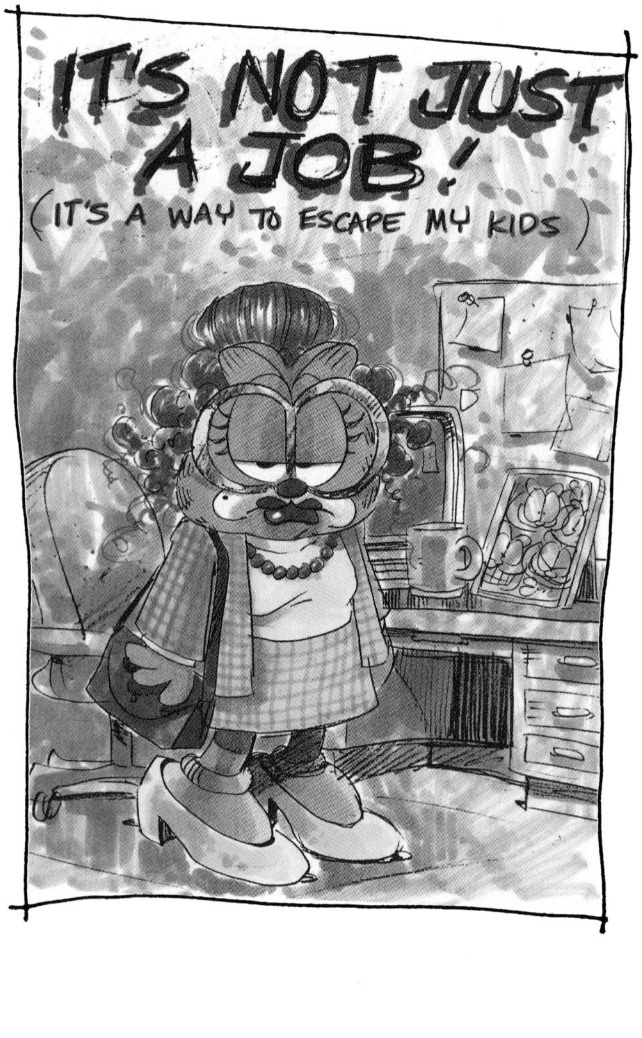
IT'S NOT JUST A JOB!
(IT'S A WAY TO ESCAPE MY KIDS)

I'M TOO
SEXY FOR
MY
TONGUE

EAT YOUR HEART OUT
CHIPPENDALES
PK

RISQUÉ BUSINESS

Rejected gags and sketches.

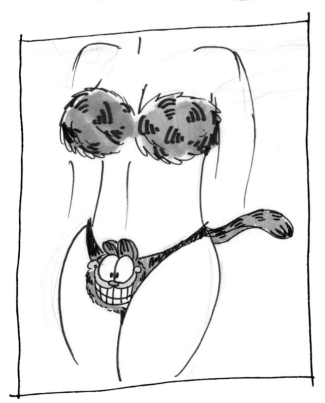

GARFIELD IN THE GROOVE
Unused musician parodies designed for T-shirts.

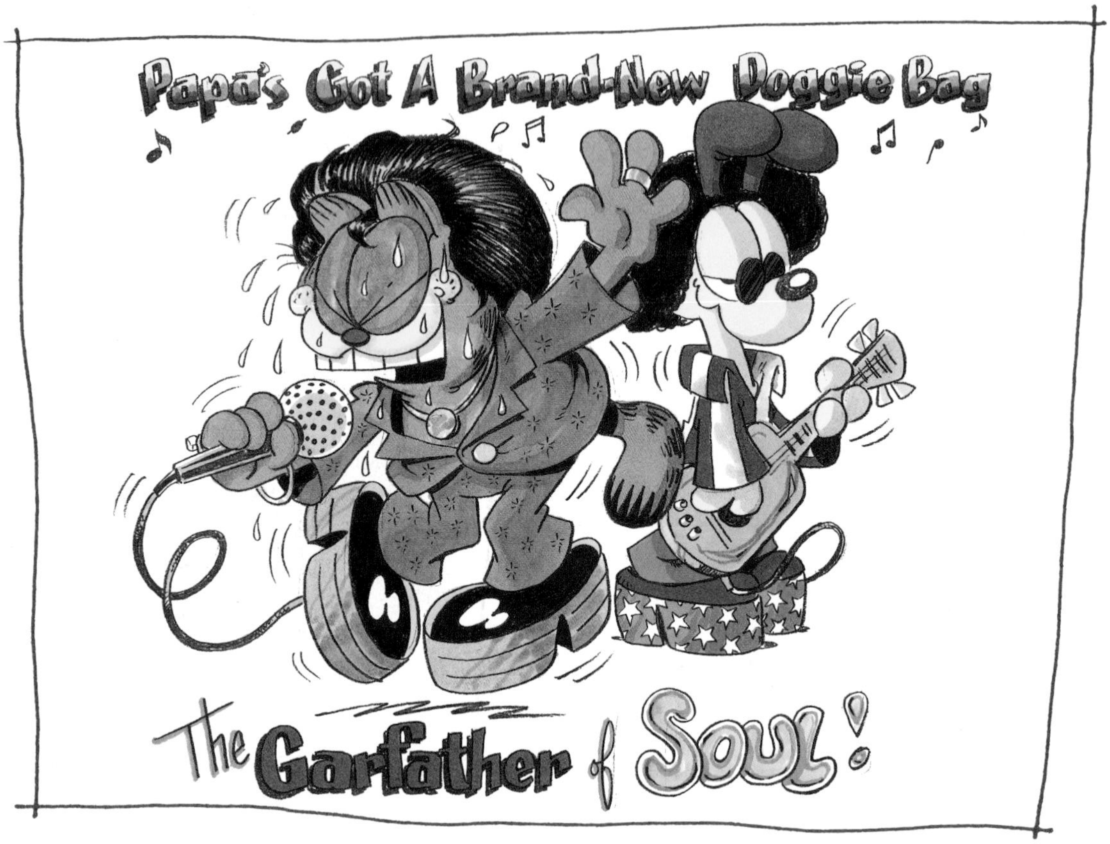
Papa's Got A Brand-New Doggie Bag
The Garfather of Soul!

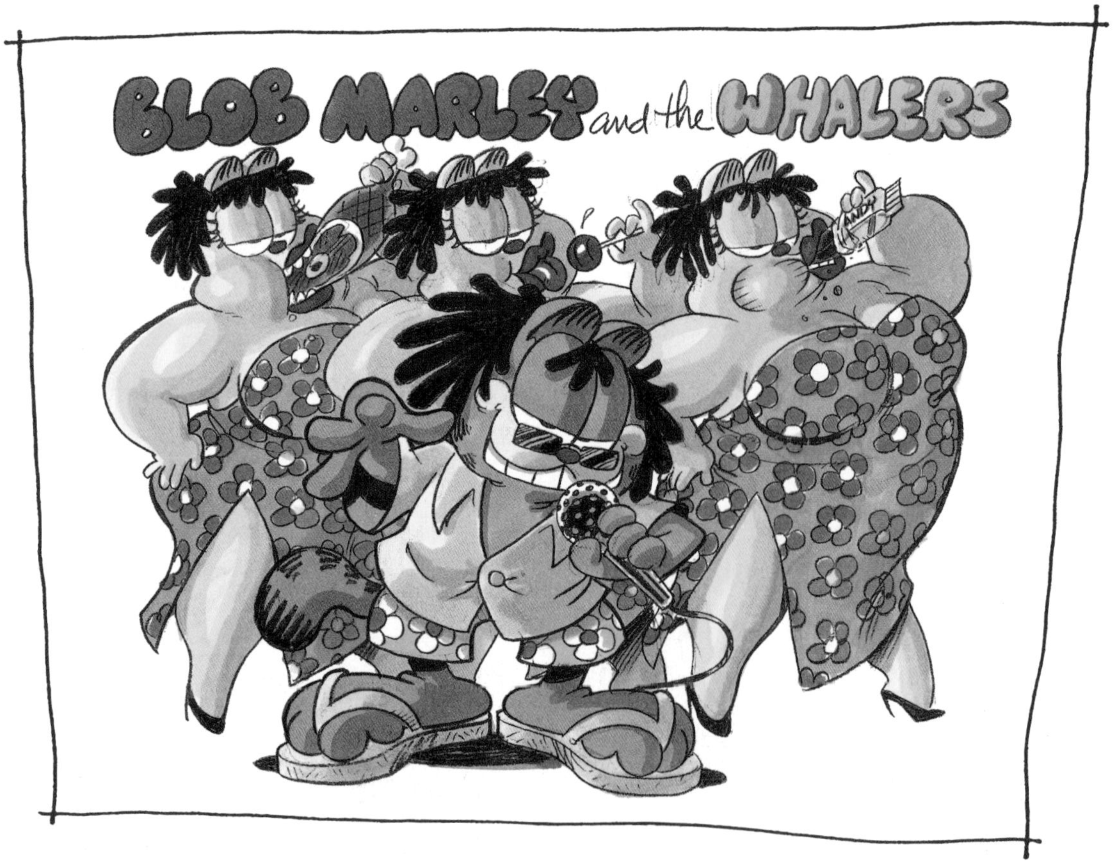
BLOB MARLEY and the WHALERS

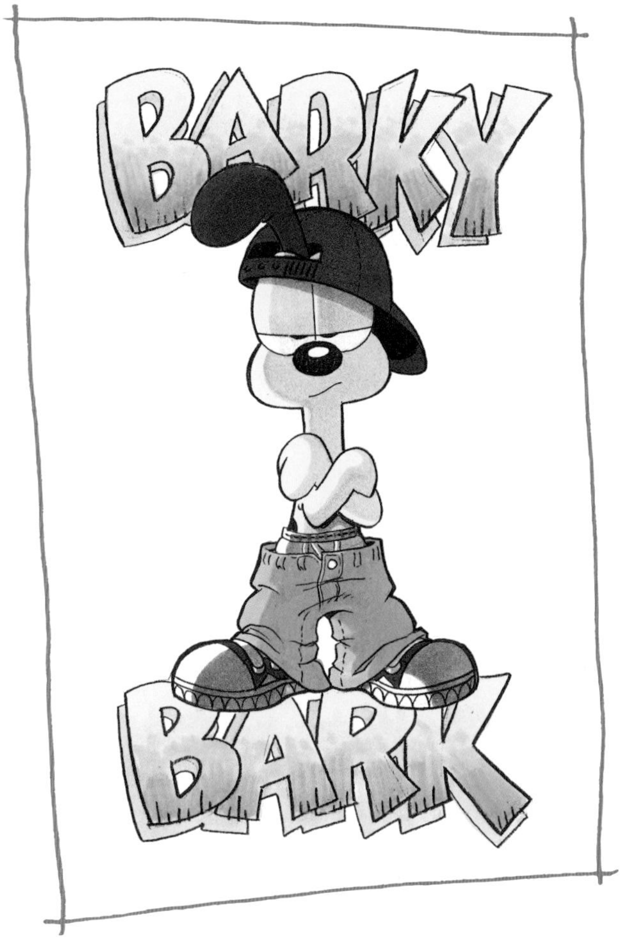
BARKY
BARK

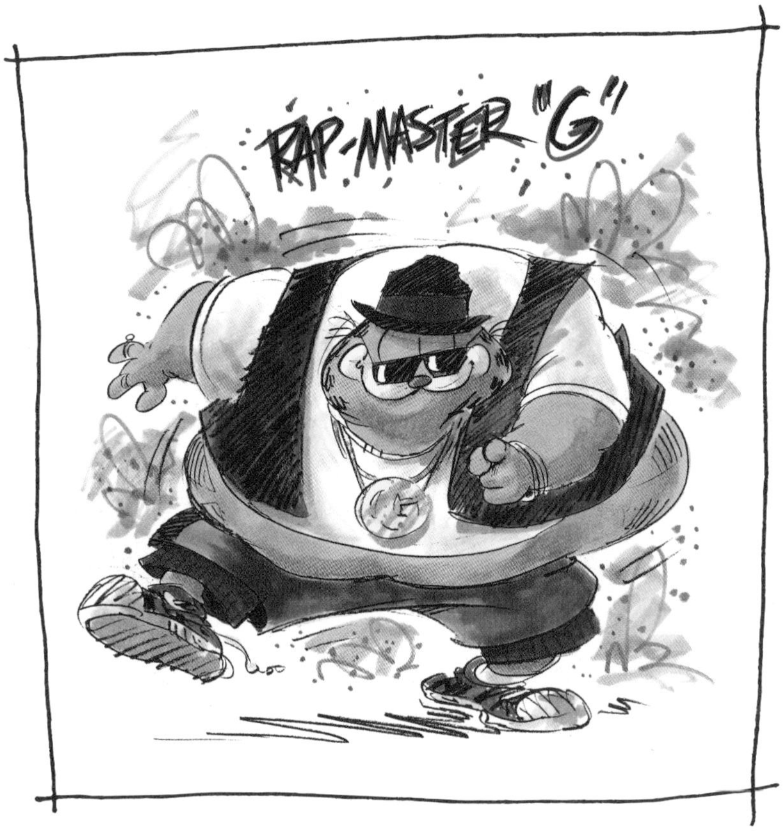
RAP-MASTER "G"

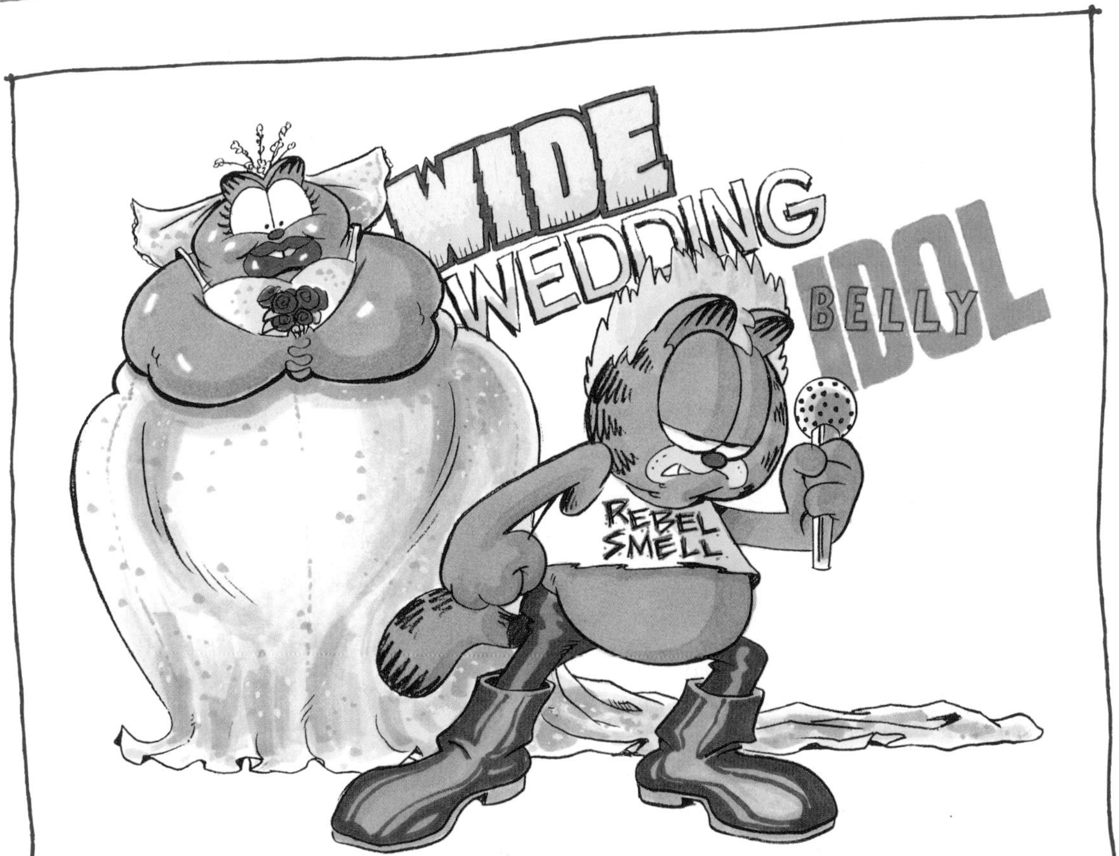
WIDE
WEDDING
BELLY
IDOL
REBEL SMELL

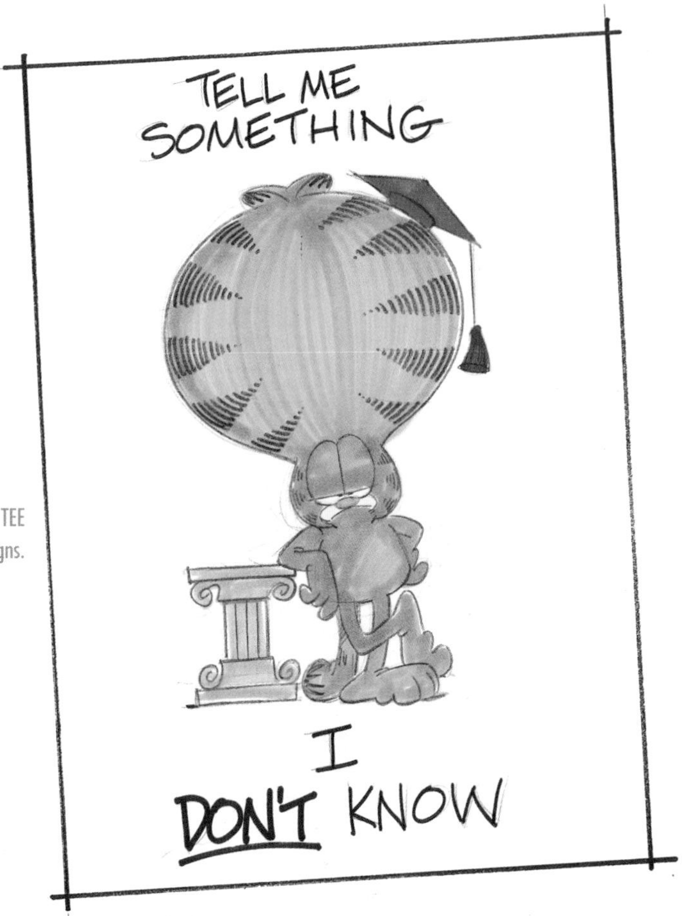
TELL ME SOMETHING
I DON'T KNOW

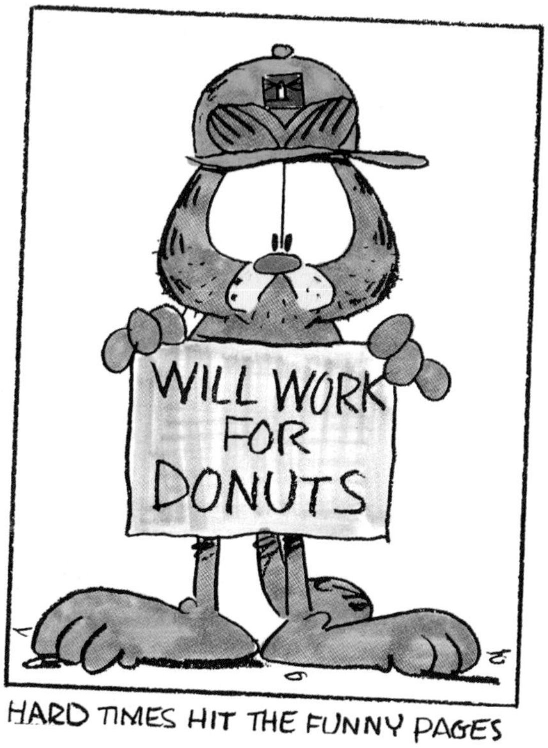
WILL WORK FOR DONUTS
HARD TIMES HIT THE FUNNY PAGES

Right: UNSUITED TO A TEE
Rejected T-shirt designs.

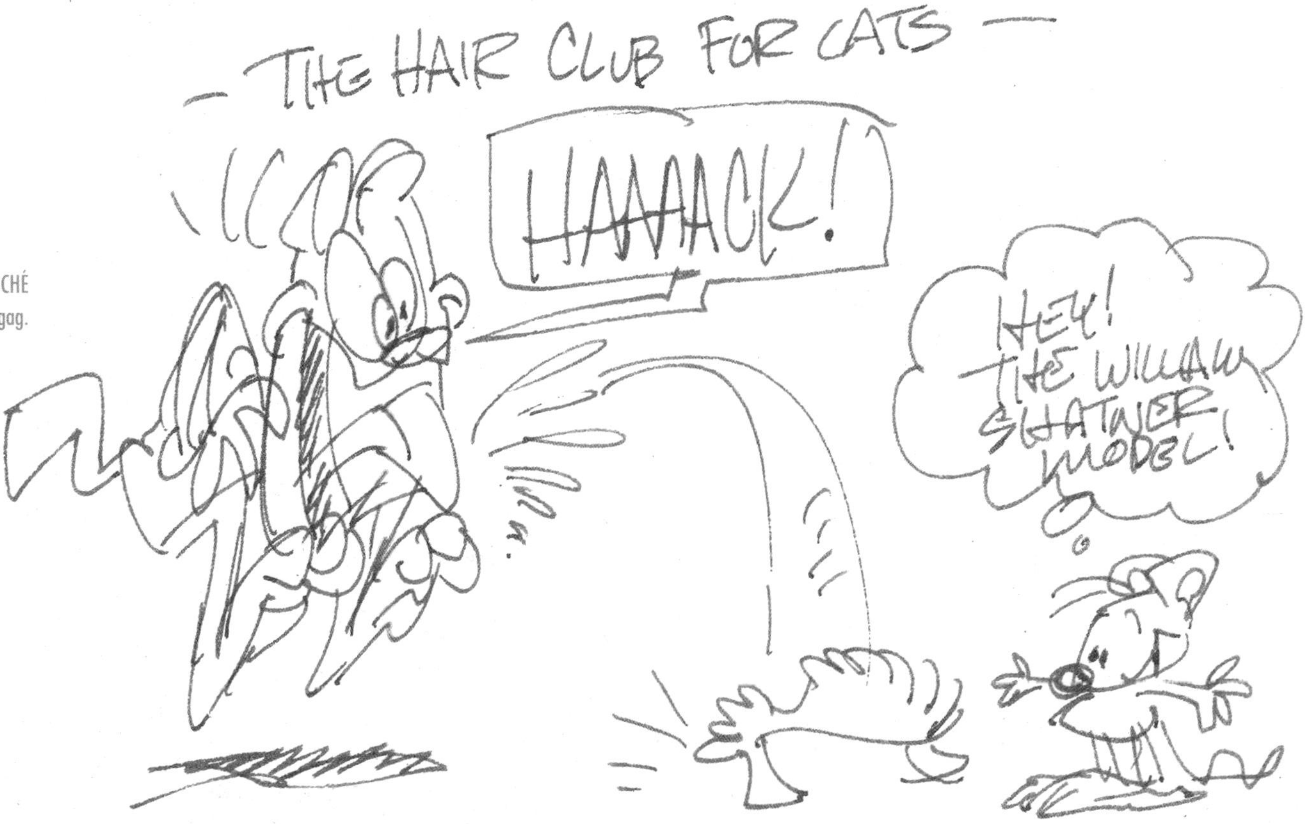
— THE HAIR CLUB FOR CATS —
HAAAACK!
HEY! THE WILLIAM SHATNER MODEL!

Right: TOUPEE TOUCHÉ
Rejected poster gag.

CLOTHES MAKE THE, ER, MAN
Garfield, Odie, and Jim dressed to thrill.

ODIE as P.M. Margaret THATCHER

Jim as Margaret Thatcher

AFTERWORD BY LYNN JOHNSTON

IT WAS THE EARLY 1980S. I'D JUST BECOME SYNDICATED, AND ONE OF THE FIRST CARTOONISTS TO WELCOME ME INTO THE BUSINESS WAS JIM DAVIS.

WE STOOD, WATCHING A PARADE OF OUR HEROES WALK BY... FILLING THE SEATS IN THE GRAND BALLROOM OF THE PLAZA HOTEL IN NEW YORK.

CARTOONISTS WE HAD LOVED, LEARNED FROM, BEEN INSPIRED BY, AND WERE HONORED TO MEET WERE GATHERED TO CELEBRATE THE ANNUAL REUBEN AWARDS EVENING; THE OSCARS OF THE INDUSTRY— AND, WE WERE THERE. JIM AND I WERE IN OUR 30S.

"LYNN," HE SAID, "ONE DAY, YOU AND I WILL BE THE OLD GUARD. YOUNG, NEW CARTOONISTS WILL COME UP TO US AND SAY "DID YOU REALLY KNOW CHARLES SCHULZ?"

I LAUGHED. COULDN'T IMAGINE THAT FAR AHEAD... COULDN'T IMAGINE US BEING THE SENIORS!

LAST YEAR, AT THE REUBEN AWARDS, A YOUNG NEW CARTOONIST CAME UP TO ME AND SAID "DID YOU REALLY KNOW CHARLES SCHULZ?—WHAT WAS HE LIKE?"

WELL, WE'RE NOT QUITE "THE OLD GUARD" YET, JIM —BUT, WE'RE WORKING ON IT. CONGRATULATIONS, MY FRIEND, ON 25 YEARS OF GARFIELD!!! —TELL HIM TO SHARE HIS CAKE!

Lynn Johnston

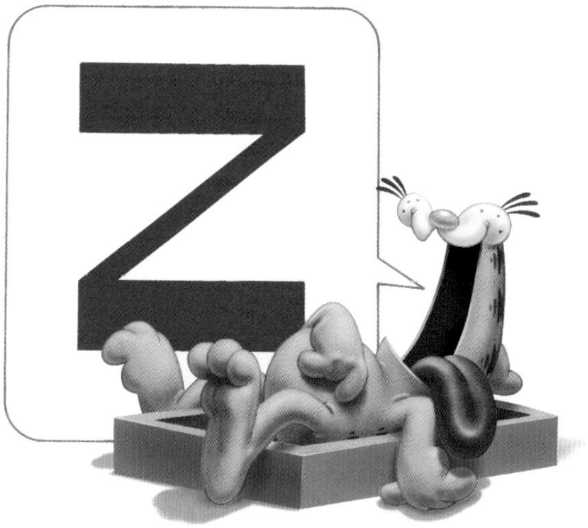
Z